Nick,

With many thanks for
the foreword

David

THE LAW OF PENSION TRUSTS

THE LAW OF
PENSION TRUSTS

David Pollard

OXFORD
UNIVERSITY PRESS

UNIVERSITY PRESS

Great Clarendon Street, Oxford, OX2 6DP,
United Kingdom

Oxford University Press is a department of the University of Oxford.
It furthers the University's objective of excellence in research, scholarship,
and education by publishing worldwide. Oxford is a registered trade mark of
Oxford University Press in the UK and in certain other countries

Published in the United States of America by Oxford University Press
198 Madison Avenue, New York, NY 10016, United States of America

British Library Cataloguing in Publication Data
Data available

Library of Congress Control Number: 2013943934

ISBN 978–0–19–967248–6

Printed and bound in Great Britain by
CPI Group (UK) Ltd, Croydon, CR0 4YY

*This book is dedicated to my wife, Louise, and
my children Jessica, Elizabeth, and Andrew.*

FOREWORD

By the Hon Mr Justice Warren

In his foreword to the 18th edition of Lewin on Trusts, Lord Walker of Gestingthorpe addressed the philosophical question of identity, referring to the *Cutty Sark* and other famous vessels when almost every timber and plank have been replaced, perhaps many times.

David Pollard's latest book raises no such conceptual difficulties. It is a spanking new vessel, made out of the most modern lightweight-but-super-strong materials and equipped with state-of-the-art navigational equipment to guide the reader through the uncharted waters of developing trust law as well as the channels bounded on each side with the rocks of statutory regulation.

This book does not pretend to be a detailed commentary on the legislation nor a learned discourse on trust law as it applies to pensions trusts equivalent to Lewin. Instead, not only is it a practical book but it is also a challenging and questioning book, identifying problems here, offering solutions there. It draws attention to difficulties others may have overlooked; it helps the informed reader to see the way to avoid those difficulties and, where it is too late to do so, to find answers to them.

No book on this subject could be an easy read; indeed only a passionate pensions lawyer (or reviewer or foreword writer) would contemplate reading it from cover to cover. Lord Walker observed the stark division between those who are fascinated by and those who are stupefyingly bored by pension schemes (see the quotation at the head of the Introduction to this book) and like him I count myself among the former. This book is a unique contribution to the literature and will, I am sure, prove a source of endless stimulation for the fascinated. For the stupefyingly bored? If they could only be forced to read the Introduction, they could not but want to read more and, who knows, perhaps become converts.

I am delighted to welcome this new book and to recommend it to all those practising, be they lawyers, actuaries, accountants, or others, in the pensions world.

Nicholas Warren
July 2013

PREFACE

Pension schemes resemble cricket, or horse racing, or poker—the list could be extended almost indefinitely—in that either you are fascinated by them or you find them stupefyingly boring; there is no middle ground for 'don't knows'. It will be apparent that I am not ashamed to be counted among the former faction. I hope I may have persuaded some of you that there is real interest in seeing how some long-standing trust principles are being tested in this relatively new and very important field.

> Sir Robert Walker 'Some Trust Principles in the Pensions
> Context' in AJ Oakley (ed), *Trends in Contemporary Trust Law*
> (Clarendon Press, 1996) 134

Family trusts are now a shrinking enclave designated as 'private client' work, and pensions trusts, burdened by increasingly complex regulatory statutes, are another enclave reserved for pensions specialists.

> Lord Walker of Gestingthorpe *Futter v HMRC*
> [2013] UKSC 26 at [15]

Pensions law is fascinating.

Pension schemes are both massively important socially (as a method of delivering retirement income) and massively interesting for lawyers—very complicated and often with a great deal at stake.

Sadly pension schemes have not attracted much in the way of legal writing, compared to (say) employment or trust law (save as an example of a commercial trust as part of a trust law course).

Academic lawyers do not come across them much. Practitioners are (in the main) usually too busy to write much.

Pension schemes are not generally taught as a subject at universities or law schools, so the first time that a lawyer may interact with them is in private practice (during a training contract etc). The Association of Pension Lawyers (APL) works strongly to fill this gap by its programme of seminars and conferences. Its website is a first port of call for papers and talks on issues. In Australia the annual Superannuation Law conference generates much helpful learning.

Reflecting its social importance, much of pensions law now has a statutory overlay, in particular the Pensions Acts 1995 and 2004 and underlying regulations.

This book looks at a variety of issues in pensions law, focusing primarily on the common law principles. The statutory provisions are not ignored and are covered as applicable, but are not generally the primary focus of the discussion.

This book is an analysis of aspects of trust law and how it applies to occupational pension schemes as commercial entities.

The book brings together academic analysis of various aspects of occupational pension schemes established under trust, focusing in the main on common law driven issues. It looks in depth at tricky areas of pensions law outside statute, such as trustees' obligations to employers, how spouses and dependants rank as beneficiaries, implied duties owed by employers.

It analyses the decided cases on the areas chosen, including decisions out of the UK where relevant. It comments on how trust law should apply to pension schemes in light of their differing nature to 'traditional' family settlements.

Trusts

In the UK, private sector occupational pension schemes are, in the main, established as trusts. So, in the same way as for directors of corporations, many of the basic principles and obligations are derived from trust law. But trust law that must be applied to the special circumstances of occupational pension schemes.

This book looks at various areas of pensions law and how they inter-relate with general trust and common law.

Space[1] and time mean that there is much that this book does not cover: for example funding, investment, Pensions Regulator moral hazard powers, winding-up, statutory debt on the employer (s 75). The issue of challenges to trustee decisions (and the extent of the rule in *Hastings-Bass*) is, at the time of writing, in some flux following the decision of Lord Walker in the Supreme Court (in *Pitt/Futter v HMRC*).

This book focuses on occupational pension schemes established under trust.

An overview of the UK legal position

The case law in the UK in relation to pensions is in a state of flux. When I first started in the pensions field, back in the 1980s, there were three well-known UK pensions cases.[2] These three were *Cowan v Scargill*,[3] *Imperial Foods*,[4] and *Courage*.[5]

Since then there has been a comparative explosion in both legislation and case law. From a position where there were few if any barristers who understood anything about pensions, we now have a (still relatively small) group of pension specialists. There is a very much larger range of pension specialists in solicitors' firms. The amount of case law has much expanded.

What are the factors behind this? The following seem to me to be relevant:

- There is potentially a lot of money involved in pension schemes. Particularly where final salary (defined benefit) schemes are involved, the amount at stake in relation to surpluses (or deficits) can be huge. The costs of litigation are also large but the huge amounts at stake can justify them.
- Members have become more aware and the public generally have become more aware of the value of their pension rights. Following Robert Maxwell's death, the discovery of a big

---

[1] The initial drafts came in at 215,000 words, well over the 140,000 word target.
[2] We were wrong—there were other cases. See eg the 1937 House of Lords case, *Tibbals*, mentioned in Ch 15.
[3] *Cowan v Scargill* [1985] Ch 270, [1984] 2 All ER 750 (Sir Robert Megarry V-C).
[4] *Re Imperial Food Ltd's Pension Scheme* [1986] 2 All ER 802, [1986] 1 WLR 717 (Walton J).
[5] *Re Courage Group's Pension Schemes, Ryan v Imperial Brewing and Leisure Ltd* [1987] 1 All ER 528, [1987] 1 WLR 495 (Millett J).

hole in the pension schemes focused everyone's mind. It made pensions front-page news in a way that they had not been before.

- There are more lawyers who specialize in this area. That seems to mean that more points are taken and more disputes raised.
- The creation of the post of Pensions Ombudsman has meant that members can bring their disputes before a judicial process with no fear as to costs should they lose. This has meant the many disputes which might well not previously have got as far as the courts (because of the cost fear) have been taken forward.
- The courts are 'moving the goal posts'. The courts generally have moved away from the policy in the 1940s and 1950s of strict interpretation of documents and statutes towards a more purposive approach to interpretation.

The last point deserves more explanation. Led by the House of Lords, the courts have moved away from a literal construction. They try to make more 'practical sense' of statutes and documents. In addition there has been the rise of the implied term of trust and confidence in relation to employer powers, the rise of judicial review in administrative law matters etc.

Clearly we are in a much more active stage for the judiciary than was the case in the years following the Second World War. This may mean that the judges feel better able to dispense 'justice' in an individual case, but as we all know it inevitably means that there is less certainty for others. Hence the need for litigation. Some of this arises from the increased statutory regulation, much of it giving rise to problems in practice. Questions of statutory interpretation tend to arise.

How Will the Judges Act?

The net effect of all this is that it is becoming more and more difficult to predict how the judiciary will react in any particular situation. The judiciary in England and Wales is generally very clever, but has little experience of pensions (with some notable exceptions, in particular Sir Nicholas Warren, Dame Sarah Asplin, and Lord Walker, with the newly appointed Christopher Nugee). This probably makes them relatively cautious about establishing general principles away from traditional trust law. They are concerned that they do not know the full ramifications of a particular ruling. This means that they will undoubtedly be more reluctant to overrule or not follow an earlier case.

The paucity of UK decisions makes it, in my view, highly relevant to look at decisions in other jurisdictions.

Pensions Law as 'Interesting'

One of the fascinations of doing pensions law in the UK (sadly it does not seem that we are ever going to be called 'super lawyers' in the same way as Australian lawyers practising superannuation law) is the technical issues that it constantly raises. In practice it is a combination involving:

- many technical areas: specific pensions law, trusts, tax, employment, insolvency etc;
- a lot of money often at stake;
- a collective element in that it involves both trustees and employers who can have differing perspectives;
- trustees who are constrained by fiduciary duties—this means they are pushed to 'get it right' and may feel they cannot take a commercial view; and

- a multitude of schemes—there is no single template in the UK for the establishment of a pension scheme and so there are a number of schemes with a number of different structures.

Add into this an increasing tendency by the government and Parliament to tinker with the system in many ways (sometimes pretty unhelpfully) and you have a recipe for a fascinating area of the law.

I am conscious that my clients may not appreciate this as much as I do. I sometimes tell them that this is an 'interesting' issue and then comment that the last thing they want to hear is their lawyer describe something as interesting.

There has been an increase in decided case law litigation and legislation in the UK, but some of the basic principles remain as elusive as ever. Legislation tends to be pretty rare and still in the basic 'common law' areas—eg contract, trust, tort.

Looking Overseas

So it is with pleasure that I try to look at case law from other jurisdictions where it is still relevant. Although there are now more UK cases than when I started, we still need to look at other jurisdictions when we can.

In practice I do turn to the Australian case law when I can. There are a number of reasons for this:

- the common law systems are still pretty closely aligned—although legislation tends increasingly to differ (more on this below);
- there is ready access to a lot of Australian materials on the internet; and
- I appreciate the quality of the judiciary in Australia.

Other relevant jurisdictions include Ireland, New Zealand, South Africa, and Canada.[6] But for some reason they either seem to generate less case law (at least that is relevant to me) or I am a bit more dubious about how to apply it in the UK context. This is particularly true in relation to Canada where their development of the concept of fiduciary duties and obligations seems to me to be moving in different directions to those in the UK (and probably Australia).

Help

Many people have helped with this book and given useful comments and advice, including Jonathan Hilliard, Tim Cox, Derek Sloan, Alex Chiang, and Louise Pollard. Particular thanks go to Sir Nicholas Warren for the foreword and to my colleagues at Freshfields Bruckhaus Deringer: Dawn Heath, Charles Magoffin, Kathleen Healy, Leanne Turner, Andrew Murphy, Alice Greenwell, Suhasini Gunasena, Sara Chambers, Lindsay McLeod, Alex Fricke, Harriet Sayer, Julia Chirnside, Alison Chung, Hannah Machin, Jim Arnold, Ila Bhate, and Tom Westwell.

The errors, of course, remain my own.

The law is stated as at 1 August 2013.

David Pollard

---

[6] I worked for three years in Singapore, but sadly have yet to find a pensions case from there (although I did recently find one on insolvency law for my paper to the APL on 'Who is connected or associated?').

AUTHOR BIOGRAPHY

Other books by David Pollard:

- *Corporate Insolvency: Employment and Pension Rights*
- *Freshfields on Corporate Pensions Law 2013* (co-editor)
- *Freshfields on Corporate Pensions Law 2012* (co-editor)
- *Guide to the Pensions Act 1995* (co-editor)

David Pollard is a solicitor and a partner in the city firm, Freshfields Bruckhaus Deringer LLP, based in London. He has advised on pensions law for over 25 years.

David is a leading practitioner in pensions law, having been chairman of the Association of Pension Lawyers (APL) from 2001 to 2003.

He is the author of the leading book *Corporate Insolvency: Employment and Pension Rights* 5th edn (2013), and the co-editor of the books *Guide to the Pensions Act 1995* and *Freshfields on Corporate Pensions Law 2013*. He has contributed chapters to looseleaf books on Employment law, Insolvency law, and Pensions law.

He is also the co-editor of the journal *Trust Law International*.

In 1998, David was awarded the Wallace Medal by the Association of Pension Lawyers (APL) for excellence in communicating pensions issues. David has also been a vice-chair of the Industrial Law Society (ILS).

David graduated from St John's College, Cambridge with a BA in Maths and Law. He has been a solicitor since 1980 and a partner with Freshfields since 1990. He worked in the Freshfields office in Singapore from 1984 to 1987.

CONTENTS

TABLE OF CASES

TABLE OF LEGISLATION

STATUTORY INSTRUMENTS

LIST OF ABBREVIATIONS

Legislation

PA	Pensions Act
PSA	Pension Schemes Act
SI	Statutory Instrument
SIS Act	Superannuation Industry (Supervision) Act 1993 (Aus, Cth)
SSPA	Social Security Pensions Act
UCTA	Unfair Contract Terms Act

Courts/Tribunals

CA	Court of Appeal
CJEU	Court of Justice of the European Union (including the ECJ)
DC	Divisional Court
DP	Determinations Panel (of the Pensions Regulator)
EAT	Employment Appeal Tribunal
ECJ	European Court of Justice, now part of the Court of Justice of the European Union
ET	Employment Tribunal
HL	House of Lords (replaced as a judicial body by the Supreme Court from October 2009)
PC	Privy Council
SC	Supreme Court
UT	Upper Tribunal

Judges

C	Chancellor (replaced the Vice-Chancellor from October 2005)
CJ	Chief Justice (High Court)
J	Justice (High Court)
JSC	Justice of the Supreme Court
LJ	Lord Justice (Court of Appeal)
MR	Master of the Rolls
P	President
PO	Pensions Ombudsman
V-C	Vice-Chancellor (replaced by the Chancellor from October 2005)

Other Bodies

APL	Association of Pension Lawyers
DSS	Department of Social Security (became the DWP in June 2001)
DTI	Department of Trade and Industry (became BERR in June 2007)
DWP	Department for Work and Pensions
FMLC	Financial Markets Law Committee
HMRC	Her Majesty's Revenue and Customs
Opra	Occupational Pensions Regulatory Authority (replaced by the Pensions Regulator in April 2005)

| PPF | Pension Protection Fund |
| TPR | the Pensions Regulator |

Journals

ABR	Australian Bar Review
ASLB	Australian Superannuation Law Bulletin
CLJ	Cambridge Law Journal
Conv	Conveyancer and Property Lawyer
J Eq	Journal of Equity
LQR	Law Quarterly Review
MLR	Modern Law Review
PCB	Private Client Business
TLI	Trust Law International

Case References

AC	Appeal Cases
ACLC	Australian Company Law Cases
ACLR	Australian Company Law Reports
All ER	All England Law Reports
ALR	Australian Law Reports
BCC	British Company Cases
BCLC	Butterworths Company Law Cases
CCPB	Canadian Cases on Pensions and Benefits
Ch	Chancery
CLR	Commonwealth Law Reports (Australian)
CSOH	Court of Session (Outer House)
DLR	Dominion Law Reports (Canadian)
ECR	European Court Reports
Eq	Equity
EWCA	England and Wales, Court of Appeal
EWHC	England and Wales, High Court
FCA	Federal Court of Australia
HCA	High Court of Australia
ICR	Industrial Case Reports
IR	Irish Reports
IRLR	Industrial Relations Law Reports
ITELR	International Trust and Estates Law Reports
JLR	Jersey Law Reports
KB	King's Bench
NSWLR	New South Wales Law Reports
NZLR	New Zealand Law Reports
NZSC	New Zealand Superannuation Cases
OPLR	Occupational Pensions Law Reports
P	Probate
P&CR	Property and Compensation Reports
PBLR	Reports on the Perspective online service
PLR	Pensions Law Reports
QB	Queen's Bench

SC	Scottish Cases
SCR	Supreme Court Reports (Canada)
SLR	Singapore Law Reports
SLT	Scots Law Times
TLR	Times Law Reports
UKHL	United Kingdom, House of Lords
UKPC	Privy Council
UKSC	United Kingdom, Supreme Court
VR	Victorian Reports (Australian)
WLR	Weekly Law Reports
WN	Weekly Notes
WTLR	Wills and Trusts Law Reports

See generally the index 'Cardiff Index to Legal Abbreviations' (maintained by Cardiff University) at <http://www.legalabbrevs.cardiff.ac.uk>.

1

WHAT IS AN OCCUPATIONAL
PENSION SCHEME?

Structure

This book looks at various aspects of the law governing private sector occupational pension schemes in the UK. **1.1**

This Chapter looks at the structure of such schemes: **1.2**

(a) the general structure of occupational pension schemes;
(b) the statutory definitions, both before and after 2005;
(c) an outline of the benefit, legislation and tax structures

Introduction

Broadly, the major occupational pension schemes, in the private sector, are: **1.3**

(a) established as a trust by an employer (or group of employers);

1

(b) envisage benefits being provided out of the trust to employees and former employees of the employer (and their spouses, civil partners, and dependants);

(c) registered with the tax authorities, Her Majesty's Revenue and Customs (HMRC) under the Finance Act 2004.

1.4 Given that the bulk of the membership (and assets) in the UK of occupational pension schemes are in such arrangements, this book focuses on them (unless otherwise stated). Other types of employer pension provision are possible, including:

(a) unregistered schemes (ie without tax registration)—examples are top-up promises, not restricted by tax limitations;

(b) public sector arrangements—usually established under statute and may be unfunded (eg the state pension or the civil service pension schemes) or funded (eg the Local Government Pension Scheme).

The Structure of Pension Schemes

1.5 It is important to note that generally UK occupational pension schemes are established so that the primary obligation to provide the relevant retirement benefits (pension/lump sum) rests with the trustees and not with the employer.

1.6 The structure could, fairly easily, have been framed instead so that the trust assets were a security device. The primary obligation to pay the pensions could have rested with the employer, with the trust merely providing a funded form of security to ensure that obligation was ultimately met.

1.7 This alternative structure can be seen in:

(a) the German pension system (where pensions payable by employers are generally simple debt obligations, although with security in the form of compulsory insurance); and

(b) in some UK state pensions (eg the Civil Service Pension Scheme, the Teachers Pension Scheme, the Fire Services Pension Scheme etc) where there are no underlying assets and the pension remains an unsecured obligation of the relevant state body.

1.8 Clearly then an occupational pension scheme will have a trust obligation to pay benefits at a relevant level to members of the pension scheme (employees and ex employees) and (depending on the terms of the scheme) to their spouses and dependants.

1.9 These obligations are generally payable at some time in the future. The actual amount that will be needed to meet the obligation is not known at today's date (at least in the case of defined benefits as opposed to defined contribution benefits).

1.10 It is clear that at any one time the level of assets held within the pension scheme (shares and land etc) may, on an actuarial estimate, be considered to be more (or less) than the underlying anticipated future liability. This gives rise to a potential surplus or deficit in the fund.

Tripartite Structure

A good way of looking at a typical occupational pension scheme structure is to view it as a **1.11** tripartite relationship between the employer, the trustee, and the member[1]:

This three way relationship involves: **1.12**

(a) a trust instrument (usually a deed) establishing a trust (and generally dealing with the relationship between the employer and the trustees). It will also specify the benefit structure, perhaps in a separate set of rules (usually attached to the trust deed[2]);

(b) a contractual employment relationship between the employer and the member; and

(c) a classic trust/beneficiary relationship between the trustees and the member, also governed by the trust deed.

Figure 1.1 below shows this.

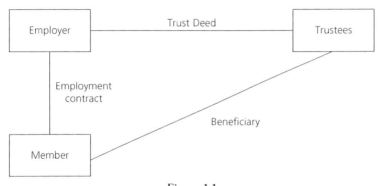

Figure 1.1

Even this tripartite relationship has its areas of difficulty: **1.13**

(a) Is the relationship between the trustees and the employer governed by contract?

(b) Do variations to the trust deed or benefits amount to a variation of the employment contract requiring the agreement of the affected members?

(c) If the employer and a member agree a change in benefits, does this bind or apply to the trustees? A point considered by Neuberger J in *South West Trains v Wightman*.[3]

(d) What is the nature of the contractual implied duty of mutual trust and confidence between an employer and employee?[4]

   (i) Is this duty enforceable against the employer by the trustees as well as by members?

   (ii) Is the implied duty of mutual trust and confidence enforceable after the employment relationship ends?

(e) Is there a contract between the member and the trustees?

---

[1] See eg Wood J in the EAT in *Walden Engineering Co v Warrener* [1992] OPLR 1, [1993] IRLR 420 and Sir Robert Walker 'Some Trust Principles in the Pensions Context' in AJ Oakley (ed), *Trends in Contemporary Trust Law* (Clarendon Press, 1996) 124.

[2] References in this book to the trust deed or the rules are to this trust instrument.

[3] [1997] OPLR 249. See Ch 15 (Contract overriding trust).

[4] See Ch 13 (Employers' powers: the implied duty of trust and confidence).

1.14 However, practitioners will realize that the tripartite structure above is often rather simplistic. Additional factors include:

(a) the inclusion of a separate principal company[5] in relation to centralized (or group) schemes;

(b) the fact that in many cases the trustee is a company;[6]

(c) does it make a difference that some of the members will no longer be current employees of any relevant employer?[7] Do the same legal relationships arise where members are pensioners and deferred members?

The structure now starts to look more complicated – a more complicated diagram shows this in figure 1.2 below.

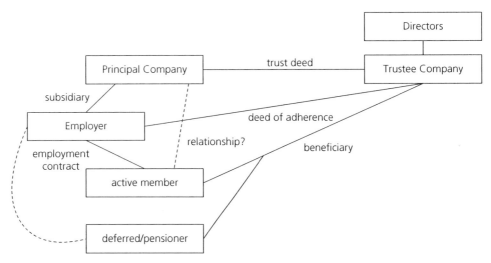

Figure 1.2

1.15 This adds its own potential issues:

(a) Does the principal company owe any duties to the members?

(b) Is the implied duty of mutual trust and confidence enforceable by members against only their employer? Or is it also enforceable against a principal company? Is this affected by the lack of an employment relationship?

(c) What duties (if any) does the principal company owe to the participating employers?

(d) If the principal company does not actually employ anyone, is it still an 'employer' for the purposes of the pensions legislation?[8]

1.16 The issue goes further—the structure needs to add in other parties, such as:

(a) advisers (lawyers, actuaries, auditors, administrators, fund managers, custodians, etc);

(b) directors of companies, insolvency practitioners, etc

---

[5] Effectively the scheme sponsor (and usually the company that established the scheme). The title will vary from scheme to scheme. The term 'principal employer' is common.

[6] See Ch 4 (Corporate trustees) and Ch 5 (Liabilities of directors of corporate trustees).

[7] See eg the discussion in *Merchant Navy Ratings Pension Fund Trustees Ltd v Chambers* [2001] All ER (D) 84 (Feb), [2001] OPLR 321, [2001] PLR 37 (Blackburne J).

[8] The issue of identifying a 'statutory' employer (ie an entity that counts as an employer for the purposes of the pensions legislation) is a difficult one. For three (contrasting) first instance decisions, see *Hearn v Dobson* [2008]

The chart becomes even more complicated – the chart in figure 1.3 demonstrates this.

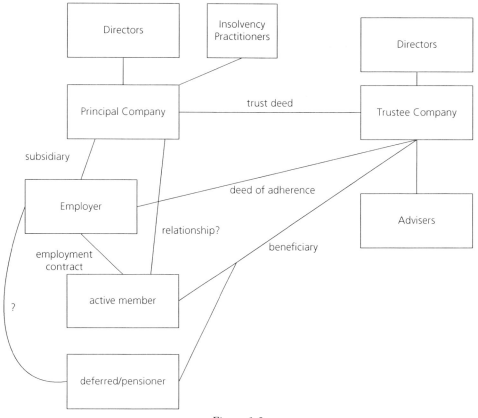

Figure 1.3

And even more—what of the position of secondary beneficiaries, that is spouses or dependants who may get benefits on the member's death?[9] **1.17**

Statutory Definition of OPS

The term 'occupational pension scheme' is used throughout the pensions legislation (in particular in the Pension Schemes Act 1993 and in the Pensions Acts 1995 and 2004). The definition in section 1 of the Pension Schemes Act 1993 applies in both the Pensions Acts 1995[10] and 2004.[11] The definition in the tax legislation differs.[12] **1.18**

EWHC 160 (Ch) (Morgan J); *Cemex UK Marine Ltd v MNOPF Trustees Ltd* [2009] EWHC 3258 (Ch) (Peter Smith J); and *PNPF Trust Co Ltd v Taylor* [2010] EWHC 1573 (Ch) (Warren J). These are discussed in *Freshfields on Corporate Pensions Law 2013* (ed D Pollard and C Magoffin) (Bloomsbury Professional, 2013) Ch 2.

[9] See Ch 8 (Pension trusts: the position of spouses and dependants).
[10] See Pensions Act 1995, s 125(5).
[11] See Pensions Act 2004, s 318(1).
[12] See Finance Act 2004, s 150 for a definition of both 'pension scheme' and 'occupational pension scheme'.

Pensions legislation: definition before 2005

1.19 Before September 2005, the term was defined in section 1 of the Pension Schemes Act 1993[13] as follows:

> 'occupational pension scheme' means any scheme or arrangement which is comprised in one or more instruments or agreements and which has, or is capable of having, effect in relation to one or more descriptions or categories of employment so as to provide benefits, in the form of pensions or otherwise, payable on termination of service, or on death or retirement, to or in respect of earners with qualifying service in an employment of any such description or category.

1.20 This definition is quite wide: it covered not only traditional funded retirement schemes, but also life assurance and small self-administered schemes. It was not limited to schemes with revenue approval or tax registration.

1.21 The Court of Appeal discussed the definition in *Parlett v Guppys (Bridport) Ltd*[14] and in *Westminster City Council v Haywood (No 1)*.

1.22 In 1997 in *Westminster City Council v Haywood*[15] Millett LJ (as he then was) observed that the definition of occupational pension scheme is a very wide definition. However, Millett LJ in fact refused to give the section 1 definition the wide application it had been given by Robert Walker J at first instance. He held that, despite the width of the words 'scheme' and 'arrangement' in section 1, the council's severance and compensation scheme and its super-annuation scheme could not together be taken as one 'occupational pension scheme' but rather were two schemes for the purposes of section 1.

1.23 In 1999 in *City & County of Swansea v Johnson*,[16] Hart J upheld a decision of the Pensions Ombudsman that an industrial injury scheme was an occupational pension scheme. Hart J held that a local authority regulation providing unquantified injury benefits regardless of length of service was nonetheless an occupational pension scheme. The key to the decision was Hart J's view that 'qualifying service' as used in the definition of occupational pension scheme meant no more than 'such service as qualifies'. This was followed by the Court of Appeal in *Parlett*.

1.24 The *City of Swansea* case opened up the possibility that permanent health insurance policies (which normally pay out benefits without regard to length of service) constitute occupational pension schemes. The determination of this is likely to depend on the terms of the scheme, in particular whether the employee received the benefit after termination of employment. If so, it would fall within the definition of an occupational pension scheme. If the employee technically remains in service while claiming the benefit, it would likely not constitute an occupational pension scheme. However, the changed definition from 2005 (see 1.28 below) now does not refer to 'qualifying service', but instead to reaching a particular age, retiring, or leaving service.

1.25 In *Parlett v Guppys (Bridport) Ltd*,[17] the Court of Appeal referred to both *Westminster* and *City of Swansea* and held that a resolution passed at the annual general meeting of a company providing for payment of a pension to the former managing director qualified as being an occupational pension scheme.

---

[13] Formerly the Social Security Act 1973, s 51(3)(a) and the Social Security Pensions Act 1975, s 66(1).
[14] [1999] OPLR 309, CA.
[15] [1998] Ch 377, [1997] OPLR 61, CA at 66C.
[16] [1999] Ch 189 (Hart J).
[17] [1999] OPLR 309, CA.

In *Bus Employees Pension Trustees Ltd v Harrod*,[18] Scott V-C (as he then was) held that a trust, **1.26** the National Bus Pension Fund, which had wound-up had ceased to be an occupational pension scheme within the statutory definition in section 1. This was on the basis that although the trustee had a claim for the return of funds paid to the Secretary of State for Transport, this was not enough to constitute the scheme as an occupational pension scheme. Scott V-C held:

> This is not a case, in my opinion, of an uncompleted winding up. It is a case of a believed complete winding up. It may be that there is no asset of any sort comprised in the fund. The cause of action sued on in the breach of trust action is defended and may yet prove to be ephemeral. In my judgment, in a case such as this where the winding up has been apparently completed and the members apparently paid off and all that is left is a contested cause of action for breach of trust, there is, for the time being at least, nothing that 'is capable of having effect so as to provide benefits in the form of pensions' etc. In the present state of affairs, neither fund, in my view, comes within the section 1 definition. It may do, if and when money is received by the trustee from the Secretary of State; but it does not, in my opinion, come within the definition now.

In 2000 in *Creak v Lincoln National*,[19] the Pensions Ombudsman looked at the definition of **1.27** an occupational pension scheme in section 1 and held that it did not cover a long-term disability plan where the benefits would cease no later than the member's normal retirement date.

Pensions legislation: definition after 21 September 2005

With effect on and from 22 September 2005 (the date the EU IORP Directive came into **1.28** force), the definition of occupational pension scheme in section 1 of the Pension Schemes Act 1993 was amended by section 239 of the Pensions Act 2004. Following further amendment in 2007, it now reads:

(1) 'occupational pension scheme' means a pension scheme—
  (a) that—
    (i) for the purpose of providing benefits to, or in respect of, people with service in employments of a description, or
    (ii) for that purpose and also for the purpose of providing benefits to, or in respect of, other people, is established by, or by persons who include, a person to whom subsection (2) applies when the scheme is established or (as the case may be) to whom that subsection would have applied when the scheme was established had that subsection then been in force, and
  (b) that has its main administration in the United Kingdom or outside the EEA States,[20] or a pension scheme that is prescribed or is of a prescribed description;
  . . .
(4) In the definition in subsection (1) of 'occupational pension scheme', the reference to a description includes a description framed by reference to an employment being of any of two or more kinds.
(5) In subsection (1) 'pension scheme' (except in the phrases 'occupational pension scheme', 'personal pension scheme' and 'public service pension scheme') means a scheme or other arrangements, comprised in one or more instruments or agreements, having or capable of having effect so as to provide benefits to or in respect of people—
  (a) on retirement,
  (b) on having reached a particular age, or
  (c) on termination of service in an employment.

---

[18] [2000] Ch 258, [1999] 2 All ER 993 (Scott V-C) at 271.
[19] (2000) 29 June, J00394 (Farrand PO).
[20] The words 'EEA states' were substituted for the words 'member States' from 26 November 2007: Occupational Pension Schemes (EEA States) Regulations 2007 (SI 2007/3014), reg 2, Sch, para 1(a).

1.29   The Interpretation Act 1978[21] includes definitions of 'EEA States' and the 'EEA Agreement':

'EEA agreement' means the agreement[22] on the European Economic Area signed at Oporto on 2nd May 1992, together with the Protocol adjusting that Agreement signed at Brussels on 17th March 1993, as modified or supplemented from time to time.

'EEA state', in relation to any time, means—

(a)   a state which at that time is a member State; or
(b)   any other state which at that time is a party to the EEA agreement.

1.30   The definition in section 1 of the Pension Schemes Act 1993 (as substituted by the Pensions Act 2004) is very wide and covers both funded and unfunded schemes and tax registered or unregistered schemes (Revenue approved and unapproved schemes before 6 April 2006 and the changes under the Finance Act 2004).

It includes an element of 'purpose'—the extent of this was discussed by Morgan J in *Dalriada Trustees Ltd v Nidd Vale Trustees Ltd* [2013] EWHC 3181 (Ch) (decided in October 2013, too late to be considered in this book). The issue was whether some types of scheme are not occupational pension schemes (because of the purpose for which they were set up) and so potentially not within the powers of the Pensions Regulator.

The definition in PSA 1993 is widened by regulations. The Pension Schemes (Categories) Regulations 2005[23] provide (in reg 2) for three descriptions of pension scheme to be occupational pension schemes. These are:

(a)   schemes established by a person other than an employer of persons benefiting from the scheme, but in respect of whom such employers contribute to the scheme;
(b)   pension schemes established under the North/South Co-operation (Implementation Bodies) (Northern Ireland) Order 1999[24] (which might not otherwise be occupational pension schemes because they do not have their main administration in the United Kingdom); and
(c)   schemes fulfilling the criteria set out in the definition of 'public service pension scheme' in section 1(1) of the Pension Schemes Act 1993 (except the requirement to be an occupational pension scheme).

Non-pension arrangements covered?

1.31   It may be that the definition could also cover various other arrangements set up by employers to benefit employees and not normally considered to be pension schemes. Examples are:

(a)   redundancy plans—these usually apply on a dismissal. This may not count as 'retirement', but will count as 'termination of service';
(b)   profit-sharing schemes, savings plans and medical plans—these are more likely to apply during service rather than on retirement or termination;
(c)   an industrial injury plan or post-retirement medical plan—these look likely to qualify (eg see *City of Swansea*,[25] on the old definition).

---

[21]   Schedule 1, as amended by the Legislative and Regulatory Reform Act 2006, s 26(1).
[22]   For an updated text of the EEA Agreement, see <http://www.efta.int/legal-texts/eea.aspx>.
[23]   SI 2005/2401.
[24]   SI 1999/859.
[25]   [1999] Ch 189 (Hart J).

Thus Robert Walker J at first instance in *Westminster City Council v Haywood* [26] considered **1.32** that a severance and compensation scheme could constitute an occupational pension scheme (for the purposes of the jurisdiction of the Pensions Ombudsman):

> There are to my mind a number of indications that Westminster's severance and compensation scheme, even though funded in a different way, could and should be regarded as part of the same scheme as the pension scheme (in the stricter sense). The definition in s1 of the 1993 Act recognises that a scheme may be comprised in more than one instrument. It also contemplates that a scheme will or may provide 'benefits, in the form of pensions or otherwise, payable on termination of service, or on death or retirement'. This treatment of benefits payable on 'termination of service' as potentially different from those payable on 'retirement' suggests that payments of compensation for loss of office are seen as properly within the scope of an occupational pension scheme. The same thought seems to be the explanation of the otherwise puzzling reg 7(2), [27] inserted by amendment in 1993, of the Transfer of Undertakings (Protection of Employment) Regulations 1981, SI 1981/1794.

On appeal, [28] Millett LJ reversed the actual decision of Robert Walker J on the basis that the sev- **1.33** erance scheme was a separate scheme from the main pension scheme, but that the employee could not bring a complaint to the Pensions Ombudsman about the severance scheme because he was not in 'pensionable service'. Millett LJ commented:

> the relationship between the wide definition of 'occupational pensions scheme' and the narrower jurisdiction conferred on the Pensions Ombudsman by reference to an 'authorised complainant' (being a person entitled to 'long service benefits') was not fully explored before us; but it is strongly arguable that the jurisdiction of the Pensions Ombudsman is limited to the investigation and determination of complaints by persons entitled to long service benefits as such, ie in relation to their long service benefits.

In practice many (but not all) of the requirements in the pensions legislation only apply **1.34** to an occupational pension scheme which has tax registration. Other non-tax registered schemes [29] are not caught. But exceptions to this (where non tax-registered schemes are caught) include:

(a) preservation and revaluation (Pension Schemes Act 1993);
(b) the prohibition on forfeiture etc (Pensions Act 1995, section 91); and
(c) the jurisdiction of the Pensions Ombudsman to hear complaints (Pension Schemes Act 1993); and
(d) the jurisdiction of the Pensions Regulator to monitor trustees (Pensions Act 2004).

This may be why the issue has not arisen in many cases to date.

Changes in the 2005 definition

The post-2005 definition is in some respects wider than the previous definition of occupa- **1.35** tional pension scheme in the Pension Schemes Act 1993. The requirement for benefits to be payable by reference to 'qualifying service' has gone.

---

[26] [1996] 2 All ER 467 (Robert Walker J) at 477.
[27] Now reg 10(2) of TUPE 2006.
[28] *Westminster City Council v Haywood* [1998] Ch 377, [1997] 2 All ER 84, CA at 94.
[29] Particularly those with less than 100 members (the limit in the EU IORP Directive).

1.36 Instead the scheme must provide benefits 'on retirement,[30] on having reached a particular age, or on termination of service in an employment'. A scheme will be an occupational scheme if it is established for the purpose of providing benefits to or in respect of people in employments in a description (or for such persons and others). This seems to allow a scheme including self-employed people to be an occupational pension scheme.[31]

1.37 Conversely the definition is narrower in other respects. The post-2005 requirement is that the scheme must have its 'main administration' in the United Kingdom or outside the member states. The intention here is that pension schemes that have their main administration in another EU or EEA member state are not regulated by the UK legislation (instead they will be regulated primarily by the authorities in the relevant member state).

1.38 The term 'main administration' is not defined in the 1993 Act,[32] but is taken from the underlying EU IORP Directive[33] (where it is similarly undefined, but used alongside 'registered office'—not a concept applicable to trusts).

1.39 In a UK context it seems most likely to apply to the place that the trustees meet and carry out their functions,[34] rather than where the underlying scheme administration (eg processing pensions, making payments etc) is carried out. The Pensions Regulator guidance on Cross Border schemes[35] states: 'If a scheme has trustees in the UK and is set up under UK law, it can be taken to have its main administration in the UK.'

1.40 One side-effect of the 2005 change to the definition is that occupational pension schemes that have their main administration outside the UK but in another EU or EEA member state will not be occupational pension schemes and so not within various provisions of the UK legislation. In many cases this exclusion seems illogical.[36] Conversely, occupational

---

[30] The term 'retirement' is not defined further. It can cause difficulties—see eg various cases on the meaning of this term when used in scheme rules: *Hoover Ltd v Hetherington* [2002] EWHC 1052 (Ch), [2002] OPLR 267 (Pumfrey J); *AGCO Ltd v Massey Ferguson Works Pension Trust Ltd* [2003] EWCA Civ 1044, [2004] ICR 15, [2003] OPLR 199, CA; and *Venables v Hornby* [2003] UKHL 65, [2004] 1 All ER 627, HL. Discussed by Sarah Asplin QC and Christopher Nugee QC, 'Retires, retiring, retired' (APL seminar, April 2004). Most recently see *Re Sea Containers Services Ltd* [2012] EWHC 2547 (Ch); [2012] PLR 569 (Hildyard J).

[31] Before 6 April 2006, participation of a self-employed person was not allowed by the Inland Revenue if tax approval was to be obtained for the scheme. But the tax position changed in April 2006 when the pensions tax simplification provisions in the Finance Act 2004 came into force.

[32] The same term is used in ss 252 to 255 and 293 and 294 of the Pensions Act 2004 (provisions also reflecting the EU IORP).

[33] Directive 2003/41/EC of the European Parliament and of the Council of 3 June 2003 on the activities and supervision of institutions for occupational retirement provision.

[34] This is similar to the view taken by HMRC when looking at the tax status of overseas schemes (where s 150(7) of the Finance Act 2004 refers to where a scheme is 'established'). HMRC's manual states: 'Normally, a scheme will be treated as established in the country where its registered office and main administration is, or, if there is no registered office, where its main administration is. The scheme's location of main administration is where the scheme's decisions are made. In the case of a trust-based scheme that would normally be determined by reference to where the scheme trustees are resident' (RPSM14101030).

[35] Under ss 287 to 295 of the Pensions Act 2004, and the Occupational Pension Schemes (Cross-border Activities) Regulations 2005 (SI 2005/3381).

[36] For example reg 10 of the Transfer of Undertakings (Protection of Employment) Regulations 2006 (SI 2006/246) exempts an OPS (using the 1993 Act definition) from the automatic transfer principle. The definition used for the purposes of the Financial Services legislation expressly amends the 1993 Act definition of OPS to exclude para (b)—the member state wording (so that it covers an OPS wherever it has its main administration)— see the definition in reg 3(1) of the Financial Services and Markets Act 2000 (Regulated Activities) Order 2001 (SI 2001/544, as amended by SI 2006/1969). Recent amending regulations have amended a specific piece of pensions legislation to allow transfers to a scheme established in a member state—see the Occupational and Stakeholder Pension Schemes (Miscellaneous Amendments) Regulations 2013 (SI 2013/459).

pension schemes with main administration outside the EU and EEA will still be within the definition.

The definition is wide enough that an occupational pension scheme can cover: 1.41

(a) an arrangement for a single person; or
(b) an informal oral promise.[37]

Death benefits and occupational schemes

It is common for occupational pension schemes to include provisions for benefits to be paid   1.42
following the death of the member/employee. These include payment of lump sum death
benefits and pensions to survivors (spouse or dependants of the member).

The old (pre-2005) definition in section 1 of the Pension Schemes Act 1993 included an   1.43
express reference to benefits payable on death. The new definition inserted by the Pensions
Act 2004 does not. But a scheme which provides death benefits will still be an occupational
pension scheme if it provides retirement benefits as well.

But, based on the IORP, section 255 of the Pensions Act 2004 includes a prohibition on   1.44
occupational pension schemes having any activities other than 'retirement-benefit activities',
defined broadly to mean activities relating to retirement benefits. These are defined in
section 255(5):

> 'retirement benefits' means—
> (a) benefits paid by reference to reaching, or expecting to reach, retirement, and
> (b) benefits that are supplementary to benefits within paragraph (a) and that are provided on
>   an ancillary basis—
>   (i) in the form of payments on death, disability or termination of employment, or
>   (ii) in the form of support payments or services in the case of sickness, poverty or need, or
>   death.

In February 2006, the DWP stated that it considered that this prohibition prevents occupa-   1.45
tional pension schemes from providing death benefits other than as ancillary to the provision
of retirement benefits for the particular member. If this interpretation is correct,[38] it will
mean that occupational pension schemes should cease providing benefits for members only
on death (eg life cover only members). Such benefits would need to be provided by a separate
scheme (which will not qualify as an occupational pension scheme). The Pensions Regulator
issued guidance on this in June 2006.[39]

Other statutes

In some statutes the term 'occupational pension' or 'pension scheme' is used but not   1.46
defined—see for example the provisions in the Insolvency Act 1986 relating to liabilities

---

[37] For example the determination of the Pensions Ombudsman in *Wads v Alex Kennedy Ltd* (2010) 15 April, 77420/1 (King PO).
[38] It seems rather bizarre, especially considering the comment of the then DWP minister, Baroness Hollis, in the House of Lords' debate on what became this section that 'The clause does not prevent occupational pension schemes that are subject to it undertaking any current business' (House of Lords, 14 September 2004).
[39] TPR Guidance on 'Lump-sum death benefits' (June 2006). See <http://www.thepensionsregulator.gov.uk/guidance/guidance-death-benefits.aspx>.

under adopted employment contracts[40] or relating to the definition of an associated person.[41] In practice the courts are likely to follow the definition in section 1 of the Pension Schemes Act 1993.

1.47 Most (but not all) of the Trustee Act 2000 does not apply to 'pension schemes'. These are defined (section 36) as an occupational pension scheme (within the meaning of the Pension Schemes Act 1993) established under a trust and subject to the law of England and Wales.

Summary of Retirement Benefits

1.48 The rest of this chapter goes on to give a summary of:

(a) the types of retirement benefit provision in the UK; and
(b) occupational pension schemes in more detail.

Types of retirement benefit provision

1.49 Retirement benefits in the UK are provided through a combination of state (social security) benefits and supplementary arrangements.

1.50 Supplementary arrangements are those providing benefits over and above those provided by the state. As UK social security benefits are comparatively low, supplementary provision is common.

Social security

1.51 Employers and employees are required to make contributions to the state social security system. Among the benefits this provides are two principal retirement benefits:

(a) the state basic pension, a flat-rate pension to which all individuals who have made sufficient National Insurance Contributions (NICs) are entitled; and
(b) the State Second Pension (S2P), an additional earnings-related element. This was previously the State Earnings-Related Pension Scheme (SERPS).

1.52 State pension age was 60 for women and 65 for men, but from 2010 it has become 65 for everyone except women born before 6 April 1955, for whom there is a sliding scale of state pension ages. The Pensions Act 2011 will raise the state pension age further, so that from October 2020 the state pension age will rise to 66.

1.53 Instead of simply supplementing state benefits, an occupational (ie employer-sponsored) or personal pension scheme may currently[42] also provide benefits which replace those provided by S2P. This is known as contracting out (of S2P) and was popular in the UK when generous rebates applied. Where a scheme is contracted out, employers and employees pay reduced rate NICs (see Contracting out of state benefits, below).

---

[40] See s 44 of and Sch B1, para 99 to the Insolvency Act 1986—discussed in Ch 35 (Carrying on business—adopted employment contracts) in D Pollard, *Corporate Insolvency: Employment and Pension Rights* 5th edn (Bloomsbury Professional, 2013).

[41] Section 435, Insolvency Act 1986, discussed in *Re Thirty-Eight Building Limited (No 1)* [1999] 1 BCLC 416 (Hazel Williamson QC). See Pollard (2013).

[42] The government announced in 2012 its intention to end contracting-out from a future date. The Pensions Bill 2013 had its first reading before the House of Commons on 9 May 2013.

Supplementary provision

Retirement benefits to supplement the state benefits may be provided via occupational pension schemes or personal pension plans. (Note that in the UK the words 'scheme' and 'plan' are used interchangeably.) Since October 2001, new stakeholder pension schemes (usually personal pensions) have also been available. **1.54**

DB and DC occupational pension schemes

Occupational pension schemes are retirement benefit arrangements sponsored and administered by or on behalf of an employer. There are two main types. **1.55**

(a) Defined benefit (DB): benefits are determined by reference to a pension of a target amount at normal retirement age, which is normally related to the amount of the member's annual pay and length of service with the employer. There are two common types known as 'final salary' and 'career average'.
(b) Defined contribution (DC): only the level of the contributions required from the employer/employee is specified. The benefits ultimately paid out will depend on what those contributions will buy (hence the other common name for these schemes, 'money purchase').

DB schemes are described further below. **1.56**

In a DC scheme (or section), the contributions are invested. When the member retires, the value of the accumulated fund is used to provide the member with an income for life (usually by buying an annuity from an insurance company). **1.57**

DC schemes present less risk for employers, as contributions are stable (typically, a fixed percentage of the employee's salary). As a result they have become much more popular in recent times and most new pension schemes will be DC. Many employers have closed their DB schemes to new members and now offer DC arrangements. **1.58**

Such an arrangement may be an occupational pension scheme, or could take the form of a group personal pension plan (GPP)—discussed below. **1.59**

It is possible to have a hybrid occupational pension scheme, providing both salary-related and money purchase benefits. There are various types of hybrid scheme: some offer different types of benefit structure to different categories of employees or have a single DB or DC structure coupled with an underlying guarantee of the other type. Some even start off as DC plans, but switch to DB benefits when the employee reaches a certain age. **1.60**

Some employers offer a separate scheme (or a separate section in the main scheme) for highly remunerated employees, providing a higher level of benefits than the level received by other employees (often known as an executive scheme or section). **1.61**

The regime applying to occupational pension schemes is considered in more detail later in this chapter. **1.62**

Personal pension schemes

The alternative to an occupational pension scheme is a personal pension scheme. This is a contract between an individual and a personal pension scheme provider—typically an insurance company or bank. It is always a money purchase arrangement. **1.63**

1.64 An active member of an occupational pension scheme used (before the tax rules changed in 2006) only to be able to contribute to a personal pension scheme in very limited circumstances. Historically, personal pension plans were taken out by individuals acting alone, particularly those who were self-employed or who had opted out of their employer's occupational pension scheme. However, it is becoming more common for employers to offer group personal pensions (GPPs). Under this arrangement the employer agrees to pay contributions to a personal pension scheme if it is taken out with a particular provider which offers special terms to the employees of that employer. The plan remains personal to the individual.

Stakeholder schemes

1.65 As a result of UK government concerns that many workers in the UK did not have any supplementary pension provision, a new type of scheme was introduced in 2001, aimed especially at lower paid employees and those who change employers frequently.

1.66 A stakeholder scheme is a type of DC pension arrangement similar to a personal pension. It is usually administered by a third party such as an insurance company, and its administration charges are capped by law at 1 per cent of the fund value per annum.

1.67 Before October 2012, each employer in the UK with five or more qualifying employees needed to provide access to a stakeholder scheme for its employees. However, the employer does not have to contribute to the stakeholder scheme. An employer may be exempt even from these requirements if it already provides an occupational scheme or GPP which satisfies certain criteria (eg it offers membership to any employee over age 18 with at least three months' service who has earnings above a certain level and, in the case of a GPP, the employer contributes at least 3 per cent of pay).

1.68 Employees do not have to join the stakeholder scheme nominated by their employer, but are free to choose any stakeholder scheme available on the market.

1.69 The stakeholder pension regime will terminate as auto-enrolment obligations (see below) are bought in.

Auto-enrolment

1.70 Phased in from 2012, there is to be a general requirement for all employers to auto-enrol employees in a qualifying pension arrangement (Pensions Act 2008). Employees and the state (by tax relief) will also contribute. Employees will be able to opt out of this requirement. A qualifying pension arrangement can be either an occupational pension scheme or a personal pension.[43]

Occupational pension schemes: legislation

1.71 The principal statutes governing occupational pension schemes are the Pension Schemes Act 1993, the Pensions Act 1995, and the Pensions Act 2004. There is also a wealth of regulations. As private sector occupational pension schemes are normally set up under trust, trust law is also relevant.

1.72 Much (but not all) of the legislation only applies to private sector schemes if they are (or have been) tax registered.

---

[43] See *Freshfields on Corporate Pensions Law 2013* (ed Pollard and Magoffin, 2013).

Tax: registered schemes

Favourable tax treatment is available for occupational pension schemes if they are registered with (before 5 April 2006, approved by) the UK tax authority, Her Majesty's Revenue and Customs (HMRC), previously called the Inland Revenue. To qualify, the scheme must comply with requirements which are set out in the Finance Act 2004 and monitored by HMRC. **1.73**

With a registered occupational pension scheme an employer can claim relief against corporation tax for its contributions and employees are not (subject to not exceeding the annual allowance) taxed on those contributions. **1.74**

Members (and, following the member's death, spouses etc) pay income tax on their pension when they receive it (but lump sums are tax-free up to certain limits). **1.75**

The new pensions tax regime came into force on 6 April 2006, under the Finance Act 2004. The key elements of this are: **1.76**

(a) There is a single lifetime allowance on tax-advantaged pension saving; for the tax year 2010/11 this was £1.8 million (the lifetime allowance) but it reduced to £1.5 million for tax year 2012/13. The government announced in December 2012 that it will seek a further reduction to £1.25m for 2014/15.
(b) If contributions exceed the lifetime allowance, tax is charged on the excess at 25 per cent (55 per cent if the excess benefits are paid as a lump sum).
(c) Tax relief is given on a member's contributions in a period up to 100 per cent of UK earnings up to a limit which in 2010/11 was £255,000 (the annual allowance). This has reduced for the tax year 2011/12 to £50,000 (detailed provisions are in the Finance Act 2011). The government announced in December 2012 that it will seek a further reduction to £40,000 for 2014/15.
(d) The member is liable to pay income tax on the value of any benefit accrual in a relevant year exceeding the annual allowance (before 2011/12, this did not apply in the year that the benefits are taken in full).

Regulators

The Pensions Regulator

Occupational pension schemes are overseen by the Pensions Regulator (TPR), which was established on 6 April 2005 by the Pensions Act 2004. **1.77**

TPR enforces compliance with pensions legislation. It has powers to investigate schemes suspected of not fulfilling their legal obligations, to disqualify individuals from being trustees of pension schemes and to impose fines. **1.78**

TPR replaced the previous regulator, the Occupational Pensions Regulatory Authority (Opra). TPR's aims include protecting members' benefits and taking steps to reduce the likelihood of claims being made against the Pension Protection Fund (see below). It has much wider, more proactive powers than Opra had, including powers to impose contribution rates where these cannot be agreed between trustees and employers; to investigate schemes and to freeze schemes under investigation; to direct employers, trustees and others to take certain steps. **1.79**

1.80   In some circumstances TPR can require third parties who are 'connected or associated' with an employer in relation to an underfunded DB scheme to make contributions to it (known as TPR's 'moral hazard' powers).

1.81   There are also requirements under the Pensions Act 2004 for certain parties to make reports to TPR to help it in carrying out its functions.

Pension Protection Fund

1.82   The Pension Protection Fund (PPF) was established from 6 April 2005 to compensate members of DB pension schemes where the sponsoring employer is insolvent and leaves unfunded liabilities in a pension fund that commences winding up after 5 April 2005.

1.83   Certain existing pensions in payment will receive full compensation, but with reduced future increases, while other benefits will be subject to a compensation cap. The PPF is financed by a levy on DB schemes by reference to the number of members they have. The levy includes a flat-rate levy and a risk-based levy, which will be determined by reference to, among other things, the funding level of the scheme, the investments, and the financial strength of the employer.

Pensions Ombudsman

1.84   The Pensions Ombudsman is an independent public official who can investigate and decide complaints of maladministration against trustees or employers and disputes about the way that pension schemes are run. A complaint to the Pensions Ombudsman is normally based on written submissions rather than oral hearings.

1.85   Unlike court proceedings, a complaint to the Pensions Ombudsman does not put the member at risk of having costs awarded against him if his complaint fails.

Trusts and Trustees

1.86   An occupational pension scheme is usually set up under trust in order to qualify as a registered scheme with the tax-privileged status described above. A trust is a legal arrangement under which cash and assets are given to trustees (administrators with fiduciary duties, eg duties of good faith) to hold and manage for the benefit of third parties, known as beneficiaries (broadly, the employers, the members of the scheme and those entitled to benefits after a member's death). The assets of the trust are usually entirely separate from those of the employer, so that the trust's assets are protected from the employer's creditors.

1.87   Where a scheme or plan is established under trust, it is the trust that is responsible for providing benefits. The employer does not have direct liability for benefits, but only an obligation to fund the trust to provide the benefits. The scheme and the trust are effectively the same thing.

1.88   A pension scheme's trustees may be individuals or a company (a corporate trustee[44]). Although the trustees, or directors of the trustee company, may be employees of the sponsoring employer, the duties of the trustees are owed to the beneficiaries. The principal duty on trustees is to exercise their powers for a proper purpose, which usually means in the best interests of the beneficiaries.[45] Failure to comply with trustee duties may lead to a personal claim against the

---

[44]   See Ch 4 (Corporate trustees).
[45]   See Ch 9 (Trustee powers: proper purpose) and Ch 10 (Trustees' duties to employers).

trustee. This may force the trustees into conflict with the employer. Employee trustees have some protections against dismissal on the grounds of their trustee activities.

The administrative procedures of the trust, the duties and powers of the trustees and employers, and the benefits to be provided are set out in detail in a trust deed and rules. In addition to the duties and powers conferred by the trust deed, trustees have duties and powers under general trust law and specific pensions legislation, in particular the Pensions Act 1995 and the Pensions Act 2004, which may override the trust deed. **1.89**

By statute, certain powers and responsibilities under the pension scheme may belong exclusively to the trustees. Where the law does not specify who should have certain powers and responsibilities, the trust deed should make this clear. Some powers and responsibilities may belong exclusively to the trustees, whereas others may belong exclusively to the principal employer (see Employers below) or may need to be exercised jointly by both parties. **1.90**

Member-nominated trustees

To encourage member representation, sections 241 to 243 of the Pensions Act 2004 require most schemes to include at least one-third of the trustee board to be persons nominated or selected by the scheme members as trustees. In the case of a corporate trustee, this requirement applies instead to the directors of the trustee company. **1.91**

Employers

A scheme may be set up for the employees of a single employer or as a centralized or group scheme for the employees of more than one employer. Most registered UK occupational pension schemes have a designated principal employer. This is normally the main employer participating in the pension scheme. The principal employer usually holds key decision-making powers in connection with the scheme. **1.92**

Other employers that participate in the scheme are known as participating employers. To participate, an employer must usually be in the same corporate group as the principal employer. Participating employers may have certain powers in relation to their own employees. **1.93**

In the UK there are also industry-wide pension schemes—large occupational schemes for non-associated employers. These primarily occur in the former nationalized industries. These schemes differ in some respects from conventional occupational schemes and specific advice should be taken if dealing with such schemes. **1.94**

DB Schemes

Defined benefit (DB) schemes provide a pension based on certain fixed factors (eg a formula related to the employee's salary and period of service). Salary for pension purposes (pensionable salary) is commonly restricted to basic pay, or basic pay plus specified fluctuating amounts (eg certain bonuses). **1.95**

There are currently three main types of DB arrangement (the DWP consulted in November 2012 on more variants including 'defined ambition'). **1.96**

Final salary schemes

1.97 These provide a pension based on a stated fraction or percentage of the employee's final pensionable salary (eg 1/80th or 1/60th) for each year of pensionable service. Often the final pensionable salary will be, say, an average of pensionable pay over the last three years before leaving service. Pensionable service normally means the most recent period of service (employment) from the date of joining the pension scheme.

Career average revalued earnings schemes (CARE Schemes)

1.98 These provide a pension based on an average of the employee's pay over his working life. In the current economic climate, an increasing number of employers are considering changing to this basis for new employees.

Cash balance schemes

1.99 In these schemes the benefit is defined as a lump sum (calculated as a percentage of pay and service) which is then converted to a pension at retirement (often by purchase of an annuity from an insurance company). Contributions are typically credited to an interest-bearing account as a percentage of the employee's pay.

Membership and Benefits

1.100 Pension scheme members are usually issued with a members' booklet which summarizes the benefit provisions of the scheme. Generally, if something in the booklet conflicts with something in the trust deed and rules, it is what the trust deed and rules say that counts legally, but there are circumstances in which booklets or announcements can confer rights on, or bind, members—see Chapter 17 (Amendments).

1.101 The typical benefits payable on retirement are a pension (which is taxed) and a cash lump sum (which is tax free up to certain limits). The lump sum may be provided in addition to the pension or in exchange for part of the amount of pension ('commutation') or a combination of both—this will depend on the rules of the relevant pension scheme.

1.102 Under current law, membership of an occupational pension scheme cannot be made compulsory under the contract of employment.[46]

Retirement at normal retirement date

1.103 The scheme rules will usually specify a normal retirement date (NRD) for members.

Early retirement

1.104 Benefits may be taken before NRD where permitted by the scheme rules. However, the early retirement pension is often reduced by an actuarial factor to reflect the cost of having to pay the benefits over a longer period. The Finance Act 2004 lays down restrictions on the early payment of benefits: broadly, benefits may not be taken before age 55 except in

---

[46] Pension Schemes Act 1993, s 160. This is subject to an exception for schemes only providing death benefits for that member: reg 3 of the Pension Schemes (Voluntary Contributions Requirements and Voluntary and Compulsory Membership) Regulations 1987 (SI 1987/1108).

circumstances of serious ill-health (for some scheme members transitional provisions can mean that a reduced age can still apply). Where early retirement is due to ill-health, many schemes waive the actuarial reduction, although this can be expensive.

Late retirement

Scheme rules may allow a member to defer taking his pension beyond his NRD, though many provide that this must be not later than the day before the member's 75th birthday (the tax laws used to apply special provisions from age 75, although these have been changed by the Finance Act 2011). **1.105**

The benefits payable on late retirement will be greater than if the member had retired at NRD, either because an actuarial increase is applied to take account of late payment or because his employment after NRD continues to count for accrual of pension benefits. **1.106**

Leaving service

Under the Pension Schemes Act 1993, if an individual leaves employment after at least two years' pensionable service in an occupational pension scheme, his or her accrued benefits (the benefits built up in the scheme) are vested, meaning that the employee has an entitlement to those benefits (starting at normal pension age), even if they are not payable immediately. Some schemes allow earlier vesting.[47] **1.107**

A member with at least three months' but less than two years' pensionable service has the right to request either a transfer payment from the scheme to another registered pension scheme or a refund of the contributions he or she has paid into the scheme (but not to any contributions paid by the employer). **1.108**

A member who leaves the service of the employer and whose pension has vested may leave his or her benefits in the scheme until he or she reaches retirement age, becoming a deferred pensioner under the scheme. At NRD benefits will be based on the pensionable salary at the time of leaving pensionable service, revalued on a statutory basis. Alternatively, he or she may choose to require a transfer value to be paid (representing the value of their accrued benefits) from the previous employer's scheme to a personal pension scheme or to the new employer's scheme, provided it is a suitable pension arrangement and is willing to accept the transfer. **1.109**

Scheme amendments

UK law (Pensions Act 1995, section 67 as amended by the Pensions Act 2004) protects the accrued benefits of occupational pension scheme members. Schemes are permitted to make a rule change that could have a detrimental effect on the rights a member has acquired in the scheme, but only provided certain steps are taken and requirements are met. The two routes to amendment under section 67 (though a combination can be used) are: **1.110**

- obtaining written consent from each affected member (which has to be done in the case of certain specified amendments); or
- meeting the 'actuarial equivalence' requirements: certain conditions must be met when calculating the actuarial value of subsisting rights, and the scheme actuary must give an appropriate certificate.

---

[47] The Pensions Bill 2013 will, if enacted, provide that DC benefits have immediate vesting—ie the two-year qualifying period will not apply.

Death benefits

1.111 Typically, schemes also provide benefits on the death of a member, usually dependants' pensions, and, on death in service, a lump sum. Some or all of these benefits are often funded by relevant insurance.

1.112 Lump sum death benefits are often paid under discretionary trusts. This means that the trustees of the scheme have a discretion to decide to whom the benefits are payable and in what proportions, and as a result no tax is payable.

Funding and Contributions

Contributions

1.113 Occupational pension schemes may be contributory (meaning that the employees pay contributions as well as the employer) or non-contributory (only the employer contributes), though non-contributory schemes are rare today. The employee contribution rate, if any, will be set out in the rules of the scheme, and will usually be a fixed percentage of pensionable salary from time to time.

1.114 Usually DB schemes will be balance of cost schemes, where the employer pays the remaining contributions necessary to meet the balance of the costs of the scheme. In DC schemes, employer contributions are usually at a flat rate, but may vary, for example according to the level of employee contributions (there may be an element of employer matching of the employee's contributions) or the member's age (in which case employer contributions are said to be age-related).

Funding

1.115 The amount that an employer is required to contribute to a DB scheme is determined by a combination of the rules of the scheme and overriding statutory requirements. Scheme rules will give the trustees and/or the company the power to determine contribution rates. The amount required will vary with the scheme's funding position and the economic climate. Many UK pension funds which enjoyed funding surpluses in the 1990s and suspended employer contributions are now experiencing significant deficits.

1.116 In addition, a change in the statutory calculation basis of the liabilities of pension schemes has meant that schemes which were in surplus on the old statutory basis could now be underfunded on the new, higher, buyout basis. The buyout basis tests whether there would be sufficient assets to secure liabilities if the scheme was wound up and all benefits bought out with insurance policies.

1.117 A trustee-appointed actuary is required to assess the funding position of the scheme regularly. The actuary, in assessing the funding position, uses a variety of assumptions to value the assets and liabilities of the scheme at different points in time. The assumptions used are of two types: demographic (eg mortality rates) and economic (such as inflation, pay rises, and interest rates).

1.118 The statutory funding regime (Part 3 of the Pensions Act 2004) envisages that usually[48] funding valuations and ongoing contributions will be agreed between the trustees and

---

[48] Special rules apply for some schemes, eg where the trust deed gives the trustees the power to fix contributions unilaterally. See Sch 2 to the Occupational Pension Schemes (Scheme Funding) Regulations 2005 (SI 2005/3377).

the employers. If not agreed, the Pensions Regulator has a statutory power to specify what should apply.

The trustees are required periodically to prepare a schedule of contributions, which must be **1.119** certified by an actuary, showing separately the rates and due dates for all contributions payable by the employers and any compulsory contributions payable by members. There are strict rules on when the contributions must be paid into the scheme and penalties for failure to comply.

If there is a funding surplus (currently unlikely), a contribution holiday (suspension or reduction **1.120** of contributions) may be possible. In effect, all or part of the surplus is used to defray the employer's contributions. An excessive surplus in a scheme (calculated on a very conservative basis) used (before April 2006) to prejudice the tax treatment of the scheme unless promptly reduced, though it is fairly unusual to find such surpluses. However, repayments of surplus to the employer from registered schemes are permitted only in very restricted circumstances and are subject to high tax rates.[49]

DC schemes are not subject to these funding requirements, though a payment schedule is **1.121** required showing when contributions are due, and again, penalties apply for late payment.

Investments

A pension fund is typically invested in a mixture of investments: equities, fixed-term securities, **1.122** real estate, and cash to meet the scheme's liability profile. There is a good degree of investment freedom in the UK, though the Pensions Act 2004 has implemented the investment requirements of the EU Occupational Pension Schemes Directive (IORP) by, for example, prohibiting most trustees from borrowing money (save for temporary liquidity) and requiring trustees and fund managers to exercise their powers of investment or discretions in a manner calculated to ensure the 'security, quality, liquidity and profitability' of the portfolio.

The pension scheme's trustees are required to produce a statement of investment principles **1.123** (or SIP) setting out their investment policies and their attitude to risk, and must also appoint an investment manager to manage the investments (the employer may not dictate investment strategy). The 2001 Myners Review of Institutional Investment proposed a code of best practice for dealing with investments.

Generally speaking, tax registered pension schemes enjoy tax-free growth on all investment **1.124** returns, except for dividends on UK equities, where the fund may not reclaim corporation tax already deducted by the issuer.

Contracting out of State Benefits

Employees may opt out of S2P (the earnings-related portion of the state scheme) by joining a **1.125** pension scheme that is contracted out. The pension scheme then provides additional benefits known as contracted-out benefits in place of the state benefits.

For service before April 1997, guaranteed minimum pensions (GMPs) applied to members **1.126** of schemes contracted out on a salary-related basis. GMPs are minimum benefits to which

---

[49] See Ch 20 (Employers and surpluses).

the member is entitled from the scheme in lieu of the state pension. Legislation provides for minimum annual increases to GMPs.

1.127 Since April 1997, pension schemes contracted out on a salary-related basis must comply with a statutory reference scheme test. The benefits provided by the pension scheme must be assessed by the actuary as likely to be broadly equivalent to, or better than, a hypothetical reference scheme. These benefits are called 'Section 9(2B) benefits'. It is a more flexible test than the old GMP system.

1.128 DC schemes (including personal pensions) used to be able to contract out by providing 'protected rights': pension rights derived from minimum payments made to the member's individual account and certain other payments including age-related rebates paid by the UK government. The amount of benefit payable is not guaranteed.

1.129 It was also possible to have a contracted out mixed-benefit scheme, where one section of the scheme was contracted out on the (salary-related) reference scheme test basis and another on the (money purchase) protected rights basis.

1.130 Contracting out on a DC basis was abolished from April 2012.

1.131 On 14 January 2013, the government announced that it is proposing, as part of its move to a single-tier state pension, that contracting-out on a salary-related basis will also be abolished. This will take effect from April 2017, at the earliest. The Pensions Bill to achieve this was introduced in Parliament on 9 May 2013.

2

PENSION TRUSTS AND GENERAL TRUST LAW

Introduction

This chapter looks at the inter-relation of pension trusts with general trust law. It looks at: **2.1**

(a) why the material private sector pension schemes are established as trusts;
(b) the contrast with private family trusts;
(c) applying general trust rules and the flexibility of trust rules;
(d) whether private trust rules apply to pension schemes.

The question the courts on occasion need to address is how far the general trust law principles **2.2** (mainly framed in relation to private trusts) should be applied (if at all) in relation to pension trusts.[1]

---

[1] David Hayton, 'Pension Trusts and Traditional Trusts, Drastically Different Species of Trusts' [2005] Conv 229; Graham Moffatt, 'Pension Funds: A Fragmentation of Trust Law' (1993) 56 MLR 471; M Scott Donald, 'What Contribution Does Trust Law Make to the Regulatory Scheme Shaping Superannuation in Australia?'—a paper on the Australian Prudential Regulatory Authority (APRA) website: <http://www.apra. gov.au>; Robert Walker: 'Some Trust Principles in the Pensions Context'—chapter in AJ Oakley (ed), *Trends in Contemporary Trust Law* (Clarendon Press, 1996), also in [1996] PLR 107; Lord Millett, 'Pension Schemes and Trusts—The Tail Wagging the Dog' (2000) 14 TLI 66 (the 2000 Annual Lecture to the Association of Pension Lawyers); Margaret Stone, 'The Superannuation Trustee: Are Fiduciary Obligations and Standards Appropriate?' (2007) J Eq 167. Ralph E Scane QC, 'Occupational pension schemes: is the trust an adequate mode of provision?' in Donovan Waters (ed), *Equity Fiduciaries and Trusts, 1993* (Carswell, 1993); Alastair Hudson 'The Regulation of Trustees' in M Dixon and G Griffiths, *Contemporary Perspectives on Property, Equity and Trusts Law* (Oxford University Press, 2007); Karen Mumgaard, chapters 45 to 48 in Geraint Thomas and Alastair Hudson, *The Law of Trusts* 2nd edn (Oxford University Press, 2010); Ian Pittaway, 'Pension Funds—Is a Separate Branch of Trust Law Evolving?' (1990) 4 Trust Law & Practice 156; Lord Browne-Wilkinson, 'Equity and its Relevance to Superannuation Today' (1992) 6 TLI 119; Sir John Vinelott, 'Pensions Law and the Role of the Courts' (1994) 8 TLI 35; Scott Charaneka, 'Legal Darwinism: The Evolution of a New Trust Species' (2000) 11 Insurance Law Journal 1; Marina Milner, 'Pension Trusts: a New Trust Form' [1997] Conv 89; Eileen Gillesse, 'Pension Plans and the Law of Trusts' (1996) 75 Canadian Bar Review 221 and 'Pension Plans, Fiduciary Duties, and the Thorny Question of Disclosure' (2011) 90 Canadian Bar Review 517; and

Why a Trust?

2.3   The major private sector[2] occupational pension schemes are clearly established as trusts.

Legislation and tax

2.4   Establishment under trust has since September 2005[3] been a requirement for occupational pension schemes under the Pensions Act 2004. Section 252 requires an occupational pension scheme that has its main administration in the UK to be 'established under irrevocable trusts'[4] before the trustees or managers accept any funding payment.[5] It must also have written rules in force stipulating the benefits under the scheme, and any conditions subject to which benefits under the scheme accrue.

2.5   Before then, in order to obtain tax approval, the relevant tax legislation[6] required (before April 2006) that schemes were established under trust.

2.6   In the private sector by far the vast bulk of the assets held by occupational pension schemes is held within trusts. The trust performs three main purposes:

(a)   the assets are separated out from those of the employer. Should the employer become insolvent, the assets held within the trust should not be available for the employer's general creditors;[7]

(b)   third parties, such as a spouse or dependant, can be given directly enforceable rights in equity against the trustees. Until the Contracts (Rights of Third Parties) Act 1999, such third party rights could not be conferred in contract as a matter of English law;[8]

(c)   there is a clear payment by the employer when it makes contributions to the trust. This should enable the employer to get a deduction for tax purposes. Indeed, it is for this reason that many older occupational pension schemes include an express prohibition on payment of any sums back to the employer.[9] This may be found either within the scheme itself or as an express limitation of the amendment power. This becomes relevant as a background issue in considering the interpretation of such trust instruments.

Alternatives to a trust?

2.7   This is not to say, of course, that the trust is the only solution in this area. Clearly it would have been possible to have established a new statutory framework for pension scheme

---

M Scott Donald, 'What's in a Name? Examining the Consequences of Inter-legality in Australia's Superannuation System' (2011) 33 Sydney Law Review 296.

  [2]   Public sector pension schemes are sometimes established by legislation.

  [3]   The date that the EU pensions directive, IORP, came into force.

  [4]   The meaning of the term 'irrevocable' in this context is unclear. Given the express statutory refund provisions in ss 37 and 76 of the Pensions Act 1995, it does not preclude refunds of surplus to the employer—see Ch 20 (Employers and surpluses).

  [5]   There are exceptions in the Occupational Pension Schemes (Trust and Retirement Benefits Exemption) Regulations 2005 (SI 2005/2360). Broadly these cover (a) schemes with less than 100 members and not tax registered, and (b) those established in the public sector.

  [6]   See s 592(1) of the Income and Corporation Taxes Act 1988.

  [7]   Eg *Re Kayford Ltd* [1975] 1 All ER 604 (Megarry J) and *Heritable Reversionary Co Ltd v Millar* [1892] AC 598, HL. This is subject to the operation of the usual potential clawback provisions (eg for preferences or transactions at an undervalue under the Insolvency Act 1986).

  [8]   Although the contractual position was different under Scottish law.

  [9]   See Ch 17 (Amendment powers) and Ch 20 (Employers and surpluses).

obligations. However this would probably have ended up with much the same obligations imposed as those under a trust—namely someone holding assets under particular obligations to both the members and the employer.

This can be seen, by way of example, in the statutory regime established for local government **2.8** pension schemes. Such schemes are not established under trust, but instead the assets remain held by the relevant local authority. However, the assets can only be used for the purpose of paying superannuation benefits or the financial costs of administration of the funds.[10]

In practice it is not clear that the use of a separate statutory structure would give rise to **2.9** any different duties on the person or persons holding the assets. The courts have generally imposed fiduciary duties on such persons by whatever name they are called, whether it be trustees, company directors, or members of a local authority in relation to pension assets.[11]

One can easily see the temptation for the Revenue in fixing on an existing structure, the **2.10** trust, when looking for appropriate ways in which to limit the tax relief applicable to pension contributions.

Contrast with Private Trusts

Having decided on the use of a trust, the question then is how far the standard principles **2.11** applicable to a trust, developed in the context of private family settlements, remain applicable to a commercial trust such as a pension scheme.

Members not volunteers

In a private trust there is usually an element of gift (or 'bounty'). The settlor has provided prop- **2.12** erty to be held for beneficiaries as a gift. The courts have recognized in a series of judgments that the members of a pension scheme are not volunteers but instead have paid[12] for their interests under the scheme by contributing and by working for the employer.[13]

Clearly this must influence the attitude of the courts towards the obligations of trustees. **2.13** Presumably the fact that the spouse and dependants of the member have not themselves purchased the interest in the scheme should not affect the position. The member has in effect purchased these rights for them with his or her labour.

---

[10] See reg L1 of the Local Government Pension Scheme Regulations 1995 (SI 1995/1019). Discussed in the chapter 'Public Service Schemes' in Freshfields, *The Guide to the Pensions Act 1995* (Tolley Publishing, 1995).

[11] See eg *Martin v City of Edinburgh District Council* [1988] SLT 329, [1989] PLR 9 (CSOH, Lord Murray) and *Westminster City Council v Haywood* [1996] 2 All ER 467 (Robert Walker J).

[12] On pensions as deferred pay, see the discrimination cases, in particular *Barber v Guardian Royal Exchange* C-262/88 [1991] 1 QB 344, [1990] ECR I-1889, ECJ.

[13] See eg *Smithson v Hamilton* [2007] EWHC 2900 (Ch), [2008] 1 All ER 1216 (Sir Andrew Park); *Betafence v Veys* [2006] EWHC 999 (Ch) (Lightman J); *Sieff v Fox* [2005] 1 WLR 3811 (Lloyd LJ); *Stannard v Fisons Pension Trust Ltd* [1992] IRLR 27, CA at para 34; *Mettoy Pension Trustees Ltd v Evans* [1990] 1 WLR 1587 (Warner J) at 1618; *Imperial Group Pension Trust Ltd v Imperial Tobacco Ltd* [1991] 2 All ER 597 (Browne-Wilkinson V-C); *Mihlenstedt v Barclays Bank* [1989] IRLR 522, CA and *McDonald v Horn* [1995] 1 All ER 961, [1994] OPLR 281, CA at 290G. In Australia see *Finch v Telstra Super Pty Ltd* [2010] HCA 36, (2010) 242 CLR 254, HC Aus at para [33]; *Alcoa of Australia Retirement Plan Pty Ltd v Frost* [2012] VSCA 238; *Asea Brown Boveri* [1999] 1 VR 144 (Beach J); *Lock v Westpac Banking Corporation* [1991] PLR 167, (1991) 25 NSWLR 593 (Waddell CJ) at 601–2; and *Uncle v Parker* (1995) 55 IR 120 (Santow J) at 123. From New Zealand: *Cullen v Pension Holdings* [1992] PLR 135, (1993) 1 NZSC 40, 293 (McGechan J).

2.14 In *Finch v Telstra Super Pty Ltd*,[14] the High Court in Australia considered the position of trustees of a pension fund (called a superannuation fund in Australia). The case involved whether the trustees owed a duty to make a decision on a factual issue (in this case whether a member qualified for an incapacity benefit) with 'properly informed consideration'.

2.15 The High Court held that this duty was potentially greater than the obligation on a trustee of a private trust or (potentially) where the decision was not factual, but instead a true discretion. The High Court considered that reasons for this heightened duty included:[15]

  (a) the issue concerned a factual determination, not a true discretion in the private trust sense;[16]
  (b) the superannuation scheme was one of a larger employer;
  (c) for some people their superannuation is their greatest asset apart from their houses;
  (d) employer provided superannuation is part of the remuneration of employees. The legitimate expectations of employees are therefore high. And so is the 'general public importance of them being sound';
  (e) pensions have a public significance, shown by the tax benefits granted to relevant schemes and the mandatory requirements (in Australia) for employers to contribute; and
  (f) the relevant superannuation legislation imposes standards.

2.16 In light of this, the High Court held that superannuation trustees should not be 'largely immunised from judicial control without clear contrary language in the relevant trust instrument'. A provision in the trust deed for decisions of the trustee to be in its 'absolute and uncontrolled discretion' was not enough. The standards laid down in the leading Australian private trust case on trustee discretions, *Karger v Paul*,[17] did not apply to superannuation trusts.

Applying General Trust Rules

2.17 The strong argument is that by utilizing a trust structure, the parties to the scheme (effectively the employer in the first instance) must be taken to have wanted to be governed by established trust principles, in particular those formulated for private trusts. This has then received the sanction of Parliament. If different rules were to apply then the parties were at liberty to set them out specifically in the trust instrument.

2.18 To the extent that Parliament has intervened (eg in relation to disclosure by pension trustees to members in the 1996 Disclosure Regulations[18]), it must be taken to have legislated as far as it wanted and not to have intended that any greater obligation should apply to pension trusts over and above those that are applicable to private trusts.

2.19 The contrary argument is that trustees are essentially performing a public function. They are making decisions in relation to benefits of members. Members are entitled to expect that

---

[14] [2010] HCA 36, (2010) 242 CLR 254, HC Aus. Followed in *Alcoa of Australia Retirement Plan Pty Ltd v Frost* [2012] VSCA 238, Vic CA and *Sharp v Maritime Super Pty Ltd* [2012] NSWSC 1350 (Ward J).
[15] At paras [32] to [35].
[16] Citing *Dwyer v Calco Timbers Pty Ltd* [2008] HCA 13, (2008) 234 CLR 124, HC Aus, at 138–9.
[17] [1984] VR 161 (McGarvie J).
[18] SI 1996/1655. See Ch 18 (Disclosure of documents by trustees).

trustees are free and open about these matters. Perhaps an analogy could be drawn with the decision of public authorities both in questions of when their decisions may be reviewed and on the need for them to give reasons.[19]

The difficulty with the last argument is that essentially these rights and benefits spring out of **2.20** contractual matters. Classically it could not be said that one contracting party has a right to expect the other contracting party to reveal documents or reasons for decisions etc. Clearly, just thinking about this issue in the context of a purchaser of goods indicates how far the courts would have to move in order to find such obligations here.

Given that trusts have been part of English law for a number of centuries, it is rather **2.21** surprising to find that many of the basic issues relating to them are unsettled. Perhaps, in a pensions context, this is because pension trusts have only comparatively recently generated many reported cases.

Flexibility of Trust Law

It is clear that trust law is flexible. The same rules should not apply in all situations. **2.22**

In 1995 in *Target Holdings v Redferns*,[20] Lord Browne-Wilkinson held: **2.23**

> But in my judgment it is in any event wrong to lift wholesale the detailed rules developed in the context of traditional trusts and then seek to apply them to trusts of quite a different kind. In the modern world the trust has become a valuable device in commercial and financial dealings. The fundamental principles of equity apply as much to such trusts as they do to the traditional trusts in relation to which those principles were originally formulated. But in my judgment it is important, if the trust is not to be rendered commercially useless, to distinguish between the basic principles of trust law and those specialist rules developed in relation to traditional trusts which are applicable only to such trusts and the rationale of which has no application to trusts of quite a different kind.

Earlier in 1991, Browne-Wilkinson V-C (as he then was) had held in the pensions case, **2.24** *Imperial Group Pension Trust v Imperial Tobacco*:[21]

> There remains the submission of Mr Topham, for the employed members, which I accept. Pension scheme trusts are of quite a different nature to traditional trusts. The traditional trust is one under which the settlor, by way of bounty, transfers property to trustees to be administered for the beneficiaries as objects of his bounty. Normally, there is no legal relationship between the parties apart from the trust. The beneficiaries have given no consideration for what they receive. The settlor, as donor, can impose such limits on his bounty as he chooses, including imposing a requirement that the consent of himself or some other person shall be required to the exercise of the powers.

> As the Court of Appeal has pointed out in *Mihlenstedt v Barclays Bank International Ltd* [1989] IRLR 522 a pension scheme is quite different. Pension benefits are part of the consideration which an employee receives in return for the rendering of his services. In many cases, including the present, membership of the pension scheme is a requirement of employment.

---

[19] Eg the comment by Lloyd LJ in *Pitt v Holt* [2011] EWCA Civ 197, [2012] Ch 132, CA at para [114] that in relation to review of decisions by trustees 'Pension trusts and charities may well each be different in some respects, as may be discretionary trusts for a very large class, such as that at issue in *Re Baden's Deed Trusts*'. This potential for distinction was not discussed by Lord Walker on appeal: [2013] UKSC 26.

[20] [1996] AC 421, [1995] 3 All ER 785, HL.

[21] [1991] 1 WLR 589, [1991] 2 All ER 597 at 605.

> In contributory schemes, such as this, the employee is himself bound to pay his or her contributions. Beneficiaries of the scheme, the members, far from being volunteers have given valuable consideration. The company employer is not conferring a bounty. In my judgment, the scheme is established against the background of such employment and falls to be interpreted against that background.

2.25 So are pension trusts different from family trusts so that separate trust law rules should apply?

Pension Schemes are Different

2.26 The legislation relating to trusts generally, now includes many provisions stating that they do not apply to pension schemes—see Chapter 3 (Pension Trusts and Statute). For example, occupational pension schemes are not subject to the limits on the life of a trust under the rule against perpetuities.[22]

2.27 Arguments in favour of a differing approach for pension trusts can draw support from the general flexibility of trust law as indicated in the decision of the House of Lords in *Target Holdings v Redferns*.[23] This was not a pension case, but in the passage already quoted Lord Browne-Wilkinson was clearly indicating that the courts should be relatively flexible in construing commercial trusts. There may well be certain circumstances where the classic trust doctrines are inapplicable.

2.28 Lord Browne-Wilkinson had previously, when Vice-Chancellor, commented on the position of pension trusts in *Imperial Tobacco*[24] (in the passage already quoted).

2.29 There are other comments in the cases to the same effect.[25] However, clearly moving from established trust principles is not a step to take lightly.

Private trusts are different

2.30 Given the use of a trust structure and the lack of any real intervention by legislation, the position rests on an analysis of case law. But it is not certain that existing case law for private trusts can always be taken as a realistic guide for pension trusts.

2.31 Private family trusts operate in a separate tax environment than occupational pension schemes (at least those with tax registration). In practice, in many private trusts there are undesirable tax implications if the settlor retains an interest in the trust.

2.32 For example, many private trusts are set up with the aim of reducing inheritance tax. By placing assets in a trust, they are no longer part of the settlor's estate on his or her death. But anti-avoidance legislation aims to ensure that the settlor cannot 'have his cake and eat it'.

---

[22] Section 2(4) of the Perpetuities and Accumulations Act 2009 exempts 'relevant pension schemes' (defined in s 15 to include an occupational pension scheme under s 1 of the Pension Schemes Act 1993). Before 6 April 2010 contracted-out schemes and those with tax registration were excluded under s 163 of the Pension Schemes Act 1993 and the Personal and Occupational Pension Schemes (Perpetuities) Regulations 1990 (SI 1990/1143). These were repealed from 6 April 2010 by the 2009 Act.

[23] [1996] AC 421, HL.

[24] [1991] 2 All ER 597, [1991] 1 WLR 589 (Browne-Wilkinson V-C) at 597.

[25] Eg Vinelott J in *British Coal* [1995] 1 All ER 915 at 925, 'It is dangerous to import concepts which have been developed in the field of private trusts created by the bounty of a settlor or testator and apply them uncritically in the field of pension funds.'

Assets held within a trust will be deemed still to form part of the settlor's estate for inheritance tax purposes if there is a 'reservation of benefit' or the settlor has a general power of disposal.[26] So with this in mind, it is unusual to see a private trust have any form of retained control by the settlor, or any requirement for the settlor to commit further funds or assets.[27]

But these are precisely two of the key attributes of occupational pension schemes. And in the case of tax registered occupational pension schemes, there is no adverse tax effect for the trusts or the employers if the settlor (employer or member) retains some form of control or interest. **2.33**

The situation for private trusts sometimes leads to tricky contortions by the courts. In *Fuller v Evans*,[28] a settlor had set up a trust for his children and included a standard provision saying that he was not to derive any benefit 'directly or indirectly' from the trust. The settlor then got divorced and a term of the divorce decree was that he must pay the children's school fees. The trustees were concerned that if they used the trust funds to pay the school fees, this would have the effect of indirectly benefiting the settlor (because he would no longer have to pay them). Lightman J held that such a course of action by the trustees would *not* infringe the 'no benefit' clause. The trustees would be obliged to exercise their powers in the best interests of the beneficiaries (here the children), but provided they did so, any incidental and unintended benefit to the settlor could be ignored. **2.34**

Applying General Trust Principles

How does the background to a pension trust impact on the rights and duties of the employer and the rights and duties of the trustees? The Courts do not seem as yet to have resolved this in a very coherent way. In addition, even if classical trust principles are to be followed, on examination these are themselves less clear than may be thought. **2.35**

There are three potential categories[29] that the courts can apply to a particular trust rule: **2.36**

   (i) apply general trust law to pension schemes in the same way as to a family trust;
  (ii) do not apply the general trust law duty at all, or instead a lesser version; or
 (iii) apply a greater duty than would apply to a private trust.

For example, the issue of disclosure by trustees of 'trust documents'. The general rule in relation to a classic family trust is itself rather obscure.[30] How then is it to be applied (if at all) in relation to pensions trusts? There are perhaps three options: **2.37**

1. apply the same rule to family trusts and pension trusts, with the additional statutory disclosure obligations applying as well;

---

[26] Eg ss 102 to 102C of the Finance Act 1986.
[27] See the comments of Lord Browne-Wilkinson on this in his paper to the Australian Superannuation conference 'Equity and its Relevance to Superannuation Today' (1992) 6 TLI 121 and Neil Kandelaars, 'The Relationship Between Trustee, Member and Participating Employer of a Superannuation Fund' (1999) 13 TLI 210 at 217.
[28] [2000] 1 All ER 636 (Lightman J).
[29] See eg Richard Nobles in his review at (1991) MLR 165 of Nigel Inglis-Jones, *The Law of Occupational Pension Schemes* (Butterworths, 1989).
[30] See Ch 18 (Disclosure of information by trustees).

2. given the existence of specific statutory disclosure obligations, consider that the implied disclosure obligation applicable to family trusts has no application to pension trusts; or

3. consider that trustees have a greater disclosure obligation (eg to give reasons) in relation to pension trusts and compared with family trusts on the basis that the members have paid for their benefits by working.

2.38 It is in theory open to a judge to follow any of the three options made above.

An example—trustee disclosure obligations

2.39 The first option, treating pension trusts and family trusts the same—so that in effect both obligations apply—was followed in the UK in relation to disclosure obligations by Rattee J in *Wilson v Law Debenture*.[31]

2.40 In *Wilson v Law Debenture* it was argued that pension trustees should owe a greater disclosure obligation to pension beneficiaries than is owed by private trustees. Rattee J rejected this argument. In effect, Rattee J held that the parties had chosen to use a trust structure and this implied use of standard trust rules. If Parliament wished to impose greater disclosure obligations it could (and has) done so. It was not for the courts to extend the obligation further.[32] The parties involved in setting up the trust must be taken to have been aware of what the obligations would be (by reference to classic family trusts) and it would be unfair for the courts to extend this.[33]

2.41 Rattee J stated:[34]

> It would . . . be wrong in principle to hold that long-established principles of trust law as to the exercise by trustees of discretions conferred on them by their trust instruments, in the context of which parties to a pension scheme such as the present entered into those schemes, no longer apply to them and that the trustees are under more onerous obligations to account to their beneficiaries than they could have appreciated when appointed, on the basis of the current trust law as it has stood for so long.

2.42 Doubts however have been cast on this actual decision (that pension trustees did not need to give reasons) and it is still open whether this will actually remain true in relation to the specific issue being addressed by Rattee J.[35] There are indications in the courts that they will look for trustees to give reasons or draw inferences if they do not.[36] *Target Holdings* could perhaps be seen as supporting an approach to give rise to greater disclosure.[37]

---

[31] [1995] OPLR 103, [1995] 2 All ER 337 (Rattee J).

[32] See also Ch 3 and the similar reasons given in the employment area by the House of Lords in *Johnson v Unisys* [2001] UKHL 13, [2003] 1 AC 518, HL. A former employee claimed damages for breach of contract by reason of the manner of his dismissal. The House of Lords rejected this claim on the basis that this would circumvent the statutory unfair dismissal regime (which included limits on liability etc).

[33] See also in Australia *Caboche v Ramsay* (1993) 119 ALR 215 at 228, 233 where Gummow J commented that the ordinary law of trusts and property should apply to pension schemes.

[34] [1995] 2 All ER 337 at 348.

[35] See Sir Robert Walker, speaking, extra-judicially, in his chapter 'Trust Principles in the Pensions Context' in AJ Oakley, *Trends in Contemporary Trust Law* (Oxford University Press, 1996), also in [1996] PLR 108. However, Rattee J's decision was supported in *Thomas on Powers* (Sweet & Maxwell, 1998) 372.

[36] See eg the comments of Robert Walker J in *Scott v National Trust* [1999] 4 All ER 705 at 718c and of the Court of Appeal in *Edge v Pensions Ombudsman* [2000] Ch 602, [1999] 4 All ER 546, CA at 571.

[37] See generally Ch 18 (Disclosure obligations). Discussed by Hugh Arthur in *Pensions and Trusteeship* (Sweet & Maxwell, 1998) Ch 6 and by Sir Robert Walker, speaking extra judicially, in his paper 'Some Trust Principles in the Pensions Context' in *Trends in Contemporary Trust Law* (Oxford University Press, 1996), also in [1996] PLR 108.

The third option, namely to consider that there should be no implied trust law disclosure **2.43**
duty at all on pension trusts (on the basis that Parliament has already intervened and the
courts should not build on that) is unlikely to be followed in the UK. The statutory
disclosure obligations mainly relate to provision by trustees of benefit details (and core documents). It can stand alongside an implied disclosure obligation for other matters not covered
by the statute (eg trustee reasons, investment decisions etc).

Other examples

In 1994 in *Schmidt v Air Products of Canada*,[38] the majority of the Supreme Court in Canada **2.44**
held that normal trust principles apply to a pension plan which has been impressed with a
trust. In that case, there could be no revocation of the trust (to allow funds to flow back to the
employer) unless this had been expressly reserved in the trust instrument. Cory J held that
'when a pension fund is impressed with the trust, that trust is subject to all applicable trust
or principles'.

However, 12 years later in *Buschau v Rogers Communications Inc*,[39] the Supreme Court dis- **2.45**
tinguished *Schmidt* and held that the general trust law principle of the rule in *Saunders v
Vautier* was 'not easily incorporated into the context of employment pension plans'. This was
for various reasons (see Chapter 16), including that applying the common law in *Saunders v
Vautier* would be inconsistent with the underlying legislation—see further Chapter 3.

As already mentioned, in 2010 in *Finch v Telstra Super Pty Ltd*,[40] the High Court in Australia **2.46**
considered that trustees of a superannuation fund owed a duty to make a decision on a factual issue (in this case whether a member qualified for an incapacity benefit) with 'properly
informed consideration'. This duty was held to potentially be greater than the obligation on
a trustee of a private trust or (potentially) where the decision was not factual, but instead a
true discretion.

The High Court considered that reasons for this heightened duty included:[41] **2.47**

(a) the issue concerned a factual determination, not a true discretion in the private trust
    sense;[42]
(b) the superannuation scheme was one of a larger employer;
(c) for some people their superannuation is their greatest asset apart from their houses;
(d) employer provided superannuation is part of the remuneration of employees. The legitimate
    expectations of employees are therefore high. And so is the 'general public importance of
    them being sound';
(e) pensions have a public significance, shown by the tax benefits granted to relevant schemes
    and the mandatory requirements (in Australia) for employers to contribute; and
(f) the relevant superannuation legislation imposes standards.

In light of this, the High Court held that superannuation trustees should not be 'largely **2.48**
immunised from judicial control without clear contrary language in the relevant trust

---

[38] (1994) 115 DLR (4th) 631, Can SC.
[39] (2006) SCC 28, Can SC.
[40] [2010] HCA 36, (2010) 242 CLR 254, HC Aus. Followed in *Alcoa of Australia Retirement Plan Pty Ltd v
Frost* [2012] VSCA 238 and *Sharp v Maritime Super Pty Ltd* [2012] NSWSC 1350 (Ward J).
[41] At paras [32] to [35].
[42] Citing *Dwyer v Calco Timbers Pty Ltd* [2008] HCA 13, (2008) 234 CLR 124, HC Aus, at 138–9.

instrument'. A provision in the trust deed for decisions of the trustee to be in its 'absolute and uncontrolled discretion' was not enough. The standards laid down in the private trust case on trustee discretions, *Karger v Paul*,[43] did not apply to superannuation trusts.

Conclusion

2.49 The courts are developing the position over time. A degree of flexibility will apply. The case law will develop as it always has: incrementally. But this will only be a gradual process and often limited to those aspects where a different approach is necessary. Dealing with the rights and duties of an employer may well be one example of where this is necessary.

2.50 Some guidance can be given by the existing cases:

(a) disclosure obligations on trustees—general rules apply;

(b) trust companies can be used (and direct liability of directors to beneficiaries is limited)—same for pensions and private trusts;[44]

(c) trust deed amendments and surplus refunds—adapt to the position of pension trusts;[45]

(d) winding-up a trust—*Saunders v Vautier* does not apply;[46]

(e) employer discretions—separate *Imperial* duty;[47]

(f) appointment and removal of trustees—not a fiduciary power in pension trusts;[48]

(g) conflict of interest rules—likely to be overridden by the trust instrument or an exemption implied;[49] and

(h) level of trustee decision making and court review—unclear if different from private trusts.[50]

2.51 Broadly, a situation by situation approach emerges. It is suggested:

(a) normal trust rules will apply in most cases;[51]

(b) normal trust rules are flexible in any event and so may adapt;[52]

(c) trust rules will not apply if otherwise this would be inconsistent with the purpose of pension trusts[53] or the relevant legislation;[54] and

(d) trust deed interpretation will depend on the relevant trust deed—this is the same as for private trusts, but the background circumstances of a pension scheme (in particular the tax) are relevant.[55]

---

[43] [1984] VR 161 (McGarvie J).

[44] See Ch 5 (Liability of directors of corporate trustees).

[45] See Chs 17 (Amendment powers) and 20 (Employers and surpluses).

[46] See Ch 16 (*Saunders v Vautier* and pension trusts).

[47] See Ch 13 (Employer powers: the implied duty of trust and confidence).

[48] See Ch 12 (Employer powers to appoint and remove trustees).

[49] See Ch 6 (Conflict issues for pension trustees) and *Edge v Pensions Ombudsman*.

[50] Pension trusts were not covered one way or the other by the Supreme Court in *Pitt v HMRC* [2013] UKSC 26, SC. *Finch v Telstra* [2010] HCA 36, (2010) 242 CLR 254, HC Aus (see 2.14 above) was concerned with a factual decision, not a benefit discretion.

[51] *Wilson* [1995] OPLR 103.

[52] *Target Holdings* [1996] AC 421.

[53] Eg Employer powers—Imperial duties etc. See Ch 11.

[54] *Buschau v Rogers Communications Inc*—see Ch 3.

[55] *Finch v Telstra* [2010] HCA 36, (2010) 242 CLR 254, HC Aus and *Stevens v Bell* [2002] EWCA Civ 672, [2002] OPLR 207, CA. See Ch 17 (Amendment powers).

3

PENSION TRUSTS AND STATUTE

How are Pensions Trusts Affected by Statute?

Private sector[1] occupational pension schemes are clearly established as trusts. But they are **3.1** also increasingly governed by specific pensions legislation, in particular the Pensions Schemes Act 1993 and the Pensions Acts 1995 and 2004. The trend is for general trust legislation not to apply automatically to pension schemes (eg the Trustee Act 2000).

Clearly, the pensions legislation applies to govern the scheme and to bind the trustees. **3.2** The legislation is, in the main, made overriding (ie it applies regardless of the terms of the trust[2]).

This chapter looks at how the existence of these statutory requirements may affect how **3.3** general trust law applies to occupational pension schemes. Should the application of general trust law be modified, not just by reason of the underlying nature of pension schemes (see Chapter 2), but also by reason of the existence of a relevant statute?[3]

Exemptions from General Trust Statutes

There is not a huge amount of general legislation on trusts, but what there is has increasingly **3.4** exempted or excluded pension trusts. For example:

(a) Occupational pension schemes are not subject to the limits on the life of a trust under the rule against perpetuities. Section 2(4) of the Perpetuities and Accumulations

---

[1] Public sector pension schemes are sometimes established by legislation.

[2] The main exception is that the preservation requirements originally in the Social Security Act 1973 and now in the Pension Schemes Act 1993 are not overriding—see Warren J in *Re IBM Pension Plan* [2012] EWHC 2766 (Ch) and later *Re IBM Pension Plan (No 2)* [2012] EWHC 3540 (Ch).

[3] See Andrew Burrows, 'Common Law and Statute' (2012) 128 LQR 232; William Gummow, 'The Common Law and Statute' in *Change and Continuity: Statute, Equity and Federalism* (Clarendon Press, 1999); J Beatson,'Has the Common Law a Future?' [1997] CLJ 291 and 'The Role of Statute in the Development of

Act 2009 exempts 'relevant pension schemes' (defined in s 15 to include an occupational pension scheme under s 1 of the Pension Schemes Act 1993).[4]

(b) Much of the Trustee Act 2000 does not apply to occupational pension schemes (as defined in the 1993 Act)—see s 36.

  (i) The investment provisions in Parts 1, 2, and 3 of the 2000 Act do not apply nor does Part 4 in so far as it confers power to appoint nominees and custodians or, in relation to investment functions, an agent—ss 36(3), (5) and (8) (on the basis that occupational pension schemes are covered by their own code in the Pensions Act 1995[5]).

  (ii) Conversely, the general duty of care may apply to the trustees of occupational pension trusts in relation to matters other than investment, agency for investment purposes, and the appointment of a nominee or custodian—s 36(2) and pension trustees may delegate non-investment functions under Part 4—s 36(5).

  (iii) However, for the protection of pension scheme beneficiaries, pension trustees are expressly prohibited from using the powers in Part 4 to delegate any function to the scheme employer or to a person who is connected with, or an associate of, the scheme employer—s 36(6). In practice pension scheme trustees are unlikely to use the powers in Part 4 but instead rely on an express power in the trust deed (so that the limits in Part 4 do not apply).

3.5 The most recent legislation did not exclude pension schemes. The Trusts (Capital and Income) Act 2013 dealt with apportionment rules for trusts as between income and capital. The Act applies to pension trusts (ie they are not excluded) but it is very unlikely to impact on pension schemes (the issue of such an apportionment rarely if ever arises). The Act also only applies to new trusts and is subject to any contrary provision in the trust.

3.6 Conversely, the older trust legislation contained no exemptions for pensions trusts. For example, the Trustee Act 1925 and the Trustee Investments Act 1961 both apply to pension trusts. But in the main, they are default provisions and so the powers and obligations would only apply subject to anything to the contrary in the trust deed.[6] Most pension schemes would in many areas (eg investment powers) have extended provisions in their trust deed.

Impact of Statute on Common Law Developments

3.7 There is much specific pensions legislation. Clearly, the existence of pensions legislation impacts on the pension scheme as imposing (in the main) a core minimum of duties and obligations.

Common Law Doctrine' (2001) 117 LQR 247; Paul Finn, 'Statutes and the Common Law' (1992) 22(1) University of Western Australia Law Review 7; and P Atiyah, 'Common Law and Statute Law' (1985) 48 MLR 1. See also Reinhard Zimmermann, 'Statuta Sunt Stricte Interpretanda? Statutes and the Common Law: A Continental Perspective' [1997] CLJ 315 and GN Gunasekara, 'Judicial Reasoning by Analogy with Statutes: Now an Accepted Technique in New Zealand' (1998) 18 Statute Law Review 177.

  [4] Before 6 April 2010 contracted-out schemes and those with tax registration were excluded under s 163 of the Pension Schemes Act 1993 and the Personal and Occupational Pension Schemes (Perpetuities) Regulations 1990 (SI 1990/1143). These were repealed from 6 April 2010 by the 2009 Act.

  [5] See the explanatory notes to the 2000 Act, which comment that 'Trustees of occupational pension schemes are in a special position'.

  [6] See eg s 3(1) of the Trustee Investments Act 1961 and, in relation to the power of appointment of trustees under the 1925 Act, *LRT v Hatt* [1993] OPLR 225 (Knox J).

But this can also impact on the general common law position, for example general trust and contract law.

Employment law example

For example, in the field of employment law, there is a vast statutory structure in the UK **3.8** dealing with unlawful discrimination (sex, race, disability) and unfair dismissal and redundancy (retrenchment). Does this mean that the courts should not seek to develop the common law duties in relation to contracts etc but leave it instead to Parliament?

This approach was rejected by the House of Lords in one case, *Malik v BCCI, Mahmud v BCCI*.[7] **3.9** In this case, the House of Lords considered that it was appropriate to approve and take forward the development of the implied term of mutual trust and confidence between employers and employees.

It is noticeable that the House of Lords expressly considered that the common law should **3.10** supplement the statutory provisions (in the UK aside from the unlawful discrimination cases, generally the statutory jurisdiction of courts and tribunals to grant remedies only applies where there has actually been a dismissal, ie a termination of the employment relationship either expressly or following a breach of contract).

But there are limits as to how far the common law will be developed. In *Johnson v Unisys*,[8] the **3.11** House of Lords held that an employee could not claim a breach of the implied duty of trust and confidence to claim damages on his or her dismissal.

Such a claim would negate the careful statutory scheme for unfair dismissal established by **3.12** statute. A former employee claimed damages for breach of contract by reason of the manner of his dismissal. The House of Lords rejected this claim on the basis that this would circumvent the statutory unfair dismissal regime (which included limits on liability etc).

The limits of this 'exclusion area' are still being worked out—see *Eastwood v Magnox Electric plc*[9] **3.13** and *Edwards v Chesterfield Royal Hospital NHS Foundation Trust*.[10]

Statute influencing common law

In some cases the common law will be influenced by statute—what Professor Beatson and **3.14** Gummow J call the 'analogical force' of the statute.[11]

An example is the position taken by the courts in relation to exclusion clauses in contracts. **3.15** In *Photo Production v Securicor*,[12] Lord Wilberforce commented that the existence of statutory regulation[13] of exclusion clauses in one area (consumer contracts) was an indication by the legislature that contracts outside the scope of the legislation should be allowed to include clauses apportioning risks as the parties saw fit.

---

[7] [1998] AC 20, HL.

[8] [2001] UKHL 13, [2003] 1 AC 518, HL.

[9] [2004] UKHL 35, [2005] 1 AC 503, HL.

[10] [2011] UKSC 58, [2012] 2 AC 22, SC. See the discussion by Catherine Barnard and Louise Merrett in 'Winners and Losers: *Edwards* and the Unfair Law of Dismissal' [2013] CLJ 313.

[11] William Gummow, 'The Common Law and Statute' in *Change and Continuity: Statute, Equity and Federalism* (Clarendon Press, 1999); J Beatson 'Has the Common Law a Future?' [1997] CLJ 291 and 'The Role of Statute in the Development of Common Law Doctrine' (2001) 117 LQR 247.

[12] [1980] AC 827, HL at 843.

[13] The Unfair Contract Terms Act 1977.

3.16 In some cases the courts will limit the impact of a common law right or duty in order to ensure that a statutory regime is not sidestepped. A particularly stark example, in the related employment area *Johnson v Unisys*,[14] is discussed at para 3.11 above.

3.17 A similar example is found in the law of nuisance. No common law remedy applies if this would defeat statute. In *Marcic v Thames Water Utilities Ltd*[15] the House of Lords held that the common law of nuisance could not impose obligations on a statutory sewerage undertaker inconsistent with the statutory scheme of the Water Industry Act 1991. In this case, the claimed action in nuisance ignored the statutory limitations on the enforcement of sewerage undertakers' drainage obligations. The House of Lords held that an important purpose of the enforcement scheme in the 1991 Act was that individual householders should not be able to launch proceedings in respect of failure to build sufficient sewers. Individual householders could bring proceedings in respect of inadequate drainage only when the undertaker had failed to comply with an enforcement order. The existence of a parallel common law right would 'set at nought' the statutory scheme, effectively supplanting the role the independent regulator was intended to discharge.

3.18 In relation to trusts (and hence closer to pension schemes), in *Armitage v Nurse*,[16] the Court of Appeal considered the impact of an exoneration clause in a private trust. Millett LJ gave the leading judgment and held that it was up to Parliament to enact legislation if there was to be regulation of exclusion provisions in relation to trustees. There was no reason for the common law to invalidate clauses excluding negligence or even gross negligence.[17]

Application to Pension Schemes

3.19 The UK pensions legislation generally does not contain a code setting out the fundamental rights and duties of trustees.[18] In particular, it does not contain a general description of the general fiduciary duties of trustees—for example, a duty of care in relation to investment or how to decide amongst different classes of beneficiary or how to deal with surpluses or deficits etc. These are all left to matters of the general law and questions of interpretation of the underlying trust instruments. This is in contrast to the general codification of the position of directors (under the Companies Act 2006) and the position of superannuation trustees in Australia.[19]

3.20 There are some glosses:

(a) the pensions legislation generally overrides the trust provisions (if inconsistent).[20] Unlike (say) the general trust law (or the Trustee Act 1925), the legislation cannot be contracted-out of under the trust instrument.[21] The legislation is not a default rule, but instead an override;

---

[14] [2001] UKHL 13, [2003] 1 AC 518, HL.

[15] [2003] UKHL 66, [2004] 2 AC 42, HL.

[16] [1998] Ch 241, CA at 256.

[17] This principle should apply to pension schemes—the Law Commission has considered the issue of exoneration clauses and recommended no changes (Law Com No 301, June 2006). Parliament has enacted a specific limitation for pension schemes in one area—investment duties (Pensions Act 1995, s 33)—see further Ch 14 (Trustee indemnities and exonerations).

[18] Contrast in Australia, the Superannuation Industry (Supervision) Act 1993 (Cth) (the SIS Act). See M Scott Donald 'Regulating for Fiduciary Qualities of Conduct' (2013) J Eq (forthcoming).

[19] Under the Superannuation Industry (Supervision) Act 1993 (commonly called the 'SIS Act').

[20] Pensions Act 2004, s 306 and Pensions Act 1995, s 117.

[21] Contrast where the legislation expressly allows this—by expressly referring to the terms of the pension schemes—eg Pensions Act 1995, s 32 (decisions by a majority); Pensions Act 1995, s 34 (power to make

(b) any duty of care (whatever it is) in relation to investment matters cannot be excluded or reduced by the trust instrument.[22] In the UK employers can be given many powers under the trust deed. There is a narrow statutory provision limiting this in relation to investment powers (s 35 of the Pensions Act 1995 provides that any provision in a scheme for the consent of the employer is overridden).

3.21 It can be argued that a large amount of pensions legislation is already in place. The courts should recognize this and adapt how general trust, contract, or common law is applied to pensions schemes.

3.22 Relevant factors to be considered by the courts are:

(a) pension benefits are provided under a trust, but are purchased by the members (in effect as deferred pay);
(b) discrimination legislation in and under the Equality Act 2010 generally applies to pensions and (rather oddly) to pension trustees; and
(c) for many people their pension benefits are their greatest asset (apart from their houses).

3.23 The courts are also likely to consider as background the social policy behind pensions and the tax benefits usually available.[23]

3.24 In some cases the courts will limit the impact of a common law right or duty in order to ensure that a statutory regime is not sidestepped. Thus, as mentioned above in *Johnson v Unisys*,[24] the House of Lords held that an employee could not claim a breach of the implied duty of trust and confidence to claim damages on his or her dismissal. Such a claim would negate the careful statutory scheme for unfair dismissal established by statute.

3.25 This is, however, difficult to predict. A modification of the common rule will be only in limited cases. In practice unless the two are inconsistent, the courts are more likely to construe the statute so that any common law duty (on trustees or employers) is not supplanted, but instead the two exist side by side.

Disclosure—*Wilson v Law Debenture*

3.26 In *Wilson v Law Debenture*[25] it was argued that pension trustees should owe a greater disclosure obligation to pension beneficiaries than is owed by private trustees. Rattee J rejected this argument. In effect, Rattee J held that the parties had chosen to use a trust structure and this implied use of standard trust rules. If Parliament wished to impose greater disclosure obligations it could do (and has done) so. It was not for the courts to extend the obligation further.[26]

---

investments); and Pensions Act 2004, ss 241–243 (terms of arrangements for MNTs or MNDs to be decided by the trustees, within limits).

[22] Pensions Act 1995, s 34.
[23] See eg *Stevens v Bell* [2002] EWCA Civ 672, [2002] OPLR 207, CA and Ch 17 (Amendment powers) on interpretation issues.
[24] [2001] UKHL 13, [2003] 1 AC 518, HL.
[25] [1995] OPLR 103, [1995] 2 All ER 337 (Rattee J).
[26] See also Ch 3 and the similar reasons given in the employment area by the House of Lords in *Johnson v Unisys* [2001] UKHL 13, [2001] 2 All ER 801. A former employee claimed damages for breach of contract by reason of the manner of his dismissal. The House of Lords rejected this claim on the basis that this would circumvent the statutory unfair dismissal regime (which included limits on liability etc).

3.27 The parties involved in setting up the trust must be taken to have been aware of what the obligations would be (by reference to classic family trusts). Despite the point that the members had paid for the benefits, it would be unfair of the courts to extend this.

3.28 Rattee J stated:[27]

> It would . . . be wrong in principle to hold that long-established principles of trust law as to the exercise by trustees of discretions conferred on them by their trust instruments, in the context of which parties to a pension scheme such as the present entered into those schemes, no longer apply to them and that the trustees are under more onerous obligations to account to their beneficiaries than they could have appreciated when appointed, on the basis of the current trust law as it has stood for so long.

> I accept Mr Warren's submission that if any such amendment to the law of trusts as applied to pension schemes is to be made it should be made by the legislature, either by regulations made under or by the extension of s 113 of the Pension Schemes Act 1993 in which Parliament has already addressed the question of the extent to which members of a pension scheme should be entitled to information relating to the scheme's administration.

Doubts have, however, been cast on this actual decision (that pension trustees did not need to give reasons) and it is still open whether this will actually remain true in relation to the specific issue being addressed by Rattee J.[28] There are indications in the courts that they will look for trustees to give reasons or draw inferences if they do not.[29]

Funding?—*British Vita* and *Pilots*

3.29 For example, the Pensions Act 2004 includes specific provisions on the funding of relevant occupational pension schemes. In two cases, *Pilots*[30] and *British Vita*,[31] Warren J had to consider the impact of the statutory provisions on a provision in the scheme trust deed dealing with funding.

3.30 Clearly the statutory provision operated as a minimum, but did it operate to remove any inconsistent provision in the scheme—for example one giving the trustee power to fix contribution rates (without any need for employer or Regulator consent)?

3.31 Despite both:

(a) a ministerial statement to that effect at the time the Pensions Bill 2004 was in Parliament, and

(b) the existence of specific legislation dealing with application of the funding rules where the trustee had a discretion over funding,

Warren J held that the trust deed provision still applied—alongside the statutory provision.

---

[27] [1995] 2 All ER 337 at 348.

[28] See Sir Robert Walker, speaking, extra-judicially, in his chapter 'Trust Principles in the Pensions Context' in AJ Oakley, *Trends in Contemporary Trust Law* (Oxford University Press, 1996), also in [1996] PLR 108. However, Rattee J's decision was supported in *Thomas on Powers* (Sweet & Maxwell, 1998) 372.

[29] See Ch 18 (Disclosure obligations) and for example the comments of Robert Walker J in *Scott v National Trust* [1999] 4 All ER 705 at 718c and of the Court of Appeal in *Edge v Pensions Ombudsman* [2000] Ch 602, [1999] 4 All ER 546, CA at 571.

[30] *PNPF Trust Co Ltd v Taylor* [2010] EWHC 1573 (Ch) (Warren J).

[31] *British Vita Unlimited v British Pension Fund Trustees Ltd* [2007] EWHC 953 (Ch), [2008] 1 All ER 37 (Warren J).

Saunders v Vautier in Canada—*Buschau*

Conversely, in Canada in *Buschau v Rogers Communications Inc*,[32] the Supreme Court held that the general trust law principle of the rule in *Saunders v Vautier* was 'not easily incorporated into the context of employment pension plans'. **3.32**

This was for various reasons (see Chapter 16), including that applying the common law in *Saunders v Vautier* would be inconsistent with the Canadian pensions legislation. **3.33**

Standard of decisions—*Finch v Telstra*

As mentioned in Chapter 2, in Australia, in 2010 in *Finch v Telstra Super Pty Ltd*,[33] the High Court looked at the existence of the legislation on pensions in deciding on the extent of the duties of trustees of a pension fund (called a superannuation fund in Australia) when making a decision on a factual issue (in this case whether a member qualified for an incapacity benefit). The High Court held that the trustees should make the decision with 'properly informed consideration'. This duty was held to potentially be greater than the obligation on a trustee of a private trust or (potentially) where the decision was not factual, but instead a true discretion. **3.34**

The High Court considered that reasons for this heightened duty included the fact that superannuation schemes were already subject to statutory regulation. The court considered that superannuation (the Australian term for pensions) has a public significance, shown by the tax benefits granted to relevant schemes and the mandatory requirements (in Australia) for employers to contribute, and held:[34] **3.35**

> Because of the potentially lengthy time periods over which superannuation savings are accumulated, it was natural, and it is now in many instances mandatory, for a trust mechanism to be employed. These funds have increasingly come under detailed statutory regulation. The government considers that the taxation advantages of superannuation should not be enjoyed unless superannuation funds are operating efficiently and lawfully.

In light of this, the High Court held that superannuation trustees should not be 'largely immunised from judicial control without clear contrary language in the relevant trust instrument'. A provision in the trust deed for decisions of the trustee to be in its 'absolute and uncontrolled discretion' was not enough. The standards laid down in the private trust case, *Karger v Paul*[35] did not apply to superannuation trusts. **3.36**

Conclusion

The statutory position, in particular the pensions statutes and legislation and the tax position, are factors which the courts will have in mind when reaching decisions on interpretation or on the standards and duties on trustees or employers. They may cause some deviation from the general trust and contract rules, but these are likely to be only in limited cases. **3.37**

The comments of Rattee J in *Wilson* continue to resonate. **3.38**

---

[32] 2006 SCC 28, Can SC.
[33] [2010] HCA 36, (2010) 242 CLR 254, HCA. Followed in *Alcoa of Australia Retirement Plan Pty Ltd v Frost* [2012] VSCA 238, Vic CA and *Sharp v Maritime Super Pty Ltd* [2012] NSWSC 1350 (Ward J). See Ch 2 (Pension trusts and general trust law).
[34] At paras [32] to [35].
[35] [1984] VR 161 (McGarvie J).

4

CORPORATE TRUSTEES

Corporate Trustees

Introduction

4.1 This chapter discusses the issues that arise in practice if the choice is made to have a trustee company[1] for an occupational pension scheme instead of a group of individual trustees. This chapter[2] looks at:

(a) the different types of corporate trustee and the advantages and disadvantages in practice of having a corporate trustee;

(b) some of the specific implications of the pensions legislation in relation to corporate trustees.

4.2 Chapter 5 looks in more detail at the potential liability of directors of a corporate trustee.

---

[1] For the historical position, see DR Marsh, *Corporate Trustees* (Europa Publications, 1952).
[2] This chapter is derived largely from part of a chapter in *Tolley's Pension Law* (LexisNexis).

Types of Corporate Trustee

A private sector registered occupational pension scheme will be set up under trust (see s 252 **4.3** of the Pensions Act 2004 on the need to be set up under an irrevocable trust). When setting up or running such a pension scheme under trust, a trustee is needed.

For smaller (usually insured) schemes it has been quite common to use the employer company **4.4** itself as sole trustee. This is still legally possible, although it does not represent best practice. For example, the Occupational Pensions Regulatory Authority (Opra) (the predecessor of the Pensions Regulator) commented in 1999 in its bulletin[3] that it preferred to see separate corporate trustee bodies or named individuals as trustees. Using the company as sole trustee can lead to a blurring of the distinction between the powers and duties of the employer on the one hand and the powers and duties of the trustees on the other.

There are three different types of trustee bodies considered in this chapter, these are: **4.5**

(a) a set of individuals;
(b) a trust corporation; or
(c) a trustee company.

Alternatively, a combination of these can be used (eg an independent trust corporation with **4.6** individual trustees).

Trust corporation

A trust corporation is a company which is given special status under the Trustee Act 1925 **4.7** and the Law of Property Act 1925. The definitions in both Acts state:

> 'trust corporation' means the Public Trustee or a corporation either appointed by the Court in any particular case to be a trustee, or entitled by rules made under sub-section (3) of section four of the Public Trustee Act 1906, to act as custodian trustee.

The main general provision is set out, in reg 30(1)(b) of the Public Trustee Rules 1912,[4] as **4.8** any corporation which:

(a) is established under the laws of the UK or any other member state of the EU;
(b) is empowered by its constitution to undertake trust business in England and Wales;
(c) has one or more places of business in the UK; and
(d) is either:
    (i) incorporated by special Act of Parliament or royal charter; or
    (ii) registered under the relevant Companies Act (or in another member state of the EU) having a capital of not less than £250,000 of which not less than £100,000 has been paid up (or its equivalent in other currencies); or
    (iii) is registered in the UK or any relevant member state as an unlimited company and which has one of its members which is a company within any of the previous classes.

---

[3] Opra Bulletin Issue 9, May 1999, at p 10.
[4] SI 1912/348, as substituted by SI 1975/1189 and as amended.

4.9　This is a pretty stringent test to comply with. Most companies which act as trustees will not be trust corporations within the definition: those which are include bank trustees or the larger professional trustees.

Trustee company

4.10　More common is the situation where a specialist company has been set up to act as a trustee. This could be either a:

(a) professional trustee company—eg charging a fee but set up by some independent person, for example pensioneer trustees for small self-administered schemes (SSASs) or independent trustees formed for the purpose of acting as independent trustees on insolvency;[5] or

(b) specifically incorporated trustee company for an individual trust, often a subsidiary of the principal employer with a small issued share capital (say £100) or perhaps a company incorporated by guarantee.

4.11　This chapter focuses on the position of these 'subsidiary' trustee companies. They can be distinguished from more independent trustee companies on the basis that they do not charge a fee and tend to act as trustee of only one scheme (or only the schemes of one employer).

4.12　The decision for the sponsoring employer of a pension scheme when setting up the scheme (or at some stage later), assuming that no form of 'independent' trustee is needed, is whether to have the relevant individuals (directors of the employer, members of the scheme, etc) act as personal trustees or whether they should instead be directors of a specifically incorporated trustee company.

Trustee company compared to trust corporation

4.13　The main distinctions between a trustee company and a trust corporation are:

(a) A sole trustee company cannot give a valid receipt for capital monies on the sale of land, whereas a trust corporation can (Trustee Act 1925, s 14 and Law of Property Act 1925, s 27).

(b) If a trustee wishes to retire, but only the statutory powers of retirement under s 39 of the Trustee Act 1925 are applicable,[6] this will only be effective if there are either two persons or a trust corporation remaining as trustees after the retirement (see the wording of ss 39 and 37(2) of the Trustee Act 1925). These provisions were amended by the Trusts of Land and Appointment of Trustees Act 1996. The requirement before the change in the 1996 Act was for two 'individuals', not for two 'persons'. The effect of the change seems to be that now a corporation or company can be included, as the term 'person' generally includes a company (Sch 1 to the Interpretation Act 1978)—see Mann J in *Jasmine Trustee Ltd v Wells & Hind*.[7]

---

[5] Under ss 22–26 of the Pensions Act 1995. See D Pollard, *Corporate Insolvency: Employment and Pension Rights* 5th edn (Bloomsbury Professional, 2013) Ch 53 'Independent trustee obligations'.

[6] Retirement under an express power in the trust is not caught by the s 39 limitation—see *LRT Pension Fund Trustee Co Ltd v Hatt* [1993] OPLR 225 (Knox J).

[7] [2007] EWHC 38 (Ch), [2007] 1 All ER 1142 at [21] (Mann J).

Incorporating a Trustee Company

Since 1992, it has been possible to have only one shareholder in a private limited company— **4.14**
see the Companies (Single Member Private Limited Companies) Regulations 1992.[8]
Accordingly, a company (whether limited by shares or by guarantee) can be formed now by
one member—see ss 7 and 38 of the Companies Act 2006.[9] Section 7 of the Companies Act
2006 allows companies to be formed by one member, whereas s 38 provides that any law that
applies to companies formed by two or more persons applies with relevant modifications to
companies formed by one person.

Use of the name 'Trust' in the company requires the approval of the Department for Business, **4.15**
Innovation and Skills (BIS)—see the Company, Limited Liability Partnership and Business
Names (Sensitive Words and Expressions) Regulations 2009.[10]

Consent is normally easily given if it is clear that the company will only act as trustee of **4.16**
pension trusts of a related employer, eg the XYZ Pension Trust Co Ltd. For more information,
see Chapter 3 of Companies House Guidance Booklet GP1, Incorporation and Names.[11]

Regulation 3(1)(b) of the 2009 Regulations only refers to the 'possessive forms of those **4.17**
words and expressions' and the Companies Registry has previously confirmed orally over the
telephone that use of the word 'Trustee' does not require approval.

Memorandum and articles of association

The trustee company will need a set of constitutional documents (usually a memorandum **4.18**
and articles of association).

The memorandum should include the usual powers (eg to operate a bank account), but it is **4.19**
preferable for the primary object to be to act as a trustee. This can be general, but it is helpful
to give a particular power to act as a trustee of a pension scheme.

For companies formed on or after 1 October 2009 the default articles of association will be **4.20**
the model articles provided under the Companies Act 2006—see ss 19–20 of the Companies
Act 2006 and the Companies (Model Articles) Regulations 2008.[12] For companies formed
before October 2009, the articles of association are usually based on the relevant Table A—
see s 8 of the Companies Act 1985 and the Companies (Tables A to F) Regulations 1985.[13]

Various regulations in the Model articles or Table A may need to be amended; for example, **4.21**
the following provisions may be useful:

(a) A provision enabling alternate directors—this will need to tie in with the member-
nominated director (MND) provisions.[14]
(b) A provision incorporating the MND provisions (and any alternative arrangements)
(see further below).

---

[8] SI 1992/1699.
[9] Formerly s 1(3A) of the Companies Act 1985 (as amended by SI 1992/1699).
[10] SI 2009/2615, as amended, replacing the Company and Business Names Regulations 1981 (SI 1981/1685).
[11] December 2012. See <http://www.companieshouse.gov.uk/about/pdf/gp1.pdf>.
[12] SI 2008/3229.
[13] SI 1985/805, as amended.
[14] See ss 241–243 of the Pensions Act 2004 and later in this chapter.

    (c) A provision providing for a director to lose office automatically on becoming disqualified from acting as a pension trustee (eg under s 29 of the Pensions Act 1995) (see later in this chapter).

    (d) Amendments to regs 85 and 86 of 1985 Table A and reg 14 of the 2008 Model Articles so that any interest of a director as a member of the pension scheme or in the employer does not need notification or does not prevent the director from voting or counting towards a quorum at meetings of the directors.

4.22 On the last point, quorum and conflicts, the director will still be required (at risk of a criminal penalty) to declare any interest under s 182 of the Companies Act 2006.[15] For duties that arise on or after 1 October 2008, s 177 of the Companies Act 2006 requires directors to disclose their interest in proposed transactions or arrangements. Breach of this duty under s 177 has the same consequence as breaching a common law or equitable duty and does not make the director criminally liable—see s 178 of the Companies Act 2006.

4.23 Regulation 14 of the 2008 Model Articles does not require a declaration of interest by a director but it does restrict the ability of the director to participate in the decision-making process unless the interest arises from 'arrangements pursuant to which benefits are made available to employees and directors or former employees and directors of the company or any of its subsidiaries which do not provide special benefits for directors or former directors'.

Appointing a Trustee Company

4.24 Care should be taken when arranging for the appointment of a trustee company which is not a trust corporation.

4.25 If the statutory powers of appointment and removal of trustees are to be used, s 37(1)(c) of the Trustee Act 1925 can cause problems if there was only one trustee originally appointed and a sole trustee will not be able to give a valid receipt of all capital money. This would clearly be the case where trusts include land.[16]

4.26 It was previously unclear how far the problems caused by s 37(1)(c) of the Trustee Act 1925 could be excluded by express provision in the relevant trust instrument (utilizing s 69(2) of the Trustee Act 1925). However, it is now clear that an express provision in the trust instrument will be effective—see the decision of Knox J in *LRT Pension Fund Trustee Co Ltd v Hatt*.[17]

4.27 If the pension scheme has individual trustees, their replacement by a corporate trustee needs to comply with the provisions of ss 241–243 of the Pensions Act 2004[18] dealing with member-nominated trustees and directors. In practice, a change from individuals to a corporate trustee (with the same individuals as directors now) should be consistent with any existing MNT arrangements (merely replacing them with equivalent MND arrangements).

---

[15] Formerly s 317 of the Companies Act 1985.

[16] Trustee Act 1925, s 14(2) and Law of Property Act 1925, s 27.

[17] [1993] OPLR 225 (Knox J). The remaining problems in this are discussed by Michael Jacobs 'To Be or Not to Be…Trustee Act 1925, s 37(1)(c) Revisited Again' (1993) 7 TLI 73.

[18] And the Occupational Pension Schemes (Member-nominated Trustees and Directors) Regulations 2006 (SI 2006/714).

Foreign companies

There seems to be no reason why foreign companies may not be trustees of UK-based pension **4.28** schemes. However, if the foreign company is the sole trustee, it may not be resident in the UK. A registered scheme under the Finance Act 2004 is required to have a tax administrator who is resident in the UK, EU or EEA (Finance Act 2004, s 270).

Trustee company: limited by shares or guarantee?

The most common type of company is one limited by shares. The other alternative would be **4.29** to have a company which is limited by guarantee. A company limited by shares is perhaps easier as it is clearer who is the beneficial owner of the shares (hence whether the company is owned by the principal employer or someone else).

One problem with the company limited by shares is that something has to be done with the **4.30** issued share capital (ie it could be paid and put into a bank account somewhere or lent back to the holding company). If to be held by the directors, the shares need to be transferred on a director ceasing to hold office.

Who Should Own the Trustee Company?

There are two main possibilities for the ownership of a specialized trustee company formed **4.31** for an individual scheme. These are:

(a) the trustee company could be a wholly-owned subsidiary of the principal employer or sponsor; or
(b) the trustee company could be owned by its directors (eg as its shareholders or as the members of a company limited by guarantee).

There are a number of points which arise when considering ownership of the trustee company. **4.32**

(a) Ownership by the principal employer obviously gives more control to the principal employer to use its shareholding to appoint or remove directors (although this will be subject to the MND provisions—see later in this chapter). Conversely it may look less independent to the members.
(b) Ownership by the principal employer used to mean that shares held by the trustee company (as part of the assets of the scheme) would count towards the 3 per cent limit for disclosure of substantial shareholdings under Pt VI of the Companies Act 1985. This section has now been repealed, but issues remain under the Disclosure and Transparency Rules (see 4.68 later in this chapter).
(c) Ownership by the principal employer (or another group company) is helpful if it is wanted to put the assets of the scheme in a common investment fund with the assets of another scheme of that employer or with the employer itself. The difficulty is whether such a common investment fund is regulated so that the operator requires authorization under the Financial Services and Markets Act 2000. There is an exemption in para 10 of the Schedule to the Financial Services and Markets Act 2000 (Collective Investment Schemes) Order 2001[19] where each of the participants (ie the trustees) is

---

[19] SI 2001/1062.

a body corporate in the same group as the operator (ie the operator of the common investment fund).

(d) Ownership of shares (or a company limited by guarantee) by the directors requires some mechanism for dealing with change of shareholding when directors change (eg die or resign etc). This can be built into the articles of association if desired.

(e) Ownership of the trustee company by the principal employer may allow the trustee to be included in the group registration for VAT purposes (see discussion later in this chapter). This is relatively uncommon.

(f) Ownership of the trustee company by the principal employer may make it easier to include the trustee company (and its directors) within a group insurance policy of the employer (eg directors' and officers' insurance).

(g) Ownership of the trustee company as a subsidiary of the principal employer will mean that the provisions of the Companies Act 2006 will need to be considered if the assets of the pension scheme are to include shares in the parent.

  (i) Such employer-related investment is generally limited to 5 per cent of the fund in any event (Pensions Act 1995, s 40[20]).

  (ii) But if any parent shares are to be held, one of the exemptions to the general prohibition in s 136 of the Companies Act 2006[21] on a subsidiary becoming a member of its holding company needs to apply. Sections 138–140 of the Companies Act 2006[22] contain various exemptions for pension trustees, allowing such a holding provided (broadly) that the employer has only a residual interest in the trust property (or an interest as a result of the exercise of a charge or lien to obtain the discharge of a monetary obligation owed by a member of the scheme).

(h) If the trustee company is a subsidiary of the principal employer, this will mean that the directors of the trustee company are directors of an associated company, ie a subsidiary of the employer. This can mean that various restrictions apply under the Companies Acts on transactions with directors.

  (i) Section 235 of the Companies Act 2006 (qualifying pension scheme indemnity provision) provides an exemption for pension schemes from the restrictions (contained in s 232(2) of the Companies Act 2006) on companies indemnifying their directors or directors of associated companies against certain liabilities.

  (ii) An employer in the same group as the trustee company (eg in the scheme trust deed) will be able to indemnify directors against liabilities incurred in connection with the company's activities as trustee of the scheme. However, this indemnity cannot provide protection against a liability arising from a fine imposed in criminal proceeds, a penalty from a regulatory authority or liability incurred by the director defending criminal proceedings in which he is connected.[23]

(i) If the trustee company is a subsidiary of the principal employer, this will mean that it is potentially liable for obligations of the employer under the UK carbon reduction commitment (CRC) scheme. All members of a group of companies are jointly and severally

---

[20] See Ch 19 (Employer-related investment).
[21] Formerly s 23 of the Companies Act 1985.
[22] Formerly Sch 2 to the Companies Act 1985.
[23] Section 256 of the Pensions Act 2004 also prohibits indemnities out of the assets of a pension trust to the extent that they cover criminal fines or civil penalties under pensions legislation. See further Ch 14 (Trustee indemnities and exonerations).

liable for the obligations of the group under the CRC scheme—Art 24 of the CRC Energy Efficiency Scheme Order 2011.[24]

Advantages and Disadvantages of a Separate Trustee Company

Advantages

The advantages of having a trustee company include the following. **4.33**

Reduced formality

There is less formality involved when there is a change of a trustee director as compared to a **4.34** change in a personal trustee. The legal title to assets and contracts etc remains with the trustee company where there is a change of director. This means that there is no need to seek to novate contracts or transfer assets.

There is an automatic vesting of most assets under s 40 of the Trustee Act 1925 in the case of **4.35** individual trustees; however, this does not cover some assets, eg land held on lease and shares. Problems are minimized by the use of custodians holding legal title. Section 40 of the Trustee Act 1925 only applies where the appointment of the new trustee is by deed.

There is less need for deeds of appointment or removal, and therefore fewer deeds are involved **4.36** all together.

Reduced need for relevant notifications

There is also less need to make relevant notifications of any change in the trustee board. All **4.37** that is required is a notification to the Companies Registry (within 14 days). In the case of individual trustees, notifications must usually be made to HMRC (tax registered schemes), the National Insurance Contributions Office (contracted-out schemes), and the Pensions Regulator (tax registered schemes—within 12 months)—see 4.80 below.

Appointment and removal of trustees

The duties and the responsibilities of the party (usually the employing company) in appoint- **4.38** ing and removing company directors (ie the director of the trustee company) is clearer than the position as a matter of trust law in relation to the appointment and removal of trustees.

It has been argued that the power to appoint a trustee is a fiduciary power that must be **4.39** exercised in the interests of the beneficiaries to the scheme—see the nineteenth-century decisions of Kay J in *Re Skeats' Settlement*[25] and the Court of Appeal in *Re Shortridge*.[26] But this is misconceived—see Chapter 12 (Employer powers to appoint or remove trustees). In any event, the argument that the power is fiduciary is much less likely to apply to the appointment or removal of directors (even if they are directors of a company that just operates as a trustee company).

Avoiding problems of s 34 of the Trustee Act 1925

Using a trustee company avoids the problem under s 34 of the Trustee Act 1925, of being **4.40** unable to have more than four trustees of a settlement of land.

---

[24] SI 2010/768, as amended. See further, *Freshfields on Corporate Pensions Law 2013* (ed D Pollard and C Magoffin) (Bloomsbury Professional, 2013) Ch 11.5.
[25] (1889) 42 ChD 522 (Kay J).
[26] [1895] 1 Ch 278, CA.

Majority voting

4.41 Companies generally provide full majority voting by directors. Clearly, the articles can provide for something else (eg weighted voting for directors in some circumstances), as can a particular trust instrument. The general rule for individual trustees is that they must act unanimously unless they are authorized to do otherwise by the trust instrument: see *Luke v South Kensington Hotel Co.*[27] The position here has been amended by s 32 of the Pensions Act 1995 (discussed later in this chapter).

Easier to get deeds executed

4.42 It is generally easier to get deeds executed. Once a matter has been approved by the board it usually needs only the signatures of two directors, a director and secretary, or one director provided that a witness attests the signature. There is no need to involve all the directors. It should be noted that company directors are generally obliged to assist in the carrying out of a board resolution, even if they abstained or voted against: see Millett J in *Re Equiticorp International plc.*[28]

The shelter of corporate personality

4.43 It seems clear that the directors of the trustee company can shelter behind the separate corporate personality of the trustee company at least in relation to ordinary creditors (eg fund managers, third party contractual, creditors etc). This is discussed further in chapter 5 (Liability of directors of corporate trustees).

Flexibility of Pensions Act 1995 provisions

4.44 There may be advantages in terms of the flexibility of the various provisions in the Pensions Act 1995. Again, some of these are discussed further later in this chapter.

Transactions between directors and the company

4.45 Certain transactions between directors and the company are prohibited by the Companies Act 1985.

(a) For example, loans to directors entered into before 1 October 2007 were prohibited by s 330 of the Companies Act 1985. For loans entered into on or after 1 October 2007, s 197 of the Companies Act 2006 requires shareholder approval.

(b) Transactions are voidable if entered into in excess of the board's powers and involve directors (see s 41 of the Companies Act 2006[29]).

(c) Certain other transactions require shareholder approval (eg substantial property transactions involving directors).[30]

4.46 If directors of the employer company were also individual trustees, these sections could cause difficulty in relation to certain types of transaction between the employer company and the individual trustee.

4.47 Although these restrictions generally extend to persons connected with a director or associated with a director, a pension trustee company will not normally be connected or associated with a director. This is because usually the directors will not control the trustee company for this purpose.

---

[27] (1879) 11 ChD 121, CA.

[28] [1989] 1 WLR 1010, [1989] BCLC 597 (Millett J).

[29] Formerly s 322A of the Companies Act 1985.

[30] See ss 190–195 of the Companies Act 2006 for transactions entered into on or after 1 October 2007 and s 320 of the Companies Act 1985 for transactions entered into before that date.

In general, a trustee of a trust which includes, among its beneficiaries, the director or his **4.48** family is to be treated as connected (see s 252(2)(c) of the Companies Act 2006) with the director. But this is expressly stated not to apply to a pension scheme—see the final words to s 252(2)(c). For a discussion of complexities in this area see the decision of Hazel Williamson QC in *Re Thirty-Eight Building Ltd*.[31]

Subsidiary companies can hold shares in employer holding company

Companies which are subsidiaries of the employer are allowed to hold shares in the employer **4.49** holding company. Residual interests held under a pension scheme are disregarded for the purposes of the prohibitions on subsidiaries holding shares in their parent companies under Pt 18, Ch 1 of the Companies Act 2006.[32]

Delegation

Delegation by individual trustees is generally not permitted unless expressly authorized by **4.50** the trust instrument (which in practice is common for pension schemes) or, in relation to investment matters, by s 34(2)(a) of the Pensions Act 1995 to a fund manager. There is also an implied delegation power by using agents etc in Pt IV of the Trustee Act 2000, restricted in relation to occupational pension schemes by s 36.

Conversely, delegation by boards of directors of companies (including corporate trustees) **4.51** is generally permitted and will usually be expressly dealt with under the articles of association if not elsewhere (see further the discussion of s 34 of the Pensions Act 1995 at 4.124 below).

Extension of insurance cover

Directors' and officers' insurance cover may be easier to extend to directors of a subsidiary **4.52** trustee company.

(Before December 2002) avoiding s 716 of the Companies Act 1985 limitations

Commercial activities (eg partnerships) used (before December 2002) generally to be pro- **4.53** hibited if more than 20 people were involved—see s 716 of the Companies Act 1985. There were exceptions made for various professional partnerships.

If a pension scheme wished to invest in a partnership venture, each of the trustees would have **4.54** counted towards this 20-person limit. A trustee company was more advantageous as it would have only counted as one participant.

This limit was removed, however, with effect from 21 December 2002 by the Regulatory **4.55** Reform (Removal of 20 Member Limit in Partnerships etc) Order 2002.[33]

Disadvantages

The various disadvantages of a trustee company include the following. **4.56**

Separate trustee to give receipts

There is a need to appoint a separate trustee to give receipts for the proceeds of sale or other **4.57** capital monies arising under a trust for sale of land (Trustee Act 1925, s 14 and Law of Property Act 1925, s 27).

---

[31] [1999] 1 BCLC 416, [1999] OPLR 319 (Hazel Williamson QC, sitting as a deputy High Court judge).
[32] Formerly ss 23, 145, 146, and 148 of the Companies Act 1985 and Sch 2 to the Companies Act 1985.
[33] SI 2002/3203.

Slightly more paperwork

4.58   There is more paperwork involved with a trustee company, although this is not terribly onerous. For example, there is a need to submit returns to the Companies Registry.

Preparation of accounts

4.59   Accounts need to be produced and, unless a view is taken that the company is dormant for this purpose, audited.

4.60   A trustee company may well qualify as being a dormant company although the members of the pension scheme may not be impressed to view the trustee company's accounts and see that it is dormant—for financial years beginning on or after 6 April 2008, see ss 480 and 1169 of the Companies Act 2006.[34]

4.61   A dormant company is exempt from the requirements in the Companies Act 2006 to have audited accounts. Before 26 May 2000 a special resolution was needed.[35] Under the Companies Act 2006, directors will need to provide a statement that the members have not required the company to obtain an audit of its accounts.

4.62   In relation to financial years beginning before 1 October 2007, a company exempt from the accounts requirements was also exempt from the requirement to appoint auditors.[36]

4.63   However, under s 242 of the Companies Act 1985, and s 441 of the Companies Act 2006 for financial years beginning on or after 6 April 2008, a dormant company is still required to deliver (unaudited) accounts to the Registrar of Companies.

4.64   From 1 October 2008, dormant companies have been exempted from the requirement for laying accounts before the company in a general meeting under s 241 of the Companies Act 1985—the obligation was repealed in relation to private companies from 1 October 2008.[37]

4.65   For financial years ending on or after 1 October 2007, private companies are no longer required to hold annual general meetings under the Companies Act 2006, and consequently there is no longer a requirement to lay accounts before a general meeting.[38]

4.66   The finding that the trustee company is dormant for this purpose assumes that the transactions of the pensions scheme (eg paying pensions, receiving contributions, dealing in investments etc) are not treated for accounting purposes as transactions of the trustee company. This seems logical (given that all these transactions involve trust property) even in the case of contractual obligations of the pension scheme (which are entered into by the trustee with a right of indemnity out of the trust assets). This position seems to be accepted by most accounting firms.

---

[34] For accounts and reports for financial years beginning before 6 April 2008, see s 249AA of the Companies Act 1985, as inserted by the Companies Act 1985 (Audit Exemption) (Amendment) Regulations 2000 (SI 2000/1430).

[35] Section 250(1) of the Companies Act 1985, as inserted by the Companies Act 1989.

[36] See s 388A of the Companies Act 1985, as inserted by the Companies Act 1989 and substituted by SI 1994/1935.

[37] See s 1295 of and Sch 16 to the Companies Act 2006.

[38] See s 238A of the Companies Act 1985 (as inserted by the Companies Act 2006 (Commencement No 3, Consequential Amendments, Transitional Provisions and Savings) Order 2007 (SI 2007/2194)) and s 424 of the Companies Act 2006 for the time period for sending out accounts.

The pension scheme itself will need to draw up accounts in the usual way—see the Occupational **4.67** Pension Schemes (Requirements to Obtain Audited Accounts and a Statement from the Auditor) Regulations 1996.[39] These are not submitted to the Companies Registry.

Declaration of interest in shares of PLCs

Before 20 January 2007, under Pt VI, ss 198–220 of the Companies Act 1985 persons holding **4.68** (generally) over 3 per cent of the issued share capital in a public company used to be required to make notifications of their interest. It was clear that in using a trustee company, the individual directors were not (without more) to be taken as interested in shares held by the trustee company. Accordingly, they did not have to aggregate any interest held by the trustee company (eg by the pension scheme) with their personal shareholdings.

These provisions were repealed by s 1295 of and Sch 16 to the Companies Act 2006 as from **4.69** 20 January 2007.

Under Chapter 5 of the Disclosure Rules and Transparency Rules Sourcebook (DTR5.1) **4.70** and ss 89A–89L of the Financial Services and Markets Act 2000,[40] a person who acquires or disposes of shares that are admitted to trading on a regulated or prescribed market is required to notify the issuer if the person's percentage of those voting rights, either as a shareholder or through direct or indirect holding of financial instruments, exceeds or falls below 3, 4, 5, 6, 7, 8, 9, or 10 per cent (the thresholds are different in the case of a non-UK issuer).

In using a trustee company, the individual directors are (without more) unlikely to be **4.71** considered to hold indirect voting rights in the shares held by the trustee company—see DTR5.2.1R. Accordingly, they do not have to aggregate any interest held by the trustee company (eg by the pension scheme) with their personal holding.

Under s 203(2) of the Companies Act 1985 (before its repeal), a body corporate which had **4.72** control of the trustee company was deemed to be interested in shares held by the trustee company (even if held on trust for the pension scheme). In the usual situation where the trustee company is a wholly-owned subsidiary of one of the employers, this would mean that the employer (and any other companies having control of the employer) would be treated as being interested in shares held by the trustee company. This seemed anomalous.[41]

A body corporate will also be obliged under DTR5.1.2R to notify the issuer if there is a relevant **4.73** change in the body corporate's voting rights. If the trustee company is a subsidiary of the employer, this raises the issue that the employer will be considered to control the trustee company (see DTR5.2.2(G) and the glossary) and so will be treated as the indirect holder of the indirect voting rights in the shares held by the trustee company (DTR5.2.1(e)).

Limitation clauses

It is prudent to check that any exclusion or limitation clauses affecting the general liability **4.74** of trustees are expressly stated to apply to directors of a trustee company. This is discussed further in Chapter 5.

Less transparency

There is perhaps less transparency. Individual trustees may be more visible to employees etc.

---

[39] SI 1996/1975.
[40] Inserted by Pt 43 of the Companies Act 2006.
[41] See further D Pollard, 'Occupational Pension Schemes: Disclosure of Interests in Shares under Part VI of the Companies Act 1985' (1996) 17 Company Lawyer 272.

4.75 *Registering charges*

4.76 If the trustee company scheme grants a mortgage or charge over any of its assets or the assets of the scheme, this will usually require registration at the companies registry—s 859A of the Companies Act 2006.[42] Section 859J also provides that the trust company may also file a statement that it is acting as a trustee (this does not seem to be compulsory).

Impact of the Pensions Act 1995

4.77 The implications of the Pensions Act 1995 must be considered, for example the member-nominated trustee regime. Use of a trustee company will probably involve slightly more work because changes will need to be made to the articles of association etc. This is considered further later in this chapter at para 4.108.

Need for 'usual residential address' of directors

4.78 Before 1 October 2009, s 289 of the Companies Act 1985 required that details of the 'usual residential address' of each director be included in the details filed at Companies Registry (using form 288). Some directors could, however, claim an exemption. This only applied to directors who were at risk of violence.[43]

4.79 Section 163 of the Companies Act 2006 came into force on 1 October 2009 and allows directors to use a service address instead of their 'usual residential address' on the company's register of directors. This can be stated to be 'The company's registered office'.[44] The director's residential address will still need to be provided to Companies House under s 12 of the Companies Act 2006 but this information will not be publicly available for inspection.[45] Section 165 of the Companies Act 2006 also requires companies to keep a register of the director's usual residential address; however, s 162 of the Companies Act 2006 does not require these details to be made available for public inspection.

4.80 The general requirement to provide public disclosure of the residential address of a director is a distinction from the position of individual trustees, for whom the only registration requirement is with the Pensions Registry, now operated by the Pensions Regulator, where there is no requirement for residential addresses to be given.

Higher penalties levied by the Pensions Regulator

4.81 The maximum civil penalties that the Pensions Regulator can levy are generally greater for trustee companies than they are for individual trustees. See, for example, s 10(2)(a) of the Pensions Act 1995, which fixes a maximum civil penalty of £5,000 for individuals and £50,000 in other cases (ie including companies).

More difficult to entrench trustee structure

4.82 It is more difficult to entrench a particular trustee structure in the trust deed governing the pension scheme (eg providing for half the directors of the corporate trustee to be elected by the members). Such a provision cannot bind the trustee company (even if a party to the trust deed). The issue needs to be dealt with indirectly by a provision that a trustee can only act

---

[42] As inserted from 6 April 2013 by the Companies Act 2006 (Amendment of Part 25) Regulations 2013 (SI 2013/600).
[43] See the Companies (Particulars of Usual Address) (Confidentiality Orders) Regulations 2002 (SI 2002/912).
[44] See s 163(5) of the Companies Act 2006.
[45] See ss 242 and 1087 of the Companies Act 2006.

or be appointed if it complies with the relevant requirements or requiring the employer to ensure that the trustee company complies with the relevant requirements.

For examples see: **4.83**

(a) clause 2A of the Trust Deed governing the Railways Pension Scheme, as set out in the Railways Pension Scheme Order 1994;[46]

(b) clause 1B of the British Coal Staff Superannuation Scheme, as set out in the British Coal Staff Superannuation Scheme (Modification) Regulations 1994;[47] and

(c) clause 3(1) of the Industry-Wide Coal Staff Superannuation Scheme, as set out in the Industry-Wide Coal Staff Superannuation Scheme Regulations 1994.[48] This requires that the articles of association of any new trustee include provisions providing for the appointment of a committee of management including four to be appointed under rules agreed with organizations representing substantial classes of employees.

Disqualification of directors

If one director becomes disqualified from acting as a trustee (eg becomes bankrupt), the **4.84** trustee company is also disqualified (while that director remains on the board)—see s 29 of the Pensions Act 1995 (see Ch 7). The risk of this applying is reduced by a provision in the articles of association providing for a director automatically to cease to hold office if he or she becomes disqualified.

Formerly reduced protection under the Insurance Companies Act 1982

There is now no difference in the level of protection given to trustees as policyholders of an **4.85** insurance company on the insolvency of the insurer.

Use of a trustee company (instead of an individual trustee) used to give a reduced protec- **4.86** tion under the Insurance Companies Act 1982 and the Policyholders Protection Act 1975 on the liquidation of a relevant insurance company with whom the trustees had taken out insurance.

The use of corporate trustees did not affect the protection available in relation to long-term **4.87** business of the insurance company (eg annuities and investment policies etc). However, in relation to general business (eg liability insurance, fire insurance etc) protection was only available under the Insurance Companies Act 1982 if the policyholder was a 'private policy-holder'. This was defined in s 6(7) of the Insurance Companies Act 1982 as an individual or partnership or other incorporated body of persons all of whom are individuals. It seemed that where any of the trustees was a company (even when acting with individuals) none of the trustees was able to claim the protection of the Act—see the decision of the House of Lords in *Scher v Policyholders Protection Board (No 2)*.[49]

The position changed with the replacement of these Acts by the Financial Services and **4.88** Markets Act 2000 (FSMA 2000). The Financial Services Compensation Scheme (FSCS) applies if a UK insurer gets into financial difficulties. The FSCS is broadly a fund established under the FSMA 2000 that compensates policyholders for various losses.

---

[46] SI 1994/1433.
[47] SI 1994/2576.
[48] SI 1994/2973.
[49] [1994] 2 AC 57, HL.

4.89 With regard to general business, in relation to pension scheme trustees there is now no distinction in the protections given to individual trustee policyholders and corporate trustee policyholders. Any trustee (corporate or individual) of an occupational pension scheme of an employer which is a 'large company', 'large partnership', or 'large mutual association' will not receive the benefit of being able to claim for compensation from the FSCS.

4.90 Under the FSCS, a 'large company' is a company that is not a 'small company' under s 382 of the Companies Act 2006 (for accounts and report related to the financial years beginning on or after 6 April 2008).[50] Broadly, a small company is one which satisfies two or more of the following conditions:

(a) a turnover of not more than £5.6m pa for the financial year ending 5 April 2008, and not more than £6.5m pa for financial years ending on or after that date;
(b) a balance sheet total of not more than £2.8m for the financial year ending 5 April 2008, and not more than £3.26m for financial years ending 6 April 2008 or later; and
(c) not more than 50 employees (this is unchanged under the Companies Act 2006).

4.91 Section 383 of the Companies Act 2006 is relevant (and adds additional conditions for qualification as a small company) if the company is a parent company.

4.92 All pension scheme trustees are, though, normally able to claim in relation to long-term insurance. Under the FSCS the exclusion of trustees of pension schemes for large companies does not apply in relation to long-term insurance (see r 4.3.2R).

4.93 There are still some exclusions under the FSCS (eg directors or managers of the insurance company in default), but these will only apply in special circumstances. There are special rules under the FSCS dealing with claims by trustees (eg dealing with the position if the beneficiary of the trust getting the benefit of any claim would themselves be an excluded person)—see rr 12.6.1–12.6.7.

Potential for prohibition on corporate directors

4.94 There may be a problem in using a corporate trustee if it is desired to have a company (eg an independent trustee corporation) as one of the directors. This was allowed under the Companies Act 1985. The government's White Paper on modernizing company law (published in July 2002) stated that it intended to legislate to prohibit companies from acting as directors, but after representations were made, this was not subsequently enacted as part of the Companies Act 2006.

4.95 Sections 154 and 155 of the Companies Act 2006 allow corporate directors, but from 1 October 2008 the company must have at least one director who is a natural person, and this requirement is met if the office of director is held by a natural person as a corporate sole or otherwise by virtue of an office.

4.96 The Companies Act 2006 requirement to have at least one natural person acting as director does not apply to companies until 1 October 2010 if on 8 November 2006 none of the company directors were natural persons, and s 282 of the Companies Act 1985[51] (requirement as to number of directors) was complied with in relation to the company.[52]

---

[50] Formerly s 247 of the Companies Act 1985 (as amended).
[51] Or Art 290 of the Companies (Northern Ireland) Order 1986.
[52] For this transitional provision see Sch 4, Pt 3, para 46 to the Companies Act 2006 (Commencement No 5, Transitional Provisions and Savings) Order 2007 (SI 2007/3495).

VAT

VAT can be quite a confusing issue. There can be some VAT implications in having a corporate **4.97** trustee and including it in a group registration with the employers (although in practice this is unusual).

Trustees of occupational pension schemes will incur various expenses (eg advisers' fees, invest- **4.98** ment managers' fees etc) on which they will be charged VAT. Generally, under the VAT notice on Funded Pension Schemes,[53] HMRC allows the employer to recover input VAT of the trustees of an occupational pension scheme of that employer. This applies whether the trustee is a company or individual trustees. This is subject to various conditions, including that a VAT invoice has been addressed to the employer (see paragraph 5 of VAT notice 700/17/96).

However, this practice is subject to various limitations. The services rendered to the trustees **4.99** must relate to the management of the pension scheme and not to investment matters[54] (see paragraphs 4–7 of VAT notice 700/17/96).

It is possible for a corporate trustee, which is owned by the employer, to be included within **4.100** the employer's VAT group. This would mean that it would be possible for VAT to be recovered on other invoices rendered to the trustees, outside those relating to the management of the scheme covered by VAT notice 700/17/96 (eg investment management fees).

In one case, *Midland Bank plc v Customs & Excise*,[55] the employer managed to structure the **4.101** pension arrangements so that the investment advice etc was made to the employer (rather than to the trustees). This was in the context of the scheme which provided for the employer to perform 'the functions of choosing and reviewing the investment comprised or to be comprised' in the pension fund and to 'appoint a suitable investment manager to provide investment management and advice'. In these circumstances the VAT Tribunal held that the employer could recover the VAT input tax it had paid to the investment managers etc, and that it did not need to charge VAT on its own supply of the advice to the trustees (as there was no consideration for this). This route is probably unavailable since the Pensions Act 1995 came into force, which requires investment matters to be the responsibility of the trustees and not the employer (see s 35(4) of the Pensions Act 1995).

In practice, it is not normally worth trustees considering registering individually for VAT **4.102** purposes (although this may be more relevant with significant land transactions following the change to VAT in this area). A trustee registered for VAT would be able to get a deduction on the fees payable by it (eg to advisers), but there may then be an onward VAT charge on the trustee supplying the advisers' services to the scheme—see the decision of the First Tier Tribunal in *JIB Group Ltd v HMRC*,[56] following the decision of the VAT and Duties Tribunal in *Capital Cranfield Trustees v HMRC*.[57]

Conversely, if a trustee company was established as a subsidiary of the employer (which is **4.103** itself VAT registered), the trustee company could be included within the employer's VAT group.[58] In this case all the companies within the group are treated as one entity for the purposes of paying and recovering VAT.

---

[53] VAT notice 700/17/96 Value Added Tax—Funded Pension Schemes.
[54] But see now the ECJ decision in *Re PPG Holdings BV* (Case C-26/12) (2013) 18 July.
[55] [1993] VATTR 525.
[56] [2012] UKFTT 547.
[57] [2008] UKVAT V20532.
[58] See s 43(3) of the Value Added Tax Act 1994 as to the relevant definition of control.

4.104 The advantages and disadvantages of such a group registration are listed below.

(a) The ability of a VAT group to recover all its VAT depends on the level of its exempt supplies etc compared to its other vatable supplies. The pension scheme may well have a significant level of exempt supplies (eg dealings in securities). This could affect the percentage level of recovery of the VAT group as a whole.

(b) Conversely, including the trustee company in the VAT group may allow recovery of investment management expenses (not within VAT notice 700/17/96). See, for example, *BOC International Ltd v Customs & Excise.*[59]

(c) Including a trustee company within a VAT group of the employer would allow supply of services by another company within the employer's group to be free of VAT. This could be helpful if the employer is a member of the financial services group with its own fund manager etc.

(d) The rules relating to group registration for VAT purposes generally impose joint and separate liabilities on each of the members of a VAT group for the VAT liabilities of the group (through its representative member). This could be an issue if this liability meant that the assets of the pension scheme could be attacked by HMRC in order to settle the employer's VAT liabilities. However, HMRC has indicated that it will not make a claim against the assets of a pension trust. Paragraph 15 of VAT notice 700/17/96 states:

> 15 Liability to meet the VAT debts of the representative member
>
> All members of a group registration are jointly and severally liable for the tax due from the representative member. In the event of that member being unable to meet the VAT debt of the group, each group member will, as a general rule, be liable for the amount of the debt arising during the period that they were members of the group. However, where a corporate trustee is included in a group registration, Customs are advised that this liability does not extend to the assets of any trust, eg a pension fund of which the corporate trustee is the trustee, except to the extent the group VAT debt is attributable in whole or in part to the administration of the trust.

Impact of the Pensions Act 1995 and Pensions Act 2004

4.105 The Pensions Act 1995 and the Pensions Act 2004 generally refer to various obligations on trustees. In doing this, the natural interpretation is that they must be referring to the trustee itself (ie the trustee company) and not to the individual directors.

4.106 Indeed, the Acts in various places clearly go on to refer to directors of trustee companies, for instance:

(a) s 242 of the Pensions Act 2004 (previously ss 18 and 19 of the Pensions Act 1995) dealing with member-nominated directors of corporate trustees;

(b) s 3(2)(e) of the Pensions Act 1995 dealing with prohibition orders against certain directors of trustee companies;

(c) s 10(5) of the Pensions Act 1995 dealing with civil penalties against directors of trustee companies; and

(d) s 115 of the Pensions Act 1995 dealing with potential liability of directors for offences by bodies corporate.

---

[59] [1982] VATTR 84.

The Pensions Bill that led to the Pensions Act 1995 did not originally draw these distinctions **4.107** very carefully. The position of corporate trustees was only dealt with through (relatively late) amendments to the Bill during its passage through Parliament. This means that, in practice, the Pensions Act 1995 does not deal terribly well with the position of corporate trustees in a number of respects.

Member-nominated directors

Sections 16–21 of the Pensions Act 1995 dealt with the position of member-nominated **4.108** trustees and member-nominated directors. Section 18 dealt with member-nominated directors and applied where there is a corporate trustee and 'the company is connected with the employer or prescribed conditions are satisfied'. In these circumstances the trustee company needed to arrange for compliance with ss 18 and 19 dealing with member-nominated directors.

The Occupational Pension Schemes (Member-nominated Trustees and Directors) Regulations **4.109** 1996[60] (the 'MNT Regulations'), as amended, confirmed in reg 4(1)(a) that if each trustee is a company (ie so that s 18 of the Pensions Act 1995 applies—see reg 5 of SI 1996/1216) then there was no need to go down the member-nominated trustees route in ss 16 and 17.

These sections (and regulations) were repealed and replaced (during 2006) by ss 241–243 of the **4.110** Pensions Act 2004. The new provisions are much less prescriptive than the 1995 Act provisions (although they require that at least one-third of the directors are member-nominated). The 2004 Act is clearer that the requirements in s 242 (and any relevant regulations) have effect to override the memorandum and articles of association of a corporate trustee (s 306(4) and (5)).

Liability of directors under the Pensions Act 1995

In general, relevant fines and penalties under the Pensions Act 1995 and the Pensions Act **4.111** 2004 will be imposed on the trustee, ie the trustee company. However, there is provision for this liability to flow through to the directors of a trustee company in certain circumstances.

For example, s 10(5) entitles the Pensions Regulator to levy a civil penalty against a director **4.112** of a trustee company if the company would be so liable for a penalty and the relevant act or omission of the trustee company 'was done with the consent or connivance of, or is attributable to any neglect on the part of', any director.

A similar provision applies under s 115 in relation to criminal offences under Pt I of the **4.113** Pensions Act 1995 and under s 309 of the Pensions Act 2004. The effect of these provisions is discussed in the next chapter.

Prohibition

If a trustee company was prohibited from acting as a trustee on a particular trust scheme **4.114** under s 3 of the Pensions Act 1995 (as originally enacted), that prohibition used to be extendible by Opra to a director of the company if Opra was satisfied that the acts or defaults giving rise to those circumstances were committed with the consent or connivance of, or attributable to any neglect on the part of, the director. It would appear that, under s 3(2)(e), if the director had resigned quickly enough on the trustee company being prohibited then

---

[60] SI 1996/1216.

it may not have been possible for Opra to make an order under that section. This section referred to a person who 'is' a director of a company which is prohibited. A director who was prohibited under s 3 could then be disqualified from acting as a trustee of any pension scheme under s 29(3)(a) of the Pensions Act 1995.

4.115 But s 3 has now been replaced by new provisions under the Pensions Act 2004, and these no longer deal specifically with directors.

Disqualification

4.116 Section 29 of the Pensions Act 1995 generally deals with disqualification of trustees of any occupational pension scheme established under trust (see further Chapter 7 (Regulator powers to appoint, remove, or disqualify trustees)).

4.117 In relation to a corporate trustee, it is clear that the trustee company is disqualified under s 29 of the Pensions Act 1995 if any director of the company is disqualified under s 29 (see s 29(1)(c)). This could cause problems for trustee companies. It may not be very easy to find out if a particular director has in fact become disqualified. Failure to know that an individual has been disqualified does not seem to be a defence to the criminal offence under s 30(3) of the Pensions Act 1995 of acting as a trustee while disqualified. In addition, disqualification automatically triggers the company ceasing to be a trustee (although there appears to be a saving under s 30(6) for things done while purporting to act as a trustee).

4.118 It would be prudent for trustee companies to change their articles of association to include an express provision providing that an individual director will cease to hold office on ceasing to be qualified to act as a trustee (under ss 29, 3 or 4 of the Pensions Act 1995 or otherwise).

4.119 There seems to be a bit of a timing conundrum here. Will the courts regard the cessation of acting as a director as preceding the disqualification under s 29(1)(c) of the Pensions Act 1995 in relation to the trustee company, or will they regard it as being too late, ie that once a bankruptcy order is made against the director this has the effect of automatically causing the trustee company to cease to be a trustee albeit that the director also ceases (at the same time or later) to be a director of the trustee company? This second solution seems impractical (although presumably it would be open to the sponsoring employer etc to arrange to reappoint the trustee company).

Time off for employee trustees

4.120 One example of the problems with the position of a trustee company arises under ss 58–60 of the Employment Rights Act 1996.[61] These give general protections (rights to time off and no unfair detriment etc) to employees who are trustees of a pension scheme of the employer.

4.121 As originally enacted, the sections did not apply to employees acting as directors of a corporate trustee. Changes were made by the Welfare Reform and Pensions Act 1999.[62] This amended the 1996 Act so that it expressly covers employees who are acting as directors of a trustee company. The amendments apply from 25 April 2000.

---

[61] Which consolidated and replaced ss 42–46 of the Pensions Act 1995.
[62] Schedule 2, para 19.

Conflicts of interest—s 39 of the Pensions Act 1995

Section 39 of the Pensions Act 1995, the 'Drexel' provision, allows trustees to exercise powers **4.122** even though they are also members. This was enacted following the decision of Lindsay J in *Manning v Drexel Burnham Lambert*[63]—see the discussion by Scott V-C in *Edge v Pensions Ombudsman.*[64]

The section only refers to trustees and not to directors of corporate trustees. The rest of the **4.123** Pensions Act contains numerous distinctions between a trustee who is a company and one where individuals are trustees. It is unlikely that a court would construe s 39 so as to cover directors of a corporate trustee (although they may well find an implied provision to the same effect—see *Edge v Pensions Ombudsman* and Chapter 6 (Conflict issues for pension trustees)).

Delegation by trustees—s 34 of the Pensions Act 1995

Section 34 of the Pensions Act 1995 deals with delegation by trustees of investment **4.124** powers and limits to whom they can be delegated. As was pointed out by the Legislative and Parliamentary Committee of the Association of Pension Lawyers (APL) to the then Department of Social Security, the limits on delegation are not expressed to apply to any 'delegation' by corporate trustees to some of the directors or to other agents.

In practice, a company can only act through its agents (eg the directors or others). On this **4.125** basis it is logical that as a matter of law a decision by the board of directors of a trustee company that (say) an investment committee (of the directors or including non-directors) is authorized to take decisions on investment matters is not actually a delegation but rather a method of formalizing how the trustee company itself will take the relevant decision. The decision is an internal corporate matter (involving the fixing of the appropriate person within the corporation) rather than a formal external delegation.

Appointment of advisers

Section 47 of the Pensions Act 1995 deals with the requirement for various advisers to be **4.126** appointed by the trustees. This includes the auditor, the actuary and, in practice, the fund manager and the legal adviser.

It seems easier to use a corporate trustee in this context to avoid any question of whether or **4.127** not any such appointments (and they are required by regulations to be in writing) need to be renewed if there is a change of individual trustees.

The practice to date seems to be not to require the renewal of these appointments even where **4.128** there is a change of individual trustees. This seems right, but the position is clearer for a corporate trustee.

---

[63] [1994] OPLR 71, [1995] 1 WLR 32 (Lindsay J).
[64] [1998] 2 All ER 547 (Scott V-C).

Trustee indemnities

4.129 Section 256 of the Pensions Act 2004 (replacing s 31 of the Pensions Act 1995) prohibits indemnities out of the assets of the scheme in relation to fines or penalties imposed on any 'trustee or manager' under the Pensions Act 1995 or the Pension Schemes Act 1993.

4.130 It may be arguable that nothing in s 256 prohibits any such payments being made to indemnify directors of corporate trustees for such fines or penalties. However, again a purposive approach would operate to extend this prohibition. As against that, breach of s 256 is a criminal offence (see s 256(5) of the Pensions Act 2004) and so a strict construction may be more appropriate.[65]

Trustee meetings

4.131 Section 32 of the Pensions Act 1995 provides for an amendment of the general trust law rule (discussed above) that trustees must generally make decisions unanimously (as recommended by the Pension Law Reform Committee,[66] chaired by Professor Goode, which preceded the Pensions Act 1995).

4.132 In practice, such provisions are normally amended by the trust instrument in relation to pension schemes. Section 32(1) allows the trust instrument to provide otherwise.

4.133 Section 32 appears to be relatively inflexibly drafted in that it states: 'Decisions of the trustees of a trust scheme may, unless the scheme provides otherwise, be taken by agreement of a majority of the trustees.'

4.134 It should be noted that the requirement is that the majority of the trustees must agree any decision, not merely the majority of the trustees present at the relevant meeting. In addition, there is no provision envisaged for a casting vote (eg the chairman). Decisions of trustees will, therefore, differ in this respect from decisions of company directors (see eg reg 88 of Table A, SI 1985/805).

4.135 It is perhaps unclear whether trustees who have been disqualified or removed under ss 3, 4, or 29 of the Pensions Act 1995 can still count towards quorums etc for this purpose. There are savings for the actions of such trustees—ss 6(3) and 30(5). Would these savings still apply if all parties were aware of the disqualification? Section 32(2)(a) also allows for the trustees to fix a quorum for meetings, unless the scheme provides otherwise.

4.136 Again, it would be prudent for the trust instrument to provide otherwise in that it is unclear whether physical presence is required under s 32(2)(a) or whether presence by proxy or at the end of a telephone or video link would suffice.

4.137 Section 32(2)(b) of the Pensions Act 1995 provides that:

> notice of any occasions at which decisions may be so taken must, unless the occasion falls within a prescribed class or description, be given to each trustee to whom it is reasonably practical to give such notice.

---

[65] See further, Ch 14 (Trustee indemnities and exonerations).
[66] CM 2342.

It is unclear how far this extends—what is an occasion 'at which decisions may be so taken'? **4.138** The 1996 Scheme Administration regulations[67] specify certain minimum requirements for such a notice. In particular, reg 10 of these regulations says it must be in writing and sent not less than ten days before the meeting.

Generally, the difficulties with s32 of the Pensions Act 1995 mean that it is probably easier **4.139** to use a trustee company so that s 32 will not apply. Instead, provisions as regard majority voting and notice of meetings will be governed by the provisions of the articles of association of the trustee company.

Record keeping

Regulations under this section can require trustees to keep records of their meetings. **4.140** Regulation 13 of the 1996 Scheme Administration Regulations requires records to be kept of various matters including the date and time of all meetings, who was present, and the decisions made. It seems clear that these requirements do not apply to a meeting of the board of directors of a corporate trustee. Instead, the (minimal) requirements of the articles (eg Table A) and the companies legislation will apply.

Whistle-blowing and notification

Section 70 of the Pensions Act 2004 (replacing s 48 of the Pensions Act 1995) contains a **4.141** wide requirement to whistle blow to the Pensions Regulator. This extends to a trustee and to any person 'involved in the administration of such a scheme'. Section 70(3) then goes on to give an immunity from breach of duty where a report is lodged under s 70 (excluding any legal adviser in relation to matters (broadly) subject to legal professional privilege— see s 311).

It seems clear that a director of a corporate trustee would fall within the category of 'any **4.142** person involved in administration of such a scheme' and so within s 70.

Section 69 contains an obligation on the trustee to notify the Pensions Regulator of various **4.143** events. This obligation falls on the trustee, not on a director. But the Pensions Regulator has power to levy a civil penalty under s 10 of the Pensions Act 1995 for failure to comply with either s 69 or s 70. As discussed above, a director of a corporate trustee can be held responsible under s 10 if he or she is the cause of the failure.

Assignment, forfeiture etc

Section 91 of the Pensions Act 1995 deals with the inalienability of an occupational pension. **4.144** There are various exceptions to this principle contained in s 91(5).

Section 91(5)(e) includes an exception for a charge or lien or set off against a person's benefit **4.145** for the purpose of discharging monetary obligations due from the person in question to the scheme arising out of a criminal, negligent, or fraudulent act or omission by him or 'in the case of a trust scheme of which the person in question is a trustee, arising out of a breach of trust by him'.

Again, it is unclear whether this would extend to some sort of default by a director of a trustee **4.146** company. Arguably, if such a director is liable as an accessory (see Chapter 5 (Liability of

---

[67] Occupational Pension Schemes (Scheme Administration) Regulations 1996 (SI 1996/1715).

directors of corporate trustees)) then there has been a breach of trust by him and so the section should apply.

Pensions Ombudsman

4.147 The Pensions Ombudsman has jurisdiction to hear complaints of maladministration and disputes of fact or law.[68]

4.148 The regulations clarify that such claims can also be brought by members against an administrator. This is defined (in relation to an occupational pension scheme) as meaning: 'any person concerned with the administration of the scheme'. This means that a wide range of persons are potentially within the jurisdiction of the Pensions Ombudsman and this probably includes directors of a trustee company.

4.149 The then Pensions Ombudsman indicated in his Annual Report for 1996/97 that he considers this wording to be wide enough to catch directors of a trustee company. Subsequently, the Pensions Ombudsman has held that directors of a corporate trustee are administrators and so within his jurisdiction—see the determination in April 1999 in *Globe v Jas F&C Carter Ltd*.[69]

4.150 The Pensions Act 1995 extended the jurisdiction of the Pensions Ombudsman to include complaints by (and not just against) trustees in some cases. Section 157 referred to a complaint by 'the trustees' so it seems that the jurisdiction required action by all the trustees, not just a minority dissenting trustee.

4.151 Section 146(1)(e) of the Pension Schemes Act 1993 was inserted by the Child Support, Pensions and Social Security Act 2000. It allows the Ombudsman to determine disputes between individual trustees of the same occupational pension scheme. This would not seem to allow disputes between directors of a corporate trustee to be heard.

4.152 Section 146(1)(g) of the Pension Schemes Act 1993 allows the Ombudsman to determine questions relating to the carrying out of functions by a sole trustee. The question must be referred to him by or on behalf of the sole trustee—s 146(1A)(e) of the Pension Schemes Act 1993. It seems that this is most naturally construed as requiring any reference to the Ombudsman to have been authorized by the sole trustee. In the case of a corporate trustee this will be by a resolution of the board of directors. Thus it seems not to allow a single director to refer a dispute with the other directors to the Ombudsman (unless they also resolve that the matter should be referred).

Trustee knowledge and understanding

4.153 There are separate obligations under s 248 of the Pensions Act 2004 for a trustee company to ensure that each relevant individual who exercises any function of the trustee company is conversant with the documents of the scheme and has knowledge and understanding of the law of pensions and trusts and principles relating to funding and investments. These obligations are similar to those for individual trustees under s 247, but it is noticeable that they

---

[68] Section 146 of the Pension Schemes Act 1993 and the Personal and Occupational Pension Schemes (Pensions Ombudsman) Regulations 1996 (SI 1996/2475, as amended).

[69] (1999) 22 April, F00060 (Farrand PO) at para 36. On the jurisdiction of the Pensions Ombudsman in relation to administrators, see the decision of the Court of Appeal in *R (on the application of Government Actuary's Department) v Pensions Ombudsman* [2013] EWCA Civ 901, [2013] All ER (D) 259 (Jul), CA.

extend to all individuals acting for the trustee company in relation to the scheme, not just the directors and officers.

The Occupational Pension Schemes (Trustees' Knowledge and Understanding) Regulations **4.154**
2006[70] allow individual trustees and directors of a trustee company a grace period after their first appointment in which to comply with this duty. This does not apply if:

(a) he is an independent trustee who meets the requirements of s 23(1) of the Pensions Act 1995; or

(b) he was appointed as a consequence of holding himself out as having expertise in any of the matters listed in s 248(5) of the Pensions Act 2004 or in any regulations made under para (c) of that section.

---

[70] SI 2006/686.

5

LIABILITY OF DIRECTORS OF CORPORATE TRUSTEES

5.1 An occupational pension scheme established as a trustee will need a group of individuals to act as the controlling body—either as individual trustees or as directors of a corporate trustee. Using a corporate trustee has become more common and has many advantages (see the preceding chapter).

5.2 This chapter[1] looks at how the personal liability position of relevant individuals differs if they are directors of a trustee company, compared to being individual trustees.

Individual Trustees v Directors

5.3 Where individuals are appointed to act as trustees themselves, they owe personal liabilities to contractual creditors of the trust (in the absence of an exclusion in the relevant contract)—see *Muir v City of Glasgow Bank*,[2] and for a more recent example, *Marston Thomas and Evershed plc v Benn*.[3]

---

[1] This chapter is derived largely from part of a chapter in *Tolley's Pension Law* (LexisNexis), which itself was derived from D Pollard, 'Pension Schemes: Corporate Trustees' (2000) 14 TLI 2. On the position in Australia, see PF Hanrahan, 'Directors' Liability in Superannuation Trustee Companies' (2008) 2 J Eq 204 and the talk by Justice Ashley Black, 'Understanding the Impact of Recent Cases on Directors Duties' (2012) Simply Super conference—on the NSW supreme court website: <http://www.supremecourt.lawlink.nsw.gov.au/agdbasev7wr/supremecourt/documents/pdf/black_2012.02.24.pdf>.

[2] (1879) 4 App Cas 337, HL. In Australia, see *Octavo Investments Pty Ltd v Knight* [1979] HCA 61, (1979) 144 CLR 360, HC Aus at 367; *Vacuum Oil Co Pty Ltd v Wiltshire* [1945] HCA 37, (1945) 72 CLR 319, HC Aus at 335, 324. In relation to tort liabilities see *JA Pty Ltd v Jonco Holdings Pty Ltd* [2000] NSWSC 147, (2000) 33 ACSR 691 (Santow J).

[3] (1999) *The Times*, 18 May, [2007] WTLR 315 (Chadwick J).

Similarly, an individual trustee will be personally liable to provide the relevant benefits envisaged by the trust instrument (although these will normally be limited by the trust instrument to the assets in the trust) and will be fully personally liable for a breach of trust (subject to any relevant exoneration provision). **5.4**

Is the position of the individual any better where he or she is merely a director of a trustee company rather than specifically a trustee? Can the individual shelter behind the separate legal personality of the trustee company? **5.5**

The answer is that the position of the individual is improved where he or she is a director as opposed to being a trustee. However, it cannot be said that the individual escapes all responsibility insofar as the actions of the trustee company affect creditors and/or beneficiaries of the trust. **5.6**

Creditors

Generally, liabilities will be incurred by the trustee company to individual creditors, for example under contracts. On usual principles, directors of the trustee company will not be liable to those creditors save in extreme circumstances—see *Salomon v Salomon & Co Ltd.*[4] **5.7**

Given that a trustee company commonly has only a very small issued share capital and small personal (as opposed to trust) assets, the directors would obviously need to consider the solvency position of the trustee company at the time the liabilities are entered into. The trustee company will usually have an indemnity for liabilities properly incurred by it out of the trust assets (see eg Trustee Act 2000, s 31 and Chapter 14 (Trustee indemnities and exonerations)). Usually this will mean that the trustee company is solvent. **5.8**

If solvency becomes a problem (eg because the trust assets are insufficient) the directors must consider their position under the insolvency legislation, particularly in relation to wrongful trading (Insolvency Act 1986, s 214) and fraudulent trading (Insolvency Act 1986, s 213). **5.9**

There is also an expanding line of recent judicial authority imposing duties on directors to consider the interests of creditors in the position where the company's solvency is in question.[5] **5.10**

Section 170 of the Companies Act 2006 makes it clear that director's duties under the Act are owed to the company. Section 172 of the Companies Act 2006 says a director must act in the way he considers, in good faith, would be most likely to promote the success of the company for the benefit of its members as a whole having regard to various matters including the interest of the company's employees and the need to foster the company's business relationships with suppliers, customers, and others. **5.11**

Liability to trust beneficiaries

Where a company acts as a trustee, clearly in practice the actual decisions in relation to the trust will have to be made by individuals. Commonly those individuals will be directors or employees of the trustee company. **5.12**

---

[4] [1897] AC 22, HL.
[5] *Winkworth v Edward Baron Development Co Ltd* [1987] 1 All ER 114, HL; *West Mercia Safetyware v Dodd* [1988] BCLC 250, CA; and *Re Pantone 485 Ltd* [2002] 1 BCLC 266 (Richard Field QC).

5.13 Clearly if the trustee company commits a breach of trust as a result of such a decision, the company itself will be liable, in the usual way, to the beneficiaries and others affected. This will be subject to the terms of any relevant clause in the trust instrument limiting or excluding liability (generally these will be effective save for actual fraud (ie dishonesty)—see *Armitage v Nurse*[6]).

5.14 However, are the individuals who actually made the decision (or omitted to act in the case of an omission) on the part of the trustee company also potentially liable, or can they shelter behind the corporate personality of the trustee company and so escape all personal liability altogether?

Basis for Liability to Beneficiaries

5.15 A director or employee could potentially become personally liable to a beneficiary by the following six different routes.

(a) Through a direct fiduciary duty owed to beneficiaries by directors of corporate trustees.

(b) Through a direct tort duty owed to beneficiaries by directors of corporate trustees.

(c) By an accessory liability, ie as a third party who dishonestly procures or assists in a breach of trust (by the trustee company).

(d) An indirect duty, eg as a fiduciary or a duty of care in tort or contract, ie that the individual director owed a duty to the trustee company. This can then be enforced by the company itself (eg through its liquidator) or arguably the benefit of the claim based on breach of that duty is an asset of the trust and so could be enforced by the new trustees and/or by a beneficiary. Lindsay J in *HR v JAPT*[7] called this a 'dog-leg claim'.

(e) By the corporate veil of the trustee company being disregarded and pierced.

(f) By statute operating to impose direct liabilities for criminal fines and penalties onto directors and officers.

5.16 Case law indicates that routes (a), (b), and (e) are unlikely to be available in most circumstances. However, routes (c), (d), and (f) will usually apply to define the legal duties owed. Below is a more detailed discussion of the six bases for personal liability.

Direct fiduciary duty

5.17 This would, in effect, be a claim that a director of a company which is also a trustee is automatically liable for any breaches of trust by the trustee company.

5.18 There was some support for a direct approach in two unreserved judgments of Dankwerts J in the 1950s: *Re French Protestant Hospital*[8] and *Abbey and Malvern Wells Ltd v Ministry of Local Government*.[9] In these cases Dankwerts J held that (in effect) directors owed direct fiduciary duties to beneficiaries of the trust of which the company was trustee. These two cases were supported, to a degree, by comments of Vinelott J in *Re Thompson's Settlement*.[10]

---

[6] [1998] Ch 241, CA and see Ch 14 (Trustee indemnities and exonerations).
[7] [1997] OPLR 123 (Lindsay J).
[8] [1951] Ch 567 (Dankwerts J).
[9] [1951] Ch 728 (Dankwerts J).
[10] [1986] Ch 99 (Vinelott J).

However, both judgments of Dankwerts J are unreserved and do not seem well argued. More **5.19**
recently in *HR v JAPT*,[11] Lindsay J pointed out that the earlier Court of Appeal authorities of
Wilson v Lord Bury[12] and *Bath v Standard Land*[13] had not been cited to Dankwerts J. In both
these cases the Court of Appeal had held (by a majority in the *Bath* case) that directors were
not as such liable for breaches of trust by the trustee company.

In the *HR* case the plaintiffs' counsel sought to distinguish these two Court of Appeal decisions **5.20**
by arguing that they should not apply to the case of a trustee company that administers only
one trust and has only a very small issued share capital. However, Lindsay J considered that
he was not, without more, able to depart from the clear expressions of principle of the Court
of Appeal.

Lindsay J also considered two Australian decisions: Finn J in *Australian Securities Commission* **5.21**
v AS Nominees[14] and Walters J in *Hurley v BGH Nominees Ltd.*[15]

Lindsay J did not refer to other Australian authorities that can be seen as supporting the *Bath* **5.22**
approach—see *Galladin Pty v AimNorth Pty Ltd*;[16] and *Jeffrey v NCSC*.[17] He did discuss, in a
later part of the judgment, another Australian case, *Young v Murphy*.[18]

Accordingly, Lindsay J held:[19] **5.23**

> In my judgment neither subsequent English authority nor Commonwealth authority enables
> me to distinguish *Bath*…There is a broad principle, as Cozens-Hardy MR described it in
> *Bath* at page 627, that the directors of a trust company stand in a fiduciary position only to
> the company itself not to strangers dealing with the company and not even where the stranger
> is able to describe himself as a beneficiary of the trust of which the company is trustee. Whilst
> exceptional facts can be envisaged, as Finn J suggested and as *Barnes v Addy* (as I shall come
> to) illustrates, in which a finding of a fiduciary relationship between a beneficiary and the directors
> of the trustee company may be justified, I do not see the facts here relied on in argument,
> consisting only of directors purporting to act as such and acting (alleged carelessness apart)
> as one might expect directors of a trustee company to act, to be sufficient to enable any such
> a finding. In other words, at any rate at first instance and so long as *Bath* stands, I regard this
> way of putting the Plaintiffs' case as unarguable.

This seems right as a matter of principle. It seems wrong to impose an automatic liability, **5.24**
effectively as a guarantor, on directors of a trustee company regardless of their involvement
in the particular circumstances.

Subsequent cases have followed this approach. In Guernsey, the Royal Court has held, in **5.25**
Cross v Benitrust International (CI) Ltd,[20] that a director of a trustee company does not owe
automatically a direct fiduciary duty to a beneficiary of a trust. The judge followed the decision of the Court of Appeal in *Bath v Standard Land*.

---

[11] [1997] OPLR 123 (Lindsay J).
[12] (1880) 5 QBD 518, CA.
[13] [1911] 1 Ch 681, CA.
[14] [1996] PLR 297, (1995) 13 ACLC 1822 (Finn J).
[15] [1984] 10 ACLR 197 (Walters J).
[16] (1993) 11 ACLC 838 (Perry J).
[17] (1989) 7 ACLC 556 (Wallace, Brinsden, and Pidgeon JJ).
[18] (1994) 12 ACLC 558, [1996] VicRp 19, [1996] 1 VR 279 (Brooking, Phillips, and Batt JJ).
[19] *HR v JAPT* [1997] OPLR 123 (Lindsay J) at 133.
[20] (1998/99) 2 OFLR 32.

5.26   More recently, in 2008, in *Gregson v HAE Trustees Ltd*,[21] Robert Miles QC held in a case involving a private trust (and not a pension scheme) that there was no question of a direct fiduciary duty owed by directors of a trustee company to beneficiaries, again following the decision of the Court of Appeal in *Bath v Standard Land*. He also held that a 'dog leg' claim was not arguable in the case where the trustee company was the trustee of several trusts.

5.27   Similarly in Australia, it has been consistently held that directors of a corporate trustee do not generally owe fiduciary duties to trust beneficiaries. In *McEwen v Combined Coast Cranes Pty Ltd*[22] Young CJ in Eq said:

> Of course there is the problem as to how far the directors of the trustee or how far Trevor and Terry could be personally liable if there was a liability in this connection. The stronger view appears to be that it is only in very rare circumstances that the directors of a trustee company being agents of the company are personally liable for the defaults.[23]

5.28   To similar effect is the observation of Brereton J in *Fay v Moramba Services Pty Ltd*:[24]

> There is significant authority against the proposition that directors of a trustee company owe a fiduciary duty to the beneficiaries merely by reason of their position as directors.[25]

5.29   Perhaps it could be argued that trust beneficiaries are not in the same position as normal contractual creditors, since such creditors are voluntary creditors as they take the risk of dealing with a limited liability company. Conversely, trust beneficiaries can be seen as involuntary claimants and so deserve greater protection. However, this argument would also apply in relation to other involuntary claims, eg claims based on tort. This argument seems likely to be very difficult to sustain following the decision of the Privy Council in *Re Goldcorp Exchange: Liggett v Kensington*.[26]

5.30   As an alternative, it could be argued that it would be right to impose such an automatic liability only in the case of specific trustee companies set up in relation to one trust and with a very limited capital. This was argued by counsel in *HR v JAPT*,[27] drawing a contrast with the earlier Court of Appeal decisions.[28] Conversely, perhaps only those directors actually involved in the relevant decision with knowledge of the relevant facts could be held directly liable.

---

[21] [2008] EWHC 1006 (Ch), [2008] 2 BCLC 542 (Robert Miles QC, sitting as a deputy High Court Judge).

[22] [2002] NSWSC 1227, (2003) 44 ACSR 244 (Young CJ in Eq) at 251 [54].

[23] Citing: *Bath v Standard Land Co Ltd* [1911] 1 Ch 618; *Hurley v BGH Nominees Pty Ltd* (1982) 31 SASR 250; *Re James* [1949] SASR 143, [1949] ALR 367; Young CJ's own decision in *Glandon Pty Ltd v Strata Consolidated Pty Ltd (No 3)* (unreported, SC(NSW), Young J No 4258/1988, 4 June 1990, BC9002364); and the paper by HAJ Ford and IJ Hardingham, 'Trading Trusts: Rights and Liabilities of Beneficiaries' in PD Finn (ed), *Equity and Commercial Relationships* (Law Book Co, 1987), 48 at 60ff.

[24] [2009] NSWSC 1428 at [29] (Brereton J). See also *Hackett v Nambucca Valley Quarries Pty Ltd* [2012] NSWSC 1189 at [35] (Gzell J).

[25] Citing: *Australian Securities Commission v AS Nominees Ltd* [1995] FCA 1663, (1995) 62 FCR 504, 522 (Finn J); *Young v Murphy* [1996] 1 VR 279, 301–2 (JD Phillips J); *Pope v Butcher* (1996) 20 ACSR 37; *Collie v Merlaw Nominees Pty Ltd* [1998] VSC 203, [96] (Byrne J); cf *Hurley v BGH Nominees Pty Ltd* (1984) 2 ACLC 497, which was to the contrary, but is criticized in RI Barrett, 'Recent Cases' (1985) 59 ALJ 46, 47.

[26] [1995] 1 AC 74, PC. See in particular Lord Mustill at 104D, but compare the comments at 109H based on 'swollen assets' and 'involuntary creditors etc'. Similarly, the Supreme Court in Canada: *Sun Indalex Finance LLC v United Steelworkers* (2013) SCC 6, SC Can.

[27] [1997] OPLR 123 (Lindsay J).

[28] See also *Gregson v HAE Trustees Ltd* [2008] EWHC 1006 (Ch), [2008] 2 BCLC 542 (Robert Miles QC).

However, both these approaches involve drawing a line at some stage. When would a director **5.31** be held to have sufficient knowledge? When would a trustee company be considered to be under-capitalized for this purpose? It must be better in the interests of certainty to keep the line clear. Indeed, as counsel pointed out in the *HR* case, it is difficult to see why the questions of 'accessory' liability can arise in relation to directors (as many of the leading cases involved) if the direct fiduciary liability route is available.

The comments in *Wilson* were approved in 1991 by the Privy Council in *Kuwait Asia v* **5.32** *National Mutual Life Nominees.*[29]

In *Gregson v HAE Trustees Ltd*,[30] Robert Miles QC (sitting as a deputy High Court Judge) **5.33** held that there was no question of a direct fiduciary duty owed by directors of a trustee company to beneficiaries, following the decision of the Court of Appeal in *Bath v Standard Land.*[31]

To some extent the argument in favour of a direct fiduciary duty (rejected in the *HAE* and **5.34** *HR* decisions) rests on treating the directors of a trustee company as being the decision makers in practice and so should be treated as if they were trustees. This, however, would be to ignore the corporate status of the trustee company.[32] Support of this 'no direct fiduciary duty approach' (recognizing the status of the corporate entity) is given by the recent decision of the High Court in Australia in *Montevento Holdings Pty Ltd v Scaffidi.*[33]

In *Montevento* the High Court held (overturning a majority decision in the Western Australia **5.35** Court of Appeal) that an individual with the power of appointment of trustees was allowed to appoint a company in which the individual was the sole director and all the shares in which were owned by the appointor. The High Court held that the trust deed clearly distinguished between individuals and corporations and that this meant that the appointment was not contrary to an express limitation in the power of appointment (which provided that 'so long as any individual Appointor is a Beneficiary that individual shall not be eligible to be appointed as a Trustee').

Direct tort duty

The plaintiffs in *HR v JAPT*[34] argued that a director of a trustee company could owe direct **5.36** duties in tort to the beneficiaries in the following two ways:

(a) By the imposition of a duty to act with care and skill on those who take upon themselves to act for others, following comments of the House of Lords in 1995 in *Henderson v Merrett Syndicates Ltd*[35] and *White v Jones.*[36]

---

[29] [1991] 1 AC 187, PC.
[30] [2008] EWHC 1006 (Ch), [2008] 2 BCLC 542 (Robert Miles QC).
[31] [1911] 1 Ch 681, CA.
[32] See eg the House of Lords in *Salomon v A Salomon & Co Ltd* [1897] AC 22, HL and, more recently, the Supreme Court in *Holland v Revenue and Customs Comrs* [2010] UKSC 51, [2011] 1 All ER 430, SC, holding that where an individual (A) who was a director of a company (B) that was itself a director of a second company (C), this meant that B was the director of C and that A was not a de facto director of C within the wrongful trading provisions in s 212 of the Insolvency Act 1986 on the insolvency of C.
[33] [2012] HCA 48, HC Aus.
[34] [1997] OPLR 123 (Lindsay J).
[35] [1995] 2 AC 145, HL.
[36] [1995] 2 AC 207, HL.

(b) On the basis that directors can be personally liable in tort for actions of their company—following cases such as the decision of the Court of Appeal in *Williams v Natural Life Health Foods Ltd* [37] (later in any event reversed on appeal[38]).

5.37 However, Lindsay J considered that no such tort liability could arise here. He considered that arguments based on an imposition of a duty of care where persons act for others in tort could only apply where there was otherwise a lacuna in the law which would be unjust. For example, in *White v Jones* the projected beneficiaries of the deceased would have no claim open to them against the negligent solicitor unless a tortious duty was involved. Lindsay J in *HR v JAPT* considered that he:

> cannot read the broad language as intended impliedly to override long established existing principles as to the identification, outside the identified lacuna, of as between whom fiduciary relationships exist or as to the identity of he who should be taken to have been the actor who should have assumed responsibility and who, on that account, became vulnerable to a claim.

5.38 Here there was no lacuna in the law and to hold otherwise would in effect be to overturn the well-established principles of separate corporate personality (and liability) found in *Salomon v Salomon*.[39] Accordingly, this argument did not have any prospect of success.

5.39 The second argument was based on the principle that where a tort has been committed by a company, the court has, by reference to special facts, felt able to impose liability on the director or directors personally concerned. Lindsay J discussed what was then the recent decision of the Court of Appeal in *Williams v Natural Life Health Foods*[40] (itself discussing the New Zealand decision in *Trevor Ivory v Anderson*[41]). In this case a director was held personally liable for a misrepresentation made by the company in a leaflet issued to clients.

5.40 However, in *HR v JAPT*[42] Lindsay J considered that the decision in *Williams* depended largely on the fact that the action was based on the various (misleading) claims made by the company which were stated to be based on the direct personal experience of the director concerned and that director's personal involvement in his company. In *HR v JAPT* the activity of the director was:

> activity of the kind which one might expect of a director of such a company. Although the line is hard to describe and will sometimes be hard to see, I do not see [the director] as here over-stepping the line between the area in which identification of a director's acts with his company is the basic premise and that area in which it can be recognised that the director's acts involve an assumption of personal liability.

5.41 The correctness of Lindsay J's remarks was borne out by the later reversal by the House of Lords of the decision of the Court of Appeal: see *Williams v Natural Life Health Foods*.[43]

---

[37] [1997] 1 BCLC 131, CA.
[38] See *Williams v Natural Life Health Foods Ltd* [1998] 2 All ER 638, HL.
[39] [1897] AC 22, HL.
[40] [1997] 1 BCLC 131, CA.
[41] [1992] 2 NZLR 517, NZCA.
[42] [1997] OPLR 123 (Lindsay J).
[43] [1998] 2 All ER 638, HL. Note, however, the criticism of this decision in Ross Grantham and Charles Rickett, 'Directors' Tortious Liability: Contract, Tort or Company Law?' (1999) 62 MLR 133. Alan Berg, in his note, 'Accessory Liability for Breach of Trust' (1996) 59 MLR 443 wondered why Mr Tan, the director in *Royal Brunei Airlines v Tan* [1995] 2 AC 378 (discussed later in this chapter) was not in fact the subject of a claim in tort in any event. The answer may be that the Law Lords seem to be reluctant to impose a direct tort duty (see *Williams* [1998] 2 All ER 638, HL).

In New Zealand in *McNulty v McNulty*,[44] Osborne AJ referred to *HR v JAPT* and *Trevor* **5.42**
Ivory Ltd v Anderson[45] and would have struck out a claim in tort (if pleaded) by a beneficiary
against a director of a trustee company.

Later cases have sought to fix liability on directors for torts they have committed when **5.43**
acting on behalf of the company. But generally some direct tort or involvement seems to
be needed—see *Standard Chartered Bank v Pakistan National Shipping Corpn*[46] (deceit and
fraudulent representation).

A director is not liable, however, if he did no more than carry out his constitutional role in **5.44**
the governance of the company—see *MCA Records v Charly Records*.[47]

Accordingly, neither of the direct tort routes are likely to be available to beneficiaries. **5.45**

Accessory Liability

In the 1870s, the House of Lords in *Barnes v Addy*[48] made it clear that a third party can be **5.46**
directly liable to beneficiaries of a trust in some circumstances where the third party has been
involved in a breach of trust by the trustee, ie has procured or assisted the breach of trust.
This accessory liability does not require the third party to have benefited personally nor to
have received any trust property.

The extent of such accessory liability was considered by the Privy Council in *Royal Brunei* **5.47**
Airlines v Tan.[49] The Privy Council stated that dishonesty is required on the part of the third
party and that there is no requirement for the trustee itself to be dishonest. The case involved
a claim against the managing director of a travel agency company. The director was held
liable because he had arranged for trust money held by the company for the airline plaintiff
to be paid away in breach of trust and this was dishonest on his part. This decision has
generally been welcomed. However, reservations have been expressed about the nature of the
'dishonesty' that is required to found liability.[50]

Royal Brunei was a decision of the Privy Council and so, in theory, was not strictly binding **5.48**
on courts here.[51] However, the decision has been followed in various cases in England and
Wales, including now in the House of Lords in *Twinsectra v Yardley*.[52]

---

[44] [2011] NZHC 1173 at [88]–[91] (Osborne AJ).
[45] [1992] 2 NZLR 517, NZCA.
[46] [2003] 1 AC 959, [2003] 1 All ER 173, HL. See also in New Zealand, *Body Corporate 202254 v Taylor*
[2008] NZCA 317, [2009] 2 NZLR 17, NZCA.
[47] [2003] 1 BCLC 93, CA. See also *Standard Chartered Bank v Pakistan National Shipping* [2003] 1 AC
959, HL; *Koninklijke Philips Electronics NV v Princo Digital Disc GmbH* [2004] 2 BCLC 50 (Pumfrey J); and
Societa Esplosivi Industriali SpA v Ordnance Technologies Ltd [2007] EWHC 2875 (Ch), [2008] 2 All ER 622
(Lindsay J).
[48] (1874) LR 9 Ch App 244, HL.
[49] [1995] 2 AC 378, PC.
[50] See the notes by Peter Birks (1996) LMCLQ 1 and Alan Berg (1996) 59 MLR 443.
[51] See eg the Court of Appeal in *Sinclair Investments (UK) Ltd v Versailles Trade Finance Ltd (in admin)*
[2011] EWCA Civ 347, [2012] Ch 453. The Court of Appeal can have problems when looking at conflicting
decisions. See Matthew Conaglen and Richard Nolan, 'Precedent from the Privy Council' (2006) 122 LQR
349 and Richard Nolan, 'Bribes: A Reprise' (2011) 127 LQR 19.
[52] [2002] 2 AC 164, HL.

Royal Brunei dishonesty

5.49 Lindsay J in *HR v JAPT* considered the statement of the law by the Privy Council in *Royal Brunei Airlines v Tan*. Lindsay J pointed out that:

(a) *Royal Brunei* dishonesty is governed by an objective rather than a subjective standard (but see now the decision of the House of Lords in *Twinsectra*);

(b) it is not dependent on the lower/higher moral standards of the individuals concerned, although regard may be had to some personal attributes such as the experience and intelligence of the individuals concerned;

(c) carelessness is not as such dishonesty; nor is imprudence, although imprudence may be carried recklessly to such lengths as to call in question the honesty of a person concerned; and

(d) acting in reckless disregard of others' rights or possible rights can be a tell-tale sign of this kind of dishonesty.

5.50 According to Lindsay J it is '*Royal Brunei* dishonest' for a person:

unless there is a very good and compelling reason, to participate in a transaction if he knows it involves a misapplication of trust assets for the detriment of the beneficiaries or if he deliberately closes his eyes and deliberately chooses not to ask questions so as to avoid his learning something he would rather not know and then for him to proceed regardless.

5.51 Lindsay J then discussed the meaning of this:

in other words, as I understand the judgment in the case, Royal Brunei dishonesty so far as concerned with risk is not directed to the taking of risk in relation to one's own position but with the taking of a risk which is 'commercially unacceptable' because it might jeopardise the position of others. However, on the facts of this case, [the director] could hardly say that his activity as a director of the [trustee company] could reasonably be thought not to affect any one but that trust company.

5.52 Following this the House of Lords ruled, in *Twinsectra v Yardley*,[53] that there is some subjective element needed in order to show dishonesty in this context. The majority held (Lord Millett dissenting on this point) that it must be established that:

(a) the third party's conduct was dishonest by the ordinary standards of reasonable and honest people; and

(b) the third party realised that by those standards his or her conduct was dishonest.

5.53 There is some further discussion of this difficult issue by the Court of Appeal in the exoneration case of *Walker v Stones*[54] and by the Privy Council in *Barlow Clowes International Ltd (in Liquidation) v Eurotrust International Ltd*.[55]

---

[53] For commentary on *Twinsectra*, see N Richardson (2002) 16 TLI 174.

[54] [2000] 4 All ER 412, CA.

[55] [2005] UKPC 37, [2006] 1 All ER 333, PC. See Joachim Dietrich, 'The Liability of Accessories under Statute, in Equity, and in Criminal Law: Some Common Problems and (Perhaps) Common Solutions' (2010) 34 Melbourne University Law Review 106; Steven Elliott and Charles Mitchell, 'Remedies for Dishonest Assistance' (2004) 67 MLR 16 and Pauline Ridge, 'Justifying the Remedies for Dishonest Assistance' (2008) 124 LQR 445.

In *Stokors SA v IG Markets Ltd*,[56] a case dealing with potential liability of employees for a **5.54** breach of trust, Field J discussed the trilogy of *Royal Brunei*, *Twinsectra*, and *Barlow Clowes* and held[57] that the various principles could be derived from the authorities:

(1) It is not necessary for the Court to establish whether or not the defendant considered that he was acting dishonestly. Instead, the defendant's knowledge of the transaction has to be such as to render his participation contrary to normally acceptable standards of honest conduct.[58]

(2) An honest person does not deliberately close his eyes and ears, or deliberately not ask questions lest he learn something he would rather not know and then proceed regardless where there may be a misapplication of trust assets to the detriment of beneficiaries.[59]

(3) A dishonest state of mind may consist in suspicion combined with a conscious decision not to make inquiries which might result in knowledge.[60]

(4) In a commercial setting dishonesty can be found on the basis of commercially unacceptable conduct.[61]

(5) Acting in reckless disregard of others' rights or possible rights can be a tell-tale sign of dishonesty.[62]

(6) Recklessness is a species of dishonest knowledge and is therefore relevant to the Court's consideration of dishonesty in this context. 'Not caring' does not mean 'not taking care', rather it means indifference to the truth. The moral obliquity of this position is in the wilful disregard of the importance of truth.[63]

(7) Someone can know, and can certainly suspect, that he is assisting in a misappropriation of money without knowing that the money is held on trust or what a trust means.[64]

Dishonesty may well be difficult to prove. Dishonesty must be specifically pleaded— **5.55** see *Armitage v Nurse*[65] and *Brown v Bennett*.[66] A high standard of proof of dishonesty is required—see eg the decision of the Court of Appeal in *Heinl v Jyske Bank (Gibraltar) Ltd*.[67] There is a good summary of these issues by Charles Mitchell in the chapter on 'Assistance' in the book *Breach of Trust*.[68]

For example, in Australia in *Compaq Computer Australia Pty Ltd v Merry*,[69] Finkelstein J held **5.56** that directors of a company did not have sufficient knowledge of breach of the terms of an agreement to segregate sale proceeds and place them in a separate account. In *Stokors*, Field J

---

[56] [2013] EWHC 631 (Comm) (Field J).
[57] At para [9].
[58] *Barlow Clowes* at [15].
[59] *Royal Brunei* at 389G.
[60] *Manifest Shipping Co Ltd v Uni-Polaris Insurance Co Ltd* [2001] UKHL 1, [2003] 1 AC 469, HL at 515.
[61] *Royal Brunei* at 390G, 'The individual is expected to attain the standard which would be observed by an honest person placed in those circumstances. It is impossible to be more specific. Knox J captured the flavour of this, in a case with a commercial setting, when he referred to a person who is 'guilty of commercially unacceptable conduct in the particular context involved': see *Cowan de Groot Properties Ltd v Eagle Trust Plc* [1992] 4 All ER 700, 761'.
[62] *Royal Brunei* at 390G.
[63] Applied by Hamblen J in *Brown v InnovatorOne plc* [2012] EWHC 1321 at [1055].
[64] *Twinsectra* at [19] (Lord Hoffmann).
[65] [1998] Ch 241 at 251, CA.
[66] [2002] 2 All ER 273 (Neuberger J).
[67] [1999] Lloyd's Rep 511, CA.
[68] P Birks and A Pretto (eds), *Breach of Trust* (Hart Publishing, 2002) 188–91.
[69] [1998] ALR 1 (Finkelstein J).

held that on the facts the employees did not have sufficient knowledge of any breach of trust and so were not liable as accessories.

5.57   Conversely, Hart J at first instance in a pensions case, *Wakelin v Read*,[70] considered that the Pensions Ombudsman had good grounds for considering a director (Mr Read) of a company which was the trustee of a pension scheme to have been dishonest in relation to sale and leaseback of property that had resulted in a big loss to the scheme. He held (at para 37) that:

> The finding that Mr Read was oblivious to the conflict of interest, the fact that the investment was obviously fraught, the fact that Mr Read and his co-directors plunged into the transaction 'eyes shut ears stopped', and the fact that the transaction represented a commercially unacceptable risk in that it jeopardised the position of the beneficiaries, are all independent of the finding that the leaseback was a sham, and, taken together, compel the conclusion that Mr Read was dishonest in the Royal Brunei sense.

5.58   On appeal, the Court of Appeal[71] held that the issue of dishonesty should be referred back to the Pensions Ombudsman to determine the factual issue of dishonesty.[72]

5.59   The *Royal Brunei* principle can extend to dishonestly assisting a breach by a company director of his duty to the company—see the Court of Appeal in *Brown v Bennett*.[73]

Exclusion clauses

5.60   It is unclear whether a director (or other third party) could be liable as an accessory if there is in fact no breach of trust because the trustee can rely on an exemption clause. Lord Nicholls in *Royal Brunei Airlines v Tan*[74] stated:

> These examples suggest that what matters is the state of mind of the third party sought to be made liable, not the state of mind of the trustee. The trustee will be liable in any event for the breach of trust, even if he acted innocently, unless excused by an exemption clause in the trust instrument or relieved by the court.

5.61   It would therefore seem arguable that a director may be liable even if the trustee company is not. In practice it is likely that if a director is dishonest, the trustee company will be treated as dishonest (as happened in *Royal Brunei* itself).

5.62   Emily Campbell argued, in her article 'Dishonest Assistance: To Plead or Not to Plead',[75] that, in the light of Lord Nicholls' remarks, if an exoneration clause is 'worded in such a way as to preclude a breach of trust from having occurred, then any claim against a third party in dishonest assistance is bound to fail'.

5.63   Charles Mitchell in his chapter on 'Assistance'[76] notes the potential distinction between clauses that exclude any duty arising on the trustee company in the first place from those

---

[70] [1998] OPLR 147, [1998] PLR 337 (Hart J).

[71] *Wakelin v Read* [2000] OPLR 277, CA.

[72] For an example in Australia of a director being held liable where there was a breach of trust by the company (acting as trustee of a unit trust), see *Re S & D International Pty Ltd (No 4)* [2010] VSC 388 (Robson J).

[73] [1999] 1 BCLC 649, CA.

[74] [1995] 2 AC 378, PC at 385.

[75] December 1998, Trusts & Estates Journal.

[76] See Birks and Pretto (eds), *Breach of Trust*, 159 and 208. See also Parker Hood, *Principles of Lender Liability* (Oxford University Press, 2012), para 8.107.

clauses that just limit the liability. But he goes on to argue that even in the second case a third party (ie here a director) might escape liability on the ground that:

> dishonest assistants are jointly and severally liable with the wrongdoing trustees or fiduciaries whose breaches of trust they assist, with the consequence that the release of the trustee or fiduciary should also operate to release those with whom he is jointly and severally liable.

In New Zealand in *McNulty v McNulty*,[77] Osborne AJ referred to *HR v JAPT* and struck out **5.64** a claim being made against a director of a trustee company. He held, at para [77], that the director could rely on the exclusion clause (in favour of the trustees, including the trustee company) allowing conflicts. Osborne AJ held:

> [76] By reason of my finding in relation to GCA [the trustee company], namely that GCA had not committed a breach of fiduciary duty by acting in an arguably conflicted situation because cl14.1 permitted such an event, Mr Gowing [the director] can be in no different a position. The plaintiffs pleaded that he was the person responsible for directing the professional trustee company. If he thereby personally had an arguable responsibility as a matter of trust law to carry out the terms of the trust, then he equally had the benefit (or burden) of clauses by which the trust deed defined or limited responsibilities.

> [77] I would therefore find on this ground alone that the second cause of action as against Mr Gowing is untenable.

It would be prudent to provide in any trust deed for any exclusion clause to be expressly **5.65** stated to apply to trustee directors. It is unlikely, however, that any exclusion clause will have a wider scope and cover 'dishonesty' (see Chapter 14).

In 1999, Nicholas Warren QC (as he then was) suggested in an article 'Trustee Risk and **5.66** Liability'[78] that one reason to include directors of a corporate trustee within an exclusion clause is to cover the potential divergence between the 'subjective' dishonesty that Millett LJ (as he then was) held in *Armitage v Nurse*[79] could not be covered by an exoneration clause and the 'objective' dishonesty held by Lord Nicholls in *Royal Brunei* as sufficient to fix liability on a third party (such as a director).

It seems that the directors of a trustee company are probably able to rely on an exclusion **5.67** clause (or indemnity) that refers to them even though they are (in most cases) not parties to the trust deed. It seems to the author to be best to consider the directors as able to enforce the provisions in their favour on the basis that they are, to that extent, beneficiaries of the pension trust. Mummery LJ commented in *Wakelin v Read*[80] that any attempt to make the director (Mr Read) liable as joint tortfeasor with the trustee company would be met by reliance on the exoneration clause in the trust deed (which was expressly stated to cover directors, officers, and employees of a corporate trustee).

The Contracts (Rights of Third Parties) Act 1999 means that for contracts entered into after **5.68** 11 May 2000 directors may be able to rely on these provisions as a matter of contract law even though they may not be a party to the deed or rules. This would require the trust provisions to be construed as a contract (which seems unlikely—see for example the Law Commission's

---

[77] [2011] NZHC 1173 (Osborne AJ).
[78] (1999) 13 TLI 226 at 238.
[79] [1998] Ch 241, CA.
[80] [2000] OPLR 277, CA at 285G.

consultation paper No 171 on Trustee Exemption Clauses at paras 2.60 to 2.64 and the Court of Appeal on the Unfair Contract Terms Act 1977 in *Baker v JE Clark & Co*[81]). See further Chapter 14 (Trustee indemnities and exonerations).

Indirect Fiduciary Duty or Duty of Care (A 'Dog-Leg' Claim)

5.69 Directors (and to a lesser extent employees) owe a range of duties to their company or employer (ie the trustee company). These include fiduciary duties based on their office as directors, various statutory duties (including, importantly, duties in relation to wrongful and fraudulent trading; see ss 213 and 214 of the Insolvency Act 1986) and, in the case of executives and executive directors, contractual (and tortious) duties in relation to their position as employees.

5.70 The duty of care and skill of a director was historically set at a relatively low level, following the 1925 decision of Romer J in *Re City Equitable Fire Insurance Co*.[82]

5.71 Generally, there is an implied term (under s 14 of the Supply of Goods and Services Act 1982) in contracts for the supply of a service that, where the supplier is acting in the course of the business, the supplier would carry out the service with reasonable care and skill. However, this does not apply to the provision of services to a company by a director of the company in his capacity as such—see the Supply of Services (Exclusion of Implied Terms) Order 1982.[83]

5.72 However, the courts have recently been extending the liability of directors (in particular non-executive directors such as the non-professional directors of a trustee company) owed to the company.[84] Directors of trustee companies can clearly be liable to the company for a breach of these duties. For example, in *Bishopsgate Investment Management v Maxwell (No 2)*,[85] the Court of Appeal held that a director was liable to a trustee company (in this case a fund manager) for breach of his fiduciary duty in signing documents without making enquiries.

5.73 The Companies Act 2006 enacts various general duties on directors (see ss 171–177). This includes a general duty of skill and care duty:

> 174 Duty to exercise reasonable care, skill and diligence
> (1) A director of a company must exercise reasonable care, skill and diligence.
> (2) This means the care, skill and diligence that would be exercised by a reasonably diligent person with—
>   (a) the general knowledge, skill and experience that may reasonably be expected of a person carrying out the functions carried out by the director in relation to the company, and
>   (b) the general knowledge, skill and experience that the director has.

---

[81] [2006] EWCA Civ 464, [2006] PLR 131, CA.
[82] [1925] Ch 407 (Romer J) at 427.
[83] SI 1982/1771.
[84] See eg *Re Continental Assurance Co PLC* [1997] 1 BCLC 48 (Chadwick J); *AWA Ltd v Daniels* (1995) 13 ACLC 614, NSWCA; *Re Property Force Consultancy Pty Ltd* (1995) 13 ACLC 1051 (Derrington J, Queensland Supreme Court); *Norman v Theodore Goddard* [1991] BCLC 1028 (Hoffmann J); *Re D'Jan of London* [1994] BCLC 561 (Hoffmann LJ); *Ginora Investments v James Capel & Co* (1995) 10 February (Rimer J); and *Bairstow v Queens' Moat Houses PLC* [2000] 1 BCLC 549, (Nelson J). Other cases are usefully collected in Peter Willoughby, *Misplaced Trusts* (Gostick Hall Publications, 1999) 80.
[85] [1994] 1 All ER 261, CA.

Directors of a trustee company may also incur liabilities under the Companies Acts, for **5.74** example if they engage in wrongful trading or fraudulent trading (see ss 213 and 214 of the Insolvency Act 1986). This could easily be the case where their actions result in the trustee company incurring liabilities (eg a breach of trust) where it does not have the assets to meet them (eg because its indemnity out of the assets in the pension scheme is not available).

However, it seems likely that these direct statutory liabilities are probably owed directly only **5.75** to the liquidator of the trustee company and are not available to be transferred to a new trustee as trust assets.[86]

Clearly these duties can be enforced by the trustee company, particularly if it has suffered loss **5.76** as a result of their breach by the director concerned, for example if the trustee company has become liable for breach of trust. However, can this claim be enforced by the new trustee of the relevant trust without going through the old trustee company?

HR v JAPT

In *HR v JAPT*[87] Lindsay J considered arguments that the director of the trustee company **5.77** owed a duty of care (fiduciary duty or a tortious duty) to the trustee company. By breaching that duty the trustee company suffered a loss, namely a claim by the beneficiaries of the pension scheme. It was argued that the claim by the trustee company against the director is an asset of the pension scheme which has, therefore, passed to the current trustees.

Lindsay J pointed out that the current trustees were appointed by deed and so s 40(1)(b) of **5.78** the Trustee Act 1925 had effect to vest the new trustees with the assets of the trust (including the claim against the director).

The defendant director argued that the proper means of enforcing any such duty would be **5.79** by the trustee company itself bringing an action against him. The plaintiffs (current trustees and the beneficiaries) could force the trustee company to bring such action by driving it into liquidation and then requiring the liquidator to take such an action. The proceeds would then, in effect, pass to the pension scheme as the main creditor of the corporate trustee.

Lindsay J pointed out that there could well be limitation difficulties against such a process. **5.80** However, Lindsay J thought it was arguable that such an indirect claim, based on a fiduciary or tort duty, could be brought by the present trustees or by the beneficiaries of the scheme. Lindsay J relied on comments of Lord Nicholls in *Royal Brunei* where he discussed the position of agents of the trustees. Lord Nicholls had said:[88]

> For the most part they will owe to the trustees a duty to exercise reasonable skill and care. When that is so, the rights flowing from that duty form part of the trust property. As such they can be enforced by the beneficiaries in a suitable case if the trustees are unable or unwilling to do so.

---

[86] *Re Yagerphone* [1935] Ch 392 (Bennett J); *Re MC Bacon (No 2)* [1991] Ch 127 (Millett J); *Re Oasis Merchandising Services* [1997] 1 All ER 1009, CA; and *Re Ayala Holdings Ltd (No 2)* [1996] 1 BCLC 467 (Knox J).
[87] [1997] OPLR 123 (Lindsay J).
[88] [1995] 2 AC 378, PC at 391.

5.81   Lindsay J thought it was at least arguable that such indirect or 'dog-leg' claims by beneficiaries could also be made against directors. He considered the decision of the Supreme Court of Victoria in *Young v Murphy*[89] in which Phillips J (with whom Booking and Batt JJ agreed) seemed to hold against any such indirect claim. However, Lindsay J distinguished the decision in *Young* on the basis that he thought that the decision there rested in part on the particular form of pleading and in part on the particular facts.

5.82   Lindsay J seems to have treated it as a factual matter that in *Young* it could not be said that the directors owed their duties 'only in relation to some particular trust or trusts', whereas in the *HR* case the trustee company was only ever trustee of one trust.

5.83   In effect Lindsay J said that he was: 'not confident that the reasoning involved in *Young* cannot be distinguished, if not on the pleadings alone then on the facts'. Accordingly, the point was arguable and so striking out would not be ordered.

5.84   Lindsay J went on to analyse the level of care that was involved. He thought it was clear that any duty owed by the director would be on the 'yardstick of his being a director' rather than on a different one of his being a trustee. He also dismissed the argument that allowing such a 'dog-leg' claim may discourage individuals from accepting office as directors. He dismissed this as only being relevant if the trustee company is insubstantial and uninsured and stated that: 'if all that is discouraged is the use of insubstantial uninsured trust companies, that would be a discouragement many might think timely enough'.

5.85   Lindsay J pointed out that the alternative (of allowing the trust company to enforce the director's duty) would involve extra complication and expense (perhaps needing a liquidator to be appointed). It could also give rise to limitation problems. It should be noted that there may also be difficulties in allowing certain statutory claims to be transferred.

5.86   There is authority in the UK that certain claims given to a liquidator (eg to bring an action under s 214 of the Insolvency Act 1986 for a contribution by a director to the assets of the company by reason of wrongful trading) cannot be assigned to a third party: see the decision of the Court of Appeal in *Re Oasis Merchandising Services Ltd*,[90] distinguishing (on the basis of differently worded statutory provisions) the decision of Drummond J in the Australian Federal Court in *Re Movitor Pty Ltd*.[91]

5.87   Subsequent to the *HR* case, in Victoria in *Collie v Merlaw Nominees Pty Ltd*,[92] Byrne J followed *Young v Murphy* and held that a substitute trustee had no right to sue a director of a former trustee for breaches of statutory and fiduciary duty. *HR v JAPT*[93] was not mentioned by Byrne J in this case.

Gregson

5.88   The most recent UK case is one involving a private family trust (and not a pension scheme). In *Gregson v HAE Trustees Ltd*,[94] Robert Miles QC held that there was no question of a direct fiduciary duty owed by directors of a trustee company to beneficiaries, following the decision

---

[89] [1996] 1 VR 279, (1994) 12 ACLC 558, Supreme Court of Victoria.
[90] [1997] 1 All ER 1009, CA.
[91] [1995] 19 ACSR 440 (Drummond J).
[92] [1998] VSC 203 (Byrne J).
[93] [1997] OPLR 123 (Lindsay J).
[94] [2008] EWHC 1006 (Ch), [2008] 2 BCLC 542 (Robert Miles QC, sitting as a deputy High Court Judge).

of the Court of Appeal in *Bath v Standard Land* [95] (see above). He also distinguished *HR v JAPT* and held that a 'dog-leg' claim was not arguable in the case where the trustee company was the trustee of several trusts.

In *Gregson*, Robert Miles QC held that in the absence of dishonesty, a beneficiary is unable to **5.89** bring a claim against a director trustee on behalf of a trustee company. The *Gregson* case involved a discretionary family trust, the beneficiaries of which included the issue of the settlor's grandparents, a group to which the claimant in this case belonged. During the life of the trust, trust property had consisted wholly of shares in the family furniture business, Courts. In 2004 Courts entered administration, was found to be insolvent, and its shares became worthless. The claimant instituted proceedings against the trustee company and the trustee directors alleging that the trustee company had breached its duty to review and diversify its investment of scheme assets (and to take advice on the same).

The claimant pleaded that the trustee company had an action against the trustee directors for **5.90** this breach of duty and that this claim was held on trust for beneficiaries, effectively allowing a beneficiary to enforce the trustee company's potential action against the director in its stead (again, a 'dog-leg' claim). Ultimately Robert Miles QC determined that in the absence of dishonesty, a beneficiary is unable to bring a claim against a director trustee on behalf of a trustee company.

It is difficult to conclude that the concept of a 'dog-leg' claim has now been fully rejected **5.91** by the courts. The judge in *Gregson* distinguished *HR v JAPT* and held that a 'dog-leg' claim was not arguable in that case because the trustee company was the trustee of several trusts. In the *HR* case the trustee company was only ever trustee of one trust. Also, the *Gregson* case did not involve a pension scheme trust company so whether the features of such an arrangement would better lend itself to support the concept of a 'dog-leg' claim is unclear.

McNulty

In New Zealand, in *McNulty v McNulty*,[96] Osborne AJ followed the decision of Lindsay J in **5.92** the *HR* case and held that a claim against a director of a corporate trustee should be struck out as on the facts no direct fiduciary duty or tort duty arose on the director.

A 'dog-leg' claim could give rise to some issues about whether any exoneration clause applicable **5.93** to the trustee can be relied on by the director. It seems to me that this should be possible. The liability of the director can be no greater than the loss suffered by the trustee company, which is itself limited by the exoneration clause.[97] Statutory provisions limiting the ability of a director to exclude or restrict his liability to the company for breach of duty would not impact on this analysis (see s 532 of the Companies Act 2006, formerly s 310 of the Companies Act 1985). Nevertheless, it is common for exoneration clauses to be stated expressly to extend to directors of a corporate trustee.

---

[95] [1911] 1 Ch 681, CA.
[96] [2011] NZHC 1173 (Osborne AJ).
[97] See *McNulty v McNulty* [2011] NZHC 1173 at [76] (Osborne AJ).

Piercing the Corporate Veil

5.94 In some (limited) cases, the courts are prepared to pierce the corporate veil and ignore the separate existence of the company—see the Supreme Court in *VTB Capital plc v Nutritek International Corpn.*[98] In *Prest v Petrodel Resources Ltd*,[99] the Supreme Court held that piercing of the corporate veil would only be allowed when a person is under an existing obligation or liability or subject to an existing legal restriction which he deliberately evades, or the enforcement of which he deliberately frustrates by interposing a company under his control. The court may then pierce the corporate veil, but only for the purpose of depriving the company or its controller of the advantage that they would otherwise have obtained by virtue of the company's separate legal personality. Usually some degree of deception or fraud will be needed.

5.95 In *HR v JAPT*[100] the plaintiffs argued that the separate legal personality of the trustee company should be disregarded and instead the directors seen as the only real parties to the relevant transactions. However, Lindsay J held that this was not possible. There had never been any deception as no one had been deceived into thinking that the trustee company was other than it was:

> an asset-less, income-less corporate entity with no function other than the management and administration of the Scheme, a function necessarily carried out by individuals on their behalf... No concealment of any relevant fact is pleaded.

5.96 Nor was there any evidence of 'a device or sham or cloak'. Accordingly, Lindsay J held that any case based on this argument was quite hopeless.

5.97 There is also an analogy with the reasoning of the Supreme Court in the recent decision in *Holland v Revenue and Customs Commissioners.*[101] The case dealt with the position of an individual (A) who was acting as a director of a company (ZCo) that was itself a corporate director of another company (KCo). The Supreme Court held (Lord Walker and Lord Clarke dissenting) that A was acting solely in his capacity as a director of ZCo and so was not a de facto director of KCo.

Statutory Liabilities

5.98 In some jurisdictions (eg Jersey, Guernsey, and the Turks and Caicos Islands) legislation makes the directors of a trustee company liable as guarantors for the liabilities of the trustee company. This is subject to the ability of the courts to give relief if the director was unaware of the breach without being reckless or negligent. There is no such general statutory provision in the UK.

5.99 However, in the UK, where statutes impose criminal fines and penalties on companies, they commonly include a provision allowing those penalties to apply to the directors and officers

---

[98] [2013] UKSC 5, [2013] 2 WLR 398, SC.
[99] [2013] UKSC 34, [2013] 3 WLR 1, per Lord Sumption at [35].
[100] [1997] OPLR 123 (Lindsay J).
[101] [2010] UKSC 51, [2011] 1 All ER 430, HL.

of the company if the relevant act 'was done with the consent or connivance of, or is attributable to any neglect on the part of', any director or officer.[102]

This can apply to directors or officers of trustee companies. For example, under the Pensions **5.100** Act 1995 fines and civil penalties are generally imposed on the trustee, ie the trustee company.

However, there is provision for this liability to flow through to the directors of a trustee **5.101** company in certain circumstances. For example, s 10(5) of the Pensions Act 1995 entitles the Pensions Regulator to levy a civil penalty against a director of a trustee company if the company would be so liable for a penalty and the relevant act or omission of the trustee company 'was done with the consent or connivance of, or is attributable to any neglect on the part of', any director. A similar provision applies under s 115 in relation to criminal offences under Pt I of the Pensions Act 1995 and under s 309 of the Pensions Act 2004 in relation to offences under that Act.

---

[102] See the discussion of this issue (in relation to insolvency practitioners) in D Pollard, *Corporate Insolvency: Employment and Pension Rights* 5th edn (Bloomsbury Professional, 2013) Ch 15. See also David Bergman, 'Corporate Conniving and Directors' Duties' (1999) New Law Journal 1436.

6

CONFLICT ISSUES FOR
PENSION TRUSTEES

I find the idea that a person who has the power to distribute a fund amongst a class which includes himself should be able to apply the fund or any part of it for his own benefit . . . outrageous.

Mr Justice Vinelott (1993)

In the modern world, conflicts of interest cannot be avoided. They can, however be managed. As long as trustees are aware of the potential for conflict and know what is required of them as trustees, they will be able to carry out their trustee duties to the best of their abilities.

The Pension Law Reform Committee[1] (Chaired by Professor Goode)
(September 1993)

---

[1] CM 2342.

[The] difficulty is this. All four of the trustees whose proposals are put before me and whose discretion is being exercised are...themselves beneficiaries whose benefits under the Scheme are thereby augmented. I should expect any intelligent layman interested enough to have read so far to say 'so what?'...

Mr Justice Lindsay (1994)

The notion that, when the discretionary power of amendment is exercised so as to increase an existing benefit or add a new benefit, the member trustees must be excluded from benefit is, in my opinion, quite simply ridiculous.

Sir Richard Scott V-C (1998)

Introduction

This chapter looks at conflict of interest issues[2] for pension trustees (and directors of a corporate trustee). It reviews: **6.1**

(a) the implied general law restriction on conflicts for fiduciaries, including when there is a conflict and the possible 'two hats' rule;
(b) its application to pension trustees and a review of the main pensions cases;
(c) the position of company directors (where there is a corporate trustee);
(d) potential exceptions, including express provisions, implied authorizations and other defences;
(e) the impact of majority voting provisions;
(f) whether a conflict exclusion can be added by amendment; and
(g) the issues if a senior officer of an employer is to be on the trustee board.

Conflicts of interest or duty are endemic in pension schemes trusts. Trustees (or directors of trustee companies) are usually employees or officers or even shareholders of the employer (or its parent). Trustees are also often members of the pension scheme. The trustee company may be a subsidiary of the employer.[3] **6.2**

Conflicts of interest can potentially have very severe effects. If one is found and is not relieved by a relevant authorization, equity intervenes in a number of severe ways. Commonly: **6.3**

(a) the relevant transaction is voidable by a beneficiary;
(b) the relevant trustee is also personally liable to the beneficiaries for breach of trust;
(c) the counterparty to the transaction (eg the company) will probably have knowledge of the facts giving rise to the conflict and hence breach of trust. Even if unaware of the legal consequences that follow, it seems that the counterparty will hold any relevant assets on constructive trust (and may also be personally liable for breach of trust); and
(d) the beneficiaries may apply to court to have the trustee removed or this may be a ground for the Pensions Regulator to appoint a further trustee or remove a conflicted trustee.[4]

---

[2] See Malcolm Fitzsimons, 'Managing Pension Scheme Trustee Conflicts of Interest' (2006) 20 TLI 211; Institute of Chartered Accountants in England and Wales (ICAEW) guidance, 'Acting as a Trustee for the Pension Fund of Your Employer' (June 2007); Philip Bennett, 'Coping with Conflict' (2004) The Treasurer 27 (May); Pensions Regulator guidance, 'Conflicts of Interest' (October 2008); Matthew Conaglen, *Fiduciary Loyalty: Protecting the Due Performance of Non-Fiduciary Duties* (Hart Publishing, 2010), Ch 6.
[3] See Ch 4 (Corporate trustees).
[4] See eg the *Telent* determination by the Pensions Regulator in November 2007 (TM/3573). In May 2013, the Financial Conduct Authority (FCA) banned a non-executive director of two mutual societies from acting because she had not disclosed a conflict of interest.

6.4 The Pension Law Reform Committee,[5] chaired by Professor Goode, which preceded the Pensions Act 1995 discussed conflict issues. It reviewed the position on conflicts of interest, particularly with the employer. It recommended that:

> It is inevitable that there will be some conflict of loyalties. Trustees appointed by management frequently hold key positions within the company, whilst trustees appointed by members may feel obligations to those who appointed them. It is unrealistic to imagine that individual trustees will be able to leave behind entirely their other roles while acting as trustees. In the modem world, conflicts of interest cannot be avoided. They can, however, be managed. As long as trustees are aware of the potential for conflict and know what is required of them as trustees, they will be able to carry out their trustee duties to the best of their abilities.

General Default Rule for Fiduciaries

6.5 It is a general default rule applicable to a fiduciary that he should not put himself in a position where his duty and interest (or duty and another duty) may conflict.[6] However, there must be more than the remote possibility of a conflict of interest.[7]

6.6 It is possible to exclude or modify the usual equitable rule on conflicts of interest:

(a) by an express provision in the trust instrument;[8] or

(b) with express informed consent of the beneficiaries; or

(c) with implied consent or agreement;[9] or

(d) by implication, for example, if the trust is established with an initial trustee who has a conflict of interest (see *Sargeant v National Westminster Bank plc*[10]) or if such a conflict is implicit—eg in the division laid down in the trust deed between employer and member nominated trustees (see Scott V-C in *Edge v Pensions Ombudsman*,[11] subsequently upheld by the Court of Appeal[12]).

6.7 A conflict can be relieved by applying to court in advance—*Manning v Drexel Burnham Lambert*.[13]

6.8 If there is a real conflict (eg if the company is trustee and the trustee has a discretion to augment benefits with any sums remaining falling to the company), then some decisions reach an extreme view that this may disqualify the company (through its insolvency practitioner and perhaps anyone else) from exercising the fiduciary powers.[14]

---

[5] Pension Law Reform, *The Report of the Pension Law Review Committee* (Chairman: Professor Roy Goode) (September 1993) CM 2342, para 4.5.14.

[6] *Phipps v Boardman* [1967] 2 AC 46, HL and *Kelly v Cooper* [1993] AC 205, PC.

[7] See the discussion by Edward Nugee QC (sitting as a Deputy High Court judge) in *Re Wallace Smith & Co Ltd* [1992] BCLC 970 at 987 of *Re Esal (Commodities) Ltd* [1989] BCLC 59, CA and *Re Arrows Ltd* [1992] BCC 121 (Hoffmann J).

[8] See eg *Bray v Ford* [1896] AC 44, HL. See also *Dale v IRC* [1954] AC 11 at 27, HL.

[9] *Kelly v Cooper* [1993] AC 205, PC. But the Court of Appeal has recently held that this may be limited— *Rossetti Marketing Ltd v Diamond Sofa Co Ltd* [2012] EWCA Civ 1021, [2013] 1 All ER (Comm) 308, CA.

[10] (1990) P&CR 518, CA.

[11] [1998] Ch 512 (Scott V-C).

[12] [2000] Ch 602, CA.

[13] [1994] OPLR 71, [1994] PLR 75 (Lindsay J).

[14] See eg in a pensions context, *Mettoy Pension Trustees Ltd v Evans* [1991] 2 All ER 513 (Warner J) and *Re William Makin & Son Ltd* [1993] OPLR 171 (Vinelott J). On insolvency practitioners, see D Pollard, *Corporate Insolvency: Employment and Pension Rights* 5th edn (Bloomsbury Professional, 2013) Ch 47.

The duties imposed on fiduciaries are generally onerous. There is a duty not to profit out of **6.9** the trust and not to be in a position of where there is a conflict of interest. This is explained to apply in circumstances which seem very rigorous and, almost, unfair. Trust cases such as *Keech v Sandford*,[15] *Regal (Hastings) Ltd v Gulliver*,[16] and *Boardman v Phipps*[17] all underline the jealous nature of the equitable duties imposed on trustees and other fiduciaries.

A trustee may have some protection for any breach of trust claim if there is a suitable exonera- **6.10** tion clause in the trust deed. But these commonly do not apply to an intentional breach and so may not be available (see Chapter 14).

General Fiduciary Principles

The starting point for this section is the House of Lords' speeches in *Aberdeen Railway* and **6.11** *Bray v Ford*.

Lord Cranworth LC in *Aberdeen Railway Co v Blaikie Bros*[18] held that there was a strict duty **6.12** on a fiduciary not to have a conflicting interest. It was no defence to a claim to show that the underlying contract being complained of was still fair.

He stated: **6.13**

> The general question, whether a director of a railway company is or is not precluded from dealing on behalf of the company with himself, or with a firm in which he is a partner. The directors are a body to whom is delegated the duty of managing the general affairs of the company. A corporate body can only act by agents, and it is of course the duty of those agents so to act as best to promote the interests of the corporation whose affairs they are conducting. Such agents have duties to discharge of a fiduciary nature towards their principal. And it is a rule of universal application, that no one, having such duties to discharge, shall be allowed to enter into engagements in which he has, or can have, a personal interest conflicting, or which possibly may conflict, with the interests of those whom he is bound to protect. So strictly is this principle adhered to, that no question is allowed to be raised as to the fairness or unfairness of a contract so entered into. It obviously is, or may be, impossible to demonstrate how far in any particular case the terms of such a contract have been the best for the interest of the cestui que trust, which it was possible to obtain. It may sometimes happen that the terms on which a trustee has dealt or attempted to deal with the estate or interests of those for whom he is a trustee, have been as good as could have been obtained from any other person—they may even at the time have been better. But still so inflexible is the rule that no inquiry on that subject is permitted.

In *Bray v Ford*[19] a solicitor who was a governor of a charitable college charged profit costs **6.14** for his professional services under the mistaken belief that the memorandum of association allowed him to do so. Lord Watson said that the respondent was not:

> legally justified in charging and accepting payment of full professional remuneration in respect of services rendered by him to the college in his capacity of solicitor . . . the respondent was neither entitled to charge profit costs in respect of these services, nor to retain them when received by him. Such a breach of the law may be attended with perfect good faith, and it is, in

---

[15] *Keech v Sandford* (1726) Sel Cas Ch 61, 2 Eq Cas Abr 741, 25 ER 223, LC.
[16] *Regal (Hastings) Ltd v Gulliver* (1942) [1967] 2 AC 134n, [1942] 1 All ER 378, HL.
[17] *Boardman v Phipps* [1967] 2 AC 46, HL.
[18] (1854) 2 Eq Rep 1281, (1854) 1 Macq HL 461 at 471–2, HL.
[19] [1896] AC 44 at 48, HL.

my opinion, insufficient to justify a charge of moral obliquity, unless it is shown to have been committed knowingly or with an improper motive.

6.15 Lord Herschell said:[20]

> It is an inflexible rule of a court of equity that a person in a fiduciary position, such as the respondent's, is not, unless otherwise expressly provided, entitled to make a profit; he is not allowed to put himself in a position where his interest and duty conflict. It does not appear to me that this rule is, as has been said, founded upon principles of morality. I regard it rather as based on the consideration that, human nature being what it is, there is danger, in such circumstances, of the person holding a fiduciary position being swayed by interest rather than by duty, and thus prejudicing those whom he was bound to protect. It has, therefore, been deemed expedient to lay down this positive rule. But I am satisfied that it might be departed from in many cases, without any breach of morality, without any wrong being inflicted, and without any consciousness of wrongdoing.

6.16 These passages are quoted again and again in later cases.[21]

6.17 Where a potential fiduciary has a potential conflict, and the appointor does not know this, one old 1823 case, *Peyton v Robinson*[22] held that the potential appointee should tell the appointor before being appointed, otherwise he or she cannot afterwards exercise a discretionary authority for his or her own benefit.

Member Trustees

6.18 One obvious source for the trustees (or directors of a corporate trustee) are the members of the scheme itself, ie take some or all of the trustees from among the employees (and ex-employees) who are members of the scheme (and hence beneficiaries of the pension trust).

6.19 The Pensions Act 1995[23] added a requirement for, in general, at least one-third of the trustee board to be elected by the members (or alternative arrangements put in place). The Pensions Act 2004[24] replaced the 1995 Act provisions with new provisions requiring arrangements to be put in place to secure at least one-third of the trustee board to be member elected or nominated (alternative arrangements are no longer possible). The 1995 Act also included:

(a) an express provision allowing member trustees to keep their benefits;[25] and
(b) for a trustee to have unfair dismissal protection if dismissed for a reason relating to his or her functions as a trustee of an occupational pension scheme.[26]

6.20 Member trustees will have a conflict of interest where they are given a discretion if the effect of the exercise of that discretion will be to benefit (or act to the detriment of) the member trustee's personal interest as a member.

---

[20] At 51–2.
[21] Eg by Lord Templeman in *Guinness Plc v Saunders* [1990] 2 AC 663 at 691, HL.
[22] (1823) 1 LJOS Ch 191 at 194.
[23] Sections 16 to 18.
[24] Sections 241–243 of the Pensions Act 2004. See *Freshfields on Corporate Pensions Law 2013* (ed D Pollard and C Magoffin) (Bloomsbury Professional, 2013) Ch 11.
[25] Section 39—see discussion below.
[26] Now in s 102 of the Employment Rights Act 1996. Extended to directors of a corporate trustee by the Welfare Reform and Pensions Act 1999 (inserting a new s 102(1A) into s 102). See also Ch 5 (Liability of directors of corporate trustees).

Examples of this are: **6.21**

(a) a pensioner trustee being asked by the employer to agree to a (discretionary) increase in pensions in payment;
(b) a member trustee considering augmentation of benefits on a scheme winding-up;
(c) a member trustee considering a level of bulk transfer payment (where the member trustee is included in the transfer or remains behind).

A member trustee will need to look for an exoneration or amending provision (or rely on the **6.22** statutory exemption in s 39 of the Pensions Act 1995).

Is There a Conflict?

The broad tests laid down in *Bray v Ford* and *Aberdeen Railway v Blaikie* are stated in very **6.23** rigorous terms.

Two points can be made: **6.24**

(a) First, the question arises as to whether a conflict of interest or potential conflict of interest itself gives rise to a breach of trust by the relevant trustee.
    Shepherd in his book, *Law of Fiduciaries*,[27] argues strongly that a mere conflict of interest does not of itself give rise to a breach of trust. Rather, he argues, a breach of trust arises when the trustee in fact makes a decision and favours the competing interest over and above that of the beneficiaries. A conflict of interest would, however, remain sufficient to enable a beneficiary to seek removal of the trustee.
(b) This does lead on to the second question as to where and when a conflict actually arises. Lord Cranworth LC in *Aberdeen Railway v Blaikie* referred to 'a personal interest conflicting, *or which possibly may conflict*, with the interests of those whom he is bound to protect'.

Lord Upjohn in *Boardman v Phipps*[28] referred to Lord Cranworth's comment and continued: **6.25**

the phrase 'possibly may conflict' requires consideration. In my view it means that the reasonable man looking at the relevant facts and circumstances of the particular case would think that there was a real sensible possibility of conflict; not that you could imagine some situation arising which might, in some conceivable possibility in events not contemplated as real sensible possibilities by any reasonable person, result in a conflict.

Similarly, in the slightly earlier case of *Boulting v ACTAT*,[29] Upjohn LJ (as he then was) stated **6.26** that:

A broad rule like this...must be applied realistically to a state of affairs which discloses a real conflict of duty and interest and not some theoretical or rhetorical conflict.

Lord Upjohn was dissenting in *Boardman v Phipps*. But it seems that generally commentators think that this dissent was not so much as to the law as to its particular application to the facts concerned.[30] **6.27**

---

[27] JC Shepherd, *Law of Fiduciaries* (Carswell, 1981) Chs 8 and 24.
[28] [1967] 2 AC 46 at 124, HL.
[29] [1963] 2 QB 606 at 638, CA.
[30] See eg R Meagher, W Gummow, and J Lehane, *Equity Doctrines and Remedies* 4th edn (Butterworths, 2002) para 5-065.

6.28 Certainly in later cases Lord Upjohn's comments have been followed. See for example Roskill J in *Industrial Development Consultants v Cooley*[31] and Jonathan Parker LJ in *Bhullar v Bhullar*.[32] A similar relaxation applies to company directors. They are not in breach of the statutory conflicts rule (s 175 of the Companies Act 2006) if the 'situation cannot reasonably be regarded as likely to give rise to a conflict of interest'—s 175(4)(a) of the Companies Act 2006.

Inflexible rule

6.29 Although this is stated in *Bray v Ford* to be an 'inflexible' rule, later cases have also commented that although it is strict, it is also flexible in its application.[33] Lord Wilberforce in the Privy Council in *New Zealand Netherlands Society 'Oranje' Inc v Kuys*[34] held:

> The obligation not to profit from a position of trust, or, as it sometimes relevant to put it, not to allow a conflict to arise between duty and interest, is one of strictness. The strength, and indeed the severity, of the rule has recently been emphasised by the House of Lords in *Boardman v Phipps*...It retains its vigour in all jurisdictions where the principles of equity are applied. Naturally it has different applications in different contexts. It applies, in principle, whether the case is one of a trust, express or implied, of partnership, of directorship of a limited company, of principal and agent, or master and servant, but the precise scope of it must be moulded according to the nature of the relationship.

6.30 In Australia in *Hospital Products*[35] Mason J held that the scope of a fiduciary duty was to be 'moulded according to the nature of the relationship and the facts of the case'. He went on to observe that, in some cases, 'the so-called rule that the fiduciary cannot allow a conflict to arise between duty and interest...cannot be usefully applied in the absolute terms in which it has been stated'.[36]

6.31 Again, in the High Court of Australia, Deane J in *Chan v Zacharia*[37] emphasized the dangers of an unreasonable approach:

> [O]ne cannot but be conscious of the danger that the over-enthusiastic and unnecessary statement of the broad general principles of equity in terms of inflexibility may destroy the vigour which it is intended to promote in that it will exclude the ordinary interplay of the doctrines of equity and the adjustment of general principles to particular facts and changing circumstances and convert equity into an instrument of hardship and injustice in individual cases.[38] There is 'no better mode of undermining the sound doctrines of equity than to make unreasonable and inequitable applications of them'.[39]

---

[31] [1972] 2 All ER 162 (a fuller report than at [1972] 1 WLR 443) (Roskill J).

[32] [2003] EWCA 424, [2003] 2 BCLC 241, CA. See also in Australia *Re VBN and the Australian Prudential Regulation Authority* [2006] AATA 710, (2006) 92 ALD 259 (Administrative Appeals Tribunal) at [547].

[33] See eg Deane J in *Chan v Zacharia* (1984) 154 CLR 178, cited in Meagher, Gummow, and Lehane (2002) para 5-065.

[34] [1973] 2 All ER 1222 at 1225, PC. Cited by Jonathan Parker LJ in *Bhullar v Bhullar* [2003] EWCA Civ 424, [2003] 2 BCLC 241, CA.

[35] *Hospital Products Ltd v United States Surgical Corpn* [1984] HCA 64, (1984) 156 CLR 41 at 102; see also *Maguire v Makaronis* [1997] HCA 23, (1997) 188 CLR 449 at 463–4 and *Clay v Clay* [2001] HCA 9, (2001) 202 CLR 410 at [46].

[36] *Hospital Products* [1984] HCA 64 at 102–3.

[37] *Chan v Zacharia* [1984] HCA 36, (1984) 154 CLR 178 at 205. See also *Clay* [2001] HCA 9 at [47].

[38] See *Canadian Aero Service Ltd v O'Malley* [1974] SCR 592 at 608–9; S Cretney, 'The Rationale of Keech v Sandford' (1969) 33 Conv 161 at 168ff; AJ Oakley, *Constructive Trusts* (Sweet & Maxwell, 1978), 57ff.

[39] *Barnes v Addy* (1874) LR 9 Ch App 244 at 251 (Lord Selborne LC).

In a pensions context, this can perhaps give rise to two arguments: **6.32**

(a) First, that there is no actual conflict merely because a trustee is also (say) a director of the
     employer or its holding company. At this stage, particularly while the scheme is ongoing
     the conflict is more apparent than real.

     This argument, however, reaches its limits where there are actions or negotiations between
     the trustees and the employer. For instance on scheme funding, a bulk transfer following
     an acquisition, on a return of surplus or on amendments to the pension scheme.
(b) Conversely, the references in the cases mentioned tend to be to a 'personal interest'. Finn
     in his book, *Fiduciary Obligations*,[40] distinguishes between conflicts of interest and duty
     on the one hand and conflicts of duty and duty on the other.

     Thus a transaction between a trustee (acting personally) and his trust, such as the
     sale or purchase of property, is clearly a conflict of interest and duty. Conversely where
     the trustee is acting in a situation where he owes fiduciary duties to another party (eg
     another trust or a company of which the trustee is a director) this is a conflict of fiduciary
     duties.

The rules clearly apply where there is a conflict of duty and duty.[41] Thus Lord Cozens-Hardy **6.33**
in *Moody v Cox & Hatt*[42] stated:

> A solicitor [who also acts as a trustee] may have a duty on one side and a duty on the other,
> namely a duty to his client as a solicitor on the one side and a duty to his beneficiaries on the
> other; but if he chooses to put himself in that position it does not lie in his mouth to say to the
> client 'I have not discharged that which the law says is my duty towards you, my client, because
> I owe a duty to the beneficiaries on the other side'. The answer is that if a solicitor involves
> himself in that dilemma it is his own fault.

In a pension schemes context, it is perhaps more common that a conflict of duty and duty will **6.34**
arise, rather than a conflict of duty and interest. It may well be the case in some circumstances
that the trustee/director does not merely owe fiduciary duties to the trust/trustee company,
but is also interested in the employer (or another company in its group), for instance as an
employee or an officer or a shareholder or (particularly on a winding up) as a creditor.

The 'Two Hats' Approach—Is Fair Dealing a Defence?

Generally where there is a conflict of interest and duty, ie where the trustee stands personally **6.35**
to gain from a trust, the approach is that the trustee cannot seek to uphold the transaction
merely on the grounds that it was entered into in good faith or that it represents the best that
could possibly be obtained by the trust. Thus it is clearly not a defence to say that an independent trustee would in any event have proceeded with the transaction. The transaction
remains automatically voidable by the beneficiaries.

The rationale for this rule seems to be that equity wishes to impose a stringent duty on **6.36**
trustees and is dubious of its task of seeking to investigate the commercial moralities of a

---

[40] PD Finn, *Fiduciary Obligations* (Law Book Co, 1977).
[41] For company directors, see s 175(7) of the Companies Act 2006: 'Any reference in this section to a conflict
of interest includes a conflict of interest and duty'.
[42] [1917] 2 Ch 71, CA. See also *Transvaal Lands Co v New Belgium (Transvaal) Land and Development Co*
[1914] 2 Ch 488, CA and *Hilton v Barker Booth and Eastwood* [2005] UKHL 8, [2005] 1 All ER 651, HL.

transaction—see *Transvaal Lands*.[43] There is a discussion of this strict 'self-dealing' rule in the decision of Megarry V-C in *Tito v Waddell (No 2)*.[44]

6.37   However, it seems that this automatic voidability rule may perhaps not apply where the trustee is not personally involved, but has a more remote interest. In *Tito v Waddell* this is called the 'fair dealing' rule and is stated to apply where a trustee purchases a beneficial interest from a beneficiary. The transaction is not necessarily avoidable but, in the words of Megarry V-C:

> Can be set aside by the beneficiary unless the trustee can show that he has taken no advantage of his position and has made full disclosure to the beneficiary, and that the transaction is fair and honest.

6.38   If this is the case, then it may justify the 'two hats approach'. This would acknowledge that the trustee has a conflict of interest, but uphold a transaction provided the trustee can show that the transaction is justifiable as being one which an independent trustee would have entered into. Other ways of expressing this are to say that it is on arm's length terms or that the trustee has noted that he is wearing his 'trustee hat' and ignored his other interest in making the relevant decision.

6.39   Thus *Farrar v Farrars Ltd*[45] involved a solicitor, Mr Farrar, who was one of three trustees and also solicitor to the trustees (in fact mortgagees). The property in question was sold to a company in which Mr Farrar had a small shareholding and for which he also acted as solicitor. He took no part in the negotiations. The Court of Appeal refused to set aside the transaction. The court refused to set aside the transaction on the grounds that it was invalid, no matter how fair and honest it was, but did hold that the burden was thrown upon the company of showing that the sale was fair and honest.

6.40   More recently, the Privy Council in *Tse Kwong Lam v Wong Chit Sen*[46] applied *Farrar* and held that there was no inflexible rule that a mortgagee exercising his power of sale could not sell to a company in which he had an interest. However, the mortgagee and the company had to show that the sale was made in good faith and that the mortgagee had taken reasonable precautions to obtain the best price reasonably obtainable at the time.

6.41   However, to the contrary effect, is the decision of Vinelott J in *Re Thompson's Settlement*.[47] This case involved a sale of an asset by a trust to a company which had as its directors one of the trustees and his wife. Vinelott J held that a defence of fair dealing was not available in this case. He distinguished *Farrar v Farrars Ltd* on the basis that the solicitor concerned in that case had not been a director of the company which had purchased the relevant asset (although he had been a shareholder and a solicitor to the company). However, the Privy Council decision in *Tse Kwong Lam* was not mentioned by Vinelott J, nor was it cited to him in argument. The decision in *Re Thompson's Settlement* was called a 'high water mark' on this point by Knox J in *Hillsdown* (see para 6.63 below).

---

[43]   *Transvaal Lands Co v New Belgium (Transvaal) Land and Development Co* [1914] 2 Ch 488, CA. But note the criticism in Finn [472].
[44]   [1977] Ch 106 at 240 (Megarry V-C).
[45]   (1888) 40 Ch D 395, CA.
[46]   [1983] 3 All ER 54, PC.
[47]   [1986] 1 Ch 99 (Vinelott J).

Similarly the comments of Lord Denning MR in *Boulting v ACTAT*:[48]   **6.42**

> Or take a nominee director, that is, a director of a company who is nominated by a large share-holder to represent his interests. There is nothing wrong in it. It is done every day. Nothing wrong, that is, so long as the director is left free to exercise his best judgement in the interests of the company which he serves. But if he is put upon terms that he is bound to act in the affairs of the company in accordance with the directions of his patron, it is beyond doubt unlawful...'.

See further the nominee director cases—can the nominee act in the interests of his appointor?   **6.43**
See *Kuwait Asia v National Mutual*[49] and *Re Neath Rugby Ltd; Hawkes v Cuddy*.[50]

Application to Pension Trusts

The conflicts rules have been held to apply to pension trusts—in an early case (1963) Cross   **6.44**
J held in *Re Brooke Bond & Co Ltd's Trust Deed*[51] that an insurer acting as custodian trustee of a pension fund was subject to the conflicts rules and so buy-out policies could not be purchased from the insurer.

Later pensions cases have also applied a strict conflicts rule,[52] but more recently been ready   **6.45**
to agree a relaxation[53] or to apply the fair dealing rule instead[54] or imply a relaxation into the trust deed.[55] These are discussed below.

In practice many trusts now include specific provision for dealing with conflicts—not least   **6.46**
to mitigate the absolute rule that could otherwise apply (eg striking down a decision, even though it may be possible to show that it was fair and the same decision would have been made even without the conflict). This is obviously safer than relying on the courts implying agreement or a relaxation.[56]

Certainly in a commercial context, it is noticeable that conflicts rules seem to be less rigor-   **6.47**
ously applied to company directors. For example:

(a) the companies legislation now allows a board of directors to sanction a conflict—
s 175(4)(b) of the Companies Act 2006; and

---

[48] [1963] QB 606 at 626, CA. See also *Regal Hastings v Gulliver* where Mr Gulliver was acting as a trustee.

[49] [1991] 1 AC 187, PC. See also the antipodean cases: *Re Broadcasting Station 2GB Pty Ltd* [1964–5] NSWR 1648 (Jacobs J); *Levin v Clark* [1962] NSWR 686 (Jacobs J); *Bennetts v Board of Fire Commissioners* (1967) 87 WN (Pt l) 307 (Street J); and *Berlei Hestia (NZ) Ltd v Ferryhough* [1980] 2 NZLR 150 (Mahon J).

[50] [2009] EWCA Civ 291 at [32] and [33], CA (Stanley Brunton LJ) and, at first instance, [2007] EWHC 2999 at [185]–[195] (Ch) (Lewison J). See also *Re Southern Counties Fresh Foods* [2008] EWHC 2810 at [51]–[69] (Ch) (Warren J). There is a useful summary of the position (including discussion of the Irish cases) in the article by Deirdre Ahern, 'Irish Legislative Proposals for Clarification of Nominee Directors' Best Interest Duty' [2010] 31 Company Lawyer 291.

[51] [1963] Ch 357 (Cross J).

[52] *Re William Makin & Sons Ltd* [1993] OPLR 171, [1992] PLR 177 (Vinelott J); *British Coal Corpn v British Coal Staff Superannuation Scheme Trustees* [1995] 1 All ER 912, [1993] OPLR 51 (Vinelott J).

[53] *Drexel* [1995] 1 WLR 32 (Lindsay J).

[54] *Hillsdown* [1997] 1 All ER 862 (Knox J).

[55] *Edge v Pensions Ombudsman* [2000] Ch 602, CA and see para 6.66 below.

[56] The attitude of the courts in a particular situation can be difficult to predict—contrast the decision in *Kelly v Cooper* [1993] AC 205, PC (implied contract term so estate agent not liable for failing to tell client about

(b) in a manner which has been described as somewhat 'anomalous' there is no general rule that a director of a company is prohibited as such (at least provided he or she is a non-executive director) from also being a director of a competing company—see *London & Mashonaland Exploration Co v New Mashonaland Exploration*[57] and *Bell v Lever Bros.*[58]

Pensions Conflict Cases

6.48 Since 1994, conflict issues have arisen in a number of pensions cases. In addition, there has been specific pensions legislation dealing with pension trustees (provisions for member-nominated trustees etc and a specific exemption in s 39 of the Pensions Act 1995).

6.49 The conflicts position has also received increased attention as a result of the changes made to the conflicts provisions etc in relation to directors in the Companies Act 2006 (this applies to directors of trustee companies). Furthermore, the Pensions Regulator has issued guidance in relation to conflict issues.

6.50 In practice, conflict issues have also risen up the agenda as a result of the increased powers given to trustees as against employers. In practice, trustee powers were much more limited in the past by lack of specific provision in the trust deed (eg the employer may have reserved the right to terminate contributions or set the contribution rate in any event). This has changed as a result of specific legislation both for ongoing contributions and on termination.

6.51 The result of this is that the trustees commonly now have a much greater bargaining position as regards the employer. The Pensions Regulator advises trustees to consider the strength of the employer when agreeing or setting contribution rates etc. All of this points to (potentially) more robust negotiations between employers and trustees. The employer's sanction of being able to 'walk away' from the scheme or its funding has now disappeared. This has thrown conflict issues with the employer into more stark relief.

6.52 The key pensions cases on conflicts are discussed below. The determinations panel of the Pensions Regulator also took a strict view on potential conflicts in the *Telent* determination.[59]

William Makin and *British Coal*

6.53 In *William Makin*[60] and later in *British Coal*,[61] Vinelott J was considering a position where various exercises of discretion were being proposed for approval by the court. Vinelott J held that the relevant representative beneficiaries (who were representing the members) were in a fiduciary position and could not take advantage of any benefit improvements that were being

---

confidential information) with the more recent decisions in *Hilton v Barker Booth and Eastwood* [2005] UKHL 8, [2005] 1 All ER 651, HL (solicitor in breach) and the Court of Appeal in *Rossetti Marketing* [2012] EWCA Civ 1021, [2013] 1 All ER (Comm) 308, CA (agent in furniture trade).

[57] [1891] WN 165 (Chitty J).
[58] [1932] AC 161 at 195–6, HL.
[59] 7 November 2007—see para 7.24 below.
[60] *Re William Makin & Sons Ltd* [1993] OPLR 171, [1992] PLR 177 (Vinelott J).
[61] *British Coal Corpn v British Coal Staff Superannuation Scheme Trustees* [1995] 1 All ER 912, [1993] OPLR 51 (Vinelott J).

put forward. In *British Coal*, he responded to criticism of the decision in *William Makin* on this and held[62] that:

> common sense dictates that no man should be asked to exercise a discretion as to the application of a fund amongst a class of which he is a member. He cannot be expected fairly to weigh his own merits against the merits of others.

This is a very strict view. It seems wrong for two reasons.   **6.54**

(a) First, in relation to trustees, it seems wrong if it is to support an absolute view that a trustee cannot be party to the exercise of a discretion where he or she is a potential beneficiary of that discretion. For example, a trustee elected by pensioner members should, instinctively, be able to benefit from an increase in benefits granted to all pensioners. In practice, if not covered by an express provision, it should (in a pensions context) readily be implied.[63]

(b) Secondly, the arrangement here was being approved by the court and so should be capable of approval despite any conflict issues.

Drexel

This second point was considered further by Lindsay J in *Re Drexel Burnham Lambert UK*   **6.55**
Pension Plan.[64] This case involved trustees applying to the court to approve a proposal to deal with benefits on a winding-up of a scheme. This would include additional benefits for members, including the trustees.

Lindsay J reviewed the cases on the potential conflict and commented: **6.56**

> I would expect any intelligent layman interested enough to have read so far to say 'so what'.

Lindsay J held that the general equitable prohibition on conflicts applied to pension trustees,   **6.57**
but that the general 'no conflict' duty was 'riddled with exceptions'. He referred to the Court of Appeal decision in *Sargeant* (implied authority where those who were put into the position of conflict not at their own volition) and to the Privy Council in *Kelly v Cooper* (contract can override).

Lindsay J held that it was open to the court to approve a decision by the trustees, even though   **6.58**
they were conflicted (as beneficiaries they would benefit from relevant benefit increases).[65]

The *Drexel* decision came out while the Pensions Bill 1995 was before Parliament. Amendments   **6.59**
were made and s 39 of the Pensions Act 1995 was enacted to provide for member conflicts—
see para 6.99 below.

Hillsdown

In 1996 in *Hillsdown Holdings v Pensions Ombudsman*,[66] Knox J considered a case involving   **6.60**
a pension scheme where there had been a transfer from one scheme to another scheme as part of an arrangement for a surplus refund to the employer.

---

[62] [1995] 1 All ER 912 at 925.

[63] See *Edge v Pensions Ombudsman* [2000] Ch 602, CA, discussed below.

[64] [1995] 1 WLR 32 (Lindsay J).

[65] *Drexel* was cited and followed in Australia in *Re VBN and the Australian Prudential Regulation Authority* [2006] AATA 710, (2006) 92 ALD 259 (Administrative Appeals Tribunal) at [547].

[66] [1997] 1 All ER 862 (Knox J).

6.61   One of the claims that was made was that some of the directors of the corporate trustee of the transferring scheme were also directors of the trustee of the receiving scheme and directors of the employer.

6.62   Knox J held that the self-dealing rule should apply here, but that this did not automatically invalidate the transaction. Instead, it put the onus of proving that the transaction was reasonable and proper onto the parties concerned.[67]

6.63   Knox J distinguished[68] as 'the high-water mark' the decision of Vinelott J in *Re Thompson's Settlement*.[69] In *Thompson* a transaction amounting either to an assignment or a surrender and regrant of a lease between trustees on the one hand and a company on the other was held voidable under the self-dealing rule because one of the trustees was also a director and, with his wife, majority shareholder in the company. The transaction was therefore within the self-dealing rule.

6.64   Vinelott J, in reply to an argument that the self-dealing, as opposed to the fair-dealing, rule only applied if there was a sale or purchase by trustees of trust property or something analogous to it, said:[70]

> I do not think the self-dealing rule can be so confined. It is clear that the self-dealing rule is an application of the wider principle that a man must not put himself in a position where duty and interest conflict or where his duty to one conflicts with his duty to another (see in particular the opinion of Lord Dunedin in *Wright v Morgan* [1926] AC 788 at 797) which I have cited. The principle is applied stringently in cases where a trustee concurs in a transaction which cannot be carried into effect without his concurrence and who also has an interest in or owes a fiduciary duty to another in relation to the same transaction. The transaction cannot stand if challenged by a beneficiary because in the absence of an express provision in the trust instrument the beneficiaries are entitled to require that the trustees act unanimously and that each brings to bear a mind unclouded by any contrary interest or duty in deciding whether it is the interest of the beneficiaries that the trustees concur in it.

6.65   Knox J in *Hillsdown* also commented that any conflict duty would only apply 'unless there is an express provision in the relevant trust deed permitting a trustee to act in negotiations with the employer'.

Edge

6.66   Conflicts were also considered by Scott V-C and by the Court of Appeal in *Edge v Pensions Ombudsman*.[71]

6.67   At first instance,[72] Scott V-C considered the position of those of the trustees who were members in service and so had benefited from amendments made to the scheme (with the agreement of the employer).

6.68   Scott V-C disagreed with determination of the Pensions Ombudsman that the augmentation decision was invalid as being contrary to the conflicts duty. Scott V-C held[73] that the

---

[67] [1997] 1 All ER 862 at 895 (Knox J).
[68] [1997] 1 All ER 862 at 895 and 896 (Knox J).
[69] *Re Thompson's Settlement, Thompson v Thompson* [1986] Ch 99 (Vinelott J).
[70] [1986] Ch 99 at 115.
[71] [2000] Ch 602, CA.
[72] [1998] Ch 512 (Scott V-C).
[73] [1998] Ch 512 at 540 (Scott V-C).

fact that the pension scheme trust deed required there to be member trustees (as current employees) would produce an absurd result if it meant that the member trustees must be excluded from benefit.

Scott V-C referred to the decision of the Court of Appeal in *Sargeant* and considered it was **6.69** conclusive of the conflict of interest point in relation to the scheme concerned. He held[74] that it would have been open to the draughtsman of the rules to have excluded an express provision for the member trustees to retain any benefits. But in the absence of such an express provision, it 'must be implied in order that the rules should have ordinary business efficacy'. Scott V-C held:

> The notion that, when the discretionary power of amendment is exercised so as to increase an existing benefit or add a new benefit, the member trustees must be excluded from benefit is, in my opinion, quite simply ridiculous.

Scott V-C went on to say that the issue of whether or not trustees were protected by the **6.70** *Sargeant* exception did not depend on whether or not the trustees in question have been 'pro active in seeking appointment or, in the style of the speaker of the House of Commons, have been dragged protesting into office'.

On appeal, the Court of Appeal did not deal with the particular conflict point, but indicated **6.71** that they had no doubt that Scott V-C's reasoning was correct.[75]

It was argued in the Court of Appeal that because of the conflict of interest, the trustees had **6.72** the onus of showing that the decision which they had reached was fair, referring to *Hillsdown*. The Court of Appeal rejected this holding that the situation differed from *Hillsdown* given that the rules required the representation of current employees amongst the trustee board. This meant that those seeking to challenge a decision of the trustee should bear the ordinary burden of establishing that the decision had been reached properly or the decision had been reached improperly.

Company Directors

It would seem that there should be very little difference between the position of an individual **6.73** trustee and a director of a trustee company. Both have fiduciaries owing relevant fiduciary duties and the relevant conflict rule should apply.

The general conflict rules in relation to companies and their directors have, of course, generally **6.74** been modified for many years by express provision in the articles of association of the company. Otherwise it would not be possible for directors of a company to (for example) be paid save with the agreement of the shareholders. This general implied rule is almost universally excluded by a specific provision in the articles of association. Such provisions have long been upheld by the court.

The position in relation to conflicts for directors of company trustees has now been codified **6.75** by the Companies Act 2006, including express provisions for the board of directors of a company to be able to approve certain conflicts of interest (eg by establishing a policy). See further para 6.125 below.

---

[74] [1998] Ch 512 at 540 at 541 (Scott V-C).
[75] [1998] Ch 512 at 562.

Express Provisions on Conflict

6.76 There is no reason why an express provision in the relevant trust deed dealing with conflicts would not be upheld and given full force of effect by the courts. The conflict duty and obligations are merely default rules which can be overridden by express provision in the trust deed.

6.77 Most of the cases dealing with the conflict duty include a caveat saying that the conflict issue is subject to an express provision in the relevant trust deed—see for example the House of Lords in *Bray v Ford*[76] and *Dale v IRC*.[77] This also follows from the implied authorization cases (see para 6.86 below)—eg *Kelly v Cooper*.[78]

6.78 In *Edge v Pensions Ombudsman*,[79] at first instance, Scott V-C held[80] that it would have been open to the draughtsman of the rules to have excluded an express provision for the member trustees to retain any benefits. But in the absence of such an express provision, it 'must be implied in order that the rules should have ordinary business efficacy'. An express exemption does not otherwise seem to have been considered much in a pensions context.[81]

6.79 An override is common in company articles of association (indeed paying a director would not be allowed without such a provision). It may be construed strictly.[82]

6.80 For example, in the private trust case, *Breakspear v Akland*,[83] Briggs J (as he then was) upheld an exercise of a discretion by a trustee in their own favour on the basis that there was an express provision in the trust deed allowing trustees to benefit from the exercise of a discretion. This was a private trust case, but there seems no reason why this should not apply to pension trusts.

6.81 In practice, in light of the conflict provisions in the Companies Act 2006 (which should have prompted a review by companies of conflict provisions for their directors, including trustee companies) and the Pensions Regulator's guidance on conflicts in 2008, express provisions dealing with conflicts are now commonly found both within trust deeds and articles of association of trustee companies.

6.82 These generally deal with the position of both individual trustees and directors of a trustee company (the term 'trustee board' covering both senses) providing for:

(a) members of the trustee board to be able to benefit from the scheme and the exercise of discretions;

---

[76] [1896] AC 44, HL.

[77] [1954] AC 11 at 27, HL. See also *Space Investments Ltd v Canadian Imperial Bank of Commerce Trust Co (Bahamas) Ltd* [1986] 3 All ER 75 at 77, PC.

[78] [1993] AC 205, PC.

[79] [1998] Ch 512 (Scott V-C).

[80] [1998] Ch 512 at 541 (Scott V-C).

[81] But note the brief mention in *Doyle v Manchester Evening News* [1989] PLR 47 (Judge Blackett-Ord V-C). In relation to company directors, see Vinelott J's comments in *Movitex v Bulfield* [1988] BCLC 785 (Vinelott J). Noted by Sealy [1987] CLJ 217.

[82] For example *Guinness v Saunders* [1990] 2 AC 663, HL (power on remuneration given to board of directors not within delegation to sub-committee).

[83] *Breakspear v Ackland* [2008] EWHC 220 (Ch), [2009] Ch 32 (Briggs J). Discussed in Chapter 18 (Disclosure of documents: *Schmidt v Rosewood*) on the separate disclosure issue.

(b) members of the trustee board to be able to be interested in the relevant employer (and its group), whether as an employee, officer, or shareholder;[84]

(c) members of the trustee board to be able to cease to act or to absent themselves from relevant decisions where they have conflicts of interest;

(d) declarations of conflicts of interest where necessary;

(e) there to be no duty of disclosure by members of the trustee board to the other members of the trustee board where the information has been obtained by the members of the trustee board in confidence (eg as a result of some other duty). This is discussed at para 6.165 below in relation to the potential for there being an implied duty of disclosure.

Such express provisions are helpful, given that in practice it is generally not going to be pos- **6.83** sible to obtain a waiver or consent from the individual members of any conflict. It may well be that in practice such exclusions would be implied into a trust instrument in any event (see *Edge v Pensions Ombudsman*), but in practice it is always safer to include express provisions.

Clearly trustees, once appointed (or directors of a trustee company), generally owe their **6.84** duties to the trustee company and not to their appointor—see *Kuwait Asia*[85] and Ch 5 (Liability of directors of corporate trustees).

There is no reason why a provision dealing with conflicts should be considered invalid as **6.85** somehow being contrary to a core obligation in a trust. The trustee would remain responsible in the same way as any other trustee (ie he or she should act in a fiduciary manner and not, say, at the direction of his or her appointor).[86]

Implied Authorization

It is clearly possible to argue that the nature of a pension scheme trust is such that an implied **6.86** authorization for the trustees to include officers of the principal company could be found.

This can apply from the nature of the fiduciary relationship. For example in *Kelly v Cooper*,[87] **6.87** the Privy Council held that no strict conflict duty would be applied to estate agents. It was to be expected that they may act for many customers and it would not be practical to impose an implied duty not to act for other potential sellers or purchasers.

In *Rossetti Marketing Ltd v Diamond Sofa Co Ltd*[88] a case concerning an agency for furniture **6.88** distribution, Lord Neuberger MR considered that *Kelly* should be limited (and refused to find an implied authorization in that case). He stated:

> More generally, I agree with what is said in the 19th edition of Bowstead & Reynolds (footnote 294 of para 6-045) that, particularly as 'estate agents are only imperfectly agents and are known to act for many principals', it is highly questionable whether the reasoning in *Kelly* [1993] AC 205 should be extended to other cases of agency, at least in the absence of clear evidence to support such an extension. This view is also supported by a helpful article by Joshua Getzler, LQR, 2006, 122 (Jan), 1, 7, which commends the approach of the House of Lords in the subsequent

---

[84] Often helpful given the prevalence of share options.
[85] *Kuwait Asia Bank EC v National Mutual Life Nominees Ltd* [1991] 1 AC 187, PC.
[86] See the discussion on 'core duties' in Ch 14 (Trustee indemnities and exonerations).
[87] [1993] AC 205, PC.
[88] [2012] EWCA Civ 1021 at [27], CA.

case of *Hilton v Barker Booth & Eastwood* [2005] UKHL 8, [2005] 1 WLR 567. In that case, Lord Walker referred to 'the content of the contractual duty of full disclosure being rooted in the fiduciary relationship' between principal and agent (in that case, a solicitor).

6.89 An implied authorization can also be found in individual circumstances. For example, in the private trust case, *Sargeant v National Westminster Bank plc*,[89] the Court of Appeal held that two trustees could buy trust property from the trust where the conflict of interest was known to the settlor and into which they had been placed by the terms on which the settlement was established.

6.90 Two possible arguments then arise in the case of pension schemes:

(a) the employer could, perhaps, be considered to be a settlor for this purpose. It may well have initially set up the settlement with directors as trustees. Under the argument in *Sargeant* this should mean that at least those initial trustee/directors would not be subject to conflict of interest rules. However, it may not perhaps extend to later trustees unless the argument that they have not placed themselves in a conflict is one which extends to the fact that it is the company (as settlor?) which places them in a conflict position;

(b) a wider argument could perhaps rely on what was described in *Stannard v Fisons Pension Trust Ltd*[90] by Warner J as the 'symbionic relationship between a company and its pension fund'. This is presumably a reference to the fact that the continued existence of the pension fund, in particular its funding may well depend on the trustees retaining the goodwill of the principal company. This perhaps could be viewed as an extension of the argument that there is no conflict between the principal company and the pension scheme trustees at least while the scheme and the company are ongoing.

6.91 If this is correct, a greater conflict may arise when the scheme ceases to be ongoing, ie it is being wound up (and the employer has entered insolvency proceedings)—see *Mettoy*. However, the position here has now been covered by legislation dealing with independent trustees in employer insolvency.[91]

6.92 The leading pensions case in this area is the decision of Scott V-C (as he then was) approved by the Court of Appeal in *Edge v Pensions Ombudsman*.[92] Scott V-C referred to both *Sargeant* and *Drexel* and held that an exoneration in favour of member trustees against any prohibition on their taking any benefit should be implied. He held:

> The passage from Nourse LJ's judgment [in *Sargeant*] that I have cited is, in my judgment, conclusive of the conflict of interest point in the present case. The member trustees are placed by the rules themselves in the position of conflict between interest and duty to which the Pensions Ombudsman referred. The rules require the body of trustees to include employee

---

[89] (1990) 61 P&CR 518, CA. On implied authorization, see also the Australian cases: *Princess Anne of Hesse v Field* [1963] NSWR 998 at 1009 (Jacobs J) and *Inge v Inge* [1990] VicSC 365, (1990) 8 ACLC 942 (O'Bryan J). *Sargeant* was followed in Australia in *Re VBN and the Australian Prudential Regulation Authority* [2006] AATA 710, (2006) 92 ALD 259 (Administrative Appeals Tribunal) at [547].

[90] [1992] IRLR 27, [1991] PLR 225 (Warner J).

[91] See ss 22–26 of the Pensions Act 1995, as amended by the Pensions Act 2004 (and replacing provisions in the Social Security Act 1990). See further, Pollard, *Corporate Insolvency* 5th edn (2013) Ch 53.

[92] [2000] Ch 602, CA.

members. The rules contemplate that, as trustees, the employee members will from time to time have to exercise discretions in which their duty and interest may conflict. In these circumstances there is, in my judgment, no rule of equity that requires them to account for the benefits that an entirely proper exercise of discretionary powers may produce for them. I would reach the same conclusion as a matter of construction of the rules. It would have been open to the draftsman of the rules expressly to have provided for member trustees to retain any benefits that exercises of the trustees' discretionary power to fix the level of members' contributions and discretionary power to amend the rules to provide additional benefits for members might produce. In my judgment, a provision to that effect must be implied in order that the rules should have ordinary business efficacy.

An implied term may be less likely to apply to directors, the Court of Appeal taking the view **6.93** in *Gwembe Valley Development Co v Koshy (No 3)*[93] that there was no scope for implying terms in articles of association of a company—but this may no longer apply following the Privy Council decision in *A-G of Belize v Belize Telecom Ltd*.[94]

Other Defences/Relaxations

The rule relating to conflicts of interest is subject to other potential relaxations. These are **6.94** discussed below in turn.

Consent from beneficiaries

Generally, where beneficiaries have given their informed consent (see *NZ Netherlands Society* **6.95** *v Kuys*[95]) then no breach will arise.

This is obviously impracticable in the case of a large pension scheme where not all the **6.96** beneficiaries will be of age nor yet identified. It is also likely to be impractical in relation to a small pension scheme with only a few members. The consent of discretionary recipients (eg spouse or dependants) may also be needed—but see Chapter 8 (Pension trusts: the position of spouses and dependants).

Consent of the other trustees is not usually considered to be enough (consider *Regal (Hastings)* **6.97** *v Gulliver*[96]). But the majority decision-making rule found in pension trusts could justify such a consent.[97]

In the case of a money purchase scheme, it may be that the consent or direction of the member **6.98** in relation to his or her own notional account would be enough to allow a conflict (or give a deemed indemnity[98]).

---

[93] [2003] EWCA Civ 1048, [2004] 1 BCLC 131, CA at para [56].
[94] [2009] UKPC 10, [2009] 2 All ER 1127, PC.
[95] [1973] 2 All ER 1222, PC. On informed consent, see further *Hurstanger Ltd v Wilson* [2007] EWCA Civ 299, [2007] 2 All ER (Comm) 1037, CA.
[96] (1942) [1967] 2 AC 134n, [1942] 1 All ER 378, HL.
[97] See further at para 6.111 and *Re Thompson's Settlement, Thompson v Thompson* [1986] Ch 99 (Vinelott J) at 115G.
[98] Under the principle in *Hardoon v Belilios* [1901] AC 118, PC. Applied in a pensions context in relation to a scheme with just one member: *Independent Trustee Services Ltd v Rowe* [1998] OPLR 77 at 98 (Parker J). See Ch 14 (Trustee indemnities and exonerations).

Section 39 exemption

6.99 Section 39 of the Pensions Act 1995 has provided, since coming into force on 1 January 1996, an express exemption from the conflicts rules for a trustee who is also a member. It provides that:

> No rule of law that a trustee may not exercise the powers vested in him so as to give rise to a conflict between his personal interest and his duties to the beneficiaries shall apply to a trustee of a trust scheme, who is also a member of the scheme, exercising the powers vested in him in any manner, merely because their exercise in that manner benefits, or may benefit, him as a member of the scheme.

6.100 This exemption applies to all trustees who are also members of the scheme. Section 39 was enacted following the decision of Lindsay J in *Manning v Drexel Burnham Lambert*[99]—see the discussion by Scott V-C in *Edge v Pensions Ombudsman*.[100] It does not expressly cover:

(a) directors of a corporate trustee;[101] or

(b) trustees who have some other conflict or interest (eg as a spouse of a member or as a director or employee of the employer).

6.101 If a wide approach were given to the disability that attached to directors of corporate trustees, then it would be arguable that s 39 of the Pensions Act 1995 was not wide enough to cure this.

6.102 The section only refers to trustees and not to directors of corporate trustees. The rest of the Pensions Act 1995 contains numerous distinctions between a trustee who is a company and one where individuals are trustees. It is unlikely that a court would extend the exemption in s 39 to cover directors of a corporate trustee.[102] See for example the recent decision of the High Court in Australia in *Montevento Holdings Pty Ltd v Scaffidi*[103] upholding the distinction (in the context of a trust provision) between acting as a trustee and acting as the sole director of a trustee company.

Authorization by the court: section 61 of the Trustee Act 1925

6.103 It seems that if there is a conflict of duty this can always be rectified by an application to court for authority to act. Indeed this may be the only course where the trustee is sufficiently uncertain of his position.

6.104 Section 61 of the Trustee Act 1925 also allows the court to relieve a trustee who has acted honestly and reasonably. This is quite a high standard and will not readily be available.[104] The courts have not shown themselves particularly minded to grant equitable relief to fiduciaries in this situation under s 61. Thus relief was not given in *Boardman v Phipps*[105] nor (under the equivalent provision for directors) in *Guinness v Saunders*.[106]

---

[99] [1994] OPLR 71, [1995] 1 WLR 32 (Lindsay J).

[100] [1998] Ch 512 (Scott V-C).

[101] See Ch 4 (Corporate trustees).

[102] In one determination, the Deputy Pensions Ombudsman referred to s 39 when upholding a benefit increase in favour of a trustee director who was also a member. The scheme included an express provision covering directors: *Ecart* 85837/1 (2012) 31 October (Irvine Deputy PO).

[103] [2012] HCA 48, HC Aus. See Ch 5 (Liability of directors of a corporate trustee).

[104] See Ch 14 (Trustee indemnities and exonerations). For an example of a refusal by the Pensions Ombudsman, see *McCann v Surstock* (2010) 16 August, 26791/4 (Irvine Deputy PO).

[105] *Boardman v Phipps* [1967] 2 AC 46, HL.

[106] *Guinness v Saunders* [1990] 2 AC 663, HL.

Abstain from voting

In a company context, articles of association usually provide that a director interested in a contract shall not vote at the relevant board meeting nor be counted in the quorum to consider the matter.   **6.105**

It is less common to find such provisions in pension schemes. In the absence of such a specific provision, it seems that the trustee should either take the view that he should take part in the decision, putting out of his mind any of the conflicting interests (relying on the principles mentioned earlier) or, conversely, resign as a trustee. Generally, beneficiaries are entitled to have all their trustees consider decisions (this is the basis of the unanimity rule in trustee decisions). It is not clear whether or not this is displaced by an express provision of the trust deed providing for a majority of the trustees to be able to act.   **6.106**

Exoneration clauses

Exoneration clauses in the trust deed, eg so that the trustee is only liable for conscious wilful default, may protect a trustee in a conflict situation. These clauses are usually construed against the trustee concerned.   **6.107**

One issue is that the relevant conflict will usually be known to the trustee concerned and so his or her actions are likely to be seen as deliberate or wilful and so may well not fall within the scope of the relevant exoneration provisions.   **6.108**

Another issue is that an exoneration clause, even if it applies, is likely mainly to relieve the trustee concerned from liability for breach of trust. It is unlikely to prevent the other consequences—eg invalidation of the underlying transaction.[107]   **6.109**

In addition the courts have not shown themselves particularly minded to grant equitable relief to fiduciaries in this situation under s 61 of the Trustee Act 1925 or otherwise. Thus relief was not given in *Boardman v Phipps* nor in *Guinness v Saunders*.   **6.110**

Impact of Majority Voting?

It is less clear what happens if the conflict breach is only relevant to one trustee (or director of a trustee company). In pension schemes (unlike the position of private trusts where the implied legal position is that unanimity is required[108] is usually not modified), it is usual for the pension trust instrument to provide for majority voting (of those trustees present at a meeting, subject to any relevant quorum requirements).   **6.111**

Section 32 of the Pensions Act 1995 provides for an amendment of this general trust law rule that trustees must generally make decisions unanimously. This was recommended by the Pension Law Reform Committee,[109] chaired by Professor Goode, which preceded the Pensions Act 1995.   **6.112**

In practice, pension trusts usually contain express provisions dealing with majority voting. Section 32(1) allows the trust instrument to provide otherwise.   **6.113**

---

[107] See eg Lord Walker in *Pitt/Futter v HMRC* [2013] UKSC 26 at [89], SC.
[108] *Luke v South Kensington Hotel Co* (1879) 11 ChD 121, CA; *Swale v Swale* (1856) 22 Beav 584, (1856) 52 ER 1233 (Romilly MR); *Re Butlin's Settlement Trust* [1976] Ch 251 (Brightman J).
[109] CM 2342.

6.114   The position of directors of a trustee company has long been that majority voting (of those directors present at a meeting) applies, subject to any relevant quorum requirements in the articles.

6.115   Section 32 appears to be relatively inflexibly drafted in that it states: 'Decisions of the trustees of a trust scheme may, unless the scheme provides otherwise, be taken by agreement of a majority of the trustees.'

6.116   It should be noted that the requirement under s 32 is that the majority of the trustees must agree any decision, not merely the majority of the trustees present at the relevant meeting. In addition, there is no provision envisaged for a casting vote (eg the chairman). Decisions of trustees therefore differ in this respect from most companies where the articles deal with decisions of company directors.[110]

6.117   If there is provision for majority decision and there is such a decision (perhaps ignoring any votes cast by the conflicted trustee or director), does this mean that the decision should be upheld and there be no breach? So that none of the four consequences outlined above should apply? Or alternatively the 'fair dealing' rule allowing the relevant decision potentially to be justified as being fair or the same as would have been made even without the conflict.

6.118   The fair dealing rule approach if there is majority voting (even in the absence of an express provision allowing such a conflict) gets some support from Vinelott J's comments in *Re Thompson's Settlement*:[111]

> The principle is applied stringently in cases where a trustee concurs in a transaction which cannot be carried into effect without his concurrence and who also has an interest in or holds a fiduciary duty to another in relation to the same transaction. The transaction cannot stand if challenged by a beneficiary because in the absence of an express provision in the trust instrument the beneficiaries are entitled to require that the trustees act unanimously and that each brings to bear a mind unclouded by any contrary interest or duty in deciding whether it is in the interest of the beneficiaries that the trustees concur in it.
>
> The same principle also applies, but less stringently, in a case within the fair-dealing rule, such as the purchase by a trustee of a beneficiary's beneficial interest. There, there are genuinely two parties to the transaction and it will be allowed to stand if freely entered into and if the trustee took no advantage from his position or from any knowledge acquired from it.

6.119   This seems logical (but it would be safest for the relevant trust deed or company articles to spell out the conflict).

6.120   An example is the robust decision of the Pensions Ombudsman in *Rath*,[112] where a decision by trustees on a scheme winding-up to refund surplus to the employer (and not to exercise a discretion to augment members' benefits) was upheld by the Ombudsman. A member complained that the trustees had a conflict of interest in that four out of the five trustees (at the time of the final decision) were also officers of the employer. The Ombudsman held that the appointment of an independent trustee meant that any conflict issue had been addressed (even though apparently the independent trustee did not attend the relevant final meeting).

---

[110] See eg SI 1985/805, reg 88, Table A.

[111] *Re Thompson's Settlement, Thompson v Thompson* [1986] Ch 99 at 115G (Vinelott J).

[112] *Rath v Association of Investment Trust Companies* (2009) 24 September, 27884/2 (King PO).

Can a Conflict Exclusion be Included or Changed in an Existing Scheme?

6.121 Pension trusts usually have a wide express amendment power, usually requiring the employer and the trustees to agree.[113]

6.122 Care is obviously needed before trustees agree to a change to a scheme to allow conflicts. This could be seen as giving them wider protection against the fund or the members than before. The trustees owe a fiduciary duty to exercise their powers for a proper purpose (usually in the best interests of the scheme).

6.123 One answer may be that it is considered that it is better for the trustee board to include a wide range of individuals, including those who may otherwise be caught by a potential conflict (eg members, trade unionists, company executives) or that otherwise trustees are not prepared to come forward. This latter argument was upheld by Lord Hope in the Court of Session in *Governors of Dollar Academy Trust v Lord Advocate*[114] to allow an amendment to a charity to allow for trustee insurance, to be paid out of the funds of the charity.

6.124 Such a change to an existing scheme does not require consent or certification under s 67 of the Pensions Act 1995[115]—accrued rights (ie benefits) are not affected.

Authorizing Director Conflicts in the Articles

6.125 The better view is that articles of association of a company can contain provisions authorizing a director's actual or potential conflict (avoiding the need to obtain a specific authorization by the board of directors of the trustee company under s 175, of the Companies Act 2006).

Relevant Companies Act 2006 and Table A provisions

6.126 The Companies Act 2006 provides:

(a) s 180(4)(b) provides that the general statutory duties are not infringed by anything done (or omitted) by the directors in accordance with provisions of the articles 'dealing with conflicts of interest';
(b) s 232(1) avoids any provision in articles that purports to exempt a director to any extent from any liability that would otherwise attach to him in connection with any negligence, default, breach of duty, or breach of trust in relation to the company;
(c) s 232(4) provides that nothing in s 232 prevents a company's articles from making 'such provision as has previously been lawful for dealing with conflicts of interest';
(d) reg 85 of 1985 Table A authorized directorships of 'any body corporate promoted by the company or in which the company is otherwise interested' and allows the director to keep benefits derived from the directorship.

---

[113] See Ch 17 (Amendment powers).
[114] [1995] SLT 596, CSOH.
[115] See Ch 17 (Amendment powers).

Hansard extracts

6.127 It is clear from Hansard that it was intended that anything lawful before 1 October 2008 (when these provisions in the Companies Act 2006 came into force) should continue to be lawful on and after that date.

(a) House of Lords 9 May 2006 Lord Sainsbury:

> We do not want the articles of the company to be prevented from doing what they can do now in relation to those matters which fall within [sections 175 or 176].

(b) House of Lords 23 May 2006 Lord Sainsbury:

> Two major principles have guided our approach. The first is that we cannot agree to return to the pre-1928 position, under which companies were able to include widely drafted exclusion clauses in their articles. The current law sets the balance. It is acceptable for the articles to exempt directors from liability for certain conflicts. But for the necessary protection of the company, it is not acceptable for the articles to exempt the directors from others. The second principle is that we do not want to prevent the articles doing what they can now do in relation to these matters, which fall within [s 175 or s 176]. [Section 180(4)] already enables companies to give authorisation in all the ways that they may do so at the moment. Our amendment to this provision [ie s 232(4)] expands it to make clear that the company's articles can authorise conflicts of interest. . . . Our amendment ensures that the articles are not prevented from doing anything currently possible in relation to conflicts of interest. . . . Everything that may currently be done in the articles for authorising or dealing with conflicts of interest will remain valid and can continue to be done in the future. The Bill will leave the law unchanged in this area.

Is a reg 85-type article valid after 1 October 2008?

6.128 As a result of s 232(4), a provision equivalent to reg 85 of 1985 Table A or reg 78 of 1948 Table A remains valid after 1 October 2008 because it is valid before that date. Regulation 85 and reg 78 are valid before 1 October 2008 for the following reasons:

(a) The Greene Committee report[116] (1926) recommended the introduction of statutory control on provisions protecting directors from liability. This led eventually to s 232 via s 205 of the Companies Act 1948 and s 310 of the Companies Act 1985. The Committee thought this necessary to combat the then common practice of exempting directors from liability except for 'wilful neglect or default', and other cases where directors were excused in every case other than actual dishonesty. See paras 46 and 47 of KM174786.

(b) The scope of s 205 of the Companies Act 1948 (ie the predecessor of s 232(1)) and regs 78 and 84 of Table A 1948 (now regs 85, 86, and 94 Table A 1985) was considered by Vinelott J in *Movitex v Bullfield*:[117]

> But it would be at the lowest paradoxical to find that s 205 [Companies Act 1948] conflicts with arts 78 and 84 [of 1948 Table A]. The legislature in enacting the 1948 Act must have contemplated that the modifications of the self-dealing rule in arts 78 and 84 do not infringe s 205. Accordingly, if s 205 is fairly capable of a construction which avoids that conflict, that construction must clearly be preferred to one which does not.

---

[116] For more about the Greene Committee and the history of s 232 see paras 11.46–11.51 of the Law Commission's consultation paper no 153 'Company Directors: Regulating Conflicts of Interest and Formulating Statements of Duties' (September 1998).

[117] [1988] BCLC 104 at 122 (Vinelott J). Noted by Sealy [1987] CLJ 217. The Court of Appeal referred to *Movitex* in the later case of *Gwembe Valley Development Co v Koshy (No 3)* [2003] EWCA Civ 1048, [2004] 1 BCLC 131, CA but did not cast any doubt on this issue.

How far can articles go in authorizing conflicts?

It is not clear what a provision 'dealing with' conflicts means for the purpose of s 180(4)(b). **6.129**
It can be argued that this does not extend to allowing authorization of conflicts beyond the
scope of reg 85 of 1985 Table A and that a more widely drafted provision would infringe
s 232(1). It is arguable that, on general rules of statutory interpretation, a general provision
such as s 180(4)(b) should not be taken to override the specific authorization provisions in
s 175 by sanctioning another method of authorization. This would mean that a directorship
in a company promoted by the company, or in which the company was interested, would not
have to be authorized under s 175—but others would.

The corresponding provisions in 1948 Table A were different to reg 85 of 1985 Table A—and **6.130**
wider (see italicized wording):

> 78. A director of the company may be or become a director or other officer of, or otherwise
> interested in, any company promoted by the company *or in which the company may be inter-
> ested as shareholder or otherwise*, and no such director shall be accountable to the company
> for any remuneration or other benefits received by him as a director or officer of, or from his
> interest in, such other company unless the company otherwise direct.

The Table As preceding 1948 contained no provision dealing with conflicts of interest. It is not **6.131**
clear why this provision was added to the 1948 Table A, nor why the 1948 and 1985 Table
As were different in this respect.

Under the law before and after 1 October 2008 it is possible to authorize directorships of all **6.132**
group companies—not just subsidiaries. It is not clear how far directorships outside a group
can be authorized by the articles. But if reg 78 of 1948 Table A is effective—and it should
be—then the articles could authorize a directorship of any company in which the company
is 'interested as shareholder or otherwise'.

Should a Senior Officer of the Employer be a Trustee?

The thrust of the pensions legislation has been to give greater powers to trustees of pension **6.133**
schemes. The Pensions Regulator interprets this to guide trustees towards taking a more
independent position with the sponsoring employer and 'acting like a bank'. This will mean
more negotiations between the trustees and the employer.

The rest of this chapter looks at the conflict of duty that can arise for the individuals con- **6.134**
cerned as a result and seeks to point to the factors that companies and individuals should take
into account when deciding whether or not a senior officer of the employer (eg the finance
director) should be a pension trustee.

Overview

There can be a difficult balance for an employer to strike as to whether or not a senior officer **6.135**
of an employer company (eg a director of the employer or of its parent company) should also
be on the trustee board of the employer's pension scheme.

Clearly, the role of the senior officer may result in a conflict of duty between: **6.136**

- the duty to the scheme owed as a trustee; and
- the duty owed as an employee, director, or officer of the employer.

6.137 A conflict can arise for more junior employees as well, but in practice this is less likely to be an issue. In addition, members of a trustee board may have a conflict as members of the scheme (although s 39 of the Pensions Act 1995 gives a limited approval for such member conflicts).

6.138 Pension scheme rules often (but not always) contain an express provision allowing conflicts. The articles of association of any corporate trustee company also need to be checked for any provision allowing for conflicts.

6.139 However, a senior officer who acts in breach of any duty owed to the employer and/or the trustee board would remain personally liable for such a breach.

6.140 Furthermore, a senior officer may perhaps be in breach of a duty to the scheme if he or she does not disclose to the trustee board any material information that he or she knows. It may not be a defence that this information is confidential to the company. This may not be expressly covered by the scheme rules (or the trustee's articles of association). The articles of association of a corporate trustee can be amended by the shareholders (often the employer) to make it clear that there is no automatic breach of duty in such a case. The scheme trust deed could also be amended to this effect, though this would usually have to be agreed with the trustees and may be more difficult.

6.141 A perception issue for the individual concerned would remain. How can he or she remain in a trustee meeting while possessing relevant information?

6.142 Against this has to be balanced the desire to have relatively senior and experienced individuals acting on the trustee board, particularly on issues where there is no conflict (eg in implementing an agreed investment strategy).

6.143 One solution is to have the senior officers not have any information or take part in any decisions the employer may be making. But in many cases this will be impractical.

6.144 Many companies may decide that it is better if (say) the finance director is not a trustee. This is because of the increased likelihood of a conflict issue in light of the increased powers of trustees under the pensions legislation and the views of the Pensions Regulator (eg in fixing contribution rates etc).

6.145 It may well be possible to have a senior officer (eg the Finance Director) still attend trustee meetings (as an observer, not a trustee) or even (if this is allowed by the scheme rules or the articles of the trustee company—as a technical pensions matter this can be easier for a trustee company) sit on a separate committee in some areas (this may be more difficult in the investment area).

6.146 If an actual conflict arises, this should be managed by parties—in particular by the senior officer in question. Typically this would involve abstaining from the trustee's decision-making process and not taking part in any negotiations (or being present for the relevant part of meetings). The senior officer should also formally declare the potential conflict to the rest of the trustee board.

6.147 Approaching the trustee board to discuss this issue may well lead them to consider what information flows there should generally be between the trustee and the employer. Broadly, it would be sensible for the employer and the trustee board to:

(a) agree a protocol for the supply of relevant information; and

(b) agree a formal confidentiality agreement with each set of trustees (and the individual trustee directors), so that the employer can have more assurance that any information provided to a trustee on a confidential basis is kept confidential (this can also help listed companies comply with the Listing Rules).

Level of skills needed by trustees

In a relevant defined benefit scheme, the employer is ultimately responsible for the funding. So it helps the employer having individuals on the trustee board who have a high level of commercial skills, knowledge, and experience. This is particularly important in the light of: **6.148**

(a) the powers held by pension scheme trustees (increased by the Pensions Act 2004);
(b) the employer's need to negotiate and agree with the trustee board on matters such as funding, investment, benefit changes etc. If clearance from the Pensions Regulator is needed for some corporate action, the employer may be looking for the trustee board to act speedily;
(c) the requirements on trustees to have appropriate knowledge and understanding. This is now a statutory requirement under the Pensions Act 2004. It is intended to make trustees (and trustee directors) better equipped to take decisions on key issues;
(d) the Pensions Regulator's statements that it expects pension scheme trustees to act more like commercial business managers and large creditors of the employer; and
(e) the likelihood that, over time, these increased expectations will be reflected in how the courts approach the duties of pension scheme trustees.

However, there will be concerns that on occasion a senior officer, as an officer or employee of the employer: **6.149**

(a) may be required to take actions which conflict with their roles as members of the trustee board;
(b) may be aware of information that is confidential to the employer, where it is possible that they are under a duty to disclose this to the trustee board—for example, the financial state of the employer (and its group), a proposed transaction, or the negotiating position of the employer in discussions between the employer and the trustee board.

The nature of the roles of the senior officers within the employer may mean that this could be an ongoing concern.   **6.150**

Where a trustee (or trustee director) has a potential conflict and is involved in a decision by the trustee, the main consequences could be: **6.151**

(a) the court ruling that the decision of the trustee was taken in breach of trust and therefore invalid; and/or
(b) the conflicted trustee/director being held to be in breach of his duty as a trustee (or director of the trustee).

The following questions need to be considered: **6.152**

(a) whether the senior officer can act at all as a trustee (or director of a trustee company) given the potential for conflicts summarized above;
(b) how each senior officer and the trustee board should deal with an actual conflict, ie a specific transaction or matter in which that senior officer is taking an active role on behalf of

the employer, or in relation to which the senior officer has knowledge of information confidential to the employer; and

(c) if any senior officer becomes aware of information confidential to the employer in the course of his or her duties as a director or employee of the employer (or another group company), and that information may affect decisions taken by the trustee board, whether the senior officer is obliged immediately to disclose that information to the other members of the trustee board.

Can a senior officer act as a trustee despite the potential conflicts?

6.153 The existence of potential conflicts of interest or duty will not always preclude a senior officer from acting as a trustee (or director of a trustee company) if the parties concerned—the employer and the trustee—give express consent to this or if the relevant governing documentation allows for this. In practice, this means that:

(a) The employer will need to consent to the senior officers accepting the appointment in spite of the potential conflict.
  (i) Employer consent will be implied if the trustee appointment is by the company.
  (ii) If a senior officer is employed by another group entity or is an officer of any group entity, it would be prudent to ensure that entity also gives express consent (by written agreement) and/or modifies its governing documents.
  (iii) If the senior officer is also a director of a group company, its memorandum and articles of association need to be checked to see whether they allow the potential conflict. The conflict provisions in the Companies Act 2006 will need to be considered.

(b) It is preferable if the provisions of the scheme trust deed (and the articles of association of a corporate trustee) expressly allow the senior officer's appointment in spite of the potential conflicts. If these documents do allow this, the decisions of the trustee board should not be automatically void by reason of the potential conflicts.

(c) It is preferable to check the conflict provisions to clarify that a member of the trustee board:
  (i) can act despite a conflicting duty (as well as a conflicting interest), though there is likely to be a reasonable argument that conflicting interest wording already supports this interpretation; or
  (ii) is not under an obligation to disclose confidential information to the trustee where to do so would be in breach of a duty owed to the employer (see para 6.160 below).

6.154 Pension schemes often include an exoneration clause providing that the trustee is not liable save for a deliberate breach of trust etc. The issue in a conflict situation will often be that the individual senior officer would be acting deliberately in the context of non-disclosure and so would probably not be able to take advantage of these provisions.

6.155 Separate consideration must be given to how a senior officer should act in situations where his or her duties to the employer conflict with their duty to exercise their powers for a proper purpose and in the best interests of the scheme.

How should a senior officer deal with an actual conflict?

6.156 An actual conflict of duty may exist if there were a specific transaction or matter affecting the relevant pension in which a senior officer were taking an active role on behalf of the employer, or in relation to which the senior officer had knowledge of information confidential to the employer. For example, the employer could be considering proposals to change future service pension benefits, or a transaction amounting to a Type A event for Pensions Regulator purposes (see para 6.166 below).

Commonly trust deeds and articles of association allow for decisions to be taken by a majority of directors (eg reg 88 of the 1985 Table A). **6.157**

A majority vote rule is helpful, as it means that the concurrence of a conflicted senior officer is not required for a decision to be taken by the trustee board. However, there may be a risk that a majority vote in such circumstances would not be conclusive. A court may be concerned over the degree of influence that the conflicted senior officer may have had on the trustee board's deliberations. **6.158**

There are various ways in which a conflicted senior officer could be excluded from a particular trustee board decision: **6.159**

Option	Comments
1. Resign and replace All trustee directors who are conflicted on a specific issue (eg a particular transaction in relation to which the trustee board and the employer must negotiate, and where they are involved in the employer's decision-making) resign and are replaced by new directors not involved in company decision-making on the issue.	Replacement trustee board members would be required in order to comply with minimum number imposed under scheme rules/Trustee articles of association and MNT/MND[118] requirements. Trustee board would lose benefit of the senior officer's experience and knowledge on other (non-conflicted) scheme matters.
2. Abstain from relevant meetings/votes All conflicted trustee board members could absent themselves from meetings at which the issue in question is being discussed, and abstain from voting on the matter.	This is permitted if the scheme rules or articles of the trustee allows decisions to be taken by majority vote. The number of trustees/directors deciding the matter must satisfy the quorum requirements.
3. Step aside and delegate matter to sub-committee Decision on specific transaction raising the conflict may be delegated to a sub-committee of the trustee board. All conflicted persons would be excluded from the sub-committee and from the trustee's decision-making on any negotiations, but continue to participate in other trustee/scheme matters. This would be a more formal method of excluding conflicted persons from relevant meetings than 2 above.	Formal delegation to sub-committee needs to be permitted under the scheme rules or Trustee articles of association. Formal delegation is better for managing perception of the decision-making process and for creating paper trail showing the Trustee's efforts to manage conflicts. Conflicted trustee board members would remain potentially liable for ultimate decision taken by the trustee. This would not trigger any MNT/MND implications and avoids falling below minimum number of directors imposed by articles. Trustee board would retain benefit of the current company-appointed trustees' experience and knowledge on other Scheme matters.

(Continued)

---

[118] Member-nominated trustee or member-nominated directors. An obligation under ss 241–243 of the Pensions Act 2004.

Continued

Option	Comments
4. Individual delegation to fiduciary or alternate director Each conflicted senior officer could personally delegate his or her powers and responsibilities in relation to the merger to a fiduciary agent, ie an alternate director. The agents would act for them in relation to the specific transaction, but keep all information and the trustee's position confidential. The conflicted person would continue to participate in other trustee matters but take no part in decisions on the transaction in question.	This would need to be permitted by scheme rules or trustee articles and terms of MNT/MND opt-out. This would avoid falling below any minimum number of directors imposed by articles. Each individual delegation would need to make clear that the fiduciary agent would not share information with or take instructions from the relevant trustee. The delegation would also need to ensure that the fiduciary agent is protected against liability to the same extent as the trustee/trustee directors under the Scheme rules (eg by including a mirror indemnity/limitation of liability). The conflicted person would remain liable for ultimate decision taken by the trustee board. Fiduciary agents potentially liable to the conflicted person for a decision taken which exposes the latter to liability.

Should a senior officer disclose to the trustee board information confidential to employer?

6.160 A related point is the likelihood that a senior officer, by reason of his or her role at the employer, may become aware of confidential information that is materially relevant to the trustee board (eg knowledge of the employer's negotiating position on a particular matter being discussed with the trustee board, or of the employer's possible future intentions).

6.161 This could put the senior officer in a very difficult position. Clearly, he or she would have a duty to the employer not to disclose the information without the employer's consent. There is potentially a conflict of duty, as it is possible that there is also a duty to disclose the confidential information to the other members of the trustee board.

6.162 The existence of two conflicting duties will not protect the fiduciary (in the absence of an express or implied waiver or agreement)—see for example the cases involving a solicitor with conflicting duties between clients.

6.163 In *Moody v Cox & Hatt*[119] Lord Cozens-Hardy MR held:

> A solicitor [who also acts as a trustee] may have a duty on one side and a duty on the other, namely a duty to his client as a solicitor on the one side and a duty to his beneficiaries on the other; but if he chooses to put himself in that position it does not lie in his mouth to say to the client 'I have not discharged that which the law says is my duty towards you, my client, because I owe a duty to the beneficiaries on the other side.' The answer is that if a solicitor involves himself in that dilemma it is his own fault.

6.164 This was followed more recently by the House of Lords in another solicitor case, *Hilton v Barker Booth and Eastwood*.[120]

---

[119] [1917] 2 Ch 71, CA.
[120] [2005] UKHL 8, [2005] 1 All ER 651, HL.

The decided court decisions in this area are not clear as to whether or not there is in fact a **6.165** general duty owed by a fiduciary (such as a trustee or director) to disclose to the other trustees all relevant information that he or she possesses. The Court of Appeal imposed such a duty on company directors in *Item Software (UK) Ltd v Fassihi*,[121] partly based on what is now the obligation in s 172 of the Companies Act 2006 for directors to promote the success of the company. On balance, this seems incompatible with the decision of the House of Lords in *Bell v Lever Bros* and it may still remain arguable that such a duty may not exist (at least where the trustee/director has not committed any wrongdoing).

The Pensions Regulator has stated in its guidance that it expects trustees who could be involved **6.166** on both sides of the negotiation over a material event (called a type A event) (eg those who are also senior officers):

(a) to ensure that the trustees have the appropriate information on a timely basis;
(b) to draw his fellow trustees' attention to the potential conflict; and
(c) to absent himself from trustee meetings when the issue is discussed and play no part in decision-making.

There is also a perception issue. How will it look to outsiders (eg the members) if a senior **6.167** officer has remained in a trustee meeting while possessing relevant information?

Given this, generally a senior officer should consider if he or she needs to resign or abstain **6.168** from the decision-making process, under one of the ways summarized above. However, if the conflict is likely to be a 'one-off' issue, the conflicted person may consider absenting himself from meetings.

Some lawyers argue that he or she would still be in breach of a duty of disclosure to the trustee/ **6.169** scheme. This seems overly strict.

Another way of managing this issue would be for the employer to give its express consent to **6.170** the senior officer disclosing any relevant information (including confidential information) to the other members of the trustee board. This would remove the conflict of duty—but obviously has the drawback from the company's point of view that it may not want confidential information being provided to the trustee board when this is not at a time of its own choosing.

The articles of association of the employer company also need to be checked to see if they **6.171** allow for a director to have a conflicting duty.

Conversely, the duty may apply the other way. There may be times when the trustee board **6.172** wants the relevant senior officer to keep some information confidential from the employer. In practice, in the past senior officers are often expressly used by trustee boards as a conduit for passing the views of the trustee back to the employers. In that case, no confidentiality issue arises. But there may be other (more extreme) cases where confidentiality becomes an issue.

---

[121] [2004] EWCA Civ 1244, [2005] 2 BCLC 91, CA. This decision has been described as controversial in potentially imposing a positive fiduciary duty rather than a proscriptive one—see *Brandeaux Advisers (UK) Ltd v Chadwick* [2011] IRLR 224 at [47] (Jack J) and *GHLM Trading Ltd v Maroo* [2012] EWHC 61 (Ch), [2012] 2 BCLC 369 at [193] (Newey J). It did not consider the leading Australian case on this point: *Breen v Williams* (1966) 186 CLR 71. See the criticism of *Item Software* in Australia in *P&V Industries Pty Ltd v Porto* [2006] VSC 131 (Hollingsworth J) and also in Ho and Lee 'A Director's Duty to Confess: A Matter of Good Faith?' [2007] CLJ 348. See Matthew Conaglen, *Fiduciary Loyalty* (Hart Publishing, 2010) 56.

6.173 It is also helpful to make it clear that the senior officers' duties as members of a trustee board do not require them to disclose to the other directors confidential information, where to do so would put them in breach of a duty to a third party—eg the employer. This could be done by amending the articles of association of a company trustee (if the trustee is a subsidiary of the employer, the immediate parent company could pass the necessary shareholder resolution). A change to the articles would protect the senior officers against a claim that they were personally in breach of their duties by withholding confidential information.

6.174 To be valid, the amendment would need to be a proper decision under company law. The decision to amend would be likely to be a valid one, given that the employer's motives in so acting would be to help ensure that the trustee board includes people of appropriately high calibre and experience.

6.175 A further issue would be the potential for a claim that the senior officer (or trustee company) is, by reason of a senior officer's possession of material confidential information, in breach of its duties to the scheme beneficiaries.[122] Therefore, a further precaution would be to amend the scheme trust deed to the same effect. Again, the amendment would need to be a proper decision under trust law.

6.176 An effective way of managing this perception, and any concerns of the trustee board that they may be insufficiently informed, would be to agree with the trustee a protocol for the supply of information. This should be combined with a formal confidentiality agreement between the employer and the trustee (these are becoming more common). Such agreements give the employer more comfort that any information provided to the trustee board on a confidential basis is kept confidential (and also helps listed companies show compliance with the Listing Rules). Preferably the individual trustees (or directors of a trustee company) and any advisers should also be asked to sign up to the confidentiality agreement.

---

[122] Although this may be unlikely—see Ch 5 (Liability of directors of corporate trustees).

7

REGULATOR'S POWERS TO APPOINT, REMOVE, OR DISQUALIFY TRUSTEES

Introduction

This chapter considers the powers of the Pensions Regulator under the Pensions Act 1995 in relation to occupational pension schemes to: **7.1**

(a) appoint trustees—s 7;
(b) suspend trustees from acting—s 4; and
(c) prohibit trustees from acting in relation to a particular scheme or schemes generally—s 3.

This chapter also looks at s 29 of the 1995 Act dealing with automatic disqualification of trustees (ie without any need for an order from the court or the Pensions Regulator).

These provisions all came into force on 6 April 1997, originally as powers for the Occupational **7.2** Pensions Regulatory Authority (Opra), the regulator established under the Pensions Act 1995. With effect from 6 April 2005, the provisions were amended by the Pensions Act 2004:

(a)   the Pensions Regulator was established (s 1) and replaced Opra (s 7); and

(b)   references in the Pensions Act 1995 to Opra (or the 'Authority') became references to the Pensions Regulator—s 7(2); and

(c)   amendments were made to the underlying powers in ss 3, 4, 7, and 29.

The Pensions Bill 2013 issued in draft by the government in January 2013 envisages a further change. If enacted it will add a new s 3A to the 1995 Act providing that where a person becomes prohibited from being a trustee under s 3, any company of which that person is a director will also be prohibited.

7.3   These provisions apply to all occupational pension schemes.[1] There are no exemptions for (say) unapproved schemes, one member schemes or small self-administered schemes.

In practice (of course) the provisions only apply to schemes with trustees—ie a 'trust scheme', defined[2] as one established under a trust (eg not to simple contractual promises or to various statutory schemes).

The Pre-1995 Law

Who may be a trustee?

7.4   As a matter of general law, any person—male or female, married or unmarried, human or corporate—who can hold and dispose of any legal or equitable interest in property can be a trustee. It follows that a pension scheme trustee, like other trustees:

(a)   may be a non-British subject (*Meinertzhagen v Davis*[3]);

(b)   may be resident outside the UK (although this should be considered carefully—*Re Whitehead's Will Trusts*[4]);

(c)   cannot be a minor (ie under age 18)—s 20 of the Law of Property Act 1925;

(d)   cannot be of unsound mind, if this is known to the appointor (*Re East*[5] and *Re Blake*[6]); and

(e)   may (perhaps) be a bankrupt (*Turner v Maule*[7]: bankrupt trustee unfit, but not incapable).

7.5   In 1990, the Social Security Pensions Act 1975 was amended by the Social Security Act 1990 to provide that on the insolvency of an employer there must (subject to exceptions) be an independent trustee of the employer's pension scheme. These provisions were later re-enacted in the Pensions Act 1995 and substantially amended by the Pensions Act 2004, so that the Pensions Regulator now has a discretionary power to appoint an independent trustee.[8]

7.6   However, prior to employer insolvency, it remained before April 1997[9] entirely a matter for the terms of the pension trust as to who has power to appoint and remove trustees and

---

[1]   The definition in s 1 of the Pension Schemes Act 1993 applies (see s 124(5) of the Pensions Act 1995). See further Ch 1 (What is an occupational pension scheme?).

[2]   Section 124(1) of the Pensions Act 1995.

[3]   (1844) 1 Coll 335, 63 ER 444 (Knight Bruce V-C).

[4]   [1971] 1 WLR 833 (Pennycuick V-C).

[5]   (1873) 8 Ch App 735, CA.

[6]   [1887] WN 173, CA.

[7]   (1850) 15 Jur 761. See also *Re Watts' Settlement* (1851) 9 Hare 106, (1851) 68 ER 434 (Turner V-C).

[8]   These provisions are not discussed further here. For further detail, see D Pollard, *Corporate Insolvency: Employment and Pension Rights* 5th edn (Bloomsbury Professional, 2013).

[9]   When the Pensions Act 1995 came into force, including the provisions discussed in this chapter and the member-nominated trustee provisions.

who is eligible to be a trustee. (This is, of course, subject to the supervisory powers of the courts—see below.) Often the principal employer has the express power to appoint and remove trustees. Less commonly there is provision for member or trade union nomination or an entrenched independent trustee.[10]

There is some old case authority in relation to private trusts to the effect that the power **7.7** of appointment and removal of trustees is a fiduciary power—ie it must be exercised for a proper purpose, in the interests of the scheme and not in the interests of the appointor (see *Re Skeats' Settlement*[11] and *Re Shortridge*[12]). But, as discussed in Ch 12, this does not apply to employer powers under an occupational pension scheme. Instead, the *Imperial* good faith duties will apply.[13]

Supervision by the courts

The courts operate a general supervisory function in relation to all trusts, including pension **7.8** schemes. A court may:

(a) appoint new trustees—s 41 of the Trustee Act 1925;
(b) remove trustees (*Re Chetwynd's Settlement*[14]);
(c) appoint a judicial trustee—Judicial Trustees Act 1896[15];
(d) give directions to trustees—Pt 64 of the Civil Procedure Rules[16]; and
(e) generally administer the trust—*Re Blake.*[17]

The Goode Committee

In 1993, the Pension Law Review Committee,[18] chaired by Professor Goode, commented **7.9** in its report on the merits of introducing a system of statutory authorization for pension scheme trustees. The Committee did not agree to this proposal on the grounds that trustees could not be said to be carrying on a business; also it did not think it would be practically feasible to vet individually the trustees of the many thousands of existing pension schemes.

Instead, the Goode Committee proposed a system of statutory disqualification of trustees. **7.10** Under its proposal, trustees would automatically be disqualified either if they fell within specified criteria (to be modelled on the Company Directors Disqualification Act 1986) or because they had a conflicting role within the scheme (ie as scheme auditor or actuary).

---

[10] See eg clause 3 of the Industry-Wide Coal Staff Superannuation Scheme, as set out in the Schedule to the Industry-Wide Coal Staff Superannuation Scheme Regulations 1994 (SI 1994/2973), requiring that the articles of association of any new trustee include provisions providing for the appointment of a committee of management including four to be appointed under rules agreed with organizations representing substantial classes of employees.

[11] (1889) 42 ChD 522 (Kay J).

[12] [1895] 1 Ch 278, CA.

[13] See *Imperial Group Pension Trust Ltd v Imperial Tobacco Ltd* [1991] 2 All ER 597 (Browne-Wilkinson V-C), discussed in Ch 13.

[14] [1902] 1 Ch 692 (Farwell J).

[15] See *McDonald v Horn* [1993] OPLR 183 (Vinelott J) for an example of this in a pensions context.

[16] Previously Ord 85, r 2 of the Rules of the Supreme Court. See also Practice Direction 64B.

[17] (1885) 29 ChD 913, CA.

[18] The Pension Law Review Committee (Cm2342), chaired by Professor Goode. Its report was issued in September 1993.

The Pensions Act 1995

7.11 The Pensions Act 1995 limits the freedom of pension schemes to fix their own structures for choosing trustees in four ways:

    (a) the requirements in relation to member-nominated trustees;[19]

    (b) limitations on links with the scheme auditor or scheme actuary (s 27);

    (c) the powers of the Pensions Regulator to make orders appointing (s 7), suspending (s 4), or prohibiting[20] (s 3[21]) trustees;

    (d) the automatic disqualification provisions (s 29).

7.12 Whilst the Goode Committee recommended that the criteria for trustee disqualification be modelled on the provisions of the Company Directors Disqualification Act 1986, the government in its White Paper[22] opted instead for the Charities Act 1993 model. This was reflected in the Pensions Act 1995.

Member-nominated trustees

7.13 Sections 16–21 of the 1995 Act related to member-nominated trustees (and member-nominated directors). They were the first statutory limits (outside employer insolvency) on the freedom of an occupational pension scheme to provide who has power to appoint trustees. These provisions were superseded by new provisions in the Pensions Act 2004.[23]

Auditors and actuaries as trustees: section 27

7.14 Section 27(1) of the 1995 Act provides that the trustee of a scheme and any person who is 'connected with' or an 'associate of'[24] such a trustee is ineligible to act as an auditor or actuary of the same scheme, ie the statutory scheme auditor or actuary appointed by the trustees under s 47.

Section 27 reflects the Goode Committee's opinion that the existence of the professional relationship which the actuary and auditor have with a scheme would be incompatible with trusteeship due to the potential conflicts of interests involved.

Trustee Appointment by the Pensions Regulator: Section 7

7.15 The Pensions Regulator is given power in s 7 of the 1995 Act to appoint pension scheme trustees in specified circumstances. The government made it clear in the debates in the House of Commons that restrictions were placed on this power in view of the cost which additional trustees can bring to the scheme.[25]

---

[19] Originally ss 16–21 of the Pensions Act 1995. Replaced with effect from 6 April 2005 by ss 241–243 of the Pensions Act 2004.

[20] From 1997 to 2005 Opra had a separate power to disqualify a person from acting as a trustee of schemes generally—s 29(3) of the Pensions Act 1995. This power was repealed from 6 April 2005 by the Pensions Act 2004 and, in effect, replaced by the wider powers under the substituted new s 3 of the Pensions Act 1995.

[21] Substituted with effect from 6 April 2005 by s 33 of the Pensions Act 2004.

[22] Secretary of State for Social Security, *Security, Equality, Choice: The Future for Pensions*, June 1994 (Cm2594).

[23] See *Freshfields on Corporate Pensions Law 2013* (ed D Pollard and C Magoffin) (Bloomsbury Professional, 2013) Ch 11.1 'Member-nominated trustees'.

[24] The terms 'connected with' and 'associate of' are defined by reference to the Insolvency Act 1986. They are complex—see Pollard, *Corporate Insolvency* (2013) Ch 70 'Who is connected or associated'.

[25] Minister of State for Social Security, William Hague MP, Hansard, 9 May 1995, col 107.

Power to replace trustees

Section 7(1) gives the Pensions Regulator power to appoint a new trustee in place of one it **7.16**
has removed under s 3 or where a trustee ceases to act by reason of his or her disqualification
(eg under s 29).

This enables the Pensions Regulator to act speedily to fill the gap that could otherwise occur
if, for example, a sole trustee were prohibited or disqualified.

Power to appoint additional trustees

Under s 7(3), the Pensions Regulator can appoint new trustees to a scheme where, in its **7.17**
opinion, it is *reasonable* to do so in order:

(a) to secure that the trustee board has the required expertise for the administration of the
    scheme;
(b) to secure that their numbers are sufficient for the proper administration of the scheme;
(c) to secure that the assets of the scheme are used and applied appropriately; or
(d) otherwise to protect the interests of the generality of the members of the scheme.[26]

The power under s 7(3) originally only arose if the Regulator was satisfied that it was 'neces- **7.18**
sary' to appoint a new trustee to secure the relevant matters. This is a stricter test than a test
based on (say) whether the Regulator considered it desirable (compare s 18(1)(b) of the
Charities Act 1993 giving the Charity Commissioners powers to act where they consider it
necessary *or desirable*).

The section was amended by the Pensions Act 2008[27] so that the test is now weaker: whether **7.19**
the Pensions Regulator considers it 'reasonable' to appoint a trustee. This is obviously a wider
power and enables the Regulator to act in more cases than previously.

The explanatory notes to the 2008 Act commented on this that: **7.20**

> 442. The section extends this power to allow the Pensions Regulator to appoint trustees in
> certain circumstances where it is reasonable to do so, instead of necessary. The 'necessary test'
> means that the Regulator may only appoint a trustee if it is satisfied that there is no other
> option available and it must act almost as a last resort. A 'reasonable test' would enable the
> Regulator to appoint a trustee where there are a range of options available but the appoint-
> ment is the most appropriate action for the scheme.

The Pensions Act 2008 also amended s 7 to add a new ground of appointment—if the **7.21**
appointment was reasonable 'otherwise to protect the interests of the generality of the members of the scheme'. This looks to be a more general catch-all ground that the Regulator may
seek to use. Note that it only refers to the interests of 'members' and not any others interested
in the scheme (eg employers, spouses, or dependants).

The s 7 power only extends to appointment of a trustee and not (say) to allow appointment **7.22**
of a director to an existing trustee company. This means that the Regulator's powers under
s 7 are limited to appointing a trustee alongside (or perhaps in replacement of) an existing
trustee.

---

[26] This last bullet is in s 7(3)(d) and was added with effect from 26 January 2009 by the Pensions Act
2008, s 131.
[27] Section 131.

7.23 The Pensions Regulator reports[28] that it exercised its s 7 powers 507 times in 2011/12. An example is the TPR determinations panel's determination in *Re Dalton Power Products Ltd Staff & Works Retirement and Death Benefit Scheme*,[29] where the company had been dissolved and the two remaining trustees thought they had resigned some time ago and were not willing to act. An independent trustee was appointed, with fees payable out of the fund and holding all the trustee powers.

TPR determination in *Telent/GEC 1972 Plan* (2007)

7.24 This is a good example of the Regulator's use of this power in the decision in 2007 of the determinations panel of the Pensions Regulator to review appointment of three new independent trustees.[30] The Regulator's appointment was under its power in s 7 of the Pensions Act 1995.[31]

7.25 In effect in *Telent*, the Regulator was considering its powers under s 7 before its amendment by the 2008 Act—ie if it was:

> satisfied that it is necessary to [appoint a trustee] in order. . . .
>
> (c) to secure the proper use or application of the assets of the scheme.

7.26 The trustee had raised concerns about what it considered were the proposals by the new parent company for the new strategy of the employer in relation to appointment of trustee directors and running the scheme, and in particular its investment strategy. The existing trustee was concerned that the new parent company would arrange for trustee directors to be appointed who may have a personal interest in the performance of the scheme's investments. The existing trustee said that it was concerned that such new appointments may have a conflict of interest and could seek a move to an excessively risky investment policy. Despite the new parent stating that it would support a more limited entrenchment of independent trustees, after an oral hearing, the determinations panel of the Pensions Regulator confirmed the appointment of three new trustees under the s 7 power (to hold office alongside the existing trustee company). The panel considered that a case for such appointment had been made out, even on the 'necessary' wording. The panel based this partly on the potential for a conflict of interest and partly on a fear that the prospective new parent would seek a more risky investment strategy.

7.27 The panel's determination is difficult to understand in many areas. The potential conflict and the potential shift in investment strategy seem to reflect no more than many schemes may have in place. But the panel seems to have been influenced by the position of the parent company (having been taken over) seeming to have a business model that focused on the potential to generate profit from the pension scheme rather than any other business (but again this is no more that other employers do). In addition, the new trustee board appointments seem to have been considered to raise a potential issue, because there was a concern that they may have been sympathetic to that model.

---

[28] The Pensions Regulator's Annual Report for 2011/12, App 1.

[29] TPR case ref TM9967, 8 June 2011.

[30] 7 November 2007. See the TPR website at <http://www.thepensionsregulator.gov.uk/docs/DNTelent ReasonsofDeterminationsPanel.pdf>. There is a good summary in *Pensions Law Handbook* 10th edn (Bloomsbury Professional, 2011) 103.

[31] See also the determination in August 2011 confirming the appointment of Dalreida in relation to a number of trusts based on concerns about the investments that had been made.

The panel's reasoning on conflicts[32] and the power of appointment seems wrong (and may **7.28** reflect the way the case was argued). It ignores any express provision allowing for conflicts (this would be common, but no express provision is mentioned) and, on the power of appointment, relies on the private trust case of *Re Skeat's Settlements*[33] (which is not applicable to pension trustees and on any reading is inapplicable to the issue of appointing new directors).[34] But it seems that the fiduciary nature of the power here was not challenged.[35]

The finding that the appointments were 'necessary' (despite the fact that no changes had yet **7.29** occurred and the prospective new parent did not yet have control of the employer) seems to have been pushing the jurisdiction to its extremes. Concerns about this may have been one reason for the statutory changes in the Pensions Act 2008 widening the s 7 powers.

Additional powers

As the rules of the trust may not have foreseen such an appointment, s 7(5) enables the **7.30** Pensions Regulator to include in the order appointing a trustee provisions:

(a) specifying the number of trustees in the scheme;
(b) requiring the trustee's fees to be paid by the scheme;
(c) providing for the appointment and removal of the trustee appointed.

In addition, the Pensions Regulator may include in the appointment order a provision that **7.31** the employer or the scheme (or both) is to be liable for payment of the appointed trustee's fees—s 8(1).

When the Pensions Bill was passing through Parliament in 1995, the government refused **7.32** to agree to amendments in the House of Lords limiting the trustee's fees payable under ss 7(5) and 8(1) to a reasonable amount. The then DSS Minister of State, Lord Mackay of Ardbrecknish, said[36] that a trustee charging unreasonable fees could be removed by the Pensions Regulator and 'would never again be put into a trust by the authority'.

Lord Mackay stated later:[37]

> Where [The Pensions Regulator] appoints a trustee to a scheme we do not wish to provide a means by which someone can stall the appointment by engaging in time-wasting court action over whether the fees to be charged are reasonable.
>
> It is important that the authority's power to appoint trustees is sufficiently flexible to enable it to set out the terms under which the appointment is made. We accept that, where possible, the appointee should not be a professional trustee. But there will be situations where, in order to secure the interests of scheme members, it will be necessary to appoint professional trustees. This will involve a cost which it is appropriate for the scheme to have to bear. But at the outset, the authority will agree the terms of the appointment including the level of fees to be charged. Scheme members, employers or other trustees will be free to bring to the authority's attention any concerns they have that the terms of the appointment are not being adhered to. If the

---

[32] Contrast in Australia the decision of the Administrative Appeals Tribunal overturning a disqualification by the regulator (APRA) on the basis of an alleged conflict: *Re VBN and the Australian Prudential Regulation Authority* [2006] AATA 710, (2006) 92 ALD 259 (Administrative Appeals Tribunal). Noted by Noel Davies, 'Conflicts of Interest' (2013) 24 ASLB 164.

[33] (1889) 42 ChD 522 (Kay J).

[34] See Chs 6 (Conflicts) and 12 (Employer powers to appoint trustees) on these areas.

[35] See para 17 of the determination.

[36] Hansard, 7 February 1995, col 181.

[37] Hansard, 13 March 1995, col 582.

appointee has abused his position, for example by charging excessive fees, the authority has more than adequate powers to remove the professional trustee; and it would be unlikely to use the services of such a person in the future.

7.33 Section 8(4) gives the Pensions Regulator the power to restrict the powers and duties of the trustee which it has appointed or to provide that certain powers shall be exercised by the appointed trustee to the exclusion of the existing trustees. This overrides the majority decision provisions in section 32.[38]

7.34 This power enables the Pensions Regulator, in effect, to appoint a trustee who takes over all the powers of the trustees (not dissimilar to the effect on directors of a company if an administrator is appointed under the Insolvency Act 1986). Unless the Pensions Regulator makes such an order, the powers and duties of the appointed trustee will be the same as those of the existing trustees—s 8(3).

7.35 At the time of the 1995 Bill, the government anticipated that there may in future be a need to regulate minimum standards for the trustees whom the Pensions Regulator appoints.

Section 7(6) provides that regulations can be made to describe who may and who may not be appointed by the Pensions Regulator. The then DSS Minister of State, Lord Mackay of Ardbrecknish, said[39] that:

> Where [the Pensions Regulator] takes the serious step of appointing a trustee to a scheme, there may be significant problems with the scheme's administration. That will often be the case. It is important that we are able to set down minimum standards of experience, competence and integrity for those whom the authority is able to appoint.

No regulations have been made.

There is an exception to the general duty of confidentiality owed by the Pensions Regulator,[40] so that TPR can disclose restricted information to a trustee that TPR has appointed, if this is for the purpose of enabling or assisting the trustee to exercise his functions in respect of the scheme.[41]

Suspension of Trustees: Section 4

Suspension Order

7.36 Section 4 gives the Pensions Regulator the power to suspend a trustee of a trust scheme or of a particular trust scheme or description of schemes—s 4(3). This is a means whereby the interests of beneficiaries can be protected as soon as the Pensions Regulator has a suspicion of any potential wrongdoing in the running of a scheme.

The power was similar to that given to the Charity Commissioners in relation to charity trustees by s 18(1)(i) of the Charities Act 1993.

---

[38] The provisions in s 16(7) requiring member nominated trustees to have the same powers as all other trustees were also overridden by s 8(4). There is no express override for the equivalent provision on MNTs in s 241(7) of the Pensions Act 2004, but this is framed differently and special powers under s 8(4) are unlikely to be contrary to it.

[39] Hansard, HL, 7 February 1995, col 175.

[40] Pensions Act 2004, s 82.

[41] Pensions Act 2004, s 87(6).

During Committee debates in the House of Commons on the then Pensions Bill, it was **7.37** made clear that a suspension order is to be used for the protection of the trust scheme rather than as an imputation of the integrity of the trustee. The then DSS Parliamentary Under-Secretary, James Arbuthnot MP, said:[42]

> A suspension order will always be temporary and it will not imply any wrongdoing. It will be used to protect schemes rather than to penalise trustees. The lapsing or the revocation of the order will result in the suspension being lifted. That will be automatic. No blame can or should be attached to the trustee—in much the same way as the withdrawal of charges in a criminal case clears the name of the accused.

Effectively the suspension order acts as a thinking space during which the Pensions Regulator **7.38** can decide whether it wishes to remove the trustee under its powers in s 3 (see para 7.44 below) or while proceedings go forward which could lead to automatic disqualification under s 29 (see para 7.59 below).

Unlike s 3 there is no requirement for the Pensions Regulator to give notice to the trustee concerned before determining to issue a suspension order under s 4.

Grounds

The circumstances in which a suspension order can be made are as follows: **7.39**

In relation to individuals

(a) the Pensions Regulator is considering whether to make a prohibition order under s 3;
(b) consideration is being given to the institution of proceedings for an offence involving dishonesty or deception;
(c) proceedings have been instituted for an offence involving dishonesty or deception;
(d) a petition for bankruptcy or the sequestration of his estate has been presented to the court; or
(e) an application has been made for a disqualification order under the Company Directors Disqualification Act 1986.

In relation to companies

(f) the same circumstances as individuals; and in addition
(g) a winding-up petition has been presented to the court; or
(h) any of its directors could be suspended by reason of any of the last three circumstances listed above for individuals.

Section 4(3) provides that, whilst suspended, a trustee is prohibited from exercising any **7.40** functions of a trustee in respect of any trust scheme to which the order applies. Usually the order will specify the scheme or schemes concerned. It is not clear whether an order under s 4 could extend to all occupational pension schemes of which the person named is a trustee.

The suspension order will remain in effect for the duration of the proceedings which have **7.41** caused the order to be made. However, where the suspension order is made so as to allow the Pensions Regulator to consider whether to make a prohibition order under s 3 (or based on consideration being given to the institution of proceedings for an offence involving

---

[42] Hansard, 9 May 1995, col 91.

dishonesty or deception), it will have effect for an initial period not exceeding 12 months. This may be renewed by the Pensions Regulator—s 4(2).

7.42 Section 4(6) provides that the suspension order may also contain provisions which will ensure the management of the trust's affairs are not disturbed during this temporary phase, eg in relation to the execution of instruments and dealing with rules governing trustees' proceedings (see also the quorum provisions in s 32).

7.43 If an order is made under s 7(5) passing all the powers of the trustees to the newly appointed trustee, the position of the remaining trustees is unclear. They will remain in office but not have any powers. In practice they are probably in the same position as the directors if a company enters administration or liquidation under the Insolvency Act 1986—their powers pass to the insolvency practitioner, save for a limited power to challenge the relevant appointment—see *Newhart Developments Ltd v Co-operative Commercial Bank Ltd*.[43] In *Dalriada Trustees Ltd v Faulds*[44] the remaining trustees in such a situation were awarded their costs on an indemnity basis in the construction application.

Prohibition Orders: Section 3

7.44 Under the original s 3 (before its substitution by the Pensions Act 2004), the then Regulator (Opra) used only to be able to make a prohibition order under s 3 of the 1995 Act in respect of a particular trust scheme. This was unlike the more general powers in relation to a suspension order under s 4 (see above) or a disqualification order under s 29 (see below). The new s 3 (inserted by the Pensions Act 2004 from 5 April 2005) now allows the Pensions Regulator to make a prohibition order under s 3 of the 1995 Act in respect of a particular trust scheme or a particular description of trust scheme or trust schemes in general.

Grounds

7.45 The extent of the Regulator's jurisdiction (and supervisory role) under what became the original s 3 was debated in the House of Commons at the time of the Pensions Bill in 1995. The government rejected an amendment to enable Opra to remove trustees for breaches of general trust law (and thereby to place on Opra a general duty to enforce trust law), on the basis that this was best left to the courts.[45]

7.46 The original s 3(2) only allowed Opra to prohibit a person from being a trustee of a particular scheme if:

(a) the trustee had been in serious or persistent breach of any duties under Pt I of the 1995 Act (which relates to duties of trustees of occupational schemes) or of specified provisions of the Pension Schemes Act 1993—excluding breaches of the provisions in the Acts which relate to indexation, equal treatment, and the supply of information to the Compensation Board (it was thought that both the Pensions Ombudsman and the Compensation Board were best equipped to deal with these matters);

---

[43] [1978] QB 814, CA.
[44] [2011] EWHC 3391 (Ch), [2012] 2 All ER 734 (Bean J). See Fenner Moeran at para E1.33 in *Tolley's Pension Law*.
[45] Hansard, HC, 9 May 1995, col 97.

(b) there had been a breach of another section of the 1995 Act which specifically allowed Opra to act under s 3—eg ss 28(4), 36(8).

With the change from Opra to the Pensions Regulator (with its enhanced supervisory role), **7.47** s 3 was substituted with a new, wider power with effect from 6 April 2005 by the Pensions Act 2004. The post-2005 s 3 allows the Regulator to prohibit a person from being a trustee if the Regulator is satisfied that the person is 'not a fit and proper person' to be a trustee of the scheme or schemes to which the order relates.

This 'fit and proper person' formula is used in other legislation—for example the powers of **7.48** the Financial Services Authority (FSA) to prohibit persons from exercising a regulated activity if they are not 'fit and proper'—s 56 of the Financial Services and Markets Act 2000.[46]

The Pensions Regulator issued in June 2013 a revised statement of its policies on this power, **7.49** as required by s 3(6):

Criteria for 'fit and proper persons'

The Regulator will investigate whether a trustee is a 'fit and proper person' to be a trustee of a pension scheme by looking at all the relevant information. In particular, the regulator will consider any information which concerns the trustee's:

- honesty and integrity;
- competence and capability;
- financial soundness.

General considerations

When considering the above criteria, the regulator may take into account (where relevant):

- any attempt to deceive
- any misuse of trust funds;
- any breaches of trust or pensions law if these are significant, persistent, deliberate, or contrary to legal advice received;
- if a trustee's professional charges constitute a breach of trust or demonstrate a lack of internal controls
- criminal convictions (other than those noted under section 29 of the Pensions Act 1995 ...) so far as these are not spent under the Rehabilitation of Offenders Act 1974 ... These convictions are not limited to those involving dishonesty or deception and could involve convictions for money laundering, violence or substance abuse, for example.

This is not a comprehensive list of the factors the regulator will consider when considering whether to exercise its power but it is indicative of what it could consider where relevant. One of the Pensions Regulator's statutory objectives under the Pensions Act 2004 ... is to protect the benefits of members of occupational pension schemes, and the regulator will take such actions as are necessary and proportionate to meet that objective.

Source: TPR website <http://www.thepensionsregulator.gov.uk/docs/statement-prohibition-orders-june-2013. pdf>.

---

[46] To be amended from a future date by the Financial Services Act 2012 when it comes into force (but the fit and proper concept is retained). The FSA stated its policy in relation to prohibition orders in Ch 8 of its

7.50 Where there was a corporate trustee the old (pre-2005) s 3 allowed Opra to make an order under s 3 prohibiting a company if any director of the company is prohibited from being a trustee under s 3. (This also prevented a possible loophole whereby a trustee could be prohibited under s 3 but could return by becoming a director of a trustee company.)

7.51 This was not retained in the new s 3, presumably on the basis that the new 'fit and proper' power was wide enough to deal with the situation. This seems to have been too inflexible and the Pensions Bill 2013 issued in draft for comments by the government in January 2013 would, if enacted, insert a new s 3A into the 1995 Act. This would provide that a corporate trustee becomes prohibited if any time any of its directors becomes prohibited from being a trustee of the relevant scheme under s 3. The notes to the Bill indicate that the intention is that the prohibition ceases if the relevant individual leaves the board of the company. But the effect of the prohibition is to remove the company as a trustee—proposed new s 3A(2)—with no provision for re-appointment. The safest course for a trustee company will be to include an express provision in its articles saying that a person ceases to be a director immediately before a prohibition order is made.

Effect of a prohibition or suspension

7.52 Once a person has been prohibited under s 3 (or suspended under s 4) he or she is guilty of a criminal offence if he or she purports to act as a trustee—s 6(1) of the Pensions Act 1995. But things done by the person are not invalidated—s 6(3) and they can remain liable for things done or omitted to be done—s 6(4).

7.53 The Regulator has power by order to vest trust property in the continuing trustees in consequence of an appointment or removal under the statutory powers in the Pensions Act 1995—s 9.

Procedure

7.54 The Regulator's powers under these sections (3, 4, and 7) are listed among the reserved powers under Sch 2 to the Pensions Act 2004. This means that the relevant power must be exercised by the determinations panel of the Pensions Regulator—see s 10(3) of the Pensions Act 2004.

7.55 The 'standard procedure' requires the regulator to give notice of any relevant application to be given to persons who appear would be directly affected if the relevant order was made.[47] This will almost always include the other trustees and the principal employer (as the person with power to appoint or remove trustees).

Register of prohibition orders

7.56 The Pensions Regulator is required to set up a register of persons who are prohibited under s 3[48]—s 66 of the Pensions Act 2004. The register does not list persons automatically disqualified under s 29(1). An inquirer has a right to request the Pensions Regulator to disclose

---

Enforcement Manual and has issued specific guidance on the fitness and propriety of individuals in the section of the *FSA Handbook* entitled the 'Fit and Proper test for Approved Persons' (FIT).

[47] Pensions Act 2004, s 96(2)(a). This requirement meant that the specific notice provisions in s 5 of the Pensions Act 1995 were no longer needed and this section was repealed by the Pensions Act 2004.

[48] Before April 2005, Opra was required to keep a register of persons against whom it had made a disqualification order under s 29 of the Pensions Act 1995—s 30(7) of the Pensions Act 1995.

whether a person named by the inquirer is disqualified in respect of a particular scheme (or description of schemes)—s 67(2) of the Pensions Act 2004.

The register does not extend to cover suspension orders under s 4. There seems to be no requirement that the inquirer has any interest in the scheme named. **7.57**

The register is on the TPR website[49] and lists (March 2013) some 13 persons (four of whom are companies) who are prohibited from acting for any schemes. There is a separate register for partial prohibitions, but there are no current entries. **7.58**

Disqualification: Section 29

Section 29 of the Pensions Act 1995 introduced (from 6 April 1997), for the first time in relation to occupational pension schemes, provisions dealing with the disqualification of trustees from acting as the trustee of *any* occupational pension scheme established under trust. **7.59**

Section 29 now provides for the automatic disqualification of a trustee in specified circumstances, such as bankruptcy—s 29(1). Before the amendments made on 6 April 2005 by the Pensions Act 2004, s 29 also provided for Opra to be able to disqualify by order in specified circumstances, such as if there was a prohibition order under s 3 or mental disorder—s 29(3) and (4). This power was repealed from 6 April 2005, presumably on the basis that the new wider power under s 3 made this provision unnecessary.

Section 29 is very similar to s 72 of the Charities Act 1993 (which deals with trustees of charities). **7.60**

The Pensions Regulator has power to waive a disqualification—s 29(5)—see below.

Effect of disqualification

Where under s 29 a trustee becomes disqualified or subject to a disqualification order he or she will automatically cease to be a trustee—s 30(1). **7.61**

He or she does not have to take steps to resign or be removed from the trusteeship as the trusteeship will have been ended automatically by law.

The wording of s 30(1) is a little obscure on the question of what happens to the trustee should his (or her) disqualification be removed (eg by order of the Pensions Regulator or expiry of time). The section refers to the person ceasing to be a trustee 'while he is so disqualified'. **7.62**

The better interpretation is that the removal of a disqualification does not automatically reinstate the person as a trustee. To hold otherwise would mean that the scheme would not know whether or not a permanent vacancy had occurred. This could be particularly difficult in relation to member-nominated trustees.

Nevertheless trust rules could usefully provide for the automatic removal and replacement of the trustee in such circumstances.

---

[49] <http://www.thepensionsregulator.gov.uk/regulate-and-enforce/prohibition-of-trustees.aspx>.

Automatic Disqualification: Section 29(1)

7.63 Section 29(1) provides a list of circumstances on the basis of which a trustee will be automatically disqualified from being a trustee of *any* occupational pension scheme.

7.64 Under s 29(1), an individual is automatically disqualified if:

(a) he has been convicted of any offence involving dishonesty or deception—s 29(1)(a);

(b) he has been adjudged bankrupt or sequestration of his estate has been awarded and (in either case) he has not been discharged or he is subject to a bankruptcy restrictions order or an interim bankruptcy restrictions order—s 29(1)(b);

(c) a moratorium period under a debt relief order (under Pt 7A of the Insolvency Act 1986) applies in relation to him or her is the subject of a debt relief restrictions order or an interim debt relief restrictions order (under Sch 4ZB to the Insolvency Act 1986)—s 29(1)(ba);

(d) he has made a composition with creditors and not been discharged—s 29(1)(e); or

(e) he has been disqualified as a company director under the Company Directors Disqualification Act 1986 or s 429(2)(b) of the Insolvency Act 1986—s 29(1)(f).

A company (or Scottish partnership) is automatically disqualified if any of its directors (or partners) have been disqualified on the grounds set out above—s 29(1)(c) and (d).

Offence involving dishonesty or deception: section 29(1)(a)

7.65 The disqualification is not limited to specific offences or convictions on indictment. It seems likely that, although there is no specific confirmation of this (unlike s 1(4) of the Rehabilitation of Offenders Act 1974 which provides that under that Act 'conviction' extends to include convictions outside Great Britain), the conviction does not need to be one in the UK. See the decision of the Court of Appeal (on a similar provision in the Estate Agents Act 1979) in *Antonelli v Secretary of State for Trade and Industry*.[50]

7.66 Examples of offences involving dishonesty or deception are the offences of theft and obtaining a pecuniary advantage by deception under the Theft Act 1968.

Dishonesty

7.67 In *R v Ghosh*[51]—a case on the Theft Act—the Court of Appeal held that the test for determining whether a person acted *dishonestly* is:

(a) whether his actions were dishonest according to the ordinary standards of reasonable and honest people; and

(b) if so, whether he himself realized that his actions were, according to these standards, dishonest.

Therefore, in criminal matters, the test is partly subjective: did the person realize that his actions were (viewed objectively) dishonest? The test may be more strict than the equivalent in civil law (eg dishonestly assisting a breach of trust), where it is more objective (see the Privy Council in *Royal Brunei Airlines Sdn Bhd v Tan*[52] and *Barlow Clowes International Ltd*

---

[50] [1998] 1 All ER 997, CA. Ultimately this is a question of interpretation of the relevant statute. For a contrary example (that offences overseas were not a 'crime' within the relevant statute) see the Irish Supreme Court in *McK v D* [2004] IESC 31, [2004] 2 IR 470.

[51] [1982] QB 1053, CA.

[52] [1995] 2 AC 378, PC.

v Eurotrust International Ltd,[53] decisions sandwiching a different view by the House of Lords in *Twinsectra Ltd v Yardley*[54]).

Buckley J in *Re London and Globe Finance Corpn Ltd* [55] considered that to *deceive* is to induce **7.68**
a man to believe a thing is true which is false or a thing is false which is true, contrary to what the person practising the deceit knows or believes to be the case (as modified by Lord Radcliffe in *Welham v DPP*[56]).

Deception

The term 'deception' is defined in s 15(4) of the Theft Act 1968 (for the purposes of that Act) **7.69**
as 'any deception (whether deliberate or reckless) by words or conduct as to fact or as to law, including a deception as to the present intention of the person using the deception or any other person'.

It is likely that conviction of a person for an offence which does not require dishonesty or **7.70**
deception in order for there to be a conviction will not satisfy s 29(1)(a), even if the person has been dishonest or deceived.

Disqualification applied from the date that the section came into force (6 April 1997), even **7.71**
if the conviction occurred before that date—s 29(2)(a).

Rehabilitation of Offenders Act 1974

Disqualification does not apply if the conviction is spent for the purposes of the Rehabilitation **7.72**
of Offenders Act 1974 (ROA 1974)—s 29(2)(a).

A conviction of an individual is spent for the purposes of ROA 1974 after the rehabilitation **7.73**
period under s 6 of ROA 1974 expires. It is not possible for an offence committed by a corporation to become spent under ROA 1974.

As mentioned above, the term 'conviction' as used in ROA 1974 expressly includes convic- **7.74**
tions outside Great Britain (s 1(4) of the ROA 1974).

The rehabilitation periods are set out in s 5 of the ROA 1974. They are to be amended when **7.75**
s 139 of the Legal Aid, Sentencing and Punishment of Offenders Act 2013 comes into force. The table below gives a general guide.

Sentence	Rehabilitation period	New period (for adults) under the 2012 Act
Custodial sentence of over 48 months or life	No rehabilitation period	No rehabilitation period
Custodial sentence of 30 to 48 months	No rehabilitation period	Seven years from date of conviction
Custodial sentence of six to 30 months	10 years from date of conviction	Four years from date of conviction

(Continued)

---

[53] [2005] UKPC 37, [2006] 1 All ER 333, PC.
[54] [2002] UKHL 12, [2002] 2 AC 164, HL.
[55] [1903] 1 Ch 728 at 732 (Buckley J).
[56] [1961] AC 103 at 126, HL.

Sentence	Rehabilitation period	New period (for adults) under the 2012 Act
Custodial sentence of up to six months	Seven years from date of conviction	Four years from date of conviction
Fine or other sentence	Five years from date of conviction	One year from date of conviction

Bankruptcy: section 29(1)(b)

7.76 Section 29(1)(b) applies if a trustee has been adjudged bankrupt (or sequestration of his estate has been ordered—this is a Scottish procedure) and he has not been discharged.

7.77 In practice the most relevant bankruptcy orders will be those made in Great Britain under the Insolvency Act 1986 (England and Wales) or the Bankruptcy (Scotland) Act 1985 (Scotland). However, s 29(1)(b) is not expressly limited to bankruptcies in Great Britain and the section could be held to apply to bankruptcies overseas (eg in Northern Ireland or the Republic of Ireland).

7.78 An individual (not a company) will have been adjudged bankrupt in England and Wales under the Insolvency Act 1986 (IA 1986) if a bankruptcy order has been made by the court following a petition (ss 264 and 381 of the IA 1986). The bankruptcy takes effect when the order is made and lasts until it is discharged (s 278 of the IA 1986).

7.79 Generally, a bankrupt is discharged three years after the bankruptcy order is made, unless the bankrupt had been subject to criminal bankruptcy proceedings or had previously been bankrupt within the previous 15 years or the court agrees on the application of the official receiver to extend the bankruptcy (s 279 of the IA 1986).

7.80 Disqualification will apply from the date that s 29 of the Pensions Act 1995 came into force (6 April 1997), even if the bankruptcy occurred before that date (s 29(2)(b) of the 1995 Act).

Composition, contract, or arrangement with creditors: section 29(1)(e)

7.81 Section 29(1)(e) applies if a trustee has made a composition, contract, or an arrangement with his creditors (or granted a trust deed for the behoof of his creditors—this is a Scottish procedure) and he has not been discharged.

7.82 In practice the most relevant contracts or arrangements with creditors will be those made in Great Britain under the Insolvency Act 1986 (England and Wales) or the Bankruptcy (Scotland) Act 1985 (Scotland). However, s 29(1)(e) is not expressly limited to arrangements in Great Britain under these Acts. The section could be held to apply to arrangements overseas (eg in Northern Ireland, the Republic of Ireland, or elsewhere).

7.83 Disqualification will apply from the date that s 29 of the 1995 Act comes into force (probably 6 April 1997), even if the composition contract or arrangement was made before that date (s 29(2)(c) of the 1995 Act).

Compromises or arrangements involving an individual in England and Wales will usually **7.84** be either:

(a) an individual voluntary arrangement in England and Wales under the Insolvency Act 1986 (Pt 8, ss 252–263), which is a composition in satisfaction of an individual's debts or a scheme of arrangement of his affairs; or
(b) a composition or arrangement outside the Insolvency Act 1986 requiring registration under the Deeds of Arrangement Act 1914.

Disqualification under the Company Directors Disqualification Act 1986, section 29(1)(f)

Section 29(1)(f) provides that a trustee is disqualified if a disqualification order is made under **7.85** the Company Directors Disqualification Act 1986 (CDDA 1986) (or under section 429(2)(b) of the IA 1986—see also s 12 of CDDA 1986).

Disqualification applied from the date that s 29 of the 1995 Act came into force (6 April **7.86** 1997), even if the disqualification order was made before that date (s 29(2)(d) of the 1995 Act).

Orders are made by a court under CDDA 1986 prohibiting a person from being a director **7.87** of, or concerned in the promotion, formation, or management of, a company for a specified period (s 1 of the CDDA 1986). Disqualification can be made on various grounds, including:

(a) conviction of offences in relation to companies (ss 2–5 of the CDDA 1986); or
(b) if the company became insolvent and his conduct as a director made him unfit to act (s 6 of the CDDA 1986). This can be following the report of an insolvency practitioner (s 7(3) of the CDDA 1986).

Disqualification can be for up to 15 years. The court can grant leave for a person to act as a **7.88** director even if an order is still in force (ss 1 and 17 of the CDDA 1986), but this does not discharge the order (so that person would remain disqualified under s 29 of the 1995 Act from acting as a pension scheme trustee).

Company (or Scottish partnership) where a director (or partner) has been disqualified

This is an example of the maxim 'a rotten apple will rot the whole barrel'. It attracted some **7.89** debate in 1995 in the committee stage in the House of Commons.[57] The consequences of disqualification of one director for the remaining directors of the company are quite dramatic. The Act does not provide any mechanism for removing the director from the company, as the government felt this was a matter best dealt with by the company itself or alternatively the DTI.

Companies who act as trustees should consider seeking to avoid the problem by including **7.90** in their articles of association a provision for the automatic removal of a director if he or she becomes disqualified, prohibited, or suspended under the 1995 Act.

It is unclear how the timing on this works. If the articles provide for a director to cease to **7.91** hold office on an order being made (or becoming disqualified) does this protect the company

---

[57] Hansard, 9 May 1995, cols 87–92.

(ie does the removal of the director take effect first so that the company does not become disqualified)?

7.92 It seems likely that this should be effective. Alternatives are to provide that:

(a) the removal occurs when relevant proceedings are commenced etc (see the list in s 4), but this may be too early; or

(b) the removal is deemed to take effect immediately before the disqualification event—but how will you know that it is going to occur? At least this gives a pointer to the relevant judge to allow the company to continue.

Effect of disqualification

7.93 Section 30(1) provides that a trustee who becomes disqualified under s 29 has the effect of removing him as a trustee. Disqualified people will not have to take steps to resign on the removal from their trusteeship because it will have been ended automatically by law. It may, however, be appropriate for the trust instrument to indicate that a trustee will automatically retire on becoming disqualified under the 1995 Act.

Sanctions

7.94 A person who purports to act as a trustee of an occupational pension scheme while disqualified under s 29 will be guilty of a criminal offence—s 30(3). In order to protect the interests of the trust and those dealing with it, his or her acts will not become invalid merely because of the contravention—s 30(5). These provisions are similar to those in s 6 in relation to prohibition or suspension under ss 3 or 4 (see above).

Suspension, Prohibition, and Disqualification Orders: Common Provisions

7.95 There are a number of common provisions relating to the making of suspension, prohibition, and disqualification orders by the Pensions Regulator which deal in particular with:

(a) the form of the order;

(b) the revocation or waiver of the order;

(c) the timing of the circumstances taken into consideration by the Pensions Regulator in making the order;

(d) the vesting of property; and

(e) sanctions for breach of the order.

Form of the order

7.96 As mentioned above, the powers of the Pensions Regulator under ss 3 and 4 (and its waiver power under s 29(5)) are reserved matters, meaning that the relevant decision needs to be made by the determinations panel of the Pensions Regulator. Once it has made a determination, a written notice must be sent to 'such persons as appear to them to be directly affected'. This will include:

(a) the person against whom the order is made;

(b) (probably) the other trustees; and

(c) (probably) the primary employer of the scheme.

The notice must specify (reg 2):   **7.97**

(a) the determination made;
(b) the reasons for that determination;
(c) the right to apply for a review; and
(d) the time limit for making such an application.

There is a right under s 96(3) of the Pensions Act 2004 to appeal to the Upper Tribunal **7.98**
against the Pensions Regulator's decision. This operates as a new hearing and is not just a
review of the previous decision—s 103. An appeal must normally be made within 28 days
or later if the Tribunal allows.[58] Orders of the regulator through the determinations panel do
not normally take effect until the appeal period has expired—s 96(5), but this does not apply
to orders under ss 3, 4, or 29—s 96(6) of the Pensions Act 2004.

Revocation

The person against whom an order is made will always have the right to apply to the Pensions **7.99**
Regulator to have the order reviewed or revoked (ss 3(3), 4(5), and 29(5) of the Pensions
Act 1995).

Even where a person is automatically disqualified under s 29(1) he can apply for a notice in **7.100**
writing waiving his disqualification—s 29(5).

There are no time limits imposed on the making of an application. The Pensions Regulator **7.101**
is unlikely to grant a waiver or revocation lightly since the purpose of these provisions is to
prevent people who have shown financial incompetence or dishonesty in the past from being
in control of pension funds.

Decisions of the Charity Commissioners may serve as a useful starting point or guidance in **7.102**
this area. Volume 1 of *Decisions of the Charity Commissioners* (1993) sets out a list of issues
they would consider when deciding whether to waive the disqualification of a trustee. The
following matters may be relevant in the case of a pension fund trustee:

(a) the specific nature of the offence in respect of which the disqualification arises;
(b) the gravity of the offence and the sentence passed by the court;
(c) the seriousness of the bankruptcy or composition;
(d) whether the applicant is prohibited from acting as a director of any company under the
     CDDA 1986 and, if so, whether leave has been given under the Act for him to act as a
     director of any other company; and
(e) the views of the other trustees.

An example of an application to the use of the power in s 29(5) to waive a disqualification is **7.103**
given in Summary 3 in Opra Bulletin 1 (January 1997). The Pensions Regulator refused to
waive the disqualification of a trustee convicted of multiple fraud offences.

An example of the use of the power in s 3 is given in Summary 10 in Opra Bulletin 1 (January **7.104**
1997). This concerned a scheme with currently only one member who had also been the
trustee but who had become automatically disqualified. Opra decided to grant the waiver to

---

[58] Paragraph 5 of Sch 3 to the Tribunal Procedure (Upper Tribunal) Rules 2008 (SI 2008/2698, as amended).

the applicant in respect of any scheme of which he was the sole member. The board gave the following reasons for its decision:

(a) the administrators of the scheme had confirmed that the applicant had always acted absolutely properly as a trustee of the scheme;

(b) the applicant's conduct before and after his criminal conviction, and his character, gave the board reason to believe that it was acceptable to grant the waiver;

(c) the waiver was limited to apply only to a class of schemes where the sole member was the applicant.

7.105 The revocation of an order will enable a trustee to continue or to begin to act as trustee only after the date of the revocation. In all cases, the 1995 Act provides that revocation of the order will not affect anything done before that time. As a result, any breach of the order whilst it was in force remains an offence by the trustee.

7.106 If the governing trust deed (or articles of association of a trustee company) provides for a trustee (or director) to vacate office on becoming disqualified, prohibited or suspended, the revocation of the relevant order (or grant of a waiver) will not (unless the trust deed (or articles) so provides) have effect to reinstate the person as a trustee (or director).

Vesting of property

7.107 Under s 9 of the 1995 Act, the Pensions Regulator is given the same jurisdiction and powers as are exercisable by the High Court as regards the vesting and transferring of property to trustees which may result from changes in the composition of the trustee board consequent upon an order being made under ss 3 or 7.

7.108 This could include an order vesting property in the remaining trustees. In practice the removed trustee should execute any transfers needed. If the assets are held by a nominee (or custodian) for the trustees from time to time, no vesting order will be needed.

Breach of order

7.109 Where a prohibition, suspension, or disqualification order is made or a trustee becomes disqualified, he or she should immediately cease to take any further part in the affairs of the pension scheme. If a person continues to act as trustee he or she will be committing an offence for which they could be prosecuted.

On a summary conviction an individual would be liable to a fine not exceeding the statutory maximum (£5,000) and on conviction on indictment to a fine or imprisonment or both—ss 6(1) and 30(3).

7.110 The pension trust and those who deal with it will be protected from the effects of such a breach. Sections 6(3) and 30(5) of the 1995 Act provide that things done by a trustee in breach of ss 3, 4, or 29 will not be invalid merely because of that.

8

PENSION TRUSTS

The Position of Spouses and Dependants

Introduction

The primary beneficiaries under a pension scheme are clearly the members and the employers. **8.1** Schemes commonly also extend benefits to the spouse and dependants of a member. Normally these benefits are payable only following the death of the member.

8.2 This chapter looks at the position of the spouse and dependants of a member as 'secondary beneficiaries' under a pension scheme.[1] What is the nature of the duties (if any) owed by the scheme trustees and employers to these secondary beneficiaries?

8.3 The benefits payable to the member have clearly been earned by the member's employment. Many cases make the point that the member is not a volunteer.[2] Clearly also the benefits payable to the secondary beneficiaries form part of the benefits that the member has earned. They form part of the member's benefits—for example they form part of the member's 'accrued rights' under the Pensions Act 1995. Section 124(2) defines a member's accrued rights as the rights 'which have accrued to *or in respect of* him ...'. The italicized words are clearly intended to include benefits payable to secondary beneficiaries.[3]

8.4 What control does the member have over these benefits? Can the trustees or employer safely act in the interests of the member (or with his or her consent) to the detriment of all or a particular secondary beneficiary? What weight should the trustees give to the member's wishes when considering distribution of a lump sum death benefit?

8.5 This is a fairly fundamental question and not much discussed.[4]

The structure of pension schemes

8.6 As discussed in Chapter 1 (What is an occupational pension scheme?), one way of looking at a typical occupational pension scheme structure is to view it as a tripartite relationship between the employer, the trustee and the member.[5] Figure 8.1 below gives a diagrammatic view.

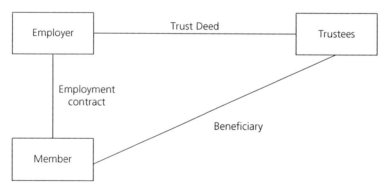

Figure 8.1

---

[1] Robin Ellison has pointed out that the issue of the rights of family members have an impact under EU law as well. This can arise when considering the rights of the family of a worker if (say) the worker exercises a right to work in another member state. These rights are known as 'derived rights'.

[2] See eg *Mettoy Pension Trustees v Evans* [1991] 2 All ER 513, [1990] 1 WLR 1587 (Warner J) and Ch 17 (Amendment powers).

[3] See eg the discussion of this point in paras 10.1.1 and 10.3.1 of the joint opinion of April 2000 of Nicholas Warren QC (as he then was) and Paul Newman on s 67 of the Pensions Act 1995 to the Institute of Actuaries (see <http://www.actuaries.org.uk/research-and-resources/documents/s67-pensions-act-1995-opinion>).

[4] See, however, D Pollard, 'Pension Trusts: The Position of Spouses and Dependants' (2002) 16 TLI 74, based on a talk to the APL conference in November 2001.

[5] See eg Wood J in the EAT in *Walden Engineering Co v Warrener* [1992] OPLR 1, [1993] IRLR 420.

This three-way relationship involves: **8.7**

(a) a trust instrument (usually a deed) establishing a trust (and generally dealing with the relationship between the employer and the trustees);
(b) a contractual employment relationship between the employer and the member; and
(c) a classic trust/beneficiary relationship between the trustees and the member, also governed by the trust deed.

This is still a simplistic view of the complexities of the pension structure—see Chapter 1   **8.8**
(What is an occupational pension scheme?).

Secondary Beneficiaries

A further complication is obvious. Most occupational pension schemes will not have the   **8.9**
member as the sole recipient of retirement benefits. Most (if not all) schemes will also envisage
benefits being payable following the death of a member (either in service or in retirement) to
the member's spouse (or registered civil partner) and/or dependants.

It is not a requirement to have these benefits, but in practice it would be unusual not to have   **8.10**
them. A pension payable to the spouse is a requirement if the scheme is to be contracted-out
(under the Pension Schemes Act 1993) of the state second pensions (S2P) or the state earnings
related pension scheme (SERPS).[6]

Adding these potential beneficiaries into a chart from Chapter 1 shows how complicated   **8.11**
things become—see figure 8.2 below.

This chapter looks at the implications for pension schemes (and the various duties and   **8.12**
relationships between the parties) of these secondary beneficiaries, ie the member's spouse
or civil partner,[7] future spouse (or civil partner), and dependants etc.

How does the existence of the secondary beneficiaries impact on the underlying relationships?

The situation here is where the secondary beneficiaries are essentially contingent beneficiar-   **8.13**
ies only, ie their benefits depend upon the individual concerned surviving the member.
Before 2006, Inland Revenue approved pension schemes would not generally allow benefits
to be paid to such a secondary beneficiary while the member is still alive.[8] The new tax rules
from 6 April 2006 generally envisage tax charges if benefits are not authorized payments.
This allows for pensions to the spouse, civil partner, or dependants following the death of the
member—see Finance Act 2004, Sch 28, Pt 2,[9] but not generally before.

---

[6] See eg s 17 of the Pension Schemes Act 1993 in relation to guaranteed minimum pensions for widows and widowers from schemes contracted out before 6 April 1997 on a salary-related basis.

[7] In this chapter, references to a spouse should be taken to include a civil partner registered under the Civil Partnership Act 2004. Discrimination against a civil partner (eg only to include married spouses) will, in an employment or pensions context, usually be illegal discrimination on the grounds of sexual orientation under the Equality Act 2010, although there is an exemption in Sch 9, para 18 for pension benefits relating to service before 5 December 2005 (the date the 2004 Act came into force).

[8] There are exceptions following bankruptcy or suspension while the member is in prison.

[9] Particularly the definition of 'dependant' in para 15.

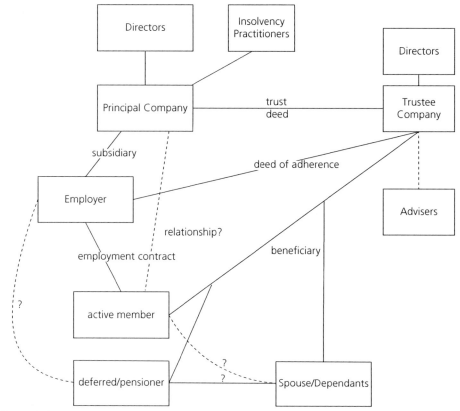

Figure 8.2

8.14 This means that this chapter does not look at a situation where a spouse has obtained a sharing order from the court[10] (as part of divorce or nullity proceedings) and so has become a primary beneficiary in his or her own right.

Who are secondary beneficiaries?

8.15 In practice for tax registered schemes, beneficiaries who can be paid a pension are limited to the spouse or civil partner and the dependants of the (deceased) member are eligible.

8.16 It is common for a pension scheme to envisage a benefit being payable following the member's death as of right to the surviving spouse and/or children (under age 18 or older than that if undergoing full-time education or disabled) of the member. As mentioned above, some sort of spouse's pension is a requirement if the scheme is to be contracted-out under the Pension Schemes Act 1993.

8.17 Discretions are often given to trustees to give benefits to other dependants as well (or in substitution for the benefit payable to the spouse or children).

8.18 It is sometimes argued that failure to provide a pension as of right to an unmarried 'partner' (ie not a spouse or registered civil partner) of a member constitutes indirect discrimination

---

[10] Under the powers in the Welfare Reform and Pensions Act 1999.

on the basis of sexual orientation[11] or is contrary to the non-discrimination rule in the Human Rights Act 1998.[12] In practice, much of the case law upholds being able to treat marriage as a special status.[13] Even if not, some form of discrimination would seem in principle to be likely to be objectively justified. There remains the issue that the 'partner' will not be as readily identifiable in the same way as a spouse (there will be no legal certificate proving the status). Accordingly the trustees will look for some degree of certainty. The easiest potential measure may be a nomination by the member him or herself.

The tax laws broadly have no restrictions for registered pension schemes on the recipients of payment of *lump sum* benefits following the death of a member.[14] The tax legislation allows lump sum benefits to be paid (as an authorized payment) to any third party, whether or not a spouse or dependant. In practice it is common for pension scheme deeds to set out a fairly large class of potential beneficiaries (including the spouse, dependants, and relatives of the member and any person benefiting under the member's will) automatically. The member can then add to the class by notice in writing to the trustees before his or her death.[15] **8.19**

The trustees are commonly given a discretion to choose amongst the class thereby established as to who is to receive all or part of the lump sum payable upon death. The member will usually also be asked to indicate his (non-binding) wishes. A discretionary trust is used on the basis that it adds flexibility (eg if the member's circumstances have changed since the date of the wishes form or will etc). It also clearly avoids any risk of the lump sum being treated as part of the member's estate for inheritance tax purposes.[16] **8.20**

Impact of Secondary Beneficiaries

How then do the secondary beneficiaries impact on the relationships between the principal parties: the member, the employer, and the trustees? **8.21**

The purpose of this chapter is to examine the impact on these relationships. **8.22**

There may well be circumstances where the employer and the trustees wish to act for the benefit of the member or in reliance on the consent of the member. Can they do so without running any risk of a claim from a secondary beneficiary? **8.23**

---

[11] It is probably not sex discrimination—see *Grant v South West Trains* C-249/96, [1998] ECR I-621, ECJ and *Secretary of State v MacDonald* [2001] IRLR 431 (Ct of Sess).

[12] Ie on the grounds of status under Arts 1 and 14 of the First Protocol. See the decisions of Treacy J to that effect in Northern Ireland in *Re Brewster* [2012] NIQB 85 and *Re Morrison* [2010] NIQB 51, dealing with pension schemes established by legislation.

[13] Eg *Shackell v United Kingdom* (2000) 27 April, ECHR; *Burden v United Kingdom* [2008] STC 1305, [2008] All ER (D) 391 (Apr), ECHR.

[14] Finance Act 2004. There were (under the pre-2006 tax regime) some restrictions in special cases: eg for controlling directors.

[15] Providing the member can add to the class only by notice received *before death* is a useful protection against fraud—what if someone 'discovers' a direction from the member after death?

[16] Note, however, that including a provision binding trustees to distribute the lump sum as directed by the member would seem *not* to make the lump sum form part of the member's estate for inheritance tax purposes. This is provided the member could not nominate him or herself or the estate. It would be prudent to ensure that any binding direction by the member complied with the attestation requirements of the Wills Act—although this is another topic.

Examples of problem areas

8.24   Examples of this situation include:

(a)   The trustees acting to invest assets representing money purchase benefits in investments chosen by the member. Could the trustees be liable to the secondary beneficiaries if they follow the member's request or direction and the investments concerned do not do as well as they could have done? Is this more of an issue where the member chooses a particularly speculative investment?

(b)   On retirement a member chooses to use money purchase assets to buy a single life annuity (ie with no benefits for secondary beneficiaries). Can the trustees properly act on the member's request?

(c)   The member asks the trustees and the principal company to agree to a scheme amendment changing the benefits under the scheme. Instead of a pension being paid automatically to the spouse, the member asks that the pension be paid instead to another dependant. Perhaps the member and the spouse have separated but are not willing (perhaps for religious reasons) to divorce. If the scheme provides that a benefit is payable to the spouse automatically (with no provision for it to be redirected by the trustees), can the trustees and the company properly agree to this request (eg by including a discretion to redirect or allowing the member to nominate who is to receive the pension)?[17]

(d)   The employer and the member wish to agree to commute all benefits into a lump sum. Is the consent of the member alone enough for this? If not, then even if the current spouse consents, how does this deal with the fact that there could potentially be a future different spouse (eg if the current spouse dies or there is a divorce and the member remarries). Such total commutation may be an issue in revenue approved schemes in relation to trivial commutation (ie an annual pension of less than £260 a year or in cases of serious ill health) or in unapproved schemes (where the total commutation of pension is often desired by the parties as a clean break following a termination of employment etc).

8.25   Total commutation of benefits to a lump sum is quite common in US plans. However, in many cases the Internal Revenue Code requires a joint life annuity to be given unless the member *and his or her spouse* elect otherwise.[18] This is presumably in order to avoid the risk of the member taking all the money and spending it, leaving the spouse destitute. There are specific rules about when spouse consent is not needed (eg if the member is single—and can prove it—or if the spouse cannot be located[19]).

8.26   The trustees are asked to act in a manner which is in the interests of the member, but not necessarily of the secondary beneficiaries. Does the member's interest outweigh that of the secondary beneficiaries? For example, a proposal that would benefit the employer (and hence indirectly the active members).

---

[17]   There is no issue under s 67 of the Pensions Act 1995, because the member is consenting. Note that any change would have to be subject to the relevant contracting-out requirements if the scheme is contracted-out of the state second pension (under PSA 1993).

[18]   Section 401(a)(11) of the Internal Revenue Code.

[19]   The plan administrator needs to make proper enquires about this. It is not enough to rely on a letter from the member—*Lester v Reagan Equipment Co Profit Sharing Plan* 1992 WL 193499 (ED La 1992).

The trustees want to distribute the death lump sum by acting on the expression of wishes **8.27** recently signed by the member to the exclusion of other potential beneficiaries. What weight should the trustees give to those wishes?[20]

The company wants to be able to agree a surplus refund even though it may be contrary to **8.28** the trust deed or potentially a breach of trust. Can the company and the trustees proceed with unanimous member consent? Or is the consent of the secondary beneficiaries needed too?

Position of the Employer

The relationship between the employer and a secondary beneficiary is a bit clearer. **8.29**

Contract

The secondary beneficiary has never been employed by the employer. The rights of a second-**8.30** ary beneficiary are contingent on and derived from the rights of the member.

In practice this means that there is no direct contractual relationship between an employer **8.31** and a secondary beneficiary. It is difficult to see that the employer can do anything other than treat the member as the sole contacting party. In any event the rights of a member against the employer are in any event usually viewed as fairly limited.[21] Perhaps the greatest right at present is to enforce the implied mutual duty of trust and confidence.[22]

It is unlikely that any direct contractual rights will be given to secondary beneficiaries by the **8.32** Contracts (Rights of Third Parties) Act 1999. This is because many employment contracts will predate the Act (which is not retrospective). Even for those contracts made after 10 May 2000, there will often be no direct contractual obligation on the employer other than to make membership of the scheme available to the member.

This probably means that the mutual duty of trust and confidence, as an implied contractual **8.33** term, is not enforceable by the secondary beneficiaries. However, this probably does not matter if the duty is enforceable by the trustees in any event.[23]

Secondary beneficiaries may be able to enforce any contractual duty if they also happen to be **8.34** the personal representatives of the member's estate—eg *Beswick v Beswick*.[24]

---

[20] In Australia there are many cases of the Superannuation Complaints Tribunal overruling a decision by trustees to follow the member's wishes and instead ordering payment to what the tribunal considers to be a more deserving relative. This has resulted in amending legislation in Australia allowing schemes the option of providing that the member's expression of wishes is binding on the trustees. The wish form has to comply with various formalities (eg it must not be more than three years old and must be signed before two adult witnesses)—see s 59(1A) of the Superannuation Industry (Supervision) Act 1993 (as amended in 1999) and regs 6.17A and 6.17B of the SIS Regulations.

[21] See D Pollard and N Randall, *Pensions as a Contractual Right* (Industrial Law Society, 2002); Paul Stannard, 'Pensions as an Employment Right', 1992 APL Conference; and Duncan Buchanan, 'Pensions—A Contractual Right?', 2001 APL Conference.

[22] See Ch 13 (Employer powers: the implied duty of trust and confidence).

[23] It seems to follow from *Imperial Tobacco* [1991] 1 WLR 589 (Browne Wilkinson V-C) that the duty is owed to trustees as well. Notwithstanding this, it has been argued that the implied duty is *not* in fact enforceable by trustees (on the basis that it was not necessary for the decision in *Imperial Tobacco* to have the duty enforced by the trustees). See Ch 13 (Employer powers: the implied duty of trust and confidence).

[24] [1968] AC 58, HL.

Tort

8.35 Does the employer owe any duty of care in tort to secondary beneficiaries? Any loss would be economic, so there would need to be a special relationship for a negligence duty to arise under the principles relating to negligent mis-statement in *Hedley Byrne v Heller*.[25] It does not seem to me that the employer's relationship with the secondary beneficiaries should fall into this class. It would also be difficult for a secondary beneficiary to show detrimental reliance.

8.36 However, in *White v Jones*,[26] the House of Lords held a solicitor liable in tort to a potential beneficiary under a will where the solicitor had negligently failed to prepare the will before the testator died. Lord Goff held that reliance by the intended beneficiary was not necessary. The law would give the intended beneficiary a remedy to avoid a lacuna in the law. The principle in *White v Jones* has been applied in a pension context.

Gorham v British Telecommunications plc

8.37 *Gorham v British Telecommunications plc*[27] involved a claim by the dependants of a deceased employee against BT (his former employer), the pension scheme trustees, and a financial adviser. The employee had been wrongly advised by a financial adviser tied to an insurer, Standard Life, to take out a personal pension. He had not been advised that it would have been better to enter the employer's scheme.

8.38 About 10 months later this advice was corrected by the adviser, but the employee did not then seek to join the employer's scheme as (seemingly) he misunderstood the booklet issued to him by the employer. He seems to have thought that he was in the employer's scheme anyway because the booklet said that he would be automatically entered into the scheme unless he signed an opt-out form. At first instance, the judge found that he thought he was in the pension scheme because he had not formally opted out by returning a signed opting-out form. This was despite the fact that on joining BT the employee had asked the employer to opt-out from the pension scheme and no pension contributions had ever been deducted from his pay.

8.39 On the employee's death, the pension scheme refused to pay any benefits and the dependants (widows and children) sued.

8.40 At first instance, Judge Raymond Jack QC (sitting as a High Court Judge) held[28] that the employer[29] did owe a duty of care to dependants in relation to the explanatory literature given to the member, but that in the circumstances there was no breach of that duty by the employer. As Pill LJ stated[30] (in the later appeal to the Court of Appeal by the financial adviser):

> The case against BT and the trustees of the BT pension scheme was based on their reaction to the failure to send to them the completed opting-out form and upon the allegedly misleading contents of their pensions literature. The judge rejected the claim, holding that 'there was no

---

[25] [1964] AC 465, HL.

[26] [1995] 2 AC 207, HL.

[27] [2000] 4 All ER 867, CA.

[28] On 29 January 1999.

[29] There was no claim that the trustees of the pension scheme owed a duty of care—see p 23 of the judgment. Instead, the claim against the trustees was based on estoppel based on the wording of the booklet.

[30] See [2000] 4 All ER 867 at 875.

need for the literature to say that, if he [Mr Gorham] failed to return the opting-out form but his instruction to opt out was nonetheless acted on, he would not be a member'. The judge did however hold that BT owed the plaintiffs a duty of care:

'In my judgment, where an employer provides information to an employee in connection with pension matters and the information is relied upon by the employee to the ultimate detriment of his dependants on his death, the law should recognise a duty to the dependants.'

The judge cited the speech of Lord Browne-Wilkinson in *White v Jones* [1995] 2 AC 207 at 274.

Judge Jack held the financial adviser to be liable for the loss of dependants' pension resulting **8.41** from the initial advice, but not the loss of the death in service lump sum. This was because Mr Gorham could have re-joined the BT scheme when he received the correct advice—his dependants would then have been eligible for the death in service lump sum, but not the dependants' pension (because he died before the end of the two-year qualifying period for the dependants' pension under the rules of the BT scheme).

The dependants appealed against the ruling against the financial adviser, but not against **8.42** the judgment that the employer and trustees were not liable. On the appeal,[31] the Court of Appeal agreed that the financial adviser owed a duty of care to the dependants of the employee in relation to the advice given to the employee.

Pill and Schiemann LJJ, however, held that the duty was limited. They agreed with Judge **8.43** Jack that the financial adviser was not liable for the lump sum loss after the correct advice had been given.

In *White v Jones* the House of Lords drew a distinction with the case of someone intending **8.44** to make a gift while still alive. Even if the solicitor were negligent, there would be no loss as the donor could still make the gift. This point would be relevant in the case of any purported duty owed to secondary beneficiaries while the member is still alive.

Pill LJ commented (at 876): **8.45**

Before leaving *White v Jones*, I mention the inter vivos gift which Lord Goff ([1995] 2 AC 207 at 262) contemplated when considering the conceptual problems involved. As a result of a solicitor's negligence, the instrument conferring the gift is not effective for its purpose and the mistake comes to light during the lifetime of the donor, after the gift to the intended donee should have taken effect. In such circumstances, Lord Goff concluded, the intended donee would not have any claim against the solicitor because the donor is able to put matters right, if he sees fit. In putting it in that way Lord Goff was, as I understand it, dealing with causation. The prospective donee has no claim because the donor had the opportunity to perfect the gift but chose not to do so. What Lord Goff regarded as the real reason for concern, namely that 'the only person who may have a valid claim has suffered no loss and the only person who has suffered a loss has no claim', did not arise. It does, however, arise in the present case.

Sir Murray Stuart-Smith dissented on this point. He would have held the financial **8.46** adviser liable for the loss of the lump sum as well, despite the correcting advice (unlike Judge Jack, both Schiemann LJ and Sir Murray Stuart-Smith would have reduced any award to reflect the contributory negligence of Mr Gorham after the correct advice had been given).

---

[31] [2000] 4 All ER 867, CA.

8.47   The decision of the Court of Appeal does not relate to the employer or trustees, so it must still be arguable that they are in a different position to a financial adviser. However, in practice the Court of Appeal did not comment adversely on Judge Jack's finding against the employer.

8.48   The Court of Appeal also discussed the issue of any conflict of interest between the employee and his dependants.

8.49   Pill LJ stated[32] that:

> Inevitably in insurance contracts of this kind, there is a potential conflict of interest between the customer and his dependants. One customer will wish to do the best he can for himself, by way of a pension during his lifetime. Another will sacrifice, to the full extent he can, his interests to those of his dependants. The existence of the duty cannot in my view depend on the category into which the customer falls or on how far along the spectrum of providing for his dependants he travels. I do not see the conflict of interest as an obstacle to the creation of a duty of care to the dependants however. The duty is not one to ensure that the dependants are properly provided for. It is, in the present context, a duty to the dependants not to give negligent advice to the customer which adversely affects their interests as he intends them to be.

8.50   Schiemann LJ agreed:[33]

> Like Pill LJ, I am not troubled by Sir Murray Stuart-Smith's concern…about a conflict of interest. This concern, I think, arises by approaching the question as one of a duty owed by the adviser to intended beneficiaries and then asking what is the scope of the duty owed by the adviser to the intended beneficiaries? However, the assumption of responsibility to beneficiaries in cases such as the present does not operate to widen the scope of the duty but merely to widen the number of those who can sue in respect of any breach. That was I believe the approach of Lord Goff, who in White v Jones [1995] 2 AC 207 at 268, states that the assumption of responsibility will of course be subject to the terms of the contract between the solicitor and the testator.

8.51   Sir Murray Stuart-Smith commented:[34]

> There is one other aspect of this question which has caused me some concern. It is not difficult to imagine a situation where there is a conflict of interest between the investor and his dependants. For reasons of his own, which may be good or bad, he may wish to enhance his own pension at the expense of his wife's. In such a situation plainly someone in Mr Cornwell's position cannot owe a duty of care both to the investor (which he undoubtedly does) and also to the wife.

> But should not the possibility of such conflict deter the courts from imposing a duty of care towards the dependants? It is quite clear that there was no such conflict in this case. I think Mr Palmer is right when he submits that it will be reasonably clear on the facts of a particular case that there is such a conflict. There will perhaps be borderline cases where the factual decision is not easy; but I do not think that should deter the courts from imposing a duty where there is clearly no such conflict. Accordingly I agree with the judge that Standard Life was under a duty of care towards the claimants.

8.52   There is no discussion in any of the judgments whether the benefits payable to dependants are payable as of right or only as a result of the exercise of a discretion by the trustees of the pensions scheme (lump sums are likely to only be payable if the trustees exercise a discretion).

---

[32] At 877.
[33] At 881.
[34] At 883.

This does not seem to have made any difference to the existence of the duty of care. There is a comment at the end of Pill LJ's judgment[35] that:

> At the very end of the hearing, it was for the first time contended that there might be a duty to Mrs Gorham without there being a duty to the infant children. Even if that argument is permitted, I see no merit in it on the present facts and upon an application of the principle in *White v Jones*. The widow and the infant children were equally dependent and their position cannot be distinguished.

The judgments do not imply a duty on employers (or trustees) to give advice. They **8.53** merely support the principle that if advice or information is in fact given, it must not be negligent.[36]

Trustees: conflicting principles

The position is more difficult for trustees. There is no easy answer to the rather fundamental **8.54** issues raised by the examples given above. There are two conflicting principles at play:

- That the pension benefit package belongs to (and should be under the control of) the member. It derives from the contract of employment. It is a benefit derived from the work of the member as an employee. Hence in one sense the benefit is deferred pay—for the member. The member has agreed (as part of the arrangement with the employer), that part of the benefit is payable to the spouse (or other secondary beneficiaries). However, it remains at heart a benefit of, and earned by, the employee/member.
- Against this, a trust structure has been adopted. Indeed, one of the reasons for having a trust structure was probably to be able to give enforceable rights to the secondary beneficiaries. Prior to the Contracts (Rights of Third Parties) Act 1999 it was much more difficult (at least in England and Wales[37]) to give such rights to persons not party to the employment contract. The beneficiaries of the trust clearly include the secondary beneficiaries. They are contingent beneficiaries—they will only benefit if they live longer than the member. There may be a double contingency: many benefits are not payable as of right but require an exercise of a discretion by the trustees. However, they are beneficiaries and, as such, entitled to the usual rights to enforce the trust etc.[38]

Member Priority Over Secondary Beneficiaries

The better view is that the courts should hold that the interests and the rights of the member **8.55** should be seen as paramount. The primary responsibility of the trustees is to the member, not the secondary beneficiaries. In effect, a consent or direction given by the member should be binding on the secondary beneficiaries.

This only applies while the member is alive. Once the member dies, the secondary benefi- **8.56** ciaries become actual beneficiaries, not contingent beneficiaries. Their consent is now what is needed.

---

[35] At 879.
[36] See *University of Nottingham v Eyett* [1999] 2 All ER 437 (Hart J); *Outram v Academy Plastics* [2000] PLR 283, [2000] IRLR 499, CA; and *Wirral Borough Council v Evans* [2001] OPLR 73 (Evans-Lombe J).
[37] The position was different in Scotland.
[38] See *IRC v Gartside* [1968] AC 553, HL.

8.57 The reasons for this approach are:

(a) It matches the instinctive view that practically everyone has of how pension schemes are set up and should work. The benefits derive from the employment contract with the employee/member. They are primarily for the benefit of the member. They should be susceptible to arrangements made by the member. The other beneficiaries are effectively secondary, deriving their benefit in the right of or in respect of the member (but not actually directly benefiting before the member dies). Another way of expressing this is to say that the primary purpose of the scheme is to provide benefits to and in respect of the member.[39] The member can be seen to be one of the settlors of the scheme.[40]

(b) In very many cases, the ultimate level of benefit payable out of the pension scheme will depend on decisions that have been made by the member. For example, in the case of a final salary scheme, the ultimate benefit would depend on the final salary earned by the member. If the member agrees (say) a particular level of pay or (say) chooses not to work overtime, this may well adversely affect the ultimate level of benefit. However, it is difficult to see that any of the secondary beneficiaries would have a claim against the member or the employer in these circumstances.

Similarly if the member chose to resign and no longer remain in employment, this will affect the benefits. Again it is difficult to see the secondary beneficiaries having a right of action against anyone in these circumstances.

Lastly, the member may well have the choice about certain benefits. For example whether or not to pay AVCs or whether or not to contribute to a money purchase scheme at a particular level (thereby attracting matching contributions). Again it is difficult to see a court holding that there was any duty on the employee (or the employer) in the circumstances to any potential secondary beneficiary.

8.58 This instinctive view of the structure is reflected in the statutory arrangements. These assume in many cases that the benefits belong to the member.

Statutory Framework

8.59 The statutory framework generally assumes that the member is the primary beneficiary and can bind the secondary beneficiaries.

Section 67: amendments

8.60 Section 67 of the Pensions Act 1995 protects entitlements and accrued rights. Generally these cannot be varied adversely without the consent of the trustees and the consent of the *member* (if alive[41]). If the member gives his or her consent, there is no further requirement under s 67 to look beyond this and seek the consent of the secondary beneficiaries as well.

---

[39] See eg the comment at para 4.1.15 of the Goode Report (1993): 'Occupational pension schemes are established primarily for the benefit of members and should therefore be run on this basis.' It does go on to say that 'It is the duty of the trustees to have regard to the interests of all categories of beneficiary, and of dependants where covered by the scheme rules . . .'

[40] See eg *Brooks v Brooks* [1995] 3 All ER 257, HL and *Air Jamaica v Charlton* [1999] 1 WLR 1399, PC—note that in the latter case any funds remaining were returned to the *members* (or their estates) as original contributors and not to any secondary beneficiary.

[41] For the position after the member's death—see discussion at para 8.75 below.

Such consent could of course be very difficult to obtain in practice (how would the scheme identify all spouses?). Often it would be impossible (eg to obtain the consent of minors and potential future beneficiaries).

Transfers-out: Pension Schemes Act 1993

The statutory transfer provisions in Ch 4 of Pt 4 of the Pension Schemes Act 1993 give a right **8.61** to the member to require the trustees to make available a cash equivalent as a transfer-out of a scheme to another arrangement.

The member can exercise the statutory transfer right and transfer the cash equivalent into a **8.62** personal pension which does not provide any benefits to the spouse or dependants (or to a particular spouse or dependant). The trustees could *not* refuse such a request—it would be the valid exercise of a right given to the member alone by the legislation.

Not all members have a statutory transfer right (those within one year of normal pension age **8.63** or who are pensioners do not for example). However, many schemes include non-statutory transfer provisions giving the trustees power to transfer with the consent of the member alone (this begs the question of whether they owe a duty to the other dependants as well in the circumstances).

If the statutory transfer right is exercised, the trustees are given a statutory discharge (s 99(1) **8.64** of the Pension Schemes Act 1993):

> the trustees . . . shall be discharged from any obligation to provide benefits to which the cash equivalent related . . .

Section 91 of the Pensions Act 1995: member surrender

Section 91 contains various prohibitions on surrender, assignment, forfeiture, etc of benefits. **8.65** However, s 91(5)(b) expressly allows the member to surrender benefits in exchange for the grant of other benefits.

This seems to allow the member to surrender (say) a spouse pension in exchange for (say) a **8.66** lump sum or a greater member pension. By 'allow' in this context, it seems that the section does not prohibit such an arrangement if it is allowed for by the scheme. It does not confer a freestanding statutory power of surrender if there is not one already in the scheme. See also para 8.77 below on liens.

Self-investment: section 40 of the Pensions Act 1995

The prohibition on employer-related investment under s 40 of the Pensions Act 1995 did not **8.67** (before the changes made in 2010) apply in relation to investments representing voluntary contributions where the *member* has consented in writing to that investment—see reg 13(4) of the Occupational Pension Schemes (Investment) Regulations 2005.[42] See Chapter 19 (Employer-related investment).

---

[42] SI 2005/3378. Formerly reg 6(5) of the Occupational Pension Schemes (Investment) Regulations 1996 (SI 1996/3127). Regulation 13(4) was revoked from 23 September 2010 by the Occupational, Personal and Stakeholder Pensions (Miscellaneous Amendments) Regulations 2009 (SI 2009/615). See Ch 19 (Employer-related investment).

Surplus refunds: section 37 of the Pensions Act 1995

8.68 Section 37 deals with payments of surplus to an employer—see Chapter 20 (Employers and surpluses). It imposes various pre-conditions that must be satisfied before such a payment can be made. These include a requirement that the trustees of the scheme must agree to the exercise of the relevant power—s 37(2).

8.69 The requirements also include that:

> the trustees are satisfied that it is in the interests of the *members* that the power be exercised in the manner so proposed—s 37(4)(b).

8.70 It is significant that the requirement relates only to the interests of the members. There is no reference to considering the interests of secondary beneficiaries, save where they are actually presently entitled to the payment of benefits[43] (eg following the member's death).

Financial Services and Markets Act 2000

8.71 The financial services legislation[44] generally requires day-to-day control of investment decisions in relation to the management of pension scheme investments to be with an authorized person. This obviously raises a potential problem in relation to money purchase benefits where in practice the trustees follow investment choices made by the member.

8.72 The SIB,[45] in its guidance in relation to the operation of the old legislation, dealt specifically with this issue. It considered that trustees would not be making day-to-day investment decisions where they invested assets of a pension scheme in order to match their liabilities by reference to the instructions of the member. The SIB stated, in its Guidance Release[46] issued in March 1988, that this would not be managing assets. In effect the SIB seems to have considered that the investment represented assets belonging to the member.

General Rights in Legislation

8.73 Statute clearly gives a primary role to members—*not* secondary beneficiaries. The term 'member' is defined[47] in a way that clearly excludes a secondary beneficiary.[48] This is true even after the member has died and a pension has started payment to the secondary beneficiary.

8.74 Many statutory rights are limited to members. So secondary beneficiaries do not get the chance to vote for member-nominated trustees;[49] only members need to be notified about surplus refunds[50] or failure to pay contributions.[51]

---

[43] See reg 2 of the Occupational Pension Schemes (Payments to Employers) Regulations 1996 (SI 1996/2156) extending the meaning of member for this purpose.

[44] See Art 4 of the Financial Services and Markets Act 2000 (Carrying on of Regulated Activities by Way of Business) Order 2001, replacing, from 1 December 2001, s 191 of the Financial Services Act 1986.

[45] The Security and Investments Board—the precursor of the Financial Services Authority.

[46] SIB Guidance Release 2/88 (March 1988): 'The Financial Services Act 1986—Pensions Advice and Management'.

[47] See s 124(1) of the Pensions Act 1995.

[48] Although the definition of deferred member could be better—it does not refer to someone who has pensionable service, but instead refers to a person who has accrued rights. This is circular, as the definition of accrued rights itself refers to a member—see Hugh Arthur, *Pensions and Trusteeship* (Sweet & Maxwell, 1998) 211.

[49] See ss 241–243 of the Pensions Act 2004 and previously ss 16–21 of the Pensions Act 1995.

[50] Pensions Act 1995, s 37(4)(e).

[51] Pensions Act 1995, s 59(1).

Some statutory rights are extended to secondary beneficiaries, but these are pretty limited **8.75** and usually only apply after the member's death—for example:

(a) the 1996 Disclosure Regulations give limited rights to a spouse or to a beneficiary (defined as 'a person, other than a member of the scheme, who is entitled to the payment of benefits under the scheme'—as such it probably only means current pensioners) to general information about the scheme.[52] This includes copies of the basic scheme information, copies of deeds etc, annual reports and actuarial reports etc. It does not include any right to individual information[53] (eg a benefit statement). These rights are limited to members (and prospective members);

(b) after the member's death, s 67 of the Pensions Act 1995 envisages that, in relation to scheme amendments, instead of the consent of the member, the consent of the survivor of the member is needed;[54]

(c) members are clearly entitled to complain to the Pensions Ombudsman. Secondary beneficiaries can too, but only after the member's death. The definition of 'actual or potential beneficiaries' who can bring complaints includes 'the widow or widower, or any surviving dependant, of a deceased member of the scheme'.[55]

Generally only members can use the internal dispute resolution (IDR) procedure required **8.76** by s 50 of the Pensions Act 1995. However, after the member's death, the IDR procedure is available to the 'widow, widower or surviving dependant of a deceased member'.[56]

Lien/forfeiture for member debt

It is unclear whether the crime etc of a member can operate to forfeit not only the benefits **8.77** payable to the member personally but also those payable to the relevant secondary beneficiaries.

For reasons that are not very clear, the Goode Committee[57] recommended that it should **8.78** not.[58] This was accepted by the government in its White Paper[59] following the Goode Report. However, the wording ultimately adopted in s 91(5)(d) of the Pensions Act 1995 does not follow this line. As originally drafted it allowed a charge or lien over the member's *accrued rights* (which would include the benefits for the secondary beneficiary).

The wording of this section was, however, amended by the Welfare Reform and Pensions Act **8.79** 1999[60] (with effect from 1 December 2000). It now only allows a set-off or lien to apply to the 'entitlement or right' of the 'person in question' instead of to his or her 'accrued rights'. Section 93 dealing with forfeiture has been similarly amended.

---

[52] See the Occupational Pension Schemes (Disclosure of Information) Regulations 1996 (SI 1996/1655), regs 3, 4, 6, and 7.

[53] See reg 5 of the 1996 Disclosure Regulations.

[54] Consent requirement in s 67B(5) (as added by the Pensions Act 2004) and the definition of 'affected member' in s 67A(5). Before the 2004 Act changes on 6 April 2006, the original provisions in the 1995 Act were to similar effect.

[55] Pension Schemes Act 1993, s 146(7).

[56] See reg 3(1)(b) of the Occupational Pension Schemes (Internal Dispute Resolution Procedures) Regulations 1996 (SI 1996/1270).

[57] Pension Law Review Committee, whose report was issued in September 1993 (Cm 2342).

[58] See para 4.14.32 and recommendation 166.

[59] See 'Security, Equality, Choice: the Future for Pensions' (Cm 2594, June 1994).

[60] See paras 57–59 of Sch 12.

8.80 It is not clear whether or not the 'entitlement or right' of a member will include the potential benefits of the relevant secondary beneficiaries. It seems likely that the intention behind the change in wording was to catch pension credits granted to an ex-spouse following a divorce sharing order,[61] but the change may be construed as going further than this.[62] The better view is that, even under the changed wording, if a member commits a relevant act (eg a crime) and has his or her pension forfeited, this also operates to forfeit any pension payable to the member's spouse and dependants.

Conclusion in Relation to the Statutory Framework

8.81 Aside from the potential change made to the lien provision, the statutory framework clearly identifies the member as the primary beneficiary. It gives only limited rights to secondary beneficiaries (and then generally only after the member's death). This is a strong argument supporting the dependent nature of the rights of the secondary beneficiary.

8.82 Against this, it can be argued that the rights of secondary beneficiaries can arise under relatively old deeds. It is not uncommon for a scheme to have been established many years ago, well before the modern wave of legislation (starting with the Social Security Act 1973). How can those rights be considered against a later legislative framework?[63]

8.83 There are two responses to this point:

(a) first, the legislative framework is an illustration of how the legislature perceived pension schemes to operate. Hence it is evidence of the instinctive view mentioned above;

(b) secondly, some of the rights granted (in particular the transfer out right now in the Pension Schemes Act 1993) are overriding and affect all members. Even if the secondary beneficiaries previously had greater rights, they have been changed by the later legislation.

What are the arguments against?

8.84 The secondary beneficiaries are clearly beneficiaries of the trust. Indeed, that is probably one reason why the trust structure has been used (to get around problems that used to exist with privity of contract). As such the presumption should be that they are entitled to all the protections available to beneficiaries. It would be a radical shift in trust law to reduce or remove those rights.

8.85 Even in relation to the employment contract, it is less obviously the case that the secondary beneficiaries do not have rights against the employer. Since the passing of the Contracts (Rights of Third Parties) Act 1999, it has been possible for the employer and the employee to agree as part of the employment contract to confer direct benefits on third parties such as secondary beneficiaries. If they have done this in a way that complies with the Act, the secondary beneficiaries will be able to enforce these rights against the employer.[64] If such

---

[61] See the explanatory notes to the amending legislation, the Welfare Reform and Pensions Act 1999.

[62] See Warren J in *IBM United Kingdom Pensions Trust v IBM United Kingdom Holdings Ltd* [2012] EWHC 2766 (Ch) at [463]–[474].

[63] See Lord Hoffmann in *International Power v Healy* [2001] UKHL 20, [2001] 2 All ER 417 at [55] on not construing deed provisions by reference to later amendments.

[64] There is an exclusion in s 6(3)(a) of the 1999 Act that rights cannot be granted so as to be enforceable against the employee by third parties. However, this does not prevent rights being enforceable against the employer by third parties.

third party rights have been created they cannot be rescinded or varied etc save in compliance with the 1999 Act (eg through an express variation provision in the contract itself or where the court considers that the whereabouts of the third party cannot reasonably be ascertained or he is mentally incapable).[65]

Is it a protection for the trustees or the employer if the amendment power in the trust deed **8.86** allows for amendments with the consent of the member? If trustee consent is needed as well, it begs the question about whether the trustees should give their consent if the amendment could adversely affect the secondary beneficiaries even if the member has consented. Schemes which require the consent of all affected persons before accrued rights can be changed are in even more difficulty!

Case Law

What then does the case law say? How have the judges dealt with this issue? **8.87**

Saunders v Vautier

Clearly, classic trust law envisages that the secondary beneficiaries are contingent beneficiaries— **8.88** with all that implies. For example, any attempt to vary the trust (not relying on an express amendment power) would mean that the consent of all adult beneficiaries, including contingent beneficiaries, would be needed. This is the rule in *Saunders v Vautier*.[66]

The Court of Appeal looked at this in relation to a small pension scheme—see *Thorpe v* **8.89** *Revenue and Customs Commissioners*.[67] This case involved a sole member claiming to terminate a scheme. This was challenged by the Revenue and it was held that *Saunders v Vautier* did not apply because of the interests of the secondary beneficiaries.

In some circumstances, if there are beneficiaries who cannot give their consent (eg if they are **8.90** minors) the court may be able to give consent on their behalf under the Variation of Trusts Act 1958.

Pension schemes are different

Chapter 2 (Pensions trusts and general trust law) looks at whether pension schemes should **8.91** be treated differently to private family trusts on this point?

Arguments in favour of a differing approach for pension trusts draw support from the **8.92** decision of the House of Lords in *Target Holdings v Redferns*.[68] This is not a pension case. However, Lord Browne-Wilkinson stated:[69]

> Even if the equitable rules developed in relation to traditional trusts were directly applicable to such a case as this, as I have sought to show, a beneficiary becoming absolutely entitled to a trust fund has no automatic right to have the fund reconstituted in all circumstances. Thus, even applying the strict rules so developed in relation to traditional trusts, it seems to me very doubtful whether Target is now entitled to have the trust fund reconstituted. But in my

---

[65] See s 2 of the Contracts (Rights of Third Parties) Act 1999.
[66] (1841) Cr & Ph 240. See Ch 16 (*Saunders v Vautier*).
[67] [2010] EWCA Civ 339, [2010] STC 964, CA.
[68] [1996] AC 421, HL.
[69] [1996] AC 421 at 435.

judgment it is in any event wrong to lift wholesale the detailed rules developed in the context of traditional trusts and then seek to apply them to trusts of quite a different kind. In the modern world the trust has become a valuable device in commercial and financial dealings. The fundamental principles of equity apply as much to such trusts as they do to the traditional trusts in relation to which those principles were originally formulated. But in my judgment it is important, if the trust is not to be rendered commercially useless, to distinguish between the basic principles of trust law and those specialist rules developed in relation to traditional trusts which are applicable only to such trusts and the rationale of which has no application to trusts of quite a different kind.

8.93 Are the rights of secondary beneficiaries part of the 'fundamental principles of equity' within this quote?

8.94 Lord Browne-Wilkinson was clearly indicating that the courts should be relatively flexible in construing commercial trusts. There may well be certain circumstances where the classic trust doctrines are inapplicable. I consider that this is one of those cases.

8.95 This is one of the circumstances where the court should take such a flexible attitude. To do so would fit in better with how people instinctively regard pension trusts.

South West Trains

8.96 The most relevant case in this area is the decision of Neuberger J (as he then was) in *South West Trains Ltd v Wightman*.[70]

8.97 This case involved an amendment to the contract of employment between the employer and the employee. A change was agreed between the employer and the relevant trade union representing the member train drivers. This was approved by a ballot of the train drivers.

8.98 Part of the change agreed was the restructuring of the contract of employment so that some allowances were consolidated into basic pay. It was appreciated by the employer at the time that this could raise potential problems in relation to the pension scheme as the allowances were currently non-pensionable, but the scheme rules envisaged that all basic pay would be pensionable.

8.99 Accordingly, special provision was made for the changes to the contract of employment to include an express agreement that the element of basic pay representing the consolidated allowances would only be pensionable for future service (from the date of the change). Thus basic pay would form two parts. Current basic pay and the new allowance basic pay. Current basic pay would be pensionable for all service, but the allowance-based basic pay would only be pensionable for future service (ie pensionable service before the date of the change would not be a factor in relation to the allowance basic pay).

8.100 This change was part of the package of changes agreed to the contract of employment. But when the employer asked the trustees to amend the pension scheme to reflect the agreement, the change was disputed by various members. Accordingly, an application was made to the court as to whether it was proper for the trustees to agree to amend the trust to reflect the benefit structure agreed in the contract of employment.

---

[70] [1997] OPLR 249, [1998] PLR 113 (Neuberger J). See also Ch 15 (Contract overriding trust: *South West Trains*).

Various groups of beneficiary were joined as representative beneficiaries. These included **8.101** a member representing all other members of the scheme (and secondary beneficiaries for them) who had not agreed to the restructuring. They were affected on the basis that unless the changes were made, the scheme would be in financial difficulty.

The train drivers, as the members whose contracts had been changed, were one class. Also **8.102** joined, as a separate class, were the spouses and other secondary beneficiaries of this group of members. They were represented by Mrs Wightman, the wife of the member representing the train drivers. However, she had the same legal representation as Mr Wightman, the member representing the train drivers.

Ultimately, the decision turned on: **8.103**

(a) whether the change to the pension benefits was binding on the members as having properly been incorporated into the contract of employment (answer: yes);
(b) whether the amendments were contrary to s 67 of the Pensions Act 1995 (answer: the 1995 Act did not apply because the amendments had been agreed in the contract of employment before 6 April 1997); and
(c) whether the amendments contravened specific protection legislation for the railway pension scheme (answer: no).

Unfortunately one of the issues, namely whether the member could validly agree to a reduc- **8.104** tion of benefits even though the spouse and secondary beneficiaries had not agreed, was not addressed in the judgment. Neuberger J merely noted (at 274):

> **Dependants**
>
> It will be recalled that Mrs Wightman was joined as second defendant; this was in order to represent all the dependants of the drivers. I have not dealt with the provisions of the [schemes and the railway legislation] relating to dependants of employees, but, as one would expect, they are all concerned to give or protect pension rights not merely of employees, but also of their dependants. Mr Etherton [counsel for the train drivers and their dependants] has accepted that any conclusions which I reach on the four questions which I have determined apply equally to the drivers' dependants as they do to drivers, and accordingly it is unnecessary to consider that aspect further.

This case supports the view that spouses and secondary beneficiaries do *not* have a claim. If **8.105** they really did have such a claim, then it would have been pushed harder in the *South West Trains* case.

Estoppel cases: *Icarus* and *Engineering Training Authority*

In *South West Trains*, Neuberger J also mentioned[71] the estoppel cases, *Icarus (Hertford) v* **8.106** *Driscoll*[72] and *Engineering Training Authority v Pensions Ombudsman*.[73] Neuberger J mentioned these cases when summarizing the argument of counsel for the other (non-driver) members that it could be said to have been assumed in these cases that a contract with the member would effectively bind the trustee.

In *Icarus*, the employer issued an announcement in 1978 that the accrual rate under the **8.107** scheme would reduce for future service (the scheme ceased to be contracted-out from 1/60th

---

[71] At 271.
[72] [1990] PLR 1 (Aldous J).
[73] [1996] OPLR 167, [1996] PLR 409 (Carnwath J).

or 1/80th to 1/270th and that members would cease to contribute. No formal amendment was ever made to the scheme deeds, so when the scheme came to be wound-up the trustee wanted to know whether benefits should be payable as envisaged under the deed (the higher rate) or at the lower rate envisaged in the announcement.

8.108 Aldous J held that the announcement should apply. He stated (at para 15) that:

> All the parties to the scheme, namely the plaintiff, the Prudential and the members, have since 1978 proceeded on the basis that the rate of accrual was 1/270th and they cannot now go back on it. Further I believe it would not be unjust or unfair to hold them to that. In fact it would be odd for me to decide that the rate was 1/60th or 1/80th when all the parties had accepted and worked on the basis that it was 1/270th.

8.109 *Icarus* supports the member priority view. Clearly the announcement would not have been given to the secondary beneficiaries. Yet they were, in effect bound by the acquiescence and agreement of the members. The point about the existence of the secondary beneficiaries is not raised expressly in the judgment, but it is clear that Aldous J was aware that there were such benefits and potential beneficiaries. He mentions the existence of widow's annuities (see para 3) and goes on to make a representation order (at para 29) covering secondary beneficiaries as follows:

> Finally I have to decide whether it be right to order that a defendant be appointed to represent all persons other than the plaintiff [ie the employer/trustee] who may be or become beneficiaries under the trust of the scheme. I have had the advantage of argument from counsel for the plaintiff and the defendant and I believe this is a proper action to which to make the representation order sought. The potential beneficiaries are numerous and it would not be reasonable for them to all be joined as defendants. I believe that the matters raised under the originating summons are proper to decide as between the plaintiff and the defendant in a representative capacity.

8.110 In *Engineering Training Authority* the employer decided to make an employee, Mr Stubbs, redundant. The redundancy would take effect a few months before Mr Stubbs' 50th birthday. Mr Stubbs pointed out to the employer that he would get enhanced benefits if he was allowed to stay in employment until age 50. An agreement was reached between Mr Stubbs and the employer that Mr Stubbs would remain as an employee until after his 50th birthday (although not actually working for most of that time), would receive an ex gratia lump sum and would then retire on an immediate pension slightly in excess of £10,000 pa. This £10,000 figure was an immediate pension (ie with no actuarial reduction for early payment), but it did not reflect an enhancement (of 6⅔rds added years) that was envisaged by the pension scheme rules for members retiring by reason of redundancy over age 50.

8.111 After he retired, Mr Stubbs brought a claim before the pensions ombudsman that he was entitled to the extra pension attributable to the 6⅔rds added years under the rules. The ombudsman agreed with the claim, holding that Mr Stubbs was entitled to the added years under the rules, given that he had not expressly waived the added years element.

8.112 Carnwath J overturned this ruling. He held that the agreement between Mr Stubbs and the employer was intended to cover the added years point.[74] Carnwath J held[75]:

> Mr Stubbs understood that the calculation was based on his accepting a pension without the 6⅔ years' enhancement. That was confirmed in his letter to the Ombudsman. His complaint

---

[74] Contrast Jonathan Parker J in *Spooner v British Telecommunications plc* [2000] OPLR 189.
[75] At 175E.

was not that the agreement had been misconstrued, but that he had been 'coerced' into signing it.

In effect then the member's agreement was held to bind the trustees and hence the secondary **8.113** beneficiaries (although no such secondary beneficiaries are mentioned). However, this point does not seem to have been argued. Earlier, counsel for the ombudsman had agreed that if the agreement had this effect, then the employer could not be compelled to contribute to fund for the added years and the trustees could not be accountable to Mr Stubbs.

Seifert

There is also the rather difficult Court of Appeal decision in *Seifert v Pensions Ombudsman*.[76] **8.114** This involved a claim by an individual about his pension benefits. He had left employment and then received a misleading quotation from a director of the employer (also a trustee) about the level of benefits he could be expected to receive if he took immediate early retirement. Accordingly, he delayed his decision until the point was sorted out. However, in the interim, the employer went into insolvent winding up, as did the scheme. The priority order under the scheme meant that the individual would have had a better claim if he had been a current pensioner than he did as being a deferred pensioner. The individual complained to the Ombudsman who upheld the claim and ordered that he should receive a pension as though he had been a current pensioner. This was overturned by Lightman J in the High Court, but the decision of the Ombudsman was reinstated by the Court of Appeal.

This is a difficult decision. It is difficult to see why the Court of Appeal felt that the trustees **8.115** to the pension scheme (now an independent trustee) were bound by a misleading statement made apparently by the employer (or perhaps by individuals in their capacity as previous trustees) to the employee. Perhaps it can be argued that the case is authority for the fact that arrangements or relationships between the employer and the employee can be binding on the trustees. This judgment is not very satisfactory.

Commonwealth Cases

In various commonwealth cases, the courts have looked at situations where member consent **8.116** for a proposal (eg to change the trust or refund surplus) is required. Generally they have looked for the consent of all the members and all spouses (or at least an overwhelming majority of them). The courts have approved proposals even where not all members have agreed. This is based on the relevant variation of trust legislation in each jurisdiction. This seems to give greater powers to the courts than the equivalent in England and Wales, the Variation of Trusts Act 1958.

Canada: *Sandwell, Bentall, Continental Lime*, and *Buschau*

There are various cases from British Columbia that could be seen as giving some insight. **8.117** They relate to an application to the court to approve an amendment to a pension scheme to allow a negotiated package to go ahead. The package involved using surplus to increase benefits, together with a refund of surplus to the employer (even though the refund was contrary to the trust instrument). The package was agreed to by most of the plan members (but

---

[76] [1997] OPLR 395, CA.

not all). The application to court was to approve the package under the British Columbian equivalent of the English Variation of Trusts Act 1958.

8.118 In *Re Sandwell & Co Ltd and Royal Trust Corpn of Canada*[77] there was a substantially over-funded defined benefit plan.[78] There was no requirement that the surplus be used to increase the benefits of the participants. In the ordinary course it could remain in the fund, offsetting the need for future contributions by the employer, but on termination the surplus would belong to the remaining participants and would be divided pro rata among them.

8.119 All active and retired participants consented to the proposal to use the surplus to enhance the benefits of the participants and refund to the employer any surplus remaining after enhancing the benefits, so long as the refunded balance did not exceed the amount applied to enhance the benefits of the participants. Court approval was necessary because there was a class of potential participants known as 'contingent beneficiaries' who were unascertained, and in some cases unborn.

8.120 Approval was granted by the Court of Appeal on the basis that, since this arrangement appeared to be of benefit to the groups being considered, this was just the type of situation for which the Trust Variation Act was intended.

8.121 Carrothers JA for the court said:[79]

> The interest of a contingent beneficiary is dependent upon participation in the plan by the participant through whom that uncertain interest is derived. By the same token, the uncertain interest of the contingent beneficiary is perforce enhanced along with the enhancement of the pension benefits to the participant through whom the interest derives. The interest of a contingent beneficiary is in succession to the participant and is for the most part the result of a designation by that participant. The interest of a contingent beneficiary is dependent upon an uncertain event or condition which may never happen or be performed, or which may not happen or be performed until after the exhaustion or extinction of the pension benefits.
>
> In my view the potential interests of the contingent beneficiaries are so remote and uncertain that it is unreasonable and unnecessary that an attempt be made to consult them about the new plan. The consent of the participants in whose shoes they may ultimately stand is enough.

8.122 These comments support my view. However, it should be noted that they are expressed in the context of an application to court for approval by the court under the relevant legislation. It could be argued that this statement is really meant as a guide to whether or not the court should agree to a variation under the statutory power.

8.123 In *Re Versatile Pacific Shipyards and Royal Trust Corpn of Canada*[80] the members did not unanimously approve the proposed variation which would have given the members half of the large surplus with the other half going to the company. The company was in serious financial difficulty and some of the company's portion of the surplus was to be used for severance pay. The surplus, on termination, would belong to the members, but the decision whether to terminate rested entirely with the employer.

---

[77] (1985) 17 DLR (4th) 337 (BCCA).

[78] This description is taken from the judgment of Sigurdson J in the later *Bentall* case—see below.

[79] At 341.

[80] (1991) 84 DLR (4th) 761 (BCSC). Again this description is taken from the judgment of Sigurdson J in the later *Bentall* case—see below.

Chief Justice Esson did approve the variation but the question of the court's jurisdiction to vary the trust in these circumstances was not argued or discussed. He said:[81]   **8.124**

> The court appointed Royal Trust, which had been trustee of the fund for some years, to also be representative of the members who agreed to the settlement and to advise the court. Some 90% or more of the present members have approved the settlement in writing. They represent substantially more than 90% of the fund's obligations.
>
> There clearly will be a benefit to them if the settlement goes through in that there will be a substantial increase in their entitlement. In return, of course, they will lose whatever chance there might be of benefiting from the distribution of the full surplus if that were ever to come about, but for reasons made clear in the material and in the submissions, that seems to be a most remote contingency. The practical truth seems to be that there would be a real risk of the surplus being used in other ways of no benefit to the current members who I think are the persons whose interests should be given the greatest weight here.

In *Bentall Corpn v Canada Trust Co* (1996) 26 BCLR (3d) 181, (1996) 13 CCPB 77 Sigurdson   **8.125**
J allowed the application. Only seven out of the 279 members in the plan did not positively consent to the proposal.

Sigurdson J considered that the court had power to approve the package on behalf of the   **8.126**
non-consenting members. This was on the basis that the Canadian statute (unlike the English Act) allowed the court to consent on behalf of contingent beneficiaries (and the members were held to be contingent beneficiaries in relation to any claim to surplus).

There is no mention in the judgment about secondary beneficiaries (perhaps there were none   **8.127**
under the plan or their interests were seen as the same as the relevant member).

In *Continental Lime v Canada Trust Co*,[82] Shaw J followed *Bentall* and agreed to a similar   **8.128**
proposal. This time only one out of the 90 members failed to consent in writing. The Public Trustee opposed the proposal on behalf of contingent beneficiaries who may be minors or persons as yet unborn or incapacitated individuals.

In *Buschau v Rogers Cablesystems*,[83] Newbury JA touched on the *Saunders v Vautier* issue.   **8.129**
He stated

> It may even be that the requirements of *Saunders v Vautier* cannot be met if the Premier Plan is considered on its own, since there may be contingent beneficiaries—for example, the heirs and family members of deceased employees—whose consent may not be obtained. But that question is not before us.

In *Buschau v Rogers Cablesystems*[84] on appeal to the Supreme Court, it was held that *Saunders*   **8.130**
v Vautier did not apply to a pension scheme. Partly this was because of the legislation, but partly it was on the basis of the secondary beneficiaries having not consented.

New Zealand: *Philips* and *Capral*

Re Philips New Zealand Ltd[85] is also a case involving the universal consent of the members.   **8.131**
In *Philips* the issue was agreement to a refund of surplus to the company. This was prohibited

---

[81] At 762.
[82] (1998) 19 CCPB 160 (1998) 4 December (Shaw J). Available on the web at <http://www.courts.gov.
bc.ca>.
[83] (2001) 26 CCPB 47, BCCA.
[84] 2006 SCC 28, (2006) 9 ITELR 73 Canadian Supreme Court. See Ch 16 (*Saunders v Vautier*).
[85] [1997] 1 NZLR 93, (1996) 1 NZSC 40,368 (Baragwanath J).

by the scheme rules. Baragwanath J held that such a refund was, however, allowed with the unanimous consent of all the members. It seems from the judgment that there were in fact no benefits under the scheme to secondary beneficiaries. Baragwanath J distinguished the earlier case of *Re Lyell*[86] on that ground.

8.132 The later case of *Capral Fiduciary Ltd v Ladd*[87] was on similar facts. Here, however, there were secondary (presumably death) benefits. Consent had been obtained from all the members and from the current spouse of each member.

8.133 Nicholson J referred to the *Philips* case and held that he could give consent to the proposal on behalf of all future spouses. He had power to do this under s 64A of the Trustee Act 1956, the equivalent in New Zealand of the UK Variation of Trusts Act 1958 provided the court was satisfied that the proposal was not to their detriment.

8.134 Nicholson J considered that a future spouse would be likely to have consented to the proposal. The proposal clearly benefited the member and so hence the family unit, including any potential future spouse. He stated:[88]

> The only likelihood of the pensions and other benefits abating is if Capral were to cease to exist or become insolvent. All concerned obviously consider this to be extremely unlikely. Benefit of the proposed distribution of surplus may accrue to future spouses indirectly by improving the welfare of the families to which these future spouses will belong.

8.135 There is no mention of benefits for children or other dependants (perhaps these benefits were not provided). In any event the same analysis would apply.

8.136 Nicholson J also held that there was no need to obtain consent from the members of the class to whom the lump sum death benefit could be distributed. These were discretionary beneficiaries—they would only receive a benefit if the trustees exercised a discretion in their favour.[89] He went on to hold that even if consent were needed, he would give it under the same statutory power.[90]

8.137 Both *Sandwell* and *Capral* clearly can be seen as giving some support to the member priority argument (that the consent of a spouse or other contingent beneficiary is not needed).

8.138 However, they do not do this expressly. Instead, the judges were able (by virtue of a statutory power) to give consent on behalf of the potential future spouses etc, so the end result was the same. There is no mention in the judgments of the argument (that the members' consent was all that was needed) having been raised. Presumably then it was not. How would the judges have reacted if it had?

Conclusion

8.139 This chapter only seeks to examine one particular aspect of the pension relationship. The actual rights of any secondary beneficiary will depend on the circumstances that are involved.

---

[86] [1977] 1 NZLR 713.
[87] (1999) 1 NZSC 40,455 (Nicholson J).
[88] At 40,460.
[89] Citing *Re Beckett's Settlement* [1940] 1 Ch 279 and *Gartside v IRC* [1968] AC 553.
[90] See *Underhill and Hayton: Law of Trusts and Trustees* 18th edn, ed David Hayton, Paul Matthews, and Charles Mitchell (LexisNexis, 2010) 477 for a discussion of a broadly similar issue under the English Variation of Trusts Act 1958.

Three situations must be distinguished:	**8.140**

(a) where the member has a right to do something (under the trust deed or statute);
(b) where the trustees have a discretion and wish to exercise it in the interests of the member (but not necessarily the secondary beneficiaries);
(c) where the member's consent is being sought for something that would otherwise be a breach of trust.

Where the member has a right to do something

In the first case, provided the power was properly granted, the member's consent or direction is something on which the trustees are forced to act. Examples are: **8.141**

(a) a choice by the member over the level of employee contributions (including voluntary contributions);
(b) a decision by the member not to join the scheme or to opt-out of membership.[91]
(c) agreement between the employer and employee about the level of future remuneration or a decision by the employee to resign employment;
(d) a transfer request under the cash equivalent provisions in the Pension Schemes Act 1993;
(e) a direction about investment of money purchase reference assets (if this right is given to the member under the trust deed);
(f) an election to commute pension on retirement (again if this is a right given to the member under the trust deed).

The trustees have no discretion.[92] They do not have to consider the interests of the secondary beneficiaries. The trustees are, in effect under a duty to act once the direction has been given. Seemingly, they do not have any duty to look to see whether the consent is properly informed etc.[93] **8.142**

Where the trustees have a discretion or power and wish to exercise it in the interests of the member (but not necessarily the secondary beneficiaries)

In the second case, the question is how the trustees exercise the discretion they have been given. **8.143**

Examples are: **8.144**

(a) agreeing to changes in the benefit structure;
(b) distributing the lump sum death benefit;
(c) agreeing to a surplus refund as part of a package of benefits (if there is power to do this under the trust deed).

---

[91] Membership cannot be made compulsory under the contract of employment—s 160 of the Pension Schemes Act 1993. For an example see *Gorham v British Telecommunications* [2000] 4 All ER 867, CA, mentioned at para 8.37 above.

[92] See eg *Pikos Holdings (Northern Territory) Pty Ltd v Territory Homes Pty Ltd* [1997] NTSC 30 (Kearney J), noted in (1998) 12 TLI 44, where Kearney J (in the Supreme Court of the Northern Territory of Australia) held the trustee of a unit trust to be in breach of trust when it failed to call a meeting of unit holders following a requisition by the 20 per cent required under the trust deed. It was no defence that the trustee considered that a meeting would not be in the best interests of the unit holders.

[93] The position may be different if the trustees are aware that the member is under some sort of disability (eg mentally incapable). In the US in *Sladek v Bell System Management Pension Plan* 880 F.2d 972 (7th Cir 1989) it was held that a wife remained a beneficiary even though the member had elected for a single life annuity. It was claimed that the member was suffering from Alzheimer's disease at the time of the election.

8.145 In many cases the interests of the member will not differ markedly from the interests of the secondary beneficiaries, as part of the family unit. For example in *Capral Fiduciary*, Nicholson J held that the changes there would benefit the family unit (including future spouses) and so could be approved by the court.

8.146 In other cases, the interests of the member and the secondary beneficiaries can diverge. For example:

(a) if the member has given an expression of wishes to trustees in relation to a death benefit; or

(b) if the member asks the trustees to agree to take away a benefit for a particular secondary beneficiary.

8.147 In these cases, it seems to me to be legitimate and proper for the trustees to exercise the discretion in the interests of the *member*. Ultimately I think it is right that the courts should construe pension trusts so that the primary rights are given to the member as opposed to the secondary beneficiaries.

8.148 In many cases it may be very difficult to get the consent of the current spouse,[94] let alone future spouses (and infant children).

8.149 It is clear that discretions must be exercised for the purpose for which they were given and not for a collateral or improper purpose. It is not necessary to treat all beneficiaries equally when exercising such a discretion—see the decision of the Court of Appeal in *Edge v Pensions Ombudsman*.[95]

8.150 The primary purpose of a pension scheme is to provide benefits for the member, not the secondary beneficiaries. The secondary beneficiaries' rights are derived from the member and secondary to those of the member.

8.151 If this is right, the trustees will be protected (from a breach of trust claim) if they exercise their discretion with the member's approval.

8.152 This line is supported by the Canadian and New Zealand cases. In effect the courts there were being asked to use their statutory powers to agree to a variation of a trust. They did so on the basis that it would benefit the member and hence the secondary beneficiaries. In *Re Sandwell*,[96] Carrothers JA was explicit about this:

> In my view the potential interests of the contingent beneficiaries are so remote and uncertain that it is unreasonable and unnecessary that an attempt be made to consult them about the new plan. The consent of the participants in whose shoes they may ultimately stand is enough.

8.153 Although the point was not argued, the end result in *South West Trains v Wightman* also supports this view.

---

[94] See the issues surrounding bank consent obtained by banks, recently discussed by the House of Lords in *Royal Bank of Scotland v Etridge (No 2)* [2001] UKHL 44, [2002] 2 AC 773.

[95] [2000] Ch 602. See also the discussion in Ch 9 and the articles by Edward Nugee QC, 'The Duties of Pension Scheme Trustees to the Employer' (1998) 12 TLI 216 and SEK Hulme QC, 'The Basic Duties of Trustees of Superannuation Trusts—Fair to One, Fair to All?' (2000) 14 TLI 130.

[96] (1985) 17 DLR (4th) 337 (BCCA).

Where the member's consent is being sought for something that would otherwise be a breach of trust

In the third case, can the trustees rely on the consent of the member as a defence to what would otherwise be a breach of trust? **8.154**

Examples would be: **8.155**

(a) acting in a manner not allowed by the trust deed (eg agreeing a package with the employer involving a refund of surplus where this is not allowed by the trust deed); or

(b) exercising a discretion or power improperly (eg for an improper purpose or without proper consideration).

In practice the second example above is really the same as the second case just discussed about how trustees exercise their discretions. Given my view of the primary purpose of the trust, the consent or approval of the member should be enough here. **8.156**

In practice then this third case is limited to cases where the amendment power in the trust deed is not wide enough to allow the action proposed (or it has not been complied with). Such cases often relate to surplus refunds. **8.157**

The nature of a pension trust is such that only the consent of the member is needed, even for such an action ultra vires the trust. However, this is a step away from traditional trust principles. It is also difficult to point to any clear case authority for such a step. The Canadian and New Zealand cases point a bit of the way, but (it will no doubt be argued) are in the context of the exercise of a statutory amendment power. So they are more like case two situations (relating to the exercise of a discretion or power). **8.158**

South West Trains v Wightman looks (at least in its end result) as the clearest authority for the view that member consent is all that is needed. However, even here, the main issue was whether the trustee should be agreeing to the exercise of the amendment power in the circumstance. So it is arguably a class two case as well. And in any event, as I have pointed out, the issue of the rights of the secondary beneficiaries was not argued before the court. **8.159**

If this would otherwise be a breach of trust, it seems that the trustee is in effect relying on a form or waiver or estoppel by the beneficiary affected (ie here the member). It may be that informed consent is needed from the member.[97] **8.160**

Even if the consent of the member does not bind the secondary beneficiaries, it should be noted that, if the member has given his consent, this (seemingly even if not fully informed) could give rise to an implied indemnity to the trustees if there is subsequently a claim for breach of trust (eg by a secondary beneficiary affected). This is the rule in *Hardoon v Belilios*.[98] **8.161**

This rule has been applied in a pensions context in *Independent Trustee Services v Rowe*.[99] Jonathan Parker J held that the principle was not confined to bare trusts but extended to a beneficiary of a small self-administered pension scheme. The beneficiary here was the sole member, but not the sole beneficiary, as his wife was a contingent beneficiary. The three trustees were the member, his wife, and an independent pensioneer trustee. The member **8.162**

---

[97] See the discussion of this in Art 95 in *Underhill and Hayton: Law of Trusts and Trustees* (2010) 1214.
[98] [1901] AC 118, PC.
[99] [1998] OPLR 77 (Jonathan Parker J). See also Ch 14 (Trustee indemnities and exonerations).

considered that the trustees had received some bad investment advice. Accordingly, at the member's request, the trustees had sued the adviser. This meant that all three trustees were personally liable for costs if the action was lost. Jonathan Parker J held that the pensioneer trustee in these circumstances was entitled to a personal indemnity from the member (but interestingly not from his wife) should the costs ultimately payable be greater than those that could be recovered from the available fund in the trust.

8.163 It is commonly said that pension trusts are deferred pay, and that the members are not volunteers. But this is not the case in relation to the secondary beneficiaries. They clearly take their rights only by virtue of their relationship to the member. As such it seems only right that they should be bound by decisions of the member.

9

TRUSTEE POWERS—BEST INTERESTS OR PROPER PURPOSE?

Introduction

This chapter[1] considers the scope of the exercise of discretions and powers by trustees of **9.1** defined benefit occupational pension schemes. Chapter 10 then goes on to look at whether or not the trustees have a duty to consider the interests of the employer.

This chapter (and Chapter 10) build on the seminal articles on this topic[2] by: **9.2**

(a) Edward Nugee QC in 1998: the duties of pension scheme trustees to the employer[3]; and

(b) the Australian, SEK Hulme QC in 2000: 'The Basic Duties of Trustees of Super-annuation Trusts—Fair to One, Fair to All?'.[4]

Pension Schemes as Trusts

As discussed in Chapter 2 (Pension schemes and general trust law), in the private sector by **9.3** far the vast bulk of the assets held by occupational pension schemes is held within trusts. This means that there are trustees with duties and responsibilities under trust law.

---

[1] An earlier version was published in (2006) 20 TLI 21. An even earlier paper was given at the annual conference of the Society of Pension Consultants (SPC) in 2004.

[2] See Xenia Frostick, 'Is There a Duty to Act in the Best Interests of Beneficiaries?' (2000) 83 Pension Lawyer 2 and Geraint Thomas, 'The Duty of Trustees to Act in the "Best Interest" of Their Benficiaries' (2008) 2 J Eq 177. In Australia, see Michael Vrisakis, 'The Best Test of (or the "Bestest") Interests of Members' (2006) 17(9) Superannuation Law Bulletin 138 and M Scott Donald, 'Best Interests?' (2008) 2 J Eq 245.

[3] (1998) 12 TLI 216, based on his 1998 lecture to the Association of Pension Lawyers (APL).

[4] (2000) 14 TLI 130.

What is the legislative background?

9.4 Trust instruments and, increasingly, statute, give various powers to pension trustees. The nature of the powers and duties of trustees must be considered in the light of what the settlor (here including the employer as the founder of the trusts) and Parliament can be considered to have intended.

9.5 Of major importance recently have been the powers and duties under the Pensions Acts 1995 and 2004, in particular:

(a) **Investment:** provision for trustees to fix the statement of investment principles (in consultation with the employers). Any requirement for employer consent is over-ridden (s 35 of the Pensions Act 1995);

(b) **Ongoing funding:** provisions for trustees to agree on scheme specific funding etc (in agreement with the employers unless (broadly) the trust instrument gives the power to fix contributions to the trustees already). If agreement is not reached, the Pensions Regulator has power to decide (ss 221–233 of the Pensions Act 2004); and

(c) **Termination funding:** An obligation on employers to fund the pension scheme on various termination events (eg scheme winding-up, employer entry into formal insolvency proceedings, employer ceasing to participate in a multi-employer scheme) (s 75 of the Pensions Act 1995, as amended). Trustees are also given power to allocate the resulting debt obligation between the employers (s 68 of the Pensions Act 1995).

Role of trustees

9.6 Employers and Parliament have chosen to use the trust structure for many pension schemes. Clearly in using a trust structure, they must have intended that the duties and obligations of the trustees should follow the obligations established by court decisions over the centuries.[5] Parliament has not chosen to lay down any rules defining how trustees generally (or pension trustees specifically) should exercise their powers.[6]

9.7 Once appointed, it is clear that trustees are not delegates of their appointors (whether employers or members). Instead they must exercise their duties and discretions as independent office holders (and not exercise their powers following instructions or directions from a third party).[7]

9.8 Clearly, trustees owe fiduciary (and other) duties to the beneficiaries of the trust. A settlor does not generally have power to enforce the trust. In his article 'Developing the Obligation

---

[5] See Ch 2.

[6] Contrast directors where the Companies Act 2006 (ss 170–181) codifies directors' duties (to a degree) and the position of superannuation funds in Australia, where s 52 of the Superannuation Industry (Supervision) Act 1993 (SIS) enacts a general duty on trustees:

> 52.2 (1) If the governing rules of a superannuation entity do not contain covenants to the effect of the covenants set out in subsection (2), those governing rules are taken to contain covenants to that effect.
>
> (2) The covenants referred to in subsection (1) are the following covenants by the trustee:
>
> (c) to ensure that the trustee's duties and powers are performed and exercised in the best interests of the beneficiaries.

[7] See eg *Kuwait Asia Bank EC v National Mutual Life Nominees Ltd* [1991] 1 AC 187, PC holding that an appointor of a nominee director was not vicariously liable for the acts of the appointee. The same position should apply for trustees.

Characteristic of the Trust',[8] Professor David Hayton argued that 'protectors' appointed by the settlor should be able to enforce a trust, having summarized the orthodox view:

The orthodox view: trusts need beneficiaries to enforce them

Of course, in English trust law as Lord Millett has stated,[9] 'It is elementary that a settlor who retains no beneficial interest cannot enforce the trust which he has created.' Once the settlor has unilaterally transferred his entire interest in particular property to his trustee this is regarded as amounting to the complete fulfilment of his purposes, so that he drops out of the picture.[10] Into the picture come the beneficiaries for whose benefit the trustee is to own and manage the trust property and who have equitable proprietary interests which enable them to trace the trust property and claim an equitable lien over any exchange product or an equitable proportionate ownership interest in such product. The trust has thus developed from a repository of the settlor's wishes to a property receptacle providing proprietary interests for the beneficiaries.[11]

Later, having become a Law Lord, Lord Millett held in *Twinsectra Ltd v Yardley*[12] that a provider **9.9** of funds to be held for a purpose on a Quistclose trust could enforce the trust and so must have more of an interest than just being a settlor:

He cannot do so as settlor, for a settlor who retains no beneficial interest cannot enforce the trust which he has created.

The primary beneficiaries of a pensions trust are clearly the employers (see Chapter 10) **9.10** and the members of the scheme—the past and present (and potentially future) employees. Spouses and dependants of members are often secondary beneficiaries (directly benefiting only following the death of the member) and so are usually regarded as being bound by actions affecting the member.[13]

But does the class of persons who are beneficiaries limit those whose interests the trustees **9.11** should take into account?

Private trusts/pension trusts

Given the use of a trust structure and the lack of any real intervention by legislation, the posi- **9.12** tion rests on an analysis of case law. But it is less clear whether existing case law for private trusts can be taken as a realistic guide for pension trusts. As discussed in Chapter 2, in *Target Holdings v Redferns*,[14] Lord Browne-Wilkinson commented (in a now much cited passage):

But in my judgment it is in any event wrong to lift wholesale the detailed rules developed in the context of traditional trusts and then seek to apply them to trusts of quite a different kind. In the modern world the trust has become a valuable device in commercial and financial

---

[8] (2001) 117 LQR 96. Professors Matthews and Parkinson have taken issue with the views of Professor Hayton. See later Jonathan Hilliard, 'On the Irreducible Core Content of Trusteeship—A Reply to Professors Matthews and Parkinson' (2003) 17 TLI 144.

[9] When a leading Queen's Counsel, in 'The Quistclose Trust: Who Can Enforce it?' (1985) 101 LQR 269 at 287.

[10] *Re Astor's ST* [1952] Ch 534 at 542 (Roxburgh J); *Bradshaw v University College of Wales* [1988] 1 WLR 190 at 194 (Hoffmann J). Also see *Goulding v James* [1997] 2 All ER 239.

[11] RMB Cotterrell in S Goldstein (ed), *Equity and Contemporary Legal Developments* (Hebrew University of Jerusalem, 1992) 302–34. Generally, see Paul Matthews, 'The New Trust: Obligations without Rights?' in AJ Oakley (ed), *Trends in Contemporary Trust Law* (Clarendon Press, 1996).

[12] [2002] UKHL 12, [2002] 2 AC 164, HL at [96].

[13] See Ch 8 and D Pollard, 'Pension Trusts: The Position of Spouses and Dependants' (2002) 16 TLI 74.

[14] [1996] AC 421 at 435.

dealings. The fundamental principles of equity apply as much to such trusts as they do to the traditional trusts in relation to which those principles were originally formulated. But in my judgment it is important, if the trust is not to be rendered commercially useless, to distinguish between the basic principles of trust law and those specialist rules developed in relation to traditional trusts which are applicable only to such trusts and the rationale of which has no application to trusts of quite a different kind.

Why Does This Matter?—Key Trustee Powers

9.13   Fundamentally in this age of deficits rather than surpluses, pension trustees often (depending on the terms of the scheme, but with some powers fixed by statute) have key powers:

(a) to set the ongoing contribution rate from the employers;[15]

(b) to be able to veto changes proposed by the employers (eg to benefits);[16]

(c) to decide the investment policy for the assets of the scheme;[17]

(d) to wind up the scheme[18] (which usually triggers an immediate funding obligation on the employers under s 75 of the Pensions Act 1995[19]);

(e) to agree transfers-out of the scheme or to transfers-in to the scheme;

(f) to decide whether any surplus arising during the scheme's life can be repaid to the employer (s 37 of the Pensions Act 1995) or (if the trust deed so provides) on a scheme winding-up.[20]

9.14   The issue can arise in other areas. For example, the scheme rules may give a member the right to retire early (before normal retirement date). Often this will involve a decision being made as to the amount of reduction to apply to the normal pension—usually to make the early payment cost neutral in actuarial terms. Many schemes give the decision as to the amount of the reduction to the trustees to fix (perhaps using words such as 'to allow for the earlier payment').

9.15   Clearly here the purpose of the power is to be cost neutral. It is not proper for the trustees to say that no reduction is in the best interests of the member concerned and so therefore none should apply.[21] Even if the scheme is otherwise well funded (and so the other members are not directly affected in a material way), this must be the right result.

9.16   Similar issues arise in cases where (say) the trustees have the power to:

(a) reduce or terminate ill-health pensions because the member has got better;

---

[15]   Under the scheme specific funding provisions in Pt 3 of the Pensions Act 2004, ongoing funding is to be fixed by the trustees with the agreement of the employers, or in default of agreement by the Pensions Regulator (but the Scheme Funding regulations provide that the trustees retain the power to fix contributions if the trust instrument already gives them this power).

[16]   This depends on the amendment power in the trust instrument, but changes to accrued rights always require the consent of the trustees (s 67 of the Pensions Act 1995), unless there is an exemption.

[17]   Sections 34 and 35 of the Pensions Act 1995.

[18]   This depends on the terms of the scheme (but the Pensions Regulator has a statutory power to wind-up under s 11 of the Pensions Act 1995).

[19]   On s 75 debts, see D Pollard, *Corporate Insolvency: Employment and Pension Rights* 5th edn (Bloomsbury Professional, 2013) Chs 57–62.

[20]   See Ch 20 (Employers and surpluses).

[21]   See Warren J in *Re IBM Pension Plan* [2012] EWHC 2766 (Ch), at [504] (provision providing for an actuarial reduction to be applied to early retirement does not allow the trustee to apply no reduction). Contrast *Universities Superannuation Scheme Ltd v Simpson* [2004] EWHC 935 (Ch) (Lloyd J).

(b) reduce the pension payable to a surviving spouse or civil partner of a member where he or she is much younger than the member;

(c) pay a pension to a dependant of the member following the member's death;[22]

(d) allocate all or part of any surplus arising on a winding-up to the employers (instead of to provide benefit improvements for the members).[23]

Fiduciary Duty

So having decided that the pension trustees owe fiduciary duties in relation to the trust bene-   **9.17**
ficiaries, we might try to guide them in their deliberations by saying that:

> Trustees have an overriding duty to act in the best interests of the members of a pension scheme.[24]

But in fact this is much too simplistic a description of the nature of the fiduciary duties owed   **9.18**
by pension trustees. It is positively misleading in many circumstances. For example:

1. Any such duty is not overriding. If (say) the trust deed prohibited investment in land, the trustees would not have power to invest in land even in circumstances where the investment would clearly be beneficial.[25] It is not possible to point to this external overriding 'duty' to override the express terms of the trust.[26] So it is more accurate to refer to the trustees as 'exercising their powers' in a fiduciary manner.[27]

2. It begs the question as to why the members are the only ones whose interests need to be considered. There are others who are beneficiaries—for example spouses[28] and dependants of members are also usually express beneficiaries under the terms of the scheme (as contingent beneficiaries if the scheme provides for benefits to be paid to them following the death of the member). And is the employer a beneficiary?

---

[22] See eg *Brown v Singer and Friedlander Pension Scheme* (2011) 28 October, 83842/1 (Irvine Deputy PO), where the underfunded state of the scheme supported no pension being awarded.

[23] See *Thrells v Lomas* [1993] 1 WLR 456 (Nicholls V-C) and *Alexander Forbes Trustee Service Ltd v Halliwell* [2003] EWHC 1685 (Ch), [2003] OPLR 355 (Hart J) discussed in Ch 10.

[24] See eg Megarry V-C in *Cowan v Scargill* [1985] Ch 270: 'The starting point is the duty of trustees to exercise their powers in the best interests of the present and future beneficiaries of the trust, holding the scales impartially between different classes of beneficiaries. This duty of the trustees towards their beneficiaries is paramount. They must, of course, obey the law; but subject to that, they must put the interests of their beneficiaries first.'

[25] Section 34(1) of the Pensions Act 1995 gives a general power to trustees to make 'investments of any kind as if they were absolutely entitled to the assets of the scheme'. This is overriding (see s 117). But s 34 expressly states that it is 'subject to any restriction imposed by the scheme'. So it does not override any express prohibition in the trust deed.

[26] See eg in Australia, *Pikos Holdings v Territory Homes Pty Ltd* [1997] NTSC 30 (Kearney J) (discussed by Vicki Vann (1998) 12 TLI 44). A charity may in some circumstances be authorized by the court to make a payment outside its objects to meet a 'moral obligation': *Re Snowden* [1969] 3 All ER 208 (Cross J) and s 27 of the Charities Act 1993. But this does not apply to a statutory provision: *Attorney General v Trustees of the British Museum* [2005] EWHC 1089 (Ch), [2005] Ch 397 (Morritt V-C). Contrast also the powers of the Charity Commission under ss 26 and 29 of the Charities Act 1993, discussed by Mark Atkinson, 'Goalkeepers are Different. What About Pension Scheme Trustees?' (2003) 17 TLI 25 at 32.

[27] To be fair this 'exercise powers' formulation is used in many of the cases. Eg Megarry V-C in *Cowan v Scargill* [1985] Ch 270. But the judge did go on in that case to refer to this duty as being 'paramount'—whatever that means (see M Scott Donald, 'Best Interests?' (2008) 2 J Eq 245 at 252). Similarly, in *Fuller v Evans* [2000] 1 All ER 636 for example, Lightman J referred to trustees *exercising powers* in the *paramount* interests of the beneficiaries.

[28] And, from 5 December 2005, when the Civil Partnership Act 2004 came into force, registered civil partners.

3. The case law points more towards trustees being required to act for a proper purpose—this may sometimes be the same as acting in the best interests of the members, but not always.

9.19 SEK Hulme quotes[29] Lord Nicholls (speaking extra-judicially) in a talk he gave in 1995:[30]

> To decide whether a proposed course is in the best interest of the beneficiaries it is necessary to decide first what is the purpose of the trust, and what benefits were intended to be received by the beneficiaries. Thus to define the trustee's obligation in terms of acting in the best interests of the beneficiaries is to do nothing more than formulate in different words, a trustee's obligation to promote the purpose for which the trust was created.

Who is a Beneficiary?

9.20 So re-formulating the duty, it is necessary to define who is a beneficiary.[31]

9.21 Slightly oddly, it is not particularly clear how to categorize a person (real or corporate) as being a beneficiary or not under a trust.[32] The main English law practitioner text on trusts is the book *Underhill and Hayton: Law of Trusts and Trustees*.[33] But it does not try to give an all-embracing definition of the term beneficiary, other than to state in its starting definition of a trust that the beneficiaries are those for whose benefit the trustees hold the trust property.[34]

9.22 This is, of course, a crucial question:

(a) Only beneficiaries can enforce a trust.[35] Even Professor Hayton in his article is arguing that protectors (ie persons other than the settlor appointed in a private trust to exercise powers etc) should only be able to enforce a trust if the trust instrument expressly says so.

(b) If an employer counts as a beneficiary under a pension scheme then its interests need to be taken into account by the trustees. If the employer is not a beneficiary then it may be that its interests positively should not be taken into account.[36] Get the answer wrong and the decision of the trustees may well be invalid—see private trust decisions of the Court of Appeal in *Re Hastings-Bass*[37] and most recently the Supreme Court in *Pitt v HMRC*.[38]

---

[29] (2000) 14 TLI 130 at 145.

[30] Published, slightly amended, in 'Trustees and their Broader Community: Where Duty, Morality and Ethics Converge' (1996) 70 Australian Law Journal 205 at 211.

[31] Cases on who is a beneficiary include *Shaw v Lawless* (1838) 5 Cl & Fin 129, 155–6; *Finden v Stephens* (1846) 2 Ph 142; *Foster v Elsley* (1881) 19 ChD 518 (Chitty J); and *Gandy v Gandy* (1885) 30 ChD 57, CA.

[32] See eg in Australia, *Yazbek v Commissioner of Taxation* [2013] FCA 39 (Bennett J) discussing the meaning of beneficiary, concluding that an object of a discretionary power is a beneficiary.

[33] *Underhill and Hayton: Law of Trusts and Trustees* 18th edn, ed David Hayton, Paul Matthews, and Charles Mitchell (LexisNexis, 2010).

[34] Article 1.1.

[35] See the comments from Lord Millett cited by Professor Hayton in his article at [2001] 117 LQR 96 mentioned above.

[36] But the interests of the employer may be relevant if it is the settlor, even if it is not a beneficiary. The law here seems confused!

[37] [1975] Ch 25, CA.

[38] [2013] UKSC 26, SC, upholding on this the Court of Appeal [2011] EWCA Civ 197, [2012] Ch 132, CA.

The main test for a financial trust such as a pension scheme would be to consider if that person **9.23**
is or might become eligible, under the terms of the scheme,[39] to receive a benefit—ie be paid
money[40] by the trustees as a benefit. So this includes:

(a) pensioners (as current recipients of cash benefits[41]);
(b) active and deferred members (as persons with a contingent interest—dependent on
    them living long enough to have cash benefits paid to them[42]);
(c) spouses, civil partners, and dependants, who may be entitled to a cash payment or pen-
    sion following the death of a member: This may be discretionary (eg most lump sum
    death benefits) or payable as of right (eg a spouse pension in a contracted-out scheme).
    Clearly, the benefit is contingent. It is only payable if the person survives the member;
(d) prospective members (and their spouses etc): It is often said that trustees owe a duty to
    consider the interests of prospective members as well as the current members. In practice
    it is difficult to see what this duty adds, save that it is more than the current membership
    who have an interest in how the scheme is managed (so perhaps the current members
    may well not be entitled to require the trust to be wound-up[43]);
(e) trustees: This is not intuitively obvious, but it seems right that trustees can benefit by
    reason of their indemnity out of the fund (as can directors and officers if the indemnity
    extends to them as well). In *Chief Commissioner of Stamp Duties v Buckle*,[44] the High
    Court in Australia confirmed the right of trustees to be indemnified out of trust assets
    against liabilities properly incurred in the administration of the trust. It held that this
    right is not a charge or encumbrance on the trust assets, but instead is a preferred benefi-
    cial interest in the trust fund.[45]

This test is quite strict in one sense. Third parties who are affected by the actions of the trus- **9.24**
tees are (presumably) not beneficiaries. So (for example) the spouse of a member (in a scheme
which does not have any spouse benefits) presumably cannot complain about the actions of
the trustees which may adversely affect the member? It is not enough that the spouse might
reasonably expect to benefit from a payment made to the member. This feels instinctively
right—see also Chapter 8 (The position of spouses and dependants).

But this may be just a recognition that the benefits payable to a spouse or dependant are **9.25**
derived through the member. He or she is the person to whom any duties are properly owed
and who has any legally enforceable claims for breach of duty by the trustees. Perhaps there
is an analogy here with the discussion by the House of Lords on derivative claims in the

---

[39] Including where this is implied by statute—eg under a pension sharing order, or, more relevantly here,
under s 77 of the Pensions Act 1995 in favour of an employer on the winding-up of a scheme. Or where a benefit is
implied under a resulting trust—see *Air Jamaica v Charlton* [1999] 1 WLR 1399, PC and Lord Millett 'Pension
Schemes and the Law of Trusts—The Tail Wagging the Dog?' (2000) 14 TLI 66.

[40] For a registered pension scheme, the tax laws generally envisage that providing a non-cash benefit—ie a
benefit in kind—to a member is an unauthorized payment and so a tax charge would arise.

[41] Ie persons with an 'entitlement' in the language used in the pensions legislation (eg s 67 of the Pensions
Act 1995)—see the Court of Appeal in *KPMG v Aon* [2005] EWCA Civ 1004, [2005] PLR 301.

[42] Broadly, persons with an 'accrued right' in s 67 terms (although for a member with less than two years'
qualifying service, the accrued right may be limited to a return of contributions).

[43] See the decision of the Supreme Court of Canada in *Buschau v Rogers Communications Inc* (2006) SCC
28, discussed in Ch 16 (*Saunders v Vautier*).

[44] [1998] HCA 4, [1998] 192 CLR 226, HC Aus.

[45] Discussed further in Ch 14 (Trustee indemnities and exonerations).

context of duties owed to a company and whether the shareholders can also have a cause of action—see *Johnson v Gore Wood & Co (No 1)*.[46]

9.26 Chapter 10 (Trustees' duties to employers) goes on to look at the position of the employer in more detail.

Purpose Test: Trust Law

9.27 Tellingly, the latest 2010 edition of *Underhill and Hayton: Law of Trusts and Trustees*[47] does not include a 'best interests of beneficiaries' test. Instead it states the purpose test. It states[48] the general principle applicable to powers of trustees:

> ...a trustee
>
> (a) must consider from time to time the exercise of his distributive and managerial discretions; ...
>
> (d) must exercise his discretions only within the scope of the terms of the relevant power and, then, only for the purposes for which the discretions were conferred on him by the settlor and not perverse to any sensible expectation of the settlor...[49]

9.28 In a pensions context, the reference to 'settlor' should be considered as being to the person who set up the trust and decided what powers should be given to the trustees, ie the employer. There are cases where the members have been considered to be the settlor,[50] but the better view is to regard both the employer and the members as settlors for different purposes.[51]

9.29 There are lots of cases on this purpose test. They are discussed in the Nugee and Hulme articles. As early as 1758, the principle was established in *Aleyn v Belchier*[52] that trust powers must be exercised for the purposes for which they were given:

> No point is better established than that a person having a power must exercise it bona fide for the end designed, otherwise it is corrupt and void.

9.30 This notion that powers must be exercised for the purposes of the trust has been supported by a number of decisions since then.[53]

---

[46] [2002] 2 AC 1, HL and, in Australia, see *Thomas v D'Arcy* [2005] QCA 68, Queensland CA.

[47] 18th edn, ed Hayton, Matthews, and Mitchell (LexisNexis, 2010). Also on proper purpose, see Matthew Conaglen, *Fiduciary Loyalty* (Hart Publishing, 2010) 44 and RC Nolan, 'Controlling Fiduciary Power' [2009] CLJ 293, 298.

[48] Article 57, p 897.

[49] Citing (see p 692), *McPhail v Doulton* [1971] AC 424 at 449, HL; *Re Hay's Settlement Trust* [1981] 3 All ER 786 at 792 (Megarry V-C); *Hayim v Citibank* [1987] AC 730 at 746, PC; *Re Beatty's Will Trust* [1990] 3 All ER 844 at 846 (Hoffmann J); and *Edge v Pensions Ombudsman* [1998] Ch 512 at 535 (Scott V-C) and on appeal [2000] Ch 602 at 627 (Chadwick LJ). See also the discussion in the same book (at p 29) on the same lines on the position of a fiduciary power.

[50] *Brooks v Brooks* [1996] AC 375, HL; *Air Jamaica v Charlton* [1999] 1 WLR 1399, PC.

[51] This is also the view of Daniel Fischel and John H Longbein, 'ERISA's Fundamental Contradiction: The Exclusive Benefit Rule' (1983) 55 University of Chicago Law Review 1105 at 1118.

[52] (1758) 1 Eden 132, 28 ER 634.

[53] See eg *The Duke of Portland v Topham* (1864) 11 HL 32; *Fouche v The Superannuation Fund Board* (1952) 88 CLR 609; *Re Courage Group Pension Scheme* [1987] 1 WLR 495; and *Thrells v Lomas* [1993] 1 WLR 456 (Nicholls V-C), in addition to the cases discussed below.

Lord Browne-Wilkinson summarized the position in *Westdeutsche Landesbank Girozentrale* **9.31**
v Islington LBC:[54]

> (i) Equity operates on the conscience of the owner of the legal interest. In the case of a trust,
> the conscience of the legal owner requires him *to carry out the purposes for which the property*
> *was vested in him* (express or implied trust) or which the law imposes on him by reason of
> his unconscionable conduct (constructive trust) (my emphasis).

In a pensions context, see for example Millett J in *Re Courage Pension Schemes*:[55]   **9.32**

> It is trite law that a power can be exercised only for the purpose for which it is conferred, and
> not for any extraneous or ulterior purpose. The rule-amending power is given for the purpose
> of promoting the purposes of the scheme, not altering them.

And Knox J in *Hillsdown Holdings v Pensions Ombudsman*:[56]   **9.33**

> …powers may not be exercised for a purpose or with an intention beyond the scope of or not
> justified by the instrument creating the power.

And this purpose test is mirrored for company directors—see eg *Howard Smith v Ampol*.[57]   **9.34**
Sections 171 and 172 of the Companies Act 2006 came into force on 1 October 2007
(enacting a DTI White Paper on reform of company law[58]) and now impose express statutory duties on directors including:

171 Duty to act within powers
A director of a company must—

> (a) act in accordance with the company's constitution, and
> (b) only exercise powers for the purposes for which they are conferred.

172 Duty to promote the success of the company

> (1) A director of a company must act in the way he considers, in good faith, would be most
> likely to promote the success of the company for the benefit of its members as a whole, and
> in doing so have regard (amongst other matters) to—
> (a) the likely consequences of any decision in the long term,
> (b) the interests of the company's employees,
> (c) the need to foster the company's business relationships with suppliers, customers and
> others,
> (d) the impact of the company's operations on the community and the environment,
> (e) the desirability of the company maintaining a reputation for high standards of busi-
> ness conduct, and
> (f) the need to act fairly as between members of the company.
> (2) Where or to the extent that the purposes of the company consist of or include purposes
> other than the benefit of its members, subsection (1) has effect as if the reference to promot-
> ing the success of the company for the benefit of its members were to achieving those
> purposes.
> (3) The duty imposed by this section has effect subject to any enactment or rule of law requir-
> ing directors, in certain circumstances, to consider or act in the interests of creditors of the
> company.

---

54 [1996] AC 669, [1996] 2 All ER 961 at 988, HL.
55 [1987] 1 All ER 528 at 536 (Millett J).
56 [1997] 1 All ER 862 at 879 and 880.
57 [1974] AC 821, PC.
58 CM6456 (March 2005).

9.35 The analogy here is to equate the position of the scheme (not the beneficiaries) with that of the company. So to adapt s 172(1) and (3) for pension trustees:

> A trustee of a pension scheme must act in the way he considers, in good faith, would be most likely to achieve the purposes of the scheme.

What does the purpose test mean?

9.36 But finding that there is a proper purpose test only gets a trustee so far. It leads on to the question about how the trustees (or indeed a court) works out what is the purpose of a particular power.

9.37 For example:

(a) In *Courage*,[59] Millett J held that it was contrary to the purpose of the power to allow a substitution of principal employer while the change was purported to be made with a view to the retention of surplus by the holding company of the current principal employer (instead of the scheme (with its surplus) remaining with the old principal employer (which was being sold) and remaining attached to the employees[60]); and

(b) in *Hillsdown*,[61] Knox J held that it was contrary to the purpose of the transfer-out power to make a transfer to a new scheme with the purpose of allowing a surplus refund to the employer that was prohibited by the old scheme.

(c) In *British Coal*,[62] Vinelott J commented on the purpose of a pension scheme, when looking at an amendment power:

> The employer, if he has a power of amendment, is entitled to exercise it in any way which will further the purposes of the pension scheme to ensure that the legitimate expectations of the members and pensioners are met without, so far as possible, imposing any undue burden on the employer or building up an unnecessarily large surplus. The employer himself has an interest in maintaining a pension fund which is satisfactory to existing and attractive to future employees, and he has an interest in ensuring that it is effectively managed, for example in seeing that the powers of investment are confined within proper limits, if necessary by amendment, and that they are properly exercised. If the assets of the scheme are so large that all legitimate expectations of the members and pensioners can be met without continued contribution by him at the rate originally provided, he can by amendment reduce or suspend contributions for a period.

9.38 In *Re Manisty's Settlement*[63] (not a pensions case), Templeman J commented:

> In practice, the considerations which weigh with the trustees will be no different from the considerations which will weigh with the trustees of a wide special power. In both cases reasonable trustees will endeavour, no doubt, to give effect to the intention of the *settlor* in making the settlement and will derive that intention not from the terms of the power necessarily or exclusively, but from all the terms of the settlement, the surrounding circumstances and their individual knowledge acquired or inherited. In both cases the trustees have an absolute discretion and cannot be obliged to take any form of action, save to consider the exercise of the power and a request from a person who is within the ambit of the power (emphasis added).

---

[59] *Re Courage Group's Pension Schemes* [1987] 1 All ER 528, [1987] 1 WLR 495 (Millett J).
[60] But see the later gloss by Blackburne J in *Merchant Navy Ratings Pension Fund Trustees Ltd v Chambers* [2002] ICR 359, [2001] OPLR 321.
[61] *Hillsdown Holdings v Pensions Ombudsman* [1997] 1 All ER 862 (Knox J).
[62] *British Coal Corpn v British Coal Staff Superannuation Scheme Trustees* [1995] 1 All ER 912 (Vinelott J).
[63] [1974] Ch 17 at 26 (Templeman J).

Purpose of a Pension Scheme

SEK Hulme put forward[64] the nature of a pension trust as follows: **9.39**

> A superannuation deed is and it reflects a balancing operation; a reconciliation, agreed to by all parties, of economic interests which in their starkest expression lead the members to seek the maximum amount of benefits at the minimum cost to themselves and lead the employer to seek to confer the minimum amount of benefits at the minimum cost to itself; in a more civilised statement, a reconciliation, seen by all parties as fair to themselves, of the demands of members and the willingness of the employer; a scheme for the provision of benefits to the members at a cost to the employer and perhaps also to members, the expression of both being accepted as fair to all concerned.

A simpler purpose test is proposed as: **9.40**

> The purpose of a defined benefit occupational pension scheme is to provide the stated and accrued relevant benefits to (and in respect of) the members at a cost acceptable to the employer.

Some comments on this formulation: **9.41**

(a) 'defined benefit': because different principles apply to money purchase or defined contribution (DC) benefits. In a DC plan, there is less obviously a cost to the employer beyond the agreed contribution rate (although there could be if there were, for example, fraud by the trustees[65] or the employer had given an indemnity to the trustees);

(b) 'stated benefits': because the scheme is to provide the benefits stated.[66] Any augmentations or benefit increases may well impose extra costs on the employers. In practice most schemes require the consent of the employer for such discretionary benefits (save perhaps on a scheme winding-up), so the employer can look after its own interests when deciding whether or not to give consent. But some schemes do not include this (or give an unfettered power to the trustees—eg to fix the reduction applicable on early retirement). This cost principle should apply here.

(c) 'accrued benefits': because many parties would envisage a primary duty on trustees to look after the accrued benefits of member—not any future service benefits. But this is a more contentious point.

(d) 'to and in respect of the members': to clarify that the benefit derives from the member's employment. As between the member and any spouse or dependant who may also benefit, the member is the primary beneficiary.[67]

(e) 'cost acceptable to the employer': this allows room for the employer to agree an action that may incur extra cost—eg a benefit increase or a change in investments from 'risky' equities to 'less risky' bonds.

Some might want to add at the end of the test: **9.42**

> balancing the interests of the employers and the members.

---

[64] See (2000) 14 TLI 130 at 136.
[65] See regs 10–13 of the Occupational Pension Schemes (Employer Debt) Regulations 2005 (SI 2005/678) containing an obligation on employers to contribute to money purchase schemes if a deficiency arises through fraud etc.
[66] See eg the comments of Chadwick LJ in *Edge v Pensions Ombudsman* [2000] Ch 603 at 623, CA.
[67] See Ch 8 (Position of spouses and dependants).

9.43   Without having tested it in a survey, many (most?) of those involved with occupational pensions would recognize and agree with that test as setting out their views on the purpose for which a pension scheme was established and has been operated.

9.44   It might be said that this is all quite interesting, but in relation to an existing scheme such a purpose cannot now be expressly included in the scheme documents. Clearly an express purpose statement on the lines above could be added into a new scheme, but these are not very common.

9.45   That is true, but the case law does make it clear that the purpose of a scheme can be changed over time—see the comments of Millett J (as he then was) in *Courage*,[68] citing *Thellusson v Viscount Valentia*,[69] a case involving the Hurlingham Club where a club had changed its objects over time.

9.46   The purpose outlined above is, it is suggested, in fact already the current purpose of most occupational defined benefit pension schemes. So this purpose is already in place without any need to be expressly stated (and there must be scope for including such a statement in new trust deeds for existing schemes).

Edge v Pensions Ombudsman

9.47   Chadwick LJ in *Edge v Pensions Ombudsman*[70] (in a paragraph divided up for ease of reading) confirmed this:

> In examining the contention that, in exercising their power to amend the rules, the trustees were subject to a duty to act impartially as between individual or classes of beneficiaries—in the sense relied upon by the ombudsman—it is important to have in mind the circumstances in which the need for amendments arose and the nature of those amendments. A convenient starting point is rule 3:
>
> > The main purpose of the scheme is the provision of retirement and other benefits for employees of training boards and successor bodies who are members of the scheme. The trust fund is to be constituted and maintained by means of periodical and other contributions to be made by the members and by the employers in accordance with the rules.
>
> At the risk of stating the obvious, that 'main purpose' rule embodies three concepts which are fundamental to a pension scheme of this nature.
>
> - First, the purpose of the scheme is to provide the retirement and other benefits to which the members, pensioners, and dependants are entitled under the rules. The scheme is a 'defined benefits' scheme: the benefits are fixed by the rules. The scheme is not set up as a unit trust, under which the members would be entitled to a proportionate share in the fund.
> - Second, the fund out of which the benefits are to be provided is constituted and maintained by means of periodic payments. The amount of those payments will depend not only on the rate of contributions but also on the number of members in service from time to time who are contributors and on the number of employers who continue to participate. In that sense the fund is dynamic. Although it will be possible, at any given time, to measure the value of the assets then held in the fund, and to measure the liabilities which then have to be met out of those assets (on the basis of termination), that is not a particularly useful exercise unless termination is seen to be

---

[68] [1987] 1 All ER 528 at 537 (Millett J).
[69] [1907] 2 Ch 1, CA.
[70] [2000] Ch 603 at 623, CA.

imminent. What is required is an actuarial valuation of the assets, present and future, taking into account the contributions which are to be made by employers and members over the remaining life of the fund; and an actuarial valuation of the liabilities which will have to be met as employees in service retire and become pensioners (or die and leave dependants).

- Third, the task of the trustees is to maintain a balance between assets and liabilities valued on that actuarial basis; so that, so far as the future can be foreseen, they will be in a position to provide pensions and other benefits in accordance with the rules throughout the life of the scheme. That task is to be performed by setting appropriate levels for employers' and members' contributions. If that task could be performed with perfect foresight there would be no surpluses and no deficits. But, because the task has to be performed in the real world, surpluses and deficits are bound to arise from time to time and prudent trustees will aim to ensure that the likelihood of surplus outweighs the risk of deficit. Nevertheless, it is no part of the trustees' function, in a fund of this nature, to set levels for contributions which will generate surpluses beyond those properly required as a reserve against contingencies.

The purpose test proposed above is not inconsistent with any 'sole purpose' or 'main purpose' **9.48** requirement to provide retirement benefits that might have been required before April 2006 by the Inland Revenue[71] or by the terms of a scheme. It is also consistent with:

- s 252 of the Pensions Act 2004, requiring that an occupational pension scheme must be established under an irrevocable trust; and
- the requirements in s 255 of the Pensions Act 2004 for the activities of an occupational pension scheme to be limited to 'retirement-benefit activities'.

Saying that the benefits must be those stated and must be at a cost acceptable to the employer **9.49** still leaves the benefits as being solely retirement benefits. See for example the decision of the House of Lords in *Fraser v Canterbury Diocesan Board of Finance*[72] that a school remained for the purpose of educating children of the poor of a particular parish even though it may have included (in later years) some children from a neighbouring parish and some children of more wealthy parents.

Foster Wheeler

The 'fair balance' approach as between members and the employer is also supported by the **9.50** Court of Appeal decision in *Foster Wheeler v Hanley*.[73] That case was mainly concerned with interpreting amendments made to a pension scheme.

The Court of Appeal held that the relevant amendment should still take effect in relation to **9.51** future service (and that an unwieldy blue pencil approach should not apply), even though this would result in lower benefits for some members, on the basis that this was a fairer result.

---

[71] See para 1.4 of the last version of the Revenue practice notes, IR12 (2001) dealing with discretionary approval under the Income and Corporation Taxes Act 1988 before their replacement (from 6 April 2006) by the registration concept under the Finance Act 2004:

> In exercising its discretion to approve schemes, the Board require them to be bona fide established for the sole purpose of providing relevant benefits, and continued approval will be dependent on that sole purpose being maintained.

[72] [2005] UKHL 65, [2006] 1 AC 377, HL.
[73] [2009] EWCA Civ 651, [2010] ICR 374 at [36], CA.

9.52 Arden LJ stated:

> By conferring a windfall on members with mixed NRDs, the judge's solution did not satisfy the principles which I have identified. It is unfair to the company and potentially unfair to other members of the scheme.

ITS v Hope

9.53 Similarly, the 'best interests of the members' test is (in effect) rejected by the rather difficult decision of Henderson J in *Independent Trustee Services v Hope*.[74] That case involved a group of members who were concerned that their benefits would be capped if the scheme entered the Pension Protection Fund (PPF). This group presented a plan to the trustees designed to get better benefits for them but not to reduce the benefits of the remaining members.

9.54 The arrangement would involve the trustee making a transfer payment (at a full level) in respect of the capped members. This would reduce the solvency remaining in the scheme (ie it would be more than a 'share of fund'), but the remaining members would not be adversely affected as the scheme would enter the PPF and their benefits would be provided up to the same protected level (as if the transfers out had not taken place).

9.55 A simple 'best interests of the members' purpose test would clearly be satisfied (the transferring members would be better off, the remaining members would be unaffected). The trustees were still concerned that the PPF would be affected and so applied to court (with the PPF and the Pensions Regulator also being represented).

9.56 Henderson J held that the transfer payments would be invalid as being made for an improper purpose. This is a clear decision that the 'best interests' purpose is not overriding or the main purpose test.

9.57 The facts of this case are unusual because the employer had become insolvent without triggering PPF protection and the trustees were the only creditors who had an interest in forcing a further insolvency event. This gave the trustees an unusual ability to control when the employer would suffer a 'qualifying insolvency event', without which the scheme could not enter the PPF. Therefore they had sufficient time to formulate a buy-out proposal before the qualifying insolvency event. Usually the employer itself or another contingent creditor would trigger the insolvency event, which would leave the trustees with insufficient time to formulate a buy-out. The judge acknowledged that 'typically, a period of between 15 and 24 months is needed' for a buy-out.

9.58 Standing back, it seems reasonable (as the judge decided) to protect the PPF in the specific circumstances of this case. Having said that, Henderson J was obviously struggling to find a legal way of reaching his decision. The members pointed out that Parliament has enacted a range of protections for the PPF, but did not think it necessary to block this route.

9.59 The problem with the judgment is that it raises many uncertainties. Henderson J wanted to deter any future attempt to 'take advantage of the existence of the PPF' and held that there was a 'principled basis upon which the court can intervene to nip behaviour of this kind in the bud'. So this decision could have wider relevance. For example, this case may prevent the trustees of a scheme that is funded below the PPF protected level from taking a 'Las Vegas

---

[74] [2009] EWHC 2810 (Ch), [2010] ICR 553 (Henderson J). On the potential for the interests of the PPF to be considered, see Andrew Simmonds QC, 'The Pension Protection Fund—18 Months On' (2007) 21 TLI 150.

'gamble' by making high-risk investments knowing that even if the investments fail, the scheme members will still be protected up to the PPF level.

If this case has wider application, Henderson J's reliance on the 'public interest' arguments **9.60** creates some uncertainty. It is not clear when this principle can be invoked in the future. For example, it may not always be clear when trustees are allowed to take the PPF into account:

(a) when buying out benefits with an insurer;
(b) when allocating assets during a partial wind-up (eg if only some sections of the scheme are eligible for PPF entry);
(c) during a scheme merger (trustees compare the PPF level before and after the merger);
(d) when commuting pensions for cash (eg when considering the commutation rates available); or
(e) when investing the scheme's assets. But this decision will probably not affect buy-ins, because a buy-in policy will still be an asset of the scheme that is available to the PPF.

An odd aspect of *ITS v Hope* is that the judge did not explain why a different approach to **9.61** transfers-out was adopted by the Court of Appeal in the earlier case of *Easterly v Headway*[75] (in *ITS*, Henderson J did not even refer to this case). In *Easterly*, the Court of Appeal allowed a different 'cunning plan'—that is, for the trustees to carry out a partial buy-out that increased the employer's liability to the scheme. Perhaps there may be less public interest in protecting an employer than in protecting the PPF? But it would have been better if the judgment in *ITS v Hope* had at least dealt with this.

The safest course of action for trustees will be to ask themselves whether it would be reason- **9.62** able for them to make a particular decision even if the PPF did not exist. Trustees should carefully minute these decisions so that they can later prove that the PPF's existence was not a factor in their decision. If trustees cannot ignore the PPF's existence, they will need advice based on the specific facts of their situation.

In a more recent case, *Dalriada Trustees Ltd v Faulds*,[76] Bean J followed a similar proper pur- **9.63** pose approach to an investment power (this time to invalidate actions by trustees seemingly designed to get around tax rules).

Conclusion

The case law clearly supports a proper purpose test that usually requires trustees to seek to **9.64** exercise their powers in what they consider to be the best interests of the scheme. They usually need to balance the interests of the members against those of the employer. Often this may give a wide discretion,[77] but broadly means that they need to act 'fairly'.[78] An approach solely (say) favouring the members (with their dependants etc) may well be an improper purpose, unless the employer agrees.

---

[75] [2009] EWCA Civ 793, [2010] ICR 153, CA. Nor in *ITS* did Henderson J refer to the leading case on transfer payments, the decision of the Privy Council in *Wrightson Ltd v Fletcher Challenge Nominees Ltd* [2001] UKPC 23, [2001] OPLR 249, PC.

[76] [2011] EWHC 3391 (Ch) (Bean J).

[77] See eg *Wrightson Ltd v Fletcher Challenge Nominees Ltd* [2001] UKPC 23, [2001] OPLR 249, PC.

[78] See *Foster Wheeler v Hanley* [2009] EWCA Civ 651, [2010] ICR 374, CA and the end of Ch 10 below.

10

TRUSTEES' DUTIES TO EMPLOYERS

Introduction

10.1 This chapter builds on Chapter 9 (which looked at the scope of the duties of trustees of defined benefit occupational pension schemes) and looks at whether or not the trustees of a defined benefit occupational pension scheme have a duty to consider the interests of the employers.

10.2 This chapter aims to build on the seminal articles on this topic[1] by:

---

[1] See also Xenia Frostick, 'Is There a Duty to Act in the Best Interests of Beneficiaries?' (2000) 83 Pension Lawyer 2 and Geraint Thomas, 'The Duty of Trustees to Act in the "Best Interest" of their Beneficiaries' (2008) 2 Journal of Equity 177. Further, in Australia, see Pam McAlister, 'The Changing Winds of Superannuation— Relief for Employers?' (2000) 11 Journal of Banking and Finance Law and Practice 100; Lisa Butler, 'A Reply to the Changing Winds of Superannuation—Relief for Employers?' (2000) 11 JBFLP 284; Michael Vrisakis, 'The Best Test of (or the "Bestest") Interests of Members' (2006) 17(9) Superannuation Law Bulletin 138; and M Scott Donald, 'Best Interests?' (2008) 2 Journal of Equity 245. In the US see John H Longbein and Daniel

(a) Edward Nugee QC in 1998: 'The Duties of Pension Scheme Trustees to the Employer';[2] and

(b) the Australian, SEK Hulme QC in 2000: 'The Basic Duties of Trustees of Superannuation Trusts—Fair to One, Fair to All?'.[3]

Why does this matter?

As mentioned in Chapter 9, fundamentally in this age of deficits rather than surpluses, pension trustees often (depending on the terms of the scheme, but with some powers fixed by statute) have various key powers and discretions in relation to a scheme, in particular about funding and investment.   **10.3**

Fiduciary Duty

As discussed in Chapter 9, the trustees must exercise their powers and discretions in accordance with their fiduciary duties. Usually this means for a proper purpose—often this will be in line with what is the best interest of the scheme, and through that the beneficiaries. So it becomes important to know how far the employer is a beneficiary under the scheme and how far its interests should be taken into account.   **10.4**

So where does this leave an employer?   **10.5**

What does the Regulator say?

The Occupational Pensions Regulatory Authority (Opra)[4] issued a guide for pension scheme trustees[5] which clearly envisaged that employers are included within scheme beneficiaries. The guide stated that beneficiaries included the employer. Conversely the guidance from the Pensions Regulator on notifying breaches of the law[6] ignores the employer as beneficiary issue altogether, merely referring to a duty to act for the benefit of all beneficiaries.   **10.6**

In its more recent (May 2006) statement on how the Pensions Regulator will regulate the funding of defined benefits,[7] the Regulator seems to seek to draw a balance between seeking increased security for benefits (by getting as much funding as possible into a scheme) and the interests of employers in not tying up funds. If, for example, trustees were envisaged as exercising their powers solely in the interests of members, why would it be appropriate for the Regulator to allow funding below a very safe measure (eg insurance buy-out cost?). But the guidance states: **10.7**

> The technical provisions trigger will help us identify those schemes where we may take a closer look at how the trustees have determined their technical provisions. In setting this trigger we have taken into account:

Fischel, 'ERISA's Fundamental Contradiction: The Exclusive Benefit Rule' (1983) 55 University of Chicago Law Review 1105.

[2] (1998) 12 TLI 216, based on his 1998 lecture to the Association of Pension Lawyers (APL).

[3] (2000) 14 TLI 130.

[4] Opra was abolished from 5 April 2005 and replaced by the Pensions Regulator (Pensions Act 2004, s 1).

[5] Previously available on the Pensions Regulator website in the Opra archive section.

[6] Paragraph 28 of the code.

[7] Previously on the Regulator's website.

that neither Government, legislation nor the regulator require ongoing schemes to fund to the solvency (full buy-out) level whereby all accrued liabilities could be secured immediately by the purchase of insurance policies (Hansard: Standing Committee B, Tue 23 March 2004 (Morning), Pensions Bill (2004)—Ninth Sitting).

10.8   Later the Regulator seems to take the narrow view—that the interests of members are best served by the support of a strong company (but this of course begs the question if the company can afford more):

> Our position is that the best means of delivering the members' benefits is usually for the scheme to have the continued support of a viable employer. Therefore, when considering the reasonable affordability of a recovery plan, we will pay particular attention to the future viability of the sponsoring employer, recognising the balance between paying down pension fund deficits now and employers investing in the business.[8]

10.9   Broadly, the issues of the level of funding for pension schemes is a matter of policy. Parliament (and the government) have decided in the Pensions Act 2004 to pass the responsibility for this policy issue to trustees (and the Pensions Regulator) without giving any indication of what level of funding is appropriate. So no wonder the Regulator (and trustees) are struggling to work out what duties have been imposed.

10.10   The government announced in 2012 that it intended to modify the statutory objectives of the Pensions Regulator in relation to scheme funding (under Pt 3 of the Pensions Act 2004) so that it includes an objective to consider the ability of the employer to pay. The proposed new objective is set out in the Pensions Bill put forward in May 2013:[9]

> in relation to the exercise of its functions under Part 3 only, to minimise any adverse impact on the sustainable growth of an employer.

Employer as an Express Beneficiary

10.11   Often the employer is an express beneficiary under the pension scheme in any event. That is to say that the terms of the scheme envisage the employer being paid an amount under the scheme.

10.12   The main examples are:

(a)   the employer may benefit from any surplus funds remaining on an ultimate winding-up of the scheme[10] (either expressly under the trust deed or, under s 77(4)(b) of the Pensions Act 1995, if benefits have been secured in full and assets remain undistributed[11]);

(b)   the scheme may include provisions allowing payment of a surplus to the employer even while the scheme is ongoing. This is allowed by the tax rules (there is a specific tax charge) and regulated by s 37 of the Pensions Act 1995;[12] and

---

[8]   See also para 13 of the May 2013 funding statement by the Pensions Regulator.
[9]   First reading on 9 May 2013.
[10]   See the discussion of this in relation to the employer as a beneficiary in Richard Nobles, *Pensions Employment and the Law* (Clarendon Press, 1993) 74.
[11]   Broadly, a statutory provision providing for payment to the employer if otherwise funds would go to the Crown as *bona vacantia* (because the trust instrument expressly prohibited payments to the employer). See recommendations 18 and 19 of the Goode Committee (1993) CM2342. For an example of *bona vacantia* see *Re ABC Television* (1973) [1989] PLR 21.
[12]   See Ch 20 (Employers and surpluses).

(c) charges and liens over the assets of the scheme in favour of the employer (for some liabilities owed by members to the employer) are allowed by the pensions legislation and the tax laws.[13]

Winding-up surpluses

Here the decision of Nicholls V-C (as he then was) in *Thrells Ltd (1974) Pension Scheme v Lomas*[14] is instructive. This involved a scheme that was winding-up. There was a surplus available after all required benefits had been provided and a discretion was given to the trustee to augment benefits (up to the then revenue limits), with any balance remaining being paid to the employer. The employer was the sole trustee and the liquidator (recognizing a conflict) surrendered his power to augment benefits to the Court.   **10.13**

The Vice Chancellor decided that the Court would exercise the discretion to increase benefits in the manner in which a trustee could be expected to act, having regard to all the material circumstances. These circumstances included the position of the employer. Nicholls V-C listed the material circumstances as including: **10.14**

 (i) the scope of the power;
 (ii) the purpose of the power;
 (iii) the source of the surplus;
 (iv) the size of the surplus and the impact of the statutory pension indexation provisions;
 (v) the financial position of the employer; and
 (vi) the needs of the members of the scheme.

It may well be that in practice most defined benefit pension schemes are currently in deficit on a winding-up basis. That is to say that their current level of assets is less than the actuary estimates that would be needed to secure all the benefits by purchasing matching annuity policies with an insurance company. So the employer's prospects of any payment to it on a winding-up may currently be remote.   **10.15**

Even if there is no express provision for surplus refund on a winding-up, one may be implied under a resulting trust—see the Privy Council in *Air Jamaica v Charlton*.[15]   **10.16**

Ongoing surpluses

In the UK it seems that the courts have not felt any difficulty in allowing a payment out of an ongoing pension scheme to an employer under an express provision. The main issue has been whether or not the express provision was effective: **10.17**

(a) to allow a scheme to be made to cancel payments that would otherwise have become payable—*National Grid v Mayes*;[16] or
(b) given restrictions in an amendment power—see eg *Harwood Smart v Caws*;[17] or
(c) given restrictions in the scheme itself—eg *Hillsdown Holdings v Pensions Ombudsman*.[18]

---

[13] See *Freshfields on Corporate Pensions Law 2013*, ed D Pollard and C Magoffin (Bloomsbury Professional, 2013) and D Pollard, 'Employers' Liens on Pension Benefits' (2002) Journal of Pensions Management (June).
[14] [1993] 1 WLR 456, [1993] 2 All ER 546 (Nicholls V-C).
[15] [1999] 1 WLR 1399, PC.
[16] [2001] 1 WLR 864, HL.
[17] [2000] OPLR 227, [2000] PLR 101 (Rimer J).
[18] [1997] 1 All ER 862 (Knox J)

10.18 Ultimately in 2001 Lord Hoffmann in *National Grid v Mayes*[19] commented (emphasis added):

> 16 The question is one of construction, to be answered according to familiar principles. The pension scheme background is of course very important. On the other hand, some of the matters put forward as relevant by Mr Inglis-Jones on behalf of the National Grid members seemed to me of marginal significance. For example, he said that the main purpose of the scheme was to provide pensions for the employees. That I would certainly accept. But then he said that it would be inconsistent with such a purpose to make payments or the equivalent of payments to the employer. In relation to a surplus, this does not seem to me to follow. A surplus is (by definition) money in excess of what is needed to effect the main purpose of the scheme. Next, Mr Inglis-Jones said that it must be borne in mind that part of the surplus was funded by contributions from the employees. Indeed, the whole of the funding may be said to be either their contributions or payment for their services. No doubt considerations of this kind have influenced the implication of an implied term of good faith, *but they cannot displace the fact that the scheme confers the power to make arrangements upon the employer and no one else*. In some schemes the power is more evenly distributed but in this one it is not. Mr Inglis-Jones's submissions would lead to the conclusion that the employer cannot act in his own interests, but the implied term does not go so far. Once it is accepted that he can act in his own interests, and that the extent to which he is doing so in this case cannot be criticised, I do not see the relevance of the way in which the surplus was funded.
>
> 17 Mr Inglis-Jones then said that while it might be reasonable for the employer to suspend his future contributions, the release of accrued liabilities, or actual payment of money to himself, would imperil the security of the fund. An actuarial surplus, he said, was notional and evanescent, here today and (with the slightest change in assumptions) gone tomorrow. That argument, as it seems to me, is really an argument against doing anything about a surplus at all. From the point of view of the adequacy of the fund, there is no difference between paying money to the employer and paying it in the form of (for example) extra benefits to classes of employees. Both result in there being less money in the fund. Clause 14(5) in my view does not require the employer to be sceptical about the actuarial certificate. Caution is a matter for the actuary in certifying the surplus and certifying the arrangements as reasonable. The employer's duty is simply to make them.

10.19 Indeed, standing back, it is difficult to see why the English courts have allowed surplus refunds to employers out of ongoing schemes if they did not consider the employer to be a beneficiary. The UK pensions legislation clearly envisages that refunds may be made (eg s 37 of the Pensions Act 1995).

10.20 By contrast, in 1992 in Canada, the Canadian Supreme Court held in *Schmidt v Air Products*[20] that (for example) any interest of the employer to a payment out of a pension scheme must be expressly reserved in the trust instrument (and cannot be included later by using the amendment power). This looks odd to English lawyers. The English courts have not felt the need to follow the Canadian Courts on this 'interest' or 'reservation' point.

Employer as Quasi-Beneficiary

10.21 Given the employer's funding obligations to the scheme (both under statute[21] and (often) the trust deed), in my view an employer should be considered to be a quasi-beneficiary of

---

[19] [2001] 1 WLR 864 at 869, HL.
[20] [1992] 2 SCR 611, [1995] OPLR 283, Can SC.
[21] See, on a scheme winding-up etc, s 75 of the Pensions Act 1995 (as amended). On an ongoing basis, funding rates are fixed for relevant schemes by the 'scheme specific funding' provisions in Pt 3 of the Pensions

the scheme even in the absence of an express payment provision (whether out of an ongoing scheme or as a form of resulting trust on winding-up).

An employer should be looked on as a beneficiary even if it does not receive a direct monetary benefit out of the assets of the scheme. Instead, the employer is an indirect or quasi-beneficiary. Its obligations (eg to fund the scheme) are reduced if the trustees comply with their duties (eg achieve a greater investment return). **10.22**

This reduction of a payment obligation to the trust should result in the same beneficiary status as a positive payment obligation out of the trust. **10.23**

The position can be contrasted with the private trust case of *Fuller v Evans*[22] (mentioned at para 10.39 below), because there the indirect benefit of the settlor (having his children's school fees paid by the trust reduced the legal or moral obligation on the settlor) was outside the scheme. In a pension trust it is the obligation of the employer to fund the scheme and so it is directly affected by the actions of the trustee. **10.24**

This view is supported by both Edward Nugee and SEK Hulme in their articles mentioned at the beginning of this chapter. Fischel and Langbein reached a similar view in their article 'ERISA's Fundamental Contradiction: The Exclusive Benefit Rule' when looking at the position of pension plans under the US pensions legislation, ERISA.[23] **10.25**

Canada: the *Buschau* case

In Canada, the Court of Appeal in British Columbia did not look at this argument with favour. It decided that, in the context of the particular plan, an employer was not a beneficiary under a defined benefit pension plan—see *Buschau v Rogers Communications Inc.*[24] The Court of Appeal held that the employer in that case had no standing to object to an agreement between all the members and beneficiaries of the plan to terminate and wind-up the plan (under the rule in *Saunders v Vautier*[25]). The Supreme Court upheld the ultimate decision[26] (but mainly on the basis that *Saunders v Vautier* had been impliedly excluded by the legislation). **10.26**

This was in the context of a plan that excluded the employer from any monetary benefit under the plan (although it had retained the right to amend or terminate the plan). If the plan had given the employer the right to all or part of any surplus on termination or while it was ongoing, the court would have held that the employer was a beneficiary for this purpose ([51]). **10.27**

Buschau was a Canadian case decided in the light of the 2002 decision of the Canadian Supreme Court in *Schmidt v Air Products*.[27] In *Schmidt*, the Canadian Supreme Court had **10.28**

Act 2004. These statutory obligations do not apply to all occupational pension schemes. There are various (complicated) exclusions—see D Pollard, *Corporate Insolvency: Employment and Pension Rights* 5th edn (Bloomsbury Professional, 2013).

[22] [2001] 1 All ER 636 (Lightman J).
[23] (1983) 55 University of Chicago Law Review 1105 at 1119—see fn 3 above. See also Sarah Lacey and Geoff Topham, 'The Powers and Duties of Pension Scheme Trustees' in *Tolley's Pension Law* (LexisNexis, looseleaf) para E2.38.
[24] [2004] BCCA 80, (2004) 6 ITELR 919 (CABC).
[25] (1841) 49 ER 282, affirmed (1841) 41 ER 482.
[26] 2006 SCC 28, 269 DLR (4th) 1. See further Ch 16 (*Saunders v Vautier*).
[27] [1992] 2 SCR 611, [1995] OPLR 283.

held that the ability of an employer to reduce its contributions to a plan (by taking a contribution holiday) was still allowed. It held that it did *not* amount to an interest in the trust for this purpose.[28]

10.29 In *Buschau*, the Supreme Court of Canada overturned the decision of the Court of Appeal and held that the active members cannot terminate the plan by acting unanimously (but without the agreement of the employer). In *Buschau v Rogers Communications Inc*,[29] the Supreme Court of Canada held that it was not possible for all the active members of a pension scheme to resolve to terminate and wind up the scheme using the rule in *Saunders v Vautier*, despite the opposition of the employer company.

10.30 The Supreme Court reached this decision based on considering that:

(a) the rule in *Saunders v Vautier* is, for pension schemes, displaced by the Canadian pensions legislation;
(b) employers establish pension plans because doing so suits their interests and they have the 'right not to have their management decisions disturbed'; and
(c) the social purpose of pension plans would be defeated if members could require early distribution of assets.

10.31 The decision looks at the interests of the employer.[30] It also goes on to say that the interests of future spouses etc need to be taken into account and their consent will also be needed.[31]

10.32 LeBel, Deschamps, Fish, and Abella JJ held:

30 Third, employers establish plans because it is in their interest to do so. Under normal circumstances, they have the right not to have their management decisions disturbed. In contrast, the common law trust allows no room for the settlor's interest. Although the particular circumstances of this case may lead to the conclusion that the employer no longer has a legitimate interest in the continuation of the Plan, a blanket statement that the employer has no interest conflicts with the usual expectations of parties to a pension plan.

10.33 McLachlin CJ and Bastarache and Charron JJ held:

92 The Plan clearly states then that it is the employer who may amend and terminate the Plan and that it is the employer's expectation that the Plan and Trust will continue indefinitely. In such circumstances, there could be no reasonable expectation on the part of RCI or the members that the Trust could be terminated by the members, over RCI's objections, in order that the members might obtain the surplus. The application of the rule in *Saunders v Vautier* would contradict the reasonable contractual expectations of the parties because beneficiaries who can collapse a trust under *Saunders v Vautier* can, with the consent of the trustees, collectively agree to vary its terms. The rule would permit members of a pension plan to unilaterally vary its terms without the employer's consent.

10.34 This seems a sensible decision insofar as it relies on the need for employer consent as well—consistent with the argument that the employer is effectively a beneficiary. But the Supreme Court was fairly tentative in going that far.

---

[28] See *Buschau* in the Court of Appeal at [57], citing *Schmidt v Air Products* at p 654. See also in South Africa, the similar comments of Marais JA in *TEK Corpn Provident Fund v Lorentz* 1999 (4) SA 884, discussed in Ch 20 (Employers and surpluses).
[29] 2006 SCC 28, [2006] 1 SCR 973, (2006) 9 ITELR 73, (2006) 269 DLR (4th) 1, Canadian Supreme Court.
[30] Eg [30] and [94].
[31] See [99].

Conversely, the argument that the consent of future spouses etc is needed seems rather **10.35** unhelpful (and contrary to my argument that the member can give consent in right of the spouse etc).

Previously, in *Atco Lumber v Leech*[32] Sigurdson J in British Columbia had held that an **10.36** employer, as settlor, had no standing to bring a claim for breach of trust against the trustees of a long-term disability trust, even though the trust was funded by the employer. This seems an odd decision, but may have been determined by the concession by the employer that it was not a beneficiary.[33] An appeal to the British Columbia Court of Appeal[34] failed, partly on the grounds that the law had changed as a result of the decision of the Supreme Court in *Buschau*, but also on jurisdiction grounds (so the beneficiary issue was not discussed).

UK—the surplus cases

In the UK, the courts have envisaged that trustees and employers could negotiate over surplus— **10.37** eg Millett J in *Courage*[35] and Knox J in *Hillsdown*.[36] This seems to accept that the employer is a beneficiary.

The Court of Appeal in *Stevens v Bell* [37] (discussed further at para 10.62 below) while holding **10.38** that a surplus refund could not be made out of the particular ongoing scheme, did this on the basis of a specific restriction in the scheme. It does not seem to have been raised before the court that such a refund would not be allowed on the basis that it would be outside the scope of the scheme, because the employer is not a beneficiary.

But compare the decision of Lightman J in the private trust case *Fuller v Evans*.[38] In looking **10.39** at the effect of clause 12, the 'no benefit for the settlor' clause in the trust, he held:[39]

> The first stage is to consider what the position would have been if the settlement had not included cl 12. In that situation in the exercise of the power in question in this case (as in the exercise of all other powers) the trustees would be required to have regard exclusively to the interests of the beneficiaries, and could not seek by the exercise or non-exercise of the power to promote the interests of anyone else, and most particularly the settlor. It would be open to the trustees to decide that the power be exercised though the effect would be to relieve the settlor in whole or in part of his obligations under the consent order, but they could not set out to benefit the settlor by affording him relief in this way. If the exercise of the power was in the best interests of the beneficiaries, the trustees might exercise the power though the exercise incidentally relieved the settlor in whole or in part from his obligations, but they could not allow the perceived advantage to the settlor to be a factor favouring its exercise.

Reading this passage with 'employer' instead of 'settlor' is enough to show that the position **10.40** of pension trusts looks very different from those of private trusts.[40]

---

[32] (2006) BCSC 524, 52 CCPB 131 (Sigurdson J).
[33] See [31].
[34] (2007) BCCA 238.
[35] [1987] 1 All ER 528 (Millett J).
[36] [1997] 1 All ER 862 (Knox J).
[37] [2002] EWCA Civ 672, [2002] OPLR 207, [2002] All ER (D) 301 (May), CA.
[38] [2000] 1 All ER 636 (Lightman J).
[39] At [5].
[40] See further the discussion on fraud on a power in relation to pension schemes in G Thomas and A Hudson, *The Law of Trusts* (Oxford University Press, 2004) 591 and 592, stating that 'occupational pension schemes are fundamentally different'.

Analogy with duties owed by company directors to creditors

10.41 There is an expanding line of recent judicial authority imposing duties on directors to consider the interests of creditors in the position where the company's solvency is in question.[41]

10.42 Although the position is not absolutely clear, the better view is that this duty is owed to the company, not direct to the creditors. In 'Directors Taking Into Account Creditors' Interests',[42] Andrew Keay concludes that:

> An examination of the recent case law demonstrates that while most courts have resisted the view that directors owe an independent duty to creditors of their companies, they have confirmed that directors do owe a duty to their companies to take account of the interests of creditors when companies are in some sort of financial difficulty.

10.43 In *Peoples Department Stores Inc v Wise*,[43] the Canadian Supreme Court held that, in Canada at least, while directors do not owe fiduciary duties to creditors (instead solely to the company), they do owe a duty of care to creditors which creditors may enforce.

PPF as a beneficiary

10.44 An analogy can be drawn between the employer (as scheme funder) and the Pension Protection Fund (PPF) as potential provider of the PPF level of protected benefits if the employer enters an insolvency process and the scheme funding is insufficient. If such a situation is likely, do the trustees owe any duty to (say) invest with the interests of the PPF in mind? Or do they owe a duty to exercise their investment powers solely in the interest of the members? So should the trustees adopt a risky investment strategy on the basis that if it does well, the members may benefit. But if it does badly, the members still get the PPF protected benefits through the PPF?

10.45 It seems that the interests of the PPF need to be considered at least as a question of 'proper purpose' on transfer—*Independent Trustee Services Ltd v Hope*.[44] And this points to a similar analysis to the position of the employer. But others have argued to the contrary.[45]

10.46 There may be a distinction in that if a scheme enters the PPF there is a statutory assignment to the PPF board of all the assets of the scheme.[46] Arguably this may include a right to bring an action against the trustees for breach of trust committed by them before the transfer. But

---

[41] See *Winkworth v Edward Baron Development Co Ltd* [1987] 1 All ER 114, HL; *West Mercia Safetyware v Dodd* [1988] BCLC 250, CA; and *Re Pantone 485 Ltd* [2002] 1 BCLC 266.

[42] (2003) 24 Company Lawyer 300. See also Razeen Sappideen, 'Fiduciary Obligations to Corporate Creditors' (1991) Journal of Business Law 365; A Keay, 'Another Way of Skinning the Cat: Enforcing Directors' Duties to Creditors' (2004) 17 Insolvency Intelligence 1; and A Keay, 'Formulating a Framework for Directors' Duties to Creditors: An Entity Maximisation Approach' [2005] CLJ 614.

[43] [2004] 3 SCR 461, 2004 SCC 68. Andrew Keay comments on this case in 'Directors' Duties—Do Recent Canadian Developments Require a Rethink in the United Kingdom on the Issue of Directors' Duties to Consider Creditors Interests?' (2005) 18(5) Insolvency Intelligence 65–8.

[44] [2009] EWHC 2810 (Ch), [2010] ICR 553 (Henderson J). See the discussion in Ch 9.

[45] Before the *ITS* decision, see Keith Webster, 'Investment Risk' (APL conference, 2005); and Ian Greenstreet—e-mail to the author. Ian Greenstreet referred to various cases on the potential for a tort duty in favour of the PPF, citing *Andrew v Kouniss Freeman* [1999] 2 BCLC 641 (Civil Aviation Authority successfully sued auditors on the basis that in renewing the airlines licence the CAA had relied on the accounts and the auditors had assumed a duty of care to the CAA) and *Law Society v KPMG Peat Marwick McLintock* [2000] 4 All ER 540, CA (auditors failed to uncover extensive fraud which subsequently resulted in 300 claims against the Law Society compensation fund. The auditors unsuccessfully argued that no duty of care arose. The Court held that it was clearly foreseeable that failure to identify fraud could result in loss to the Law Society).

[46] Pensions Act 2004, s 161.

such a cause of action is by no means clear (is it an asset of the trust or of the members?) and it begs the question of whether the trustees were acting in breach of trust in the first place. In *HR v JAPT*[47] it was left open as to whether there could be such an action by a successor trustee against a director of an earlier corporate trustee.[48]

Employer as beneficiary

So where the employer is a beneficiary, express or quasi, the trustees must owe some duty to consider its interests.[49] There is nothing unusual in this—trustees of private settlements have long been used to balancing the competing interests of life tenants with remaindermen. Is there anything different in a pension trust? **10.47**

This is the same conclusion as was reached by Messrs Nugee and Hulme in their articles. Indeed it seems difficult to find anyone, other than fairly vague off-the-cuff judicial remarks, willing to support a different view (save perhaps in the state of Victoria, as we shall see). **10.48**

Having the employer as beneficiary is one reason why it is common to have the employer as a party to any construction hearing involving the scheme. Other than *Cowan v Scargill*[50] itself (and the absence of the employer is commented on by both Edward Nugee and SEK Hulme), the almost universal practice seems to be for the employers to be joined to any proceedings (or themselves be plaintiffs). Contrast the position of private trusts where it is very unusual to join in the settlor in any dispute. **10.49**

Purpose of a Pension Scheme

Chapter 9 discusses the purpose of a pension scheme and suggests (following the lead of SEK Hulme[51] from Australia) the nature of a pension trust as: **10.50**

> The purpose of a defined benefit occupational pension scheme is to provide the stated and accrued relevant benefits to (and in respect of) the members at a cost acceptable to the employer.

How Does This Apply in Practice?

The precise extent to which trustees have to consider the interests of employers as well as members/employees in the exercise of a power or discretion is unclear. **10.51**

There seems to be a wide view and a narrow view as to how far trustees can take account of the interests of the employer. **10.52**

(a) *Wide view*
   The wide view allows trustees to consider the interest of the employer as a beneficiary (or quasi-beneficiary) under the plan. It emphasises the requirement for the trustees' powers to be exercised for the purposes for which they were conferred (see above); for the purposes of the trust.

---

[47] [1997] OPLR 123, [1997] PLR 99 (Lindsay J)—see Ch 5 (Liability of directors of corporate trustees).
[48] See also Ian Greenstreet, 'Should Trustees be More Like Bankers?: The Changing Role of Occupational Pension Scheme Trustees' (2005) 19 TLI 3.
[49] Or at least to take account of its interests when looking at the purpose of the scheme and the relevant power—see Ch 9.
[50] [1985] Ch 270 (Megarry V-C).
[51] See (2000) 14 TLI 130 at 136.

(b) *Narrow view*

The narrow view considers that trustees must only act in the interests of the members (and contingent beneficiaries). This allows the employer's interests to be considered only when that benefits the members. It rejects the argument that a pension trust should properly be regarded as a 'purpose trust'.

10.53 The next part of this chapter reviews the relevant law and then considers it in relation to the following two examples:

(a) How should trustees exercise their discretion whether or not to agree to an amendment requested by the employer that would reduce future service benefits (assuming that there is no legal prohibition to the proposed amendment)?

(b) To what extent can and should the trustees take into account the interests of the employer when deciding whether to move investments from equities to gilts?

10.54 A firm of actuaries, Hewitt Bacon & Woodrow, usefully summarized this issue in their look at the role of the actuary in a pension scheme.[52] They distinguish between the role of the actuary:

(a) as a *calculator* (merely providing figures as required—eg to check compliance with a statutory standard such as the MFR). This corresponds to the role of a trustee who has no powers or discretions, eg but is instead merely concerned to check that a minimum level of funding has been provided;

(b) as an *advocate*—ie the narrow view where the role of the trustee is to represent solely the interest of the members; or

(c) as a *broker*—to work with the employer in partnership, eg to find the broadly 'fairest' solution, balancing all interests.

Wide View—Trustees Should Take into Account the Interests of Employers

10.55 The wide view regards the scheme as being for the purpose of providing relevant benefits for and in respect of past, current, and future employees. The trustees must exercise their powers for the purposes for which they were conferred and for the purposes of the plan.

10.56 This means that it would be legitimate for trustees to consider the interests of the employer in appropriate circumstances. In fact, some of the cases go so far as to suggest that the interests of the employer are a relevant factor which the trustees must take into account.

Edge v Pensions Ombudsman

10.57 The clearest exponent of this view is probably Chadwick LJ in 1999 giving the unanimous judgment of the Court of Appeal in *Edge v Pensions Ombudsman*.[53] He says of the trustees:[54]

They must, for example, always have in mind the main purpose of the scheme—to provide retirement and other benefits for employees of the participating employers. They must consider the effect that any course which they are minded to take will have on the financial ability

---

[52] *Financial Times*, 6 September 2004.
[53] [2000] Ch 602, [1999] 4 All ER 546, CA.
[54] At 626.

of the employers to make the contributions which that course will entail. They must be careful not to impose burdens which imperil the continuity and proper development of the employers' business or the employment of the members who work in that business.

And later[55] he held:

10.58

The matters to which we have referred are not to be taken as an exhaustive or a prescriptive list. It is likely that, in most circumstances, pensions trustees who fail to take those matters into account will be open to criticism. But there may well be other matters which are of equal or greater importance in the particular circumstances with which trustees are faced. The essential requirement is that the trustees address themselves to the question what is fair and equitable in all the circumstances. The weight to be given to one factor as against another is for them.

The *Edge* decision was made in the context of a discussion of use of surplus (in an ongoing scheme). It could be argued that Chadwick LJ's remarks should be considered in that context. If that were the case, then a line would have to be drawn between decisions where it is appropriate to consider the interests of the employer and decisions where it is not.

10.59

More recently, in *Alexander Forbes Trustee Service Ltd v Halliwell* [56] Hart J accepted (here in the context of use of a surplus in a winding-up) the argument that the trustees are required to consider the interests of the employer was applied:

10.60

It was submitted that the Ombudsman had overlooked the fact that in exercising its discretion over surplus the trustees were not bound solely to consider the interest of the members but were entitled and indeed bound to consider the interests of the employers as well: indeed, if its obligation was solely to consider the interests of the members it was difficult to see how any surplus could have been allowed to return to the employers at all.

In my judgment those criticisms of the Ombudsman's determination are justified.

See also *Harding v Joy Manufacturing Holdings Ltd*,[57] where the Inner House of the Court of Session referred to *Edge* and approved a merger proposal with one-third of the surplus going on benefit improvements and all the assets transferring to a new scheme. It was acknowledged that this would benefit the employer.

10.61

Stevens v Bell

Stevens v Bell[58] also supports the wide view. This was a case on the width of the powers given to the trustees and the actuary under the Airways Pension Scheme. The scheme rules gave the actuary (appointed by the trustee) the power to fix a scheme to deal with surplus if the trustee and the employer could not agree.

10.62

Lloyd J (as he then was) held[59] that the actuary could take into account the interests of the employer when deciding on the scheme[60]:

10.63

Question
10. If the answer to 5 above is 'yes', what, on the true construction of Clause 11(b), are the powers and duties of the appointed actuary to whom such a scheme is referred in default of

---

[55] At 627.
[56] [2003] EWHC 1685, [2003] OPLR 355 (Hart J) at [22] and [23].
[57] 2000 SLT 843, [2001] OPLR 235, CSIH. See discussion in Ch 20 (Employers and surpluses).
[58] [2001] OPLR 135, [2001] PLR 99 (Lloyd J), [2002] EWCA Civ 672, [2002] OPLR 207, CA. Sometimes cited as *British Airways Pension Trustees Ltd v British Airways plc*.
[59] [2001] OPLR 135, [2001] PLR 99 (Lloyd J).
[60] See [56] of the judgment of Lloyd J and [35] of the judgment of Arden LJ in the Court of Appeal.

agreement between the Management Trustees and the Employer and, in particular, whether and to what extent the appointed actuary is entitled or obliged to take into account the interests of the Employer in directing the form of the scheme to be adopted?

Answer

The appointed actuary has to consider the proposals by the Management Trustees and those put forward by the Employer, and either side's objections to the other's proposals, and has to ensure that he is properly informed as to the circumstances of the scheme, and must then decide whether and, if so, how the Management Trustees' proposed scheme ought to be modified so as to be the appropriate scheme to be put into effect in the circumstances, being fair and reasonable having regard to the interests of all concerned: members, pensioners and others, such as dependants, as well as the Employer.

10.64 This supports the wide view since it must be true that it can only be legitimate for the actuary to take account of the interests of the employer if it is legitimate for the trustees (whom the actuary advises) to do so.

10.65 The decision of Lloyd J was the subject of an appeal. The Court of Appeal (having the advantage of the later decision of the House of Lords in *National Grid* [61]) reversed Lloyd J in part.[62] But question 10 was not the subject to appeal (and was not discussed in the Court of Appeal's judgment[63]).

10.66 There are some comments of relevance in the Court of Appeal judgments. Arden LJ stated (at [153]):

> Mr Green[64] submits that the employer is a legitimate object of the discretion under clause 11(b). He goes further and submits that, as this is a balance of cost scheme, if there is a surplus that must mean that the employer has paid more than he was bound to do, and that there is nothing objectionable in refunds to the employer out of surplus during the currency of the scheme. This argument is reinforced by the requirement for the trustees to obtain the consent of the employer to which the surplus is attributable (see clause 11(b)). But it does not I think follow from the fact that this is a balance of cost scheme that the employer should be repaid its contributions out of surplus before the scheme has terminated as opposed to when the scheme terminates. I note that in the Wrightson case Lord Millett's remarks were directed to the situation arising on a final dissolution. Indeed Mr Green eschews the proposition that the employer has any vested proprietary claim to the assets of the scheme while ongoing. It has merely a prospective and contingent right (contingent, that is, on the scheme being dissolved and assets being available for distribution to the employer under clause 19); this right may simply be a 'floating equity' which may or may not crystallise (see *Commissioner of Stamp Duties (Queensland) v Livingstone* [1965] AC 694). The absence of a vested proprietary right while the scheme is ongoing is consistent with the impermanent nature of surplus discussed above. Accordingly, it is at least a possible construction of the APS Trust Deed that the employers' contributions once made are to remain in the scheme and to remain there as security for the members unless and until the scheme is brought to an end. The question however is: what is the true interpretation of the scheme?

Phoenix Ventures

10.67 In *Re Phoenix Venture Holdings Ltd (Company No 2692 of 2005)*[65] Sir Andrew Morritt V-C had to consider a challenge by a participating employer in a group scheme to an allocation

---

[61] *National Grid Co plc v Mayes; International Power plc (formerly National Power plc) v Healy* [2001] UKHL 20, [2001] 2 All ER 417, [2001] ICR 544, HL.
[62] [2002] EWCA Civ 672, [2002] OPLR 207, CA.
[63] See comment at [129] in Arden LJ's judgment.
[64] Counsel for British Airways, the employer.
[65] [2005] EWHC 1379 (Ch) (Morritt V-C).

of the s 75 debt payable on the winding-up of the scheme. The company was the only remaining employer in the MG Rover Group Pension Scheme that was not in formal insolvency proceedings.

The trustee was concerned that the scheme would not be eligible for the Pension Protection **10.68** Fund (PPF) unless all the employers were placed in a formal insolvency process (eg liquidation or administration). So the trustee apparently had an incentive to fix a large amount as payable by the company so that this could form the basis for an insolvency petition. The trustee passed a resolution allocating the s 75 debt on a joint and several basis. The allocation was purportedly made under a power in the scheme rules and under the statutory power under s 68 of the Pensions Act 1995.

The Vice-Chancellor held that the challenge by the company succeeded on the technical **10.69** basis that the purported allocation made by the trustees was actually not within the terms of the allocation powers they had given themselves.

Interestingly, the judgment also looks briefly at the issue of whether such an allocation could **10.70** have been challenged by the company as being improper (eg because it did not take account of the company's interest). The Vice-Chancellor held that these issues raised serious points that would deserve a trial of the issues.

Other cases

In *Re K&J Holdings, Pinsent Curtis v Capital Cranfield* [66] the Court of Appeal commented **10.71** that power to require 'appropriate' contributions (having taken advice from the actuary):

> would not entitle the trustees to demand a contribution for the purpose of building up a surplus and to fund increases to benefits payable to members under the Scheme.[67]

But the Court of Appeal held that it would have been open to the trustee to have demanded **10.72** the buy-out cost of providing benefits after a termination notice had been served by the employer.[68]

A wide view is also supported by the comments of the Court of Appeal in *Foster Wheeler*[69] **10.73** (trustee to act fairly so no 'windfall' benefit improvements) and Henderson J in *Alitalia*[70] (funding rule does not require funding to buy-out).

In Australia, the wide view is also supported by the 1991 decision of Waddell CJ in New **10.74** South Wales in *Lock v Westpac Banking Corpn*[71] (another case involving the use of surplus). He stated[72] that:

> It seems to me that . . . the trustees, while they had a duty to act in the interests of the members, were entitled to take into consideration the interests of the Bank . . . in considering whether or not to consent to the proposed amendment of the deed. If they were satisfied on reasonable

---

[66] [2005] EWCA Civ 860, [2005] 4 All ER 449, CA.
[67] Mummery LJ at [25].
[68] Mummery LJ at [25], Smith LJ at [33].
[69] *Foster Wheeler v Hanley* [2009] EWCA Civ 651, [2010] ICR 374 at [36], CA. See Ch 9 (Trustee powers—proper purpose).
[70] *Alitalia-Linee Aeree Italiane SPA v Rotunno* [2008] EWHC 185 (Ch) (Henderson J).
[71] (1991) 25 NSWLR 593, [1991] PLR 167 (Waddell CJ in Eq). Noted in (1992) British Pension Lawyer, January.
[72] At 610.

grounds that the overall package was a resolution in the interests of the parties…which was fair to both the Bank and the members, they were in my own opinion entitled to consent…

10.75 Pam McAllister comments on this case that 'As the Bank [the employer] did not have any legal, equitable or contingent interest in the surplus, it appears that Waddell CJ (in Eq) used the term "interests" in a broad non-technical sense'.[73]

10.76 Further support for the wide view can be found in private trust cases. In the *Hastings-Bass*[74] case it was held that trustees could take account of the interests of the settlor in exercising their discretions. This was followed in *Abacas Trust Co v Barr*.[75]

10.77 In *Hillsdown Holdings v Pensions Ombudsman*,[76] Knox J commented:

> In this case the mode of application of the surplus, once ascertained pursuant to r 23(a), was a matter for the FMC trustee alone, subject to consultation with the actuary. Hillsdown was not in a position to ask for a share of the surplus as a term of giving its consent because its consent was not needed. That is not to say that the FMC trustee should have cut itself off altogether from and ignored the principal employer under its scheme; but there is a very wide gulf between active bargaining for substantial financial payments and consultation with a view to ensuring that pension fund trustees take a decision which fits in, so far as practicable and permissible, with an employer's industrial strategy.

Statute

10.78 It is noticeable that there has generally been no attempt by Parliament to legislate for how trustees generally or pensions trustees in particular are to exercise their powers (and this cannot be through any shortage of available legislative opportunity). So it is noticeable that:

(a) Trustees are directed to consult with employers over the statement of investment principles (SIP)—s 35(5) of the Pensions Act 1995. And failure to do so can invalidate the SIP—see *Pitmans Trustees Ltd v Telecommunications Group plc*.[77]

(b) The new scheme specific funding regime under the Pensions Act 2004 generally envisages agreement between the trustees and the employer on the matters required (statement of funding principles, recovery plan, schedule of contributions etc)—ss 221–233 of the Pensions Act 2004.[78]

(c) From April 2006, the Pensions Act 2004 has required arrangements to be in place to secure that at least ⅓rd of the trustees of a pension scheme (or directors of a corporate trustee) to be elected or chosen by the members, so leaving up to ⅔rds to be appointed as provided by the scheme (usually by the employer).[79] If a pension scheme is to be run

---

[73] See P McAllister, 'The Changing Winds of Superannuation—Relief for Employers?' (2000) 11 Journal of Banking and Finance Law and Practice 100 at 102 fn 23. For a response, see Lisa Butler, 'A Reply to "The Changing Winds of Superannuation—Relief for Employers?"' (2000) 11 JBFLP 284.

[74] *Re Hastings-Bass (deceased): Hastings v Inland Revenue Commissioners* [1974] 2 All ER 193, CA.

[75] *Re Barr's Settlement Trust, Abacus Trust Co (Isle of Man) v Barr* [2003] 1 All ER 763 (Lightman J). But note that Lightman J's decision in *Fuller v Evans* [2000] 1 All ER 636 (cited at para 10.39 above) seems to support a more narrow view.

[76] [1997] 1 All ER 862 at 890 (Knox J).

[77] [2005] OPLR 1, [2004] PLR 213 (Morritt V-C).

[78] The Occupational Pension Schemes (Scheme Funding) Regulations 2005 (SI 2005/3377) alter this for a scheme where the trustees currently fix the ongoing contribution rate, so that the trustees retain a unilateral power over these matters, but with an express obligation to consult the employers—Sch 2, para 9.

[79] Pensions Act 2004, ss 241–243, applying from 6 April 2006. From 1997 until then, alternative arrangements approved by the members (under the regulations made under ss 16–21 of the Pensions Act 1995) could have resulted in a lower proportion of member-nominated trustees.

solely for the benefit of members alone (to the exclusion of the employer), why has Parliament not enacted that there must be 100 per cent member-nominated trustees?

Narrow View—Trustees Must Take Account of Only the Interests of the Members

A narrower view would be to regard trustees as mainly being concerned with looking after **10.79** the interests of the members (and contingent secondary beneficiaries). The argument then is that they should ignore the interests of the employers save insofar as it potentially has an adverse affect on the members.

Case law

Although (rather surprisingly) the interests of the employer were not directly considered, in **10.80** *Cowan v Scargill*[80] Megarry V-C commented in relation to the exercise of investment powers by trustees of a pension scheme:

> Powers must be exercised fairly and honestly for the purposes for which they are given and not so as to accomplish any ulterior purpose, whether for the benefit of the trustees or otherwise.

Asea Brown Boveri

The leading case here is probably the decision in Victoria of Beach J in *Asea Brown Boveri*.[81] **10.81** Beach J suggested that:

> In my opinion trustees of the Superannuation Fund owe a duty of loyalty exclusively to the members. It does not follow from that, however, that a trust deed can never be altered to meet the interest of the employer. Trustees are free to negotiate with a employer for a package of amendments that may include benefits to the employer if in the opinion of the trustees that would benefit the members.

Beach J refused to follow the decision of the English Court of Appeal in *Edge*. **10.82**

Invensys

Subsequently in Australia, Byrne J has followed the decision in *Asea Brown Boveri*. In *Invensys* **10.83** *Australia Superannuation Fund Pty Ltd v Austrac Investments Ltd*[82] Byrne J had to consider a request by trustees for confirmation that they could reach a deal with the employer—a refund of surplus in exchange for benefit improvements. The question arose as to whether this was compatible with the pension trust and in particular the covenant implied under s 52(2)(c) of the Superannuation Industry (Supervision) Act 1993 (the SIS Act) which is as follows:

Section 53 covenants to be included in governing rules

52—(1) Governing rules taken to contain covenants. If the governing rules of a superannuation entity do not contain covenants to the effect of the covenants set out in subsection (2), those governing rules are taken to contain covenants to that effect.

---

[80] [1985] Ch 270 at 288D. See the commentary on *Cowan v Scargill* in Paul Watchman, Jane Anstee-Wedderburn, and Lucas Shipway, 'Fiduciary Duties in the 21st Century: A UK Perspective' (2005) 19 TLI 127.
[81] [1999] 1 VR 144 (Beach J). See at the end of the judgment, at 161.
[82] (2006) 198 FLR 302, [2006] VSC 112 (Byrne J).

(2) The covenants. The covenants referred to in subsection (1) are the following covenants by each trustee of the entity:

> . . .

> (c) to ensure that the trustee's duties and powers are performed and exercised in the best interests of the beneficiaries.

10.84 Byrne J held that the proposed surplus refund was allowed, but followed the narrow view expressed by Beach J in *Asea Brown Boveri*, holding:

> 108 Paragraph (c) then speaks of the interests of beneficiaries. In the SIS Act, beneficiary is a defined term:
>
> > 'beneficiary', in relation to a fund, scheme or trust, means a person (whether described in the governing rules as a member, a depositor or otherwise) who has a beneficial interest in the fund, scheme or trust and includes, in relation to a superannuation fund, a member of the fund despite the express references in this Act to members of such funds;
>
> It was common ground that the members of the Trust are beneficiaries. Counsel for the Trustee submitted that the employers in this case had a sufficient interest in the Fund to bring them, too, within this definition. Accordingly, it was contended, the Trustee was entitled and indeed obliged to have regard to their best interests as well as to those of members.
>
> 109 Counsel for certain of the defendants argued for a different construction of beneficiary, contending that, as a matter of construction, it did not include the employers. This appears to be the view taken in the APRA letters where 'beneficiaries' is treated as the equivalent of 'members'. This cannot be correct, if only because under the Trust Deed dependants of deceased members may be beneficiaries. Nevertheless, I was urged by all parties not to enter upon this debate and to proceed on the basis that the employers are not beneficiaries for the purposes of paragraph (c). I am content to do so without expressing any concluded view upon the matter. I will, for ease of reference, adopt the approach of APRA and treat the covenant in question as one directed for the benefit of members by which expression I include past and present and potential future members.
>
> 110 The first question for consideration is whether, having regard to the covenant inserted by s 52(2)(c), it is proper for the Trustee to make any distribution in favour of a non-beneficiary. How might such a distribution which involves the disbursement of a fund which might in other circumstances be paid to beneficiaries be in the best interest of those beneficiaries?
>
> 111 There are many answers to this. In *Asea Brown Boveri Superannuation Fund No.1 Pty Ltd v Asea Brown Boveri Pty Ltd*, Beach J concluded that the Trustee had a duty to act in the interests of the members of the fund only; it had no duty to act in the interests of the employer. This conclusion has been subject to some criticism[83] but, as a judge at first instance, I accept it as a statement of the law which I must apply. But this does not mean that the Trustee might not confer a benefit on the employers, if, in the opinion of the Trustee, this would be of benefit to the members. In the present case there is no certainty that the members might do better if less than $49.8M were distributed to the employers. It may be that, if the proposal involved a reduction in this payment, the employers would withdraw their support, with the consequence that there would be no distribution of surplus to anybody or that there would be a lengthy and expensive and uncertain litigation to resolve the impasse. The evidence before me shows that the Trustee has good grounds for such an apprehension. If only for this reason, I conclude that the Trustee is entitled, consistent with its proper concern for the best interests of the beneficiaries, to make a payment of part of the surplus to the employers.

---

[83] SEK Hulme, 'The Basic Duty of Trustees of Superannuation Trusts—Fair to One, Fair to All?' (2000) 14 TLI 130; D Pollard, 'Trustees' Duties to Employers: The Scope of the Duty of Pension Trustees' (2005) 20 TLI 21 at 49.

112 Second, the Trustee has formed the view that its duty to members with respect to the surplus, having regard to the nature of the trust, is to make a payment which is generous but not extravagant and that this payment would consume only $36M of the surplus. No criticism is directed to this decision.

113 Third, the covenant inserted by s 52(2)(c) is a covenant of the Trust Deed. The Deed including this covenant must accord with the legislative scheme which contemplates, in certain circumstances set out in s 117(5) that a payment might be made to employers. Nor is such a possibility seen in the statute to be inconsistent with the Trustee's obligations under s 62.

Other cases

In England, Elias J (as he then was) seems to have accepted counsel's submissions that trustees would be expected to act in the interests of members in agreeing whether or not to wind up a plan: *Hagen v ICI Chemicals*.[84] He was looking at a claim by Mr Hagen and other employees that they had been misled by ICI in relation to the pension benefits on offer following a transfer to Kvaerner. The ICI scheme did not have a power for it to be discontinued by the employer. The new Kvaerner scheme did. **10.85**

In New Zealand in *Re UEB Industries Ltd Pension Plan*[85] it was held that powers are to be exercised for the purpose for which they are conferred. But, like *Cowan v Scargill*, it also refers to the exercise of powers for the benefit of the beneficiaries so, again, it could also support the narrow view in appropriate circumstances. **10.86**

As SEK Hulme comments in his article, the narrow view seems to have evolved from case law (i) to the effect that pension scheme trusts are not purpose trusts[86] (thus refuting the arguments that powers should be exercised to promote the purposes of the trust) and (ii) dealing with balancing the interests of beneficiaries *inter se*.[87] **10.87**

What Will the Employer Do if Agreement is Not Given?

In many situations where trustees are being asked to consider agreeing to amendments requested by the employer, even if a narrow view is taken, the question remains whether the trustees could reasonably reach the decision that agreeing to the amendments is in the interest of the members. It may well be the case that if the trustees do not agree to the amendment, then there may well be a serious risk of a loss of support by the employers for the pension scheme. **10.88**

The employer may indicate that it may consider other options (but will be mindful of not making a threat that could breach the *Imperial Tobacco*[88] implied mutual duty of trust and confidence[89]). The employer's powers could include: **10.89**

(a) closing the scheme to future accruals; or

---

[84] [2002] IRLR 31 (Elias J).

[85] [1990] 3 NZLR 347 (Gault J), on appeal [1992] 1 NZLR 347, [1991] PLR 109, NZCA.

[86] See the Supreme Court of Canada in *Schmidt v Air Products* [1994] 2 SCR 611, SC Can.

[87] Citing *James Miller Holdings v JD Graham & Others* [1977–78] ACLC 30, [1992] PLR 165 (McGarvie J) and the decision of the Supreme Court of New South Wales on 13 October 1988 in *Austchem Nominees Pty Ltd v AC Hatrick Chemical Ltd*.

[88] [1991] 1 WLR 589 (Browne Wilkinson V-C). See Ch 13 (Employers' powers: the implied duty of trust and confidence).

[89] It seems to follow from *Imperial Tobacco* that the mutual duty of trust and confidence is owed to trustees as well. Notwithstanding this, it has been argued that the implied duty is *not* in fact enforceable by trustees (on the basis that it was not necessary for the decision in *Imperial Tobacco* to have the duty enforced by the trustees), but enforceability by trustees seems to be too well entrenched now. See Ch 13.

(b) winding-up the scheme—see for example on employer's powers to terminate employment in the Privy Council in *Reda v Flag Ltd*;[90] or

(c) limiting future increases in pay that is pensionable. This seems to be within the employer's unilateral powers, if there is no contractual right to a relevant pay rise (such a contractual right would be unusual).[91]

10.90 In practice an employer is now very unlikely to take any action which would trigger a winding-up of the scheme. Regulations under s 75 of the Pensions Act 1995 (which came fully into force in March 2004) mean that a debt will be triggered on the employer if the assets in the scheme are not enough to meet the full buy-out cost in respect of any scheme which begins winding-up after 11 June 2003. This was a major shift in the balance of power between employer and trustees. In practice it lead to the views of the Pensions Regulator that the trustees should in some circumstances treat themselves in the same way as a bank with an unsecured loan to the employer.

Statute/Regulator views

10.91 There are some references in statute to the need of trustees (or the Pensions Regulator) to consider the interests of members (and not others, eg employers or dependants etc).

(a) Section 37 of the Pensions Act 1995 deals with payment to employers. This is only allowed if the trustees agree and they must be satisfied that it is 'in the interests of the members' to agree to do this.[92]

(b) Section 11(1)(c) of the Pensions Act 1995 gives the Pensions Regulator the power to order the winding-up of a pension scheme if it is satisfied that this is 'necessary in order to protect the interest of the generality of the members of the scheme'.

(c) The Pensions Act 2004 gives objectives to the Pensions Regulator to seek to protect the benefits for members and also to reduce the risk of claims on the Pension Protection Fund (PPF).[93] But later the Pensions Regulator is also told, when exercising a regulatory function, to take account of the effect of its decisions on all those 'directly affected' (including presumably employers[94]).

10.92 The Pensions Regulator seems to be looking at the narrow view. Its guidance and public pronouncements indicate that trustees of defined benefit schemes with a deficit (and it is difficult to think of a scheme which will not have a deficit on the buy-out basis under s 75 of the Pensions Act 1995) should treat themselves as creditors of the employers in the same way as banks.

10.93 David Norgrove, the then chair of the Pensions Regulator commented in a speech in May 2005 to the National Association of Pension Funds:[95]

Here I would mention another word in what we want to be, and that is commercial. In making our decisions we are required to take into account the effect on jobs, the jobs of people who are not members of schemes as well as those who are. Generally this will point in the same

---

[90] [2002] UKPC 38, [2002] IRLR 747, PC.
[91] See *South West Trains v Wightman* [1997] OPLR 249, [1998] PLR 113 and *NUS Superannuation Fund v Pensions Ombudsman* [2002] OPLR 17, [2002] PLR 93.
[92] Section 37(4)(b). See further on s 37, Chapter 20 (Employers and surpluses).
[93] Pensions Act 2004, s 5.
[94] Pensions Act 2004, s 100(2).
[95] 12 May 2005.

direction as the objective of ensuring that benefits can be paid. After all, bankrupt companies cannot make pension contributions and neither can people who are unemployed. But we have already faced cases where an operation would go under if it could not leave its pension scheme behind, allowing it to fall into the PPF. We have agreed in those cases that a new company, without the pension scheme, should be created in order to preserve employment. But this has been on the condition that the pension scheme and therefore the PPF should benefit from any recovery by taking a stake in the new company, a larger stake, though still falling short of control, where no new money was going in, and a smaller stake where we were following banks or others who were putting in further investment.

The reference to bankruptcy is an indication that the Regulator was supporting the narrow **10.94** view. It begs the question of the view that the Regulator will take if the employer is sufficiently strong to be able to pay a large amount into the scheme (without a risk of insolvency). Should the trustees/Regulator be looking for funding up to (say) a buy-out level—or should they take into account the need to keep the employer strong? This is a fundamental question (which Parliament seems to have pushed onto trustees and the Pensions Regulator rather than enact a funding standard itself).

The government issued a consultation paper on this issue in January 2013. The DWP asked **10.95** for evidence as to whether the statutory objectives of the Regulator should be amended to provide for it to consider the financial position of employers. The specific question is 'What would be the advantages of a new statutory objective for the Pensions Regulator to consider the long term affordability of deficit recovery plans to sponsoring employers?'. A proposed new objective is included in the Pensions Bill (presented for first reading in May 2013)—see para 10.10 above.

The consultation paper on funding issued at the end of October 2005 by the Pensions **10.96** Regulator is noticeable for saying very little about the ability of trustees to have regard to the interests of the employer when negotiating on funding matters. There is some discussion around looking at the ability of the employer to pay, but that seems to be having regard to the affordable cost rather than the 'acceptable' cost referred to in the primary purpose suggested above (see para 10.50 above).

There are references in this consultation document to wanting strong employers: **10.97**

> While we will want to make sure that recovery plans provide the best possible mechanism for protecting scheme members within a realistic timeframe, we will also need to have regard to what the employer can reasonably afford. Indeed, we take the issue of affordability very seriously, and recognise that there will be a number of schemes which trigger our attention, but where regulatory intervention would not be appropriate because of the position of the sponsoring employer. We recognise that the best guarantee that members' benefits will be paid is a strong employer standing behind the scheme.[96]

But generally this consultation document proceeds on the basis that strong employers should **10.98** fund pension schemes as quickly as the employer can reasonably afford:[97]

> The length and profiling of the recovery period are key factors affecting the security of members' benefits. Trustees should aim for any shortfall to be eliminated as quickly as the employer can reasonably afford. The longer the recovery period the greater the chance that

---

[96] See p 4.
[97] See p 44.

the sponsoring employer will default on its payments to the pension scheme. Default is most likely because of a weakening employer and in extreme cases its insolvency.

10.99 See also the draft policy *Statement* in Ch 7:[98]

> Taking these factors into account, we may consider intervention if: . . . (ii) the recovery period is less than ten years and we consider that the financial position of the employer is such that it could reasonably clear the shortfall in a shorter period, bearing in mind the strength of the funding target (technical provisions).

10.100 The consultation document seems to look very much at the narrow view of considering only the interest of the employers to the extent that this impacts on the interests of the members.

10.101 In practice the Pensions Regulator's views are consistent with its role of protecting members' benefits and the PPF. And these views are likely to weigh heavily with trustees. But it is noticeable that there is no requirement (or protection) in the legislation for trustees to comply with direction or wishes of the Pensions Regulator. So in theory, trustees could be held to be liable for a breach of duty even if they just follow the guidance (or a specific direction) from the Pensions Regulator.

10.102 This is to be contrasted with the position of charity trustees who are able, under the Charities Act 1993, to get a confirmation from the Charity Commission approving actions that the trustees are considering taking. For example, under s 26, an action can be authorized by the Charity Commissioners:

> where it appears to the Commissioners that any action proposed or contemplated in the administration of a charity is expedient in the interests of the charity.

10.103 If approved, the charity trustees are protected from breach of trust claims if they take the action.[99] Note that this refers to 'the interests of the charity', not the interests of the beneficiaries.

Investment: the IORP Directive

10.104 For investment matters, the EU Directive on Institutions for Occupational Retirement Provision (the IORP Directive) points to the narrow view. Article 18 deals with investment rules and states:

> 1. Member States shall require institutions located in their territories to invest in accordance with the 'prudent person' rule and in particular in accordance with the following rules:
>
> (a) the assets shall be invested in the best interests of members and beneficiaries. In the case of a potential conflict of interest, the institution, or the entity which manages its portfolio, shall ensure that the investment is made in the sole interest of members and beneficiaries. . . .

10.105 Article 6 defines a member as 'a person whose occupational activities entitle or will entitle him/her to retirement benefits in accordance with the provisions of a pension scheme' and beneficiary as 'a person receiving retirement benefits'. This looks to mean that the term beneficiary is arguably defined in the IORP Directive to exclude the employer.

---

[98] Paragraph 3.16 at p 69.

[99] See ss 26 and 29 of the Charities Act 1993 and Mark Atkinson, 'Goalkeepers Are Different. What About Pension Scheme Trustees?' (2003) 17 TLI 25 at 32.

This has been enacted in the UK by regulations under s 245 of the Pensions Act 2004. **10.106** Regulation 4(1) and (2) of the Occupational Pension Schemes (Investment) Regulations 2005[100] provide:

> 4.—(1) The trustees of a trust scheme must exercise their powers of investment, and any fund manager to whom any discretion has been delegated under section 34 of the 1995 Act (power of investment and delegation) must exercise the discretion, in accordance with the following provisions of this regulation.
>
> (2) The assets must be invested—
>> (a) in the best interests of members and beneficiaries; and
>> (b) in the case of a potential conflict of interest, in the sole interest of members and beneficiaries.

Regulation 4(11) then defines beneficiary in a way that seems intended to exclude an **10.107** employer:[101]

> 'beneficiary', in relation to a scheme, means a person, other than a member of the scheme, who is entitled to the payment of benefits under the scheme.

It remains to be seen how this will be interpreted by the Courts. Increasingly the level of risk **10.108** being undertaken by a pension scheme is a matter in which the employer has a great interest (see further the discussion below).

It may be that this limitation (not reflected in any other statutory provision) allows the **10.109** interest of the employer still to be something that the trustees should take into account (in a similar manner to the finding mentioned at para 10.39 above of Lightman J in *Fuller v Evans* in relation to a 'no benefit' provision in a private trust).

Examples of Issues[102]

Turning to some examples, following *Edge* and *Halliwell*, should the employer's interests be **10.110** taken into account on the basis that it is also a beneficiary? Or, following *Cowan v Scargill* and *Asea Brown Boveri*, should the trustees limit any consideration of the interests of the employers to circumstances where the interests of the employers have a direct benefit for the members?

Amendment to Reduce Future Service Benefits

The Pension Law Reform Committee[103] (chaired by Professor Goode) reported in 1993. It **10.111** recommended that changes to accrued rights should be limited by statute (this was subsequently enacted as s 67 of the Pensions Act 1995). But it commented that employers should be able to change future pension benefits. To limit employers too much would be to make pension provision too inflexible. The Committee commented (at p 282):

---

[100] SI 2005/3378.

[101] Although query if it does so. Employers can directly benefit by way of payment under schemes, as outlined above.

[102] See Ian Greenstreet, 'Should Trustees be More Like Bankers?: The Changing Role of Occupational Pension Scheme Trustees' (2005) 19 TLI 3 and 'Voting for Christmas—The Legal Issues' (APL conference, June 2005); and Isabel France, 'Pension Scheme Rule Amendments—Getting It Right' (2004) 18 TLI 202.

[103] CM 2342.

Amendment detrimental to future rights

4.6.16 We believe that it would be unreasonable not to allow the employer to procure changes to the pension scheme for future service. To insist that the terms on which pension rights accrued did not change (and that in consequence the scheme could not be wound up) for any employee who was a member of the scheme at the point of change would make pension provision extremely inflexible. Pension schemes are established by the voluntary act of the employer, who should equally be free to stop providing pensions, or to change the way in which they are provided. Locking employers in to a single pattern of provision would be a major disincentive to their making any provision at all. The employer's ability to procure such changes would, of course, be subject to the scheme rules, employment law and the contract of employment.

4.6.17 Since scheme members are no longer required to join or remain in the scheme, it is open to them to decide to make alternative arrangements after any amendment is made. However, as the future expectations of at least some scheme members would be reduced by this kind of amendment we believe that they should be given, say, a month's advance notice before the amendment takes effect so that they have the opportunity to decide whether or not they wish to remain in the amended scheme.

10.112 So what have the courts said? At first blush it seems difficult to reconcile the decisions.

10.113 Both *Edge* and *Halliwell* related to the use of surplus. Use of surplus relates directly to the financial interests of the employer. A reduction in future service benefits clearly has cost implications for the employer. Particularly in the current market where many employers argue that it is not financially viable to continue to provide defined benefits on the generous basis which they have done in the past. With that background, it is difficult to see how *Edge* could be distinguished in this context. Of course the interests of the employer would be one of many relevant factors (some of which are referred to in Chadwick LJ's judgment in *Edge*) and it would be a matter for the trustees what weight they attributed to the various factors.

10.114 *Asea Brown Boveri* is more directly on point since it related to the exercise of the power of amendment. Here the trustees could only take account of the interests of the employer where this benefited members, ie by negotiating a package which benefited the members and the employers. *Hagen v ICI* suggests that the interests of the employers can only be taken into account where the employer is in dire financial circumstances.

10.115 Interestingly, although leading authorities for the argument that trustees must consider only the interests of the beneficiaries, both *Asea Brown* and *Invensys* acknowledge the interests of the employer as a relevant factor but then seek to limit the circumstances in which or extent to which the trustees can take it into account.

10.116 Does it make any difference if (say) an amendment power is a joint power and not a unilateral power of the trustees? It is perhaps arguable that, because the power is joint, the trustees need not take into account the interests of the employer because it does that for itself. However, it is clear from the first instance judgment of Sir Richard Scott V-C in *Edge*[104] that trustees are not required to make a commercial deal. He held:

> If the trustees had chosen to adopt such a starkly confrontational role as is suggested by the submission, they would have been entitled to do so. But their failure to do so did not, in my judgment, take them outside the spectrum of possible stances that a reasonable body

---

[104] [1998] Ch 512 (Sir Richard Scott V-C).

of trustees could properly adopt. They were not obliged to deal with the employers at arm's length as if bargaining over some commercial deal.[105]

The natural extension of this concept is that trustees do not have to adopt a negotiating position which is likely to involve putting forward a position which the employer is likely to find unattractive. In the Court of Appeal in *Edge*,[106] Chadwick LJ made two comments which illustrate this. **10.117**

> the Ombudsman criticised the trustees for making such recommendations as they felt to be fair to everyone involved in the funds. His criticism suggests that, for the trustees to escape censure, they should have put forward proposals that they did not think were fair to the employers. We find that an astonishing proposition.

Chadwick LJ then referred to the fact that the case involved the trustees putting forward proposals which the employers would be likely to find attractive and commented that: 'they were entitled to take the view that half a loaf was better than no bread'. **10.118**

The rebuttal to the argument that the employer is there to look after its own interests therefore is that the trustee can and should consider the interests of the employer to ensure that it adopts a realistic approach and to maintain goodwill to ensure that the half a loaf (as opposed to no loaf) is obtained. The question introduced by *Asea Brown Boveri* is whether this is only a legitimate course of action where the employer's financial position is extreme. **10.119**

Statutory power

There will be a statutory power for trustees (with the agreement of the employer) to reduce future service benefits if the scheme specific funding arrangements (eg technical provisions and recovery plan) cannot be agreed—s 229(2) of the Pensions Act 2004. Although this arises in the rather different context of a statutory power to amend, presumably the trustees' duty to beneficiaries as to their exercise of that power would remain the same, and it perhaps provides a useful suggestion that seen at least against the background of the need to secure past benefits, future service changes may well be reasonable. **10.120**

Finance Act changes

In 2004 the government seemed to think that changes to future service benefits are allowed. Thus Ruth Kelly MP (then the Financial Secretary to the Treasury) commented in the debates in relation to pensions tax simplification in what became the Finance Act 2004 that trustees could properly agree to amend schemes to keep benefits capped by current revenue limits even though these limits were to be removed by the tax simplification. She stated:[107] **10.121**

> Under trust law, trustees will have a fiduciary duty to act in the best interests of all the beneficiaries. They would simply be fulfilling that duty and acting in line with trust law if they changed scheme rules to allow the scheme to move into the simplified regime without losing upper limits on payable benefits or becoming liable to make unauthorised payments.

---

[105] See also the comments of the Court of Session in *Harding (Trustees of Joy Manufacturing Holdings Ltd Pension and Life Assurance Scheme)* [1999] OPLR 235, CSIH (noted in (1999) 13 TLI 255), referring to Scott V-C in *Edge*.

[106] [2000] Ch 603 at 634, CA.

[107] Debates on the Finance Bill, Standing Committee: 22 June 2004, Hansard col 657.

Decisions in Relation to the Investment Policy

10.122   Regardless of what the trust deed may say, the obligation to determine the investment policy is placed on the trustees by the Pensions Act 1995. The Pensions Act 1995 recognizes the interests of the employer in that it requires the trustees to consult with the employer about the statement of investment policy—s 35(5)(b). In addition, the trustees' power to make decisions in relation to investment matters may not be restricted by reference to the consent of the employer—s 35(4).

10.123   Assuming for these purposes that (say) the trustees are satisfied that equities will outperform gilts in the long term and the trustees are satisfied that there is no prospect of the scheme being wound-up in the near future, is it appropriate for the trustees to take account of the financial interests of the employer in setting the investment strategy? Or should the trustees be concerned only for the interests of the beneficiaries (which, on one analysis, would favour increased security and therefore arguably would favour investment in gilts and fixed interest securities)?

10.124   Unfortunately the decisions which relate directly to the exercise of the investment power (of which there are surprisingly few) are relatively unhelpful. Broadly, they support the idea that the powers should be exercised for the purposes for which they were given (and should not be influenced by personal or moral views) and should be exercised to benefit the beneficiaries by maximizing return.[108] Perhaps surprisingly, the cases focused on the interests of the members that might be derived from generating surplus rather than the interests of the employers in being able to provide the same (or greater) benefits at less costs if the fund return were greater.

10.125   In the current environment where schemes are more likely to be in deficit than surplus and schemes are even more unlikely to be sufficiently funded to meet liabilities on a winding-up (without additional funding from employers which is now required unless the employer is in liquidation or the wind-up commenced before 11 June 2003),[109] it is arguable that security is more important to members than the possibility of generating surplus.

10.126   The IORP Directive (see para 10.104 above) includes a prudent man test (interestingly prudence is not expressly stated in the later UK Investment Regulations[110]). This may lead trustees to be more cautious on risk. But note that in a private trust context, the more recent claims against trustees that have reached court have been concerned with arguments that trustees have been over cautious—eg a failure by trustees to move out of bonds and into equities—see *Nestle v National Westminster Bank*[111] and, in New Zealand, *Re Mulligan*.[112]

---

[108]   See *Cowan v Scargill* [1985] Ch 270 (Megarry J); *Martin v City of Edinburgh District Council* 1988 SLT 329 (CSOH); [1989] 1 PLR 9; *Harries (Bishop of Oxford) v The Church Commissioners* [1992] 1 WLR 1241, [1993] 2 All ER 300. But there may be a contrast with the earlier cases focusing on avoidance of risk—*Re Whiteley* (1887) 12 App Cas 727 at 733 'avoid all investments...attended with hazard'; *Re Godfrey* (1883) 23 ChD 483 at 493 acknowledging that a 'prudent degree of risk' is appropriate; and *Nestle v National Westminster Bank* [1994] 1 All ER 118, CA noting that (broadly) a trustee is to be judged not on lost return but on success in securing the trust fund.

[109]   This is the statutory debt under s 75 of the Pensions Act 1995. Regulations from 15 February 2005 removed the previous exception for an employer in liquidation—although such employers may not have the resources to meet the buy-out costs. See Pollard, *Corporate Insolvency: Employment and Pension Rights* 5th edn (2013) Ch 57.

[110]   Occupational Pension Schemes (Investment) Regulations 2005 (SI 2005/3378).

[111]   [1993] 1 WLR 1260, [1994] 1 All ER 118, CA.

[112]   *Hampton v PGG Trust Ltd* [1998] 1 NZLR 481 (Panckhurst J).

Many trustees are adopting a cautious approach and increasingly moving towards greater **10.127** security. On the principles laid down in *Edge* and *Halliwell*, the trustees should at least consider the interests of the employers when making these decisions. This is supported by the fact that even though this may be a unilateral trustee decision, it is one in relation to which the trustees are required by the Pensions Act 1995 to consult the employer.[113]

It may be possible in these circumstances to distinguish the cases which support the narrow **10.128** view on the basis that they related to joint powers and the decisions concerned did directly impact on the interests of the members. With the new requirement on employers to fund full buy-out costs, the members' benefits should not be at risk unless the employer does not have the financial backing to meet any winding-up debt.

The additional security that may be found in the Pension Protection Fund (under the **10.129** Pensions Act 2004) should also be a factor for trustees.[114]

The increased powers of trustees (under statute) means that this issue is coming to be investi- **10.130** gated by the courts.

In *Pitmans Trustees Ltd v Telecommunications Group plc*[115] the employer argued that the adoption **10.131** of a gilts matched investment policy by the trustees took place for an improper purpose, namely to increase the amount payable by the employer under s 75 of the Pensions Act 1995.

Sir Andrew Morritt V-C held (on other grounds) that a valid gilts matched policy had not **10.132** been adopted. But he went on to deal with this other argument briefly by saying:

> the adoption of the revised statement of investment principles was plainly done with the intention that a gilts-matching policy be adopted. The fact, if it be one, that one of the motives for such an adoption was to maximise the Trustees' claim under s.75 would not vitiate the exercise of the power.

Strictly this was not necessary for his decision. This may be no more than an appreciation **10.133** that trustees can ask for the increased s 75 buy-out debt if a winding-up is likely (eg *Capital Cranfield*). In practice it is unlikely that the Vice-Chancellor was intending to cast aside the case law built up over many years on issues of improper use of powers. But it perhaps gives an indication of the difficulties that employers may face in seeking to set aside decisions of trustees.

Tort Duty

Does the trustee owe any duty of care in tort to the employer? Any loss would be economic, **10.134** so there would need to be a special relationship for a negligence duty to arise (under the principles relating to negligent mis-statement in *Hedley Byrne v Heller*[116]). It seems to be fairly easy to show that a trustee's relationship with the employers, as the ultimate funders of a defined benefit scheme, should fall into this class.

---

[113] See reg 2(2)(b) of the Occupational Pension Schemes (Investment) Regulations 2005 (SI 2005/3378).

[114] But this causes some problems in analysis. Do trustees owe a duty to the PPF? Or do they have a higher duty to beneficiaries? See Ch 9 and Henderson J in *Independent Trustee Services Ltd v Hope* [2009] EWHC 2810 (Ch), [2010] ICR 553 and Andrew Simmonds QC, 'The Pension Protection Fund—18 Months On' (2007) 21 TLI 150.

[115] [2004] EWHC 181 (Ch), [2005] OPLR 1, [2004] PLR 213 (Sir Andrew Morritt V-C).

[116] [1964] AC 465, HL.

10.135 In *White v Jones*,[117] the House of Lords held a solicitor liable in tort to a potential beneficiary under a will where the solicitor had negligently failed to prepare the will before the testator died. Lord Goff held that reliance by the intended beneficiary was not necessary. The law would give the intended beneficiary a remedy to avoid a lacuna in the law.

10.136 The principle in *White v Jones* has been applied in a pension context. *Gorham v British Telecommunications plc*[118] involved a claim by the dependants of a deceased employee against BT (his former employer), the pension scheme trustees, and a financial adviser. The employee had been wrongly advised by a financial adviser tied to an insurer, Standard Life, to take out a personal pension. He had not been advised that it would have been better to enter the employer's scheme. The Court of Appeal held that a financial adviser could owe a duty in tort to dependants.

10.137 In *HR v JAPT*[119] the plaintiff (a new trustee) was claiming against the directors of a previous trustee. One ground for the claim was that the directors of a trustee company owed a duty of care in tort to the intended beneficiaries falling within the *White v Jones* principle. Lindsay J did not view this argument with favour.

10.138 Lindsay J held that no such duty could arise here. He considered that arguments based on an imposition of a duty of care in tort where persons act for others could only apply where there was otherwise a lacuna in the law which would be unjust. For example in *White v Jones*, the projected beneficiaries of the deceased would have no claim open to them against the negligent solicitor unless a tortious duty was involved.

10.139 Lindsay J felt[120] that he:

> cannot read the broad language as intended impliedly to override long established existing principles as to the identification, outside the identified lacuna, of as between whom fiduciary relationships exist or as to the identity of he who should be taken to have been the actor who should have assumed responsibility and who, on that account, became vulnerable to a claim.

10.140 In *HR v JAPT*, there was no lacuna in the law and to hold otherwise would in effect be to overturn the well-established principles on corporate personality such as that found in *Salomon v Salomon*.[121] Accordingly, Lindsay J held that this argument did not have any prospect of success.

10.141 JD Heydon has argued that a trustee should not have a concurrent liability in tort.[122] But that seems to be in the context of a claim by a direct beneficiary, not by an employer.

Contract

10.142 It seems unlikely that trustees would owe a contractual duty to employers. There may, under the trust deed, be a contractual obligation on employers to contribute—see eg the decision of the Privy Council in *Air Jamaica v Charlton*[123] and Patten J in *MNOPF Trustees Ltd v FT*

---

[117] [1995] 2 AC 207, HL.
[118] [2000] 4 All ER 867, CA. Discussed in Ch 5 (Liability of directors of corporate trustees).
[119] [1997] OPLR 123 (Lindsay J). See Ch 5 (Liability of directors of corporate trustees).
[120] At 135C.
[121] [1897] AC 22, HL.
[122] 'The Negligent Fiduciary' [1995] 111 LQR 1. Discussed by Nicholas Warren QC (as he then was) in 'Trustee Risk and Liability' (1999) 13 TLI 226 at 230.
[123] [1999] 1 WLR 1399, PC.

Everard & Sons Ltd.[124] Does this imply a duty of care on the trustees if they have to fix the contribution rate or invest the contributions received? Perhaps only in a multi-employer scheme if the trustees have power to apportion contributions among the employers—perhaps a duty to act at least in good faith is implied.[125]

Conclusion: Trustees Acting Fairly

Overall, the best view is that trustees must act fairly, balancing the primary interests of the members (and their secondary beneficiaries) against the rights and interest of the employers (as funders of the scheme). This is supported by the Court of Appeal in *Foster Wheeler v Hanley*.[126] Arden LJ commented **10.143**

> By conferring a windfall on members with mixed NRDs, the judge's solution did not satisfy the principles which I have identified. It is unfair to the company and potentially unfair to other members of the scheme. I am reinforced in this view by the fact that Mr Spink's submissions did not give any reasons to justify the windfall element as such of the judge's solution. In my judgment, the windfall element constituted a fatal flaw.

This can be seen as similar to the duty imposed on trustees in a private family settlement to decide on investment strategy, balancing the interests of the life tenant with the ultimate remaindermen. **10.144**

A similar balancing exercise is envisaged from local authorities when (say) deciding between transport users and ratepayers when fixing on a transport policy—see Lord Wilberforce in *Bromley v Greater London Council*:[127] **10.145**

> ... the G.L.C. owes a duty to two different classes. First, under its responsibility for meeting the needs of Greater London, it must provide for transport users: these include not only the residents of London, but persons travelling to and in London from outside (e.g. commuters) and tourists. Most of these will not pay rates to the G.L.C. Secondly, it owes a duty of a fiduciary character to its ratepayers who have to provide the money.

This discretion has pretty wide bounds. For example in *Wrightson v Fletcher Challenge*,[128] the Privy Council held that pension trustees had a wide discretion (when considering the amount of a transfer payment to a new scheme). The issue here was how the trustee decided on an appropriate transfer payment to be paid to a new fund following an employer (Wrightson) ceasing to participate (following its demerger from the Fletcher Challenge group). The deed provided that: **10.146**

> there shall be deemed to be a dissolution of such part of the Plan as the Trustee determines to be appropriate to the Participating Company.

[124] [2005] EWHC 446, [2005] PLR 225 (Patten J).
[125] By analogy with the duties on an agent bank in a syndicated loan arrangement—on the duties of agent banks, see *Redwood Master Fund Ltd v TD Bank Europe Ltd* [2002] EWHC 2703 (Ch), [2006] 1 BCLC 149 (Rimer J). But to the contrary see Neil Kandelaars, 'The Relationship Between Trustee, Member and Participating Employer of a Superannuation Fund' (1999) 13 TLI 210 at 225.
[126] [2009] EWCA Civ 651, [2010] ICR 374 at [36], CA.
[127] [1983] 1 AC 768 at 815, HL.
[128] [2001] UKPC 23, [2001] OPLR 249, PC. Oddly not mentioned in later transfer cases, *Independent Trustee Services v Hope* [2009] EWHC 2810 (Ch), [2010] ICR 553 (Henderson J) and *Dalriada Trustees Ltd v Faulds* [2011] EWHC 3391 (Ch) (Bean J). See Ch 9.

10.147 Lord Millett gave the Privy Council's judgment. He upheld the decision of the trustee to agree with the remaining employer and not to pass any share of surplus to the leaving employer's new pension fund. However, he felt the point was finely balanced:

> The Trustee is not entitled to allocate to the withdrawing company so much of the Fund 'as it thinks fit', but so much 'as is appropriate' to the company in question. This limits the matters of which the Trustee can take account, but in their Lordships' opinion it does not dictate the choice between a share of fund and a benefits based approach. The circumstances attendant on a partial dissolution are many and various, and their Lordships think that it would have been unwise to fetter the Trustee's discretion to choose between the rival approaches in any way, even by indicating a presumptive 'starting point'. Accordingly, they agree with the Court of Appeal that the Trustee should approach the determination of the part of the Plan attributable to the withdrawing company with an open mind, and without adopting any presumption as to the adoption of one or other of the rival approaches.

> 30 Their Lordships have considered the rival arguments in relation to the manner in which the Trustee exercised its discretion, and consider that the Court of Appeal came to the right conclusion. The surplus was relatively small and might well disappear in a short period of time should market conditions deteriorate. The Trustee was entitled to take the view that no part of it should be allocated to the Wrightson scheme. While some of the arguments which the Trustee considered might appear to be irrelevant to the exercise of its discretion, most of them had been raised by Wrightson and the Trustee could not be criticised for responding to them.

10.148 All of this leaves trustees very much up in the air. The amounts at stake are pretty large. On one side will be the employers, anxious not to have to pay too much too soon into a scheme; on the other the Pensions Regulator and the Pension Protection Fund (to say nothing of the members), who will be looking back over the actions of the past trustees—partly with a view to seeing if there is a potential claim.

11

EMPLOYER POWERS—NON-FIDUCIARY

Introduction

This chapter looks at: **11.1**

(a) What does it mean if a power is described as a fiduciary power?
(b) Are powers held by employers generally fiduciary?
(c) What do the pensions cases say?

What is a Fiduciary Power or Duty?

The term 'fiduciary duty' draws its ambit from the context and from the position of the parties.[1] **11.2**

Robert Walker J (as he then was) at first instance in *National Grid v Laws*[2] summarized the **11.3**
position when discussing the limits on an employer power under a pension scheme (in this
case to direct use of a surplus):

> 88 … The content of every fiduciary obligation is not the same. To say that a person is a
> fiduciary is the beginning, not the end, of analysis, as Frankfurter J observed in *SEC v Chenery
> Corporation* (1943) 318 US 80, 85–6. The *Imperial Tobacco* duty of good faith does (as appears
> from the examples mentioned above) prohibit the exercise of powers for collateral (and so
> improper) purposes. There is a similar prohibition on the exercise of a fiduciary power. To that
> extent, the content of the two types of duty does overlap. Nevertheless there is an essential
> distinction between the two, in that the *Imperial Tobacco* duty does not prevent the employer

---

[1] See generally, Matthew Conaglen, *Fiduciary Loyalty: Protecting the Due Performance of Non-fiduciary Duties*
(Hart Publishing, 2010) 258, 259, 260, and 268. There is also a good explanation in A Stafford QC and S
Ritchie, *Fiduciary Duty—Directors and Employees* (Jordans, 2008) Ch 1.
[2] [1997] OPLR 207, [1997] PLR 157 (Robert Walker J).

from looking after its own financial interests, even where they conflict with those of members and pensioners; see *Imperial Tobacco* [[1991] IRLR 66, 77]. I am driven to the conclusion that the Ombudsman, in his reference to National Grid preferring its other interests, lost sight of that essential distinction.

11.4 In *Bristol and West Building Society v Mothew*,[3] Millett LJ (as he then was) held:[4]

Breach of fiduciary duty

Despite the warning given by Fletcher Moulton LJ in *In re Coomber; Coomber v Coomber* [1911] 1 Ch 723, 728, this branch of the law has been bedevilled by unthinking resort to verbal formulae. It is therefore necessary to begin by defining one's terms. The expression 'fiduciary duty' is properly confined to those duties which are peculiar to fiduciaries and the breach of which attracts legal consequences differing from those consequent upon the breach of other duties. Unless the expression is so limited it is lacking in practical utility. In this sense it is obvious that not every breach of duty by a fiduciary is a breach of fiduciary duty. I would endorse the observations of Southin J in *Girardet v Crease & Co* (1987) 11 BCLR (2d) 361, 362:

> The word 'fiduciary' is flung around now as if it applied to all breaches of duty by solicitors, directors of companies and so forth ... That a lawyer can commit a breach of the special duty [of a fiduciary] ... by entering into a contract with the client without full disclosure ... and so forth is clear. But to say that simple carelessness in giving advice is such a breach is a perversion of words.

These remarks were approved by La Forest J in *LAC Minerals Ltd v International Corona Resources Ltd* (1989) 61 DLR (4th) 14, 28 where he said:

> ... not every legal claim arising out of a relationship with fiduciary incidents will give rise to a claim for breach of fiduciary duty.

11.5 This has been applied to directors—see *Gwembe Valley Holdings v Koshy*[5] and *Ultraframe (UK) Ltd v Fielding*.[6]

11.6 Matthew Conaglen in his book *Fiduciary Loyalty*[7] comments that much of the case law supports the view that:

> fiduciary duties arise when it is legitimate to expect that the fiduciary will 'act for and on behalf of' the other party to the relationship—'in the interests' of that party—and will do so to the exclusion of his own interest.

11.7 Conaglen cites (among others) the *Imperial Tobacco* case[8] and the decision of the High Court in Australia in *Hospital Products v US Surgical Corpn*[9] that there is no fiduciary duty where the whole purpose of the arrangement is that the other party can act in its own interests.

11.8 Conaglen comments[10] that there must be an expectation that the relevant party will put aside its own interests, citing *Global Container Lines v Bonyad Shipping*[11] and *Arklow Investments v Maclean*.[12]

---

[3] [1998] Ch 1, CA.

[4] [1998] Ch 1 at 16. Recently followed in *John Youngs Insurance Services Ltd v Aviva Insurance Service UK Ltd* [2011] EWHC 1515 at [75] (TCC) (Ramsey J).

[5] [2004] EWCA Civ 1048, [2004] 1 BCLC 131, CA.

[6] [2005] EWHC 1638 (Ch) (Lewison J).

[7] (Hart Publishing, 2010) 260.

[8] *Imperial Group Pension Trust Ltd v Imperial Tobacco Ltd* [1991] 2 All ER 597 (Browne-Wilkinson V-C). Discussed in Ch 13 (Employer powers: implied duty of trust and confidence).

[9] (1984) 156 CLR 41, HC Aus, at 63–4, 72–3, 122–4, and 144–6.

[10] At 259.

[11] [1998] 1 Lloyd's Rep 528 at 545 (Rix J).

[12] [2000] 1 WLR 594 at 598, PC.

Proper purposes[13]

Powers given to third parties (eg trustees or government ministers) are often considered by the courts to be subject to an implied limitation that they may only be exercised for a proper purpose.[14] **11.9**

Personal powers

Powers can be categorized (broadly) as being personal or fiduciary.[15] Edwin Simpson in his chapter on 'Conflicts' in the book *Breach of Trust*[16] commented: **11.10**

> Such a rule [the self or fair dealing rules] is not needed in the context of personal powers, since the donees of such powers have no fiduciary duties in relation to their exercise, and so the question of conflict of duty and interest does not arise.

In a footnote, he goes on: **11.11**

> Personal powers are subject to the doctrine of fraud on the power and may be regarded as fiduciary in the sense that there is a duty to the beneficiaries interested in default of their exercise not to exercise such powers otherwise than for an authorized object of the power: *Mettoy Pension Trustees Ltd v Evans* [1990] 1 WLR 1587, 1613G–1614A. But if the donee of a personal power is, as a matter of construction of the power, an object of it, there is nothing in the doctrine of fraud on the power which precludes an exercise of the power in favour of the donee: *Taylor v Allhusen* [1905] 1 Ch 529; *Re Penrose* [1933] Ch 793.

See also the discussion in the book by David Maclean *Trust and Powers*.[17] **11.12**

The limitation implied in an employment context, ie the implied duty of trust and confidence—sometimes described as a 'good faith' duty—is *not* the same as a fiduciary power. For example an employer can exercise the power in its own interests (which is not the case with a fiduciary duty or power). See eg Browne-Wilkinson V-C in *Imperial Tobacco*.[18] **11.13**

Matthew Conaglen in his book *Fiduciary Loyalty*[19] makes the point that good faith may be a part of a fiduciary duty, but is not the same as a fiduciary duty. Conaglen goes on to say[20] that: **11.14**

> The important point is that in these various cases the courts have been careful to make clear that a duty of good faith, when it is recognised, is not a fiduciary duty. One can identify numerous instances of that point being emphasised by courts which have recognised duties of good faith.

Conaglen cites various cases,[21] including the House of Lords' decisions in the employment case of *Johnson v Unisys*[22] and the pensions case of *National Grid v Mayes*.[23] **11.15**

---

[13] On proper purposes, see Ch 9 (Trustee powers: best interests or proper purpose) and Conaglen, *Fiduciary Loyalty* (2010) 44, and RC Nolan, 'Controlling Fiduciary Power' [2009] CLJ 293 at 298.

[14] See Ch 11 and *Independent Trustee Services Ltd v Hope* [2010] 1 ICR 553 at 571 (Henderson J).

[15] *Underhill and Hayton: Law of Trusts and Trustees* 18th edn, ed David Hayton, Paul Matthews, and Charles Mitchell (LexisNexis, 2010) paras 1.76 *et seq*.

[16] P Birks and A Pretto (eds), *Breach of Trust* (Hart Publishing, 2002) 87.

[17] (Sweet & Maxwell, 1989) 107–9.

[18] *Imperial Group Pension Trust Ltd v Imperial Tobacco Ltd* [1991] 2 All ER 597 (Browne-Wilkinson V-C). And more recently in a pensions context, *Prudential Staff Pensions Ltd v The Prudential Assurance Co Ltd* [2011] EWHC 960 (Ch), [2011] All ER (D) 142 (Apr) (Newey J) and in Australia *KCA Super Pty Ltd as Trustee of the Superannuation Fund known as 'KCA Super' (No 2)* [2011] NSWSC 1301 (Brereton J).

[19] (Hart Publishing, 2010) 42–4.

[20] See p 43.

[21] See p 43 fn 62.

[22] [2001] UKHL 13, [2003] 1 AC 518 at [24].

[23] [2001] UKHL 20, [2001] 1 WLR 864 at [11].

Pension Trusts—Employer Powers

11.16 It is common in pension trusts for the trust deed to include an express provision for the sponsoring employer (usually called a Principal Employer or a Principal Company—in a group situation there seems to be no requirement for it actually to be an employer) to have various important powers, including to be able to appoint and remove trustees of the pension scheme.

11.17 These commonly include powers:

(a) to agree the ongoing funding rate;
(b) to agree to amendments (this could be unilateral[24]);
(c) to appoint or remove trustees (subject to the statutory member-nominated trustee (MNT) provisions[25]);
(d) to limit investment decisions (now overridden by the Pensions Act 1995[26]);
(e) to wind-up the scheme;
(f) to agree augmentations; and
(g) to agree transfers in/transfers out.

General Rule

11.18 Powers held by an employer will, of course, be fiduciary if it happens also to be the trustee (and the trust deed gives those powers to the trustee).[27]

11.19 It is clear that the general position in relation to pensions trusts is that employer powers are not fiduciary. There is a whole raft of case law on this, which stems from the key *Imperial Tobacco*[28] case.

11.20 In *Imperial Tobacco*, Browne-Wilkinson V-C (as he then was) made a clear distinction (in relation to a power to give consent) between:

(a) a good faith obligation in exercising powers, where the employer is subject to the mutual duty of trust and confidence (but can take into account its own interests), and
(b) a fiduciary power.

11.21 He held:[29]

> The question as framed in the originating summons asks, first, whether the right to give or withhold consent is a fiduciary power. In the event, neither Mr Howell QC, for the pensioner members, nor Mr Topham, for the employee members, felt able to contend that this was a fiduciary power. I need therefore say no more on this issue than that I agree with the

---

[24] But in practice subject to the limitations on amendments adversely affecting accrued or subsisting rights under s 67 of the Pensions Act 1995.

[25] See ss 241–243 of the Pensions Act 2004.

[26] See s 35(5) of the Pensions Act 1995.

[27] See eg *Icarus (Hertford) Ltd v Driscoll* [1990] PLR 1 (Aldous J); *Re William Makin & Sons Ltd* [1993] OPLR 171 (Vinelott J); and *Polly Peck International plc v Henry* [1998] OPLR 323, [1999] 1 BCLC 407 (Buckley J).

[28] *Imperial Group Pension Trust Ltd v Imperial Tobacco Ltd* [1991] 2 All ER 597 (Browne-Wilkinson V-C).

[29] At 604–5.

concession: if this were a fiduciary power the company would have to decide whether or not to consent by reference only to the interests of the members, disregarding its own interests. This plainly was not the intention.

Nor did Browne-Wilkinson V-C consider a reasonableness test to be appropriate (at 605): **11.22**

I can see no necessity to engraft an implied limitation of reasonableness onto the company's right to refuse consent under cl 36. On the contrary, there are many good reasons why such limitation should not be implied. As Mr Mowbray QC, for the company, pointed out, in all pension schemes, including this one, the company has a direct personal interest in how the scheme is to operate for the future. Any change in benefits may well be reflected in the company having to make increased contributions. What is 'reasonable' from the point of view of the company may be unreasonable viewed through the eyes of the pensioners. Which viewpoint would the court have to adopt in testing reasonableness? Would the court have to seek to balance the reasonableness of both viewpoints? In the context of a pension scheme, a test of unreasonable withholding of consent would be unworkable.

And later (at 607) he commented: **11.23**

First, in my judgment the relevant question is not whether the company is acting reasonably. As I have said, where the interests of the company and the members are in direct conflict, it is impossible to say, for example, that the company is acting in breach of its obligations just because it would be reasonable to rely on the existing surplus as a basis for consent to an increase in the pension benefits beyond the guaranteed 5% minimum. It must be open to the company to look after its own interests, financially and otherwise, in the future operation of the scheme in deciding whether or not to give its consent.

In the *National Grid*[30] case in 2001, Lord Hoffmann looked at arguments about a power held **11.24**
by the employer to decide what should happen if a surplus was revealed. He commented:

[11] The judge held that the ombudsman had interpreted the implied duty of good faith too strictly. The employer was not a trustee. He was entitled to act in his own interests provided that he had regard to the reasonable expectations of the members. The arrangements satisfied that requirement. On this point the members now accept that the judge was right.

In *British Coal*[31] in 1993, Vinelott J held that a unilateral power of amendment held by the **11.25**
employer was not a fiduciary power and could be exercised by the employer in its own interests (at least while the scheme was ongoing and not winding-up). He referred to *Mettoy* and cases dealing with powers exercisable by insolvency practitioners and held:

However this may be, the position is quite different when the question relates to the exercise of a power of amendment of a pension fund which has not been wound up. The employer, if he has a power of amendment, is entitled to exercise it in any way which will further the purposes of the pension scheme to ensure that the legitimate expectations of the members and pensioners are met without, so far as possible, imposing any undue burden on the employer or building up an unnecessarily large surplus. The employer himself has an interest in maintaining a pension fund which is satisfactory to existing and attractive to future employees, and he has an interest in ensuring that it is effectively managed, for example in seeing that the powers of investment are confined within proper limits, if necessary by amendment, and that they are properly exercised.

---

[30] *National Grid Co plc v Mayes; International Power plc (formerly National Power plc) v Healy* [2001] UKHL 20, [2001] 2 All ER 417, HL.
[31] *British Coal Corpn v British Coal Staff Superannuation Scheme Trustees Ltd* [1995] 1 All ER 912 at 926 (Vinelott J). *British Coal* was overruled by the House of Lords in *National Grid*, but not on this point.

11.26 In *Hillsdown Holdings plc v Pensions Ombudsman*[32] Knox J was dealing with an appeal from the Pensions Ombudsman about a merger of pension schemes and a refund of surplus to the employer, Hillsdown. He referred to the good faith obligation on employers under the *Imperial Tobacco* case and held that this applied to the powers of the employer in relation to the adherence of new employers in to the scheme and to the fixing of the employer contribution rate. Knox J held (at 890):

> The other power which Hillsdown had was to suspend or determine its contributions under r 35. Clearly that power was given to it for its own benefit and there can be no question of fiduciary duty being owed in relation to its exercise.

11.27 Most recently in England, in *Prudential Staff Pensions Ltd v Prudential Assurance Co Ltd*,[33] Newey J followed *Imperial Tobacco* in looking at the extent and nature of the duties of an employer when deciding whether or not to exercise its discretion about whether or not to agree to discretionary pension increases under a pension scheme. He held:

> [140] The obligation of good faith is rooted in employment law's implied duty to preserve trust and confidence. It was by reference to the latter duty that Browne-Wilkinson V-C justified the former, explaining that the duty as to trust and confidence applied 'as much to the exercise of [an employer's] rights and powers under a pension scheme' as to an employer's other rights and powers. In *Johnson v Unisys Ltd*, Lord Steyn observed (in para 24) that the *Imperial* case 'did not involve trust law and the employer was not treated as a fiduciary'; the case, Lord Steyn opined, 'was decided on principles of contract law'.

11.28 And Newey J held later:

> [146] My own view is that members' interests and expectations may be of relevance when considering whether an employer has acted irrationally or perversely. There could potentially be cases in which, say, a decision to override expectations which an employer had engendered would be irrational or perverse. On the other hand, it is important to remember that powers such as that at issue in the present case are not fiduciary. As a result, the donee of the power is, as Mr Tennet pointed out, entitled to have regard to his own interests when making decisions... That fact must limit severely the circumstances in which a decision could be said to be irrational or perverse.

> [147] Had the power at issue been a fiduciary one, it would have been incumbent on Prudential to have regard to the correct considerations. *Edge v Pensions Ombudsman* [2000] Ch 602, [1999] 4 All ER 546, [2000] 3 WLR 79, for example, illustrates that a person exercising a fiduciary power must do so 'giving proper consideration to the matters which are relevant and excluding from consideration matters which are irrelevant' (see 627). I do not think that there is any similar obligation in relation to a power such as the one with which I am concerned. With such a non-fiduciary power, the court will, as it seems to me, consider whether, overall, a decision was irrational or perverse, not whether regard has been had to particular matters.

11.29 There is some authority in Canada that employer powers are not fiduciary—see, in Alberta, *Lloyd v Imperial Oil*.[34] *Imperial Tobacco* has been followed in Australia in a pensions context—for example the surplus case of *Lock v Westpac Banking Corpn*[35] and more recently in relation to changes in benefits—*KCA Super Pty Ltd as Trustee of the Superannuation Fund known as 'KCA Super' (No 2)*.[36]

---

[32] [1997] 1 All ER 862 (Knox J).
[33] [2011] EWHC 960 (Ch) (Newey J).
[34] 2008 ABQB 379 (Whittman ACJ).
[35] (1991) 25 NSWLR 593 (Waddell CJ in Eq).
[36] [2011] NSWSC 1301 at [67] (Brereton J).

In Australia in the *KCA Super* case[37] Brereton J was considering the position of a trustee when **11.30** faced with a proposal from the employer to change the benefits under the scheme, pointing out its alternative powers to wind-up the scheme. Brereton J held that the express power given to the company to dissolve the scheme was not a fiduciary power:

> 54 There is no reason to doubt that the Company, if lawfully able to do so, will pursue the alternative course of fund dissolution if the trustee's consent is not forthcoming. The question is whether the Company is lawfully able to do so.

> 55 The terms of the Company's power to dissolve the Fund, conferred by clause 48 of the Trust Deed, are not subject to any express limitation. I agree, as opined by Senior and Junior Counsel for the Trustee in their joint advice, that there is no reason to conclude that the Company is bound by any fiduciary obligation in exercising its powers under the Trust Deed, and is therefore at liberty to act in its own interests.

Brereton J went on to refer to *Imperial Tobacco* and to consider (at [61]) that it was 'doubtful **11.31** in the extreme' that the company would be a breach of good faith.

Imperial Tobacco—good faith

It is clear from the *Imperial Tobacco* case (and the later *Prudential* case) that any duty on **11.32** an employer to act in good faith, or consistently with an implied duty of trust and confidence, does not make the employer a fiduciary. See generally Matthew Conaglen in his book *Fiduciary Loyalty*,[38] citing *Re Courage*[39] and also *National Grid v Laws*,[40] *National Grid v Mayes*,[41] and *Johnson v Unisys*.[42]

Some exceptional cases

Employer powers can be categorized as fiduciary in two cases—these are clearly very restrictive **11.33** and exceptional cases:

(a) where the employer is also a trustee and the relevant power is clearly given to it in that capacity (eg *Icarus*,[43] discussed below); or

(b) where (perhaps) the power was previously held by the trustees and the scheme was amended so that the power passed to the employer in circumstances where otherwise the change would be struck down. This is the decision of Warner J in *Mettoy*.

Mettoy

In 1990 in *Mettoy Pension Trustees Ltd v Evans*[44] a power of the company to consent to aug- **11.34** mentations in a winding-up was held by Warner J to be fiduciary. However, this was in the unusual circumstances that the previous provisions had vested this augmentation power in the trustees and there was no evidence that the trustees had considered the implications of the change when agreeing to amend the scheme.

---

[37] *KCA Super Pty Ltd as Trustee of the Superannuation Fund known as 'KCA Super' (No 2)* [2011] NSWSC 1301 (Brereton J).
[38] At p 43.
[39] [1987] 1 WLR 495 at 514 (Millett J).
[40] [1997] OPLR 207 at 227 (Robert Walker J).
[41] [2000] ICR 174 at [42], CA.
[42] [2001] UKHL 13, [2003] 1 AC 518 at [24].
[43] *Icarus (Hertford) Ltd v Driscoll* [1990] PLR 1 (Aldous J).
[44] [1990] 1 WLR 1587, [1991] 2 All ER 513 (Warner J).

11.35 On *Mettoy*, the comments of Robert Walker J[45] (as he then was) at first instance in *National Grid*[46] are to be preferred:

> The judgment of Warner J in *Mettoy* contains a very clear and thorough analysis of all the authorities cited to him, but these did not and could not include *Imperial Tobacco* (which was decided in December 1990, a year after *Mettoy*). Although Warner J was in that case persuaded that the employer's power (to augment benefits in the winding-up of the scheme) was fiduciary, his judgment attached a great deal of weight to the insubstantial and almost illusory character of the power if it were not fiduciary (see [1990] 1 WLR especially at p 1615F). Had *Imperial Tobacco* been decided earlier and been cited in *Mettoy*, Warner J might possibly have come to a different conclusion as to whether the employer's power should be classified as fiduciary. At any rate it is the *Imperial Tobacco* duty that has received much more attention in later cases.

11.36 Matthew Conaglen in his book *Fiduciary Loyalty*[47] comments[48] that *Mettoy* is 'generally considered to have been wrongly decided on this point' (citing Robert Walker J's judgment in *National Grid*).

Two Odd Cases—*Noel Penny* and *Scully*

11.37 There are two more recent pensions cases, *Noel Penny* and *Scully*, where limits were discussed in relation to an employer power to consent to use of surplus. Both cases involved a winding-up of a pension scheme where a surplus would remain after benefits had been secured in full. In both cases some limits on employer powers were found, but they either do not address the issue (Judge Purle in *Noel Penny*) or are difficult to understand in context (the Privy Council in *Scully*).

Noel Penny (Turbines) Ltd—point not really argued

11.38 In 2008 in *Bridge Trustees Ltd v Noel Penny (Turbines) Ltd*[49] Judge Purle QC followed *Mettoy* and held that a power to distribute surplus given to the employer was a fiduciary power. He further held that the purpose of the statutory regime was to remove from the employer the power to distribute a surplus. This meant that the court could appoint a new trustee to exercise the power (the company had ceased to be in receivership, so the obligation under the Pensions Act 1995 to have an independent trustee had ended).

11.39 Judge Purle QC cited *Mettoy*, but no other case, in deciding this part of the judgment.

11.40 Judge Purle QC's comments—that the employer's power in relation to surplus could be seen as fiduciary—are odd and need to be treated with care. The company did not appear and was not represented before the court.[50] Judge Purle does not refer to the other cases on employer powers (eg *Imperial Tobacco*), nor to the comments by Robert Walker J in *National Grid* (see above).

---

[45] As Robert Walker QC he had been one of the counsel in *Mettoy*.

[46] *National Grid v Laws* [1997] OPLR 207 at 227 (Robert Walker J). See also David Hayton, 'Trust Law and Occupational Pension Schemes' [1993] Conv 283 at 292.

[47] (Hart Publishing, 2010).

[48] See p 44, fn 69. See also Hayton, 'Trust Law and Occupational Pension Schemes' 283 at 292.

[49] [2008] EWHC 2054 (Ch) (Judge Purle QC sitting as an additional Judge of the High Court).

[50] This means that the decision should not usually be cited in court—para 6 of the Practice Direction (Citation of Authorities) [2001] 2 All ER 510.

Scully v Coley

In *Scully v Coley*[51] the Privy Council dealt with an appeal from Jamaica concerning the **11.41** destination of a surplus on the winding-up of a pension scheme that had been established by Gillette. The main thrust of the decision concerns the meaning of who is a member of the scheme, but the Privy Council also briefly commented on the nature of employer's powers. Lord Collins gave the judgment and commented:

> 47 The final question is whether the provision that the allocation by the Administrator under Rule 12(c) is 'subject to the approval of [Gillette]' gives Gillette a fiduciary power to withhold approval, with the consequence (say the respondents) that the trustees could make no allocation, which would then be left to the court: *McPhail v Doulton* [1971] AC 424 at 457.

> 48 This question was raised in argument before Brooks J and the Court of Appeal, but was not the subject of decision. On this point the Board is satisfied that the appellants are right. The argument between the parties was centred on the question whether the power was a fiduciary power, and their Lordships were referred to several cases on the distinction between a power in relation to which the duty of the employer was limited to a duty of good faith and a power in respect of which the employer was a fiduciary and which was to be exercised solely in the interests of the objects of the power: *Icarus (Hertford) Ltd v Driscoll* [1990] PLR 1; *Mettoy Pension Trustees Ltd v Evans* [1990] 1 WLR 1587; *Imperial Group Pension Trust Ltd v Imperial Tobacco Ltd* [1991] 1 WLR 589; *Re William Makin & Son Ltd* [1992] PLR 177; *British Coal Corp v British Coal Staff Superannuation Scheme Trustees* [1994] ICR 537 (overruled on other grounds in *National Grid Co plc v Mayes* [2001] UKHL 20, [2001] 1 WLR 864 (HL)).

> 49 The question is not primarily whether the power is a fiduciary power (as the respondents say) or an administrative power (as the appellants say), since there is no necessary contrast between the two. In *Weinberger v Inglis* [1919] AC 606 (a decision which it would now be impossible to justify on the facts: the General Purposes Committee of the Stock Exchange was held entitled to exclude British naturalised subjects of German origin from membership) the power to admit persons to membership was held (at 640) to be both an administrative power and a fiduciary power. The real question is what is the purpose for which the power was granted. It is not necessary to decide in what circumstances Gillette could withhold approval of allocation under Rule 12(c). The reason is that their Lordships are satisfied that the power to withhold approval could not be used to alter the allocation to the 'then Members' and thereby to vary the Rules. There is already an express power in Rule 12(a) to change, modify or discontinue the Plan at any time. Gillette has not done so, and their Lordships consider it difficult (as the Board did in *Air Jamaica Ltd v Charlton* [1999] 1 WLR 1399, at 1411) to see how the Plan could lawfully be amended once it had been discontinued. Gillette has been kept informed at all times of the intentions of the Administrator and of the trustees, and is a party to these proceedings. *Gillette's failure to withhold approval cannot be regarded as a refusal to exercise a trust power so as to give the court the power to vary the provisions for allocation* (emphasis added).

Unfortunately, the decision of the Privy Council in *Scully* does not give much guidance as **11.42** to the reason why the employer in that case (Gillette) could not withhold its consent to the use of the surplus to increase benefits for members. The reference to *Air Jamaica* is unhelpful as that was a case where the employer was seeking to exercise an amendment power after a winding-up had started. The distinction between 'administrative' and 'fiduciary' powers seems odd as well—the real difference is between fiduciary and non-fiduciary (ie personal or

---

[51] [2009] UKPC 29, PC.

beneficial) powers (regardless of whether they are being used for 'dispositive' or 'administrative' purposes—this seems to be the rationale for the decision in the 1919 *Weinberger* case that the power to remove a member was both administrative and fiduciary).

11.43   Here the distribution of surplus for benefit increases for the members depended on Gillette giving its consent. Absent consent, the trust instrument envisaged no increase in member benefits (and so the surplus would presumably go somewhere else or perhaps move to a resulting trust).

11.44   The essential reasoning seems to be in the last part cited above, that Gillette had not become involved in the proceedings and so may be taken to have impliedly consented. The final comment cited above confirms (if anything) that the employer power (to give or withhold consent) was not fiduciary—'Gillette's failure to withhold approval cannot be regarded as a refusal to exercise a trust power so as to give the court the power to vary the provisions for allocation.'

11.45   If the general rule is that employer powers under or in connection with a pension scheme are not fiduciary, are there any exceptions and why is the power to appoint so special?

Challenges

11.46   It seems clear that if the answer is that the powers of an employer are fiduciary, then it will be easier for this to be challenged by a member or third party. For example, fiduciary powers are generally only exercisable in the interests of the trust and not in the interests of the power holder. The trustee-like duty to consider the proper exercise of the power (and not to take account of irrelevant factors etc), or at least to take proper advice, is limited to the exercise of a fiduciary power.

11.47   The precise limits of this 'proper consideration' obligation—at least as regards fiduciaries—are the subject of the *Hastings-Bass*[52] line of cases. Most recently the Supreme Court has ruled on this (in a non-pensions context) in *Pitt v HMRC*,[53] upholding the Court of Appeal in *Pitt v Holt*.[54] Similar issues are exercising the courts in Australia.[55] The Court of Appeal's reasoning in *Pitt v Holt* has been followed in a later pensions case.[56]

11.48   In *Sieff v Fox*,[57] Lloyd LJ commented on the distinction between powers held beneficially (less subject to review) and those held by trustees (ie fiduciary powers). He held:

> [112] Of course, *Scroggs v Scroggs*[58] was the converse of this case, in one sense, in that there the power was given to a beneficiary, and was not a fiduciary power, whereas the requirement of

---

[52]   *Re Hastings-Bass, Hastings-Bass v IRC* [1975] Ch 25, [1974] 2 All ER 193, CA and *Mettoy Pension Trustees v Evans* [1990] 1 WLR 1587 (Warner J).
[53]   *Pitt v HMRC, Futter v HMRC* [2013] UKSC 26, SC.
[54]   *Pitt v Holt; Futter v Futter* [2011] EWCA Civ 197, [2011] 2 All ER 450, CA. The decision of the Court of Appeal was upheld on this point: [2013] UKSC 26, SC. See the discussion by Teresa Rosen Peacocke, 'Liability of Professionals Retained by Settlors and Trustees Following Pitt v Holt/Futter v Futter' (2011) 25 TLI 125.
[55]   See the High Court in *Finch v Telstra Super Pty Ltd* [2010] HCA 36, HCA and *Manglicmot v Commonwealth Bank Officers Superannuation Corpn* [2010] NSWSC 363 (Rien J).
[56]   *Prudential Staff Pensions Ltd v The Prudential Assurance Co Ltd* [2011] EWHC 960 (Ch), [2011] All ER (D) 142 (Apr) (Newey J).
[57]   [2005] EWHC 1312 (Ch), [2005] 3 All ER 693 (Lloyd LJ, sitting as a judge of the High Court). Overturned by the Court of Appeal in *Pitt v Holt*, but not on this point.
[58]   *Scroggs v Scroggs* (1755) 1 Amb 272, 27 ER 182, (1755) 2 Amb 812, 27 ER 513 (Lord Hardwicke LC).

consent was vested in trustees. Here the power was exercisable by trustees, and a beneficiary (Lord Howland) had a non-fiduciary ability to give or withhold consent, as did the settlor, the Marquess of Tavistock. Apart from the fact that the exercise of the power itself in the present case is subject to duties which did not apply directly to the father's power in *Scroggs v Scroggs*, it does not seem to me that this reversal of roles makes a difference to the question whether the consent was vitiated in the circumstances. *AMP (UK) Ltd v Barker*[59] was similar to this case in this respect, since the trustees had the power and NPI's consent was required as employer.

Conflict

Can the Employer exercise the power in its own interests? Can it appoint a trustee who has a connection with the employer (eg a director of the employer)? If the power is fiduciary, then the main constraint is that it must be exercised in the sole interests of the scheme (and not in the power-holder's own interest). **11.49**

Conversely, if the power is not fiduciary, the employer can exercise it in its own interests, subject to the *Imperial Tobacco* duty (the implied duty of trust and confidence)—see eg *Imperial Group Pension Trust Ltd v Imperial Tobacco Ltd*[60] and *Prudential Staff Pensions Ltd v The Prudential Assurance Co Ltd*[61] (see Ch 13). **11.50**

Insolvency Practitioners

Can an insolvency practitioner (administrator, administrative receiver, or liquidator) appointed in relation to the employer exercise the power on behalf of the employer? Or is this a power that does not pass to an insolvency practitioner, but instead stays within the residual area of competency of the board of directors? **11.51**

This is discussed further in Ch 12 below,[62] but the issue is more complex if the power is fiduciary (it is less clear that such a power would be an asset of the employer and so may be less likely to not pass under the control of an insolvency practitioner). **11.52**

Transfer

Can the power be transferred or can the employer agree contractually with a third party how to exercise the power? This looks more difficult if the power is fiduciary. The doctrine of not fettering discretions is more likely to arise if the power is fiduciary. **11.53**

The holder of a personal power can also agree with a third party on how to exercise it. Conversely the general rule is that a fiduciary power must be exercised at the proper time and so cannot be fettered or released (unless expressly authorized).[63] **11.54**

---

[59] [2001] OPLR 197 (Lawrence Collins J).
[60] [1991] 2 All ER 597 (Browne-Wilkinson V-C).
[61] [2011] EWHC 960 (Ch), [2011] All ER (D) 142 (Apr) (Newey J).
[62] See also D Pollard, *Corporate Insolvency: Employment and Pension Rights* 5th edn (Bloomsbury Professional, 2013) Ch 47 'Pensions and other trusts'.
[63] See *Underhill and Hayton: Law of Trusts and Trustees*, para 57.7, citing *Re Wills' Trust Deed, Wills v Godfrey* [1964] Ch 219 (Buckley J).

12

EMPLOYER POWERS TO APPOINT
OR REMOVE TRUSTEES

Summary

12.1 Employers usually have an express power under the terms of an occupational pension scheme to appoint or remove the trustees. It is often commented that in relation to a family trust, a power to appoint or remove trustees is fiduciary and some extend this to apply to an employer power in an occupational pension scheme as well. This chapter focuses on the power of an *employer* to appoint or remove trustees and concludes that the power is not fiduciary.[1]

The confusion stems broadly from the old trust cases, in particular *Re Skeats' Settlement*, a **12.2** decision of Mr Justice Kay from 1889 in relation to a private family settlement.

This chapter: **12.3**

(a) reviews the case law, noting that the rationale for a fiduciary power depends on the circumstances of the case;
(b) notes that even in relation to private settlements, the cases indicate that powers held by beneficiaries are less likely to be fiduciary;
(c) points out that for commercial trusts (like pension scheme or unit trusts), the private trust cases look less applicable, given:
   (i) the ongoing interests of the employer in the scheme,
   (ii) that generally employer powers under pension schemes are not fiduciary;
   (iii) the categorization of the employer as a beneficiary; and
   (iv) the existence of other limits on employer's powers (in particular the implied good faith limits under the 1991 *Imperial Tobacco* case);
(d) concludes that a power to appoint or remove trustees held by an employer should not be considered subject to a fiduciary duty, save in unusual cases where the employer is also the trustee;
(e) notes that the terms of the trust instrument can clarify that the power is not fiduciary (and argues that an amendment can be made to achieve this); and looks at the position on the appointment of other fiduciaries (eg directors or insolvency practitioners) and notes that the position is even clearer that there is no fiduciary duty. This will apply to directors of a trustee company as well.

Why Does This Matter?

Pension trustees increasingly have wide powers that can impact on the trust and the liabilities **12.4** (and funding obligation) of the employers.

Some of these powers are given by the trust instrument (to which the employer will have **12.5** agreed, although perhaps some time ago and in a different regulatory environment).

Other powers are given to trustees by legislation (and apply regardless of any contrary provi- **12.6** sion in the trust instrument)—for example:

(a) to decide on investment strategy (with any employer consent requirement being overridden)—ss 34 and 35(5) of the Pensions Act 1995;
(b) to decide on payment of any surplus to the employer (before the scheme winds up)—s 37 of the Pensions Act 1995;

---

[1] D Pollard, 'Appointment and Removal of Trustees—A Fiduciary Power?' (1991) 37 British Pension Lawyer 1; D Pollard and D Heath, 'The Power of Employers to Appoint or Remove Trustees of Occupational Pension Schemes: Is it Fiduciary' (2011) 25 TLI 184.

(c) to agree with the employer on the actuarial valuation and ongoing funding (Pt 3 of the Pensions Act 2004), with the Pensions Regulator having power to decide if agreement cannot be reached—s 231 of the Pensions Act 2004;

(d) to give consent under the scheme amendment power to amendments detrimentally affecting accrued rights (even if the amendment power in the scheme does not require this)—s 67E(1) of the Pensions Act 1995.

12.7 So increasingly a number of employers may have relatively strained relationships with the trustee boards and perhaps particularly sometimes with independent trustees. For example if the employer feels that the trustee board is taking an excessively cautious or excessively member-friendly approach.

12.8 In those circumstances, where an employer is frustrated with the trustee board, it is not surprising that it may consider if it can exercise the power to appoint and remove all or some of the trustees. What then are the constraints on such an employer power? Can a decision by the employer be challenged (eg by a member or the other trustees)?

Challenges

12.9 It seems clear that if the answer is that the powers of an employer are fiduciary, then it will be easier for this to be challenged by a member or third party. For example, fiduciary powers are generally only exercisable in the interests of the trust and not in the interests of the power holder, the trustee-like duty to consider the proper exercise of the power (and not to take account of irrelevant factors etc) or at least to take proper advice, is limited to the exercise of a fiduciary power.

12.10 The precise limits of this 'proper consideration' obligation—at least as regards fiduciaries—are the subject of the *Hastings-Bass*[2] line of cases. Most recently the Court of Appeal has ruled on this in a non-pensions context in *Pitt v Holt*[3] and was upheld by the Supreme Court.[4] *Pitt v Holt* has been followed in a later pensions case.[5]

Conflict

12.11 Can the employer exercise the power in its own interests? Can it appoint a trustee who has a connection with the employer (eg a director of the employer)? If the power is fiduciary, then the main constraint is that it must be exercised in the sole interests of the scheme (and not in the power holder's own interest).

12.12 Conversely, if the power is not fiduciary, the holder can exercise it in his own interests—see eg *Imperial Group Pension Trust Ltd v Imperial Tobacco Ltd*[6] and *Prudential Staff Pensions Ltd v The Prudential Assurance Co Ltd*[7] (discussed further below and in Chapter 13).

---

[2] *Re Hastings-Bass, Hastings-Bass v IRC* [1975] Ch 25, CA.
[3] *Pitt v Holt; Futter v Futter* [2011] EWCA Civ 197, [2011] 2 All ER 450, CA. Upheld on this point by the Supreme Court [2013] UKSC 26, SC. See the discussion on the CA decision by Teresa Rosen Peacocke, 'Liability of Professionals Retained by Settlors and Trustees Following Pitt v Holt/Futter v Futter' (2011) 25 TLI 125.
[4] Similar issues are exercising the courts in Australia—see the High Court in *Finch v Telstra Super Pty Ltd* [2010] HCA 36 and *Manglicmot v Commonwealth Bank Officers Superannuation Corpn* [2010] NSWSC 363 (Rien J).
[5] *Prudential Staff Pensions Ltd v The Prudential Assurance Co Ltd* [2011] EWHC 960 (Ch) (Newey J).
[6] [1991] 2 All ER 597 (Browne-Wilkinson V-C).
[7] [2011] EWHC 960 (Ch) (Newey J).

Insolvency practitioners

Can an insolvency practitioner (administrator, administrative receiver, or liquidator) **12.13** appointed in relation to the employer exercise the power on behalf of the employer? Or is this a power that does not pass to an insolvency practitioner, but instead stays within the residual area of competency of the board of directors?

This is discussed further below, but the issue is more complex if the power is fiduciary (it is **12.14** less clear that such a power would be an asset of the employer and so may be less likely to not pass under the control of an insolvency practitioner).

Transfer

Can the power be transferred or can the employer agree contractually with a third party how **12.15** to exercise the power? This looks more difficult if the power is fiduciary. The doctrine of not fettering discretions is more likely to arise if the power is fiduciary.

The holder of a personal power can also agree with a third party on how to exercise it. **12.16** Conversely the general rule is that a fiduciary power must be exercised at the proper time and so cannot be fettered or released (unless expressly authorized).[8]

Who Can Appoint or Remove?

There are perhaps five main different bodies that can appoint or remove trustees of an occu- **12.17** pational pension scheme set up under trust:

(a) the employer (or principal employer);
(b) the trustee board itself;
(c) the members;
(d) the court;
(e) the Pensions Regulator.

Even this is not a full list—there could conceivably be another third party with an express **12.18** power to change trustees—eg a trade union or works council (this looks more like an employee appointment) or an independent third party (eg the President of the Law Society or the Lord Chief Justice).

This chapter is mainly going to look at the position of a principal employer. But it is worth a **12.19** preliminary look at the other four main potential appointors.

The trustee board itself

It is generally clear that where a power is held by trustees it is fiduciary in nature. The office **12.20** of trustee is the paradigm fiduciary position. There can be some issues about identifying if a power is held in a trustee capacity or instead is held by a person in a different capacity. For example, if the employer is also appointed as the sole trustee then it will exercise its powers *qua* trustee in a fiduciary manner—see for example *Icarus (Hertford) Ltd v Driscoll*.[9]

---

[8] See *Underhill and Hayton: Law of Trusts and Trustees* 18th edn, ed David Hayton, Paul Matthews, and Charles Mitchell (LexisNexis, 2010) para 57.7, citing *Re Wills' Trust Deeds* [1964] Ch 219.
[9] [1990] PLR 1 (Aldous J).

12.21 Note that member-nominated trustees (or member-nominated directors) can only be removed with agreement of all the other trustees—s 241(6) of the Pensions Act 2004.

12.22 It seems clear that the other trustees must exercise their power to give consent to a removal in a fiduciary manner. For example, in *Lee v Chou Wen Hsien*[10] the Privy Council held that a power in the articles of association of a company for the other directors to remove a director is a fiduciary power. Lord Brightman held:[11]

> Their Lordships are in agreement with the majority of the Court of Appeal that the power given by article 73 to directors to expel one of their number from the board is fiduciary, in the sense that each director concurring in the expulsion must act in accordance with what he believes to be the best interests of the company, and that he cannot properly concur for ulterior reasons of his own. It does not, however, follow that a notice will be void and of no effect, and that the director sought to be expelled will remain a director of the board, because one or more of the requesting directors acted from an ulterior motive.

The members

12.23 Selection (including election) by members of an occupational pension scheme of a number of member-nominated trustees (MNTs) has statutory backing—ss 241 to 243 of the Pensions Act 2004. If the method chosen is an election, it would be odd to categorize the power of a member to vote as 'fiduciary'. Employees are not normally fiduciaries as against the employer[12] (although this can apply in senior positions[13]).

12.24 Would a court (if there was a challenge) have to look at the motives and interests of all voting members? And could a member (or the employer or other trustees) challenge an appointment if a particular individual had made statements to particular 'constituents' about how they would act in their role as trustee, eg by protecting particular member interests?

12.25 An example of this could be the 2011 British Airways pension trustee elections. According to press reports three member-nominated trustees resigned as a result of the trustee board's decision in relation to the RPI/CPI switch. Two of those were re-elected—one of whom is quoted in the press[14] as confirming that he will:

> continue to argue the case for the restoration of RPI increases.

12.26 This could well have formed part of his trustee election manifesto.

12.27 This seems only right and proper for an election. The notion of this being somehow a 'fiduciary' power does not fit at all well.

12.28 The very existence of legislation requiring MNTs can be seen as a vindication of the argument that the employer retains a non-fiduciary power to appoint the rest of the trustee board. The Goode Report[15] (which led to the original MNT provisions in the Pensions Act 1995) did not discuss any limits on the employer's power to appoint the remainder of the trustee board.

---

[10] [1984] 1 WLR 1202, [1985] BCLC 45, PC.

[11] [1985] BCLC 45 at 50, PC.

[12] See eg *Caterpillar Logistics Services (UK) Ltd v de Crean* [2012] EWCA Civ 156, [2012] 3 All ER 129, CA.

[13] See *Nottingham University v Fishel* [2000] ICR 1462, [2000] IRLR 471 (Elias J) and later cases.

[14] Eg BBC News, 8 August 2011: 'BA pensioners seek to restore RPI link. Captain Cliff Pocock has been re-elected as an APS trustee. Members of a big BA pension scheme have elected three trustees who have pledged to restore pension increases in line with the retail prices index (RPI)' <http://www.bbc.co.uk/news/business-14445866>.

[15] Report of the Pension Law Review Committee (September 1993) CM2342.

The Pensions Regulator

The Pensions Regulator has statutory powers to prohibit or suspend trustees etc: ss 3–9 of the **12.29** Pensions Act 1995—see Chapter 7. It also has power to appoint an independent trustee on the employer entering an insolvency process—s 23 of the Pensions Act 1995.[16]

It would be odd to describe this Regulator power as 'fiduciary'. Given that it is statutory, presum- **12.30** ably it must be exercised for the purpose for which it was given and in line with the Regulator's general statutory objectives[17] (eg to minimize claims on the Pension Protection Fund).

Having said that, the Regulator, as a public body, is subject to public law duties in relation **12.31** to its powers. In practice these may be to a similar effect as a fiduciary power and subject to judicial review etc.

There is an interesting example of the Pensions Regulator using its appointment powers in **12.32** the 2007 decision of the Determinations Panel in the *Telent* case[18] (discussed further below).

The court

The courts retain a general supervisory power in relation to trusts and can appoint and **12.33** remove trustees under that jurisdiction.[19] Obviously this is subject to the usual requirement that the power must be exercised in a judicial manner. In one sense it would be odd to describe this as fiduciary, although the judicial process may be to the same effect.

The court will look to the wishes of the creator of the trust (if expressed in or to be inferred **12.34** from the instrument creating the trust) and consider whether the appointment will promote or impede the execution of the trust. The court will not appoint a trustee with a view to the interests of some of the beneficiaries in opposition to those of others—*Re Tempest*[20] and *Mohammed v Khan*.[21]

For a decision in Singapore on whether the court can review a nomination of a new trustee **12.35** made by a trustee seeking to retire—see Chan Sek Keong J in *Yusof bin Ahmad bin Talin v Hong Kong Bank Trustee (Singapore) Ltd*.[22]

Express power to appoint or remove trustees

Sometimes this power is stated in terms that 'the power of appointment and removal of trustees **12.36** is vested in the Principal Company'.

This is not happy wording as it seems to be a reference to the statutory power of appoint- **12.37** ment and removal of trustees under Pt 3[23] of the Trustee Act 1925. It is far better if a power

---

[16] See D Pollard, *Corporate Insolvency: Employment and Pension Rights* 5th edn (Bloomsbury Professional, 2013) Ch 30 'Independent trustee obligations'.

[17] Pensions Act 2004, s 5.

[18] One the TPR website at <http://www.the pensions regulator.gov.uk/docs/DNTelentReasonsof DeterminationsPanel.pdf>.

[19] Trustee Act 1925, s 41 and *Letterstedt v Boers* (1884) 9 App Cas 371. See generally 70.15 and 71.32 in *Underhill and Hayton: Law of Trusts and Trustees* for a description of the Court's powers. For an Australian summary, see JD Heydon and MJ Leeming, *Jacobs' Law of Trusts in Australia* 7th edn (LexisNexis Butterworths, 2006) paras [1585] and [1586].

[20] (1866) 1 Ch App 485, CA.

[21] [2005] EWHC 599 (Ch), [2005] All ER (D) 41 (Feb).

[22] [1989] SGHC 31, [1989] SLR 358.

[23] Sections 34–40, in particular s 36.

is worded just that the Principal Company 'may' appoint or remove trustees[24] from time to time (perhaps by deed[25]).

12.38 It is clearly important to know whether or not a trustee has been properly appointed (or removed). Subsequent actions of a trustee body will probably be invalid if proper notice of meetings etc has not been given to all trustees and one has been omitted because of an (erroneous) belief that he had ceased to act.[26] This may be more of an issue if the relevant trust instrument does not expressly provide for majority voting[27] (such an express majority voting provision is common in pensions trust deeds and see now s 32 (Decisions by majority) of the Pensions Act 1995).

12.39 It may be that if there has been an error in the appointment or removal of trustees, this could be regarded as impliedly cured by a later deed[28] executed by the principal company which makes it clear who it thinks is a trustee—see for example Scott J (as he then was) in *Davis v Richards & Wallington*.[29] A change of trustees in a deed[30] can also operate as an implied use of the amendment power under the scheme and so override limitations in the appointment power—see Knox J in *LRT v Hatt*.[31]

Power to appoint or remove trustees is special

It could be said that it is a major power to be able to control the identity of the trustees.[32] But it is no more major than other powers—such as the power to amend or determine scheme funding. As mentioned below, once appointed, a trustee has the full range of fiduciary duties regardless of who did the appointing. So the power of appointment or removal does not deserve any special status.

1977: Some support from Australia: PD Finn

12.40 PD Finn[33] in his classic book *Fiduciary Obligations*[34] clearly considers *Skeats' Settlement* to be wrong on the fiduciary point. He refers to the case and continues (at para 273):

> As has been seen, every fiduciary office exists for the benefit of its beneficiaries. It is equally clear that a donee should only appoint a person whom he considers to be fit to discharge the duties of the office—including the fiduciary duties. But a 'fiduciary power'? This description has gained some currency. But it is by no means an accepted usage, and can only be a cause for confusion.

---

[24] This has the advantage of being shorter too.

[25] There is no overriding legal requirement for new trustees to be appointed by deed. But an appointment under a deed does mean that there is an implied vesting of trust property in the new trustee under s 40 of the Trustee Act 1925.

[26] But interestingly note the comments on this point made by the Privy Council in the company director case, *Lee v Chou Wen Hsien* [1984] 1 WLR 1202, [1985] BCLC 45, mentioned earlier.

[27] For a recent case upholding an action by a trustee board where a majority only signed a document, see Vos J in *HR Trustees Ltd v Wembley plc (in liquidation)* [2011] EWHC 2974 (Ch).

[28] Or whatever else is needed under the relevant power.

[29] [1991] 2 All ER 563, [1991] 1 WLR 1511 (Scott J).

[30] Or whatever else is needed under the amendment power.

[31] [1993] OPLR 225, [1993] PLR 227 (Knox J). See the discussion in the article by Patrick O'Hagan, 'Mistake and the Implied Exercise of Powers' (2010) 24 TLI 3.

[32] See eg Robert Ham in *Tolley's Pensions Handbook* 2nd edn (1995) in the chapter on Pension Scheme Trusts.

[33] Now Mr Justice Finn, a judge of the Federal Court in Australia.

[34] PD Finn, *Fiduciary Obligations* (Law Book Co, 1977).

Trustees for debenture holders for example can have a power to appoint a director. As a power given to them virtute officii it is governed by their fiduciary obligation and must be exercised in the interests of their beneficiaries—the debenture holders. Do they, as Kay J. suggests, also owe a fiduciary duty to the company? It is considered that this supposed 'fiduciary duty' means no more that that they must not commit a fraud upon their power. They must not for example put the office up for sale to the highest bidder, or appoint a puppet for themselves. As this example illustrates a power to appoint may be governed by a fiduciary obligation—but because it is given to a fiduciary virtute officii.

Interestingly, the constraints suggested by Finn are not unlike those among the implied duty **12.41** of good faith discussed in the later *Imperial Tobacco* case (see below). Despite this, the text books have continued to argue for a fiduciary nature.[35] They also make the point that the issue turns on construction of the trust instrument and that this can clarify the nature of any relevant duties.[36]

Haydon and Leeming[37] state that an express power to remove trustees is unusual today, but **12.42** that a modern example is the power of unit holders to remove the trustee of a unit trust. They state that 'depending on the terms of the trust deed' such a power 'may not be fiduciary, although it could not be exercised fraudulently' (citing *Fitzwood Pty Ltd v Unique Goal Pty Ltd*[38]).

1889: Mr Justice Kay Deals with a Family Trust: *Re Skeats' Settlement*

The root authority for the proposition that a power to appoint or remove trustees is fiduciary **12.43** is the decision of Kay J in *Re Skeats' Settlement*.[39]

This case involved a marriage settlement where the husband and wife (who were not trustees) **12.44** were given power to appoint 'any other person or persons to be a trustee or trustees ...'. The husband and wife purported to exercise that power by appointing two new trustees, one of which was the husband himself.

Kay J (in an unreserved judgment[40]) held that the appointment was invalid. His reasoning **12.45** for this proceeded on the general ground that the power to appoint trustees is a fiduciary power which could not be exercised for the benefit of the donee and must be exercised in the best interests of the beneficiaries. The appointment by the donee of himself was not in the best interests of the beneficiaries. Kay J also went on to hold that, in addition, the express power to appoint any 'other' person precluded the appointment of one of the donees of the power himself.

---

[35] *Underhill and Hayton: Law of Trusts and Trustees*, para 71.11; Lynton Tucker, Nicholas Le Poidevin, and James Brightwell, *Lewin on Trusts* 18th edn (Sweet & Maxwell, 2008) paras 13-44 and 14-39; *Law of Pension Schemes* (looseleaf) (Sweet & Maxwell, 2006 release) 3006–9; Geraint Thomas and Alastair Hudson, *The Law of Trusts* 2nd edn (Oxford University Press, 2010) 638, para 22.39; Fenner Moeran, *Tolley's Pensions Law* (looseleaf) (Issue 57, January 2010) Ch E1. Contrast para E.1A.15 in Ch E.1A (Corporate Trustees) by Pollard making the point that appointment or removal of directors of a corporate trustee is clearly not fiduciary.
[36] See *Underhill and Hayton: Law of Trusts and Trustees*, para 71.12.
[37] Heydon and Leeming, *Jacobs' Law of Trusts in Australia* (2006) 351.
[38] (2001) 188 ALR 566 at [98]–[99]. Discussed below.
[39] (1889) 42 ChD 522.
[40] Given impressively quickly. The new trustees were appointed on 18 July 1889 and the challenge was heard (and judgment given) by Kay J on 8 August 1889.

12.46   Although *Skeats' Settlement* could be regarded as a decision on the latter narrow point only, Kay J clearly proceeded on the general basis that the power of appointment was fiduciary. He held (at 526):

> The question whether such an appointment is valid or not depends, I think, as has been said in argument, very much upon whether the power is to be treated as a fiduciary power or not. Now I take that question first. The ordinary power of appointing new trustees, *under a settlement such as this* of course imposes upon the person who has the power of appointment the duty of selecting honest and good persons who can be trusted with the very difficult, onerous, and often delicate duties which trustees have to perform. He is bound to select to the best of his ability the best people he can find for the purpose. Is that power of selection a fiduciary power or not? I will try it in this way, which I offered as a test in the course of the argument. Suppose, as happens not unfrequently, that trustees, under the terms of the deed of trust, are entitled to remuneration by way of annual salary or payment. Could the person who has the power of appointment put the office of trustee up for sale, and sell it to the best bidder? It is clear that would be entirely improper. Could he take any remuneration for making the appointment? In my opinion, certainly not. Why not? The answer is that he cannot exercise the power for his own benefit. Why not again? The answer is inevitable. Because it is a power which involves a duty of a fiduciary nature; and I therefore come to the conclusion, independently of any authority, that the power is a fiduciary power. The case cited before Lord Eldon seems expressly to confirm that view. Lord Eldon did treat it as a power in the exercise of which the appointor had a fiduciary duty to perform, which he could not exercise in any way for his own benefit, and in exercising which he was bound to do the best in the interests of the cestuis que trust whose trustee he was appointed. I therefore come without any hesitation to the conclusion that this power is of a fiduciary nature (emphasis added).

12.47   The case before Lord Eldon LC referred to by Kay J is *Webb v The Earl of Shaftesbury*.[41] However, it can be argued that *Webb* is not particularly strong authority for the general proposition as it seems arguable (the report is not very clear) that the relevant appointor in the case before Lord Eldon was himself a trustee and was therefore clearly subject to fiduciary duties.

12.48   If that was where the case law rested, the issue would not, even for family settlements, be very clear. *Skeats' Settlement* is admittedly a decision of a strong judge (Mr Justice Kay went on to become Lord Justice Kay). However, it is a first instance decision only and is therefore, as a matter of strict precedent, persuasive rather than binding in later High Court actions. It is also an unreserved judgment. In addition, it seems to rely in part on a previous decision of Lord Eldon that it may be possible to distinguish.

Appointing yourself: *Re Newen*

12.49   Kekewich J followed Kay J in *Re Newen, Newen v Barnes*.[42] This case appears to have concerned the exercise of a power to appoint new trustees exercisable by the administrators of the last remaining trustee of a settlement. *Skeats' Settlement* was followed to the extent that the donees of the power were held not to be entitled to appoint themselves.

12.50   But in *Montefiore v Guedalla*[43] the executors of the surviving trustee were authorized to appoint a new trustee, and Buckley J held that they might appoint one of their number, following the decision of Chitty J in *Tempest v Lord Camoys*[44] in preference to *Skeats*. It remained

---

[41] (1802) 7 Ves Jun 481, 32 ER 194 (Lord Eldon LC).
[42] [1894] 2 Ch 297 (Kekewich J).
[43] [1903] 2 Ch 723 (Buckley J).
[44] (1888) 58 L T 221 (Chitty J).

unclear prior to the Trustee Act 1925 to what extent the donee of a power of appointing new trustees could appoint himself.[45]

In *Scaffidi v Montevento Holdings Pty Ltd*[46] the Court of Appeal of Western Australia commented: **12.51**

> 146 Even where the language is wide enough to permit the appointor to appoint himself or herself as trustee, it is a 'very salutary' or 'most salutary' rule that the power should only be exercised to that end in 'exceptional circumstances' or 'special circumstances': *Montefiore v Guedalla* (725, 726); *In re Christina Brown* (93–94); *In re Power's Settlement Trusts* [1951] Ch 1074, 1080.

Some earlier cases

Three other cases have been cited.[47] However two of these, *Peatfield v Benn*[48] and *Sugden v Crossland*[49] concerned the exercise of powers of appointment and removal exercisable by trustees. The third case, *Pepper v Tuckey*[50] is a clearer authority in that the Lord Chancellor refused to sanction the exercise of a power of removal of a trustee. This was on the basis that it had been improperly exercised as the intention was to remove the trustee because he would not agree to a particular investment. The report in Jo & LaT (Jones & La Touche) is very short.   **12.52**

1895: The Court of Appeal Comments on the Position of Lunatics: *Re Shortridge*

That is not where the case law rested in the 1890s. There is further authority in support of the general proposition for private trusts in *Skeats' Settlement*. This is the Court of Appeal decision (given later in the same year as *Newen*) in *Re Shortridge*.[51]   **12.53**

This case involved a woman who was entitled to a life interest under a settlement. The settlement provided that she could, on any of the trustees dying, appoint other persons to be trustees of the settlement. The woman became of unsound mind and the question arose as to whether the Court had power to authorize another person to exercise the power of appointing new trustees on behalf of the woman. The relevant statutory power was that contained in s 128 of the Lunacy Act 1890 which applied to powers 'vested in a lunatic, in the character of trustee or guardian'.   **12.54**

---

[45] *Underhill and Hayton: Law of Trusts and Trustees* para 71.66, pointing out that s 36(1) of the Trustee Act 1925 now expressly authorizes the donee of a power to appoint himself, citing *Re Skeats*, *Re Newen*, and *Re Shortridge*. It points out that the statutory power does not allow the donee to appoint himself to be an additional trustee where no vacancy exists—*Re Power's Settlement Trusts* [1951] Ch 1074. See also *Jacobs' Law of Trusts in Australia* para [1512] citing an Australian case that allowed for self-appointment: *Re Christina Brown* (1921) 22 SR (NSW) 90.
[46] [2011] WASCA 146 (Murphy and Buss JJA and Hall J).
[47] In 1990 by Nigel Inglis-Jones QC in his book *The Law of Occupational Pension Schemes*. This has now become the looseleaf, *Sweet & Maxwell's Law of Pension Schemes* (Sweet & Maxwell).
[48] (1853) 17 Beav 522, 51 ER 1137.
[49] (1856) 3 Sm & Giff 192, 65 ER 620.
[50] (1844) 2 Jo & LaT 95, 7 IR Eq 572.
[51] [1895] 1 Ch 278.

12.55 The Court of Appeal (Lord Halsbury and Lindley and Smith LJJ) in a brief (unreserved) judgment followed the decision of Kay J in *Skeats' Settlement* and held that the power to appoint new trustees is a fiduciary power, therefore falling within the section.

12.56 Lord Halsbury[52] held:

> …the somewhat hypercritical objection that a power of appointing new trustees is not a power 'vested in a lunatic in the character of trustee or guardian' within the meaning of sect. 128 of the Lunacy Act, 1890, is abundantly satisfied by the decision of Mr. Justice Kay in *In re Skeats' Settlement*.

12.57 This decision feels right on the specific statutory point. But there was no discussion of the underlying rationale for the power being fiduciary.

Re Bowmer and *In Re X*

12.58 In relation to exercise by the court of powers of appointment held by a lunatic, the Court of Appeal in *Re Shortridge* referred to the earlier cases to the same effect of *Re Bowmer*[53] and *In Re Blake*[54] (cited in the later case of *In Re X*[55]). All these reports are very short and do not discuss the point in detail.

Why is an Employer Power Not Fiduciary?

12.59 So there is a clear (but unreserved and lacking in clear explanation) first instance decision in a private trust case, which has been followed by a later Court of Appeal decision on a statutory point (but without looking at the reasoning).

Judgment in *Skeats* not a statute

12.60 It is clear that we must not treat judgments as if they were statutes. For example, Mummery LJ in *Bridge Trustees Ltd v Yates*:[56]

> [57] A cautious cliché about judgments on the construction of statutes: they should not be read, construed or applied as if they were themselves statutes. Obviously a judgment on the construction of a statute cannot constitutionally substitute itself for the statute. However, when a court's reading of a statute clarifies it by explaining its purpose, structure and language and by discussing instances of how it actually works in practice, the temptation in later cases is to cite from the judgment in preference to quoting from the statute. But the function of the courts is always to interpret the statute, not to construe a judgment about it as if it had itself become a part of, or a replacement for, the statute in question.

12.61 This was repeated by Lord Walker in the Supreme Court[57] in 2011:

> [59] The discussion of *KPMG* contains some very pertinent observations, at paras 57 to 59, about the role of precedent in statutory construction. As the report is readily available it is unnecessary to repeat them. Their general tenor (with which I whole-heartedly agree) is that judgments on statutory construction are not to be read as if they were themselves statutes, and

---

[52] At 283.
[53] (1859) 3 DeG & J 658, 44 ER 1423.
[54] (1887) WN 173.
[55] [1894] 2 Ch 415.
[56] [2010] EWCA Civ 179, [2010] ICR 921 at [57].
[57] *Bridge Trustees Ltd v Yates (Secretary of State for Work and Pensions intervening)* [2011] UKSC 42, [2011] ICR 1069, SC.

that apparently wide propositions may have to be read in the context of the particular facts of the case to which they related.

Reasons given in *Skeats* do not apply to pension trusts

The decision in *Skeats* itself is clearly stated only to apply 'under a settlement such as this'—ie **12.62** to a marriage settlement. So does it apply to commercial trusts such as pension schemes? See generally Chapter 2.

The reference by Kay J to sale of rights seems odd in a pensions context. If it applied, it would **12.63** prevent a transaction under which an employer sold its business and agreed (as part of the transaction) to transfer its role as principal employer to the purchaser. Such a prohibition would be strange and perverse. It would operate to remove a potential way of protecting members and beneficiaries on such a business sale. Indeed, it would run directly contrary to the comments made by Millett J (as he then was) in the *Courage* case[58] to the effect that a substitution of principal employer should not separate the scheme from its members:

> In my judgment, the validity of a power of substitution depends on the circumstances in which it is capable of being exercised and the characteristics which must be possessed by the company capable of being substituted while the validity of any purported exercise of such a power depends on the purpose for which the substitution is made. The circumstances must be such that substitution is necessary or at least expedient in order to preserve the scheme for those for whose benefit it was established; and the substituted company must be recognisably the successor to the business and workforce of the company for which it is to be substituted.

Note that selling a right to be appointed as a trustee may seem odd in a non-pensions con- **12.64** text—for example it is an offence in New South Wales—see s 249E of the Crimes Act 1900.[59]

See further Chapter 2 for a discussion of how far general trust principles apply to pension **12.65** schemes.

More Recent UK Cases

1983: *IRC v Schroder*

In the 1983 case of *IRC v Schroder*[60] Vinelott J had to consider a trust where the settlor had **12.66** the power of appointing new trustees on a vacancy and a committee had power to remove trustees. The committee was also appointed by the settlor. The Revenue contended[61] that the settlor fell within a charging section in the Taxes Act as he was 'able in any manner whatso-ever, and whether directly or indirectly, to control the application of the income of the Trust'.

Vinelott J rejected this contention holding that the powers to appoint and remove members **12.67** of the committee and the trustees were fiduciary and could not properly be used to 'pack' the committee or change the trustees. He gave no reasons for this. *Skeats' Settlement* was not referred to in the judgment, but is mentioned in the decision by way of case stated of the special commissioners.[62]

---

[58] *Re Courage Group's Pension Schemes; Ryan v Imperial Brewing and Leisure Ltd* [1987] 1 All ER 528 (Millett J) at 542.
[59] *Lewin on Trusts* 18th edn (Sweet & Maxwell, 2008) makes a similar point at para 14-39.
[60] [1983] STC 480 at 500 (Vinelott J).
[61] At 500.
[62] See 487.

12.68 The authority of this case on this issue is weakened even further by the later comment[63] that in order to fall within the relevant section of the Taxes Act the settlor must have been in:

> a position to ensure that the trustees would act in accordance with his wishes without themselves giving any independent consideration and accordingly to act in breach of their fiduciary duty.

12.69 Thus it seems that even if the settlor's power to appoint and remove trustees was not fiduciary the decision would not have changed.

1990: *Mettoy*

Similarly in *Mettoy*[64] Warner J mentioned in passing[65] that the power given to the principal employer to appoint trustees 'is of course fiduciary'. Again no reason for this is given. *Skeats' Settlement* had been cited in argument by counsel.[66]

Appointment of Fiduciaries in Other Spheres

12.70 In other areas, outside trusts, where the appointment of fiduciaries is concerned, the courts have given clear indications that the power to appoint is not subject to fiduciary limitations (the person appointed becomes, of course, subject to fiduciary duties when appointed).

Directors

12.71 In relation to company directors, in the 1990 case of *Kuwait Asia Bank v National Mutual Life Nominees Ltd*,[67] the Privy Council held[68] that:

> in the absence of fraud or bad faith . . . a shareholder or other person who controls the appointment of a director owes no duty to creditors of the company to take reasonable care to see that directors so appointed discharge their duties as directors with due diligence and competence. . .

> The liability of a shareholder would be unlimited if he were accountable to a creditor for the exercise of his power to appoint a director and for the conduct of the director so appointed. It is in the interests of a shareholder to see that directors are wise and that the actions of the company are not foolish; but this concern of the shareholder stems from self-interest and not from duty.

12.72 Vinelott J in *IRC v Schroder*[69] also commented that the power to appoint or remove directors is non-fiduciary:

> In *Lee v IRC* Mr Lee had power to appoint and remove directors. That power was not a fiduciary power. He could have appointed himself. Assuming Quebec law to be the same as English law, directors do not owe any fiduciary duty to the shareholders. They are trustees of their powers for the company.

12.73 Clearly, directors (once appointed) are in a fiduciary position in a similar way to trustees. This points to the argument by analogy that the power to appoint trustees is not necessarily

---

63 At 505b.
64 [1990] 1 WLR 1587.
65 At 1620.
66 See 1591.
67 [1991] 1 AC 187, [1990] 3 All ER 404, PC.
68 [1990] 3 All ER 404 at 422 and 423.
69 [1983] STC 480 at 503c (Vinelott J).

fiduciary, particularly outside the 'private trust' sphere (although perhaps it could be argued that companies are more commercial entities than even commercial trusts such as pension scheme trusts).

Articles of association can confer power to appoint directors to a third party—*Woodlands* **12.74**
Ltd v Logan.[70] Such a power is not constrained by any fiduciary or other duty and may be exercised in the shareholders' own interests—*Santos Ltd v Pettingell*.[71]

A court will recognize a right delegated under the articles—*British Marac Syndicate v Alperton* **12.75**
Rubber Co.[72]

Shareholders can generally vote in their own interests,[73] but some cases indicate that they **12.76**
need to have regard to class interests (*Re Holders Investment Trust*[74]) and there may be a broad principle to exercise voting powers in what they bona fide believe to be the interests of the company—*Standard Chartered Bank Ltd v Walker*[75] and *Gore Browne* at 21[9].[76] See also Jenkins LJ (as he then was) in *Re HR Harmer Ltd*:[77]

> It cannot be denied that the holder of the majority in voting power of the shares in a company may, broadly speaking, appoint any person he thinks fit as director, and the appointment cannot be challenged merely on the ground that he might have found some more suitable person than the person he selected, or that the person he selected was his friend; but I take it that the majority shareholder's power of appointing directors must within broad limits be exercised for the benefit of the company as a whole and not to secure some ulterior advantage.

But generally there are no fiduciary obligations on a shareholder (so he can vote that he can **12.77**
purchase property from the company even if also a director).[78]

A nominated director should ignore the interests and wishes of the bank/nominator— **12.78**
Kuwait Asia Bank Ltd v National Mutual Life.[79] But in *Re Neath Rugby Ltd*, it was held at first instance that while nominee's primary loyalty is to the company, he can take account of the interests of appointor. The Court of Appeal upheld this:[80]

> An appointed director, without being in breach of his duties to the company, may take the interests of his nominator into account, provided that his decisions as a director are in what he genuinely believes to be the best interests of the company…

A nominated director can also pass information to a nominating outside party (unless **12.79**
confidential)—*Harkness v Commonwealth Bank of Australia*.[81]

---

[70] [1948] NZLR 230 (Cornish J).
[71] (1979) 4 ACLR 110 (Rath J, NSW). See *Gore-Brown on Companies* at 13[2].
[72] [1915] 2 Ch 186.
[73] *Northern Counties Securities Ltd v Jackson & Steeple Ltd* [1974] 2 All ER 625, [1974] 1 WLR 1133 (Walton J) and *Re ICI Ltd, Carruth v Imperial Chemical Industries Ltd* [1937] AC 707, HL.
[74] [1971] 1 WLR 583 (Megarry J).
[75] [1992] 1 WLR 561, CA.
[76] See also the Hong Kong decision in *Sunlink International Ltd v Wong Shu Wing* [2010] 5 HKLRD (Harris J) holding that shareholders must not exercise their voting rights irrationally in a way which will destroy the economic value of other shareholders' shares. Noted by William Wong (2011) 127 LQR 522.
[77] [1959] 1 WLR 62, CA.
[78] See *Gore-Browne on Companies* at 15[11A] and *North-West Transportation v Beatty* (1887) 12 App Cas 589 (PC); *Pender v Lushington* (1877) 6 ChD 70; *Burland v Earle* [1902] AC 82 at 94; and *Dominion Cotton Mills v Amyot* [1912] AC 546.
[79] [1991] 1 AC 187, PC.
[80] [2009] EWCA Civ 261 at [33].
[81] (1993) 12 ACSR 165 (NSW).

Insolvency practitioners

12.80 Similarly, a receiver, when appointed over a company by the holder of a floating charge, is in a fiduciary position as regards the company.

12.81 However, the courts have made clear that the bank holding the relevant debenture under which the receiver is appointed is under no duty of care in making the appointment.

12.82 It seems that an appointment of a receiver could be challenged if made in bad faith. In considering whether or not to appoint a receiver, the bank does not owe the chargor any duty of care, and a decision by the bank to exercise its power to appoint a receiver cannot be challenged except perhaps on grounds of bad faith. The bank/chargee may have a duty as to the manner in which it exercises the power (eg to take reasonable care not to appoint an incompetent), but a bank/chargee who is contractually entitled to appoint a receiver is free to do so to protect its own interests and it is under no duty to refrain from exercising its rights merely because doing so may cause loss to the company or its unsecured creditors.[82]

12.83 Again it could be argued that these cases could be distinguished on the basis that a receiver is not an ordinary fiduciary. He or she continues to owe some duties to the appointor.[83] But this does not seem to be a crucial distinction.

Pension Cases Since 1990

Icarus (Hertford) Ltd v Driscoll

12.84 In *Icarus (Hertford) Ltd v Driscoll*[84] the company set up a pension plan and was also the sole trustee. The trust instrument included power for the Principal Employer to decide on surplus. Aldous J held that where the words 'Principal Employer' were used, this denotes it is acting as trustee. So power is exercisable by it 'in a fiduciary capacity' (para [23]).

12.85 Robert Walker J commented in *National Grid*[85] that this is a case where the decision 'depended on the employer being an actual and express trustee, not a quasi-trustee'.

Re William Makin & Sons Ltd

12.86 In *Re William Makin & Sons Ltd*[86] the company was also sole trustee of a pension scheme. Vinelott J held that this meant that the powers of the company were mainly fiduciary power. The powers cannot be exercised by a liquidator because of conflict—paragraph 18. But it was also held that the statutory power was not wide enough and so cannot be exercised by receiver—paragraph 19.

---

[82] See *Downsview Nominees Ltd v First City Corpn* [1993] AC 295, [1993] 3 All ER 626, PC; *Medforth v Blake* [2000] Ch 86, CA; *Shamji v Johnson Matthey Bankers* [1986] BCLC 278; and *Re Potters Oils Ltd (No 2)* [1986] BCLC 98.

[83] *Gomba Holdings UK Ltd v Minories Finance* [1989] BCC 27 and *Gomba Holdings UK Ltd v Homan* [1986] 3 All ER 94.

[84] [1990] PLR 1 (Aldous J).

[85] [1997] PLR 157, [1997] OPLR 207 at [24] (Robert Walker J).

[86] [1992] PLR 177 (Vinelott J).

Simpson Curtis Pension Trustees Ltd v Readson

In *Simpson Curtis Pension Trustees Ltd v Readson*,[87] the Company went into receivership. Later **12.87** the directors of original trustee resigned. The company (by receiver) appointed Simpson Curtis (SC) as (independent) trustee. Simpson Curtis issued a writ against original trustee and five of its directors. The defendants argued that SC had not been validly appointed and so writs were invalid, raising three arguments:

(a) the power to appoint/remove was not an 'asset' of the company and so did not fall within the charge;
(b) the power was fiduciary and therefore could not be exercised by a receiver (*Mettoy*);
(c) the receiver should not exercise the power because of a conflict of interest (see *Mettoy*).

It was conceded that Simpson Curtis was a suitable and worthy person to be appointed.

Judge O'Donoghue (sitting as Deputy High Court Judge) held that Simpson Curtis was validly **12.88** appointed. The power was not an 'asset' but fell within powers in Sch 1 to the Insolvency Act 1986, so can be exercised by receiver. Simpson Curtis conceded that the power to appoint 'is fiduciary to the extent that it must be exercised bona fide for the benefit of the cestui que trust and must not be used by an appointer for his own gain or benefit. In such a case the Court would readily interfere to declare any such appointment void' (p238G). Judge O'Donoghue referred to Street CJ in *Re Edgar*[88] and agreed with *Law of Occupational Pension Schemes* (Nigel Inglis-Jones):

> It is one thing to say that a power is fiduciary power. It is another to decide what that means in the context of any particular power ... (p239C).

(Judge O'Donoghue held) that the power was not really within category 2 in *Mettoy* (fiduciary power in the full sense) but instead 'subject to constraints'. Anyway the legislation had later moved so that it is now a statutory power (s 57C of the Social Security Act 1990) for an administrative receiver. He also held that here there was no actual conflict. The trustee (once appointed) owes separate fiduciary duties—see Vinelott J in *Schroder v IRC*. There was no reference to *Skeats*.[89]

Independent Pension Trustee Ltd v LAW Construction Co Ltd

In *Independent Pension Trustee Ltd v LAW Construction Co Ltd*,[90] Lord Hamilton (in the **12.89** Outer House of the Court of Session) dealt with a challenge to the appointment of trustees and change of principal employer. LAW Construction was principal employer (PE) of a pension scheme. In April 1992 an administrative receiver was appointed over LAW Construction.

On 14/17 August 1992 directors of LAW Construction and other employers (some in **12.90** receivership, some not) purported to change the PE to LAW Holdings (not in receivership) and on 17/21 August LAW Holdings purported to appoint Hymans Robertson Trustees Ltd as the trustee.

---

[87] [1994] OPLR 231 (Judge O'Donoghue sitting as Deputy High Court Judge).
[88] (1972) ACLC 27 (Street CJ).
[89] Tim Cox in the commentary on this case in the OPLR reports [2004] OPLR 231 at 241, mentions *Skeats* and says the fiduciary label is unhelpful. He refers to the trust and confidence 'constraints' on employers.
[90] [1996] OPLR 259 (Lord Hamilton, CSOH).

12.91 On 22 August the receivers of LAW Construction purported to appoint Independent Pension Trustee Ltd (IPT) as trustee. The case was brought by IPT and defended by LAW Construction (acting through its directors— the receiver took no part).

12.92 IPT claimed that the appointment of Hymans Robertson was invalid on three grounds:

(a) only receivers can exercise powers, no change to LAW Holdings as PE involved;

(b) power to appoint a new PE was vested in LAW Construction 'as a trustee of the power' so could only be exercised by independent trustee (s 57D(5) of the Social Security Pensions Act 1975);

(c) parties did not act in good faith and for a proper purpose.

12.93 Lord Hamilton held that ground 1 was correct. The powers passed to the receiver. Grounds 2 and 3 were not relevant but were discussed anyway and held not correct.

12.94 Tim Cox commented in the OPLR report commentary on the case (at p 269) that there is nothing wrong in a person using power of appointment if a trustee is sympathetic to the appointer:

> This seems entirely proper since, if there is a conflict between the interests of employers and members it is clearly right that the interests of both sides should be represented in any discussion about how the trustees should exercise their powers.

Denny v Yeldon

12.95 In *Denny v Yeldon*[91] Jacob J held that the company could properly give up power to appoint trustees and pass it to the trustees.

> The company's pension scheme seems to me to be an intimate part of the company's affairs (p118E).

He cited *Re Edgar* and *Simpson Curtis* and went on to discuss the then current (but now repealed) statutory powers/duty for an insolvency practitioner and independent trustees.[92]

Mitre Pensions v Pensions Ombudsman[93]

12.96 This case looked at the issue of whether or not a power exercisable by the employer is held by it 'as trustee of the power' within s 25(2)(b) of the Pensions Act 1995 (dealing with the power of an independent trustee appointed where the company has entered an insolvency process). Presumably this provision was designed to catch fiduciary powers such as those found by Warner J as a matter of interpretation in *Mettoy Pension Trustees Ltd v Evans*[94]—see above. In particular, it has been argued that the effect of this section is that an employer power to appoint and remove the other trustees vests in the independent trustee.

12.97 In *Mitre Pensions Ltd v Pensions Ombudsman*[95] a dispute had arisen between the independent trustee and the two other trustees about their benefits as members. Eventually this went to

---

[91] [1995] OPLR 115 (Jacob J).
[92] For a discussion of the previous statutory position (now changed from April 2005) see D Pollard, *Corporate Insolvency: Employment and Pension Rights* 2nd edn (Butterworths, 2000) Ch 13.
[93] [2000] OPLR 349 (CSIH).
[94] [1991] 2 All ER 513 (Warner J).
[95] [2000] OPLR 349, 2000 GWD 22-868 (Inner House, Ct of Sess).

the Pensions Ombudsman who criticized the independent trustee. On appeal by the independent trustee, the Inner House of the Court of Session commented (at para [16]):

> While the Ombudsman had suggested, in paragraph 41, that the appellants should have investigated taking steps to have EAF and JAF removed as trustees, the appellants had no power to remove them. Removal of trustees is dealt with in the Trust Deed and only the principal employer can remove trustees. Reference was made to *Mettoy Pension Trustees Limited v Evans* [1990] 1 PLR 9 at page 43.[96] However, the appellants could not reasonably have concluded that they had, without doubt, the power to remove the other two trustees simpliciter. Section 121(2) of the Act[97] was so obscure that the appellants could not have been confident of their right to remove the other trustees without being challenged in court. In any event, all that the Ombudsman said was that the appellants should have investigated the possibility.

Polly Peck International plc v Henry

In *Polly Peck International plc v Henry*,[98] Buckley J held that administrators can exercise fiduciary and non-fiduciary powers in relation to an occupational pension scheme. So he refused to allow the company (in administration) to resign as trustee (it could not charge expenses to the pension fund) and be replaced by an independent trustee (who could charge for its services). **12.98**

Buckley v Hudson Forge

In *Buckley v Hudson Forge*[99] the company entered into receivership and then liquidation. Under the terms of the pension scheme, the company was also the trustee (an independent trustee was later appointed by the court in its place). **12.99**

Lloyd J held that the receiver (appointed out of court) was in a different position to an administrator (who is an officer of the court) and so could not have arranged for the company to decide (before the new trustee was appointed) on exercise of the power under the scheme given to the trustee (ie a fiduciary power) to augment benefits. **12.100**

Chirkinian v Larcom Trustees

Michael Furness QC (sitting as a Deputy High Court judge) commented in *Chirkinian v Larcom Trustees*[100] on the appointment of a trustee (of an employee benefit trust) by a company acting through its liquidator. The comments were obiter. He seems to have accepted that a liquidator could make the appointment, but stated that any appointment of a trustee by a liquidator needed to be solely for the benefit of the relevant beneficiaries. He commented: **12.101**

> 18 Finally, I wish to mention the question of the validity of the appointment of the Respondent as trustee. In the course of argument I asked Mr Arnfield if he was challenging the validity of that appointment, and he told me that on the evidence available he did not feel able to do so. For that reason I have disregarded this issue in deciding on the merits of this appeal. It is, however,

---

[96] This section of the judgment in *Mettoy* discussed whether or not a power held by an employer is a fiduciary power.

[97] Pension Schemes Act 1993, s 121(2) dealt with powers exercisable by the independent trustee and was replaced (in the same terms) by the Pensions Act 1995, s 25(2).

[98] [1998] OPLR 323, [1999] PLR 135, [1998] All ER (D) 647, [1999] 1 BCC 407 (Buckley J). See Pollard, *Corporate Insolvency: Employment and Pension Rights* (2013) para 26.33.

[99] [1999] OPLR 249, [1999] PLR 151 (Lloyd J).

[100] [2006] EWHC 1917, [2006] All ER (D) 403 (Jul), [2006] BPIR 1363, [2006] WTLR 1523 (Michael Furness QC, sitting as a Deputy High Court judge).

an aspect of this case which has troubled me, for two reasons. The first is that the authorities show that a liquidator can only appoint a trustee if it is in furtherance of his statutory powers to do so. On this point see *Mettoy Pension Trustees Ltd v Evans* [1990] 1 WLR 1587 at 1616 and, more pertinently, *Simpson Curtis Pension Trustees Ltd v Readson Ltd* [1994] PLR 289. Secondly, even if the liquidator did have the power to make the appointment in this case, it appears from the Simpson Curtis case that, at least in English law, the power must be exercised solely for the benefit of the beneficiaries. In the absence of evidence I accept that it is possible that the appointment of the Appellant was made by the liquidator for entirely altruistic reasons. However, if the reason for the appointment of a UK resident trustee in place of the original offshore trustee was to facilitate a claim to recover the assets the appointment would arguably be invalid.

TPR determination in *Telent/GEC 1972 Plan*

12.102   In 2007 the determinations panel of the Pensions Regulator reviewed the appointment by the Pensions Regulator of three new independent trustees.[101] The Regulator's appointment was under its power in s 7 of the Pensions Act 1995.

12.103   Section 7(3) now reads:

> (3) The Authority may also by order appoint a trustee of a trust scheme where they are satisfied that it is reasonable[102] to do so in order—
>
> > (a) to secure that the trustees as a whole have, or exercise, the necessary knowledge and skill for the proper administration of the scheme,
> >
> > (b) to secure that the number of trustees is sufficient for the proper administration of the scheme,
> >
> > (c) to secure the proper use or application of the assets of the scheme, or
> >
> > (d) otherwise to protect the interests of the generality of the members of the scheme.

12.104   In effect in *Telent*, the Regulator was considering if it was:

> satisfied that it is necessary to [appoint a trustee] in order . . .
>
> > (c) to secure the proper use or application of the assets of the scheme.

12.105   The trustee had raised concerns about what it considered were the proposals by the new parent company for the new strategy of the employer in relation to appointment of trustee directors and running the scheme, and in particular its investment strategy.

12.106   The Regulator's determinations panel referred to fiduciary nature of power to appoint and cited *Skeats*, but ultimately it made its decision on the back of the power in s 7.

Is *Skeats* Applicable to Pension Schemes?

12.107   *Skeats* and *Shortridge* were both decisions relating to a private family settlement—not a commercial trust such as a pension scheme.[103] Kay J himself in *Skeats' Settlement* clearly had

---

[101] On the TPR website at <http://www.thepensionsregulator.gov.uk/docs/DNTelentReasonsof DeterminationsPanel.pdf>. There is a good summary in the *Pensions Law Handbook* 9th edn (Bloomsbury Professional, 2010) 103.

[102] This used to say 'necessary', but the word 'reasonable' was substituted from 26 January 2009: Pensions Act 2008, s 131(1)(a).

[103] Or a unit trust—see the Australian decision in *Fitzwood v Unique Goal* (2001) 188 ALR 566 (Finkelstein J).

regard to the type of trust before him. Would these decisions be followed today in relation to a pension trust?

There are many cases on the application of trust law to pension schemes—see Chapter 2 **12.108** (Pension trusts and general trust law).

There seems to be no good reason (despite the reasoning used by Kay J in *Skeats' Settlement*) **12.109** why a power to appoint or remove trustees should be singled out as being of such importance that it should (unlike other employer powers—see Chapter 11) be considered to be fiduciary.

Private Trust Cases—Protectors

It has become relatively common for offshore trusts to include reserve powers for a settlor **12.110** (could cause tax problems) or for a 'protector'.

The powers commonly given to a protector are similar to that for an employer under **12.111** a pension scheme (see eg the list in *Underhill and Hayton: Law of Trusts and Trustees*, para 1.79).

So the question can arise as to whether powers held by a protector are fiduciary? For example: **12.112**

(a) Can a protector be replaced by the court?
(b) When can the exercise of powers be challenged?

There has been a trickle of cases on protectors (mainly outside the UK). Each depends on **12.113** their own circumstances and facts (in particular the terms of the relevant trust instrument). But, some themes or principles can be seen:

(a) if the protector is also a beneficiary:
   (i) powers probably not fiduciary;[104]
   (ii) but some comments that fiduciary elements could apply to power to appoint/remove Trustees;[105]
(b) if the protector is not a beneficiary:
   (i) can be a strong presumption of fiduciary nature;[106]
   (ii) this can apply to the settlor as well;[107]
   (iii) depends on the settlement and its purpose;
   (iv) categorization can be clarified by the trust deed.

---

[104] Non-fiduciary: *Rawson Trust v Perlman* [1990] 1 BOCM 135 (Bahamas); *Re Internine and Intertraders Trusts* (2005) [2010] WTLR 443, Jersey; *Re Z Trust* [1997] CILR 248. Limited fiduciary nature: *Re the Circle Trust: HSBC International Trustee Ltd v Wong* (2006) 9 ITELR 676 (Henderson J) Cayman Islands. Fiduciary (but not discussing the issue): *Carmine v Ritchie* [2012] NZHC 1514 at [66] (Gilbert J).
[105] *Re the Circle Trust: HSBC International Trustee Ltd v Wong* (2006) 9 ITELR 676 (Henderson J) Cayman Islands; *Re Papadimitriou* [2004] WTLR 1141 (Deemster Cain, Isle of Man).
[106] *In the Matter of the A Trust* [2012] JRC 169A; *Steele v Paz* [1993–95] Manx LR 426 (CA); *Von Knieriem v Bermuda Trust Co Ltd* (the *Star Trusts* case) [1994] Bda LR 50, (1996) 1 BOCM 116, Bermuda SC (Meerabux J)—fiduciary; *Re Bird Charitable Trust: Basel Trust Corpn (Channel Islands) Ltd v Ghirlandina Anstalt* (2008) 11 ITELR 157; *Birt, Bullen and Liddiard (Jersey)* (2008)—Jersey. See Matthew Conaglen and Elizabeth Weaver, 'Protectors as Fiduciaries: Theory and Practice' (2012) Trusts & Trustees 1, Andrew Holden, *Trust Protectors* (Jordans, 2011) and Mark Hubbard, *Protectors of Trusts* (Oxford University Press, 2013).
[107] *Re Osiris* (1999) 2 ITELR 404, [2000] WTLR 933 (Deemster Cain) Isle of Man—fiduciary.

Australian Cases

12.114 The case law in Australia refers to *Skeats*, but with an important exception for commercial trusts.

Fitzwood Pty Ltd v Unique Goal

12.115 *Fitzwood Pty Ltd v Unique Goal*[108] involved the removal of a trustee of a unit trust by a vote of the unit holders. At first instance (the point did not arise on appeal), Finkelstein J held (at para [98]):

> I am prepared to accept that a power of removal of a trustee may be a fiduciary power that must be exercised for the benefit of the beneficiaries and not for the benefit of the donee of the power, at least when the donee is not a beneficiary, although much will depend upon the terms of the trust instrument: *In re Skeats' Settlement* (1889) 42 Ch D 522, 526; *Inland Revenue Commissioners v Schroder* (1983) STC 480, 500. However, it is not likely that such an obligation will be imposed when it is the beneficiary that has been given the power of removal. In that circumstance it may usually be assumed that the beneficiary is entitled to act in his own interests when exercising the power.

Scaffidi v Montevento Holdings Pty Ltd

12.116 The later case of *Scaffidi v Montevento Holdings Pty Ltd*[109] involved a private family settlement. The court in Western Australia was more cautious than Finkelstein J in *Fitzwood*. Having cited Kay J in *Skeats*, the court continued:

> 149 Even if not correctly technically described as a 'fiduciary power' (see the discussion in Finn PD (as his Honour then was), Fiduciary Obligations (1977) [627], [644]), such a power must nevertheless be exercised bona fide for the purpose for which it was conferred: *Re Burton* (559); *Duke of Portland v Topham* [1864] EngR 339; (1864) 11 HLC 32, 54. The purpose of the power of removing and appointing trustees is ascertained by reference to the fiduciary nature of the office the object of the appointment.

12.117 So even here, the court is looking more towards a proper purpose test (than a fiduciary power). The Court of Appeal in *Scaffidi* was looking at a private trust, so not countering the comments of Finkelstein J in *Fitzwood* that:

> it is not likely that such an obligation will be imposed when it is the beneficiary that has been given the power of removal. In that circumstance it may usually be assumed that the beneficiary is entitled to act in his own interests when exercising the power.

12.118 A later Australian case (again on a private trust) considered *Fitzwood* but considered that a fiduciary obligation did arise, even where a beneficiary was the appointor (but in the event no breach of duty was found). In *Berger v Lysteron Pty Ltd*[110] Habersberger J followed Davies J in *Re Burton*[111] and held that it was important to consider the terms of the instrument. The fact that the power could transfer to a non-beneficiary and was contained in a deed of trust

---

[108] [2001] FCA 1628, (2001) 188 ALR 566 (Finkelstein J).

[109] [2011] WASCA 146 (Murphy and Buss JJA and Hall J). The Court of Appeal decision was later overturned by the High Court in *Montevento Holdings Pty Ltd v Scaffidi* [2012] HCA 48, but the fiduciary power point was not discussed (instead the decision turned on the nature of the limitation in the appointment power)—see the discussion in Ch 5.

[110] [2012] VSC 95 at [85] (Habersberger J).

[111] (1994) 126 ALR 557 (Davies J).

pointed to it being a fiduciary power. The point about the power being in the trust deed pointing to it being fiduciary may have some meaning in the context of the private trust concerned, but looks odd in the context of a pension scheme where many powers tend to be retained by the employer (and are not considered fiduciary—see Chapter 11).

Employer as a Beneficiary

12.119 Generally the Employer is a beneficiary of an occupational pension scheme—see Chapter 10 (Trustees' duties to employers). This is on the basis that:

(a) there is usually an express trust back to the employer if there is a surplus on a winding-up (and many schemes also include a power to pay surplus to the employer before a winding-up[112]);

(b) there will usually be an implied resulting trust if not express—see the decision of the Privy Council in *Air Jamaica v Charlton*;[113]

(c) the employer is the ultimate funder of a defined benefit pension scheme (either under the contribution rule in the scheme or under statute[114]) and so benefits (in having less to fund) if the scheme investments perform well.

12.120 This means that the employer is not a stranger to the trust in relation to an occupational pension scheme. This means that an employer should be treated as someone who:

• is interested in the trust;
• is a beneficiary (or at least a quasi-beneficiary) with interests.

12.121 But in any event, even if the limits on trustee duties to employers are less clear,[115] the ongoing interest of an employer in an occupational pension scheme are enough to rebut any fiduciary duty argument.

Money purchase schemes

12.122 This should apply to all occupational pension schemes, even money purchase schemes where the employer's ongoing funding obligation is more limited than for other schemes.

12.123 Even in the case of money purchase schemes, there is still an interest for employers in that the position of their employees is affected and there is still a statutory obligation on employers to fund if there is a loss caused by fraud.[116]

The Divorce Cases

12.124 The issue of fiduciary powers in relation to a power to appoint a new trustee sometimes comes up in divorce cases. A party to a marriage (say the husband) may have set up a settlement and a large amount of assets have been placed in it. The husband (as set law) has the power to

---

[112] Subject to the constraints in s 37 of the Pensions Act 1995 (as amended).
[113] [1999] 1 WLR 1399, PC.
[114] See Pensions Act 1995, s 75 and Pensions Act 2004, Pt 3.
[115] Eg Jonathan Hilliard's doubts in 'The Flexibility of Fiduciary Doctrine in Trust Law: How Far Does it Stretch in Practice' (2009) 23 TLI 119.
[116] See reg 10 of the Occupational Pension Schemes (Employer Debt) Regulations 2005 (SI 2005/678).

appoint or remove trustees. Does this mean that the assets held within the settlement should be treated as being under the control of the husband and so that the assets within the trust should be considered to form part of his assets for the purpose of divorce proceedings?

12.125 In relation to English trusts, the powers of the courts under the Matrimonial Causes Act 1973 are probably wide enough to give the courts power to look through to the trusts in direction and relation to the trust. However, where the trust is offshore, the powers may be more difficult to exercise.

12.126 In *Charman v Charman*[117] the Court of Appeal considered this point where the claim was made by the husband that the power to appoint or remove trustees was fiduciary so could not be exercised for his own benefit meaning that he did not have effective control over the trust. The Court of Appeal considered the point and cited *Skeat's Settlement*, but decided it did not need to consider the point.

Mutual Duty of Trust and Confidence

12.127 If the powers of an employer (including a power to appoint or remove trustees) are not to be viewed as fiduciary in relation to an occupational pension scheme, this does not mean that appointment/removal power is completely unfettered. It remains subject to the same 'constraints' (to use the terminology in the author's 1991 article and mentioned in the *Simpson Curtis* case) as other employers' powers.

12.128 In particular, the court has in the last two decades, generally imposed an implied duty on employers in employment contexts. This duty has been called one of 'good faith' or a 'mutual duty of trust and confidence'—see in more detail, Chapter 13 ('Employers' powers: the implied duty of trust and confidence'). It has been implied in a pensions context, beginning with the key decision in 1991 of the then Vice-Chancellor in the *Imperial Tobacco*[118] case.

Not fiduciary

12.129 As mentioned above (and in Chapters 11 and 13), this implied good faith duty is not the same as a fiduciary duty. In particular, the employer can consider and act in its own interests. See generally Matthew Conaglen in his book *Fiduciary Loyalty*,[119] citing *Re Courage*[120] and also *National Grid v Laws*,[121] *National Grid v Mayes*,[122] and *Johnson v Unisys*.[123]

12.130 Broadly an employer must not act in a way that is irrational or in a way that no reasonable employer would act. This is a severe test (see Newey J in *Prudential*).

12.131 An employer exercising an express power to appoint or remove trustees will be subject to this implied limitation. But an employer acting to get more sympathetic trustees (who once appointed are expected to act properly) is probably a proper purpose and not a breach of the implied good faith duty. Contrast on this a note on *LAW Construction* with a comment in

---

[117] [2007] EWCA Civ 503.
[118] [1991] 2 All ER 597 (Browne-Wilkinson V-C).
[119] At 43.
[120] [1987] 1 WLR 495 at 514 (Millett J).
[121] [1997] OPLR 207 at 227 (Robert Walker J).
[122] [2000] ICR 174 at [42], CA.
[123] [2001] UKHL 13 at [24].

Sweet & Maxwell's *Law of Pension Schemes*. As already mentioned, Tim Cox in the OPLR commentary on *LA2W Construction* case[124] commented:

> This seems entirely proper since, if there is a conflict between the interests of employers and members it is clearly right that the interests of both sides should be represented in any discussion about how the trustees should exercise their powers.

Conversely, in Sweet & Maxwell's *Law of Pension Schemes* (at pp 3–13) the authors comment: **12.132**

> If the principal employer were to exercise its power to remove one or more of the trustees of a scheme and to replace those trustees with others for the purpose of procuring the application of a surplus in accordance with its wishes, such a use of the power would appear wholly improper, and a fraud on a power, and would be liable to be reversed by the court.

And see the determination of the Pensions Regulator in *Telent* mentioned above. **12.133**

Express Provision in the Trust Deed

There is no reason why the position could not be clarified in the trust deed establishing a **12.134** pension scheme as to the nature of any duties imposed on an employer, including the power of appointing and removing trustees.

The cases generally make it clear that what would otherwise be implied as fiduciary duties can **12.135** be excluded in the relevant instrument—see further the decision of Warner J in *Mettoy* discussing the need to consider the nature of any discretions in the light of the trust deed as a whole and also *Bishop v Bonham*,[125] where the Court of Appeal held generally that the equitable duties which would otherwise have been implied on the part of a mortgagee could be excluded by the mortgage document. See generally *Kelly v Cooper*[126] and *Henderson v Merrett Syndicates*.[127]

Andrew Holden comments to the same effect in his book *Trust Protectors*:[128] **12.136**

> The settlor is equally free to specify that the protector holds some or all of his or her powers beneficially—that is, that the protector owes no duties whatsoever in relation to the consideration or exercise of the power, is not subject to the doctrine of fraud on a power, and can operate the power for his or her own benefit.[129]

The only limit on the ability of the trust instrument to modify the fiduciary duties which **12.137** would otherwise exist would seem to be:

(a) under statute—but none leaps to mind. Conceivably the Unfair Contract Terms Act 1977 could apply, but a provision dealing with appointment obligations does not seem to fall within what UCTA is intended to catch. In any event, UCTA is only concerned with contracts and the Court of Appeal has held in two cases in 2006 that it does not apply to trusts: *Baker v JE Clark & Co*[130]—nor to employment contracts: *Keen v Commerzbank AG*;[131]

---

124 [1996] OPLR 259 at 269 (Lord Hamilton, CSOH).
125 [1988] 1 WLR 742, CA. See also *Cowan v Scargill* [1984] 2 All ER 759 at 763 (Megarry V-C).
126 [1993] AC 205, PC.
127 [1995] 2 AC 145, HL.
128 (Jordans, 2011). See also *Underhill and Hayton: Law of Trusts and Trustees* (2010) para 71.12.
129 (Jordans, 2011) para 2.48.
130 [2006] EWCA Civ 464, [2006] PLR 131, CA.
131 [2006] EWCA Civ 1536, [2007] IRLR 132, CA.

(b) if the modification was so fundamental as to be inconsistent with the concept of the trust.[132] The limits of this principle are remarkably unclear (there is a distinct lack of cases holding that what looks like a trust in fact is not). The nature of the power to appoint or remove trustees is not so fundamental to the existence of a trust that it cannot be modified.

12.138   On this latter point, the irreducible core obligations of a trust, the case law indicates that it is a severe test. It will not apply unless the effect is to remove the core duty of honesty and good faith—see Chapter 14 (Trustee indemnities and exonerations).

12.139   Given the doubts on whether or not the power is fiduciary, it may well be considered prudent for trust deeds to contain an express provision dealing with the nature of any duties imposed on the principal company under a pension scheme trust deed.

12.140   It is, of course, a more difficult question as to whether or not such a clarificatory provision could properly be incorporated by way of amendment to an existing trust deed. In principle, there is no reason why not. Exoneration and payment clauses can clearly be included in existing trusts—they may need to be justified as being in the interests of the trust (eg if trustees would not otherwise serve)—see Lord Hope in *Dollar Academy v Lord Advocate*.[133]

Do the Private Trust Rules Apply to Pension Schemes?

12.141   See Chapter 2 (Pension trusts and general trust law).

12.142   To repeat the key comment of Lord Browne-Wilkinson in *Target Holdings v Redferns*:[134]

> But in my judgment it is in any event wrong to lift wholesale the detailed rules developed in the context of traditional trusts and then seek to apply them to trusts of quite a different kind. In the modern world the trust has become a valuable device in commercial and financial dealings. The fundamental principles of equity apply as much to such trusts as they do to the traditional trusts in relation to which those principles were originally formulated. But in my judgment it is important, if the trust is not to be rendered commercially useless, to distinguish between the basic principles of trust law and those specialist rules developed in relation to traditional trusts which are applicable only to such trusts and the rationale of which has no application to trusts of quite a different kind.

12.143   This is one of those occasions.

Trustee Companies

12.144   It is, of course, generally not uncommon for a trustee company, incorporated as a subsidiary of the principal company, to be the sole trustee of a pension scheme. This gives various benefits as regards continuity of appointments and, perhaps, some degree of protection for the directors of the trustee company from the duties they would otherwise have had had they become trustees personally. See further Chapters 4 and 5.

---

[132]   See Professor Hayton's chapter 'The irreducible core content of trusteeship' in AJ Oakley (ed), *Trends in Contemporary Trust Law* (Clarendon Press, 1996).

[133]   1995 SLT 596 (Lord Hope). Discussed by the Scottish Law Commission in its September 2003 Discussion Paper 123 on Breach of Trust at p 48. See <http://www.scotlawcom.gov.uk/download_file/view/111/>.

[134]   [1996] AC 421, [1995] 3 All ER 785, HL.

Although there was some authority in the 1950s that directors of a corporate trustee are **12.145** in a fiduciary position relating to the trust—see the two decisions of Danckwerts J in *Re French Protestant Hospital*[135] and *Abbey Malvern Wells Ltd v Ministry of Local Government and Planning*,[136] these are now considered to be inconsistent with the two older Court of Appeal decisions (not cited by Danckwerts J) in *Wilson v Lord Bury*[137] and *Bath v Standard Land*.[138]

It is now[139] clear that directors of a trustee company do not automatically owe direct fidu- **12.146** ciary duties to beneficiaries of the trust, instead they owe duties to the trustee company (although a director may, depending on the circumstances, potentially owe a direct duty if he or she aids in a breach of trust)—see *HR v JAPT*[140] and *Gregson v HAE Trustees Ltd*.[141]

If a corporate trustee is used, there is obviously more scope for the principal company to **12.147** argue that its power as shareholder to appoint and remove directors of a corporate trustee is not subject to fiduciary duties (following the *Kuwait Asia* case) even if the appointment or removal of a trustee himself is subject to fiduciary duties.

Given that a corporate trustee could be a sole trustee of several trusts and pension schemes, **12.148** it would not be very easy to apply a rule imposing a fiduciary duty on the principal company (as shareholder) in relation to appointment of directors.

Conclusion

The cases and commentary on the powers of third parties to appoint or remove trustees as **12.149** being fiduciary have often focused (at least in the UK) mainly on just citing the decision of Kay J in *Skeats' Settlement* without any analysis of whether that judgment remains applicable in a pensions context.

This chapter demonstrates that this should not apply in relation to employers and occupational pension schemes. The reasoning is that:

(a) the rationale for a fiduciary power depends on the circumstances of the case;
(b) even in relation to private settlements, the overseas cases on protectors indicate that powers held by beneficiaries are less likely to be fiduciary;
(c) for commercial trusts (like pension schemes or unit trusts), the private trust cases look less applicable, given:
   (i) it does not look appropriate to apply private trust principles to commercial trust in this area;
   (ii) the ongoing interests of the employer in the scheme;
   (iii) that generally employer powers under pension schemes are not fiduciary;
   (iv) the categorization of the employer as a beneficiary or quasi-beneficiary; and

---

[135] [1951] Ch 567.
[136] [1951] Ch 728.
[137] (1880) 5 QBD 518, CA.
[138] [1911] 1 Ch 618, CA.
[139] See Ch 5 (Liability of directors of corporate trustees) and D Pollard 'Pension Schemes: Corporate Trustees' (2000) 14 TLI 2.
[140] [1997] OPLR 123 (Lindsay J).
[141] [2008] EWHC 1006 (Ch), [2008] 2 BCLC 542 (Robert Miles QC sitting as a Deputy Judge of the High Court). Noted by Richard Nolan [2008] CLJ 472.

(v) the existence of other limits on employer's powers (in particular the implied good faith limits under the 1991 *Imperial Tobacco* case).

12.150   The terms of the trust instrument can clarify that the power is not fiduciary (and that an amendment can be made to achieve this).

12.151   In any event, the position on appointment or removal of directors of a trustee company should follow that for other fiduciaries (eg directors or insolvency practitioners) where it seems clear that there is no fiduciary duty. This will apply to directors of a trustee company as well.

13

EMPLOYERS' POWERS: THE IMPLIED DUTY OF TRUST AND CONFIDENCE— THE '*IMPERIAL*' DUTY

Introduction

13.1   The implied duty of mutual trust and confidence forms part of a fundamental re-evaluation by the courts of the mutual duties and rights between employers and employees. The implied term operates generally in an employment context[1] and also, for our purposes, applies in relation to employers' rights and discretions under an occupational pension scheme.[2]

13.2   The seminal pensions case here is the decision of Browne-Wilkinson V-C in 1991 in *Imperial Tobacco*,[3] holding that the implied term applies to employers' powers under occupational pension schemes. Later pensions cases have started to refer to this implied duty as the '*Imperial* duty'.[4]

13.3   The implied duty marks a fundamental shift by the courts.[5] In a pensions (and employment) context the development of the implied term is as great a piece of judicial law-making as the development of the law of negligence following the decision of the House of Lords in 1932 in *Donoghue v Stephenson*.[6]

13.4   However, as is often the case with judge-made law, the decision gives rise to a number of issues and questions. The full ambit and scope of the implied term will only emerge through decided cases over a number of years, probably over decades. The analogy with the law of negligence remains apt. The House of Lords clearly set out its scope in 1932, but over the past 80 or so years, a large number of decisions have followed seeking to define and explain the ambit of the duty. Examples are *Hedley Byrne*[7] in 1967 dealing with negligent mis-statement and a whole series of cases dealing with duties of local authorities (*Anns*[8] etc). Similarly, there are cases on:

(a)   the scope of the duty of care owed by accountants in relation to audited accounts (*Caparo*[9]);

(b)   whether surveyors owe duty of care to borrowers, even with a disclaimer (*Smith v Bush*[10]); and

---

[1]   See Mr Justice Lindsay, 'The Implied Term of Trust and Confidence' [2001] ILJ 1, Mark Freedland, *The Personal Employment Contract* (Oxford University Press, 2002), and Douglas Brodie, 'Beyond Exchange: The New Contract of Employment' [1998] 27 ILJ 79, 'The Heart of the Matter: Mutual Trust and Confidence' [1996] 25 ILJ 121, 'Mutual Trust and Values of the Employment Contract' [2001] ILJ 84, and *The Contract of Employment* (Thomson, 2008), Chs 8 and 9.

[2]   There is less published on pensions. See D Pollard, 'Employers' Powers in Pension Schemes: The Implied Duty of Trust and Confidence' (1997) 11 TLI 93; Philip Stear, 'Pensions, the Employment Contract and the Duty of Good Faith: Where Are We Now?' (APL seminar, November 2004), and from Australia, Anthea Nolan and Steve Godding, 'Employers' Rights and Duties in Respect of the Funds They Sponsor' (Superannuation conference 2010). More recently Meryl Thomas and Brian Dowrick, 'The Heart of the Matter – Re-Thinking Good Faith in Occupational Pension Schemes' [2007] Conv 495 and Tiziana Scaramuzza, 'Judicial deference in the application of the Imperial duty' (2013) 27 TLI (forthcoming).

[3]   *Imperial Group Pension Trust Ltd v Imperial Tobacco Ltd* [1991] 2 All ER 597 (Browne-Wilkinson V-C).

[4]   See *Procter & Gamble v Svenska Cellulosa Aktiebolaget SCA* [2012] EWHC 1257 (Ch), [2012] IRLR 733 (Hildyard J) and *IBM United Kingdom Pensions Trust Ltd v IBM United Kingdom Holdings Ltd* [2012] EWHC 3540 (Ch), (Warren J). Or the 'Imperial Tobacco duty': *National Grid Co plc v Laws* [1997] PLR 157 (Robert Walker J).

[5]   Although the seminal *Imperial Tobacco* decision was not at first seen as such by everyone. See the editorial in the November 1990 issue of British Pension Lawyer stating that 'The recent Imps decision—reported in this issue—will probably be found, some years ahead, to have been of no particular trail-blazing interest. No earth-shattering principle is enunciated. But the case marks a milestone, even so.'

[6]   [1932] AC 562, HL.

[7]   *Hedley Byrne & Co Ltd v Heller & Partners Ltd* [1964] AC 465, HL.

[8]   *Anns v Merton London Borough Council* [1978] AC 728, HL.

[9]   *Caparo Industries plc v Dickman* [1990] 2 AC 605, HL.

[10]   *Smith v Eric S Bush* [1990] 1 AC 831, HL.

(c)   whether there is a duty of care owned by employers for references (*Spring*[11]).

The list goes on.

It is clear that the implied duty of trust and confidence will perform as significant a role in   **13.5**
the pensions field. Unfortunately this means that currently there is some uncertainty. Just
as lawyers who were seeking to advise following *Donoghue v Stephenson* could not know the
precise ambit of the law of negligence, so we are currently placed in a quandary in seeking to
advise on the extent of the duty of trust and confidence. Again the law is thrown back on the
old conflict (which arises so often) between the need (particularly at the practitioner level)
for certainty and the overriding demands of 'justice'.

At one extreme, the doctrine is in such a state of development that at present it can almost   **13.6**
be said that any particular judge has a discretion as to how he or she will decide to formulate
it. There are no guarantees that another judge will follow this or indeed that the Court of
Appeal will agree. For example, in the leading employment case, *Malik v BCCI*,[12] the House
of Lords eventually overruled both the Court of Appeal and the first-instance judge and held
that there was a breach of the implied duty of trust and confidence and that the employees
could potentially claim damages based on it.

Indeed the House of Lords has commented in other cases that it can be helpful for the   **13.7**
common law to retain a degree of ambiguity. Thus Lord Wilberforce in 1967 (in a case on
covenants in restraint of trade) stated:[13]

> The common law has often (if sometimes unconsciously) thrived on ambiguity and it would
> be mistaken, even if it were possible, to try to crystallise the rules of this, or any, aspect of
> public policy into neat propositions.

We do at least have the benefit of some reasoning in the judgment, albeit relatively skimpy.[14]   **13.8**

Structure

This chapter looks at the following implications of the doctrine: **13.9**

(a)   history of the development of the term;
(b)   analysis of the pension cases that have applied it;
(c)   analysis of the term itself and some clues for the future; and
(d)   some problem areas.

Overview

The implied term of trust and confidence is sometimes called the implied duty of good faith   **13.10**
(it is discussed below how misleading this is as a description). In effect it is an implied term

---

[11]   *Spring v Guardian Assurance plc* [1995] 2 AC 296, HL.
[12]   *Mahmud v BCCI SA (in liq); Malik v BCCI SA (in liq)* [1998] AC 20, HL.
[13]   See *Esso Petroleum v Harper's Garage (Stourport) Ltd* [1968] AC 269 at 331F. More recently cited by the
Court of Appeal in *Dawnay Day & Co v d'Alphen* [1997] IRLR 442.
[14]   Compare this with the usual terse statement (devoid of much reasoning) which is all that usually emerges
from the European Court of Justice.

found by the courts as a matter of law as implied into the employment relationship. The actual term is repeated constantly in the cases as:[15]

> the employer shall not without reasonable and proper cause conduct itself in a manner calculated and likely to destroy or seriously damage the relationship of trust and confidence between employer and employee.[16]

13.11 In effect this has been used by the court in two ways.

(1) As a freestanding obligation on its own

13.12 For example, the implied term has been taken to enable an employee to claim breach of the term because of some action by (or any action) by the employer completely independent of the contract of employment. In *Malik v BCCI*,[17] for instance, an employee was able to bring an action for damages (at the time known as 'stigma damages') as he would find it more difficult to obtain work in the future because of his association with the fraudulent former employer. In many of the dismissal cases, some action by the employer against the employee has allowed the employee to claim breach of contract, and so resign on the basis of constructive dismissal, hence an unfair dismissal claim—for example an employer who yelled at his employee and abused her was held to be in breach of the implied duty and so the employee could resign and claim constructive dismissal.

(2) As a limit or fetter on an express power

13.13 In this context, the implied term operates to control a power that the employer has under the employment contract (or pension scheme).

For example an employer may have an express right to move the employee's work to another location. The implied term has been operated to limit the employer's unfettered ability to use this power. In relation to moving location, the employer must give reasonable notice etc. See eg *United Bank v Akhtar*.[18]

13.14 Not all judges like this move towards a fetter on an express power. In 1997 in *Adin v Sedco Forex International Resources Ltd*[19] Lord Coulsfield in the Employment Appeal Tribunal in Scotland clearly felt very uncomfortable with the 'so-called implied term of trust and confidence'. He could not see how the implication of such a term could be said to be necessary where it was proposed to be used to 'limit discretionary powers which an employer is given expressly'. However, these comments were given before the decision of the House of Lords in *Malik v BCCI*.

Good faith obligation in contracts generally

13.15 The implied term is part of a wider trend in contracts generally (not just pensions or employment). There is a general move away from unfettered powers or construing documents strictly, towards a more purposeful approach with implied restrictions on powers.

---

[15] But note that we should not seek to construe judicial utterances, even of the House of Lords, as if we are trying to construe a statute. See eg the comments of the Privy Council in *Royal Brunei v Tan* [1995] 2 AC 378, PC.

[16] See Lord Steyn in *Malik v BCCI* [1997] 3 All ER 1 at 15. Note that this differs from the term as defined in *Imperial Tobacco* and *Stannard v Fisons* where the reference is to 'calculated *or* likely to destroy...'. Given that Lord Steyn refers to the test as being objective (see below), no difference in the sense seems intended. The formulation used in *Imperial Tobacco* seems clearer.

[17] [1997] 3 All ER 1, HL.

[18] [1989] IRLR 507, EAT.

[19] [1997] IRLR 280, EAT.

This is part of a general move towards a good faith doctrine as part of English law (this trend can be seen in statutory versions such as the Unfair Contract Terms Act 1977 and the unfair dismissal provisions in the Employment Rights Act 1996). On the exercise of discretions in contracts generally, see the article by Richard Hooley, 'Controlling Contractual Discretion'.[20] **13.16**

Most recently, in *Yam Seng Pte Ltd v International Trade Corpn Ltd*[21] Leggatt J considered good faith in a commercial contractual context and ruled in favour of the claimant, finding that Yam Ltd was justified in terminating the contract and was able to claim damages. Leggatt J considered the extent to which elements of a duty of good faith could be implied into English law contracts and key points are: **13.17**

(a) a duty of good faith, although not implied into commercial contracts by default, can be implied based on the presumed intention of the parties and the relevant background against which the contract was made. The relevant background includes shared values and norms of behaviour taken for granted by contracting parties and these norms establish the content of any implied duty of good faith;

(b) the test of the scope of any implied duty of good faith or fair dealing is objective in the sense that it depends not on either party's perception of whether particular conduct is improper, but on whether in the particular context the conduct would be regarded as commercially unacceptable by reasonable and honest people; and

(c) contracts involving a longer-term relationship and substantial commitment require a higher degree of disclosure, cooperation, and predictable performance based on mutual trust and expectations of loyalty, which are not legislated for in the express terms of the contract, but are implicit in the parties' understanding, and are necessary to give business efficacy to the arrangements. It is too simplistic to say that good faith, honesty, and loyalty can only be implied into relationships in which fiduciary duties traditionally arise; they can arise in a wider range of relationships.

The Court of Appeal in *Compass Group UK and Ireland Ltd (t/a Medirest) v Mid Essex Hospital Services NHS Trust*[22] emphasized that whether or not there is any implied good faith obligation is very fact—and contract—specific. **13.18**

Clearly, following *BCCI*, there is an implied term in employment relationships. Are the judges then merely operating on a 'justice' basis or will this ever be an area of the law laid down by precedent and rigidly defined? The latter is likely to be right. The judges are not saying they have a general discretion to decide what they think is right in the circumstances, but instead are seeking to operate on a well-defined path. **13.19**

In a pensions context, clearly the main impact of the implied term is to limit what looks like an otherwise unfettered power held by an employer. It is no longer sufficient to point to a particular power in a trust deed (eg the power to close the scheme, the power to terminate the scheme, the power to set contributions) and to say that because this is vested in the employer or some form of employer consent is needed, the employer can exercise or refuse to exercise this power with no external controls or fetters. **13.20**

---

[20] [2013] CLJ 65. See also the section 'Implied terms and contractual discretions' at 11.65 in G McMeel, *The Construction of Contracts* 2nd edn (Oxford University Press, 2011).

[21] [2013] EWHC 111, QB (Leggatt J).

[22] [2013] EWCA Civ 200, CA.

13.21 The courts are deciding that such powers are subject to implied limitations. This is not surprising in the context of fiduciary powers held by trustees. There is a long history of construing such powers (even when expressed to be unfettered) as subject to implied restraints. For example powers must be exercised in the best interests of the members, without a conflict of interest, for a proper purpose, etc. Such limitations are less common in relation to non-fiduciary powers.

13.22 Historically the common law has shied away from imposing duties of good faith on contracting parties except in special circumstances. Partly this may be because of the difficulties the common law faces. The 'paradigm' contract law, the one we all learn at law school, seems to involve a point contract, ie a discrete contract of sale. In practice many contracts and, in particular, employment contracts and pension schemes, involve a long-standing relationship between the contracting parties. An example of a point contract would be me walking into a shop and buying a Mars bar or a Bounty bar. An example of an ongoing contract is one where there is an ongoing long-term relationship between the parties, such as an employment contract, which can last for many years.

13.23 Clearly a consumer's discretion as to whether to buy a Mars bar or a Bounty bar is unfettered It would not be open for the shopkeeper to say, after the consumer had decided on a Bounty bar, that they had taken improper considerations into account or had failed to consider that which they should have considered. Even if the consumer is acting in bad faith or arbitrarily or capriciously there is no sanction.

Common law right to act capriciously

13.24 Indeed the reluctance of the courts to interfere even with bad-faith exercises of discretions can be seen in some of the older cases (although one must wonder whether they would be followed today). For example in 1895 in *Pickles v Bradford Corpn*[23] the House of Lords held that a landowner was at liberty to sink wells on his land even though the sole purpose was to divert water from a neighbour's land. The right arises even if the landowner is acting maliciously to injure his neighbour.

13.25 Similarly in 1921 the Court of Appeal held in *Re Moore & Co and Landauer & Co*[24] that a purchaser of canned fruits was entitled to reject a shipment. The contract had stipulated for cases containing 30 tins each. The right total number of tins was delivered, but some of the cases contained only 24 tins. Rejection was allowed even though there was no difference in the market value (we must surmise that the market value of canned fruit had fallen!). This case was later described as 'excessively technical and due for fresh examination' (Lord Wilberforce in *Reardon Smith Line*[25]).

13.26 Historically, then, the courts seemed to be faced with two views. If the power was fiduciary, then there were constraints on it; if it was non-fiduciary the courts would not readily interfere with the exercise of a discretion, perhaps in the absence of fraud or criminal intent.

13.27 There are clear statements that good faith is not a part of English contract law—see *Walford v Miles*[26] and *Interfoto Picture Library Ltd v Stiletto Visual Programmes Ltd*.[27] But general

---

[23] [1895] AC 587, HL.
[24] [1921] 2 KB 519, CA.
[25] [1976] 1 WLR 989 at 998, HL.
[26] [1992] 2 AC 128, HL.
[27] [1989] QB 433, CA. See also in relation to pre-contract negotiations, *Cobbe v Yeomans Row Management Ltd* [2006] EWCA Civ 1139 at para [4], CA.

contract law may now be moving to at least imply a duty on contracting parties to exercise discretions under the contract in good faith, honestly and not arbitrarily, capriciously, or irrationally. Sometimes they refer to not acting unreasonably (in the *Wednesbury* sense—ie not in such a way that no reasonable person having the relevant discretion would act)—see the Court of Appeal decisions in *Paragon Finance plc v Nash*,[28] *Paragon Finance plc v Pender*,[29] *Socimer International Bank Ltd (in liq) v Standard Bank London Ltd*,[30] and *Gan Insurance Co Ltd v Tai Ping Insurance Co Ltd*.[31] For a fuller discussion of this move, in relation to contracts generally, see Richard Hooley, 'Controlling Contractual Discretion'.[32]

Clearly, however, the courts have now developed an implied restriction in the case of employment contracts.[33]   **13.28**

The development of the law relating to the exercise of a discretion by an employer has been **13.29** notable in the arena of bonus decision-making by employers. Whereas in the past courts might have been reluctant to interfere with even bad faith exercises of discretion, it clear from case law that has developed since 2000 that the concept of a 'bad faith' exercise of a discretion is one which sits uncomfortably with courts when considering the nature of the relationship between employer and employee.

On that basis case law has imposed limits on the power of an employer to exercise a discre- **13.30** tion which is expressed to be 'full' or 'unfettered' in contractual documentation. Even where a discretion has been widely drafted to allow the employer to take a non-exhaustive list of factors into account, case law has made it clear that:

(a) an employer must only take account of relevant matters, and no irrelevant ones. By way of illustration, in *McCarthy*,[34] the scheme rules required the remuneration committee to consider 'the extent to which the Performance Condition has been achieved at the date of termination'. The performance condition applicable to Mr McCarthy's options had been met in full, but the committee exercised its discretion to allow him to exercise only 75 per cent of his options based on Mr McCarthy's personal conduct in the last months of his employment. The Court of Appeal held that the committee had acted in breach of the rules by taking into account Mr McCarthy's conduct. This was not a factor permitted by the rules to be taken into account because it did not affect achievement of the performance condition;

---

[28] [2001] EWCA Civ 1466, [2002] 2 All ER 248.
[29] [2005] EWCA Civ 760, [2005] 1 WLR 3412, CA.
[30] [2008] EWCA Civ 116, [2008] Bus LR 1304, [2008] 1 Lloyd's Rep 558, CA.
[31] [2002] EWCA Civ 248, [2002] All ER (D) 10 (Mar), CA.
[32] [2013] CLJ 65. And see recently *Yam Seng Pte Ltd v International Trade Corpn Ltd* [2013] EWHC 111, QB (Leggatt J); *Euroption Strategic Fund Ltd v Skandinaviska Enskilda Banken AB* [2012] EWHC 584 (Comm), [2013] 1 BCLC 125 (Gloster J); and *Jacobs UK Ltd v Skidmore Owings & Merrill LLP* [2012] EWHC 3293 (TCC) (Coulson J). But emphasizing that whether or not there is any implied good faith obligation is very fact and contract specific, see the Court of Appeal in *Compass Group UK and Ireland Ltd (t/a Medirest) v Mid Essex Hospital Services NHS Trust* [2013] EWCA Civ 200, CA.
[33] And arguably also insurance contracts. For example in *Napier v UNUM Ltd* [1996] 2 Lloyd's LR 550 Tuckey J held that he could review a decision by an insurer not to pay under a permanent health policy where the policy required 'production of proof satisfactory to (UNUM) of the insured's entitlement to benefits'. He held (at p 553) 'But I do not equate the obligation to produce proof satisfactory, which is apt to describe vouching, with a stipulation that the insurer's decision to reject an adequately vouched claim cannot be disputed in the Courts on grounds other than lack of good faith. I believe that very clear words would be required to achieve this result.'
[34] *McCarthy v McCarthy & Stone plc* [2007] EWCA Civ 664, [2008] 1 All ER 221, CA.

(b) an irrelevant factor would also include taking into account unlawful grounds (such as sex, race, age, or sexual orientation);

(c) an employer must not act irrationally, perversely, or capriciously in exercising its discretion. In *Clark v Nomura*,[35] Mr Clark, a senior equity trader who had been dismissed by Nomura was not paid a discretionary bonus despite having generated significant profits for Nomura during the bonus period. Burton J found that, under the terms of Nomura's bonus scheme, Mr Clark's bonus was dependent on his performance of his contract as a senior equity trader and that the decision to give Mr Clark no bonus at all in light of his performance for the bonus period, was irrational and perverse.

(d) An employer should not act irrationally in the exercise of its discretion in respect of facts or circumstances which are similar—eg in exercising a discretion not to pay a bonus to two individuals who are employed at the same level and who are found to have engaged in the same offending conduct. It does not matter that another employer might have reached a different decision—provided that the decision reached by the employer is not a decision which no reasonable employer could have reached.[36] In *Threlfall*,[37] an employer awarded a former employee a bonus of zero on termination because of (i) the difficult economic circumstances at the time, and (ii) it was discovered that the claimant had been competing against the interests of the company. Lang J, applying *Clark v Nomura*, held that the decision was not 'so irrational or perverse that no reasonable employer would have exercised its discretion in this way. In my judgment, the decision was within the band of reasonableness'.[38]

Judicial development—retrospective

13.31 It seems that the implied duty is retrospective. It has always been there, only we (and the judges) have not known about it. Compare the situation of the National Bus trustees[39] in relation to matters which occurred in 1986, before the *Imperial Tobacco* case. The Pension Ombudsman's determination still found them liable for failing to recognize that the employer was in breach of his implied duty. This seems rather harsh (the courts themselves have recognized that earlier judgments were inconsistent with the duty), but that's the way the common law crumbles.

Statutory coverage

13.32 Can it be said that the implied term of trust and confidence should be reduced in light of the Pensions Acts? Can it be argued that Parliament has intervened to set certain standards (eg the existence of the statutory funding requirements means that no further constraints should be placed on the funding of pension schemes by employers) and it is not for the courts to develop more onerous standards?

13.33 This might well have been attractive to a less interventionist judiciary. However, it clearly will not apply today—see generally Chapter 3. The courts have developed the whole implied term of trust and confidence in employment contracts in the context of a statutory regime relating to unfair dismissal.

---

[35] *Clark v Nomura International plc* [2000] IRLR 766 (Burton J).
[36] *Mallone v BPB Industries plc* [2002] EWCA Civ 126, [2002] IRLR 452, CA.
[37] *Threlfall v ECD Insight Ltd* [2012] EWHC 3543 (QB), [2013] IRLR 185 (Lang J).
[38] [2012] EWHC 3543 (QB) at [101].
[39] *National Bus* (1996) 6 September, A10113, [1997] PLR 1, (Farrand PO).

Indeed in *Malik v BCCI*, the House of Lords considered that it was appropriate to extend the common law by analogy with a statutory provision rather than saying that the statute set down everything that was to be said and leaving it for the legislature to intervene if it saw fit. Lord Steyn cited[40] the speech by Professor Beatson in Cambridge on 'Has the Common Law a Future?'.[41] **13.34**

Uncertainty

Clearly this is a doctrine that requires 'good faith' (whatever that means—this will come up later). As such it can be difficult to argue against. Just as everyone is against sin, so everyone must normally be said to be against 'bad faith'.[42] **13.35**

However, it has to be said that the use of vague terms like this, whether in statute or in judicial development, does add a vast element of uncertainty into the law. As practitioners we are on the front line of the problems this raises in terms of being able to give advice one way or the other to clients. **13.36**

It is not just employers who are faced by this problem. It is clear that if an employer has acted in breach of the implied duty of trust and confidence, the trustees may enforce the duties. Therefore, trustees faced with (say) an employer seeking to adhere further companies to a scheme or seeking to reduce contributions should realize that this could be a breach of the duty of the trust and confidence and, if it is, require the employer not to so act. If they do not they are at risk of being held to be acting in breach of trust. (They may of course be protected by an exoneration clause.) **13.37**

History of the *Imperial* Duty and Implied Term

As Lord Steyn pointed out in *Malik v BCCI*, the implied term probably has its origin in the general duty of cooperation between contracting parties. Lord Steyn went on to point out that the implied term adds little to the employee's implied obligations to serve his employer loyally and not to act contrary to his employer's interests. **13.38**

Lord Steyn went on:[43] **13.39**

> The major importance of the implied duty of trust and confidence lies in its impact on the obligations of the employer: see Douglas Brodie 'The heart of the matter: mutual trust and confidence' (1996) 25 ILJ 121 (recent cases, commentary). And the implied obligation as formulated is apt to cover the great diversity of situations in which a balance has to be struck between an employer's interest in managing his business as he sees fit and the employee's interest in not being unfairly and improperly exploited.

Lord Steyn had already mentioned that the notion of a master and servant relationship had become obsolete. He mentioned that Lord Slynn in *Spring v Guardian Assurance plc* had noted:[44] **13.40**

> the changes which have taken place in the employer/employee relationship, with far greater duties imposed on the employer than in the past, whether by statute or by judicial decision, to care for the physical, financial and even psychological welfare of the employee.

---

[40] At p 22a.
[41] This is now published at [1997] CLJ 291.
[42] Or indeed 'maladministration'—see the comments of Robert Walker J in *Westminster City Council v Hayward* [1996] 2 All ER 467 at 480b.
[43] At p 15j.
[44] [1995] 2 AC 296 at 335, HL.

13.41 It is clear that the implied duty will not go away. All the cases which have gone to the House of Lords recently in relation to employees seem to have imposed obligations on employers. For example:

(a) *Scally v Southern Health and Social Services Board*[45] (implied term to inform employees in certain cases); and

(b) *Spring v Guardian Assurance plc*[46] (duty of care on employer to not give a negligently wrong reference).

13.42 In *Malik* Lord Steyn commented:

> The evolution of the implied term of trust and confidence is a fact. It has not yet been endorsed by your Lordships' House. It has proved a workable principle in practice. It has not been the subject of adverse criticism in any decided cases and it has been welcomed in academic writings. I regard the emergence of the implied term of mutual trust and confidence as a sound development.

Unfair dismissal

13.43 The history of the development of the doctrine can be traced back at least to the decision of the Court of Appeal in *Western Excavating v Sharp*.[47] This case concerned a claim for unfair dismissal brought by an employee. The question addressed by the Court of Appeal was how to resolve the conflicting decisions of the Employment Appeal Tribunal on the question of interpretation of the statutory unfair dismissal provisions.

13.44 In order for a right for compensation for unfair dismissal to arise, there must be a dismissal. Clearly there will be a dismissal where an employer expressly dismisses an employee. However, the statute[48] (understandably) goes on to allow an employee to resign and claim constructive dismissal in certain circumstances.

13.45 The Court of Appeal decided that the statutory provision clearly imported the normal contractual rules allowing one party (the employee) to treat a contract as terminated because of the actions of the other party (namely a repudiatory breach). The alternative construction, namely that an employee can bring an unfair dismissal claim where the employer has merely acted unreasonably, was rejected by the Court of Appeal.

13.46 Following *Western Excavating*, employees needed to be able to show a breach of a term of the contract in order to be able to bring an unfair dismissal claim in circumstances where there had not been an express dismissal. This clearly causes difficulties for employees in some circumstances.

13.47 For example if an employee has been subjected to abuse or threats, it would be difficult for him (or her) to point to an express term in the contract that has been broken by the employer. However, it would clearly be wrong to hold the employee to be bound by the contract of employment such that there was in fact no constructive dismissal. Accordingly, the courts developed the implied term by duty of trust and confidence, at least initially to allow employees to be able to bring unfair dismissal claims in these circumstances.[49]

---

[45] [1992] 1 AC 294, HL.

[46] [1995] 2 AC 296, HL.

[47] [1978] QB 761, CA.

[48] See now s 95 of the Employment Rights Act 1996.

[49] *United Bank Ltd v Akhtar* [1989] IRLR 507 (EAT) and *Lewis v Motorworld Garages Ltd* [1985] IRLR 465, CA. The Court of Appeal endorsed the implied term in *Woods v WM Car Services (Peterborough) Ltd* [1982] ICR 693, CA and in *Lewis v Motorworld Garages Ltd* [1986] ICR 157, CA.

The whole existence of the implied term can in fact be traced largely to Sir Nicolas **13.48** Browne-Wilkinson (later Lord Browne-Wilkinson). He first applied the term in the EAT in *Woods v WM Car Services (Peterborough) Ltd*, subsequently following this up with *Imperial Group Pension Trust Ltd v Imperial Tobacco Ltd*.[50] Later, the House of Lords[51] confirmed the existence of the term in *Malik v BCCI*.

Examples of breach of the implied term in an employment context

Generally in the decided employment cases the employer must have been 'nasty' in some way **13.49** towards the employee. Examples are:

(a) persistent and unwanted amorous advances (*Western Excavating*);
(b) no notice of move of workplace from Leeds to Birmingham (*Akhtar*);
(c) failure to treat seriously allegation of sexual harassment (*Bainbridge*);
(d) using foul language (*Pelamor*);
(e) giving unjustified warnings (*Walker*); and
(f) operating a dishonest and corrupt business (*Malik*).

What do the Employment Cases Say that the Term Means?

So we have the implied term: **13.50**

> the employer shall not without reasonable and proper cause conduct itself in a manner calculated and likely to destroy or seriously damage the relationship of trust and confidence between employer and employee.[52]

But what does it actually mean?

It is not a reasonableness test

This is tolerably clear. The Courts are consistent in stating that they are not imposing an **13.51** obligation on employers to act reasonably nor to do things that can later be reviewed by the Courts as being unreasonable—see *White v Reflecting Roadstuds*,[53] *Post Office v Roberts*,[54] and *Imperial Group Pension Trust v Imperial Tobacco*.[55]

This can perhaps be contrasted with some general contract cases—for example in *Braganza v BP* **13.52** *Shipping Ltd*[56] the Court of Appeal was concerned with a contract that provided for death benefits in some circumstances, but not if 'in the opinion of the company' the death resulted from the employee's wilful act. Longmore LJ held that:

> There was no dispute that where a contract gives a discretion to one of the contracting parties that discretion must be exercised honestly and on reasonable grounds. If, therefore, a death benefit is not payable if, in the opinion of the employer, the death resulted from the employee's wilful act or default, that opinion must be formed honestly and on reasonable grounds.

---

[50] [1991] 2 All ER 597 (Browne-Wilkinson V-C).
[51] Lord Browne-Wilkinson was not, perhaps oddly, in the panel that heard the case.
[52] See Lord Steyn in *Malik v BCCI* [1997] 3 All ER 1 at 15. See the comments above at para 13.10.
[53] [1991] IRLR 331, EAT.
[54] [1980] IRLR 347.
[55] [1991] 2 All ER 597.
[56] [2013] EWCA Civ 230, CA.

Longmore LJ went on to hold that the decision-maker in this case (who had considered an accident report prepared by a team for the company) could not be said to have 'positively misdirected himself in law' and it would be wrong to construe such a clause as requiring the decision-maker to take legal advice.

13.53   In *The Vainqueur José* [57] (a case which depended on the exercise of discretions by a P&I Club) Mocatta J held:[58]

> Where, as here, the success or failure of a claim depends upon the exercise of a discretion by a lay body, it would be a mistake to expect the same expert, professional and almost microscopic investigation of the problems, both factual and legal, that is demanded of a suit in a Court of law.

Mocatta J also said:[59]

> To the exercise of such discretion the common law principles must apply and these undoubtedly include fairness, reasonableness, bona fides and absence of misdirection in law.

13.54   Although not brought out in these two decisions, it seems that there may be a distinction between:

- a decision as to a factual matter (eg how did an employee die, is an employee ill) where the contract provides for a decision on this to be made by a person, as compared to
- a discretion over a non-factual matter (eg even if it is clear that an employee is ill, is there a consent for a benefit needed from the employer?).

It is easier to see that the factual decision should be subject to a reasonableness test.

But it is objective—motive is not conclusive

13.55   The test imposed is objective in the sense that it is immaterial whether the employer intended to have the impact on the employee or to break his contract—see *Malik v BCCI*,[60] *Post Office v Roberts*,[61] *Woods v WM Car Services (Peterborough) Ltd*.[62]

13.56   There is no requirement that the employee must have been aware of the conduct while he was an employee. Lord Steyn expressly rejected such a limitation in *Malik v BCCI*, overturning the Court of Appeal on this point.[63]

13.57   But motive can still be relevant. If there is in fact an intention to act (say) outrageously, the implied term will almost certainly be broken.

There does not have to be direct maltreatment of employees

13.58   In *Malik* in the Court of Appeal Morritt LJ held that the obligation:

> May be broken not only by an act directed at a particular employee but also by conduct which, when viewed objectively, is likely seriously to damage the relationship of employer and employee.[64]

---

[57] [1979] 1 Lloyd's Rep 557 (Mocatta J). Agreed by the parties in *Braganza v BP Shipping Ltd* as the applicable test (see para [13]).
[58] At p 577.
[59] At p 574.
[60] Lord Steyn at p 16g.
[61] [1980] IRLR 347.
[62] [1981] IRLR 347. See also the note by Douglas Brodie in [1996] 25 ILJ 121 at 121–2.
[63] See [1997] 3 All ER 1 at 17d–18d.
[64] See [1995] 3 All ER 545 at 550.

This was approved by Lord Steyn in the House of Lords.[65]

Damages are available

Again, in *Malik v BCCI*, the House of Lords held that the remedy for an employee where **13.59** there was a breach of the implied term was not merely to claim constructive dismissal (and hence termination of the contract of employment), but that damages were also available. Most of the earlier employment cases are concerned with claims from unfair dismissal and therefore are based on the ability of the employee to claim repudiation of the contract.

However, the doctrine has not been so limited by the House of Lords and such limitations **13.60** have not been followed in the pensions cases (see eg *Imperial Tobacco*).

Lord Nicholls stated:[66] **13.61**

Although the underlying purpose of the trust and confidence term is to protect the employment relationship, there can be nothing unfairly onerous or unreasonable in requiring an employer who breaches the trust and confidence term to be liable if he thereby causes continuing financial loss of a nature that was reasonably foreseeable. Employers must take care not to damage their employees' future employment prospects, by harsh and oppressive behaviour or by any other form of conduct which is unacceptable today as falling below the standards set by the implied trust and confidence term.

But damages for breach of the implied term are not available if the loss is connected with **13.62** dismissal (as this would interfere with and override the statutory unfair dismissal regime).[67]

Not a breach merely because the employee suffers loss

In *White v Reflecting Roadstuds*[68] the EAT held that an employer could exercise an express **13.63** power to move an employee from one department to another even though the employee would earn less as a result. Here the employer had acted with reasonable and sufficient grounds and there was no breach of the implied term.

General Description

This still does not give the practitioner much help as to when the implied term will be **13.64** broken. Evidence needs to be gathered from each of the cases in the hope that a coherent doctrine will emerge in a process akin to formulating an atomic theory.

Some help is given by the descriptions of the duty when used in the employment cases. The **13.65** employer must:

(a) be a good and considerate employer—*Woods v WM Car Services (Peterborough)*;[69]
(b) not treat employees arbitrarily, capriciously, or inequitably—*FC Gardner v Beresford*;[70]
(c) act in good faith—*Mihlenstedt, Imperial Tobacco*;

---

[65] See [1997] 3 All ER 1 at 17b.
[66] See Lord Nicholls at p 8.
[67] *Johnson v Unisys Ltd* [2001] UKHL 13, [2003] 1 AC 518, HL; *Eastwood v Magnox Electric* [2004] UKHL 35, [2005] 1 AC 503, HL; and *Edwards v Chesterfield Royal Hospital* [2011] UKSC 58, [2012] 2 AC 22, SC.
[68] [1991] IRLR 331, EAT.
[69] [1982] IRLR 413, CA.
[70] [1978] IRLR 63, EAT.

(d) not coerce the employees—*Imperial Tobacco*;

(e) not issue threats—*Hillsdown, National Bus*;

(f) not act in a way that is harsh and oppressive—*Malik*; and

(g) not give reprimands in a degrading, intimidating, or humiliating manner—*Hilton International Hotels.*[71]

13.66 The pensions cases show that the test:

(a) is not one of fairness—*Imperial Tobacco, Prudential,*[72] and *IBM;*[73]

(b) is a severe one—*Prudential*[74] and *Gogay;*[75] and

(c) is objective—*Prudential.*[76]

The Pensions Cases

13.67 How, then, is this applied in relation to discretions under or in connection with Pension Schemes?

Imperial Tobacco

13.68 In the leading judgment of Sir Nicolas Browne-Wilkinson V-C[77] in *Imperial Group Pension Trust Ltd v Imperial Tobacco Ltd,*[78] the ambit of the implied obligation was extended to cover trustees of pension schemes.

13.69 It is worth noting that Newey J commented in the later *Prudential* case[79] that:

It would make no sense to freeze-frame the duty of trust and confidence as it appeared at the date of Browne-Wilkinson V-C's decision.

13.70 It is also worth quoting the comments made by Sir Nicolas Browne-Wilkinson in *Imperial Tobacco* at some length:[80]

There remains the submission of Mr Topham[81] for the employed members which I accept. Pension scheme trusts are of quite a different nature to traditional trusts. The traditional trust is one under which the settlor, by way of bounty, transfers property to trustees to be administered for the beneficiaries as objects of his bounty. Normally, there is no legal relationship between the parties apart from the trust. The beneficiaries have given no consideration for what they receive. The settlor, as donor, can impose such limits on his bounty as he chooses, including imposing a requirement that the consent of himself or some other person shall be required to the exercise of the powers.

---

[71] [1990] IRLR 316, EAT.

[72] [2011] EWHC 960 (Ch) at [132] (Newey J).

[73] [2102] EWHC 3540 (Ch) at [18] (Warren J).

[74] Newey J at [132].

[75] *Gogay v Hertfordshire CC* [2000] IRLR 703, CA. Hale LJ at [55].

[76] See Newey J in *Prudential* at [151]. Followed by Warren J in *IBM* at [18]. In an employment context, see *Tullett Prebon plc v BGC Brokers LP* [2011] EWCA Civ 131, [2011] IRLR 42, CA.

[77] Later Lord Browne-Wilkinson. He did not sit on the panel which heard *Malik*.

[78] [1991] 2 All ER 597 (Browne-Wilkinson V-C).

[79] *Prudential Staff Pensions Ltd v The Prudential Assurance Co Ltd* [2011] EWHC 960 (Ch) at [141] (Newey J). See also Warren J in *IBM* at [17].

[80] [1991] 2 All ER 597 at 606.

[81] Geoffrey Topham, counsel for the employees.

As the Court of Appeal have pointed out in *Mihlenstedt v Barclays Bank* [1989] IRLR 522 a pension scheme is quite different. Pension benefits are part of the consideration which an employee receives in return for the rendering of his services. In many cases, including the present, membership of the pension scheme is a requirement of employment. In contributory schemes, such as this, the employee is himself bound to pay his or her contributions. Beneficiaries of the scheme, the members, far from being volunteers have given valuable consideration. The company employer is not conferring a bounty. In my judgment, the scheme is established against the background of such employment and falls to be interpreted against that background.

In every contract of employment there is an implied term—

> that the employers will not, without reasonable and proper cause, conduct themselves in a manner calculated or likely to destroy or seriously damage the relationship of confidence and trust between employer and employee . . .

(See *Woods v WM Car Services (Peterborough) Ltd* [1981] IRLR 347 approved by the Court of Appeal in *Lewis v Motorworld Garages Ltd* [1985] IRLR 465). I will call this implied term 'the implied obligation of good faith'. In my judgment, that obligation of an employer applies as much to the exercise of his rights and powers under a pension scheme as they do to the other rights and powers of an employer. Say, in purported exercise of its right to give or withhold consent, the company were to say, capriciously, that it would consent to an increase in the pension benefits of members of union A but not of the members of union B. In my judgment, the members of union B would have a good claim in contract for breach of the implied obligation of good faith: see *Mihlenstedt's case* [1989] IRLR 522 at 525, 531–532 (paras 12, 64 and 70).

In my judgment, it is not necessary to found such a claim in contract alone. Construed against the background of the contract of employment, in my judgment the pension trust deed and rules themselves are to be taken as being impliedly subject to the limitation that the rights and powers of the company can only be exercised in accordance with the implied obligation of good faith.

13.71 Browne-Wilkinson V-C was dealing with an attempted merger of two pension schemes. The trustees and the company had been in the practice of granting pension increases by amending the Scheme under clause 36. This required an amendment by the trustees with the consent of the company.

13.72 Browne-Wilkinson V-C considered the nature of the power of the company as to whether or not to give its consent to such an amendment. He held that it was neither a fiduciary power nor was it subject to a limitation based on reasonableness.

Not a fiduciary power

13.73 Browne-Wilkinson V-C stated:[82]

> if this were a fiduciary power the company would have to decide whether or not to consent by reference only to the interests of the members, disregarding its own interest. This plainly was not the intention.

No implied limitation of reasonableness

13.74 Browne-Wilkinson V-C stated that there was no implied limitation of reasonableness, ie that the Company's consent was not to be unreasonably withheld. Browne-Wilkinson V-C stated:[83]

> I can see no necessity to engraft an implied limitation of reasonableness on to the Company's right to refuse consent under clause 36. On the contrary, there are many good reasons why

---

[82] [1991] 2 All ER 597 at 604j.
[83] [1991] 2 All ER 597 at 605b.

such limitation should not be implied. As Mr Mowbray for the Company, pointed out, in all Pension Schemes, including this one, the Company has a direct personal interest in how the scheme is to operate for the future. Any change in benefits may well be reflected in the Company having to make increased contributions. What is 'reasonable' from the point of view of the Company may be unreasonable view through the eyes of the pensioners. Which viewpoint would the Court have to adopt in testing reasonableness? Would the Court have to seek to balance the reasonableness of both viewpoints? In the context of a pension scheme, a test of unreasonable withholding of consent would be unworkable.

13.75 Browne-Wilkinson V-C went on to say that employers are subject to the implied duty of trust and confidence. He called this the 'implied obligation of good faith'. In my view that is a misleading shorthand and should not be used (see discussion below[84]).

Trust and confidence

13.76 Sir Nicolas Browne-Wilkinson V-C went on to say that it was appropriate in his judgment to hold[85] that:

> The pension trust deed and rules themselves are to be taken as being impliedly subject to the limitation of the rights and powers of the Company can only be exercised in accordance with the implied obligation of good faith.

13.77 In this he distinguished the comments made by Nourse LJ in the earlier decision of the Court of Appeal in *Mihlenstedt v Barclays Bank*.[86]

When will there be a breach?

13.78 Browne-Wilkinson V-C went on (at p 607) to attempt to give further guidance as to when an employer is in breach of the employment obligation of trust and confidence, stating that:

(a) it is not a matter of reasonableness;

(b) it is open to the employer to look after its own interests;

(c) the company should exercise its rights (a) with a view to the efficient running of the scheme established by the fund and (b) not for the collateral purpose of forcing the members to give up their accrued rights in the existing fund subject to this scheme;

(d) good faith requires the company to consider proposals each time they are made. A blanket refusal may be a breach of the duty; and

(e) it would be a breach of the duty of trust and confidence to (say) act capriciously to increase the benefits of one trade union but not the members of another trade union.[87]

13.79 In the 2012 *BBC case*[88] on pensions, Warren J commented that the relevant principles 'although easy to state' are 'sometimes very difficult to apply in practice to the facts of a particular case'; and:

> …although the Vice-Chancellor in *Imperial Tobacco* went on to give some practical guidance about how the principles would work out on the ground, I do not think I am alone in finding some of the examples he gave as hard to fit within the principles.

---

[84] Note the comments of Knox J in *Hillsdown Holdings plc v The Pensions Ombudsman* [1997] 1 All ER 862 at 898g.

[85] [1991] 2 All ER 597 at 606d (Browne-Wilkinson V-C).

[86] [1989] IRLR 522, CA.

[87] [1991] 2 All ER 597 at 606c (Browne-Wilkinson V-C).

[88] *Bradbury v British Broadcasting Corpn* [2012] EWHC 1369 (Ch) at [91] (Warren J).

Later cases

The implied term has been followed in many later pension cases. The Court of Appeal **13.80** approved it in *Stannard v Fisons Pension Trust*.[89] See also Knox J in *Hillsdown*[90] and the Privy Council in *Air Jamaica v Charlton*.[91] Similarly, the Court of Appeal of New Zealand in *UEB Industries v Brabant*[92] and *Cullen v Pension Holdings*.[93] In Canada, see *Lloyd v Imperial Oil*.[94] It has, of course, been approved (in an employment case) by the House of Lords in *Malik v BCCI*.[95]

Hoover *(2002)*

In *Hoover Ltd v Hetherington*,[96] Pumfrey J held that it was not a breach of the *Imperial* duty **13.81** for an employer to refuse to consent to a pension being drawn early. This was the case even though some of the booklets had not clarified the point clearly and even though any pension payable early would be reduced for early payment. However, the employer needed to consider each case on its merits.

Pumfrey J held: **13.82**

> 53. Finally, I must consider the object of the power to consent. Mr Ham contends that the power cannot be exercised, consistently with its ostensible purpose, to save the fund against any drain represented by early payments, since a reduction factor (the early retirement factor) is applied to the benefit, and so the damage to the fund caused by early payment has already been allowed for. This power is to be exercised consistently with the general Imperial Tobacco duty of good faith, and, provided that it is fair, the Company may also look to its own interests in reducing its potential exposure. However, the obligation of good faith requires consideration of each case on its merits.

Prudential *(2011)*

In *Prudential Staff Pensions Ltd v The Prudential Assurance Co Ltd*,[97] Newey J considered **13.83** whether the employer had exercised a discretion under the scheme lawfully.

The employer's decision to restrict pensions increases to 2.5 per cent, when they had previ- **13.84** ously been awarded in line with RPI, was held not to be a breach of the employer's implied obligation of good faith. All points were decided in favour of the employer.

In particular, Newey J held that there will not be a breach of the implied duty of good **13.85** faith to members unless the employer's conduct is irrational or perverse in a serious manner. Where the decision involves the exercise of a non-fiduciary power, as in this case, the circumstances in which it could be said to be irrational or perverse will be extremely limited.

---

[89] [1992] IRLR 27, [1991] PLR 225, CA.
[90] *Hillsdown Holdings v Pensions Ombudsman* [1997] 1 All ER 862 at 889 and 890 (Knox J).
[91] [1999] 1 WLR 1399 at 1411, PC.
[92] [1992] 1 NZLR 294, NZCA.
[93] (1993) 1 NZSC 40, 293, NZCA.
[94] 2008 ABQB 379 (Whittman ACJ).
[95] [1998] AC 20, HL.
[96] [2002] EWHC 1052 (Ch), [2002] OPLR 267 (Pumfrey J).
[97] [2011] EWHC 960 (Ch), [2011] PLR 239 (Newey J).

Facts

13.86 The Prudential Staff Pension Scheme was established in 1918. There had been variation in the way that pension increases had been awarded over this period of time, but from April 1997 the statutory indexation regime applied, with the power, pursuant to the rules of the Scheme, for the employer to request that the trustee provide for additional, non-statutory increases. Until 2005, increases for each year accorded exactly with the change in the retail price index (RPI) in the year to the preceding September.

13.87 In 2005, Prudential Assurance Company, the Scheme's principal employer, took the decision to change its policy in relation to discretionary pension increases, so that in the future, rather than granting full RPI increases, discretionary increases would be based on RPI capped at 2.5 per cent (the 2005 Decision). This policy would be approved annually, and increases could be suspended, or higher increases paid, subject to the Scheme's funding position. The trustee of the Scheme brought a claim, asking for clarification on the validity of the 2005 Decision.

The claim

13.88 The trustee asked the court to consider the following points:

(a) whether the sudden change in approach to the grant of increases under the 2005 Decision had been a breach of Prudential's implied duty of good faith;

(b) clarification as to whether Prudential was estopped from denying that members were entitled to receive increases, on the basis that it had adopted a policy of providing RPI increases in the past; and

(c) whether the trustee had failed in its fiduciary duty to ascertain the scope of its powers to award pension increases, or to properly identify the considerations relevant to the exercise of such powers, with the result that the trustee's decision in relation to the award of pensions was voidable, based on the decision in *Re Hastings Bass decd*,[98] as clarified in *Pitt v Holt*.[99]

Trust and confidence/good faith

13.89 Newey J considered the *Imperial Tobacco* judgment and concluded that the 2005 Decision did not breach the obligation of good faith. It was held that the correct test to apply when deciding if an employer had breached this obligation in the pensions context is:

(a) whether the employer had acted irrationally or perversely; and

(b) whether the irrational conduct was serious.

13.90 Newey J held that, although 'members' interests and expectations may be of relevance when considering whether an employer has acted irrationally or perversely', the employer was not exercising a fiduciary power, and was therefore entitled to have regard to his own interests when making decisions.[100]

13.91 Newey J held that this is a 'severe' test.[101] It limits the circumstances in which a decision could be said to be irrational or perverse. It was further emphasized that an irrational decision

---

[98] [1975] Ch 25, CA.
[99] [2011] EWCA Civ 197, CA.
[100] Citing Robert Walker J in *National Grid v Laws* [1997] PLR 157, [1997] OPLR 207.
[101] At [132], citing Hale LJ in *Gogay v Hertfordshire CC* [2000] IRLR 703, CA at [55]. Followed by Warren J in *IBM* [2012] EWHC 3540 (Ch) at [18].

by an employer in regard to a merely trivial matter '... might not be thought to be "such as to destroy or seriously damage" the relationship between employer and members and so might involve no breach of the obligation of good faith'. These comments indicate how high the hurdle is for members to prove that an employer has breached its duty of good faith.

13.92 This decision provides some comfort to employers looking to limit discretionary pension increases, as it confirms that an employer can take its own interests into account when exercising discretionary powers in awarding pension increases, and, as explained above, it demonstrates the high threshold required for members to prove that an employer has breached its duty of good faith.

13.93 It should, however, be noted that on the particular facts in this case both the trustee and employer emphasized throughout that the RPI increases were discretionary; the Scheme rules gave Prudential discretionary rights with no explicit restrictions with regards to increases; and pensions were never increased without specific decisions to that effect being made by Prudential. It is questionable whether the same result would be reached on less clear facts.

General Guidance

13.94 It is, however, quite difficult to gain any general guidance from the cases on the circumstances when the term will be broken.

13.95 Browne-Wilkinson V-C indicated[102] in *Imperial Tobacco* his reluctance to give an indication of the effect of the obligation of good faith on 'hypothetical and unproved facts'. A similar reluctance to comment on hypothetical future cases was stated by Knox J in *Hillsdown Holdings v The Pensions Ombudsman*.[103]

13.96 Robert Walker J in *National Grid v Mayes*[104] referred to the *Imperial Tobacco* case and then went on to list some examples that had been given by Robert Ham QC (one of the counsel involved). He had suggested, by decided cases, some examples of breach of the duty of good faith:

(a) withholding consent to increased benefits for members of one trade union while granting it for members of another (see the *Imperial Tobacco case* at p597);
(b) withholding consent to an amendment increasing benefits for the collateral purpose of putting pressure on members to abandon some of their existing rights (see *Imperial Tobacco* at p599);
(c) introducing new participating employers, and so introducing large numbers of new members of a scheme, while the principal employer itself takes a contribution holiday (see *Hillsdown*[105]); and
(d) threatening to use a power to suspend contributions in order to put pressure on trustees to surrender existing powers (see the determination of the Ombudsman in the *National Bus Company* case[106]).

---

[102] See [1991] 2 All ER 597 at 607b.
[103] [1997] 1 All ER 862, [1996] PLR 427 at 466.
[104] [1997] OPLR 207 (Robert Walker J).
[105] [1997] 1 All ER 862 at 890.
[106] [1997] PLR 1, 18 at [78]–[80].

13.97 Robert Walker J went on to comment that the scope of the Imperial Tobacco duty of trust and confidence will need to be worked out in cases over the years.

13.98 He stated:

> The scope and limits of the *Imperial Tobacco* duty will no doubt be worked out, on a case by case basis, in coming years. It will probably be found to have more than one attribute in common with fiduciary duties. But it will not, I think, assist the development of the law to try to blend the two together, or to dilute the Vice-Chancellor's clear statement, in the passage already cited from *Imperial Tobacco*, that an employer can consistently with its duty of good faith have regard to its own financial interests.
>
> Once the duty is properly understood it is apparent, in my judgment, that there was no evidence before the Ombudsman to justify a conclusion that National Grid was in breach of its duty of good faith, or that the trustees of the National Grid group connived at any misuse of surplus. The trustees did indeed recommend to National Grid that the surplus should be applied on the basis of a 50:50 split rather than a 70:30 split. But National Grid decided to proceed on the 70:30 basis, and there is no ground that I can perceive for saying that in doing so National Grid was acting arbitrarily, or improperly, or otherwise in breach of good faith.

Good Faith

13.99 Although Browne-Wilkinson V-C called the implied duty of trust and confidence a 'duty of good faith', this seems not to be saying that the test is the same as 'good faith'. The Vice-Chancellor seems merely to have been using this as a shorthand.

13.100 Knox J in *Hillsdown Holdings v The Pensions Ombudsman*[107] commented:

> This implication was made by Sir Nicolas Browne-Wilkinson V-C in *Imperial Group Pension Trust Ltd v Imperial Tobacco Ltd* [1991] 2 All ER 597, the year after he decided the Vauxhall case, supra, in relation to a power to give or withhold consent to an increase in pension benefits. Sir Nicolas Browne-Wilkinson V-C used the expression:
>
>> the obligation of good faith
>
> as a form of shorthand for the implication set out above and in adopting it I should like to emphasise that it is a convenient shorthand only and in particular does not carry the implication that a failure to observe the implied obligation involved would amount to bad faith in the prejorative sense in which that expression is often used.

13.101 Accordingly, it would be better for all of us if, in future, judges and commentators did not use the 'good faith' shorthand. As we have seen above, the House of Lords has held that an intention to injure is not a necessary part of showing that there has been a breach of the implied term. Conversely, the term 'good faith' implies such a subjective test.

13.102 What does 'good faith' mean? It sounds like a subjective test—is the person acting honestly,[108] not realizing that he is mistaken? But in many civil law areas it has been taken to have a wider, more objective meaning. For example, is a person acting in good faith if he or she fails to carry out proper enquiries?

---

[107] [1997] 1 All ER 862. At p 448 in the PLR report. Note the comments of Warren J in *IBM* [2012] EWHC 3540 (Ch) at [17] that *Hillsdown* also involved a breach of trust by the scheme trustees.

[108] Even the term 'honesty' seems to have two meanings: see *Royal Brunei v Tan* [1995] 2 AC 378, PC.

In *Medirest*,[109] the Court of Appeal held that an express good faith duty was not a general **13.103** one that qualified or reinforced all of the allegations of the parties in all situations where they interact, but only applied for specified purposes. Recently, Akenhead J in the Technology & Contruction Court also took a narrow view of an express good faith clause, holding that it did not extend to acting reasonably when terminating a contract—*TSG Building Services plc v South Anglia Housing*.[110]

Who Owes the *Imperial* Duty?

There are still aspects of the implied duty of trust and confidence that remain to be worked out. **13.104**

Duty owed to former employees

It seems clear that the implied duty is owed by the employer in favour of not only its current **13.105** employees, but also its former employees. Although this can be seen as an extension of the use of implied terms, it is in line with cases such as *Spring* which confirmed that there is a duty to take care in relation to a reference for a former employee.

Duty enforceable by trustees

The implied duty is enforceable by the trustees of a pensions scheme. There is no need for **13.106** the employees to enforce it through a contract action. Arguably this follows from *Imperial Tobacco* (see above), although that case was concerned with the question of whether or not the trustees should carry out transfer requests on the basis of a consent from the members concerned. If there was a breach of the Imperial duty, arguably that invalidated the consent and so the trustees should not have carried them out. This would be different from a direct enforcement by the trustees against the employer.

Duty owed to trustees

In the *National Bus*[111] determination, the Pensions Ombudsman stated that the implied **13.107** duty is owed to the trustees as well as to the employees (and is enforceable by the trustees).

This also seems implicit in the judgments of Knox J in *Hillsdown Holdings* and of Robert **13.108** Walker J in *National Grid*.

Duty owed to non-members

It seems likely that the courts would hold that the implied duty is also owed after a member's **13.109** death to those who take benefits in respect of the member (eg spouse and dependants).

No duty owed to creditors of the employer

In *Independent Pension Trustee v LAW Construction Co Ltd*,[112] there was a conflict over who **13.110** had been appointed as a trustee. Lord Hamilton in the Court of Session held that the power to appoint and remove trustees passed to the company's receiver so the purported appointment by the directors was invalid.

---

[109] *Compass Group UK and Ireland Ltd (t/a Medirest) v Mid Essex Hospital Services NHS Trust* [2013] EWCA Civ 200, CA.
[110] [2013] EWHC 1151 (TCC) (Akenhead J).
[111] [1997] PLR 1.
[112] [1996] OPLR 259, CSOH.

13.111　Lord Hamilton went on to say[113] that he would not have held that the company owed any duty to its creditors (or the receiver) under the implied duty of trust and confidence.

Principal Employer

13.112　Does the principal employer in a group scheme owe the implied duty of trust and confidence in relation to the employees of other participating employers?

13.113　The point has not yet arisen in the cases, but it seems inconceivable that the duty would not be held to extend to other employees. Any problem is neatly avoided if it is correct that the duty is owed to the trustees as well. This would seem to cover the extreme situations where:

(a) the principal employer has no current (or even former) employees in the scheme (eg it has always been a pure holding company); or

(b) one or more of the participating companies is not connected with the principal employer (eg following a sale, during an interim period of participation in the vendor's scheme).

Liability of directors of corporate employer

13.114　If the employer breaches its implied duty of trust and confidence, it will be liable for the breach (eg in damages). Can the directors of the employer (particularly those actively involved in the breach) also be personally liable? This will obviously be of importance if the employer has become insolvent.

13.115　In practice the point does not seem to have been addressed so far. This may be because in the main the cases have involved solvent schemes and employers and the issues have usually been resolved by reversal (or prohibition) of the relevant actions (eg *Imperial Tobacco*) or a money claim on the employer (eg *Hillsdown Holdings*).

13.116　In practice given the contractual nature of the duty, it may be that the usual contractual tests for liability of an accessory will apply. But in general directors acting honestly are not liable for breaches of contract committed by the company[114] and indirect liability as an accessory is limited to direct torts—eg in practice the director should not be liable for the tort of inducing breach of contract.[115] Conversely the test based on dishonest participation in a breach of trust (see eg *HR v JAPT*[116] and *Royal Brunei v Tan*[117]) should not be applicable.

Exclusion by Contract or by the Trust Deed

13.117　Some trust deeds now include an express provision excluding the implied duty of trust and confidence.

13.118　There seems no reason why this should not be effective as against the trustees, assuming it has been validly incorporated (if it was included as an amendment, was it validly included?).

---

[113] At p 268E.

[114] *OBG Ltd v Allan* [2007] UKHL 21, [2008] 1 AC 1, HL: Lord Nicholls at [218] referring to receivers, but directors should be in the same position. See D Pollard, *Corporate Insolvency: Employment and Pension Rights* 5th edn (Bloomsbury Professional, 2013) Ch 14.

[115] But see the talk by Philip Bennett 'Trustees' Indemnities, Insurance and Exoneration Clauses' (1996) APL Conference.

[116] [1997] OPLR 123, [1997] PLR 99 (Lindsay J).

[117] [1995] 2 AC 378, PC.

The implied duty does not seem to be a core obligation that must be included in a pension trust—see generally Chapter 14 ('Trustee indemnities and exonerations') on this. The Court of Appeal in *Armitage v Nurse*[118] confirmed that exclusion clauses can be given a wide effect, provided they do not cover actual fraud or dishonesty. Generally a party cannot exclude liability for its own fraud.[119]

So any contractual exclusion could only cover the gap between 'good faith', 'capriciousness', or 'arbitrariness' and 'dishonesty' or 'fraud'. **13.119**

However, it may be more difficult to contract out of the implied duty as against the individual members. But in practice members take their benefits under a pension scheme on and subject to the terms of the pension scheme. So a provision of the scheme in effect binds the members (they cannot take the benefit of the scheme save on its terms—they cannot pick and choose or cherry-pick). **13.120**

Douglas Brodie argued in his book, *The Employment Contract*,[120] that on public policy grounds certain implied terms in law should be immune from contracting-out, arguing that there is usually an imbalance in bargaining power[121] and that the mutual duty term should be seen in the same category as the implied (statutory) obligation to take care of an employee's safety. Brodie acknowledged that to date the courts had not been prepared to go that far (citing Lord Millett in *Johnson v Unisys*[122]). **13.121**

It is likely to be a big step for the courts to hold (absent statute) that what is essentially an implied term cannot be excluded by an express term, albeit that clear wording may be needed. Holding that employers owe duties to look after the financial well-being of their employees seems likely to be fraught with danger.[123] **13.122**

In *Fish v Dresdner Kleinwort Ltd*,[124] Jack J referred to comments by Lord Steyn in *Johnson v Unisys Ltd*[125] and held: **13.123**

> Mr Goulding submitted that this showed that the obligation of trust and confidence should prevail over the express terms of the contract. I do not think so. As Lord Steyn said at the end of the paragraph, 'There is no conflict between the express and implied terms'.

The issue arose in a 1997 Ombudsman determination. In *Poole v Trustees of the Cytec Industries (UK) Ltd Pension Scheme*,[126] the Pensions Ombudsman held that the employer was not entitled to rely on the provision in the trust deed excluding any implied term or condition of mutual trust and confidence or of good faith. **13.124**

The reasoning given is typically sparse, but the Ombudsman mentioned that such a term is unusual and oppressive. He also considered that the implied duty cannot be excluded **13.125**

---

[118] [1997] 2 All ER 705, CA.
[119] *S Pearson & Son Ltd v Dublin Corpn* [1907] AC 351, HL and *HIH Casualty and General Insurance Ltd v Chase Manhattan Bank* [2003] UKHL 6, [2003] 2 Lloyd's Rep 61 at para [16], HL (Lord Bingham).
[120] (Oxford University Press, 2005).
[121] See now comments in *Autoclenz Ltd v Belcher* [2011] UKSC 41, [2011] 4 All ER 745, SC.
[122] [2003] 1 AC 518 at 549, HL.
[123] See *Reid v Rush & Tompkins Group plc* [1989] 3 All ER 228, [1990] 1 WLR, CA but note the criticism by Aline van Bever in 'An Employer's Duty to Provide Information and Advice on Economic Risks?' (2013) 42 ILJ 1.
[124] [2009] EWHC 2246 (QB), [2009] IRLR 1035 at para [35] (Jack J).
[125] [2001] IRLR 279 at para [24], HL.
[126] F00088 (1997) 16 May (Farrand PO).

by an agreement to which the member was not a party. In addition, it cannot be used to contract out of the Ombudsman's statutory jurisdiction in respect of injustice caused by maladministration.

What Does the Implied Term Mean in Practice?

13.126 As mentioned above, it is very difficult to be able to predict how an individual judge will react in any particular set of circumstances. The facts of each case must be kept in mind at all times. What seems like a wide statement applicable in many other cases may well, on reflection, turn out to be limited by the circumstances of the particular case.

13.127 There are still relatively few decided cases which refer to the implied duty of trust and confidence in a pensions setting. Even fewer of the cases have actually held that there was a breach of the implied term.

13.128 Some examples of common situations and whether the implied duty applies are given below.

Withholding consent to benefits for members of one trade union while granting it for members of another

13.129 This is the example given in *Imperial Tobacco*.[127] It is rather difficult to see this ever arising in practice. Although this example is also cited by Robert Walker J in *National Grid*, it should be noted that when the example was actually given by Browne-Wilkinson V-C in *Imperial Tobacco*, it was only in relation to a 'capricious' withholding of consent.

13.130 In practice the granting of benefits to (say) non-trade union members instead of to trade union members may well not be a breach of contract. For example in the case of *Associated Newspapers Ltd v Wilson*,[128] the House of Lords (including Lord Browne-Wilkinson) held that it was permissible for employers to offer pay rises to journalists who signed new contracts of employment (replacing collective bargaining agreements). The trust and confidence term does not seem to have been raised or indeed considered, the argument depending mainly on construction of the relevant statutory provisions.

Taking a contribution holiday

13.131 Staughton LJ in *Stannard v Fisons Pension Trust*[129] commented that a surplus might also disappear if the employer (Fisons) decreased its rate of contribution as it was free to do. However, he went on to say that 'it may even be that for Fisons to make a reduction would in some circumstances be a breach of contract with its employees', going on to refer to *Imperial Tobacco*.

13.132 With respect, on its own this is completely misguided. Parliament has, of course, legislated in the Pensions Act 1995 to lay down a minimum funding requirement. In doing this it has tried to strike a balance between security for the members and the financial position of employers. Should the Courts really be seeking now to interfere with that balance?

13.133 In practice, of course, refusing to allow employers to take contribution reductions or holidays will ultimately result in reduced funding levels as employers decide that it is not worth

---

[127] [1991] 1 WLR 589 at 597.
[128] [1995] ICR 406, HL.
[129] [1992] IRLR 27 at 32.

funding at more conservative levels if they will be unable to take advantage of any overfunding that results.

Other judges seem to have given more consideration to the issue and decided that contribution **13.134** holidays are allowed.

Knox J in *LRT v Hatt*[130] cited with approval a passage from the PLRC report of September **13.135** 1992 (the Goode Committee) about contribution reductions. In particular, Knox J considered that paragraphs 9.52–9.10 of their report contained a 'succinct and, in my view, fairly balanced, general analysis of the nature of a surplus in a pension fund'.

Knox J went on later in *Hillsdown Holdings v The Pensions Ombudsman*[131] to hold that a **13.136** rule giving power to the employer to reduce or suspend contributions operated so as to confer:

> a unilateral right on the Employers or any of them to reduce suspend or terminate their liability. No question arises of a right in the Trustees, Members or pensioners to be consulted about, let alone consent to, any exercise of that power.

Similarly, Robert Walker J in *National Grid v Laws*[132] stated, at the end of his judgment: **13.137**

> But any general exclusion of employers from surplus would tend to make employers very reluctant to contribute to their pension schemes more than the bare minimum that they could get away with. That would be unfortunate, and it would be even more unfortunate if employers were driven to abandon final salary, balance of cost schemes and were instead to turn to money-purchase schemes which may in the long term prove less advantageous to the beneficiaries.

Introducing new participating employers and so introducing large numbers of new members of a scheme, while the principal employer itself takes a contribution holiday

This derives from the comments of Knox J in *Hillsdown Holdings v The Pensions Ombuds-* **13.138** *man*.[133] It is also cited by Robert Walker J in the *National Grid* case.

This is more limited than a prohibition on all contribution reductions. However, the decision **13.139** of Knox J must be viewed in light of the particular pension trust concerned. In that case the trustees had the power unilaterally to increase benefits if there was a surplus in the scheme. In context it is difficult to see why the introduction of new employers must necessarily be considered to be a breach of the duty of trust and confidence.

To hold otherwise would mean that in many cases a merger of pension schemes will become **13.140** practically impossible—the merged scheme is almost always[134] bound to have an actuarial funding basis which is the average of the two schemes concerned and so better funded for one (and worse for the other). To say that the employer must not take advantage of this to fix a contribution rate in the merged scheme which is less than the previous contribution rate for the worse funded scheme is bizarre to say the least.

---

[130] [1993] OPLR 225 at 266 (Knox J).
[131] [1997] 1 All ER 862, [1996] PLR 427 at 434.
[132] [1997] OPLR 207 (Robert Walker J).
[133] [1997] 1 All ER 862 at 890 (Knox J).
[134] Unless the two schemes happen, coincidentally, to have identical funding positions.

Withholding consent to an amendment increasing benefits for the collateral purpose of putting pressure on members to abandon some of their existing rights

13.141 This seems to have been what Browne-Wilkinson V-C held in *Imperial Tobacco* as limb (b) of his analysis of the obligation under the implied duty of trust and confidence (and again it is cited by Robert Walker J in *National Grid*).

13.142 In relation to this limb it is rather difficult to see what the Vice-Chancellor was really saying. The judgment is full of references to the employees being asked to give up 'rights' in the existing scheme. By this it appears to be meant that the employees currently have the right to the surplus on a winding up of the existing scheme (not that this appears to be currently envisaged). This right would not apply in the new scheme. This is the 'right' that the employees are being asked to give up, albeit in exchange for some benefit improvements. Apparently this amounts to 'coercion'. It also amounts to a collateral purpose in that the company is attempting to access the relevant surplus.

13.143 This is rather difficult. Where does it differ from the situation of (say) an employer seeking to obtain agreement of the trustees to benefit improvements in exchange for a refund of surplus being made to the employer? Such a bargain would seem to be acceptable according to the decision of Millett J in *Courage*[135] and the Australian decision of Waddell CJ in *Westpac*.[136]

13.144 Indeed, in *Imperial Tobacco* the position of the employees is somewhat stronger. Their individual consent is being sought. Is it really wrong for an employer to have reached a bargain with its employee that (say) a car would be given up in exchange for other rights?[137]

13.145 Indeed, it is difficult to see why offering employees different benefits if they agree to an exchange can be said to be 'forcing them' to transfer.

13.146 With respect, it is very difficult to apply the particular circumstances outlined by the Vice-Chancellor as being a breach of the implied terms. However, in *Hillsdown Holdings* Knox J had no difficulty following *Imperial Tobacco* and distinguishing *Courage* (see para 13.160 below).

13.147 There is also the difficulty (as reflected in the final comments on p 608 of the Vice-Chancellor's judgment) that the whole question of whether or not the proposed transfers would be valid depends on the company's purpose in performing them. If it has a collateral purpose then the transfers are invalid if it does not then they are valid. It appears to be a subjective test for the company. How are the trustees to know at any one time what the purpose of the company properly is?

Refusing to consider the exercise of a power

13.148 This seems to have been what Browne-Wilkinson V-C held in *Imperial Tobacco*.

13.149 Again this seems rather odd. In the context of *Imperial Tobacco*, in effect the wrongful act by the employer was (allegedly) to state that it would never agree to future benefit improvements. This was contrary to the employer's duty to consider requests from time to time.

---

[135] [1987] 1 All ER 528 at 545 (Millett J).
[136] *Lock v Westpac Banking Corpn* (1991) 25 NSWLR 593, [1991] PLR 167 (Waddell CJ in Eq).
[137] See the example used by the Vice-Chancellor at p 608b of the All ER report.

In practice would it really make any difference to the employees if the employer said that **13.150** 'while we will of course consider matters from time to time, it is not our present intention to give benefit improvements'?

Conversely, a legitimate refusal by an employer to increase benefits, having given due **13.151** consideration to the employee's position, was upheld in New Zealand by Colgan J in *Bates v BP Oil New Zealand Ltd.*[138] This was not a breach of the implied term.

In *Walker v Sun Chemical*,[139] employees agreed to a pay cut, but later claimed that the trustee **13.152** (and employer) should have agreed to changes to the pension scheme to mitigate the pensions effect of the pay cut. The Pensions Ombudsman held that the employer had given due and proper consideration to the proposals and, after taking advice, had decided that the changes suggested would have a detrimental effect on the fund. There was no duty on the employer to make changes to the scheme to accommodate a group of members who were affected by a fall in pensionable earnings. There was no maladministration by the employer or breach of law.

Later cases make it clear that an employer must give a 'genuine and rational as opposed to an **13.153** empty or irrational exercise of the discretion'.[140]

Exercising powers after a Tupe transfer

To the extent that powers or liabilities in relation to an occupational pension scheme pass to **13.154** a transferee (purchaser) following a transfer of business (and employment) under the Tupe regulations,[141] the new employer will usually be under the same implied duties as the former employer, including the *Imperial* duty.[142]

Threatening use of power to suspend contributions in order to put pressure on trustees to surrender existing powers

As mentioned above, taking a simple contribution reduction or holiday seems to be acceptable. **13.155**

The difficulty here is the use of emotive words such as 'threat'. The determination of the **13.156** Pensions Ombudsman in the *National Bus Co*[143] case and of the decision of Knox J in *Hillsdown*[144] both indicate that an employer may be acting wrongfully if it 'makes threats' to trustees.

Quite what the distinction is between a 'threat' and an attempt to bargain or to ask trustees to **13.157** do something is unclear. It seems almost to be saying that employers should not ask trustees to do something if they realize that the trustees have powers to do something else.

In *Hillsdown*, the 'threat' seems to have been made in the context of the employer not realizing **13.158** that the trustees had the power to use the surplus shown on an actuarial valuation.

---

[138] [1996] 1 ERNZ 657, (1995) 29 September (Colgan J).
[139] M00318 (2004) 1 September (Farrand PO).
[140] *Clark v Nomura International* [2000] IRLR 766 (Burton J), an employment case, followed by Newey J in *Prudential* at [135] and Warren J in *IBM* at [18].
[141] The Transfer of Undertakings (Protection of Employment) Regulations 2006 (SI 2006/246). The liabilities that transfer are limited—see reg 10 and D Pollard, 'Pensions and Tupe' (2005) 24 ILJ 127.
[142] See comments in *The Procter & Gamble Co v Svenska Cellulosa Aktiebolaget SCA* [2012] EWHC 1257 (Ch), [2012] IRLR 733 (Hildyard J). An appeal to the Court of Appeal is pending at the time of writing.
[143] [1997] PLR 1 at 18 [78]–[80]).
[144] *Hillsdown Holdings plc v Pensions Ombudsman* [1997] 1 All ER 862 (Knox J).

13.159 In both *Hillsdown* and *National Bus*, the trustees seem to have had independent legal advice.

13.160 Knox J distinguished the decision of Millett J in *Courage*[145] to the effect that it would be acceptable for trustees to negotiate benefit improvements with the employer. But was the negotiation in *Courage* 'proper' because the surplus was in baulk (and required the agreement of both the trustee and the company to use it). In *Hillsdown*, the trustees had a unilateral power over surplus and the amendment power prohibited refunds. This seems to mean that the employer is not acting in good faith and so the exercise of the powers is 'improper'. This is the case even though the employer neither realized this nor appreciated that the trustees would be acting in breach of trust.[146]

13.161 Is this tantamount to an obligation on employers to ensure not only that the trustees are receiving legal advice (as here), but also that no mistake as to their powers is made?

13.162 The use of the term 'threat' to mean that there is a breach of the implied term seems to go much too far. What is a 'threat' and what is merely a legitimate attempt to bargain seems to be in the eye of the beholder.

Agreeing to benefit improvements for employees who have been made redundant but not for those who have resigned voluntarily

13.163 This seems eminently reasonable and it must be doubted whether anyone ever thinks to the contrary.

13.164 This view is helpfully supported by the decision of Fedak J in the Canadian case of *Mair v Stelco Inc*.[147] He considered that it was fair and reasonable for Stelco only to exercise its discretion in favour of employees who were forced by Stelco itself to retire early without the choice of refusal. There was good reason for Stelco to differentiate.

13.165 Stelco had also acted fairly and reasonably in that it had informed Mr Mair before he retired that he would not receive an enhanced pension.

Using surplus to enhance benefits and reduce redundancy costs

13.166 This should be acceptable as well. Robert Walker J in *National Grid* held that there was no breach of the implied duty where the employer had power to make such arrangements (although there is no mention in the case of the redundancy enhancements saving money for the employer).[148]

13.167 It has been argued[149] that the issue depends on whether the employer is proposing the benefit improvement in order to provide the employee with suitable retirement benefits or whether its only purpose is to save on a compensation package.

13.168 This seems to be too cautious an approach. In effect, it follows the comments made in *Hillsdown*. As mentioned above, this approach will not be followed at least in the majority of balance of cost schemes. If the trustees are prepared to agree to the augmentation (and have

---

[145] *Re Courage Group's Pension Schemes* [1987] 1 All ER 528 (Millett J).
[146] Paragraph 102 of the PLR report.
[147] [1995] 9 CCPB 140 (Fedak J).
[148] See also the comments of the Pensions Ombudsman to the same effect at [24] of his determination in *Clark v NFC plc* (8 October 1997).
[149] See the article by Monica Ma in the October 1997 issue of Pensions World.

presumably satisfied themselves about the funding position) why should such an augmentation not be made even if the employer's only reason for suggesting it is to save money? At the end of the day the purpose of the pension scheme is to provide benefits (and hence to meet obligations that the employer would otherwise have to meet out of its own funds).

Surplus refunds

It is clear that a proper negotiation between trustees and the employer about a refund of surplus with benefit improvements in exchange will not be a breach of the implied term. **13.169**

This clearly follows from the comments of Millett J in *Courage* and was allowed in Australia by Waddell CJ in *Lock v Westpac Banking Corpn*.[150] **13.170**

Refusal of pension increases

Again in principle, an employer is free to consider his own situation and refuse to consent to increases to pensions in payment.[151] **13.171**

The employer must probably give proper consideration to the circumstances on each occasion—see *Imperial Tobacco* itself and the determination of the Pensions Ombudsman in *British Airways*.[152] **13.172**

The ability of the employer to refuse to agree to pension increases because of the cost implications is supported also by some Ombudsman determinations—*Nolan v Scottish Amicable*[153] and *Parsons v Warner-Lambert (UK) Ltd*.[154] **13.173**

But care may be needed here. In *Clark v BET*[155] Timothy Walker J had to consider the amount of damages available to Mr Clark when his contract of employment was wrongfully terminated. The contract provided that: **13.174**

> The executive's salary shall be reviewed annually and increased by such amount if any as the board in its absolute discretion decide.

Timothy Walker J held that the board could not act 'capriciously or in bad faith so as to determine the increase at nil and therefore to pay Mr Clark no increase at all'. He found that other executives had in fact received increases and assessed damages on the basis that Mr Clark would have received increases of 10 per cent per annum. **13.175**

Conceivably the same ruling could be made in relation to a refusal by an employer to agree to pension increases for all or some of the members of a pension scheme when giving it to others (pension increase clauses often contain similar wording to that considered in *Clark*). **13.176**

Change of trustees

Chapter 12 deals with the power of employers to appoint and remove trustees as not being fiduciary. This power is commonly reserved to an employer (now subject to the provisions relating to member-nominated trustees in the pensions legislation). **13.177**

---

[150] (1991) 25 NSWLR 593, [1991] PLR 167 (Waddell CJ).
[151] See Newey J in *Prudential*.
[152] [1995] OPLR 369, [1995] PLR 189 (Farrand PO).
[153] D11554 (1997) 28 February (Farrand PO).
[154] F00281 (1997) 19 June (Farrand PO).
[155] [1997] IRLR 348 (Timothy Walker J).

13.178 In *Simpson Curtis Pension Trustees Ltd v Readson Ltd*[156] Judge O'Donoghue held that receivers appointed over an employer could exercise the employer's power of appointment of trustees. He considered[157] that the power would:

> seem to form more readily within the category posed by Mr David Pollard as a 'power subject to constraints'.

13.179 This is a reference to the argument that the power of appointment or removal of trustees is not fiduciary but instead is subject to some constraints, such as the implied duty of trust and confidence.[158]

Steps for employers to take to reduce the risk of a breach

13.180 Employers can take various steps to reduce the prospect of a breach:

(a) Be open with the trustees. It is helpful if there is no concealment of what is happening or why the employer is doing it.

(b) Consultation with the trustees was assumed in *National Grid v Mayes* to be helpful, even though the express terms of the power given to the employer did not require this.

(c) Negotiate with any relevant trade unions. This seems to have helped in both *LRT v Hatt* and *Lock v Westpac Banking Corpn*.

(d) Consider carefully whether or not to exercise a discretion at the appropriate time. Do not dismiss a request out of hand. This follows from *Imperial Tobacco*.

(e) Consider if costings are needed in relation to the exercise of any discretion under consideration. This helped the company in defeating a claim made before the Pensions Ombudsman in *British Airways*.

(f) Explain the reasons to those affected.[159]

(g) If asking members for consent to a change, be clear about the effect.[160]

An overall view

13.181 It may be considered that all the cases simply turn on due consideration being given by the employer towards the rights and responsibilities it owes to employees when exercising powers.

13.182 This analysis would draw a distinction between 'substantive obligations' and 'procedural rights'.

13.183 An example of this is the decision of Colgan J in the High Court in New Zealand in *Bates v BP Oil New Zealand Ltd*.[161] He referred to the implied duties of trust and confidence and good faith following *Imperial Tobacco* and the New Zealand case of *UEB Industries*.[162]

13.184 Professor Mark Freedland in his talk, 'Implied Terms and Labour Standards', given at the Industrial Law Society Conference in September 1996 also drew a distinction between

---

[156] [1994] OPLR 231, [1994] PLR 289 (Judge O'Donoghue).

[157] See p 239f of the OPLR report.

[158] See Ch 12 (Employer's power to appoint and remove trustees).

[159] In *Keen v Commerzbank AG* [2006] EWCA Civ 1536, [2007] ICR 623, CA, an employment case, Moses LJ commented that an employer will generally be required to give reasons for the exercise of a discretion otherwise 'exploitation would be all too easy'. A different approach may apply in collective situations.

[160] *Cantor Fitzgerald International v Bird* [2002] IRLR 867 (McCombe J), an employment case.

[161] [1996] 1 ERNZ 657, (1995) 29 September (Colgan J).

[162] [1992] NZLR 294, [1991] PLR 109.

substantive standards and procedural standards. He thought that the implied duty of mutual trust and confidence perhaps fell within a third category of 'general standards of behaviour or qualitative terms'. In effect, the Courts were moving down the road towards the general obligation of reasonableness, but he thought it would not go that far.

However the objective test outlined in *Malik*, combined with the finding against the employer in *Hillsdown Holdings* (even though it was not aware of any breach of trust or duty) point more towards a test which is not merely procedural, but has objective standards too. **13.185**

In practice the categorization of the test as 'severe'[163] means that it may have great similarities with the *Wednesbury* reasonableness test used in public law. Has the employer acted in a way that no reasonable employer would act (or arbitrarily or capriciously)? **13.186**

Conclusion

The implied duty of trust and confidence is perhaps the most important legal issue facing employers in relation to pension schemes. We stand at the start of the process of development by the courts of the precise meaning and extent of the duty. **13.187**

It is clear that the duty will not go away. The courts see it as a useful tool for being able to do justice. **13.188**

For practitioners, however, this means that there is currently much uncertainty. It will take many more cases before we become really comfortable with the implied duty and are able to advise confidently what it requires in any given situation. **13.189**

The old battle in the Courts between a desire to do justice and the need for certainty goes through periodic shifts. We are clearly at the stage of a major shift in favour of a court discretion. **13.190**

---

[163] Eg in a pensions context, Newey J in *Prudential*.

14

TRUSTEE INDEMNITIES
AND EXONERATIONS

Introduction

14.1 This chapter looks at the practical issues in relation to indemnities and exonerations given to trustees of pension schemes,[1] in particular looking at:

(a) the underlying legal principles and constraints; and
(b) the impact on relevant drafting.

---

[1] See Clifton Prophet, 'Protecting Pension Trustees and Fiduciaries—Exoneration and Indemnity' (2001) 15 TLI 194; Ian Greenstreet, 'Trustees Exoneration Clauses and Dishonesty in Occupational Pension Schemes' (2004) 18 TLI 132; Mark Howard, 'Pension Trustee Liability Insurance' (2011) 25 TLI 99; and Philip Bennett, 'Trustees' Indemnities, Insurance and Exoneration Clauses' (1996) APL Conference. On trustee liability generally (not just pension schemes) see David Halpern QC, 'Exoneration Clauses for Trustees and Directors and Statutory Relief from Liability' (2012) 26 TLI 32; Paul Matthews, 'The Efficacy of Trustee Exemption Clauses in English Law' (1989) 42 Conv 44; Robert Ham QC, 'Trustees' Liability' (1995) 9 TLI 21; and James Penner's chapter 'Exemptions' in P Birks and A Pretto (eds), *Breach of Trust* (Hart Publishing, 2002). See also the Law Commission report 'Trustee Exemption Clauses' (LC301, Cm6874, July 2006). For an Australian perspective, see Kevin Lingren, 'A Superannuation Fund Trustee's Right of Indemnity' (2010) 4 J Eq 85.

In the absence of a contrary provision, trustees of course can incur personal liability: **14.2**

(a) to beneficiaries, for breach of duty or breach of trust; and
(b) to third parties, under normal principles—eg for breach of contract or tort.

There are four main protections available for trustees: **14.3**

(a) an exoneration provision/indemnity out of the fund;
(b) an indemnity from the sponsoring employer;
(c) trustee insurance; and
(d) having a limited liability company act as trustee.

Exoneration and Indemnity Clauses

Exoneration clauses operate to exclude the trustee from the relevant liability. As such they **14.4**
will only apply to claims made by a beneficiary (and not claims made by a third party). They
limit potential claims by beneficiaries (eg because the wrong person is paid a benefit).

The need for an indemnity from the assets of the scheme is obvious. Where a trustee incurs a **14.5**
liability (eg to a third party, such as HMRC) the trustee is generally personally liable. A trustee
will then look to be reimbursed from the trust assets for any relevant liability.

Such an indemnity is, of course, implied in law. This is codified for trusts generally to an **14.6**
extent by s 31 of the Trustee Act 2000,[2] replacing (from 1 February 2001) s 30(2) of the
Trustee Act 1925.

Section 31 states: **14.7**

'A trustee—

(a) is entitled to be reimbursed from the trust funds, or
(b) may pay out of the trust funds,

expenses properly incurred by him when acting on behalf of the trust.

Section 30(2) of the 1925 Act stated: **14.8**

A trustee may reimburse himself or pay or discharge out of the trust premises all expenses
incurred in or about the execution of the trusts or powers.

The implied indemnity under s 30 of the 1925 Act could be excluded or modified by the **14.9**
terms of the trust—s 69(2). It is likely that the same applies to the implied indemnity under
s 31 of the 2000 Act.[3]

In a pensions case in 1998, *Polly Peck International plc (in administration) v Henry*,[4] Buckley **14.10**
J dealt with a money purchase pension scheme where the company was the trustee. The trust
provided for insurance company management charges to be paid out of the fund, but otherwise
had no express indemnity. Buckley J held that this represented a contrary intention under

---

[2] Much of the Trustee Act 2000 does not apply to occupational pension schemes—see s 36. But Pt 5 (which
includes s 31) does.
[3] On the debate in Australia about whether the implied indemnity can be excluded (which is mainly an issue
in relation to trading trusts), see Peter Edmundson, 'Express Limitation of a Trustee's Rights of Indemnity'
(2011) 5 J Eq 77.
[4] [1999] 1 BCLC 407 (Buckley J).

s 69 Trustee Act 1925, so that the implied indemnity under s 30 did not apply. In effect, the expenses of running the scheme were to be paid by the employer company.[5]

14.11 Notwithstanding the implied indemnity, it is common to include an express indemnity for trustees out of the assets of a pension scheme. There are good examples of extended exonerations and indemnities in various schemes set out in statute:

Scheme	No liability:
Civil Aviation Authority Pension Scheme[6]	'save for an act or omission which he knew to be a breach of trust and which he knowingly and wilfully committed or omitted as the case may be'.
Railways Pension Scheme[7]	unless due to 'personal conscious wrongdoing or recklessness', with professional trustees also being liable for negligence.
British Coal Staff Superannuation Scheme[8]Industry-Wide Coal Staff Superannuation Scheme[9]	'except as a result of a wilful or reckless act or omission by that person unless known by him to be a breach of trust or breach of duty in relation to the Scheme or done or omitted by him recklessly as to whether or not it is such a breach of trust or duty.' Does not apply 'to the extent that they are covered by external insurance'.
Royal Mail Pension Plan[10]	save for 'his own wilful default or neglect'.

Reasons for an express indemnity

14.12 There are perhaps two main reasons for this use of extended indemnities and exonerations:

(a) the implied statutory indemnity will only extend to liabilities *properly* incurred by the trustee;[11] and

(b) it is prudent to extend the indemnity to cover the position of a former trustee as well as an existing trustee (see further below).

14.13 The limit on the statutory indemnity to a liability 'properly' incurred by the trustee is quite limited. It is an objective test and can cause difficulties when dealing with tort liabilities (or statutory liabilities) that the trustee may have incurred as part of acting as trustee. Are such liabilities 'reasonable' or 'proper'? And if not, does the indemnity cease to apply? See the

---

[5] See also on an express indemnity superseding the implied indemnity, the Isle of Man decision, *IFG International v French* [2013] WTLR 251 (Deemster Corlett).

[6] Clauses 18.1 and 18.2 of the Trust Deed attached to the Transport Act 2000 (Civil Aviation Authority Pension Scheme) Order 2001 (SI 2001/853).

[7] Clauses 2D (exoneration) and 2F (indemnity) of the Trust Deed set out in the Schedule to the Railways Pension Scheme Order 1994 (SI 1994/1433).

[8] Clause 46(2) (indemnity) and 46(3) (exoneration) in the British Coal Staff Superannuation Scheme (Modification) Regulations 1994 (SI 1994/2576).

[9] Clause 47(2) (indemnity) and 47(3) (exoneration) in the Industry-Wide Coal Staff Superannuation Scheme Regulations 1994 (SI 1994/2973).

[10] Clause 9(7) of the deed as amended to 9 March 2012 by the Postal Services Act 2011 (Transfer of Accrued Pensions) Order 2012 (SI 2012/687).

[11] This qualification was implied into the 1925 Act. See eg *Re Beddoe* [1893] 1 Ch 547, CA; *Re Spurling's Will Trusts* [1966] 1 WLR 920 at 935 (Ungoed-Thomas J) and the mortgage case, *Gomba Holdings* [1993] Ch 171, CA. Also *Holding and Management Ltd v Property Holding and Investment Trust plc* [1990] 1 All ER 938, CA.

discussion in the Australian cases, *Gatsios Holdings Pty Ltd v Nick Kritharas Holdings Pty Ltd*[12] and contrast *Nolan v Collie*.[13]

The point is brought into stark relief if (say) a trustee incurs a liability under statute. For **14.14** example, a trustee employs an individual, but later dismisses him. The individual brings a claim for unfair dismissal and wins. The trustee is clearly liable (and any exoneration clause will not assist). But can the trustee look for an indemnity from the assets of the trust? Or is it clearly the case that they have incurred the liability improperly and so cannot (at least under the implied statutory indemnity)?

This issue is convincingly discussed by the New South Wales Court of Appeal in *Gatsios* **14.15** *Holdings v Kritharas Holdings (in Liquidation)*,[14] reaching the conclusion that it is not right to use the term 'proper' or 'reasonable' to define liabilities for this purpose.

Thus (according to the Austlii headnote): **14.16**

> Per Meagher JA:
>
> > The United States authorities which might be read as establishing either that the activity in respect of which indemnity is claimed, must be 'reasonable' and or 'proper', are limitations which do not exist in Australian law.
>
> Per Spigelman CJ:
>
> > The use of such terminology as conduct being 'proper' or 'reasonable' cannot be regarded as a test of when a trustee is entitled to receive indemnity for outgoings incurred in the course of execution of the trust. The general approach set out in both *Cotterell v Stratton* (1872) 8 Ch 295 at 302 and *Corrigan v Farelly* (1897) QLJ 105 at 111–112 are more helpful than the use of conclusory terminology of whether or not conduct was 'proper' or 'reasonable' as if it were a test.
>
> Per Mason P:
>
> > The terminology 'reasonable' and/or 'proper' conduct are terms which are notoriously open-ended and embody judgments to be made in context.

An indemnity clause can (subject to the public policy and statutory limitations discussed **14.17** below) be expressed wider so that it covers all liabilities incurred by the trustee, except (say) those incurred fraudulently or in bad faith. See for example the comment of the Court of Appeal in the mortgage case, *Gomba Holdings UK Ltd v Minories Finance Ltd (No 2)*[15] dealing with the ability of a mortgagee to add costs to the amount secured:

> Second, the many judicial references to costs 'properly incurred' make it clear that the court will examine the costs, charges and expenses sought to be added to the security and disallow those that it considers have not been 'properly incurred'. But here, too, express contractual provisions may alter what would otherwise have been the position.

To this extent an indemnity backs up any exclusion clause on liability to beneficiaries that **14.18** may be contained in the trust deed.

Any such indemnity out of the trust fund will by its nature be limited to the assets of the **14.19** scheme. It will rank behind any charge granted over those assets by the trustee, in the absence

---

[12] [2002] ATPR 41-864, [2002] NSWCA 29, NSWCA.

[13] (2003) 7 VR 287, Victoria CA. See the discussion of these cases in PW Young, CE Croft, and M Smith, *On Equity* (Lawbook Co, 2009) 496 and in Kevin Lingren, 'A Superannuation Fund Trustee's Right of Indemnity' (2010) 4 J Eq 85 at 90.

[14] [2002] NSWCA 29, NSWCA.

[15] [1993] Ch 171, CA.

of a specific provision in the charge.[16] Conversely it will rank ahead of any benefits payable to beneficiaries under the scheme—see *Chief Commissioner of Stamp Duties v Buckle*.[17]

Limits on Exonerations/Indemnities

14.20 It seems that generally exoneration or indemnity clauses will be upheld provided they do not go so far as to attempt to exclude liability for actual fraud or subjective dishonesty. There is also some doubt as to whether liability for breach of a duty in the Pensions Act can be excluded.

14.21 There may be limits on the efficacy of such clauses:

(a) Indemnities against deliberate commission of crimes are probably unenforceable as a matter of public policy.[18] This may also extend to deliberate torts (ie civil wrongs). However, in *Lancashire CC v Municipal Mutual Insurance Ltd*[19] an insurance company sought to contest liability to pay to the insured police force for its liability for exemplary damages, basing this in part on a claim that to do so would be contrary to public policy. The Court of Appeal rejected this defence holding that limitations on enforcement of insurance policies (and hence also indemnities) based on public policy should be narrowly confined.

(b) In the absence of an express reference to negligence, the courts will generally construe an exoneration or indemnity so that it will not apply to a liability caused by the negligence of the party claiming to be indemnified—*Canada Steamship Lines v R*.[20] For example in *Lutea Trustees Ltd v Orbis Trustees Guernsey Ltd*,[21] the Inner House of the Court of Session held that an exoneration clause did not cover 'culpa lata'[22] (ie gross negligence).

But the courts seem to be taking a more pragmatic view here. The Privy Council held in *Spread Trustee v Hutcheson*[23] that an exoneration clause can cover gross negligence (following *Armitage v Nurse*). And in *MIR Steel UK Ltd v Morris*[24] (not a trust case) the Court of Appeal held that the *Canada Steamship* guidelines should not be followed mechanistically.

(c) It used to be unclear whether such clauses are subject to provisions of the Unfair Contract Terms Act 1977 (UCTA). If UCTA applies then such clauses may be subject to being struck down if they do not satisfy the reasonableness test in UCTA. The answer to whether UCTA applies depends on whether or not trustees are acting in a business capacity and whether such trust liabilities can be considered to be contractual or tortious. The Court of Appeal in *Re Duke of Norfolk's Settlement Trusts*[25] considered that liabilities under a private

---

[16] *Dominion Corporate Trustees Ltd v Capmark Bank Europe plc* [2011] EWCA Civ 380, CA.

[17] [1998] HCA 4, 192 CLR 226, HC Aus. Discussed further below.

[18] Eg *Hardy v Motor Insurers Bureau* [1964] 2 QB 745, CA. See Chitty, *The Law of Contracts* 31st edn (Sweet & Maxwell, 2012) para 16-176.

[19] [1996] 3 All ER 545, CA.

[20] [1952] AC 192 at 208, PC. See also *The Emmanuel 'C'* [1983] 1 Ll R 310 and *EE Caledonia Ltd v Orbit Valve Co Europe* [1993] 4 All ER 165, CA.

[21] 1998 SLT 471, (1997) SCLR 735, (1997) 2 OFLR (ITELR) 227, CSIH.

[22] This sounds like some form of Italian coffee. However, it seems to mean gross negligence—see the comments of Millett LJ in *Armitage v Nurse* [1998] Ch 241 at 254E.

[23] [2011] UKPC 13, [2012] 2 AC 194, PC.

[24] [2012] EWCA Civ 1397, CA.

[25] [1982] Ch 61, CA. See also *Galmerrow Securities v National Westminster Bank* (1990) [2002] WTLR 125 at 155–6 (Harman J).

(non-pension) trust could not be considered to be contractual. Sir William Goodhart QC in an article in 1980[26] considered that UCTA could apply. However, this was before the *Duke of Norfolk* case and he later indicated that his view has changed.[27]

In *Baker v J E Clark & Co*,[28] the Court of Appeal upheld an exoneration clause (in a personal pension plan) applying unless there was bad faith. The Court of Appeal followed *Armitage v Nurse* and went on to hold that UCTA could not apply to trusts.

(d) An indemnity out of trust assets may well not apply if the trustee owes other amounts to the trust (eg in respect of an entirely unrelated breach)—*Re Johnson*,[29] *Re Frith*,[30] and *Re British Power Traction & Lighting*.[31] This reflects the principle that a defaulting trustee cannot claim any beneficial interest before making good his default—eg *Doering v Doering*[32] and *Re Dacre*.[33] In principle there seems no reason why this principle cannot be overridden by express wording in the trust instrument.[34]

(e) On public policy grounds indemnities or exclusions relating to the party's own dishonesty or fraud will not be upheld.[35] At the very least the court is likely to construe them very rigorously.[36]

Public Policy Limitations? Core Duties

The limits of this public policy doctrine (see (e) above) were made clear by the decision of the Court of Appeal in *Armitage v Nurse*,[37] a private trust case. There had previously been issues of whether, as a matter of law, it would be possible for an exoneration or indemnity to extend to a breach of duty by a trustee, perhaps in circumstances of negligence or, perhaps, gross negligence. **14.22**

Armitage v Nurse involved an exclusion clause exempting a trustee from liability save from 'his own actual fraud'. This was upheld by the Court of Appeal. There was no reason to cut this down as being contrary to public policy. Provided the trustee acted honestly, he would not be liable. **14.23**

Millett LJ (as he then was) held[38] that: **14.24**

> I accept the submission made on behalf of Paula[39] that there is an irreducible core of obligations owed by the trustees to the beneficiaries and enforceable by them which is fundamental

---

[26] [1980] Conv 333, repeated in Trust Law & Practice Vol 1, No 2.

[27] See AJ Oakley (ed), *Trends in Contemporary Trust Law* (Clarendon Press, 1996) 270. Note also on this point the problems as to whether or not the Unfair Contract Terms Regulations 1994, made following the EC Unfair Contract Terms Directive could apply to trusts and trustees.

[28] [2006] EWCA Civ 464, CA.

[29] (1880) 15 ChD 548 (Sir George Jessel MR).

[30] [1902] 1 Ch 342.

[31] [1910] 2 Ch 470.

[32] (1889) 42 ChD 203 (Stirling J).

[33] [1916] 1 Ch 344 at 347, CA. It does not seem to apply to a claim by a trustee to remuneration: *Galmerrow Securities v National Westminster Bank* (1990) [2002] WTLR 125 (Harman J); *Hulbert v Avens* [2003] EWHC 76 (Ch), [2003] WTLR 387 (Judge Richard Seymour QC); *Reed v Oury* [2002] EWHC 369 (Ch) at [58] (Field J).

[34] It does not seem to be overridden by the implied statutory indemnity under the Trustee Acts.

[35] *S Pearson & Son Ltd v Dublin Corpn* [1907] AC 351, HL and *HIH Casualty and General Insurance Ltd v Chase Manhattan Bank* [2003] UKHL 6, [2003] 2 Lloyd's Rep 61 at [16], HL (Lord Bingham).

[36] See eg the comments, in the context of a contractual indemnity, of Scott LJ in *Gomba Holdings UK Ltd v Minories Finance Ltd (No 2)* [1992] 4 All ER 588, CA.

[37] [1998] Ch 241, CA. Discussed by Gerard McCormack (1998) 62 Conv 100.

[38] At p 253.

[39] The plaintiff beneficiary.

to the concept of a trust. If the beneficiaries have no rights enforceable against the trustees there are no trusts. But I do not accept the further submission that these core obligations include the duties of skill and care, prudence and diligence. The duty of trustees to perform the trusts honestly and in good faith for the benefit of the beneficiaries is the minimum necessary to give substance to the trusts, but in my opinion it is sufficient.

14.25 The comments of the Jersey Court of Appeal to the same effect in *Midland Bank Trustee (Jersey) Ltd v Federated Pension Services*[40] were followed. The House of Lords refused leave to appeal from the Court of Appeal's decision in *Armitage v Nurse*.[41]

14.26 On the issue of the irreducible core obligations of a trust, the case law indicates that it is a severe test. It will not apply unless the effect is to remove the core duty of honesty and good faith—see Millett LJ in *Armitage v Nurse*;[42] Arden LJ in *Citibank NA v QVT Financial LP*[43] and most recently the majority of the Privy Council in *Spread Trustee Co Ltd v Hutcheson*.[44]

14.27 In the *Citibank* case, the Court of Appeal held that the existence of a power in the trust deed of MBIA, as guarantor of notes, to give directions to the trustee did not mean that there was not a trust. Arden LJ (giving the main judgment[45]) held:[46]

> [82] Mr Popplewell[47] submits that the effect of the structure which enables a direction to be given to the trustee by MBIA is to reduce the trustee's obligations below the irreducible minimum identified by Millett LJ in *Armitage v Nurse* [1998] Ch 241. In my judgment this is not correct. The trustee continues at all times to have an obligation of good faith, and in addition, as Mr Adkins[48] submits, there are other clauses in the trust deed where the trustee has a real discretion to exercise, for example in cl 8 of the trust deed which also confers a discretion on the trustee to give authorisations or waivers. In my judgment, while it is correct that it would be a surprising interpretation of the documentation, against which the court should lean, if the powers of the trustee were so reduced that it ceases to be a trustee at all, that point has not been reached in the present case and therefore there is no risk of recharacterising the office of trustee as something else.

14.28 Previous arguments that, as a matter of policy, an exemption clause or indemnity ought not to be effective to exclude a trustee from liability for a breach of trust involving reckless indifference or gross negligence were not accepted.

14.29 In Australia HAJ Ford and IJ Hardingham had convincingly argued[49] that an exclusion clause can extend to cover gross negligence. This also seems to have been allowed by Walton J in the preliminary judgment given in *Re Imperial Foods*.[50]

14.30 There is also some support for this approach in the decision of the Privy Council in *Viscount of the Royal Court of Jersey v Shelton*[51] (which upheld a wide indemnity in articles of association in favour of a director).

---

[40] [1996] PLR 179, [1995] JLR 352, Jersey CA.
[41] See Millett LJ in *Bogg v Raper* (1998) 1 ITELR 267.
[42] [1998] Ch 241, CA.
[43] [2007] EWCA Civ 11, [2008] 1 BCLC 376, CA.
[44] [2011] UKPC 13 (PC, Guernsey), Lady Hale and Lord Kerr dissenting. Noted by Lee Aitken in (2011) 127 LQR 503.
[45] Sir Anthony Clarke MR and Dyson LJ agreed with Arden LJ.
[46] [2007] EWCA Civ 11, [2008] 1 BCLC 376 at [82], CA.
[47] Counsel for the appellant hedge fund.
[48] Counsel for the trustee.
[49] In their chapter in PD Finn (ed), *Equity and Commercial Relationships* (Law Book Co, 1987) 57.
[50] (1986) [2007] 08 PBLR (Walton J).
[51] [1986] 1 WLR 985, PC.

In *Barnes v Tomlinson*,[52] another private trust case, Kitchin J held: **14.31**

Cl 11 of the Settlement made clear that the discretion and the powers conferred on the trustees were absolute and uncontrolled and, importantly, the trustees were not to be held liable or answerable to any beneficiary for the manner in which they exercised any such power or discretion; nor were the trustees to be held liable for any loss or damage accruing as a result of the exercise or failure to exercise any such power or discretion. Nevertheless, [the trustees] both accepted that cl 11 must be read subject to the irreducible core obligations of a trustee, namely, to act honestly and in good faith.

Kitchin J followed *Armitage v Nurse* and held:[53]   **14.32**

It has been long established that the test of honesty in the context of an express trustee is whether the trustee is conscious that he is committing a breach of duty or is recklessly careless whether he is committing a breach of duty or not: *Armitage v Nurse* [1998] Ch 241. Where the trustee is a solicitor then the issue is whether or not the trustee transgressed the normally acceptable standards of honest conduct expected from a solicitor.[54]

In *Fattal v Walbrook Trustees (Jersey) Ltd*[55] Lewison J dealt with the case of a professional   **14.33**
trustee and held that a subjective belief that a deliberate breach of trust was in the best interests of beneficiaries was not enough to protect a professional trustee from a claim of dishonesty if that belief was not also objectively reasonable. Lewison J referred to *Armitage v Nurse* and *Walker v Stones* and held[56] that to show dishonesty in the case of a professional trustee, as well as there being a deliberate breach of trust, the trustee:

(a) knows that the deliberate breach is contrary to the interests of the beneficiaries; or
(b) is recklessly indifferent to whether the breach is contrary to their interests or not; or
(c) whose belief that the deliberate breach is not contrary to the interests of the beneficiaries is so unreasonable that, by any objective standard, no reasonable professional trustee could have thought that what he did or agreed to do was for the benefit of the beneficiaries.

Lewison J referred to the comments of Sir Christopher Slade in *Walker v Stones* that the test   **14.34**
of dishonesty may vary from case to case and went on to hold[57] that:

Where the allegation of dishonesty is based on the trustee preferring his own interests to those of the beneficiaries in circumstances where there is a straight conflict between duty and interest dishonesty may be easier to establish than in a case in which the conflict is between duty and duty; and the trustee has discharged one duty in preference to another. Of course, the trustee will be in breach of trust if he prefers one duty at the expense of another, but it seems to me that it would be harder to characterise that as 'dishonest'.

---

[52] [2006] EWHC 3115 (Ch) at [75] (Kitchin J).
[53] At [79].
[54] See *Walker v Stones* [2001] QB 902, CA.
[55] [2010] EWHC 2767 (Ch), [2012] Bus LR D7 (Lewison J).
[56] At [81].
[57] [2010] EWHC 2767 (Ch) at [82] (Lewison J).

14.35   Most recently, the Privy Council (by a majority) in *Spread Trustee Co Ltd v Hutcheson*[58] followed the decision in *Armitage v Nurse*[59] and upheld an exclusion clause that excluded liability for trustees acting in good faith, ie for:

> loss of any investments made in good faith or by reason of any mistake or omission made in good faith or of any other matter or thing except wilful and individual fraud and wrongdoing on the part of the trustee who is sought to be made liable.

14.36   The beneficiaries alleged that the trustee could still be liable for gross negligence. The majority in the Privy Council held that, as a matter of English law gross negligence could be excluded, so the clause did not allow a claim based on gross negligence (and a change to the Guernsey legislation to restrict exclusion clauses so that they could not cover gross negligence was not retrospective to cover breaches alleged before the law came into force).

Meaning of Gross Negligence

14.37   If the exoneration actually refers to gross negligence, then what meaning should be given to that term?

14.38   Millett LJ commented in *Armitage v Nurse*:

> But while we regard the difference between fraud on the one hand and mere negligence, however gross, on the other as a difference in kind, we regard the difference between negligence and gross negligence as merely one of degree. English lawyers have always had a healthy disrespect for the latter distinction. In *Hinton v Dibbin* (1842) 2 QB 646, 114 ER 253 Lord Denman CJ doubted whether any intelligible distinction exists; while in *Grill v General Iron Screw Collier Co* (1866) 35 LJCP 321 at 330 Willes J famously observed that gross negligence is ordinary negligence with a vituperative epithet. But civilian systems draw the line in a different place. The doctrine is culpa lata dolo aequiparetur; and although the maxim itself is not Roman the principle is classical. There is no room for the maxim in the common law; it is not mentioned in Broom Selection of Legal Maxims Classified and Illustrated (10th edn, 1939).

14.39   In 2012 in Ireland, in *ICDL Saudi Arabia v European Computer Driving Licence Foundation Ltd*,[60] the Supreme Court of Ireland considered the meaning of 'wilful act or gross negligence' in a commercial contract. The majority in the Supreme Court agreed with the first instance judge, Clarke J, that it means 'a degree of negligence where whatever duty of care may be involved has not been met by a significant margin'. The Supreme Court was applying principles of contract interpretation common to English and Irish law.

14.40   In *Red Sea Tankers Ltd v Papachristidis (The Ardent)*,[61] Mance J (as he then was) dealt with a contract which was to be interpreted according to the law of the State of New York. Having considered the evidence regarding the law of that jurisdiction, he observed that:

> if the matter is viewed according to purely English principles of construction, ... gross negligence is clearly intended to represent something more fundamental than failure to exercise proper skill and/or care constituting negligence ...

---

[58] [2011] UKPC 13, [2012] 2 AC 194, PC. The majority were Lord Mance, Lord Clarke, and Sir Robin Auld (Lady Hale and Lord Kerr dissenting).

[59] And also the Jersey CA case, *Midland Bank Trust Co (Jersey) Ltd v Federated Pension Services* [1995] JLR 352 at 378–379, 381.

[60] [2012] IESC 55, Irish SC.

[61] [1997] 2 Lloyd's Rep 547 at 586 (Mance J).

He then held that:

> as a matter of ordinary language and general impression, the concept of gross negligence seems capable of embracing not only conduct undertaken with actual appreciation of the risks involved, but also serious disregard of or indifference to an obvious risk.

In *Tradigrain SA v Intertek Testing Systems (ITS) Canada Ltd*,[62] Moore-Bick LJ observed that **14.41** 'The term "gross negligence", although often found in commercial documents, has never been accepted by English civil law as a concept distinct from civil negligence...'.

In *Camarata Property Inc v Credit Suisse Securities*[63] Andrew Smith J followed the view of **14.42** Mance J in *Red Sea Tankers*. This was a case concerning a clause purporting to limit liability of investment advisers to cases involving 'gross negligence...fraud or wilful default...'.

Andrew Smith J referred to *Tradigrain* and *Armitage v Nurse* and noted that gross negligence **14.43** had not been recognized in English law as a concept distinct from civil negligence. He went on to state, nonetheless, that:

> The relevant question...is not whether generally gross negligence is a familiar concept in English law, but the meaning of the expression in these paragraphs of the terms and conditions...

Limits in the Pensions Legislation

Such exonerations and indemnities in relation to occupational pension schemes have since 6 **14.44** April 1997 been subject to two express limitations under the pensions legislation:

(a) Section 256 of the Pensions Act 2004[64] prohibits an indemnity out of the fund (or payment of insurance premiums by the fund) in relation to:
   (i) any criminal fines; or
   (ii) civil penalties under s 168(4) of the Pension Schemes Act 1993 or s 10 of the Pensions Act 1995.[65]
(b) Section 33 of the Pensions Act 1995 provides that any liability of a trustee (or person delegated by the trustee) for breach of an obligation under any rule of law to take care or exercise skill in the performance of any investment function cannot 'be excluded or restricted by any instrument or agreement'.

The s 33 restriction clearly applies to an exoneration provision (eg in a trust deed) and is **14.45** likely to be held to extend to indemnities to the trustee (whether out of the trust fund or from a beneficiary). This is because an indemnity looks similar in effect to an exoneration[66] and because s 33(2)(a) extends the meaning of 'excluding or restricting liability' so that it covers making the liability or its enforcement subject to restrictive or onerous conditions—an

---

[62] [2007] EWCA Civ 154 at [23], CA. For another case that has considered gross negligence in a contractual context see *JP Morgan Chase Bank v Springwell Navigation Corporation* [2010] EWCA Civ 1221, CA.

[63] [2011] EWHC 479 (Comm), [2011] 2 BCLC 54 (Andrew Smith J).

[64] Previously s 31 of the Pensions Act 1995.

[65] The Pensions Act 2004 tends to expressly refer to s 10 of the Pensions Act 1995 when dealing with a power for the Pensions Regulator to impose civil penalties. For example s 228(4) dealing with where there is a failure to make contributions under a schedule of contributions.

[66] See the comments of the Privy Council in *Viscount of the Royal Court of Jersey v Shelton* [1986] 1 WLR 985 at 991F to the effect that an indemnity has the same effect as an exoneration.

indemnity seems to fall within this (if a member claimed against a trustee, the trustee's claim to an indemnity would seem to be making the claim more onerous).

14.46   It seems likely that any exoneration or indemnity will still be effective even if it purports to cover a matter where it is ineffective by reason of the Pensions Acts limits (or the fraud/honesty public policy limit). Such absolute prohibitions tend to mean that the provision is read down, rather than becoming totally ineffective. For example in *George Mitchell (Chesterhall) Ltd v Finney Lock Seeds Ltd*,[67] Kerr LJ (as he then was) in the Court of Appeal considered that an exemption clause in a sale contract would remain effective even if it purported to exclude a condition as to title under the Sale of Goods Act 1979 which could not be excluded. He held:[68]

> ...counsel for the plaintiffs submitted that the clause was wholly void by virtue of s 55(3) in Sch 1 to the [Sale of Goods Act 1979], because its fourth sentence...purported to exclude all conditions implied by statute, including s 12 of the 1979 Act concerning the implied condition as to the seller's title. I cannot accept this submission either. Even allowing for the fact that we are dealing with an exemption clause which has to be strictly construed, it seems to me that a reasonable and businesslike construction, which gives full effect to s 55(3), is that the clause is void to the extent that it purports to exempt the defendants from the condition implied by s 12, but no further.

14.47   Having said that, a reference to the statutory limits is often included in trust deed to make it clearer that the provision is limited by the relevant legislation.

14.48   In addition, it may be arguable that an exoneration or indemnity cannot apply in relation to a breach of a provision in the Pensions Act 1995 or Pensions Act 2004. This is on the basis that s 117 of the 1995 Act provides that Pt I of the Act (and the regulations made under it) overrides any conflicting provision in the scheme. Section 306 of the Pensions Act 2004 is to similar effect in relation to the 2004 Act.

14.49   The converse argument is that ss 117 and 306 are merely meant to clarify that a duty under the relevant Act cannot be excluded (or presumably varied or modified) by a provision in the scheme (contrast s 69(2) of the Trustee Act 1925).

14.50   An alternative argument is that the 1995 Act generally does not impose any civil liability (eg to a member). Instead, it can be argued that the only sanction for breach of a provision of the Act is the penalty laid down in the Act. This is a question of divining the intention of Parliament from the Act. Somewhat bizarrely, save for sections 117 and 306, this question is not addressed expressly in the two Acts.[69]

Reduced ombudsman liability if an exoneration clause

14.51   There have been a series of cases involving appeals from the Pensions Ombudsman as to whether personal liability for awards against trustees can be made if the breach complained

---

[67] [1983] 1 All ER 108, CA.

[68] At p 122. Oliver LJ agreed on this point—p 118. Lord Denning MR did not deal with the issue. The CA decision was upheld on appeal, [1983] 2 All ER 737, HL, but this point was not considered. See D Pollard, 'The Unfair Contract Terms Act: Points When Drafting Contracts' (1987) Business Law Review 131. For other examples, see Lord Walker in *Pitt v HMRC* [2013] UKSC 26 at [13], SC.

[69] Despite a request by the APL to government (while the Bill was before Parliament) that this point be settled in the 2004 Act. For a good discussion of the difficulties in this area, see A Samuels, 'Is a Breach of Statutory Duty Actionable?' (1995) 16 Statute Law Review 225.

of is covered by an exoneration clause in the trust deed: *Miller and KC Independent Trustees Ltd v Stapleton and the Pensions Ombudsman*;[70] *Duffield v Pensions Ombudsman*;[71] and *Wild v Smith*.[72]

The cases indicate that the Pensions Ombudsman will have regard to any exoneration or indemnity available to trustees when deciding what measures to order in a determination.[73] **14.52**

The better view is that an indemnity or exoneration does not oust the statutory jurisdiction of the Pensions Ombudsman, but instead is a factor that he should consider when making a determination against a trustee. For example, if there is an indemnity out of the trust fund an order against a trustee to pay a particular benefit (or an award for distress) will result in the amount being paid out of the assets of the scheme (and hence potentially reducing other benefits or increasing the amounts payable by the employer). **14.53**

Further Interpretation Issues

Wilful default

Before its replacement in February 2001, s 30(1) of the Trustee Act 1925 also contained a protection for trustees to the extent they will not be liable in the absence of 'wilful default'. Section 31 of the Trustee Act 2000 has applied since 1 February 2001 and provides a similar indemnity. **14.54**

It is prudent not to use these words in exclusion clauses (or indemnities) given to trustees as the precise meaning of these words is the subject of some debate. **14.55**

In *Re Vickery*,[74] these words were construed as not including a mere lack of ordinary prudence or negligence. This seems to be their natural meaning. **14.56**

However, it ignores some well-established precedents in the courts of equity giving this term a meaning to include want of prudence. This seems to be just one example of equity giving unusual technical meanings to terms (different from their natural ordinary meaning). **14.57**

Accordingly, it has been argued that this case is wrongly decided and that wilful default can include negligence without any conscious wrong doing.[75] **14.58**

Ultimately, Millett LJ (as he then was) in *Armitage v Nurse*[76] held that want of ordinary prudence is not wilful default for the purpose of a trustee exoneration or exclusion clause. Millett LJ stated[77] that wilful default means a deliberate breach of trust as said in *Re Vickery* **14.59**

---

[70] [1996] 2 All ER 449, [1996] OPLR 73 (Carnwath J).
[71] [1996] OPLR 149, [1996] PLR 285 (Carnwath J).
[72] [1996] OPLR 129, [1996] PLR 275 (Carnwath J).
[73] See eg Robert Walker J in *Westminster City Council v Haywood* [1996] OPLR 95 at 110; Carnwath J in *Wild v Smith* [1996] OPLR 129 at 137; and Lightman J in *Seifert v Pensions Ombudsman* [1997] 1 All ER 214, [1996] PLR 479.
[74] [1931] 1 Ch 572 (Maugham J).
[75] See eg *Underhill and Hayton: Law Relating to Trusts and Trustees* 15th edn (Butterworth and Co, 1995) 624 and 903; John Stannard [1979] Conv 345; and Paul Matthews [1989] Conv 42. To the contrary, see Robert Ham QC at para 4.62 in *Tolley's Pensions Handbook* 2nd edn (1995).
[76] [1998] Ch 241, CA.
[77] At p 252D.

and that to establish wilful default 'nothing less than conscious and wilful misconduct is sufficient'.[78]

14.60 In *Armitage v Nurse* Millett LJ noted[79] that the expression 'wilful default' is used in the cases in two senses:

> A trustee is said to be accountable on the footing of wilful default when he is accountable not only for money which he has in fact received but also for money which he could with reasonable diligence have received. It is sufficient that the trustee has been guilty of a want of ordinary prudence (see eg *Re Chapman, Cocks v Chapman* [1896] 2 Ch 763). In the context of a trustee exclusion clause, however, such as s 30 of the Trustee Act 1925, it means a deliberate breach of trust (*Re Vickery, Vickery v Stephens* [1931] 1 Ch 572). The decision has been criticised, but it is in line with earlier authority (see *Lewis v Great Western Rly Co* (1877) 3 QBD 195, *Re Trusts of Leeds City Brewery Ltd's Debenture Stock Trust Deed, Leeds City Brewery Ltd v Platts* [1925] Ch 532n and *Re City Equitable Fire Insurance Co Ltd* [1925] Ch 407). Nothing less than conscious and wilful misconduct is sufficient. The trustee must be—
>
> > conscious that, in doing the act which is complained of or in omitting to do the act which it said he ought to have done, he is committing a breach of his duty, or is recklessly careless whether it is a breach of his duty or not. (See *Re Vickery, Vickery v Stephens* [1931] 1 Ch 572 at 583, per Maugham J)
>
> A trustee who is guilty of such conduct either consciously takes a risk that loss will result, or is recklessly indifferent whether it will or not. If the risk eventuates he is personally liable. But if he consciously takes the risk in good faith and with the best intentions, honestly believing that the risk is one which ought to be taken in the interests of the beneficiaries, there is no reason why he should not be protected by an exemption clause which excludes liability for wilful default.

14.61 This passage by Millett LJ was expressly approved by the Privy Council in *Spread Trustee*.[80] Lord Clarke (speaking for the majority) held:

> The Board agrees with counsel for the trustee that English law is clear that in this class of case it is not permissible to exclude wilful misconduct as described by Millett LJ in the above passage. As Bramwell LJ put it in *Lewis v Great Western Rly Co* (1877) 3 QBD 195 at 206:
>
> > 'Wilful misconduct' means misconduct to which the will is a party, something opposed to accident or negligence; the misconduct, not the conduct, must be wilful.
>
> Millett LJ ([1998] Ch 241 at 251) summarised his view as being that cl 15, which excluded liability for anything other than fraud—
>
> > exempts the trustee from liability for loss or damage to the trust property no matter how indolent, imprudent, lacking in diligence, negligent or wilful he may have been, so long as he has not acted dishonestly.
>
> The Board agrees.

14.62 Millett LJ in *Armitage v Nurse* and later in *Bogg v Raper*[81] held that a different meaning of wilful default would apply where a trustee has not committed any positive breach of trust but instead failed to act. Here he will be 'accountable not only for the trust funds in his hands, but also for those which he would have received if he had acted with proper diligence'.[82]

---

[78] For a discussion of this point, see Hugh Arthur, 'Exoneration Clauses after Armitage v Nurse—Where Are We Now?' (APL seminar, April 1998) and the Law Commission Consultation Paper on *Trustees' Powers and Duties* issued in June 1997.

[79] [1998] Ch 241 at 252, CA.

[80] [2011] UKPC 13, [2012] 2 AC 194 at [55], PC. The majority were Lord Mance, Lord Clarke, and Sir Robin Auld (Lady Hale and Lord Kerr dissenting).

[81] (1998) 1 ITELR 267, [1998] CLY 4592, CA.

[82] This echoes the comments made in the Law Commission Consultation Paper at para 4.15, quoting the book by RP Meagher, JD Gummow, and MJ Lehane, *Equity Doctrines and Remedies* 3rd edn (Butterworths, 1992).

In a pensions case, *Alexander Forbes Trustee Services Ltd v Halliwell*,[83] Hart J held that 'wilful **14.63** default and wrongdoing' was to be viewed so that 'wilful' qualified both 'default' and 'wrong-doing'—the composite phrase comprehends both acts of omission and of commission.

Good faith/bad faith

Bad faith is generally taken to mean not simply bad judgment or negligence but implies some **14.64** aspect of conscious doing of a wrong. See for example the comments of Lightman J in *Melton Medes Ltd v Security and Investments Board*[84] and those of the Court of Appeal in *Economides v Commercial Union Assurance Co plc*.[85]

Although, there has been some suggestion recently that good faith (and hence bad faith) can **14.65** be judged objectively, rather than subjectively as one would normally expect. For example will the courts hold that a person has been acting in good faith if he or she fails to carry out proper enquires? See the comments of Lord Steyn speaking (extra judicially) in 1996 at a conference in Malaysia.[86]

It would appear prudent, therefore, that if the phrase *bad faith* is to be used, it should be **14.66** preceded by the words *personal and conscious* to make it absolutely clear that there is to be an intention to act in bad faith and that a person's actions and intentions are to be judged subjectively.

Dishonesty

These is a term with at least two meanings. Does it involve: **14.67**

- conscious impropriety by an individual, ie knowing it is wrong? This is subjective dishonesty (this is the criminal law test—see *R v Ghosh*[87]); or
- acting by reference to an unacceptable standard (measured objectively)?—would a reasonable person have considered the action to be dishonest? See generally Lord Nicholls in *Royal Brunei v Tan*[88] and (in a pensions context) Lindsay J in *HR v JAPT*.[89]

Fraud

The term fraud seems to have several meanings. At one level is common law fraud, involving **14.68** actual moral wrong—in effect subjective dishonesty. See further the discussion in *Armitage v Nurse*.[90]

At another is so-called equitable fraud (in the sense of misusing a power). An example **14.69** is 'fraud on a power', ie using a power for a purpose for which it was not intended. This does not involve any conscious wrongdoing by the trustee—he may be acting in all innocence.

---

83 [2003] EWHC 1685 (Ch), [2003] OPLR 355 (Hart J).
84 [1995] Ch 137, [1994] PLR 167 (Lightman J).
85 [1998] QB 587, CA.
86 (1997) 113 LQR 43. See also in Australia, Kirby J in *Cannane v J Cannane Pty Ltd* (1998) 153 ALR 163 at 191–2, discussed by RD Nicholson J in *Strickland v Minister for Lands* (1998) 24 July.
87 [1982] QB 1053, CA.
88 [1995] 2 AC 378 at 389, PC. See later *Twinsectra v Yardley* [2002] 2 All ER 377, HL and *Barlow Clowes International v Eurotrust International* [2006] 1 All ER 333, PC.
89 [1997] OPLR 123 (Lindsay J). See also Ch 5 (Liability of directors of corporate trustees).
90 [1998] Ch 241, CA.

14.70 In *Armitage v Nurse*[91] an exclusion clause in a private trust exempting a trustee from liability save from 'his own actual fraud' was upheld by the Court of Appeal. It was construed as meaning the same as dishonesty (seeming to use this in the sense of knowing wrong).

Knowingly

14.71 There are evidently at least five different types of 'knowledge'—see Peter Gibson J in the *Baden* case.[92]

14.72 Knowledge can comprise any one of five different mental states which can be described as follows:

    (i) actual knowledge;

    (ii) wilfully shutting one's eyes to the obvious;

    (iii) wilfully and recklessly failing to make such inquiries as an honest and reasonable man would make;

    (iv) knowledge of circumstances which would indicate the facts to an honest and reasonable man;

    (v) knowledge of circumstances which would put an honest and reasonable man on inquiry.

14.73 Lord Nicholls later stated that he preferred to forget this classification.[93]

14.74 Care should be taken to ensure whether the knowledge relates to the act being done or to the fact that it is wrongful.

14.75 For example in *Midland Bank Trustee (Jersey) Ltd v Federated Pension Services*[94] a trustee had the benefit of an indemnity against all liabilities 'other than a breach of trust knowingly and wrongfully committed'. The trustee failed to pay the scheme assets to a new fund manager (wrongly thinking that a customer agreement was needed under the Financial Services legislation). It was sued for the loss resulting (the market rose in the meantime).

14.76 The Jersey Court of Appeal[95] held (at p 198) that this clause had two possible interpretations:

    (1) the trustee is liable if it knowingly and wilfully commits an act which amounts to a breach of trust (whether or not it knew that the act was a breach of trust); or

    (2) the trustee is only liable if it knowingly and wilfully commits an act which at the time of commission is known to it to be a breach of trust.

14.77 The court analysed a number of earlier English decisions (including a number on the meaning of 'wilful default'), but ultimately decided that the first interpretation is correct. This meant that the trustee could not in this case rely on the indemnity (it had knowingly refused to pass over the money—it did not matter that it had not realized that this was in breach of trust).

---

[91] [1998] Ch 241, CA.
[92] [1993] 1 WLR 509 at 575 (Peter Gibson J).
[93] *Royal Brunei v Tan* [1995] 2 AC 378 at 392, PC.
[94] [1996] PLR 179, [1995] JLR 352, Jersey CA.
[95] Sir Godfray Le Quesne QC, RC Southwell QC, and MJ Beloff QC.

Former Trustees

In *Seifert v Pensions Ombudsman*[96] Lightman J confirmed that former trustees remain entitled **14.78**
to take the benefit of an exoneration clause (and presumably also an indemnity) in the trust
instrument even though it does not expressly refer to former trustees. Although Lightman
J's decision was reversed on appeal,[97] this was on different grounds. This point was not
addressed by the Court of Appeal.

In principle it would seem to be unfair to exclude a former trustee from such an indemnity **14.79**
(eg against any liability to pay tax). There had previously been at least two Australian cases
confirming that the indemnity survives—see *Coates v McInnery*[98] and *All Benefit Pty Ltd v
Registrar General.*[99]

In *Agusta Pty Ltd v Provident Capital Ltd*,[100] the New South Wales Court of Appeal confirmed **14.80**
that a lien or indemnity would apply to a former trustee even after he had left office (and
transferred the trust property to a new trustee). The court held:

Lien survives a transfer to a new trustee:

43 It is necessary next to consider the consequences, as regards the trustee's preferred beneficial
interest, of a transfer of trust property by the trustee to a new trustee.

44 After such a transfer, the original trustee's preferred beneficial interest continues to subsist in
the trust property in the new trustee's hands. This was recognised by Thomas JA, Shepherdson
J and Jones J in *Belar Pty Ltd v Mahaffey* [1999] QCA 2; [2000] 1 Qd R 477 at [19]–[20]:

A trustee's right to an indemnity against trust assets in respect of expenses properly
incurred by the trustee in the conduct of the business of the trust is well recognised. In con-
ducting the business of the trust, the trustee becomes personally liable for debts incurred.

However, he is entitled to be indemnified against those liabilities from the trust assets
held by him and for the purpose of enforcing the indemnity the trustee possesses a charge or
right of lien over those assets. [*Octavo Investments Pty Ltd v Knight* [1979] HCA 61; (1979)
144 CLR 360, 367].

That is a reference to trust assets in the trustee's possession. When there is a change of
trustee with the trust assets being vested in the new trustee, the former trustee no longer has
direct access to such assets, and should make the necessary claim for indemnity against the
trustee who represents the trust.

The trustee's right of indemnity out of the trust assets is in the nature of a charge or lien
in favour of the trustee and as such takes preference or priority over claims by the cestuis que
trust. But of course when the assets have passed out of a trustee's possession the necessary
claim for a trustee's indemnity should be made against the new trustee. An unco-operative
new trustee who declined to exercise the powers to recover trust property in the hands of the
beneficiaries could be made a defendant, and orders could be made which would in effect
permit the former trustee to exercise such powers by subrogation.[101]

---

[96] [1997] 1 All ER 214, [1996] PLR 479 at 487 (Lightman J).
[97] See [1997] 4 All ER 947, CA.
[98] [1992] 10 ACLC 816.
[99] [1993] 11 ACLC 1068.
[100] [2012] NSWCA 26 at [43]–[45], NSWCA.
[101] On subrogaton by creditors to the trustee's indemnity, see *Octavo and Dowse v Gorton* [1891] AC 190,
HL. There is a good summary in Singapore: *EC Investment Holding Pte Ltd v Ridout Residence Pte Ltd* [2013]
SGHC 139 (Quentin Loh J).

45 This passage was approved by Spigelman CJ in *Gatsios Holdings Pty Ltd v Nick Kritharas Holdings Pty Ltd* [2002] NSWCA 29 at [2]. The question whether an outgoing trustee may decline to transfer trust property to the new trustee until its preferred beneficial interest has been satisfied (recently regarded by Corboy J in *Prior v Simeon (No 2)* [2011] WASC 61 as unsettled) does not arise in this case.

Nature of the Interest Given to the Trustees by an Indemnity

14.81 In *Chief Commissioner of Stamp Duties v Buckle*,[102] the High Court in Australia confirmed the right of trustees to be indemnified out of trust assets against liabilities properly incurred in the administration of the trust. This right is not a charge or encumbrance on the assets, but instead is a preferred beneficial interest in the trust fund.

14.82 This was a stamp duty case, but the reasoning will defend trustees from any claims that their indemnity could be attacked because (say) it needed to be registered as a charge over the trust assets.

14.83 In *Agusta Pty Ltd v Provident Capital Ltd*[103] Barratt JA in the New South Wales Court of Appeal summarized the position:

> The right of a trustee to be indemnified out of trust property is often described as a charge or lien: see, for example, *Vacuum Oil Co Pty Ltd v Wiltshire*;[104] *Octavo Investments Pty Ltd v Knight*.[105] In *Chief Commissioner of Stamp Duties v Buckle*,[106] the High Court preferred to regard it as a proprietary right constituting a beneficial interest enjoying priority over the beneficial interests of the beneficiaries. It is anomalous to refer to a person having a charge or lien over property of which the person is the owner. And as was emphasised by the High Court subsequently in *CPT Custodian Pty Ltd v Commissioner of State Revenue*,[107] the 'trust fund' enjoyed by the beneficiaries cannot be identified or quantified until the trustee's superior beneficial interest has been quantified and satisfied. The trustee's right is inseparable from and co-extensive with the trustee's obligations, both those already discharged but not yet reimbursed and those incurred but not yet discharged.

Legal Costs in Defending a Claim?

14.84 It seems likely that a right under an indemnity can include unsuccessful costs that the trustee has incurred in defending proceedings brought by a beneficiary, but that this is subject to the power of the court to direct that the costs cannot be recovered from the trust fund.

14.85 Arguably an express indemnity (eg allowing costs to be claimed out of the trust fund if incurred in good faith) would remove the need for the trustee to protect itself against an adverse costs order in litigation by seeking prior court approval under *Re Beddoe*.[108] But this is untested and seems to run into the issue of the court's discretion under the Civil Procedure Rules being overriding.

---

[102] [1998] HCA 4, 192 CLR 226, HC Aus.
[103] [2012] NSWCA 26 at [41], NSWCA.
[104] [1945] HCA 37, (1945) 72 CLR 319, HC Aus.
[105] [1979] HCA 61, (1979) 144 CLR 360, HC Aus.
[106] [1998] HCA 4, (1998) 192 CLR 226, HC Aus.
[107] [2005] HCA 53, (2005) 224 CLR 98, HC Aus. Discussed in Ch 16 (*Saunders v Vautier* and pension trusts).
[108] [1893] 1 Ch 547, CA.

Any indemnity is subject to the court's power to deal with costs under CPR r 46.3.[109] **14.86**
That rule provides that the 'general'[110] rule is that a trustee is entitled to be paid the
cost of his proceedings out of the trust fund to the extent not recovered from any other
person.[111]

Costs are to be assessed on the indemnity basis. An assessment on the indemnity basis means **14.87**
the court will resolve any doubt as to whether costs were reasonably incurred or were reasonable in amount in favour of the receiving party[112] (as opposed to in favour of the paying party
on the standard basis).

CPR r 46.3 does not apply if CPR r 44.5 applies (dealing with costs payable under a contract). **14.88**
An indemnity under a trust is probably non-contractual, but this should be interpreted
similarly.

The practice direction supplementing Ord 46 states (at para 1.1): **14.89**

Awards of costs in favour of a trustee or personal representative: rule 46.3

A trustee or personal representative is entitled to an indemnity out of the relevant trust fund **1.1**
or estate for costs properly incurred. Whether costs were properly incurred depends on
all the circumstances of the case including whether the trustee or personal representative
('the trustee')—
(a) obtained directions from the court before bringing or defending the proceedings;
(b) acted in the interests of the fund or estate or in substance for a benefit other than that
of the estate, including the trustee's own; and
(c) acted in some way unreasonably in bringing or defending, or in the conduct of, the
proceedings.
The trustee is not to be taken to have acted for a benefit other than that of the fund by reason **1.2**
only that the trustee has defended a claim in which relief is sought against the trustee
personally.

These provisions override the terms of the indemnity—see (on contractual indemnities) the **14.90**
Court of Appeal in the mortgage cases, *Seavision Investment SA v Evennett, The Tiburon*[113]
and *Gomba Holdings (UK) Ltd v Minories Finance Ltd (No 2)*.[114]

However, the courts will usually exercise this discretion in line with the terms of the indem- **14.91**
nity, and a simple order (as between the parties) as to the level of costs does not prevent the
trustee from claiming costs out of the fund on a higher basis under an indemnity.[115]

---

[109] The number changed from CPR r 48.4 from 1 April 2013. A similar provision was formerly RSC Ord
62, r 6(2), made under s 4(1) of the Courts and Legal Services Act 1990 (formerly s 51 of the Supreme Court
Act 1981).

[110] This seems to allow the court to have some discretion—eg to comply with the overriding objective 'to
deal with cases justly' under CPR r 1.

[111] Although there will be cases—eg involving litigation with non-parties—where the court's discretion over
costs *inter partes* does not obviously apply to the separate question of trustees being able to recover costs out of
a fund. See eg the categories outlined in *Re Buckton* [1907] 2 Ch 406 (Kekewich J) and *Singapore Airlines Ltd v
Buck Consultants Ltd* [2011] EWCA Civ 1542, CA.

[112] CPR r 44.3(3).

[113] [1992] 2 Lloyd's Rep 26, CA.

[114] [1993] Ch 171, CA.

[115] Similarly, an order confirming that the trustee can recover costs out of the fund does not prevent the
trustee claiming under an indemnity from the employer—*Alitalia-Linee Aeree Italiane SPA v Rotunno* [2008]
EWHC 185 (Ch) at [97] (Henderson J).

14.92 Millett LJ in *Armitage v Nurse*[116] held that:

> As Ungoed-Thomas J pointed out in *Re Spurling's Will Trusts* [1966] 1 All ER 745 at 758–759, it is not enough to deprive trustees of their right to recoup their costs out of the trust fund that the claim is a claim to recover money from them for the benefit of the trust. If the trustees succeed, then the claim was not well founded, and they cannot be denied their right of recoupment. I would add that even if the claim succeeds, yet they may not have so conducted themselves as to lose their right of recoupment.

Can an Indemnity be Included or Changed in an Existing Scheme?

14.93 Pension trusts usually have a wide express amendment power, usually requiring the employer and the trustees to agree.[117]

14.94 Care is obviously needed before trustees agree to a change in an existing indemnity to give them wider protection against the fund or the members than before. The trustees owe a fiduciary duty to exercise their powers for a proper purpose, usually in the best interests of the scheme. Clearly this means that they will need to justify any extension of an exoneration or indemnity—why is this for a proper purpose—ie in the best interests of the scheme?

14.95 One answer may be that otherwise trustees are not prepared to come forward. This argument was upheld by Lord Hope in the Court of Session in *Governors of Dollar Academy Trust v Lord Advocate*[118] to allow an amendment to a charity to allow for trustee insurance, to be paid out of the funds of the charity.

14.96 Such a change to an existing scheme does not seem to require consent or certification under s 67 of the Pensions Act 1995[119]—accrued rights (ie benefits) are not affected (at least prior to winding-up).

Can the solicitor who drafted the clause rely on it?

14.97 In *Bogg v Raper*[120] a solicitor had advised his client to include in his will an exoneration clause protecting the executors. The solicitor then became one of the executors. The Court of Appeal (including Millett LJ who gave the leading judgment in *Armitage v Nurse*) held that he could still benefit from the exoneration clause. It was not a sufficient benefit for the solicitor that he should be prevented from relying on it (although it would be 'otherwise if the draftsman inserted the provision without drawing the settlor's attention to it and knowing that the settlor did not realise its effect').

14.98 No challenge was made to the clause on the basis of public policy—*Armitage v Nurse* stands in the way of that. There is a discussion of the precise interpretation of the clause concerned. See also *Walker v Stones*.[121]

---

[116] [1998] Ch 241, CA.
[117] See Ch 17 (Amendment powers).
[118] [1995] SLT 596, CSOH.
[119] See Ch 17 (Amendment powers).
[120] (1998) 1 ITELR 267, [1998] CLY 4592, CA.
[121] [2001] QB 902, CA.

Indemnities from the Sponsoring Employer

It is common for a trustee, given the onerous nature of his office, also to seek an indemnity **14.99** from the employer to re-enforce the indemnity out of the assets of the scheme. The points made above in relation to an indemnity from the assets should still apply, although the public policy issues (as to whether or not a wide indemnity negates the position of being a trustee) should not be relevant.[122]

An indemnity from the employer can be wider than indemnities out of the fund. In particular, **14.100** an indemnity from an employer can cover trustee insurance and civil fines and penalties (where these cannot be paid out of the trust fund because of the Pensions Acts). They are also easier to put in place compared to an amendment to make them payable out of the fund (although this may be justifiable in some cases—see *Governors of Dollar Academy Trust v Lord Advocate*,[123] discussed at para 14.95 above).

Ultimately, of course, an indemnity is only as good as the ability of the person giving it to pay. **14.101**

Impact of section 33 of the Pensions Act 1995

It is likely that any indemnity from the employer remains subject to the limitations in rela- **14.102** tion to investment functions in s 33 of the Pensions Act 1995 (see para 14.44 above).

This is on the basis that the employer is a beneficiary of the scheme (either expressly or in a **14.103** wider sense as someone liable to top up the scheme—see Chapter 10) and the trustee owes a duty of care to the employer in relation to investment matters. This may mean that an indemnity from the employer cannot apply if it would reduce the trustee's liability to the employer (but perhaps it could apply if the liability is to the members instead).

Generally an indemnity includes implied promise not to sue: *Deepak Fertilisers & Petrochemicals* **14.104** *Ltd v Davy McKee (London) Ltd*.[124] This supports the view that an indemnity operates in the same way as an exclusion clause.

Indemnity to a director of the employer

There are several regulatory issues that do need to be considered, particularly where the trus- **14.105** tee is a director of the relevant company giving the indemnity.

Section 232 of the Companies Act 2006[125] generally prohibits indemnities from a company **14.106** to its directors. However, it is considered that indemnities to a person in his capacity as a pension trustee (or director of a trustee company) are not caught on the basis that s 232 only invalidates indemnities given to directors in relation to breach of duty 'in relation to the company'. When a director acts as a trustee he owes duties to the beneficiaries which are independent of his duties to the company.[126]

---

[122] Given that the employer is a beneficiary of a pension trust (see Ch 10), such an indemnity may be subject to the statutory limitation on indemnities in relation to investment matters in s 33 of the Pensions Act 1995. The limits on indemnities out of the fund in s 256 of the Pensions Act 2004 (formerly s 31 of the Pensions Act 1995) will not apply to restrict or prohibit such an indemnity from the employer.

[123] [1995] SLT 596, CSOH.

[124] [1999] 1 All ER (Comm) 69, CA.

[125] This replaced s 310 of the Companies Act 1985 on and from 1 October 2007.

[126] See eg the *Kuwait Asia* case [1991] 1 AC 187, PC.

14.107 *Burgoine v London Borough of Waltham Forest*[127] gives comfort that indemnities from employer companies to trustees (or directors of a trustee company) will not be struck down if the trustee is also a director of the company. Neuberger J held that s 310 of the Companies Act 1985 only applies to indemnities granted by the company itself. Indemnities granted by third parties (eg a parent company) are not caught.

14.108 This helps the case of directors of corporate trustees. It still leaves the issue of the impact of s 232 where the individual trustee is also a director of the employer (or the trustee company is an associated company with the employer). The better view here is that s 232 does not apply because the indemnity is not being given to the trustee (or trustee director) in relation to any breach of duty owed to the employer (instead it relates to a breach of duty owed to the trust).

14.109 Indemnities for directors are permitted in certain circumstances, including if they are:

(a) a permitted type of insurance; or
(b) a 'qualifying pension scheme indemnity provision' (QPSIP)—s 235. This is a provision indemnifying a director of a company that is a trustee of an occupational pension scheme against liability incurred in connection with the company's activities as trustee of the scheme.

14.110 This addresses a concern that an indemnity provided by an employer for a director of a pension scheme trustee company would be void if that person were also a director of the employer. Any indemnity in favour of the trustee directors by the trust company itself may also need to be a QPSIP (although it is arguable that this is not an indemnity from the trustee company itself but a right to claim on the fund directly).

14.111 A sponsoring company of a pension scheme can therefore use a QPSIP to indemnify a trustee director of a corporate trustee against liability incurred in connection with the company's activities as trustee of the scheme.

Requirements of a QPSIP

14.112 The QPSIP is similar to the qualifying third-party indemnity provision exemption previously available. For example, the indemnity must not cover:

(a) liability to pay a fine imposed in criminal proceedings;
(b) any sum payable to a regulatory authority as a penalty for non-compliance with a regulatory requirement; or
(c) any liability of a director in defending criminal proceedings in which he is convicted.

14.113 In contrast with a qualifying third-party indemnity provision (under s 234), QPSIPs may cover costs in defending civil proceedings brought against the director by the company or an associated company in which judgment is given against him.

14.114 QPSIPs must be disclosed in the directors' reports of the trustee company and the company providing the indemnity. A copy of the QPSIP must be kept at the registered office and available for a year after it has expired or terminated. This may involve companies keeping copies of extracts from scheme trust deeds if the QPSIP is in the trust document. In addition, shareholders have a right to request a copy of the QPSIP.

---

[127] [1997] BCC 347 (Neuberger J).

Section 190 of the Companies Act 2006[128] provides for shareholder approval to be necessary for the acquisition by a director from a company of a substantial non-cash asset over a particular value. It is considered that s 190 does not apply to the grant of an indemnity from a company to a pension trustee. The indemnity given to a director is in effect a cash asset. This is despite the extended definition of non-cash asset in s 1163 of the 2006 Act (formerly s 739(2) of the 1985 Act). Section 1163(2) does not mean that the grant of an indemnity to a director is in fact the acquisition of a non-cash asset by the director provided the indemnity is given to the director himself and the company does not discharge the director's liability to a third party direct—*Gooding v Cater*.[129]   **14.115**

Conflict of interest: The director will need to ensure that provisions relating to conflicts of interest in relation to the company are complied with. In particular, notice of the director's interest in the indemnity may need to be given to the board of directors of the company[130] and any relevant provisions (quorum, voting etc) in the articles of association must be complied with.   **14.116**

Listed companies: In relation to listed companies, consideration will need to be given to the listing rules. The grant of the indemnity to a director of the listed company or any of its associates (potentially including the trustee company if it is a subsidiary of the employer) is a transaction involving a related party, which may mean that there is a need for shareholder consent or extra disclosure requirements.[131] However, there is an exemption for an indemnity to directors (and related insurance) to the extent that it is not in contravention of the Companies Act 2006.[132] This should apply to exempt indemnities etc in favour of trustees (or directors of a corporate trustee) who are also directors of the employer or another group company.   **14.117**

Accounting points: There may also be accounting issues in relation to disclosure in the audited accounts of the company of the existence of such indemnity in favour of a director.   **14.118**

Tax issues: Generally there may also be tax considerations should payments ever actually be made by the company to trustees while they are employees of the company. In order for such payments not to be taxed, it would be necessary to show either that the liabilities incurred by the employee had been incurred necessarily in performance of his or her duties (this may be difficult) or instead that the payment was not to the individual as an employee, but rather in a different capacity (namely, a trustee).   **14.119**

Further Drafting Points

When drafting an indemnity, it should be made clear that the indemnity only applies to the extent that the trustee is not in fact able to recover from other sources. It is better if it is made clear whether an indemnity from the employer should not apply if the trustee is not able to recover from the trust fund (eg in relation to general liabilities).   **14.120**

---

[128] Replacing s 320 of the Companies Act 1985 with effect on and from 1 October 2007.
[129] (1989) 13 May (Edward Nugee QC, sitting as a deputy Judge of the High Court). Cited in *Micro Leisure Ltd v County Properties & Developments Ltd* (CSOH, Lord Hamilton) (1999) 19 January.
[130] Companies Act 2006, s 182 (formerly Companies Act 1985, s 317).
[131] Listing Rule 11.
[132] Listing Rule 11, Annex 1, Rule 5.

14.121   For example, in *Alitalia-Linee Aeree Italiane SPA v Rotunno*,[133] Henderson J held that an express indemnity from the employer was the primary obligation and applied even though the trustee also had an indemnity out of the fund. This meant that the trustee was able to claim the costs of it defending the legal proceedings (as to the meaning of the contribution rule) even though the employer's interpretation was upheld. Henderson J considered that the point was a timing one (presumably on the basis that costs taken out of the fund would reduce the fund and so ultimately increase the amounts payable by the employer). He held that this would apply even if the scheme was in surplus and would be able to meet the expense without requiring further funding.

In *Oakhurst*,[134] Gabriel Moss QC noted that counsel had conceded that an indemnity from the employer was not subject to a limit based on claiming out of trust assets first. He held that: 'After I had referred Mr Wilson to the Court of Appeal decision of *Byblos Bank SAL the Al-Khudhairy* (1986) 2 BCC 99, 549 (CA), which requires very clear evidence for such a condition precedent to be established, even where the liability is secondary, Mr Wilson very sensibly abandoned the point'.

14.122   In addition, it is now becoming common for trustees to be able to take out insurance[135] for their own liability (perhaps at the cost of the fund—if so then there probably needs to be an express power to that effect[136] or at least a provision allowing trustees to be paid).

14.123   Consideration should also be given as to whether any indemnity from the company should make it clear that it does not apply to the extent that recovery is made from an insurer.[137] This should stop an insurer which has paid on a claim made by a trustee to then bring a claim against the company (either by subrogating to the trustee's right or on the basis of a right of contribution).

14.124   When drafting the clause consider how far the clause may continue to apply even if the employer terminates liability to make contributions to the scheme. Similar issues arise in relation to any obligation on an employer to pay the expenses of the scheme. Do such obligations survive even despite an express clause allowing termination of contributions? It may be arguable (depending on the wording of the deed) that 'contributions' do not in fact include an indemnity or expense provision. Accordingly, when acting for a company, it is prudent to ensure that there is an express cross-reference to the termination provision (if this is intended).

14.125   Generally, consider how the liability of the employers (if there is more than one) is to be allocated. Are all the employers to be jointly and severally liable? If so, is this only to be as against the trustees, with liability between the employers being apportioned by someone (say the principal company?).

---

[133] [2008] EWHC 185 (Ch) (Henderson J).

[134] *Oakhurst Property Developments (Lowndes Square No 2) Ltd v Blackstar (Isle of Man) Ltd* [2013] EWHC 1363 (Ch) at [93] (Gabriel Moss QC).

[135] On trustee insurance, see Mark Howard, 'Pension Trustee Liability Insurance' (2011) 25 TLI 99.

[136] See *Kemble v Hicks (No 2)* [1999] EWHC 301 (Ch), [1999] OPLR 1 (Rimer J); *Leadenhall Independent Trustees Ltd v Welham* [2004] EWHC 740 (Ch), [2004] OPLR 115 (Park J); and *NBPF Pension Trustees Ltd v Warnock-Smith* [2008] EWHC 455 (Ch), [2008] 2 All ER (Comm) 740 (Floyd J).

[137] Eg clause 47 in the Industry-Wide Coal Staff Superannuation Scheme, as set out in the Industry-Wide Coal Staff Superannuation Scheme Regulations 1994 (SI 1994/2973).

Generally, drafters should seek express instructions from the employer before including such **14.126** an indemnity. It is not necessarily something to be included as a standard.

It is an open point how far a person seeking to challenge use of an indemnity provision by a **14.127** trustee (eg a beneficiary or the employer) could seek to have the trustee's costs taxed by the court.[138]

Power of the Court to Relieve: Section 61 of the Trustee Act 1925

The court has power, under s 61 of the Trustee Act 1925,[139] to relieve a trustee from liability **14.128** where it is believed that the trustee acted honestly and reasonably and ought fairly to be excused. For company directors, there is a similar provision in s 1157 of the Companies Act 2006.[140]

This is quite a high standard and will not readily be available. Relief is only given rarely. **14.129** Trustees will be cautious about the relief applying.[141] The trustee must be shown to have acted reasonably.[142] Merely taking advice, without more, is not necessarily a 'passport to relief' under s 61—*Marsden v Regan*.[143]

The courts have not shown themselves particularly minded to grant equitable relief (under **14.130** s 61) to fiduciaries in a conflict situation. Thus relief was not given in *Boardman v Phipps*[144] nor (under the equivalent provision for directors) in *Guinness v Saunders*.[145]

In a pensions context, relief was refused by the Pensions Ombudsman in Adams[146] and in **14.131** *McCann*.[147] Lord Hope in the Court of Session in Scotland in *Governors of Dollar Academy Trust v Lord Advocate*[148] noted the limitations of the statutory protection. He did not think that it provided a satisfactory alternative to contractual insurance cover.

However, for examples of pensions cases where relief was allowed, see *Kemp v Sims*[149] and **14.132** (under the equivalent New Zealand section) Thomas J in *Jones v AMP Perpetual Trustee Co NZ Ltd*.[150] See generally on this power, the 2011 paper 'The Repentant Trustee' by Justice PA Bergin.[151]

---

[138] See for instance *Gomba Holdings* [1992] 4 All ER 588, CA.

[139] In Scotland, see s 32 of the Trusts (Scotland) Act 1921.

[140] Previously s 727 of the Companies Act 1985.

[141] Eg relief was refused in New Zealand in the private trust case, *Re Mulligan, Hampton v PGG Trust Ltd* [1998] 1 NZLR 481 (Panckhurst J), a case on breach of trust by a professional trustee in relation to investment.

[142] See eg two Court of Appeal cases involving solicitors: *Nationwide Building Society v Davisons Solicitors* [2012] EWCA Civ 1626, CA (relief given) and *Lloyds TSB Bank plc v Markandan & Uddin (a firm)* [2012] EWCA Civ 65, [2012] 2 All ER 884, CA (relief not given).

[143] [1954] 1 All ER 475 at 482, CA.

[144] *Boardman v Phipps* [1967] 2 AC 46, HL.

[145] *Guinness v Saunders* [1990] 2 AC 663, HL.

[146] *Adams* (2009) 11 March, M00358 (King PO).

[147] *Re the SureStock Pension Scheme, McCann v Campbell* (2010) 16 August, 26791/4 (Irvine Deputy PO).

[148] [1995] SLT 596 (Lord Hope).

[149] [2008] EWHC 2579 (Ch), [2009] 034 PBLR (Norris J).

[150] [1995] PLR 53 (Thomas J).

[151] Available on the NSW Supreme Court website: <http://www.supremecourt.lawlink.nsw.gov.au/ agdbasev7wr/supremecourt/documents/pdf/bergin180211.pdf>. See also the comments in David Halpern QC, 'Exoneration Clauses for Trustees and Directors and Statutory Relief from Liability' (2012) 26 TLI 32.

Corporate Trustees

14.133 See generally Chapter 5 ('Liabilities of directors of corporate trustees'). In *HR v JAPT*[152] Lindsay J confirmed that directors of a trustee company were not automatically liable for breaches of trust committed by the trustee company (even if they were involved in it). In order for a trustee director to become directly liable to a beneficiary affected, dishonesty would need to be shown.

14.134 Dishonesty is assessed using the test in *Royal Brunei v Tan* (see above) and involves a director acting by reference to an unacceptable standard (measured objectively). For an example of the application of this to a dishonest director of a trustee company, see the decision of Hart J and the Court of Appeal in *Wakelin v Read*.[153]

Companies Act limits

14.135 Section 232 of the Companies Act 2006[154] avoids any provision (whether in the articles of association or any contract with the company or otherwise) that purports to exempt a director to any extent from any liability that would otherwise attach to him in connection with any negligence, default, breach of duty, or breach of trust in relation to the company.

14.136 Section 232(3) exempts various indemnities and s 232(4) provides that nothing in s 232 prevents a company's articles from making 'such provision as has previously been lawful for dealing with conflicts of interest'—see Chapter 6 ('Conflict issues for pension trustees').

14.137 The effect of s 232 is that an exoneration in favour of a director of a corporate trustee may be ineffective (save for the exceptions allowed). But this only applies to a liability etc of the director to the trustee company. Not to a liability in relation to (say) a beneficiary of the underlying trust. So if the trustee company has no liability (eg because of an exoneration or indemnity provision in favour of the trustee company), it will usually be the case that the individual director has no liability.

Drafting: extend exoneration to cover directors

14.138 It would be prudent to provide in the relevant scheme trust deed that any relevant exoneration or indemnity expressly covers directors of a corporate trustee.

14.139 It seems likely that the director may well not be under any liability in the first place if the trustee company can rely on the indemnity or exoneration itself—see the discussion in Chapter 5.

14.140 In New Zealand, in *McNulty v McNulty*,[155] Osborne AJ followed the decision of Lindsay J in the *HR* case and held that a claim against a director of a corporate trustee should be struck out as on the facts no direct fiduciary duty or tort duty arose on the director. The trustee company was connected with a firm of solicitors who also acted for various other beneficiaries. Osborne AJ held that the trustee company was permitted to have such a conflict by reason

---

[152] [1997] OPLR 123, [1997] PLR 99 (Lindsay J).
[153] [1998] OPLR 147, [1998] PLR 337 (Hart J) and [2000] PLR 319, [2000] OPLR 277, CA.
[154] Previously Companies Act 1985, s 310 and before that Companies Act 1929, s 129.
[155] [2011] NZHC 1173 (Osborne AJ).

of an express provision in the trust deed. Osborne AJ went on to hold that if the trustee company (GCA) was so protected, this protection must apply to the director (Mr Gowing) as well. He held, at [76]:

> By reason of my finding in relation to GCA, namely that GCA had not committed a breach of fiduciary duty by acting in an arguably conflicted situation because cl 14.1 permitted such an event, Mr Gowing can be in no different a position. The plaintiffs pleaded that he was the person responsible for directing the professional trustee company. If he thereby personally had an arguable responsibility as a matter of trust law to carry out the terms of the trust, then he equally had the benefit (or burden) of clauses by which the trust deed defined or limited responsibilities.

> I would therefore find on this ground alone that the second cause of action as against Mr Gowing is untenable.

Expressly extending any indemnity so that it covers directors is common. The aim is that it will help counter any argument that the director owes the usual corporate duties to the trustee company (which is then obliged to enforce them against the directors) and cannot take advantage of any exoneration clause (applying only to the trustee company). **14.141**

Charles Mitchell[156] noted the potential distinction between clauses that exclude any duty arising on the trustee company in the first place from those clauses that just limit the liability. But he went on to argue that even in the second case a third party (ie here a director) might escape liability on the ground that: **14.142**

> dishonest assistants are jointly and severally liable with the wrongdoing trustees or fiduciaries whose breaches of trust they assist, with the consequence that the release of the trustee or fiduciary should also operate to release those with whom he is jointly and severally liable.

Mummery LJ commented in *Wakelin v Read*[157] that any attempt to make the director (Mr Read) liable as joint tortfeasor with the trustee company would be met by reliance on the exoneration clause in the trust deed (which was expressly stated to cover directors, officers, and employees of a corporate trustee). **14.143**

It is therefore prudent practice to provide in any trust deed for any exclusion clause to be expressly stated to apply to trustee directors. It is unlikely, however, that any exclusion clause will have a wider scope and cover 'dishonesty'. **14.144**

Can the director enforce an indemnity from the fund or from the employer?

There are two main issues here: **14.145**

(a) the director is not likely to be an express party to the trust instrument—so how does he or she enforce the indemnity?
(b) the effect of the indemnity may be to exonerate the director from the liabilities he or she would otherwise owe to the trustee company. Does this run contrary to the limits in the Companies legislation?

---

156 In his chapter 'Assistance' in P Birks and A Pretto (eds), *Breach of Trust* (Hart Publishing, 2002) 159 and 208
157 [2000] OPLR 277 at 285G, CA.

14.146   In relation to the party point, this does not seem to have been raised in any of the reported cases. It seems likely that the indemnity would be enforceable by the director:

(a) against the employer on the basis that either:

  (i) the indemnity is a contractual claim and so can be enforced by the director under the Contracts (Rights of Third Parties) Act 1999.[158] This analysis does depend on the trust instrument being considered to be a contract—and so could be considered to be inconsistent with the analysis that trusts are not generally contracts and so contract law (eg the Unfair Contract Terms Act 1977 (UCTA)) does not apply—see the discussion above of the Court of Appeal decisions in *Duke of Norfolk's Settlement Trusts*[159] (where it was considered that liabilities under a private (non-pension) trust could not be considered to be contractual) and *Baker v JE Clark & Co*[160] (where an exoneration clause (in a personal pension plan) applying unless there was bad faith was upheld and it was held that UCTA could not apply to trusts); or

  (ii) the trustee is a party to the trust instrument/contract and can (and should) enforce the indemnity against the employer on the basis that it holds the right as trustee for the director;

(b) against the trust fund on the basis that either:

  (i) the director is a beneficiary of the trust (in the same way as a trustee—see *Chief Commissioner of Stamp Duties v Buckle*,[161] where the High Court in Australia confirmed the right of trustees to be indemnified out of trust assets against liabilities properly incurred in the administration of the trust. This right is not a charge or encumbrance on the assets, but instead is a preferred beneficial interest in the trust fund); or

  (ii) the trustee is a party to the trust instrument/contract and can (and should) enforce the indemnity against the trust fund on the basis that it holds the right as trustee for the director.

Indemnity from a Member: *Hardoon v Belilios*

14.147   It is also possible that a trustee will be able to take the benefit of a personal indemnity from a beneficiary (eg a member) where that member has instigated a course of action by the trustee.

14.148   This is the principle in *Hardoon v Belilios*.[162] It has been applied in a pensions context in relation to a scheme with just one member: *Independent Trustee Services Ltd v Rowe*.[163]

14.149   It is perhaps most likely to apply where there is a money purchase scheme and the member gives directions in relation to his or her account.

---

[158] The 1999 Act allows persons not identified at the date of the contract to enforce it.
[159] [1982] Ch 61, CA.
[160] [2006] EWCA Civ 464, CA.
[161] [1998] HCA 4, 192 CLR 226, HC Aus.
[162] [1901] AC 118, PC. See in Australia: *Balkin v Peck* (1998) 43 NSWLR 706, NSWCA; *Causley v Countryside (No 3) Pty Ltd* (1996), 2 September 1996, NSWCA; and *JW Broomhead (Vic) Pty Ltd v JW Broomhead Pty Ltd* [1985] VicRp 88, [1985] VR 891 (McGarvie J). Discussed in RA Hughes, 'The Right of a Trustee to a Personal Indemnity From Beneficiaries' (1990) 64 ALJ 567 and HAJ Ford, 'Trading Trusts and Creditors' Rights' [1981] Melbourne University Law Review 1, (1981–82) 13 MULR 1.
[163] [1998] OPLR 77 at 98 (Parker J).

CONTRACT OVERRIDING TRUST: *SOUTH WEST TRAINS*

This chapter looks at the position for an occupational pension scheme where an employer **15.1** and a member enter into a contract for reduced benefits. In the leading case, *South West Trains v Wightman*,[1] Neuberger J (as he then was) held such a contract to be binding on the trustee (and the member).

Contracts and Trusts

It is, of course, generally true that a contract will override a trust or fiduciary relationship. This is **15.2** clearly true in the sense that trust or fiduciary duties are often default rules and so are subject to exclusion or modification by the relevant trust instrument or contract.

---

[1] [1997] EWHC 1160 (Ch), [1997] OPLR 249 (Neuberger J).

15.3 The existence of a contract will usually mean that the fiduciary obligations must take subject to this. Lord Browne-Wilkinson held in *Kelly v Cooper*[2] (in relation to the fiduciary duties of an agent): 'The existence and scope of these duties depends upon the terms on which they are acting.'

15.4 In the same case the Privy Council approved the well-known statement in the Australian High Court of Mason J in *Hospital Products Ltd v United States Surgical Corporation*:[3]

> That contractual and fiduciary relationships may co-exist between the same parties has never been doubted. Indeed, the existence of a basic contractual relationship has in many situations provided a foundation for the erection of a fiduciary relationship. In these situations it is the contractual foundation which is all important because it is the contract that regulates the basic rights and liabilities of the parties. The fiduciary relationship, if it is to exist at all, must accommodate itself to the terms of the contract so that it is consistent with, and conforms to, them. The fiduciary relationship cannot be superimposed upon the contract in such a way as to alter the operation which the contract was intended to have according to its true construction.

15.5 In *Solicitors Indemnity Fund v Paul*[4] Mummery LJ said 'The express and implied terms of the agreement define the scope of the fiduciary duties arising from the joint venture created by it: *Kelly v Cooper*'[5].

15.6 What happens where the employer and member in relation to a pension scheme agree to a variation of the benefits that are payable out of the scheme? This will usually be contained in a contract between the member (as employee) and the employer. The trustee is not a party. Does the contract bind the member and the employer in a way that means that the trustee must operate the trust on the basis as modified in the contract?

15.7 Where the effect of the contractual agreement would be to reduce benefits, it is clear that the trustee, once having notice of the agreement, must operate the trust to comply with its terms (even if this would otherwise be inconsistent with the terms of the trust).

15.8 If the effect of the arrangement was to increase benefits, this would potentially impact on the other members of the scheme (because the liabilities would go up). Such an augmentation of benefits will almost always be expressly provided for under the terms of the scheme, but often only with the consent of the trustee (or payment of extra funds as required by the trustee). So the agreement between the member and the employer may not have direct effect under the scheme, ie it may not be effective unless the trustee consents.

15.9 It can be argued that such an external arrangement should not (even if reducing benefits) be binding on the trustee (or the pension scheme) on the basis that the trustee should follow the express terms of the scheme and not (absent a formal amendment) an external agreement.[6]

---

[2] [1993] AC 205 at 214, PC. See also in Australia *ASIC v Citigroup Global Markets* [2007] FCA 963 (Jacobson J). For a contrarian view, see Mark Leeming, 'The Scope of Fiduciary Obligations: How the Contract Informs, But Does Not Determine the Scope of Fiduciary Obligations' (2009) 3 J Eq 181.

[3] [1984] HCA 64, (1984) 156 CLR 41, 97 (High Court of Australia). Subsequently cited in the UK by the Court of Appeal in *Ranson v Customer Systems plc* [2012] EWCA Civ 841, [2012] IRLR 769 and in *Generics (UK) Ltd v Yeda Research & Development Co Ltd* [2012] EWCA Civ 726, CA.

[4] Cited by Lewison J in *Fattal v Walbrook Trustees (Jersey) Ltd* [2010] EWHC 2767 (Ch) at [111].

[5] [1993] AC 205 at 213H–215D, PC.

[6] Eg Sandip Maudgil, 'Benefit Changes and the Employment Contract' (2009) APL conference and Robert Ham QC and Jonathan Hilliard expressing doubts at an APL seminar: 'A Runaway Train or Stuck in the Sidings? South West Trains v Wightman After Bradbury and IBM' (APL seminar, 2012).

But this is misguided and clearly not what the courts have been finding. In most schemes: **15.10**

(a) the genesis of the scheme itself is an external arrangement (the underlying employment of the member by the employer);
(b) the scheme itself envisages external factors applying (eg in the case of a defined benefit scheme offering benefits based on the member's salary, the rate of salary (as from time to time agreed between the member and the employer) has a direct impact on the benefits); and
(c) an individual member has various rights under the scheme (and statute), for example to require a transfer payment to another arrangement.

Given this there seems little reason for the scheme not to give effect to an external agreement. **15.11**

It can be argued that these external factors are at least expressly provided for under the scheme. But this looks not really to be a material difference. If the trustee is already required by the governing documents and statute to look outside the four corners of the scheme at external agreements, why should it not also be bound by an express agreement to reduce benefits? **15.12**

For example, in trust law generally, the rule in *Saunders v Vautier* can allow the beneficiaries (acting together) to terminate the trust, despite any provisions of the trust (although normally trustee consent is needed if the trust is to change, rather than terminate).[7] Figure 15.1 shows this tripartite relationship. **15.13**

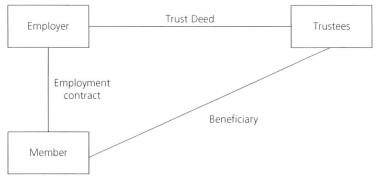

Figure 15.1

It is important to remember the basic tripartite structure involved in a pension scheme.[8] It can be easy to get confused and import trust-like duties onto the external contract (outside the trust) between the member and the employer.[9] **15.14**

It has also been argued that it is difficult for the trustee to rely on an external contract when it is not a party to that contract[10] and when the courts have shown that they are **15.15**

---

7   See Ch 16 (*Saunders v Vautier*).
8   See Ch 1 (What is an occupational pension scheme?).
9   It is arguable that Arnold J in the IMG case, *HR Trustees Ltd v German* [2009] EWHC 2785 (Ch) mixed these up in some of his obiter comments. This is discussed below.
10 Nigel Burroughs 'Pensions and External Contracts' (2012) Practical Law for Companies.

reluctant to allow changes to a trust outside the strict terms of the trust (on the basis that the trustee and the beneficiaries should be able to look to the trust instrument for its terms).[11]

15.16 The contract point seems to misunderstand that the trustees are not being asked to rely on a contract but rather to comply with it. The strict terms argument is interesting, but it seems odd in a pensions context, where many of the terms of a pension scheme are found externally, eg in statute or by looking at the underlying employment relationship (eg for amount of salary, when the employment ceases, discrimination issues). And it seems a weak reason to seek to invalidate a valid contract.

The Legal Issues

15.17 The simplest modification by an external contract is for the employer and the employee (member) in effect to agree that all or part of a pay rise will be non-pensionable. In difficult economic times, many employers who operate final salary pension schemes have been looking at ways to reduce the costs relating to those schemes.

New hires

15.18 New employees can be provided with different benefits from current employees fairly easily. All that is needed is for the offer of employment to be clear about what will be made available. This can (for example) involve closing the final salary scheme to new entrants and replacing it with a money purchase scheme.

15.19 This does not raise any legal issues—provided the practice does not result in unlawful discrimination (eg on the basis of indirect age, sex, or race discrimination).

Existing members: non-pensionable pay rises

15.20 An employer may want to reduce the costs of providing final salary benefits for existing employees.

15.21 A simple pay rise generally applies (depending on the definition of 'pensionable pay' in the scheme) to all the final salary benefits payable under a pension scheme. Employers could expressly make all or part of future non-contractual pay rises non-pensionable, or make the pay rise pensionable only on a reduced basis. For example:

- pensionable at a reduced accrual rate;
- pensionable for future service only; or
- pensionable on a money purchase basis.

15.22 In effect, the employee would be offered the pay rise on special terms. This will usually have more limited legal implications than other changes to pension benefits. It could also have a significant cost impact for the pension scheme.

---

[11] Eg the amendment cases: *Bestrustees v Stuart* [2001] OPLR 341 (Neuberger J) and at first instance *Trustee Solutions Ltd v Dubery* [2006] EWHC 1426 (Ch); [2007] 1 All ER 308 at [19] (Lewison J).

Example

Current position

An employee has 10 years' service in a 1/60th final salary pension scheme.

His salary is £15,000, so his accrued pension is:

10 × 1/60 × £15,000 = £2,500pa

Employee given a pensionable pay rise

If the employee gets a 5% pay rise (to £15,750) and works an extra year, his benefit rises to a pension of:

11 × 1/60 × £15,750 = £2,887.50pa

This is a *15.5%* rise in the benefit. This is attributable to the 10% rise in pensionable service (from 10 years to 11) and the 5% rise in pensionable pay.

Employee given a non-pensionable pay rise

If the pay rise was made non pensionable then his accrued pension is:

11 × 1/60 × £15,000 = £2,750.00pa

The increase in pension is limited to *10%* (the increase in the length of pensionable service).

This cost saving would apply to all active members, so could be significant.

The contractual position

Changing the pension benefits provided to existing employees is more difficult than changing the benefits offered to new employees, both from a legal and a human relations perspective. Existing employees may have an express or implied contractual right to be a member of the pension scheme. Even if the employer has reserved the right to terminate or amend the pension scheme at any time, the exercise of that right will be subject to the 'Imperial' duties—the implied duty of mutual trust and confidence.[12] **15.23**

Express contractual agreement with the employee will be enough to reduce benefit accrual— *Bradbury v BBC*.[13] A variation to the employee's contract allowed by collective bargaining through trade union representation can also cover pensions—*Tibbals*[14] and *South West Trains*.[15] **15.24**

Signing a contract, even where stating this to be 'under duress' (and writing this on the acceptance) will still be binding—*Hepworth Heating Ltd v Akers*.[16] **15.25**

Employees will rarely have a contractual right to a pay rise. There are therefore unlikely to be any contractual restrictions on an employer awarding a pay rise on the condition that all or part of it shall be non-pensionable. **15.26**

---

[12] See Ch 13 (Employer powers: the implied duty of trust and confidence).
[13] [2012] EWHC 1369 (Ch) (Warren J).
[14] *Tibbals v Port of London Authority* [1937] 2 All ER 413, HL.
[15] [1997] EWHC 1160 (Ch), [1997] OPLR 249 (Neuberger J). Authority from the employee to the union can be implied in some cases—see eg *Henry v London General* [2001] IRLR 132 and *Peck v FirstGroup plc* (2008) 9 October, S00537 (King PO).
[16] [2003] All ER (D) 33 (Jul), EAT.

15.27 An employee will not need to agree expressly that the pay rise is non-pensionable. There will usually be an implied consent and contract if the employee continues to work (and receive increased pay), as long as the employer makes it clear that the pay rise offer is only made on the basis that it is wholly or partly non-pensionable.

15.28 In 2002 in *Trustees of the NUS Officials' and Employees' Superannuation Fund v The Pensions Ombudsman*,[17] an employee, an official at a trade union, was sent a letter offering him a pay rise on the basis that it would be non-pensionable. He wrote back to the employer (the union) stating that he did not accept that the pay rise was non-pensionable, but he continued to work and accepted the increased pay.

15.29 On appeal to the High Court, Lightman J decided that the employee had impliedly accepted the increase in his pay on the terms set out in the employer's letter. The employee could not pick and choose. Either he took the pay rise subject to the limitation or he was not entitled to the pay rise at all. This is supported by the 1937 decision of the House of Lords in *Tibbals v Port of London Authority*.[18]

15.30 Sandeep Maugil has pointed out[19] that these decisions have perhaps two rationales:

(a) that these cases are concerned with the identification of what is pay for the purposes of the scheme. So that must be something that the employer and member must agree (as an external matter) and so the scheme (and the trustee) must operate subject to that external agreement. This was argued in *South West Trains*, but did not form the ultimate basis for the decision; and

(b) a broader principle that the courts will stop someone from claiming against a third party when he or she has contractually agreed not to and the other contracting party—here the employer—has an interest in restraining the claim. This would follow the decisions in *Snelling*[20] and *Temple*[21] and seems to have been the clear basis for the decision of Neuberger J in *South West Trains*.

Need for a Contract

15.31 The usual requirements for a contract need to be satisfied, for example consideration and an intent to create legal relations—*IMG*.[22] This will quite often be relatively easy to find in an employment relationship, but an employee signing a form which is vague (and refers to other documents such as booklets) may well not be enough—*IMG*[23] and *IBM*.[24]

15.32 In *Capita ATL Pension Trustees Ltd v Gellantely*,[25] Henderson J commented:

> For an argument based on contract to get off the ground, it would be necessary to show an intention to create legal relations, offer, acceptance and consideration: compare *South West*

---

[17] [2002] PLR 93, [2002] OPLR 17 (Lightman J).

[18] [1937] 2 All ER 413, HL. First brought to modern attention by Michael Tennet QC, 'Pensions Cases That Time Forgot' (2007) 21 TLI 125.

[19] Sandip Maudgil, 'Benefit Changes and the Employment Contract' (2009) APL conference.

[20] *Snelling v John G Snelling Ltd* [1973] QB 87 (Ormrod J).

[21] *Hirachand Punamchand v Temple* [1911] 2 KB 330, CA.

[22] *Re IMG Pension Plan: HR Trustees Ltd v German* [2009] EWHC 2785 (Ch) (Arnold J).

[23] *Re IMG Pension Plan: HR Trustees Ltd v German* [2009] EWHC 2785 (Ch) (Arnold J).

[24] *Re IBM Pension Plan* [2012] EWHC 2766 (Ch) at [482] (Warren J).

[25] [2011] EWHC 485 (Ch), [2011] All ER (D) 108 (Mar) (Henderson J).

Trains Limited v Wightman [1997] OPLR 249, [1998] PLR 113. In the present case, however, the only form of acceptance that could be relied upon would be the signature and return of the acknowledgement form at the end of the 1995 Announcement. Further, it would be hopeless to argue that merely continuing to work for the same employer after the 1995 proposed changes had in fact been implemented could constitute sufficient consideration to support a contract, given the absence of any provisions in members' contracts of employment relating to pension benefits and the general difficulty of ever persuading a court that continuing to work can constitute consideration for a variation of a contract of employment, let alone for a free-standing extrinsic contract: see for example the decision of the Employment Appeal Tribunal in *Jones v Associated Tunnelling Co Limited* [1981] IRLR 477 at paragraphs 21–23. Accordingly, a pre-requisite of any successful argument founded on contract would have to be the return of signed acknowledgement forms. The position is the same in relation to estoppel, because estoppel by representation would require a representation to be made by the members, and estoppel by convention (or conduct) would need more than mere acquiescence, and in the case of the membership of the Scheme as a whole no such representation or conduct can plausibly be identified. Again, it is only in relation to those members who signed and returned the 1995 acknowledgement form that an argument based on estoppel can properly be advanced.

An employee merely continuing to work following an announcement or notification of changes to his or her employment contract is generally not enough to show consent to the change (or a contract) unless: **15.33**

(a) the change has some immediate practical impact (and is not a change which will only apply in the future); or
(b) the change is by way of a limit to another new benefit being agreed to be provided (eg a pay rise); or
(c) the change is only referable to the new contract; or
(d) the employee is a senior employee (of 'experience and sophistication') who can be taken to have read and accepted any notice or announcement.[26]

The limit that continuing to work is not deemed acceptance of a change not having an immediate practical impact (eg a change to a pension benefit only payable at some time in the future) follows the employment law (not pensions) cases to that effect—*Jones v Associated Tunnelling Co*[27] and *Khatri v Cooperatieve Centrale Raiffeisen- Boerenleenbank.*[28] **15.34**

It is likely that a change having an immediate practical impact (eg a change in take-home pay[29] or (perhaps) a switch to an entirely new scheme[30]) will mean that continuing to work **15.35**

---

[26] *Credit Suisse Asset Management Ltd v Armstrong* [1996] ICR 882, [1996] IRLR 450 at [29], CA on an application for an interim injunction to support a restrictive covenant. But there is no fiduciary duty (even on a senior employee) requiring him or her to accept the changes proposed on the basis that they are in the interests of the company. An employee is free to contract with his employer—*Fish v Dresdner Kleinwort Ltd* [2009] EWHC 2246 (QB), [2009] IRLR 1035 at [28] (Jack J).

[27] [1981] IRLR 477, EAT (Browne-Wilkinson J). See also *Re Leyland Daf* [1995] AC 394 (Lightman J).

[28] [2010] EWCA Civ 397, [2010] IRLR 715, CA.

[29] Eg *Wilson v Lamb* [2007] All ER (D) 485 (Oct), EAT. An element of non-pensionable pay could mean that lower contributions (based on the reduced pensionable pay) are deducted/paid. The employee is likely to be held to have accepted this after quite a short period. The Court of Appeal in *Picken v Lord Balfour* [1945] 1 Ch 90 held that if the employer does not deduct, the employee must still pay (and this is a condition precedent before getting benefits).

[30] But see *FW Farnsworth Ltd v Lacy* [2012] EWHC 2830 (Ch) (Hildyard J).

is deemed acceptance and agreement to a new contract (at least if the employee does not positively object—*Rigby v Ferodo Ltd*[31]).

15.36 The employee's conduct needs to be referable only to the new contract. Elias J in *Solectron Scotland Ltd v Roper*[32] held:

> 30. The fundamental question is this: is the employee's conduct, by continuing to work, only referable to his having accepted the new terms imposed by the employer? That may sometimes be the case. For example, if an employer varies the contractual terms by, for example, changing the wage or perhaps altering job duties and the employees go along with that without protest, then in those circumstances it may be possible to infer that they have by their conduct after a period of time accepted the change in terms and conditions. If they reject the change they must either refuse to implement it or make it plain that by acceding to it, they are doing so without prejudice to their contractual rights. But sometimes the alleged variation does not require any response from the employee at all. In such a case if the employee does nothing, his conduct is entirely consistent with the original contract containing; it is not only referable to his having accepted the new terms. Accordingly, he cannot be taken to have accepted the variation by conduct.

15.37 In *FW Farnsworth Ltd v Lacy*[33] Hildyard J applied *Solectron* and held that a new contract was binding on the employee (Mr Lacy) even though it had not been signed by the employee. This was because the new contract had included new medical benefits on which the employee had claimed. This was only referable to the new contract. Both counsel agreed that to establish such consent it is for the employer to show an 'unequivocal act implying acceptance', citing Jacobs LJ in *Sallem Khatri v Cooperatieve Centrale Raiffeisen-Boerenleenbank BA*.[34]

15.38 On the evidence, Hildyard J held that the employee joining a new personal pension scheme was not unequivocally referable to the new contract. He held (at [73]):

> I would accept, that looked at singly, Mr Lacy's joinder of the scheme in fact provided for by the 2009 Contract was not voluntary and would not be sufficiently clearly and uniquely referable to acceptance of the terms of the 2009 Contract to satisfy the *Solectron* test. The circumstances I have described in paragraph 46 above seem to me to demonstrate, rather, that this act was at least in part, and probably in causative part, referable not to the exercise of a contractual entitlement but to a mandatory policy.

15.39 However, he held (at [74]) that the acceptance of the medical benefits under the new contract was referable only to that new contract:

> By contrast, in my judgment, Mr Lacy's application for PMI in the form mandated by the 2009 Contract, after he had read its terms (however speedily), and without expressing any protest or reservation, is properly to be characterised as an unequivocal act referable only to his having accepted all the terms of the 2009 Contract as and from the date of that application (in March/April 2010).

Pay bargaining

15.40 Offering a non-pensionable pay rise raises the same legal issues as any pay rise (where there is no contractual right). Legally, it would only be challengeable in limited circumstances (eg

---

[31] [1988] ICR 29, HL. A reasonable time to object will be implied: *Shields Furniture Ltd v Goff* [1973] ICR 187. An objection must be clear, but does not have to be vociferous: *Arthur H Wilton Ltd v Peebles* (1994) EAT/835/93.

[32] [2004] IRLR 4 at [30], EAT.

[33] [2012] EWHC 2830 (Ch) (Hildyard J).

[34] [2010] EWCA Civ 397, [2010] IRLR 715, CA. See also *Attrill v Dresdner Kleinwort Ltd* [2012] EWHC 1189 (QB), [2012] IRLR 553 (Owen J), upheld on appeal [2013] EWCA Civ 394, CA.

if it were unlawful sex discrimination or an attempt to force union derecognition). Provided it is carried out properly (eg with due notice), it seems unlikely to be a breach of the implied duty of mutual trust and confidence.

Collective bargaining

Of course, the issue of whether a pay rise is pensionable or non-pensionable may be the subject of collective bargaining (in the same way as the level of pay rise may be) under the employer's arrangements with unions. An obligation to negotiate on pay can include an obligation to negotiate on pensions—see the decision of the Central Arbitration Committee on this in *UNIFI v Union Bank of Nigeria*.[35]   **15.41**

The Position of the Pension Scheme

The trust deed and rules

If the employer makes a pay increase which is expressly stated to be non-pensionable, that will have implications for the pension scheme trustees.   **15.42**

The trust deed and rules of a final salary pension scheme will provide for benefits based on 'pensionable' pay or salary. This definition may be flexible and expressly allow for the employer to designate (or an employer and employee to agree) that certain elements of pay will be non-pensionable. However, the definition may not envisage this, so there may be conflict between the terms of the pay rise awarded to employees and the rules of the pension scheme.   **15.43**

Clearly, in such circumstances, it would be preferable to amend the trust deed (and, if necessary, the members' booklet) in advance to ensure consistency between the agreement reached with employees and the terms of the pension scheme.   **15.44**

However, even if this is not done, the courts have been clear that the pension trust deed will not override the pay rise terms. In 1997 in *South West Trains v Wightman*,[36] Neuberger J (as he then was) held that the trustees will be obliged in any event to administer the members' benefits and contributions in accordance with the contractual agreement reached between the employer and employees.   **15.45**

In *SWT v Wightman*, the unions had reached an agreement with the employer to provide (in the relevant collective bargaining agreement that formed part of the relevant employment contracts) that only part of a pay rise would be pensionable (and only then for future service). The union then sought to argue that the arrangement was not binding on the pension scheme. The court held that the employees were debarred from seeking pensions at a higher rate than had been agreed and that the trustees should execute a deed of amendment to regularize the position.   **15.46**

Contracting out of the state second pension

In the case of a scheme that is contracted-out of the state second pension, actuarial advice will be needed to ensure that the scheme continues to comply with the reference scheme test. Depending on the benefit level, this may not be a problem in practice.   **15.47**

---

[35] [2001] IRLR 712 (CAC).
[36] [1997] EWHC 1160 (Ch), [1997] OPLR 249, [1998] PLR 113 (Neuberger J).

Record keeping

15.48 If non-pensionable pay rises are awarded, it will be essential for the employer to maintain proper records of the pensionable and non-pensionable elements of each employee's remuneration, and make them available to the pension scheme administrators.

Do the pension scheme trustees need to consent to the change?

15.49 There are two broad approaches open to employers wishing to implement changes in relation to the pensionability of pay rises:

(a) amending the scheme rules (which most commonly requires obtaining the pension scheme trustees' consent); or

(b) entering into a contractual agreement with employees outside the pension scheme (followed by a confirmatory amendment to the scheme rules).

15.50 Pension scheme trustees may be reluctant to become involved in changes relating to pay, viewing it as part of the employee's benefits package that is more appropriately negotiated directly between the employer and its workforce. They may also be constrained by restrictions in the scheme's amendment power.

15.51 The second approach outlined above is helpful in these circumstances. This follows the principle established in *South West Trains v Wightman.*[37]

Potential Pitfalls

Check contracts of employment

15.52 Employees may have an express or implied contractual right to be members of the pension scheme or even that pay rises should be pensionable.

15.53 Whether a benefit is contractual will depend on the wording of the particular contract of employment. The general rule is that benefits promised to employees will be contractual, unless the employer clearly states that they are discretionary, ex gratia, or merely a statement of intent.

15.54 Even if employees do not have an express right to a pay rise, it could be argued that there is an implied contractual obligation on the employer to provide a particular level of pension benefit as a result of custom and practice. But this may be a difficult claim for an employee to succeed with—see eg Chapter 13 and the decision in the *Prudential* case (2011).

Express employee agreement

15.55 In terms of legal challenge, the clearest course is for an employer to obtain express employee consent to the change proposed. Express agreement will be required if the employee has a contractual right to a pensionable pay increase.

Ensure all communication is clear

15.56 Any communications with employees should make clear the pensionable (or otherwise) basis of future pay increases. Care should also be taken to ensure that no later communications

---

[37] [1997] OPLR 249 (Neuberger J).

contradict this approach. The requirement for consultation (see below) helps in meaning that non-pensionable agreements will normally have been explained to employees in advance.

Have good reasons for the decision (and document them)

Employers should not propose changes over pensionable pay without good reason. They owe an implied contractual duty of mutual trust and confidence to their employees. This means that they owe a duty of good faith (ie broadly a duty not to act in a way that is arbitrary or capricious or in which no reasonable employer would act)—see Chapter 13. **15.57**

This does not mean that an employer cannot act in its own interests but it will need to consider carefully the impact of the proposed changes and aim to be able to defend them as proportionate and reasonable. Documentation showing it has acted for valid commercial reasons and considered all available options will be helpful. Employers should also avoid giving a blanket refusal to offer future pay rises. **15.58**

Involve trustees from an early stage

Even if the trustees are not to be asked for their formal agreement to the changes, it is sensible to involve them from an early stage in the process. This will help avoid difficulties later—for example, if they are unconvinced of the existence of the contractual agreement between the employer and employees. **15.59**

Trustees are likely to seek assurances from the employer over the contractual nature of the agreement, including seeking explicit confirmations, presentations from the employer, or documentary evidence. **15.60**

Operate a thorough consultation process

The Pensions Act 2004 (and relevant regulations) impose a requirement on employers where a 'listed change' to pension benefits is envisaged. The employer is required to inform affected employees and to consult with them (or their representatives). Under the original regulations[38] it was not entirely clear whether the statutory 60-day consultation process under the Pensions Act 2004 applied to proposals to make future pay rises non-pensionable. In practice, employers were likely to want to consult as a matter of good practice. **15.61**

The original regulations did include, as a listed change a proposal 'to change, in whole or in part, the basis for determining the rate of future accrual of benefits under the scheme . . . '. It could perhaps have been argued that a change in pensionable pay was a change in the determination of the rate of future accrual. But the better view was that it was not a listed change, because the original regulations only referred to a change in the 'rate' and not, for example, the 'amount' of future accrual. **15.62**

The regulations were amended from 6 April 2010 to include a specific 'listed event' to include any change which is one to: **15.63**

> change what elements of pay constitute pensionable earnings, or to change the proportion of or limit the amount of any element of pay that forms part of pensionable earnings, for or in respect of members or members of a particular description.

---

[38] Occupational and Personal Pension Schemes (Consultation by Employers and Miscellaneous Amendment) Regulations 2006 (SI 2006/349).

15.64 This means that there should be consultation about changes in non-pensionable pay (although the limits of this obligation are still unclear—what if the rate changes each year or is from otherwise discretionary pay, such as bonuses)?

15.65 There are only limited formal sanctions that can apply to a breach of the 2004 Act consultation requirements (a civil penalty can now be charged by the Pensions Regulator[39]). The 2004 Act expressly confirms that the change will be effective, even if the consultation process is not followed.[40]

15.66 Obviously, the safest course for an employer is to consult. This may also draw out any potential concerns or even legal challenges (eg based on contractual terms or past practice).

Need for adequate record keeping

15.67 If non-pensionable pay rises are awarded, it is essential for the employer (ie its human resources department) to maintain proper records of the pensionable and non-pensionable aspects of employees' remuneration and make them available to pension scheme administrators.

The Cases

Tibbals (1937)

15.68 The decision of the House of Lords in *Tibbals v Port of London Authority*[41] is clear and authoritative. A superannuation scheme had been established under the Port of London Act 1909. This provided for a pension based on the member's 'salary or wages', which were defined to be exclusive of any 'gratuities, allowances for house or other additions'. During the First World War and after the authority paid a war bonus, making it clear throughout that this did not rank for pension.

15.69 The House of Lords held (upholding the Court of Appeal and the first instance judge) that it may not be clear as a matter of construction whether or not the war bonus was pensionable under the terms of the scheme. This did not matter because it was clear that the effect of the agreement was that the bonus was not pensionable.

15.70 Lord Roche with whom the other two members of the House of Lords agreed held (at p 417):

> The agreement held by the Court of Appeal to govern the situation was, as I see it, an agreement by the employers to pay a bonus and by the workmen to receive it, upon the terms that it should not be treated as wages within the meaning of the superannuation deed, be it for purposes of contribution or allowance. That being the agreement, to complete the picture of events it should be recalled that, not by any mistake but by virtue of the above described agreement, contributions for superannuation were made without any question for 10 years, on the basis that the bonus was not to count for the purposes of contributions, or for any purpose connected with pension, and that the scheme proceeded upon this footing. To hold that the basis could be radically altered 10 years thereafter, in 1925, at the wish of one party, would be both actuarially disturbing, and also, in my judgment, legally impermissible.

---

[39] Regulation 18A, inserted from April 2009 by SI 2009/615.
[40] Section 259(3), Pensions Act 2004.
[41] [1937] 2 All ER 413, HL. First brought to modern attention by Michael Tennet QC, 'Pensions Cases That Time Forgot' (2007) 21 TLI 125.

And later, at p 418 (refusing to consider the construction point): **15.71**

> War bonus was an unknown thing in 1903, when the superannuation deed was signed, and whether, when that bonus came into existence, the words 'other addition' were apt or not apt to describe it, or whether it was covered by those words of exclusion, may not unnaturally be a matter of some uncertainty and debate. It was such uncertainty, if not debate, which the parties, as I think, effectually resolved, and precluded by the agreement at which they arrived, when the bonus terms were discussed and arranged in advance of any actual dispute arising as to the treatment of the bonus in relation to the superannuation deed.

Tibbals is even more striking in that the scheme concerned was established under a statute. **15.72** The question of whether or not an agreement could affect a statutory right was abandoned before the House of Lords (Crossman J at first instance is stated to have held that the agreement still prevailed).[42]

South West Trains (1997)

Neuberger J (as he then was) gave the leading judgment in *South West Trains v Wightman*.[43] **15.73**

As Arnold J in the later *IMG case* summarized the case, it arose out of the privatization of **15.74** British Rail.

(a) As part of the privatization process a new pension scheme was established under which each railway business could establish its own shared cost section.

(b) One of the new businesses, SWT, duly set up a section. It also re-negotiated the terms and conditions of employment for certain categories of staff, in particular drivers.

(c) The new terms and conditions were negotiated by a working group consisting of three representatives of SWT and three representatives of the drivers' trade union ASLEF. The new terms and conditions were accepted by the union's Executive Committee and in a ballot a majority of the drivers voted in favour of them.

(d) SWT then implemented the new terms and conditions in reliance upon clause 16 of the drivers' contracts of employment, which provided that the contract was subject to terms and conditions settled from time to time under agreed collective bargaining procedures with a recognized trade union.

(e) One of the key features of the new terms and conditions was that drivers would have a pay rise to £25,000 per annum instead of £11,950 basic (and pensionable) plus allowances (non-pensionable) amounting to a further £11,000. But pensionable pay would be only £18,000.

(f) The trustee of the SWT section proposed to amend the rules of the section to give effect to this. The amendment was opposed by the drivers, who contended in essence that under the existing rules they were entitled to a pension based on the salary of £25,000 and that entitlement should not be removed by amendment. The trustee therefore applied to the court for authorization to execute the amending deed.

The application gave rise to five main issues, amongst which were whether there was a bind- **15.75** ing agreement between each driver and SWT as a result of the process by which the new terms and conditions were adopted and, if so, whether the agreement could be enforced to prevent the drivers from claiming pensions on a different basis.

---

[42] See Lord Roche at p 416.
[43] [1997] EWHC 1160 (Ch), [1997] OPLR 249, [1998] PLR 113 (Neuberger J).

15.76 Neuberger J answered yes to both of these questions. On the first point, he held[44] that the new terms and conditions, including the changes to pension rights, were within the scope of clause 16 and not excluded by a particular sentence of that clause relied on by the drivers.

15.77 On the second point, Neuberger J[45] held that it was an implied term of the agreement enforceable at the suit of SWT that the drivers would not claim pensions at a higher level than that agreed. He held[46] that it was well arguable for each of three reasons that, as a result of the contract, the trustee could refuse to pay the drivers a pension at a rate higher than that agreed even in the absence of an amendment to the rules, but did not decide the point.

15.78 Neuberger J held:

> Given my conclusion that there is a binding pensions agreement between SWT and each of the drivers, the fourth question which has to be considered is whether that agreement results in the drivers being unable to claim a pension calculated on the basis of the total number of their years of service and the whole of their final salary (ie. £25,000 subject to increase) or indeed any other basis more favourable than the aggregate of:
>   1. Part of their pension calculated on the basis of their years of service up to restructuring at £11,950 subject to increase; and
>   2. The remainder of their pension being calculated on their years of service after restructuring and £18,000 subject to increase.
> On behalf of SWT, Mr Warren contends that it is implicit in the binding pensions agreement between SWT and each of the drivers that the drivers will not claim pensions at a higher level than that agreed, and that, were the drivers to seek to claim a higher pension, SWT could obtain an injunction restraining them from doing so.
> In my judgment, that contention is well founded.

15.79 Neuberger J went on to discuss *Snelling v John G Snelling Ltd*[47] where an agreement among shareholders not to claim money off the company (not a party to the agreement) could be enforced by one shareholder against another to prevent him claiming money from the company 'by necessary implication'.

15.80 Neuberger J went on to hold:

> In the present case, I consider that it must be implicit in the contract between SWT and the drivers that the drivers would not seek from the Trustee the payment of a pension on a more generous basis than that agreed with SWT: otherwise, one very clear and obviously important aspect of the contract embodied in the restructuring proposals agreed between them would be rendered wholly nugatory. SWT's interest in its employees' pension being paid on a certain basis, as opposed to a higher basis, is direct and obvious. The greater the assets of the Section, the lower the contributions of the employer and the employee, and, accordingly, if higher pensions are to be paid, for instance, to drivers, there will be less money in the Section, and the contributions of other employees and of SWT will be correspondingly larger. Quite apart from this, I would have thought there would be a powerful argument open to other employees (such as Mr Butler) that SWT was under a duty to them to restrain the drivers from seeking a pension on a basis higher than that payable under the binding pensions agreement. While the other employees were not, of course, parties to that agreement, they would obviously suffer substantially and unfairly in terms of large increases in their contributions and (arguably) reduced pensions if it were not enforced. Given the width of the duty on SWT as discussed

---

[44] At [81]–[93].
[45] At [94]–[102].
[46] At [103]–[109].
[47] [1973] 1 QB 87 (Omerod J).

in *Imperial Group*, it seems to me that there must be a powerful case for saying that it would not merely be self-interest, but also duty to other employees, which would motivate SWT in enforcing the binding pensions agreement against the drivers.

Neuberger J considered that: **15.81**

It is, in my judgment, well arguable that, as a result of the contract between SWT and the drivers, it is not merely a matter of SWT being able to enforce the binding pensions agreement by enjoining the drivers from claiming a pension at a higher rate than that agreed between SWT and the drivers. It seems to me that, even without the intervention of SWT, it may well be that the Trustee could refuse to pay the drivers a pension at a higher rate than that agreed with SWT. There are three possible ways of arriving at that conclusion.

These three reasons were: **15.82**

(a) that the trustee could argue that any claim by a member for a pension in excess of that agreed should be dismissed as being an abuse of the process of the court—see the Court of Appeal in *Hirachand Punamchand v Temple*;[48]
(b) that in order to be a beneficiary a person must have an enforceable claim. If there was a claim for more than agreed in the contract, the trustee could successfully say that there is no basis on which the driver can demand a pension on a more favourable basis; and
(c) the level of pay for pension purposes must follow any agreement made between the employer and the employee. So the trustee must be bound—Neuberger J commented that this seems to have been assumed in two earlier cases *Icarus (Hertford) Ltd v Driscoll*[49] and *Engineering Training Authority v The Pensions Ombudsman*.[50]

Neuberger J ultimately held that he did not have to decide on these three points: **15.83**

Whether any or all of these three arguments are correct need not be decided, because it seems clear to me that, for the reasons I have given above, SWT can, would and probably should enforce the binding pensions agreement made with the drivers by restraining any driver claiming a pension on a more generous basis than that agreed under that binding pensions agreement.

Finally Neuberger J held[51] that the trustee could and should execute the amending deed.   **15.84**

Spooner (1999)

In 1999 in *Spooner v British Telecommunications plc*,[52] Jonathan Parker J held that an   **15.85**
agreement by a member to a specific level of pension as part of a redundancy package did not prevent the member from claiming that his pension benefits had been wrongly calculated. He distinguished *South West Trains v Wightman* on the basis that the redundancy agreement did not cover such a claim—the member was not aware of the claim[53] and the redundancy agreement indicated that it was granting improved benefits (not waiving other claims).

---

48 [1911] 2 KB 330, CA.
49 [1990] PLR 1 (Aldous J).
50 [1996] OPLR 167, [1996] PLR 409 (Carnwath J).
51 At [118]–[120].
52 [1999] All ER (D) 1090, [2000] OPLR 189 (Jonathan Parker J).
53 See also to similar effect on settlement wording: *BCCI v Ali* [2001] UKHL 8, [2002] 1 AC 251, HL.

NUS (2002)

15.86 In 2002 in *Trustees of the NUS Officials' and Employees' Superannuation Fund v Pensions Ombudsman*[54] Mr Allen was an employee, an official, of a trade union. He was sent a letter offering him a promotion with a pay rise, but on the basis that the pay rise would be non-pensionable. He wrote back to the employer (the union) stating that he did not accept that the pay rise was non-pensionable, but that the clear position in the trust deeds of the scheme should apply. He continued to work and accepted the promotion and the increased pay.

15.87 The employer and the employee remained disputing whether or not the pay rise was pensionable, given that the employee had never accepted the employer's position and had clearly contested it.

15.88 The Pensions Ombudsman held that this lack of consent distinguished this case from the position in *South West Trains* (where there had been agreement through the trade union). There was no implied consent from the employee merely because he continued to work (making non-acceptance clear means that merely continuing to work is not usually implied consent to a change[55]). Accordingly, the Pensions Ombudsman held that the pay rise was pensionable.

15.89 On appeal, Lightman J reversed the Ombudsman and held that the pay rise was non-pensionable. He decided that the employee had impliedly accepted the increase in his pay on the terms set out in the employer's letter. The employee could not pick and choose.[56] Either he took the pay rise subject to the limitation or he was not entitled to the pay rise at all.

15.90 Lightman J considered (at [12]):

> The primary issue between the parties relates to the contractual rights and duties of the parties.... There are three possible alternative scenarios:
>
> (i) there was simply an agreement for an unconditional increase in Mr Allen's basic wages;
> (ii) there was an agreement for an increase in his basic wages upon the terms set out in the September Letter;
> (iii) there was no change in the parties' rights and duties because there was no agreement at all.
>
> 13. If (i) is the correct analysis, Mr Allen became entitled unconditionally to an increase in his basic wages and accordingly is entitled to require RMT to make contributions as provided by the Scheme rules calculated by reference to his increased basic wages. If (ii) is the correct analysis (as is established by the decision in *South West Trains Ltd v Wightman and others* [1997] OPLR 249), the agreement reached overrides the rights of Mr Allen under the Scheme rules and RMT has been fully entitled to refuse to pay any contribution in respect of any increase granted in basic wages. If (iii) is correct, there has been no increase in wages (let alone basic wages) and accordingly no question of an increase in RMT's contributions can arise.

15.91 Lightman J went on to hold that Mr Allen would need to show an agreement with the employer that his basic wages had increased. This he could not do because the letters from the union made it clear that the pay rise was only offered on the basis that it was not

---

[54] [2002] PLR 93, [2002] OPLR 17 (Lightman J).
[55] See the House of Lords in *Rigby v Ferodo Ltd* [1988] ICR 29, [1987] IRLR 516 (not cited).
[56] A similar finding to that of the EAT in Scotland in *North Lanarkshire Council v Cowan* (2008) UKEATS/0028/07 (not a pensions case).

pensionable. Lightman J held (surely rightly) that in effect (i) was not tenable on the facts and (iii) would be an odd result (presumably requiring Mr Allen to return the amounts overpaid).

Lightman J held that (ii) applied, on the basis that Mr Allen had agreed to the package by **15.92** his conduct, even though Mr Allen had never given his express agreement to the package. He held:

> 17. Upon its true construction read as an offer, the September Letter contained two integral interdependent elements, namely the increase in wages and the provision about pension entitlement. The terms could not be severed. It was not open to Mr Allen to accept one and not the other. Mr Allen could not accept the increase without agreeing the terms as to its treatment for pension purposes. Accordingly, either Mr Allen had to agree to both or neither. If he agreed to neither, he would receive no pay increase. The only tenable interpretation of events is that by conduct Mr Allen agreed to both. For he accepted payment of the increase and both he and the RMT continued to make pension contributions on the basis that the increase did not constitute part of Mr Allen's basic salary for pension purposes.

NUS was, in effect, followed by Briggs J in *Thompson v Fresenius Kabi Ltd*[57] approving a **15.93** compromise in relation to a pension scheme on the basis that the employer could prevent future salary rises from being pensionable.

The IMG Case: *HR Trustees Ltd v German* (2009)

In November 2009 in *HR Trustees Ltd v German*[58] Arnold J held that changes made in 1992 **15.94** to the IMG pension plan (a defined-benefit (DB) pension scheme) had been ineffective to convert members' benefits from DB to defined-contribution (DC).

The judge also held that compromise agreements later entered into with members under **15.95** which they waived DB entitlements, were ineffective as contrary to s 91 of the Pensions Act 1995 (but this aspect was later reversed on appeal).

The facts

In this case, the amendment power in the IMG pension plan's 1977 deed (the 1977 Deed) **15.96** stated that: 'no amendment shall have the effect of reducing the value of benefits secured by contributions already made'. However, rules of the scheme that were introduced in 1981 (the 1981 Rules) contained a different amendment power with a less restrictive fetter.

The trustees and employer executed a deed on 3 March 1992 (the 1992 Amendment Deed) **15.97** to convert the DB scheme into a DC scheme and backdated the deed to have effect from 1 January 1992.

Prior to the purported conversion, the employees were given: memorandums and a scheme **15.98** booklet explaining the changes to the scheme; a presentation on the changes; and membership application forms to join the new DC scheme. The members returned the application forms after having signed and ticked the 'yes box'.

---

[57] [2013] PLR 157 at [38] (Briggs J). Citing *SWT*, but not *NUS*.
[58] *Re IMG Pension Plan: HR Trustees Ltd v German* [2009] EWHC 2785 (Ch) (Arnold J).

Amendment power

15.99 Arnold J held that it was contrary to the restriction in the 1977 Deed to convert DB benefits that accrued before the 1992 Amendment Deed into DC benefits. His reasons were:

(a) The fetter in the 1977 Deed was the relevant restriction that needed to be satisfied before the conversion could be ruled valid. The 1977 Deed amendment power did not give trustees the power to introduce a less restrictive amendment power in the 1981 Rules. In coming to this decision Arnold J relied on *UEB Industries Ltd v WS Brabant*[59] and *Air Jamaica Ltd v Charlton*.[60]

(b) The effect of the fetter in the 1977 Deed was to 'render ineffective the amendments made by the 1992 [Amendment] Deed in so far as they reduced the value of benefits, and in particular the future final salary benefits, which had accrued to members by virtue of their Service'. Arnold J interpreted the fetter as having that meaning by relying on a number of cases, including *Courage*[61] and *BHLSPF v Brashs*.[62]

(c) An amendment to convert such benefits from a final salary entitlement to a money purchase entitlement is permissible, but only subject to an underpin which preserves the future monetary value of the proportion of Final Pensionable Pay which the member has accrued in respect of pre-amendment Service.

(d) The 1992 Amendment Deed only converted the scheme from the date it was executed in March 1992, instead of the earlier January date. To backdate the deed to January was to treat some DB benefits as though they had always accrued on a DC basis (instead of accrued on a DB basis and then been converted into DC benefits) so was an unlawful 'attempt to re-write history'. This was also restricted by the 1977 Deed fetter.

Member agreement?

15.100 Arnold J also rejected the employer's alternative argument that even if the conversion was unlawful under the trust deed and rules the employees had contractually agreed to changes outside the scheme. The employers relied on *South West Trains Ltd v Wightman*[63] in support of their argument. Arnold J held that:

(a) Unlike the ordinary position with commercial contracts, the position in this case is 'analogous to an allegation that a contract should be inferred from conduct, and accordingly the burden of proof of intent to create legal relations is upon the proponent of the contract [the employer]'.

(b) The employer could not prove that there was an intention to create contractual relations because the:

  – memorandum and application forms directed attention to the booklet for the full details of the proposals;

  – the presentation could not create contractual relations because it was not a comprehensive statement of the proposed changes. So the employees would still be left with the understanding that the booklet explained the proposed changes;

  – the memorandums and the booklet presented the changes as already having been

---

[59] *UEB Industries Ltd v W S Brabant* [1992] 1 NZLR 294.
[60] *Air Jamaica Ltd v Charlton* [1999] 1 WLR 1399, PC.
[61] *Re Courage Group's Pension Schemes* [1987] 1 WLR 495 (Millett J).
[62] *BHLSPF Pty Ltd v Brashs Pty Ltd* [2001] VSC 512. See Ch 17.
[63] *South West Trains Ltd v Wightman* [1997] OPLR 249, [1998] PLR 113 (Neuberger J).

made (instead of being presented as proposals);
- the booklet stated that it was not comprehensive and was subject to the trust deed and rules; and
- the application form was not comprehensive, for example it did not indicate that members were being asked to give up rights they were entitled to and were protected by the 1977 Deed fetter.

(c) The position was fundamentally different from *South West Trains* because in *IMG* the agreement was contrary to restrictions contained in the scheme's trust deed and rules. Furthermore, there had been no informed consent from the members that would pre-clude them from asserting a breach, because the members had been: unaware of the fetter in the 1977 Deed; they received no advice; the effects of the proposals were not 'clearly explained' to them; they were 'not given any real choice as to whether or not to consent'; and they 'received the impression that they would not be adversely affected by the changes'.

(d) Unlike the facts of *IMG, South West Trains* only involved making future pay rises non-pensionable.

For similar reasons to those mentioned above (eg no consent), Arnold J rejected a further alternative argument that the employees had represented themselves as having accepted the changes (eg by signing the forms) and it would be unconscionable for them to act otherwise. **15.101**

Compromise agreements

In December 2010, the Court of Appeal issued its full judgment[64] overturning Arnold J in relation to one of his findings: that in relation to compromise agreements. The Court of Appeal confirmed that s 91 of the Pensions Act 1995 (which limits the surrender and assign-ment of pension benefits) is not a bar to compromising bona fide disputes over pension rights. **15.102**

Section 91 states that rights to a future pension are not permitted to be assigned, commuted, or surrendered. In the High Court proceedings, Arnold J had interpreted s 91 in such a way that any attempt to allow a member to give up their pensions entitlements would be invalid. As such, a compromise agreement between employers and employees that would affect these rights would accordingly be unenforceable. **15.103**

However, the Court of Appeal, adopting a purposive approach, has held that where the com-promise relates to a bona fide pensions dispute, its enforceability will not be restricted by s 91. **15.104**

Comments

Where an employer is seeking to rely on member agreement (under the principle in *South West Trains*) to directly agree a change with employees outside the scheme, this case suggests that, among other things, it is prudent to provide comprehensive information about the proposed changes to members. **15.105**

However, there are elements of Arnold J's decision which are difficult to reconcile with established legal principles. For example, it is unclear why a contract in these circumstances is not governed by the same rules as an ordinary commercial contract or why it is important for the members to be given a 'choice' before they can consent (see the comments below at **15.106**

---

[64] *HR Trustees Ltd v German* [2010] EWCA Civ 1349, [2011] ICR 329, CA.

para 15.137 in the later *BBC* case[65]). Furthermore, while it can be prudent to ensure that members receive advice to minimize the risk of claims for mis-selling, in this case Arnold J suggested that not obtaining advice could also vitiate consent.

15.107 Arnold J had already decided that the forms signed by the members were not contractual. Their wording was unclear and it was unclear that there was any intent to create legal relations.[66] He held that, if needed, he would have held that the employer had given consideration (by agreeing to contribute in future).

15.108 He went on[67] (strictly, given the earlier findings, this was obiter) to the effect that informed consent was needed for an agreement to override the scheme's terms, holding:

> [174] ... It is one thing to hold that an extrinsic contract may be enforced to supplement a trust deed where the deed does not contain any contrary provision. It is quite another so say that an extrinsic contract may override contrary provisions in a trust deed unless the extrinsic contract amount to consent on the part of the beneficiaries.

15.109 This is odd. The contract here was not with the trustee (where equity is traditionally protective to beneficiaries), but instead with the employer (where there is no fiduciary relationship).

15.110 Subsequently, in the *BBC* case,[68] Warren J reviewed the IMG decision and commented:

> [57] In *IMG*, the existing members of the scheme contended that there was a fundamental difference between that case and *SWT*. In the latter it was not suggested that enforcing the contract would be contrary to the terms of the trust. Arnold J observed at 172 that:
>> On the contrary, Neuberger J was inclined to accept that the trustee could and should give effect to the contract even without the amendment. One of his reasons for inclining to that view was that the extrinsic contract in that case only affected the salary to which the drivers were to be treated as entitled for the purposes of calculating their pension, which the trustees would have had to look outside the rules of the section for anyway: see *South West Trains* at 108.
>
> [58] In support of their argument, the Existing Members contended that there was no informed consent on their part which would preclude them from asserting a breach of trust. Arnold J accepted the arguments saying:
>> It is one thing to hold that an extrinsic contract may be enforced to supplement a trust deed where the deed does not contain any contrary provision. It is quite another so say that an extrinsic contract may override contrary provisions in a trust deed unless the extrinsic contract amount to consent on the part of the beneficiaries.
>
> [59] Those comments were directed at a case where the extrinsic contract did not amount to consent on the part of the beneficiaries, although it is not entirely clear what a contract without consent could be. Perhaps it means a contract where there is no vitiating element rendering it voidable. The Judge said nothing about a case where there was informed consent, whether or not the deed contains a contrary provision.
>
> [60] On the facts of *IMG*, Arnold J was not satisfied that the beneficiaries did consent, giving six reasons for that conclusion:
>> a. They were unaware of the terms of clause 7(i).
>> b. They received no advice in relation to it.
>> c. It was not clearly explained to them what was happening to their final salary benefits.

---

[65] *Bradbury v BBC* [2012] EWHC 1369 (Ch) (Warren J).
[66] At [164].
[67] At [172]–[174].
[68] *Bradbury v British Broadcasting Corpn* [2012] EWHC 1369 (Ch), [2012] All ER (D) 193 (May) (Warren J). See also the same comments in *Re IBM Pension Plan* [2012] EWHC 2766 (Ch) at [466] (Warren J).

In particular:

d. They were not told how the transfer value and additional special contributions would be calculated and the assumptions which would be employed.

e. They were not given any real choice about whether or not to consent.

f. They received the impression that they would not be adversely affected by the change.

[61] In the case before me, the situation is very different. First of all, as in *SWT*, the factor identified by Arnold J in the passage which I have set out at para 57 above, which was present in *SWT* but absent from *IMG*, is present in the case before me. Secondly, none of the six factors set out in para 60 above relied on by Arnold J (or anything like them) can be found in the case before me, with one possible exception. That possible exception is the fifth factor in relation to which Mr Stafford suggests that Members had no real choice about whether or not to consent.

[62] As to that, I would accept that the BBC ought not to be able to rely on a contract between it and a Member of the Scheme, the imposition of which would have given rise to a breach of any of the Implied Duties. Whether there has been any breach of those duties is the third issue identified in para 39 above. In contrast, if the BBC would not have been in breach of any of the Implied Duties in offering a choice to Members between, on the one hand, remaining in the New Benefits Scheme without a pay rise and on the other hand, joining CAB 2011, I do not consider that there is anything in the point which Mr Stafford makes.

Pensions Ombudsman

The approach in *South West Trains* is followed by the Pensions Ombudsman. **15.111**

In *Ahmed v National Bank of Pakistan*,[69] the member, Mr Ahmed, had signed a consent to a **15.112** change in the scheme retrospectively changing the scheme to provide for benefits (and contributions) to be calculated on basic annual salary, not gross earnings. He later complained that this was contrary to the proviso to the amendment power in the scheme deed. The Ombudsman referred to this provision:

Clause 9(1)(b) refers to not '… affecting in any way prejudicially … any rights or interests which have accrued to each prospective beneficiary …'. Prospective Beneficiaries are not defined in the Trust Deed and Rules of the Scheme but undoubtedly include the Disputant [Mr Ahmed].

But later, he held that: **15.113**

Consequently, the amendment would undoubtedly have been contrary to proviso (B) of Rule 1(c) and Clause 9(1)(b). However, in my judgment, it is plain that, with the concurrence of the Members, amendments may be made despite these provisions. Here the Disputant, and all the other members of the Scheme, chose to waive the protection otherwise afforded to them so that in substance, by confirming their agreement to the Announcement, the Members rendered the amendment to the Rules effective.

There is no reference to the decision in *South West Trains v Wightman*, but the same result **15.114** was reached. The Ombudsman considered that only the consent of the *members* was needed (despite the reference in the limitation to the amendment power to the rights or interests of *beneficiaries*). The case was a complaint by the member (and not his spouse), so it may be that the point was never raised.[70]

---

[69] (1999) 2 July, G00648 (Farrand PO).

[70] Although that point had been noted in at least one previous determination—see para 11 of E00316 (1996) 26 January (Farrand PO).

15.115 Similarly, in *Miller v Commission for the New Towns*,[71] the Ombudsman followed *South West Trains*, holding that Mr Miller could not claim to rely on the scheme rules that a bonus paid to him should be pensionable, when it had been made clear to him when the bonus arrangement was agreed with his employer that it would not be pensionable.

15.116 In 2013, the Pensions Ombudsman upheld an agreement on pay, despite claims that *SWT* should not be followed in the light of the *IMG* decision. In *Stodart v Railways Pension Trustee Co Ltd*,[72] the Deputy Pensions Ombudsman disagreed with Mr Stodart's submission, holding that an agreement with a trade union was effective, there having been lengthy negotiations with the union.

15.117 Employers will need to take care with any compromise agreements with members. Section 91 remains a difficult section. The Court of Appeal in *IMG* was helpful in overturning the judge so that it will not be an unlawful 'surrender' of a pensions right if there is a 'bona fide dispute as to the existence of those rights at the time of the agreement'.

15.118 *IMG* was also distinguished in 2010 by the Pensions Ombudsman in *Martin v IBM UK Pensions Trust Ltd*.[73] The member could not complain where the trust deed had been amended to provide for non-pensionable pay if the member expressly consented (which Mr Martin had). Clear information had been provided to Mr Martin and consideration (the pay rise) provided by the employer.

Capita v Gellately (2011)

15.119 In *Capita ATL Pension Trustees Ltd v Gellately*[74] Henderson J held that a scheme was not amended by announcements sent to members, even though some members had signed and returned an acknowledgment form. Henderson J held that where a pension scheme contains a power of amendment, the court should be very slow to permit any formalities in the amendment power to be avoided by accepting as effective an amendment which did not comply with them—see [53].

15.120 In *Gellately*, an announcement had been issued to employees purporting to equalize the normal retirement date at age 65. The members were asked to complete the form at the end of the announcement and return it as soon as possible. The announcement stated that the member had 'read the announcement' and 'understand the changes outlined'. It also provided that the member consented 'to the deduction or contributions from my earnings on the basis outlined in that announcement'. On a later issue arising, some 20 years later, the original forms could not be recovered.

15.121 However, the trustees asked the members whether they had received the form and, if they had, whether they had returned it. Of the 600 members, 109 replied to the questionnaire and 21 confirmed they had signed and returned the declaration. Henderson J referred (at [69]) to *South West Trains* and held that it would 'be hopeless' to seek to construe agreement by members continuing to work—citing *Jones v Associated Tunnelling*.[75]

---

[71] (2000) 8 February, J00141 (Farrand PO).
[72] *Stodart* 78763/3 (2013) 12 February (Irvine Deputy PO).
[73] 75663/1 (2010) 6 August (King PO).
[74] [2011] EWHC 485 (Ch) (Henderson J).
[75] [1981] IRLR 477 at [21]–[23].

Henderson J considered that, even in the case of the members that said they had returned **15.122** the form no amendment took effect by agreement. Partly this was based on the fact that the announcement itself said that it was a brief summary and indicated that formal documents would later be prepared. Henderson J held that, on the facts, no contract arose. The relevant announcement said that it was only a summary of the changes, it indicated that formal documents would be prepared (which would prevail); the information was incomplete; the parties to the contract were unclear; there was no obvious reason to have a contract—the changes could have been made by the employer with the consent of the trustees; and the form itself only claimed to be consent for increased contributions being payable.

Accordingly, Henderson J held that the announcement (and any returned declarations) were **15.123** just 'the first step in informing the membership about changes to the Scheme that were in due course to be implemented by amendment'—see [84]. A similar argument based on estoppel also failed.

Bradbury v BBC (2012)

Warren J upheld the effectiveness of both an express agreement for an element of future pay **15.124** not to be pensionable and an implied agreement (by way of a non-pensionable pay rise) in his decision in *Bradbury v British Broadcasting Corpn.*[76]

In this case Mr Bradbury, a musician with the BBC philharmonic orchestra, complained about **15.125** a BBC decision to offer a non-pensionable pay rise. This followed consultations with trade unions and members (and the trustee during 2010[77]). DB members were offered three options:

(a) pay rises with the DB pensionable pay element limited to 1 per cent;[78]
(b) to join a career average (CARE) section that was not subject to the 1 per cent cap; or
(c) to opt out of DB altogether and join a defined contribution arrangement.

Mr Bradbury chose the career average section, but later brought a complaint to the Pensions **15.126** Ombudsman that there had been a change in the definition of pensionable salary without consulting the trustees, which had adversely affected his rights under the scheme.

In October 2011, the Pensions Ombudsman found against Mr Bradbury and he appealed **15.127** to the High Court.

Warren J rejects Mr Bradbury's claim

Mr Justice Warren rejected Mr Bradbury's claim. Mr Bradbury had raised, on appeal, various **15.128** arguments about why the BBC's conduct in imposing the 1 per cent cap on DB pension increases could be challenged. These were:

(a) that imposing the cap was contrary to the trust deed and rules of the scheme;
(b) that imposing the cap was, even if the employee agreed, contrary to no assignment or surrender provisions in the Pensions Act 1995 (s 91);

---

[76] [2012] EWHC 1369 (Ch) (Warren J).
[77] Since April 2010, a proposal to limit the amount of pay that forms part of pensionable earnings has been a 'listed change' usually requiring prior consultation with employees under the Pensions Act 2004.
[78] Presumably (although this is not stated in the judgment) this was the default option if the member did not respond or did not choose the other options.

(c) that it was a breach of the implied duty of trust and confidence or the implied duty of good faith in the contract of employment; and

(d) that imposing the cap amounted to maladministration for the purposes of the Pension Schemes Act 1993.

15.129 Warren J rejected all Mr Bradbury's claims, but his judgment repays careful reading. He clearly held that:

(a) non-pensionable pay rises can be given; and

(b) this can be achieved by express agreement with the employee or by offering a pay rise on the express basis that it is non-pensionable.

15.130 But Warren J also gave a wide meaning to the protective provisions in s 91 of the Pensions Act 1995, which could cause problems in future cases.

15.131 He did not decide the question of whether the employer could be in breach of the implied duty of trust and confidence (as this had not been raised before the Pensions Ombudsman). But conversely he cast no doubt on the 2011 decision in *Prudential Staff Pensions*[79] that employers can consider their own interests and that showing a breach of the implied term is a severe test.

15.132 Warren J refused to make a finding on the implied duty of trust and confidence on the basis this had not been argued by Mr Bradbury before the Pensions Ombudsman (this leaves Mr Bradbury free to bring another claim should he want to).

Was the BBC acting contrary to the trust deed and rules of the scheme?

15.133 The rules of the scheme provided that all 'basic salary' counted as pensionable. The scheme had been amended in 2006 so that 'basic salary' was the amount 'determined by the BBC'. The BBC had argued that this meant it could determine that an element of pay is not in fact basic salary.

15.134 Warren J rejected this and said that clear words would be needed in a provision that achieved such a result. He thought that such a provision would only be sensible if it only applied in cases of doubt—para [44]. If it was to apply generally to give a wide discretion then clear words would be needed—para [64].

15.135 Such a clause would also be subject to a concern that it could in effect be exercised retrospectively (so that basic pay in one year could be recategorized as not basic pay in a later year). Very clear words would be needed for this, particularly given the terms of the BBC scheme's amendment power as used to make the amendment in 2006—paras [65]–[67].

15.136 On the main point, Warren J considered that a contract between an employer and a member would be effective to accept a pay rise on the basis that any part of it is pensionable. This would apply even if there was no such provision in the trust deed and rules—para [63].

15.137 Warren J thought that the comments of Arnold J in the *IMG* case were dealing with a very different situation, in which it was not clear when the individual members had in fact consented to the changes—para [59].

---

[79] *Prudential Staff Pensions Ltd v The Prudential Assurance Co Ltd* [2011] EWHC (Ch) (Newey J).

Is the agreement to limit pay rises contrary to section 91 of the Pensions Act 1995?

Section 91 invalidates surrenders or assignments of pension rights, save in limited circumstances. Unlike the limits on amendments in s 67, it is not limited to tax registered schemes, nor does it have a general exception for changes agreed with the member.   **15.138**

Warren J considered previous authorities on s 91 and noted that it is a wide section providing that an entitlement or 'right to a future pension' cannot be assigned, committed, or surrendered etc.   **15.139**

Having considered the cases, Warren J considered that the rights covered by s 91 do not mean just past service 'accrued' rights at the date of the change or agreement, but instead cover future service benefits as well—para [76].   **15.140**

Having said that, Warren J considered that agreeing to a reduced rate of future salary increase was not surrendering a right. Warren J considered—para [84]—that: 'his right to a future pension based on the full amount of an anticipated pay rise was no right at all; and by agreeing to a pay increase only part of which would be treated as pensionable, he did not alienate anything to which he was even prospectively entitled'.   **15.141**

Warren J agreed with the BBC's submission—para [85]—that: '... members have no right to a salary increase. Accepting a salary increase on terms that part only is pensionable does not, he submits, involve a surrender of anything; the member becomes entitled to a greater future pension, albeit one that is smaller than if the whole increase were pensionable. I agree.'   **15.142**

This is clearly helpful for future pay rises. However, Warren J's statement that future service benefits are also protected by s 91 looks quite dangerous. Would, for example, members be able to agree to opt out of a pension scheme? Why does that not amount to a surrender of benefits and so be caught by s 91? A better view is that the changes made to s 91 by the Welfare Reform and Benefit Act 1999 were only intended to clarify that pension credit following divorce was protected by the section.[80]   **15.143**

In a subsidiary argument, the BBC also argued that the purpose of the agreement was to allow a member to accrue benefits in another section of the scheme. This, the BBC argued, meant that an exception to s 91 would apply—where the agreement was for a surrender 'for the purpose of' acquiring for the member 'entitlement to further benefits under the scheme'—s 91(5)(b). However, Warren J considered that in this case the purpose of the surrender would not be the acquisition of further benefits under the scheme; instead the 'real purpose' was to achieve a larger than 1 per cent pay rise—paras [86] and [87].   **15.144**

In practice, in Mr Bradbury's case he had rejected the offer of a limited pay rise and instead chosen to join the CARE section. But Warren J held that even if he had accepted the reduced pay rise offer, it would be binding and not contrary to s 91.   **15.145**

---

[80] See the talk by Jonathan Moody (APL Summer Conference 2013).

Was the conduct contrary to the implied duty of trust and confidence?

15.146 Warren J briefly considered the leading cases on the implied duty of trust and confidence in a pensions context: *Imperial Tobacco*[81] and the more recent *Prudential Staff Pensions* case. He commented that:

> It is important to note, however, that the Implied Duties are not fiduciary duties. Nor are they duties whose scope is to be assessed by reference to concepts of reasonableness, for what seems reasonable to an employer may seem unreasonable to an employee and vice versa. Instead, an employer must not exercise its powers under a pension scheme so as seriously to damage the relationship of confidence between the employer and the employees and ex-employees; in other words there is a duty not to undermine the relationship of trust and confidence which exists between an employer and the members of a pension scheme similar to the duties arising in employment law between an employer and his employees. Indeed, the whole concept of the Implied Duties was borrowed from the concepts of employment law.

15.147 He considered that working out whether the BBC had acted in accordance with the relevant implied duties would involve a detailed factual analysis of how the BBC had reached its decision.

15.148 Warren J noted that the relevant principles 'although easy to state' are 'sometimes very difficult to apply in practice to the facts of a particular case'—para [91]; and:

> ...although the Vice-Chancellor in *Imperial Tobacco* went on to give some practical guidance about how the principles would work out on the ground, I do not think I am alone in finding some of the examples he gave as hard to fit within the principles.

15.149 These issues had not been raised before the Pensions Ombudsman and Warren J therefore decided it would be wrong for him to deal with the issue only for the first time on appeal without the employer having been given the opportunity to bring evidence.

15.150 Warren J also commented that the position in *Prudential* shows that the scope for challenge of an employer's decision is not as wide as one reading of *Imperial Tobacco* might suggest. He repeated the comment that the circumstances in which a decision could be said to be irrational or perverse are severely limited—see para [103].

15.151 Warren J commented that many employers have simply closed their schemes to any future accrual on a defined benefit basis and that 'it would be entirely unsurprising to find that the evidence gave considerable support' to submissions that this was not irrational or perverse—see para [104].

Was the action maladministration within the Pension Schemes Act 1993?

15.152 The Pensions Ombudsman has power to make a determination if he finds a case of maladministration causing injustice. Warren J considered this point did not arise at all.

15.153 If Mr Bradbury is unsuccessful on the implied duties argument it was not easy to see how he could succeed on a maladministration argument. Conversely, if he had succeeded on breach of the implied duty then it would be a logical consequence that he would also show maladministration.

---

[81] [1991] 1 WLR 589 (Browne-Wilkinson V-C).

16

SAUNDERS V VAUTIER AND PENSION TRUSTS

Introduction

The rule in *Saunders v Vautier*[1] is shorthand for the principle established in that case, namely that all the beneficiaries under a trust if of full capacity can join together and unanimously terminate the trust (even if the trustees object).[2]   **16.1**

It is clear that the rule in *Saunders v Vautier*, if it applies, allows the beneficiaries (acting together) to terminate the trust and call for the trust property to be conveyed to them. In practice, an amendment of the trust is also possible, but only if the trustees agree—*Re Brockbank*.[3]   **16.2**

Could this principle be used by the members in relation to a pension scheme (ie all the members acting together without the consent of the employer)? In practice no.   **16.3**

There have been a number of cases involving pension or superannuation schemes where the members have tried to wind-up the scheme by a form of unanimous resolution. Generally, these have failed when challenged in the courts, but different reasons have applied.   **16.4**

Application to pension schemes

This general trust law rule in *Saunders v Vautier* (that all the beneficiaries can join together to force a winding-up of a trust) is highly unlikely to apply to an occupational pension scheme, even if employer consent is given.   **16.5**

It would *not* be possible for the members of a pension scheme (and perhaps other beneficiaries—eg spouses) to join together unanimously to force the winding-up of the scheme   **16.6**

---

[1] (1841) Cr & Ph 240, 41 ER 182 (Lord Cottenham LC).

[2] See Paul Matthews, 'The Comparative Importance of the Rule in Saunders v Vautier' (2006) *122 LQR* 266. In the context of a unit trust, see Kam Fan Sin, *The Legal Nature of the Unit Trust* (Clarendon Press, 1997) 114–20.

[3] [1948] Ch 206 (Vaisey J).

over the objections of the employer (perhaps more likely as a scenario if there are only a few members remaining).

16.7 This is for four reasons:

(a) it is unlikely that the consent of all the beneficiaries, including contingent discretionary beneficiaries (eg future spouses, dependants etc), could in practice be obtained—*Thorpe v Revenue and Customs Commissioners*;[4]

(b) the employer is almost always a beneficiary of the scheme as well (and so its consent would be needed)—see Chapter 10 ('Trustees' duties to employers') and the Canadian pension case *Buschau v Rogers Communications Inc*;[5]

(c) (perhaps) a court would be likely to hold that this trust law rule does not apply to pension schemes—*Buschau*;

(d) (perhaps) the trustee is also a beneficiary (eg because of its lien over the assets) and so cannot be forced to hand over the trust assets—see the Australian High Court decision (on a unit trust) in *CPT Custodian Pty Ltd v Commissioner of State Revenue*.[6]

Consent of All Beneficiaries Needed

16.8 The Court of Appeal took a strict line in relation to a small pension scheme—in *Thorpe v Revenue and Customs Commissioners*.[7] This case involved a sole member claiming to terminate a scheme. This was challenged by the Revenue and it was held that *Saunders v Vautier* did not apply.

16.9 In *Thorpe v Revenue and Customs Commissioners*, the Court of Appeal held that the sole member of a small occupational pension scheme could not act to terminate the scheme in using the rule in *Saunders v Vautier*. Lloyd LJ gave the main judgment (unreserved) upholding the judgment in the Chancery Division and the judgment and the finding of the Special Commissioner. Dyson LJ and Sir Scott Baker agreed.

16.10 Lloyd LJ held ([22]) that the rule in *Saunders v Vautier* is well set out in *Snell's Equity*.[8]

> Although the beneficiaries cannot in general, control the trustees while the trust remains in being, or commit them to a particular dealing with the trust property, they can, if sui juris and together entitled to the whole beneficial interest, put an end to the trust and direct the trustees to hand over the trust property as they direct; and this is so even if the trust deed contains express provisions for the determination of the trust. This principle also applies where there is an absolutely vested gift made payable on a future event, with a direction to accumulate the income in the meantime and pay it with the principal; for in *Saunders v Vautier* the court declined to enforce a trust for accumulation in which no person but the beneficiary had any interest. In other words, if an accumulation is directed exclusively for the benefit of a beneficiary, the moment he is sui juris he may put an end to it and demand the property. A man who is sui juris may do what he likes with his own property.
>
> Again, where trustees are directed at their absolute discretion to pay or apply the whole or any part of the income of the fund to or for the benefit of A, and are told to pay or apply to

---

[4] [2010] EWCA Civ 339, [2010] STC 964, CA.
[5] 2006 SCC 28, [2006] 1 SCR 973, (2006) 9 ITELR 73, CanSC.
[6] [2005] HCA 53, (2005) 224 CLR 98, HC Aus.
[7] [2010] EWCA Civ 339, [2010] STC 964, CA.
[8] 31st edn (2005) para 27-25.

or for the benefit of B any part of the income not applied for A's benefit, A and B, if both sui juris, can together compel the trustees to pay the whole income as they direct, for they are the sole owners of each slice of income. But the rule does not apply if other persons have possible interests in the income, so that A and B alone could not control the trustees' application of the income.[9]

Lloyd LJ considered that the *Saunders v Vautier* principle could apply (and this was accepted by the Revenue) if 'all possible beneficiaries under a discretionary trust are identified, of full age and capacity, and all agree to the trustees to bring the trust to an end'. **16.11**

In effect, Mr Thorpe did not particularly like the fund being held within the plan (he was the only member) to be used in accordance with the Revenue rules at the time, so that benefits would be paid by way of a (taxed) pension, after a tax free lump sum had been provided. Accordingly, he arranged to give notice to the trustee that he was terminating the scheme on the basis that he was absolutely entitled to the whole beneficial interest declared by the trust deed. The Inland Revenue then made an assessment to tax under specific provisions in the Income and Corporation Taxes Act 1988 based on a cessation of approval of the pension scheme for tax purposes. **16.12**

Lloyd LJ commented that the *Saunders v Vautier* principle 'can in theory apply to a pension trust'.[10] But he went on to hold that it was clear that it did not apply on the facts of this case. The rules provided for benefits to be payable to Mr Thorpe (a limited lump sum and an annuity) on his retirement. But they went on to say that if he had died in service, then there was a discretion for the trustees to apply the lump sum to all or some of his children and his grandchildren. Similarly, if he had remarried or came to have other dependants (Mr Thorpe's wife had died and he said he was not planning to remarry) the future widow or dependant might be entitled to benefits themselves. **16.13**

Accordingly, Lloyd LJ agreed with the special commissioner that Mr Thorpe was not 'then entitled to the whole beneficial interest in the trust fund'. **16.14**

Mr Thorpe's counsel argued that the contingent benefits were only contractual and did not take effect by way of trust, but Lloyd LJ rejected this argument considering that they were rights under the beneficial trust of the scheme. They were capable of being varied (within limits).[11] Lloyd LJ commented[12] that: **16.15**

> The contingent benefits, in particular those under rule 6, arose directly under the rules which gave affect to the trusts of the scheme. They were a good deal more real than, to take an example from the books, the possibility of a 65 year old woman having a further child which in 1926 prevented the class being regarded as closed under *Saunders v Vautier*: see *Re Deloitte, Griffiths v Deloitte* [1926] Ch 56.

Interestingly, there is no discussion in *Thorpe* about the interests of the employer. Presumably, that was because Mr Thorpe was the sole director and the only shareholder of the employer. He and his wife were the only employees of the company (until Mrs Thorpe died in 1991). Following her death, Mr Thorpe was the only employee of the company and only member **16.16**

---

[9] Other cases have quoted from other trust text books—eg *Buschau* quotes from *Underhill and Hayton: Law Relating to Trusts and Trustees* and *CPT Custodian* quotes from *Thomas on Powers*.

[10] At [25].

[11] But no variation seems to have been argued here.

[12] At [25].

of the scheme. He arranged for the company to 'assign' to him all its rights under the scheme to appoint or remove trustees (Lloyd LJ queried whether this could have any legal effect[13]).

16.17 It seems relevant that in *Thorpe* it was a money purchase scheme (so with limited employer interests) and employer consent could probably be inferred anyway, given Mr Thorpe's ownership.

16.18 The principle that all the beneficiaries need to agree to a *Saunders v Vautier* arrangement probably applies to the whole scheme and not just an individual part. Even where there is a money purchase scheme, if there are several members, they may each have their own notional fund by reference to which the resulting benefits are calculated. The decision in *Thorpe* indicates that even if it was a scheme with one active member, in practice any termination is likely to be outside *Saunders v Vautier*. Depending on the terms of the scheme, if there is more than one member it may be unlikely that any single member could seek to terminate using his or her separate fund (ie without affecting the other members)—*Dalriada Trustees Ltd v Woodward*.[14]

Employer as Beneficiary

16.19 An employer having a right to a surplus on a winding-up of the scheme would clearly mean that the employer is a contingent beneficiary and so its consent would be needed for any winding-up of the scheme under *Saunders v Vautier*. The rule applies 'where there is more than one beneficiary, even although their several interests are not all immediate but successive, provided they are unanimous in wishing to end the trust'.[15]

16.20 In *Berry v Geen*[16] the House of Lords held that it could not sanction the distribution of a fund held on trust for accumulation and payment of various annuities, where it was possible that the accumulation might fail. In those circumstances, the surplus income would be undisposed of and pass on an intestacy, so that a contingent interest was held by the next of kin. The House of Lords held that it could not make the orders sought without the consent of the next of kin because to do so would or might destroy or prejudice their interests. This sounds very similar to the position of an employer in a pension scheme.

16.21 Even in the absence of the employer being the residual beneficiary on a winding-up, the interests of the employer are likely to be enough to mean that its consent is needed for a termination of the trust. This is a point made by the Supreme Court of Canada in the *Buschau* case.

Inconsistent with the Nature of a Pension Trust/Legislation

16.22 In Canada, the Supreme Court held in *Buschau v Rogers Communications Inc*[17] that the rule in *Saunders v Vautier* to terminate a trust was not 'easily incorporated' into the context of employment pension plans. This was on the basis that such plans are heavily regulated by

---

[13] At [26].
[14] [2012] EWHC 21626 (Ch) (Morritt C).
[15] RP Meagher and WMC Gummow, *Jacobs' Law of Trusts in Australia* 6th edn (Butterworths, 1997) 698.
[16] [1938] AC 575, HL. Cited by McMillan J in *Krstic v State Trustees Ltd* [2012] VSC 344.
[17] 2006 SCC 28, [2006] 1 SCR 973, (2006) 9 ITELR 73 (CanSC). Discussed by Douglas Rienzo, 'The Variation of a Pension Trust' (2010) 30 Estates Trusts & Pensions Journal 69.

statute, including specific provisions in the Canadian statute dealing extensively with the termination of plans and the distribution of assets.

The majority in the Supreme Court effectively held that it was clear from this explicit legislation **16.23** in Canada that Parliament intended the legislation to displace the common law rule. The statute must prevail over the common law rule.

The Supreme Court commented that the relevant legislation was not a complete code, but **16.24** when it dealt with a particular area—ie providing recourse to pension plan members—they should use it.

This argument based on the legislation looks to be less likely to succeed in the UK (it was **16.25** not raised in the *Thorpe* case for example). The Canadian legislation is cited in *Buschau* as providing that the consent of the Superintendant (appointed under the relevant legislation) is required before a surplus could be distributed—para [19]. The court held that this meant that Parliament intended to displace the common law rule—para [28].

The UK legislation, by contrast, does set up a statutory regulator (the Pensions Regulator) **16.26** whose role may be similar in many respects to that of the Superintendant in Canada. But in contrast to Canada, there is no statutory requirement in the UK to obtain the consent of the Pensions Regulator before distributing surplus (to members or the employer). There is a requirement for advance notice to be given to the members and the Pensions Regulator,[18] but not a consent requirement.

A minority in the Supreme Court came to the same result, but considered that trusts law **16.27** could not prevail over the governing legislation of the plan. They held that applying the rule in *Saunders v Vautier* would contradict the reasonable contractual expectation of the parties, since the terms of the plan did not give rise to a reasonable expectation that the trust could be terminated by the members over the employer's objections (so that the members might obtain the surplus). Applying the common law rule would disregard the employer's unique role in respect of the plan and the trust and circumvent the terms of the contract. The Supreme Court overturned the Court of Appeal on this issue.

For the terms of the rule in *Saunders v Vautier*, the Supreme Court quoted the definition in **16.28** *Underhill and Hayton: Law Relating to Trusts and Trustees*:[19]

> If there is only one beneficiary, or if there are several (whether entitled concurrently or successively) and they are all of one mind, and he or they are not under any disability, the specific performance of the trust may be arrested, and the trust modified or extinguished by him or them without reference to the wishes of the settlor or the trustees.

Deschamps J, giving the judgment of the majority, gave four reasons why the rule in *Saunders* **16.29** *v Vautier* could not apply.[20] She held that:

(a) pension plans are heavily regulated and the relevant legislation is inconsistent;
(b) a family trust is generally a stand alone instrument not depending on any other instruments—in contrast here the pension trust is dependent on the underlying plan for which it was created (ie the provision of the benefits);

---

[18] Pensions Act 1995, ss 37, 76. See Ch 20 (Employers and surpluses).
[19] 14th edn (1987) 628—see [21] of the judgment.
[20] At [28]–[33].

(c) the interests of the employers remain in the plan (unlike a common law trust which allows no room for the settlor's interest). She stated that: 'a blanket statement that the employer has no interest conflicts with the usual expectations of parties to a pension plan';[21] and

(d) gift or family trusts are gratuitous and accelerating the date of entitlement has no broad social consequences. However, pension trust funds are no longer generally viewed as being gratuitous and allowing them to be distributed would defeat the social purpose of preserving the financial security of employees in their retirement.

16.30 The three judges in the minority concurred in the decision, but gave slightly different reasons. They, in particular, commented that the interests of future possible spouses and common law partners would need to be obtained for the rule in *Saunders v Vautier* to apply.[22]

16.31 They also commented that pension trusts are not the same as traditional trusts and that the legal relationship with the employer needs to be taken into account:

> To permit termination of the Plan when a surplus has been realised independently of the terms of the Plan is not consistent with its object with the applicable statutory regime.[23]

16.32 Following *Buschau*, in 2010 in *Kidd v Canada Life*,[24] Perell J in Ontario approved an amendment to a pension plan, in reliance on *Saunders v Vautier* together with an approval by the Court on behalf of various categories of beneficiaries under the Variation of Trust Act.

16.33 Perell J distinguished *Buschau* as in this case the employer was agreeing to the change. Perell J noted that, at para [33] of *Buschau*, Deschamps J had stated that the rule in *Saunders v Vautier* might apply to very small pension plans. He also referenced an unreported decision of Low J to similar effect in case, *Aegon Canada Inc v Abdool*.[25]

Trustee Indemnity—*CPT*

16.34 In *CPT Custodian Pty Ltd v Commissioner of State Revenue*,[26] the High Court in Australia considered the impact of a tax on 'owners' of land on the holders of units in a unit trust.

16.35 The trustee owned three shopping centres in Victoria, each of which it held as trustee of a separate unit trust. The trustee and the designated manager were entitled to charge professional fees and recoup them out of the assets of the trusts. In one case, there was a single unit holder, in another case there was a single unit holder via an intermediate unit trust, and in the third case there were multiple unit holders.

16.36 The Commissioner assessed the unit holders for land tax on the basis that they were 'owners' of the land within the meaning of the Land Tax Act 1958. The High Court observed that the Commissioner's conduct was curious because in each case the trustee as legal owner was

---

[21] At [30].

[22] At [99].

[23] At [90].

[24] 2010 ONSC 1097 (Perell J). See also the Ontario Court of Appeal in *Lomas v Rio Algom* (2010) 316 DLR (4th) 385.

[25] (2008) 8 January (Low J).

[26] [2005] HCA 53, (2005) 224 CLR 98. In *CPT*, the High Court followed its earlier decision on the nature of the interest of a trustee in *Chief Commissioner of Stamp Duties for New South Wales v Buckle* [1998] HCA 4, (1998) 192 CLR 226, HC Aus.

liable to pay land tax and there was no question of insolvency or other difficulty in recovering the tax from the trustee as legal owner.

The High Court (unanimously) overturned the Court of Appeal and held that the unit **16.37** holder or holders were not the 'owner' of the land within the meaning of the Land Tax Act. Ultimately, the decision turned on the meaning of the word 'owner' as used in that Act.

The High Court considered whether all the unit holders under a trust were, if they acted **16.38** together, able to terminate the trust so as to become entitled to the underlying property (including land) held by the unit trust.

The High Court held that the unit holders were not 'owners' of the land held by the unit **16.39** trust. The High Court considered[27] that in order to decide whether or not someone was an 'owner' was a different question to determining whether or not a holder of a unit in a unit trust has a proprietary interest in its assets, considering the decision of the Privy Council in *Schmidt v Rosewood.*[28]

The High Court considered that, although the tax legislation referred to 'joint owners' when **16.40** looking at ownership of property, that the individual unit holders did not, together, hold any land as joint tenants nor could they be considered to be joint holders.

The High Court also considered the situation where all the units within the unit trust were **16.41** held by just one person. The Court of Appeal had held that the person should be regarded as being entitled to all of the trust assets, given that he has the power to bring the trust to an end at will and to require the transfer to him of all the assets.

The High Court disagreed with this. It referred to *Saunders v Vautier*[29] and considered that, **16.42** in Anglo-Australian law the rule has been seen to embody a 'consent principle'. The High Court referred to this as having been recently identified by Mummery LJ in *Goulding v James*[30] as follows:

> The principle recognises the rights of beneficiaries, who are sui juris and together absolutely entitled to the trust property, to exercise their proprietary rights to overbear and defeat the intention of a testator or settlor to subject property to the continuing trusts, powers and limitations of a will or trust instrument.

The High Court went on to consider[31] the rule in *Saunders v Vautier*, referring to a definition **16.43** from *Thomas on Powers:*[32]

> Under the rule in *Saunders v Vautier*, an adult beneficiary (or a number of adult beneficiaries acting together) who has (or between them have) an absolute, vested and indefeasible interest in the capital and income of property may at any time require the transfer of the property to him (or them) and may terminate any accumulation.

The High Court considered that part of the rule in *Saunders v Vautier* was that there must be **16.44** a right on the beneficiaries to have immediate payment of the trust property to them—citing

---

[27] At [16] and [17].
[28] [2003] 2 AC 709, PC.
[29] At [43].
[30] [1997] 2 All ER 239 at 247, CA.
[31] At [47].
[32] 1st edn (Sweet & Maxwell, 1998) 176.

Lightman J in *Don King Productions Inc v Warren*[33] and the Australian case of *Sir Moses Montefiore Jewish Home v Howell and Co (No 7) Pty Ltd*.[34]

16.45 The High Court went on to say that this approach to *Saunders v Vautier* would not mean that the unit holders here could require the transfer of the property to them. The Court held:[35]

> But that approach to the rule in *Saunders v Vautier* would not meet the case of the Deed considered in this litigation. In the Deed, the Manager covenanted with the Trustee (cl 23.4) to ensure that there were at all times sufficient readily realisable assets of the Trust available for the Trustee to raise the fees to which the Manager and the Trustee were entitled under cl 23.1 and cl 23.2 respectively. These stipulations made the Trustee and the Manager interested in due administration of the trusts of the Deed, in the sense identified by Kearney J in *Moses Montefiore*. Put somewhat differently, the unit holders were not the persons in whose favour alone the trust property might be applied by the trustee of the Deed.[36]

16.46 The High Court went on to say that the 19th-century formulations by the English courts of the ruling in *Saunders v Vautier* did not give consideration to the significances of the rights of the trustee under the general law to reimbursement or exoneration for the discharge of liabilities incurred in administration of the trust.

16.47 This last reason is difficult to accept. The Court of Appeal had considered that the rights of the unit holders were to call for the balance of the property (after any indemnity for costs etc had been satisfied). This seems a better analysis of the position. It is, perhaps, clearer to say that the case really turned on the tax definition of the meaning of the word 'owner' in this context.

16.48 In practice, if *Saunders v Vautier* did not apply where trustees have an indemnity, it is difficult to conceive of a trust where *Saunders v Vautier* would apply. Practically all trusts include an indemnity in favour of the trustee out of the assets for the trustees' proper expenses and liabilities (indeed this is implied under s 31 of the Trustee Act 2000—see Chapter 14).

16.49 RW White J,[37] commenting extra judicially[38] makes this point:

> The conclusion in *CPT Custodian* that 100% unit holders did not own the land is easier to accept than the premise that unit holders could not call for the transfer of the land because of an unsatisfied right of indemnity or exoneration. It is not clear why the existence of those rights should prevent unit holders from calling for a transfer. The beneficiaries' interest in the trust property is deferred to the trustee's right of indemnity, so that if they called for the transfer of the trust property where the right was unsatisfied, it would be a simple matter of realising the trust property and applying sufficient funds to satisfy the right of indemnity before distributing the remainder to the beneficiaries. Indeed, that is commonly one of the mechanisms for which a trust deed provides when a trust is to be terminated.

16.50 In *Koompahtoo Local Aboriginal Land Council v KLALC Property & Investment Pty Ltd*[39] Debelle AJ referred to *CPT* and held:

> However, I do not understand the decision in either *Buckle* or *CPT Custodian* to prevent a beneficiary who is sui juris and who has an absolute, vested and indefeasible interest in the

---

[33] [2000] Ch 291 at 321 (Lightman J).
[34] [1984] 2 NSWLR 406 at 410–11 (Kearney J).
[35] At [49].
[36] See *Blair v Curran* [1939] HCA 23, (1939) 62 CLR 464 at 498, 501; *Thomas on Powers* (1998) 380.
[37] A judge of the Supreme Court of New South Wales, Equity Division.
[38] See the NSW Court website for his paper given in May 2010 at a Higher Courts Seminar in New Zealand.
[39] [2009] NSWSC 502 (Debelle AJ).

capital and income of trust property from being able to require the termination of the trust and the transfer of the trust property to that beneficiary where a trustee has right to reimbursement and exoneration.

Conversely, in *McKnight v Ice Skating Queensland (Inc)*,[40] Chesterman J followed *CPT* and held that the trustee's indemnity meant that the beneficiary could not call for the trust assets. But he went on to hold: **16.51**

> [37] Accordingly the respondent was not, on 16 August 2007, entitled to call for the conveyance of the whole of the trust estate from the applicants, who, as trustees, may first take the sums to which they are properly entitled before it can be said that there is trust estate to which the respondent is absolutely entitled. On the other hand the termination of the trust should not be unduly delayed. It is apparent that the applicants and the respondents disagree profoundly about the manner in which the rinks are to be operated and the further land developed. Such disagreement should not be allowed to delay the respondent's right to the property. If provision is made for the applicants' claims to reimbursement the balance of the trust estate can be conveyed. See *Kemtron Industries Pty Ltd v Commissioner of Stamp Duties* [1984] 1 Qd R 576 at 587.
>
> [38] In the circumstances the appropriate course is to direct the applicants to make their claim for reimbursement within a relatively short period. The trustees may retain under their control an amount sufficient to meet their claim for remuneration but the balance can be transferred.

The *Saunders v Vautier* analysis in *CPT* has been cited in later Australian cases—for example in the family trust case *Miskelly v Arnheim*[41] and in *Re S & D International Pty Ltd (No 4)*.[42] For a case before *CPT* where a trustee of a family trust was held able to refuse to terminate a trust because of his indemnity, see *Hayman v Equity Trustees Ltd*.[43]   **16.52**

New Zealand

There are a number of New Zealand cases dealing with surplus distributions where the Court has approved a variation of trust based on unanimous consent of the members (and their spouses etc). However, all of these have involved the employer consenting as well.   **16.53**

Capral Fiduciary Ltd v Ladd[44] is a New Zealand decision involving amending a pension scheme that refers to *Saunders v Vautier*. In *Capral*, Nicholson J held that an amendment to a pension plan could be approved by the Court (acting under its statutory variation powers) to allow the plan to be amended to repay surplus to the employer. In that case, the changes were agreed by the employer and the current members and their spouses.   **16.54**

Nicholson J relied on *Saunders v Vautier* and the House of Lords' decision in *Berry v Geen*. Nicholson J also allowed *Saunders v Vautier* to be used to amend the plan rather than terminate it (following on the earlier decision in *Re Philips New Zealand Ltd*[45]).   **16.55**

---

[40] [2007] QSC 273 (Chesterman J).
[41] [2008] NSWSC 1075, [2008] 11 ITELR 311 (Hamilton J).
[42] [2010] VSC 388 (Robson J).
[43] [2003] VSC 353 (Kellam J).
[44] [1999] 1 NZSC 40,455 (Nicholson J).
[45] [1997] 1 NZLR 93, (1996) 1 NZSC 40,368 (Baragwanath J).

17

AMENDMENT POWERS

Amendment Powers

17.1 This chapter looks at the position in relation to express amendment powers included within pension schemes.[1]

---

[1] See Gino Dal Pont, 'The Amendment of Trust Deeds—A Super(Annuation) Gloss?' (2008) 31 Australian Bar Review 1; Dan Schaffer, 'Amendment Rules: Dealing With Defective Amendments' (APL 1996 conference), 'Amendment Powers—Playing Within the Rules' (APL 2000 conference); Ian Greenstreet, 'Practical Issues When Updating Your Pension Scheme Documentation' (APL 2007 conference); Isabel France, 'Pension Scheme Amendments—Getting It Right' (2004) 18 TLI 202; Richard Leigh, 'Scheme Amendments in the Light of the Pensions Act' (APL Pensions Act conference, 1997). See also in Australia, Pamela McAlister, 'Accrued Benefits—In Search of a Legal Meaning' (2000) 11 ASLB 73; Michael Mathieson, 'Secured Versus Accrued Benefits: The Brashs Case' (2002) 13 ASLB 53; David MacLean, 'Effect of an Invalid Deed of Amendment of a Superannuation Fund Trust Deed' (2001) 76 ALJ 158.

It is common (and probably completely impractical otherwise) for wide amendment powers to **17.2** be included within the trust deeds and other instruments governing an occupational pension scheme. This is because such schemes and trusts:

(a) potentially last for a long time—even if a scheme becomes closed to future new entrants, it will still be providing benefits for members (and potentially their spouses and dependants) until the last relevant member or dependant dies. Occupational pension schemes are not subject to the limits on the life of a trust under the rule against perpetuities.[2]

(b) The governing legislation and underlying tax position of occupational pension schemes is constantly changing. Starting with the Social Security Act 1973 (in relation to pensions regulation) and many finance acts (in relation to tax), it is a sign of the importance of occupational pension schemes that Parliament cannot resist making changes to the system.

(c) In some cases the legislation is overriding or specific powers of amendment are included within the legislation. However, in some it is not.

(d) The commercial needs of the employer and the members in relation to retirement provision may change over time. For example there has been an increasing shift over recent years away from a defined benefit (DB) accrual towards a defined contribution arrangements.

(e) Discrimination laws are been made directly applicable to occupational pension schemes (particularly sex discrimination and, more recently, age discrimination). These have also tended to drive scheme amendments (particularly attempts to 'equalize' benefits between male and female members following the ECJ decision in *Barber*[3]).

Having noted this, a power of amendment probably cannot be implied into a pension **17.3** scheme—for example see the Canadian case *Re Reevie and Montreal Trust Co of Canada*.[4] Some (limited) amendment powers are implied by statute.

In *Re Courage Group's Pension Schemes*[5] Millett J (as he then was) summarized this, holding **17.4** that:

> It is important to avoid unduly fettering the power to amend the provisions of the Scheme, thereby preventing the parties from making those changes which may be required by the exigencies of commercial life.

In *Stena Line Ltd v Merchant Navy Ratings Pension Fund Trustees Ltd*,[6] Briggs J at first instance **17.5** held that an amendment power in a pension scheme should be given a broad interpretation. But on appeal,[7] Arden LJ in the Court of Appeal held:

> If by 'broad interpretation' the judge meant that the power of amendment should be interpreted with greater liberality than other documents purposively construed with a view to

---

[2] The Perpetuities and Accumulations Act 2009, s 2(4) exempts 'relevant pension schemes' (defined in s 15 to include an occupational pension scheme under s 1 of the Pension Schemes Act 1993). Before 6 April 2010 contracted-out schemes and those with tax registration were excluded from the rule against perpetuities by s 163 of the Pension Schemes Act 1993 and the Personal and Occupational Pension Schemes (Perpetuities) Regulations 1990 (SI 1990/1143) (and before that see s 69 of the Social Security Act 1973). These were repealed from 6 April 2010 by the 2009 Act.

[3] See the discussion by Warren J in *Premier Foods* [2012] EWHC 447 (Ch).

[4] (1984) 46 OR (2d) 667, (1984) 10 DLR (4th) 286, Ontario CA.

[5] [1987] 1 All ER 528 at 505G (Millett J).

[6] [2010] EWHC 1805 (Ch) at [97] and [105] (Briggs J).

[7] *Stena Line Ltd v Merchant Navy Ratings Pension Fund Trustees Ltd* [2011] EWCA Civ 543 at [48], CA.

holding that an amendment is binding on Participating Employers who have not consented to it, I would disagree. In my judgment, a power of amendment should be interpreted precisely in accordance with its terms, neither more nor less.

17.6 Express powers of amendment come in many forms and most often contain restrictions or limitations. Usually, the power will be exercisable by either:

(a) the principal employer alone; or
(b) the principal employer, with the consent of the trustees; or
(c) the trustees, with the consent of the principal employer.

17.7 In practice there is no real distinction between the last two—it makes no difference in reality whether the trustee initiates the amendment (which is then agreed by the employer) or whether the employer suggests the change (which is then agreed by the trustees).

17.8 The exercise of an amendment power will mean:

(a) the employer needs to exercise the power (or give its consent) in line with the implied duties on it, in particular the implied mutual duty of trust and confidence—see Chapter 13. Its powers are not fiduciary (save in very rare cases)—see Chapter 11;
(b) the trustee board needs to exercise the power (or give its consent) in accordance with their fiduciary duties;
(c) both employers and trustees need to exercise the power for a proper purpose;
(d) the exercise needs to be carried out in accordance with any relevant formalities (eg if exercisable by deed, there is a deed);
(e) the amendment needs to be within the terms and scope of the power;
(f) the amendment needs to comply with any implied limitations;
(g) the amendment needs to comply with any express restrictions in the power; and
(h) the amendment will need to comply with the statutory limitations on amendments.

The effect of a failure to meet one or more of these requirements can differ. For example, failure to comply with a mandatory condition (eg that an amendment must be by deed) can mean that the amendment is invalid and void. Conversely some other requirements may result in an amendment only partially taking effect (eg a reduction in benefits contrary to a restriction in the amendment power in relation to past service benefits, can be effective for future service, but invalid for past service). Some other requirements do not affect the amendment at all (eg an obligation to notify members of changes) or make the amendment voidable at the discretion of the Pensions Regulator (breach of s 67 of the Pensions Act 1995).

Principles of Construction

17.9 Much of the analysis in the cases on amendment powers involves the interpretation of the power. The courts have laid down various principles for the construction of pension schemes.

Practical and purposive

17.10 In *Courage*[8] Millett J said that pension schemes should 'wherever possible be construed to give reasonable and practical effect to the scheme, bearing in mind that it has to be operated against a constantly changing commercial background...'.

---

[8] [1987] 1 All ER 528, [1987] 1 WLR 495 at 505 (Millett J).

Warner J in *Mettoy Pension Trustees v Evans*[9] held that 'the court's approach to the construc- **17.11** tion of documents relating to a pension scheme should be practical and purposive, rather than detached and literal'. This was also the approach adopted by Millett J in *Courage*.[10] This was endorsed by the Court of Appeal in *National Grid v Laws*.[11] It has been cited in many later cases, for example Henderson J in *Gellately*.[12]

In *Mettoy*, Warner J went on to say that, although there are no special rules which govern the **17.12** construction of pension scheme documents, the background facts or surrounding circum- stances in the light of which they have to be construed include four special factors:

(1) The first factor is that the members are not volunteers, and their rights have contractual and commercial origins.
(2) Secondly, the documents have to be construed in the light of Inland Revenue (now HMRC) approval requirements.
(3) Thirdly, the background facts include 'common practice from time to time in the field of pension schemes generally'.
(4) Fourthly:

> temporary and imprecise documents . . . are brought into existence as a result of the practice of the Inland Revenue and of the Occupational Pensions Board which is to recognise and give effect to such documents for statutory purposes, albeit to a limited extent. It would be inappropriate and indeed perverse to construe such documents so strictly as to undermine their effectiveness or their effectiveness for their purpose.

Professor Dal Pont has criticized[13] the 'practical and purposive' wording as not adding much **17.13** to the analysis of a provision, but instead just leading on to the adoption of a broad approach.

But the approach has been followed (and cited constantly in later cases). In *Independent* **17.14** *Trustee Services Ltd v Knell*[14] Norris J commented:

> Within the context of a pension scheme the interpretation must be one that is practical and purposive, and if more than one interpretation is possible, the correct choice may depend on the practical consequences of choosing one rather than the other.

He later cited on this point the observation of Neuberger J (as he then was) in *Bestrustees v* **17.15** *Stuart*[15] that:

> . . . A pension scheme is likely to continue for a substantial period of time and . . . those most affected by them and entitled to protection from the Trustees, the employer and indeed the court, will be people who are comparatively poor, who will not have easy access to expert legal advice, and who will not know what has been going on in relation to the management of the Scheme. In those circumstances, it seems to me that protection of the beneficiaries requires the court to be very careful before it permits a departure from the plain wording and plain requirements of the Trust Deed.

---

[9] [1991] 2 All ER 513, [1990] 1 WLR 1587 at 1610–11 (Warner J).
[10] *Re Courage Group's Pension Schemes* [1987] 1 All ER 528 at 537 (Millett J).
[11] [2000] ICR 174, [1999] OPLR 95 at 106 [41], CA.
[12] [2011] EWHC 485 (Ch), [2011] All ER (D) 108 (Mar) (Henderson J). See also the Court of Appeal in *Re K & J Holdings Ltd; Capital Cranfield Trustees Ltd v Walsh* [2005] EWCA Civ 860, [2005] 4 All ER 449, CA.
[13] Gino Dal Pont, 'The Amendment of Trust Deeds—A Super(Annuation) Gloss?' (2008) 31 Australian Bar Review 1 at 7–9.
[14] [2010] EWHC 650 (Ch) (Norris J).
[15] [2001] OPLR 341 at [34] (Neuberger J).

Stevens v Bell Principles

17.16   In 2002 in the British Airways case, *Stevens v Bell*,[16] Arden LJ (with whom Waller and Auld LJJ agreed) set out a number of interpretation principles for pension schemes including in particular the following statement:

> ...a pension scheme should be construed so to give a reasonable and practical effect to the scheme...it is necessary to test competing permissible constructions of a pension scheme against the consequences they produce in practice. Technicality is to be avoided. If the consequences are impractical or over-restrictive or technical in practice, that is an indication that some other interpretation is the appropriate one.

17.17   The next section in this chapter adapts and comments on the list of principles produced by Arden LJ.

No special rules of construction for pensions

17.18   Arden LJ held that there are no special rules of construction but pension schemes have certain characteristics which tend to differentiate them from other analogous instruments. She went on to hold, in summary:

> First, members of a scheme are not volunteers: the benefits which they receive under the scheme are part of the remuneration for their services and this is so whether the scheme is contributory or non-contributory. This means that they are in a different position in some respects from beneficiaries of a private trust. Moreover, the relationship of members to the employer must be seen as running in parallel with their employment relationship. This factor, too, can in appropriate circumstances have an effect on the interpretation of the scheme.
>
> 28. Second, a pension scheme should be construed so [as] to give a reasonable and practical effect to the scheme.... In other words, it is necessary to test competing permissible constructions of a pension scheme against the consequences they produce in practice. Technicality is to be avoided. If the consequences are impractical or over-restrictive or technical in practice, that is an indication that some other interpretation is the appropriate one.
>
> . . .
>
> 29. Third, in pension schemes, difficulties can arise where different provisions have been amended at different points in time. The effect is that the version of the scheme in issue may represent a 'patchwork' of provisions...The general principle is that each new provision should be considered against the circumstances prevailing at the date when it was adopted...Likewise, the meaning of a clause in the scheme must be ascertained by examining the deed as it stood at the time the clause was first introduced.
>
> . . .
>
> 30. Fourth, as with any other instrument, a provision of a trust deed must be interpreted in the light of the factual situation at the time it was created. This includes the practice and requirements of the Inland Revenue at that time, and may include common practice among practitioners in the field as evidenced by the works of practitioners at that time. It has been submitted to us that the factual background is only relevant if the document is ambiguous. I do not accept this submission, which is inconsistent with the approach laid down by Lord Hoffmann in *Investors Compensation Scheme Ltd v West Bromwich Building Society* [1998] 1 WLR 896.
>
> . . .

---

[16]   [2002] EWCA Civ 672, [2002] OPLR 207 at [26]–[32], CA. Sometimes cited as *British Airways Pension Trustees Ltd v British Airways plc.*

31. Fifth, at the end of the day, however, the function of the court is to construe the document without any predisposition as to the correct philosophical approach.

. . .

32. Sixth, a pension scheme should be interpreted as a whole. The meaning of a particular clause should be considered in conjunction with other relevant clauses. To borrow John Donne's famous phrase, no clause 'is an Island entire of itself'.

These are discussed in turn below: **17.19**

1 Members are not volunteers

Members of a scheme are not volunteers: the benefits which they receive under the scheme   **17.20**
are part of the remuneration for their services and this is so whether the scheme is contributory
or non-contributory. This means that they are in a different position in some respects from
beneficiaries of a private trust.[17]

The relationship of members to the employer must be seen as running in parallel with their   **17.21**
employment relationship. This factor, too, can in appropriate circumstances have an effect
on the interpretation of the scheme.

2 Give reasonable and practical effect

A pension scheme should be construed so as to give a reasonable and practical effect   **17.22**
to the scheme. The administration of a pension fund is a complex matter. It would be
'crying for the moon' to expect the draftsman to have legislated exhaustively for every
eventuality.

Millett J said in *Re Courage Group's Pension Schemes*:[18]   **17.23**

> its provisions should wherever possible be construed to give reasonable and practical effect
> to the scheme, bearing in mind that it has to be operated against a constantly changing
> commercial background. It is important to avoid unduly fettering the power to amend the
> provisions of the scheme, thereby preventing the parties from making those changes which
> may be required by the exigencies of commercial life.

Arden LJ held in *Stevens* that it is necessary to test competing permissible constructions of   **17.24**
a pension scheme against the consequences they produce in practice. Technicality is to be
avoided. If the consequences are impractical or over-restrictive or technical in practice, that
is an indication that some other interpretation is the appropriate one.

In *National Grid*,[19] where there was a choice of possible constructions, Lord Hoffmann held   **17.25**
that the correct choice depended 'upon the language of the scheme and the practical consequences of choosing one construction rather than the other'.

3 Patchwork effect

In pension schemes, difficulties can arise where different provisions have been amended at   **17.26**
different points in time. The effect is that the version of the scheme in issue may represent a

---

[17] See further Ch 2 'Pensions trusts and general trust law'.
[18] [1987] 1 WLR 495 at 505F–G (Millett J). In effect the narrow position adopted by Cross J in the old
case *Re Alfred Herbert Ltd Pension and Life Assurance Scheme Trusts* [1960] 1 All ER 618 has been superseded.
[19] [2001] OPLR 15 at 28 [53], HL.

'patchwork' of provisions: see Robert Walker J (as he then was) in the *National Grid* case[20] at first instance.[21]

17.27 Pension schemes are often subject to considerable amendment over time. The general principle is that each new provision should be considered against the circumstances prevailing at the date when it was adopted rather than as at the date of the original trust deed: see Millett J in *Re Courage*.[22]

17.28 Arden LJ held in *Stevens* that the meaning of a clause in the scheme must be ascertained by examining the deed as it stood at the time the clause was first introduced.

17.29 Later in *Alitalia*,[23] Henderson J followed Robert Walker J in *National Grid*, commenting:

> 18. It is common ground that the provisions of previous scheme documents which have been superseded may sometimes throw helpful light on the construction of the current scheme documents: see for example *The National Grid Company Plc v Laws and others* [1997] PLR 157 ('National Grid') at paragraphs [69] to [73] per Robert Walker J (as he then was). As the judge said in paragraph [72]:
>
> > The superseded provisions did at one time stand as part of the scheme, and a comparison of the old and the new may sometimes help to explain the purpose and meaning of the new provision.
>
> However, he went on to sound a salutary note of caution, with which I respectfully agree, in paragraph [73]:
>
> > I conclude that the court can, as an aid to construction, look at provisions of a pension scheme which have been superseded by an amendment. But the court should be slow to do so, both because of the inconvenience involved and because of the uncertainty (apart from exceptional cases) of deriving any useful assistance from the exercise.

17.30 In a later case, *Stena Line Ltd v Merchant Navy Ratings Pension Fund Trustees Ltd*,[24] Briggs J (as he then was) discussed the timing point further. What would the interpretation be if a clause had been incorporated on the scheme being set up, but had then been readopted without amendment in various later deeds? Did its meaning remain fixed as at the date when first adopted or could it vary gradually over time?

17.31 Briggs J referred to Arden LJ's principles in *Stevens* and held:

> 97. In my judgment the answer to this apparent conundrum is as follows.
>
> First, the starting point in relation to powers to amend pension schemes is that they should be given a broad interpretation, consistent with the need to preserve their utility over a long period of unpredictable future events, and to be of practical use in circumstances which the original framers of the power may have been unable even to imagine, at the time of its inception.
>
> Secondly, but with that important consideration in mind, the starting point for the interpretation of any particular clause in the patchwork constituted by a frequently varied pension scheme is indeed the time at which that clause is first introduced.
>
> Thirdly, the analysis does not stop there. As Arden LJ pointed out in *British Airways* at paragraph 32, a pension scheme is to be interpreted as a whole, and the meaning of any

---

[20] [1997] OPLR 207 at 223A (Robert Walker J).

[21] But note that in *National Grid* the House of Lords, Lord Hoffmann had commented that wording in other parts of the trust deed may not be appropriate to use in interpreting another clause. He commented that 'such arguments are often perilous, especially when applied to a patchwork document like the pension scheme'. This was not mentioned by Arden LJ in *Stevens*.

[22] [1987] 1 WLR 495 at 505–6 (Millett J).

[23] *Alitalia-Linee Aeree Italiane SPA v Rotunno* [2008] EWHC 185 (Ch) (Henderson J).

[24] [2010] EWHC 1805 (Ch) (Briggs J).

particular clause considered in conjunction with all other relevant clauses. Thus, a clause which is not itself amended may nonetheless take on a different meaning, or at least shade of meaning, by reference to relevant amendments introduced into the scheme at a time when the clause in question is merely repeated verbatim.

Fourthly, changes in circumstances which have occurred by the time an amendment power comes to be exercised (even if unchanged in language throughout), may affect the validity of any particular proposed exercise of that power at that later time.

98. In conclusion, I am satisfied that nothing in that analysis conflicts with the warning against any predisposition as to the correct philosophical approach: see *British Airways* at paragraph 31 and *Pilots* at paragraph 146. The wisdom of giving a prima facie broad interpretation to powers of amendment contained in pension schemes derives not from an inappropriate philosophical disposition, but from sound business common sense.

In the Court of Appeal, *Stena Line Ltd v Merchant Navy Ratings Pension Fund Trustees Ltd*,[25] **17.32** Arden LJ (with whom Toulson and Rimer LJJ agreed) held that a provision could change its meaning over time even if re-adopted without any change in subsequent deeds. The meaning was not frozen by reference to its meaning on first adoption. She held:

> [33] That passage was not directed to the situation which arises in the present appeal, where a clause in the original trust deed is adopted again when the deed is revised and replaced by a new trust deed, albeit one containing, to all and intents and purposes, the same clause and the question as to the meaning of the clause is one to be asked at the present time. Here cl 30 formed part of trust deed at all material times, but new trust deeds were adopted in substitution for the previous trust deed in 1985, 1994, 2001 and 2007. If an amendment is now proposed to deal with the current deficit, the question will be whether that amendment can now be carried out under that clause as it stands today.

> [34] I accept Mr Spink's submission that, even though the very same clause is effectively re-adopted in the same form, its meaning may change on each re-introduction if the context in which it is re-adopted is materially different. Its meaning may be narrowed, or it may equally well have been widened, because of changes in the relevant background circumstances which fall to be taken into account in interpretation. Likewise I would also accept, as did the judge in para 97 of his judgment, that it is possible that the meaning of a clause changes on re-adoption because there has been some material change in the scope or effect of some other clause in the period between its introduction and its re-introduction that has an impact on it.

In interpreting a scheme it is probably necessary to look at the previous scheme deeds—see **17.33** the comments of Lord Hoffmann in *National Grid v Mayes*[26] and the Court of Appeal in *Harris v Lord Shuttleworth*.[27]

4 In the light of the factual situation

As with any other instrument, a provision of a trust deed must be interpreted in the light of **17.34** the factual situation at the time it was created.[28]

This includes the practice and requirements of the Inland Revenue (now HMRC) at that **17.35** time, and may include common practice among practitioners in the field as evidenced by the works of practitioners at that time.[29]

---

[25] [2011] EWCA Civ 543, CA.
[26] [2001] UKHL 20, [2001] 2 All ER 417 at [22]–[24], HL. See also Robert Walker J at first instance.
[27] [1995] OPLR 79 at 89, CA.
[28] See to the same effect in a contractual context, *Crema v Cenkos Securities plc* [2010] EWCA Civ 1444, CA.
[29] See also on this *Redrow plc v Pedley* [2002] EWHC 983 (Ch), [2003] OPLR 292 at [15] (Sir Andrew Morritt V-C).

17.36 Arden LJ held in *Stevens* that the factual background is not only relevant if the document is ambiguous, citing Lord Hoffmann in *Investors Compensation Scheme Ltd v West Bromwich Building Society*.[30] In Lord Hoffmann's words:

> [i]nterpretation is the ascertainment of the meaning which the document would convey to a reasonable person having all the background knowledge that would reasonably have been available to the parties in the situation in which they were at the time of the contract.

17.37 In later contractual cases, the House of Lords and the Supreme Court have subsequently ruled to the same effect (that no ambiguity is needed) in *Chartbrook*[31] and *Rainy Sky*.[32]

17.38 In *Rainy Sky SA v Kookmin Bank*[33] Lord Clarke held:

> The language used by the parties will often have more than one potential meaning. I would accept the submission made on behalf of the Appellants that the exercise of construction is essentially one unitary exercise in which the court must consider the language used and ascertain what a reasonable person, that is a person who has all the background knowledge which would reasonably have been available to the parties in the situation in which they were at the time of the contract, would have understood the parties to have meant. In doing so, the court must have regard to all the relevant surrounding circumstances. If there are two possible constructions, the court is entitled to prefer the construction which is consistent with business common sense and to reject the other.

17.39 Arden LJ in *Stevens* also referred to *Investors Compensation Scheme*, where Lord Hoffmann also distinguished[34] the meaning of the words to be found in dictionaries from the meaning of documents:

> (4) The meaning which a document (or any other utterance) would convey to a reasonable man is not the same thing as the meaning of its words. The meaning of words is a matter of dictionaries and grammars; the meaning of the document is what the parties using those words against the relevant background would reasonably have been understood to mean. The background may not merely enable the reasonable man to choose between the possible meanings of words which are ambiguous but even (as occasionally happens in ordinary life) to conclude that the parties must, for whatever reason, have used the wrong words or syntax: see *Mannai Investments Co Ltd v Eagle Star Life Assurance Co Ltd* [1997] AC 749.

17.40 A good example of this principle is the decision of Etherton J (as he then was) in *Hearn v Younger*.[35] Etherton J held that an announcement (which may have taken effect as an amendment) referring to pension increases being given in future on pensions should be construed as not applying such increases on that part of the pension that was the guaranteed minimum pension (GMP). The parties would have taken that carve-out as understood (even though not expressly mentioned).

5 No predisposition as to a philosophical approach as to ownership of surplus

17.41 At the end of the day, the function of the court is to construe the document without any predisposition as to the correct philosophical approach.

---

[30] [1998] 1 WLR 896 at 912H, HL.
[31] *Chartbrook Ltd v Persimmon Homes Ltd* [2009] UKHL 38, [2009] AC 1101, HL.
[32] *Rainy Sky SA v Kookmin Bank* [2011] UKSC 50, [2012] 1 All ER 1137, SC.
[33] [2011] UKSC 50, [2012] 1 All ER 1137 at [21], SC.
[34] [1998] 1 WLR 896 at 913B–D, HL.
[35] [2002] EWHC 963 (Ch), [2003] OPLR 45 (Etherton J).

Arden LJ rejected submissions based on a philosophical approach. The members argued **17.42** that the 'overall approach' of the Trust Deed was favourable to the members. The employer submitted that it should be remembered that this was a balance-of-cost scheme and so the fact that there was a surplus meant that the employer had paid too much.

Arden LJ quoted Brooke LJ, giving the judgment of the Court of Appeal in the *National* **17.43** *Grid* case:[36]

> The solution to the [problem of construction in that case] lies within the terms of the scheme itself, and not within a world populated by competing philosophies as to the true nature and ownership of an actuarial surplus.

Arden LJ also referred to *National Grid* [37] in the House of Lords where Lord Hoffmann **17.44** rejected the argument of the beneficiaries of the scheme that the surplus represented their contributions or their deferred remuneration. He held that, once it was established that the employer could exercise powers conferred by a scheme in its own interests, 'I do not see the relevance of the way in which the surplus was funded'.

6 Interpret as a whole

A pension scheme should be interpreted as a whole. The meaning of a particular clause **17.45** should be considered in conjunction with other relevant clauses. Arden LJ borrowed John Donne's famous phrase, no clause 'is an Island entire of itself'.

The list of factors set out by Arden LJ has been cited and followed in many later cases, for **17.46** example: *HR Trustees v German*[38] and other cases.[39] These principles have been cited and followed in Australia—see the *Ansett* case[40] and the High Court in *Byrnes v Kendle*,[41] a private trust case.

Other Legal Interpretation Principles

Other legal principles can also apply to interpretation. **17.47**

Previous legal decisions

Generally, decisions of other courts in relation to wording in deeds are not strictly binding. **17.48** This is so even if the exact same wording is being used. This is because inevitably the other terms of the deed will differ—see Jessel MR in *New Callao Ltd*.[42]

---

[36] [1999] OPLR 95 at 108H [54], CA.

[37] *National Grid Co plc v Mayes; International Power plc (formerly National Power plc) v Healy* [2001] UKHL 20, [2001] 2 All ER 417, [2001] OPLR 15 at 22C [16], HL.

[38] [2009] EWHC 2785 (Ch) (Arnold J).

[39] *Sarjeant v Rigid Group Ltd* [2012] EWHC 3757 (Ch) (HH Judge Cooke); *Danks v Qinetiq Holdings Ltd* [2012] EWHC 570 (Ch) (Vos J); *Premier Foods Group Services Ltd v RHM Pension Trust Ltd* [2012] EWHC 447 (Ch) (Warren J); *Stena Line Ltd v Merchant Navy Ratings Pension Fund Trustees Ltd* [2011] EWCA Civ 543, CA; *PNPF Trust Co Ltd v Taylor* [2010] EWHC 1573 (Ch) (Warren J); *Independent Trustee Services Ltd v Knell* [2010] EWHC 650 (Ch) (Norris J); *Alitalia-Linee Aeree Italiane SPA v Rotunno* [2008] EWHC 185 (Ch) (Henderson J); *MNOPF Trustees Ltd v FT Everard & Sons Ltd* [2005] EWHC 446 (Ch), [2005] OPLR 315 (Patten J); *Armitage v Staveley Industries* [2006] PLR 191 at 196–7. See also the Court of Appeal in *Re K & J Holdings Ltd; Capital Cranfield Trustees Ltd v Walsh* [2005] EWCA Civ 860, [2005] 4 All ER 449, CA.

[40] *Ansett Australia Ground Staff Superannuation Plan Pty Ltd v Ansett Australia Ltd* [2002] VSC 576, 174 FLR 1 at [216] (Warren J).

[41] [2011] HCA 26, (2011) 14 ITELR 299 at [111], HC Aus.

[42] (1882) 22 ChD 484 at 488. See also *Hack v London Provincial Building Soc* (1883) 23 ChD 103 at 111; *Pedlar v Road Block Gold Mines of India* [1905] 2 Ch 427; and *Ashville Investments Ltd v Elmer Contractors Ltd* [1989] 1 QB 488 at 495.

Post-contractual conduct

17.49 In a pensions case, *Entrust Pension Ltd v Prospect Hospice Ltd*,[43] Henderson J held that the subsequent conduct of the parties could not be used as an aid to construction. He approved the statement in Lewison, *The Interpretation of Contracts*:[44]

> The court may not generally look at the subsequent conduct of the parties to interpret a written agreement. However, where the agreement is partly written and partly oral, subsequent conduct may be examined for the purpose of determining what were the full terms of the contract. In addition the subsequent conduct of the parties may be examined where an estoppel by convention is alleged; where it is alleged that the agreement was a sham; and probably for the purposes of determining the boundaries of an ambiguous grant of land.

17.50 Henderson J held that the basic principle was clearly stated by Lord Reid in *Whitworth Street Estates Ltd v Miller*:[45]

> I must say that I had thought that it is now well settled that it is not legitimate to use as an aid in the construction of the contract anything which the parties said or did after it was made. Otherwise one might have the result that a contract meant one thing the day it was signed, but by reason of subsequent events meant something different a month or a year later.

17.51 To the contrary, see Rimer LJ in *Neufeld v Secretary of State*[46] holding that the actions of the parties in relation to the performance of an employment contract can be used as a guide to the correct meaning of the contract. The contracts in *Neufeld* seem not to have been written— see para [89] and the case mainly turned on whether or not the individual was an employee or not. Special rules may perhaps apply to employment contracts when looking to determine employment status—*Autoclenz Ltd v Belcher*.[47]

Methods of Variation

17.52 There are various mechanics available for the amendment of the terms of an occupational pension scheme:

(a) an express amendment power within the scheme itself;
(b) amendment by statute or under an amendment power in a statute;
(c) amendment by express agreement between the employer and the member;
(d) amendment by announcement or augmentation

Augmentation powers

17.53 In addition to express powers of amendment (relating to the trust deed and rules etc), pension schemes usually include an express power of augmentation.

---

[43] [2012] EWHC 1666 (Ch) at [46] (Henderson J).
[44] 5th edn (Sweet & Maxwell, 2011) para 3.19.
[45] [1970] AC 583, [1970] 1 All ER 796, HL. This does not apply to oral contracts—*Maggs v Miller* [2006] EWCA Civ 1058, CA. It was also criticized by Lord Nicholls (speaking extra-judicially) in 'My Kingdom for a Horse: The Meaning of Words' (2005) 121 LQR 577 (the Chancery Bar Association Annual Lecture, March 2005).
[46] [2009] EWCA Civ 280, [2009] 3 All ER 790, CA.
[47] [2011] UKSC 41, [2011] 4 All ER 745, SC.

This is a power for the employer to be able to direct (or agree with the trustee) for increased **17.54** benefits to be payable to one or more members. Such an amendment to the standard benefit rules in a particular situation may well need extra funding (hence the common provision requiring the trustees to need to agree), or at least to be able to specify increased funding.

Such augmentation is, technically, an amendment of the terms of the pension scheme trust, **17.55** but is a standard provision in private sector occupational pension schemes. It gives increased flexibility.

To be contrasted with this would be an express agreement between the employer and the amend- **17.56** ment to *reduce* the level of benefits, in particular for future service. There is no reason in principle why such an agreement should not apply and be enforceable (binding the trustees even if they are not a party to the underlying agreement)—see Chapter 15 (Contract overriding trust).

Statutory Amendment Powers

The Occupational Pensions Board (OPB) used to have various statutory powers to amend pen- **17.57** sion schemes by issuing a modification order. Latterly these were in ss 136–142 of the Pension Schemes Act 1993. They covered modifications for various purposes, including to enable transfers-out, to dis-apply perpetuity rules, and to deal with contracting-out or winding-up. There was also a power to allow return on surplus.[48] These powers were repealed from 6 April 1997 by the Pensions Act 1995 (when Opra was replaced by the Pensions Regulator).

The Pensions Regulator has a statutory power to modify a scheme being wound-up to enable **17.58** assets remaining after the liabilities of the scheme have been fully discharged to be dis- tributed to the employer, where prescribed requirements in relation to the distribution are satisfied—s 69 of the Pensions Act 1995. There is also a statutory amendment power for the Regulator to help a scheme winding-up if the employer is in an insolvency process—s 71A of the Pensions Act 1995.[49]

There are various statutory provisions giving trustees and employers statutory powers allow- **17.59** ing the terms of occupational pension schemes (in particular the benefits) to be amended. The main ones are:

(a) **Pensions Act 1995, s 68**:[50] statutory powers for trustees to amend schemes with a view to achieving a number of listed statutory purposes. The list can be added to by statutory instrument;

(b) **Pensions Act 2004, s 229(2)**: a power for the trustee and employer to agree to reduce the accrual of future service benefits if the employer and the trustee are unable to agree on the scheme funding under the Pensions Act 2004;

(c) **Pensions Act 2004, s 251**:[51] a transitional power for trustees to modify a scheme to allow payments of surplus to an employer (the section was put in place in light of the tax changes made by the Finance Act 2004);

---

[48] See eg *Taylor v Lucas Pensions Trust* [1994] OPLR 29 (Vinelott J).
[49] Inserted by the Child Support, Pensions and Social Security Act 2000.
[50] See David Pollard, 'Section 68: The Forgotten Section?' (APL seminar, February 2001).
[51] The original section caused a number of difficulties (eg it seemed to apply to all payments to an employer, including those not taxed or at full value). Section 251 was substantially modified (and the transitional period extended) by s 25 of the Pensions Act 2011.

(d) **Equality Act 2010, s 62**: a power for trustees to make alterations to a scheme if these are required to allow it to comply with the non-discrimination rule[52] implied under s 61. The power applies if the trustees do not otherwise have the relevant power or it can only be exercised if this would be unduly complex or protracted or involves obtaining consents which cannot be obtained or can be obtained only with undue delay or difficulty. Given that the non-discrimination rule under s 61 is overriding—s 61(3), the amendment power in s 62 looks to be in order to be able to tidy up the relevant trust deed and rules;

(e) **GMP conversion**: a statutory power for trustees to amend schemes to effect conversion of guaranteed minimum pensions (GMPs)—s 24G of the Pension Schemes Act 1993 (as inserted by s 14 of the Pensions Act 2007);

(f) **Pensions Bill 2013**: the government has proposed to abolish contracting-out of the state second pension. This will impact on costs for employers, members, and schemes. The government has proposed that employers should be given a statutory amendment power to allow schemes to change to cope with this.[53]

Section 68 power

17.60 Section 68 of the Pensions Act 1995 contains a statutory power of amendment for trust-based occupational pension schemes (and stakeholder schemes). It gives trustees a statutory power to amend the terms of the scheme for various purposes. These are:

(a) to extend the class of persons eligible to receive death benefits (with employer consent);[54]

(b) to allow the scheme rules to conform with the statutory provisions for member nominated trustees[55] (Pensions Act 2004, s 241), refunds of surplus (ongoing or on winding-up) and assignment and forfeiture;[56]

(c) to allow the scheme to comply with terms and conditions laid down by the Pension Protection Fund as a condition of payment under the fraud compensation provisions (Pensions Act 2004, s 185);[57]

(d) to modify a scheme to allow an apportionment arrangement (allocating the statutory debt on employers under s 75 of the Pensions Act 1995 amongst employers in a multi-employer scheme) to be entered into;[58]

(e) to allow a scheme to deal with pension credit members following a divorce sharing order;[59]

(f) (before 6 April 2011) to amend a scheme to deal (broadly) with the effect of the changes to the tax rules from 6 April 2006 made by the Finance Act 2004;[60]

(g) to allow a scheme to remove any pre-2006 requirement for the consent of the Inland Revenue to the exercise of a power;[61]

---

[52] Discrimination for this purpose is defined in Ch 2 of Pt 2 by reference to discrimination etc because of a 'protected characteristic' (defined in Ch 1 of Pt 2—eg sex, race, age, disability, religion, or belief etc).

[53] See cl 24 and Sch 14 in the Pensions Bill introduced to the House of Commons on 9 May 2013.

[54] Section 68(2)(a) and (3).

[55] Including to allow a scheme to increase the number of trustees to deal with MNTs.

[56] Section 68(2)(b) and (d).

[57] Section 68(2)(c).

[58] Occupational Pension Schemes (Employer Debt) Regulations 2005 (SI 2005/678, as amended by SI 2010/725), reg 16.

[59] Section 68(2)(da) inserted by the Welfare Reform and Pensions Act 1999.

[60] Occupational Pension Schemes (Modification of Schemes) Regulations 2006 (SI 2006/759), reg 6.

[61] Occupational Pension Schemes (Modification of Schemes) Regulations 2006 (SI 2006/759 as inserted by SI 2010/499), reg 6A.

(h) to fix the time for priority of benefits on a winding-up following running as a closed scheme;[62]

(i) to modify a shared cost scheme to deal with extra contributions required under a recovery plan;[63]

(j) to allow a stakeholder scheme to comply with the statutory conditions to qualify as such a scheme.[64]

Section 229 power

Section 229(2) of the Pensions Act 2004 contains a power for the trustee and employer **17.61** to agree to reduce the accrual of future service benefits if the employer and the trustee are unable to agree on the scheme funding under the Pensions Act 2004. This power seems to be designed to allow trustees and employers to agree to a reduction in future service accrual, even if this is not possible under the terms of the relevant pension scheme (or, seemingly, contrary to any other restriction, including statutory protection application in some industries such as rail, coal etc).

This is a free-standing power allowing such amendments, although there is limitation in that **17.62** 'subsisting rights' (as defined in s 67 of the Pensions Act 1995) cannot be reduced. The power for the trustee and employer combines with the power of the Pensions Regulator to the same effect under s 231 of the Pensions Act 2004.

Schemes of arrangement under the Companies Act

The companies legislation has long included a power for the court to approve a scheme of **17.63** arrangement involving the members of the company or its creditors.[65] Currently this is in Pt 26 (ss 895–899) of the Companies Act 2006. This involves a company making a compromise or arrangement with its members or creditors (or any class of them).

A vote of the affected members or creditors is needed, but if approved, the arrangement is **17.64** binding on all parties (including those who did not vote or voted against) the arrangement.

If the trustee of a pension scheme is a company (which is common), the question arises as to **17.65** whether a compromise under Pt 26 could be used to amend the benefits of the members. Such a procedure would be quite useful in that a majority vote may be able to bind all members (even those who dissent or do not vote) and could give more flexibility than is allowed by an amendment power (given the s 67 limits). There would be issues in deciding on the relevant classes who get to vote, but there are safeguards in that court approval is needed.

But it is clear that a scheme of arrangement cannot be used. Part 26 only applies to 'creditors'. **17.66** Beneficiaries under a trust (such as members of a pension scheme) are not creditors of the trustee, but instead have rights as beneficiaries. In *Re Lehman Brothers International (Europe) (No 2)*,[66] the Court of Appeal held that Pt 26 could not apply to compromise the interests of trust beneficiaries.

---

[62] Occupational Pension Schemes (Winding Up) Regulations 1996 (SI 1996/3126), reg 5.
[63] Occupational Pension Schemes (Scheme Funding) Regulations 2005 (SI 2005/3377), reg 5.
[64] Welfare Reform and Pensions Act 1999, Sch 1, para 1(4).
[65] See Geoff O'Dea, Julian Long, and Alexandra Smyth, *Schemes of Arrangement: Law and Practice* (Oxford University Press, 2012).
[66] [2009] EWCA Civ 1161, [2010] 1 BCLC 496, CA.

Statutory Limitations on Amendments

17.67 Legislation also includes restrictions on the ability of a scheme to amend benefits.[67] The main limitations are:

(a) s 67 of the Pensions Act 1995: this broadly limits amendments that can be made to accrued or subsisting rights;

(b) s 37 of the Pension Schemes Act 1993: this invalidates amendments to contracted-out schemes if they would reduce accrued contracted-out rights or (in relation to future service benefits) a confirmation is not obtained from the scheme actuary;

(c) s 91 of the Pensions Act 1995 contains limits on the ability of a member to surrender or assign his or her pension rights. This probably does not apply to an amendment of the scheme (but the inter-relation of this section with the s 67 limits is unclear); and

(d) amendments discriminating between short service benefits and long service benefits are prohibited by the preservation legislation—s 72 of the Pension Schemes Act 1993.[68]

Section 67 of the Pensions Act 1995

17.68 Before April 1997 (when s 67 came into force) there was no express general restriction in the legislation on the ability of a scheme to be amended to reduce benefits. The Goode Committee recommended that such a restriction be included in legislation and s 67 of the Pensions Act 1995 was enacted. It was later substantially amended by the Pensions Act 2004. Section 67 does not have retrospective effect—see *South West Trains v Wightman*.[69]

17.69 Section 67[70] provides express restrictions on a power under a scheme to make amendments to the scheme (or indeed to the exercise a power under the scheme) which could have the effect to reduce the benefits to and in respect of a member under the scheme where those benefits are 'subsisting rights' (formerly 'accrued rights').

17.70 Such reductions are possible if the member gives written consent or if the scheme actuary is able to give a certificate of actuarial equivalence. The legislation now provides for various forms of prior notices to be given to the members of any such impending change.

17.71 Section 67 does not apply to amendments made otherwise than under the terms of the scheme (eg under a statutory power, such as that in s 68, or by court order, for example by rectification). Various changes are exempt under regulations[71]—eg inserting lien or set-off rights, modifying death benefits to deal with civil partners.

17.72 Failure to comply with the limitation in s 67 does not render the amendment void, but does make it voidable at the order of the Pensions Regulator—ss 67(2) and 67H(3).

---

[67] This is in addition to the overriding nature of most of the pensions legislation. For example, any amendment to a pension trust to provide for indexation of increases to pensions to a level below the minimum level required by s 51 of the Pensions Act 1995 would be ineffective.

[68] Formerly the Social Security Act 1973, Sch 16, para 8.

[69] [1997] OPLR 249 at 266 (Neuberger J).

[70] See Elizabeth Ovey, 'Section 67 Revisited' (APL Conference, 2012) and the joint opinion given by Nicholas Warren QC (as he then was) and Paul Newman to the Institute and Faculty of Actuaries (April 2000). Available on the Actuarial website at <http://www.actuaries.org.uk/research-and-resources/documents/s67-pensions-act-1995-opinion>.

[71] Occupational Pension Schemes (Modification of Schemes) Regulations 2006 (SI 2006/759), reg 3.

For the purposes of s 67, the legislation expressly confirms that the relevant 'subsisting rights' or 'accrued rights' are the rights applicable to a member should he or she elect to leave pensionable service.[72] This means that the benefits (which are protected) are calculated on the basis of the benefits applicable to a member who becomes a deferred member. Thus benefits only applicable to an active member (each year a lump sum death benefit) are not protected. **17.73**

In addition, it is clear that only rights are protected—not benefits payable on the exercise of a discretion (eg a lump sum death benefit payable under the terms of a discretionary trust). **17.74**

There are still a number of issues determining whether a particular benefit is protected by the s 67 restrictions. This can be difficult to determine—see for example the Court of Appeal in *AON Trust Corpn Ltd v KPMG*.[73] **17.75**

Section 37 of the Pensions Schemes Act 1993

Section 37 of the Pension Schemes Act 1993 operates to render void amendments to a scheme that affect contracted-out benefits, unless (in the case of contracted-out rights relating to service after 6 April 1997) a relevant certificate is obtained from the scheme actuary that the scheme would continue to meet the relevant benefit test for such benefits. **17.76**

Consultation

The Pensions Act 2004 also requires employers to consult in advance with affected employees (or their representatives) should amendments be proposed to benefits under an occupational scheme. The relevant amendments are those defined as a 'listed change' in the regulations.[74] **17.77**

Misstatement in Booklets/Estoppel

Pension trustees (and employers) regularly inform members of the terms of the scheme and other benefits payable under the scheme. Inevitably such information is often incomplete (it may well be expressed as only a summary of the benefits or trust instruments etc) or can be wrong (eg could overstate the level of benefit payable). **17.78**

In general, the courts have held in a number of cases that such statements or announcements etc are not generally binding on either the employer/trustee or the individual member.[75] Some form of express agreement by the employee is usually needed (eg if a benefit is reduced) and, where a stated benefit is larger than required, some form of estoppel by the employer/trustee would need to be shown for the member to succeed it making it legal enforceable. **17.79**

---

[72] Pensions Act 1995, ss 67A(6) and 124(2).
[73] [2005] EWCA Civ 1004, [2006] 1 All ER 238, CA. See also *Danks v Qinetiq Holdings Ltd* [2012] EWHC 570 (Ch), [2012] PLR 131 (Vos J).
[74] Pensions Act 2004, ss 259–261 and the Occupational and Personal Pension Schemes (Consultation by Employers and Miscellaneous Amendment) Regulations 2006 (SI 2006/349). See *Freshfields on Corporate Pensions Law 2013* (ed Pollard and Magoffin) (Bloomsbury Professional, 2013) Ch 15.
[75] See Dan Schaffer and Sarah McNally, 'Misleading Member Communications: The Last Word?' (APL seminar, September 2011); Nigel Burroughs, 'Estoppel and Pension Schemes' (APL conference, 1994); and Mark Atkinson, 'That's Not What We Meant . . . Rectification, Mistake and Estoppel' (APL spring conference, May 2001).

Benefit reduction

17.80 One of the earliest pensions cases, *Icarus (Hertford) Ltd v Driscoll* [76] gave some support that a benefit change which had been announced (benefits being reduced along with contributions being reduced) and put into effect was binding on the members who had received the announcement. This was a (perhaps rare) case of an announcement which has an immediate practical effect on the individual members (they paid lower contributions).

17.81 However, subsequent cases have been much more reluctant to find that an announced change is binding on the members by estoppel (where there has been no formal amendment to the terms of the scheme as required by the scheme amendment rule).

17.82 This is in line with the general rule adopted in employment matters that changes announced by an employer (by way of reduction are not for composition or reliability) are not generally treated as accepted and agreed by the employee merely by the employee continuing to work, unless the change had an immediate practical effect on the employee. Pension changes do not often have such a practical effect so therefore fall within this principle.

17.83 The *Icarus* case was itself doubted in a more recent case, *HR Trustees Ltd v German*. [77] Arnold J criticized *Icarus* as being 'unreasonable' and dating from the 'relatively early days of pension scheme litigation'.

17.84 In relation to detrimental amendments, estoppel binding on a member can be considered to be unlikely. Merely continuing to work after receiving an announcement is probably not enough—see *Redrow Plc v Pedley*;[78] *Trustee Solutions v Dubery*;[79] *Hodgson v Toray Textiles Europe Ltd*;[80] *Foster Wheeler Ltd v Hanley*;[81] and *Capita ATL Pension Trustees Ltd v Gellately*.[82] See also Chapter 15 (Contract overriding trust).

17.85 Later cases on benefit reduction have tended to focus on whether the terms of the relevant announcement can be a trigger of a formal amendment under the terms of the applicable amendment power.

Increased benefits

17.86 A similar principle has been applied by the courts in rather a large number of cases where a benefit has been overstated in a booklet or an announcement (ie in a manner inconsistent with the underlying trust deed and rules governing the scheme). In these cases, the courts have generally held that the terms of the booklet or announcement are usually clearly only intended as a summary of the position (perhaps with a statement included that the trust deed and rules is overriding). Examples of cases on this are *Lloyds Bank Pension Trust v Lloyds Bank*,[83] *ITN v Ward*,[84] and *Steria Ltd v Hutchison*.[85] In *Steria*, an inaccurate announcement and booklet were held not to override the position stated in the trust deed and rules.

---

[76] [1990] PLR 1 (Aldous J).
[77] [2009] EWHC 2785 (Ch) (Arnold J).
[78] [2002] EWHC 983 (Ch), [2003] OPLR 29 (Sir Andrew Morritt V-C).
[79] [2006] EWHC 1426 (Ch), [2007] 1 All ER 308, [2006] PLR 177 (Lewison J).
[80] [2006] EWHC 2612 (Ch), [2006] PLR 253 (Lewison J).
[81] [2008] EWHC (Ch), [2009] PLR 39 (Patten J).
[82] [2011] EWHC 485 (Ch), [2011] All ER (D) 108 (Mar) (Henderson J).
[83] [1996] OPLR 181 (Rimer J).
[84] [1997] PLR 131 (Laddie J).
[85] [2006] EWCA Civ 1551, CA.

The courts have generally held that, depending on the facts, a member may be able to bring a **17.87** claim based on a misleading overstatement (or indeed an over-payment[86]) based on an estoppel or change of position. Effectively this allows a person to rely on a clear representational promise where this is reasonable and equitable. Generally the member must show that his or her position is irreversible and that he or she has acted reasonably in reliance upon the representational promise.

This is a difficult test for individual members in practice to satisfy. Thus an announcement in **17.88** the booklet that in the *ITN* case that pensions would increase by 3 per cent per annum was held not to be something on which the members could rely.[87]

In *Scottish Equitable v Derby*,[88] a case involving an overpayment of benefit by the insurance **17.89** company, the member was required to repay the relevant overpayment even though he had queried it with the insurer on several occasions and had been assured that it was correctly calculated.

In *Hearn v Younger*[89] Etherton J (as he then was) held that the 'explanatory pension scheme **17.90** booklet . . . is expressed in general terms and is manifestly not intended to override the trust deed and rules'.

Members or employees will be able to show detrimental reliance on the basis of such a state- **17.91** ment only if they can show a clear action based on the statement—for example accepting a termination of employment or redundancy on the basis of a pension statement.

Interestingly, the courts have tended to find that a booklet or summary may be binding (as **17.92** part of the employment contract) in cases involving ill-health benefits (eg income protection) where the booklet does not accurately describe the underlying insurance terms.[90]

Booklets—*Steria* in the Court of Appeal

In *Steria Ltd v Hutchison*[91] the Court of Appeal overturned the Pensions Ombudsman and **17.93** the decision at first instance in the High Court and upheld the common view that disclaimers contained in scheme booklets can provide protection from claims by members that representations in a scheme booklet create a binding estoppel.

It is common for a pension scheme's administrators to issue to its members booklets and **17.94** information packs summarizing information that is relevant to its members and contained in the scheme's trust deed and rules. These member booklets generally try to simplify complex pension provisions, as well as certain aspects of pensions law.

Owing to the summary nature of the scheme booklets, inaccuracies sometimes occur between **17.95** what is contained in the scheme booklet and what the trust deed and rules actually say. Issues

[86] See *Scottish Equitable v Derby* [2001] EWCA Civ 369, [2001] 3 All ER 818, CA.
[87] Although the Pensions Ombudsman may order a payment for injury to feelings or distress (this is not usually more than £1,000 and is often in the region of £100). This can mount up to a significant sum if paid to each member.
[88] [2001] EWCA Civ 369, [2001] 3 All ER 818, CA.
[89] [2005] PLR 49 at [111] (Etherton J).
[90] See *Villella v MFI Furniture Centres Ltd* [1999] IRLR 468 (Judge Green QC) and *Jowitt v Pioneer Technology (UK) Ltd* [2003] EWCA Civ 411, [2003] ICR 1120, CA. Contrast *Crossley v Faithful & Gould Holdings Ltd* [2004] EWCA Civ 293, [2004] 4 All ER 447, CA (a senior employee who was expected to have been aware of the terms of the policy).
[91] [2006] EWCA Civ 1551, [2007] ICR 445, CA.

may subsequently arise when administrators attempt to apply the terms of the scheme rules and potentially diverge from the information provided to members in the scheme booklets.

17.96 *Steria* concerned the interaction between a member's booklet and accompanying letter and the rules of the scheme. Mr Hutchison claimed he was led to believe that, provided he had 20 years' pensionable service, he was entitled to retire from the age of 62 without an actuarial reduction to his pension. He based his claim on a letter and a booklet he received inviting him to join the relevant plan. However, under the rules of his pension scheme, the normal retirement date (NRD) was 65 and early retirement was provided only with the consent of the employer.

17.97 Importantly for the administrators of the scheme, the final page of the booklet contained a statement to the effect that members have a right to inspect the legal trust deed and rules governing the scheme and that on any question of interpretation, it was the legal documentation that prevailed over the summary booklet.

17.98 It was not until a number of years after Mr Hutchison joined the scheme that he was made aware of what the trust deed actually provided.

17.99 Mr Hutchison made a claim based on estoppel that his NRD should be age 62 as represented to him in his letter and that he should be entitled to an unreduced pension at that age. He claimed that the letter and booklet provided a clear and unambigious promise that this would be the case.

17.100 Both the Pensions Ombudsman and Peter Smith J in the High Court (on appeal) supported Mr Hutchison's arguments and held that the trustees should provide the higher amount claimed by the member. The Court of Appeal overturned the decision of the Ombudsman and the High Court. Mummery LJ stated that the main point was whether the doctrine of estoppel actually applies to the operation of an occupational pension scheme.

17.101 The judgment was based on the following key points.

    (a) There had not been a clear and unambiguous promise as alleged by the member. Although the offer letter seemed misleading, it should be read alongside the booklet, which:
        (i) defined NRD as age 65;
        (ii) stated that consent of the employer is required for early retirement; and
        (iii) stated that the legal documentation of the scheme prevails over the terms of the booklet.
    (b) The disclaimer made it impossible to rely on the statements contained in the scheme booklet.
    (c) The member had not relied on the representations to his detriment. In fact, had he not joined the scheme (and remained in his previous scheme) he would have been financially worse off.
    (d) There existed no mutual agreement or course of dealing to justify the finding of a collective estoppel.

17.102 The decision of the High Court caused a great deal of surprise to the pensions industry. The Court of Appeal's decision reaffirmed the previously established position on the use of disclaimer statements and the difficulty in proving estoppel arguments. The decision means that it will be very difficult for there to be successful claims by members based solely on a summary booklet. It particular it reaffirmed the effectiveness of disclaimer statements.

A case may still succeed if a member can demonstrate that he 'reasonably relied' on a statement **17.103** and suffered a 'detriment' as a result, especially if the statement was not associated with a disclaimer.

Conversely, shortly after *Steria*, in *R (on the application of Bradley) v Secretary of State for Work* **17.104** *and Pensions*[92] Bean J in the High Court held that the government could not rely on similar wording to defeat a claim based on maladministration based on general information and practices by the government in relation to the security of pensions schemes in insolvency. In *Bradley*, Bean J reaffirmed that a member must demonstrate reliance and detriment to succeed with a claim relating to maladministration.

However, Bean J did note in *Bradley* that the government could not rely on general dis- **17.105** claimer wording in its leaflets to prevent claims based on them. This is a potential divergence in approach from *Steria*. The future interaction between these two cases is unclear. It is worth noting that in DWP the court was predominately concerned with the extent to which the findings of the Parliamentary Ombudsman are binding on the Department for Work and Pensions.

The courts in *Steria* dealt only with estoppel issues and not with any legal arguments based on **17.106** other potential legal claims, for example maladministration causing injustice (an area where the Pensions Ombudsman has jurisdiction) or negligence.

For a (relatively rare) example of a member being able to claim based on estoppel, see Warren **17.107** J in *Catchpole v Trustees of the Alitalia Airlines Pension Scheme*[93] where the unmarried partner of a member was held to be able to rely on a misleading communication given to the member before his death.

Amending an Amendment Power

There is no reason in principle why an amendment power cannot itself be amended by **17.108** use of the amendment power. The issue turns entirely on a question of construction of the amendment power.

If there is an amendment power that merely provides that the employer and the trustees may **17.109** amend the terms of the Scheme (and the trust deed) from time to time, there seems to be no reason why that does not give power for the amendment power itself to be amended (eg to delete any requirement for the trustee to agree to future amendment or to impose a new method of amendment). A similar principle was upheld by the House of Lords in relation to legislation in *R (on the application of Jackson) v Attorney-General*.[94] The House of Lords upheld the use of the procedure in the Parliament Act 1911 to pass an Act of Parliament even though the procedure under the Parliament Act 1911 had been amended using its own provisions (by the Parliament Act 1949).

For example in *Re Smith*,[95] Lord Fraser (in the Court of Session) approved an amendment **17.110** to a pension scheme moving the amendment power from the directors of a company to its

---

[92] [2007] EWHC 242 (Admin) (Bean J).
[93] [2010] EWHC 1809 (Ch), [2010] ICR 1405 (Warren J).
[94] [2005] UKHL 56, [2006] 1 AC 262, HL. A nine Lord panel.
[95] (1969) SLT 94 (Lord Fraser).

liquidators. Lord Fraser held that the amendment was within the (wide) terms of the amendment power (and also did not infringe a limitation on amendments which prejudice the rights of members to benefits).

17.111   However, various issues can arise:

(a) is it a breach of duty for the trustee (or the employer) to agree to the amendment?—this is a general issue applicable to all uses of the amendment power;

(b) it is sometimes argued that amending a deed (or amending an amendment power) to include a further restriction etc is then invalid as being 'fetter' on the power of the trustees. However, this is misconceived in most situations. Trustees are continually 'fettering' their discretion by making and acting on decisions—for example in relation to members or investments or amendments. The equivalent point (a release of a power) was raised in *Mettoy Pension Trustees Ltd v Evans*[96] and dismissed by Warner J. It seems to add nothing to the duty point made at (a) above.

(c) It would usually be very difficult for an existing *restriction* in an amendment power to be deleted using the amendment power itself. This is sometimes raised as a reason why the amendment power cannot of itself be amended, but this would be a wider proposition.

Removing a restriction

17.112   This turns on a question of interpretation of the amendment power itself. Although the cases do not deal with this very clearly, it must be right that a limit in an amendment power cannot itself be deleted merely by using the amendment power.

17.113   By way of example, take an amendment power which includes a proviso that:

> no amendment may be made that would result in the payment back of any part of the fund to the employer.

It is not possible to delete this restriction from the amendment power using the amendment power itself. The reason for this is that the effect of the amendment (amending the amendment power) would be to contravene the restriction. The only purpose for deleting the restriction would be in order to facilitate or enable a later amendment that purported to allow a payment to the employer.

17.114   For examples of this see *HR Trustees Ltd v German*;[97] *BHLSPF Pty Ltd v Brashs Pty Ltd*;[98] and *UEB Industries Ltd v WS Brabant*.[99] In the older private trust case, *Re Bruners' Declaration of Trust*,[100] Simonds J held that a limit in the amendment power (no change to clause 3) included the implied limits in clause 3, which could not therefore be deleted.

17.115   In *Air Jamaica v Charlton*,[101] the Privy Council dealt with the position where an amendment had been made to a Jamaican pension scheme to provide for payment back of funds to the employer (despite a limit in the amendment power). Lord Millett, giving the judgment of

---

[96] [1991] 2 All ER 513 at 561h (Warner J).
[97] [2009] EWHC 2785 (Ch), [2009] All ER (D) 235 (Nov) at [125] (Arnold J).
[98] [2001] VSC 512 (Warren J).
[99] [1992] 1 NZLR 294, NZCA.
[100] *Re Brunner's Declaration of Trust, Coghill v President and Council of Cheltenham College* [1941] 2 All ER 745 (Simonds J).
[101] [1999] 1 WLR 1399, PC.

the Privy Council, commented that 'the trustees could not achieve by two steps what they could not achieve by one'.

The result is clearly correct (for the reasons given above) but the reasoning of Lord Millett in the Privy Council is too wide and difficult to understand. Take a simple example: a scheme that (say) contains a restriction in its investment power saying that none of the assets of the scheme can be invested in land. Clearly if the trustees then wanted to make an investment in land, this would be unauthorized (and a breach of trust). **17.116**

However, if there was an unfettered amendment power, it would not be contrary to the width of that power for the employer and the trustee to agree an amendment deleting the restriction in the investment power and the trustee then arranging to invest in land. This would seem unexceptional and there would be no reason for the law to say that this was not possible. However, it seems to squarely fall within the 'two steps' reasoning of the Privy Council in *Air Jamaica*, which must be regarded as wrong on this point. **17.117**

Retrospective Amendments

It is sometimes unclear whether retrospective amendments could be made to the terms of the scheme. In practice it is important to try and analyse this question by looking at whether or not what is being sought is an amendment which is: **17.118**

(a) truly retrospective in effect; or alternatively
(b) is only considered to be retrospective because, although relating to future actions (eg payment of benefits), it applies in relation to benefits which have already 'accrued' in the sense that they relate to service before the date of the amendment.[102]

Retrospective amendments to benefits already accrued (in that they relate to past service) in the sense that future payments may be increased or decreased in the future, may generally be within the express terms of the amendment power. **17.119**

The amendment power could expressly allow retrospective amendments (and many powers do this). Such a provision should be given effect—see from Australia *Graham Australia Pty Ltd v Perpetual Trustees WA Ltd*[103] and *Global Custodians Ltd v Mesh*.[104] In addition, assuming no express restriction on retrospection, a power to make retrospective amendments could probably be added in (as a clarification point) by a later amendment. **17.120**

However, the courts are naturally cautious about allowing amendments which have the effect of reducing rights which have already 'accrued' or 'vested' in some sense. In practice, retrospective amendments which reduce the level of benefits paid to or in respect of a particular member are now constrained by the limits in s 67 of the Pensions Act 1995. Such amendments cannot generally be made without member consent (or an actuarial certificate in some cases).[105] **17.121**

---

[102] See *Lord Inglewood v European Parliament*: T-229/11 and T-276/11 [2013] All ER (D) 179 (Mar) on amendments to the European Parliament pension scheme being valid on the basis that the relevant members had not reached the benefit age or had not made early retirement applications before the amendments were made.

[103] (1989) 1 WAR 65, [1992] PLR 193, Supreme Court of Western Australia.

[104] [2002] NSWSC 47 (Young CJ in Eq).

[105] There are some exceptions under the relevant regulations: the Occupational Pension Schemes (Modification of Schemes) Regulations 2006 (SI 2006/759).

17.122 However, there seems to be nothing stopping an increase (which of itself looks like a retrospective amendment in one sense) to benefits being paid in the future. Indeed, this is common in the form of (say) discretionary pension increases. For an example, see the Privy Council in the *Bank of New Zealand* case.[106]

17.123 It could be argued that the effect of such an amendment/discretionary increase is to reduce the solvency of the Scheme (its ability to pay the other benefits in future) but this does not seem to attract the statutory prohibition or limit in s 67. Nor does it seem in practice to attract a concern that such a change is for some reason outside the terms of the amendment power (as opposed to it being an issue about whether the trustees should properly agree to this, given the potential impact on funding).

17.124 The other sense of a retrospective amendment would be (say) for the trustee and the company to retrospectively authorize something that the trustee had done that was at the time a breach of trust.

17.125 Using the example given above again, if the investment power within the scheme provided that there could not be investment in land, but the trustees had gone ahead and invested in land anyway, what would be the effect of a later amendment put in place by the company and the trustee authorizing investment in land and purporting to backdate to before the investment had been made by the trustee? This is similar to the procedural/substantive divide on retrospection in legislation discussed (and rejected in favour of a 'fairness' test) by Lord Mustill in *L'Office Cherifien des Phosphates v Yamashita-Shinnihon Steamship Co Ltd.*[107]

17.126 In practice, in this example, the effect of such a retrospective amendment, if upheld, would be that the investment by the trustee would no longer be automatically a breach of trust (as being an unauthorized investment). So in effect, the company and the trustee would be waiving any breach by the trustee of the terms of the trust and the investment power.

17.127 This, of course, begs the question about why such an amendment would be a proper one to be made (given the trustee's fiduciary duty) but this may depend on the circumstances. If, for example, the value of the investment was thought to have gone up in the interim period, then it is difficult to see that there would be any damages claim and also difficult to see why it would not be appropriate to waive the breach. Conversely, if the value of the land had gone down (or not achieved the increase in value that might otherwise have been expected from authorized investments), then this may be thought to be more of an issue. However it would seem to be legitimate for the trustees (perhaps not including any conflicted trustee) and the company to decide to go ahead and retrospectively authorize the position.

17.128 There is an an example of such retrospective ratification being allowed in the pensions case, *Libby v Kennedy.*[108] Jacob J held that it was open to trustees to adopt and ratify a decision of a sub-committee of the trustees (in that case deciding on distribution of a death benefit).

17.129 In practice, many amendment powers include a provision expressly allowing amendments to be retrospective. In the absence of such a provision, then it may be that the courts would look

---

[106] *Bank of New Zealand v Board of Management of the Bank of New Zealand Officers' Provident Association* [2003] UKPC 58, 6 ITELR 142, [2003] OPLR 281, PC.
[107] [1994] 1 AC 486, HL.
[108] [1998] OPLR 213 (Jacob J). See also *Messeena v Carr* (1870) LR 9 Eq 260 (Lord Romilly MR).

to construe the amendment power restrictively in relation to retrospective amendments, particularly those to benefits as opposed to other amendments.

Note that retrospectivity in the sense of detracting from existing rights has been allowed **17.130** in relation to articles of association of companies. In *Allen v Gold Reefs of West Africa*[109] the Court of Appeal upheld an amendment to articles to impose a lien on fully paid shares. In *Society of Lloyd's v Robinson*[110] the House of Lords followed *Allen* and upheld an amendment to a trust deed that would have the effect of imposing a trust on damages claims by members of Lloyd's.

In *Doyle v Manchester Evening News*,[111] Judge Blackett-Ord V-C upheld a retrospective **17.131** amendment which had the effect of reducing benefits with retrospective effect (the definition of pensionable salary was amended to exclude certain remuneration from it). Interestingly (although not expressly cited as a factor), the amendment had (in accordance with the scheme's rules) been approved by a 75 per cent majority at a meeting of scheme members.

In *Municipal Mutual Insurance Ltd v Harrop*[112] it was held that a retrospective amendment **17.132** could not be made to correct a drafting error. But this decision is of limited precedent value as counsel had conceded that generally such retrospective amendments could not normally be made.

The test seems to be one of fairness. The Privy Council held in the *Bank of New Zealand* **17.133** case[113] that 'backdating cannot be used as a device to rewrite history'. This was followed in the pensions case, *HR Trustees Ltd v German*.[114]

It was accepted in *Harland & Wolff Pension Trustees Ltd v Aon Consulting Financial Services Ltd*[115] **17.134** that the power of amendment, which expressly permitted retrospective amendments (subject to a proviso protecting pensions in payment), had been validly exercised as a matter of domestic law to increase the normal retirement date of women in respect of a period of past service.

In a non-pensions (and non-trust) case, *Baynham v Philips Electronics (UK) Ltd*,[116] Latham J **17.135** held that an employer was unable to rely on an express contractual term which entitled it 'to vary this contract from time to time' in order to withdraw healthcare benefits from a group of pensioners after they had retired. Latham J held that the clause was only intended to cover matters such as a change in job description and could not extend to amending accrued rights of employees (in this case, post-termination healthcare cover).

More recently in a pensions case, *Dalriada Trustees Ltd v Faulds*[117] Bean J referred to the *Bank* **17.136** *of New Zealand* case and held that retrospective deeds could not be made to authorize payments out of the scheme which would otherwise be unauthorized investments.

---

[109] [1900] 1 Ch 671, CA.
[110] [1999] 1 WLR 756, HL.
[111] (1985) [1989] PLR 47 (Judge Blackett-Ord V-C).
[112] [1998] OPLR 199, [1998] PLR 149 (Rimer J).
[113] *Bank of New Zealand v Board of Management of the Bank of New Zealand Officers' Provident Association* [2003] UKPC 58, 6 ITELR 142, [2003] OPLR 281, PC.
[114] [2009] EWHC 2785 (Ch), [2009] All ER (D) 235 (Nov) (Arnold J).
[115] [2006] EWHC 1778 (Ch), [2007] ICR 429, [2006] PLR 201 (Warren J).
[116] [1995] OPLR 253 (Latham J). To similar effect, the Canadian case, *Lacey v Weyerhaeser Co* 2012 BCSC 353, [2012] 039 PBLR (035) (Saunders J).
[117] [2011] EWHC 3391 (Ch), [2012] 2 All ER 734 (Bean J).

17.137   This assumes that there is no express restriction in the amendment power that prohibits retrospective amendments (or amendments which have the effect of reducing benefits etc).

Amendment Following the Scheme Starting to Wind-Up

17.138   The courts have, in various cases, considered that the amendment power cannot generally be used (unless it specifically allows it) to make amendments (in particular to benefits) after the scheme has started to wind-up. This seems to be on the same basis as the commentary in relation to retrospective amendments generally. That is that there is a concern not to allow an amendment power to be used to take away benefits which have now in some form 'vested'. This seems to be similar to the arguments for non-retrospection in criminal legislation (see eg *Waddington v Miah*[118]).

17.139   Case law indicates that an amendment power, which does not expressly provide for it to continue beyond the start of a winding-up of a pension scheme, cannot be used during that winding-up.

17.140   An amendment power can be expressed to apply after a winding-up—see *Capital Cranfield Trust Corpn v Sagar*.[119] Indeed, there is no reason why an amendment power could not itself be amended (before the winding-up starts) to expressly provide for it to continue in effect after. The argument that an amendment power cannot itself be amended to remove a restriction probably does not apply to an implied restriction and does not apply to a restriction not on the power, but on when it can be exercised.

17.141   On the cessation of a winding-up power, see *Re ABC Television Pension Scheme*[120] and *Re Thrells Ltd (1974) Pension Scheme in liquidation v Lomas*.[121] On winding-up—see *Jones v Williams*.[122]

17.142   In *Municipal Mutual v Harrop*,[123] Rimer J commented that he probably would have found a power of amendment still to have been effective during a notice period. In *Leadenhall Independent Trustees v Welham*,[124] Park J held that a power to increase pensions did not survive commencement of the winding-up. He applied the principle in *Thrells* on this.

17.143   In *Re Edward Jones Benevolent Fund*,[125] it was held that a power of amendment survived the closure and freezing of a scheme (as opposed to its winding-up).

17.144   In *Davis v Richards & Wallington Industries Ltd*, Scott V-C suggested that the question of whether an amendment power survived termination was one of construction, and that, at least in some narrow circumstances, amendments could be made during winding-up. *Air Jamaica Ltd v Charlton* also offered some encouragement; rather than ruling out amendment

---

[118]   [1974] 2 All ER 377, HL.
[119]   [2002] OPLR 151 (Neuberger J).
[120]   (1973) [1989] 1 PLR 2 (Foster J). But reportedly to the contrary see a reputed decision also of Foster J from eight years later—*Re Bacal Pension Scheme* (1981?) as noted by Michael Tennet, 'Pensions Cases That Time Forgot' (2007) TLI 125.
[121]   [1993] 2 All ER 546, [1992] OPLR 21 (Nicholls V-C).
[122]   [1989] PLR 21.
[123]   [1998] OPLR 199 (Rimer J).
[124]   [2004] OPLR 115 (Park J).
[125]   *Re Jones (Edward) Benevolent Fund Trusts, Spink v Samuel Jones & Co Ltd* (1985) 8 March. (J Chadwick QC sitting as a Deputy Judge.)

altogether, the Privy Council said it was difficult to see how the relevant scheme could be amended 'in any significant respect' once termination had occurred.

Method of Amendment

The amendment power will, in practice, specify how it is to be exercised. For example if it requires an amendment to be made by deed, then a deed will be needed.[126] **17.145**

Many amendment powers envisage a deed (on the basis that it gives a degree of certainty as to when an amendment has been carried out). **17.146**

However, other amendment powers may envisage some other form of amendment formality. For example, a 'resolution' of the trustees or the 'consent' of the employer. In some cases it may require this to be in a written form. **17.147**

Generally, the courts look for the relevant formalities to be carried out. **17.148**

For example in a private trust case, *Re Forsters Settlement*,[127] Morton J held that where a life tenant's consent was needed to an advance of capital, the Court held that this could not be dispensed with. **17.149**

Similarly, in New Zealand in *Ritchie v Blakeley*,[128] where the power of amendment stated that any amendments to a pension scheme must have the prior approval of the relevant New Zealand regulatory authority. Although this was obtained after the amendment had been made, the New Zealand Court of Appeal held that failure to obtain approval prior to the amendment being made rendered the amendment invalid. **17.150**

In *Bestrustees v Stuart*,[129] Neuberger J held that the court should be very careful before permitting departure from the plain wording and plain requirement of a trust deed. He also held that the announcement in that case, which purported to equalize benefits, was not effective to amend the scheme; but that an amendment which purported to be retrospective but could not validly be made retrospective was nevertheless valid prospectively. **17.151**

In *Trustee Solutions v Dubery*,[130] Lewison J held that the court had no power to sanction departure from a requirement found in an amending power that an amendment be made by a document 'under hand'. **17.152**

In *Walker Morris Trustees v Masterson*,[131] Peter Smith J held that amendments were ineffective if the required actuarial certificate had not been obtained (even though the actuary would probably have been able to give the certificate if he had been asked). **17.153**

However, some more recent cases have indicated more flexibility. Where changes have been made and it seems relatively clear that they have been intended to be amendments, the courts **17.154**

---

126 Although note that a trust governed by Scottish law will interpret the term 'deed' widely and not in the same way as under English law—*Low & Bonar PLC v Mercer Ltd* [2010] CSOH 47 (Lord Drummond Young).

127 [1942] Ch 199 (Morton J).

128 [1985] 1 NZLR 630, NZ CA.

129 [2001] OPLR 341, [2001] PLR 283 (Neuberger J).

130 [2006] EWHC 1426 (Ch), [2007] 1 All ER 308 (Lewison J).

131 [2009] EWHC 1955 (Ch), [2009] All ER (D) 38 (Aug) (Peter Smith J).

have approved them. In *HR Trustees v Wembley*[132] only four out of the five trustees had signed a relevant resolution/authority in relation to a scheme amendment. Vos J held that this was a post-amendment formality and so the resolution did not have to be signed by all five trustees. Vos J applied the maxim 'equity deems that to be done which ought to be done'.

17.155 Slightly oddly, the judge did not accept an argument that as the amendment power only required a resolution, the approval of the majority of the trustees was all that was needed (given that the scheme had a majority voting provision). This could well form an alternative explanation for this decision (by analogy with company law decisions requiring directors to carry out resolutions once they have been approved by a majority—see eg Millett J in *Re Equiticorp International plc*[133]).

17.156 Conversely, where a relevant form of amendment (eg a deed) has been used, the courts are prepared to allow it to take effect as an amendment, even though the deed does not purport to be an amendment or refer to the amendment power. Examples of this are *Davis v Richards & Wallington*[134] and *LRT Pension Fund Trustee Co Ltd v Hatt*.[135]

17.157 In some cases it can be unclear whether the relevant action (eg a deed of announcement) is only intended to be a preliminary step followed by a later formal exercise of the amendment power. In *Premier Foods Group Services Ltd v RHM Pension Trust Ltd*[136] Warren J held that a 'deed of intention' was effective to be a deed of amendment.

Barber Case

17.158 Many of these issues have arisen in the context of schemes which have purported to be amended to deal with the equalization requirements that applied following the *Barber*[137] decision in 1990.

17.159 The effect of the *Barber* decision was to provide that benefits for male and female members must be equalized, at least in relation to benefits attributable to service on or after 17 May 1990 (the date of the ECJ decision). Many employers (and trustees) decided that equality of benefits was best achieved by moving the retirement age for female members up from the previous age (age 60) to the male age (age 65). Many schemes purported to do this by a simple announcement to members which would only later be formally documented in a deed of amendment (retrospectively backdating to the date of the announcement). Such retrospective amendments had been common (particularly in relation to benefits). There seemed little from a policy perspective against it. The relevant members were aware of the change and all that tended to be required was a deed executed by the trustee and the employer. This could be seen as a post-event formality.

---

[132] [2011] EWHC 2974 (Ch) (Vos J). Discussed by Paul Newman QC, 'HR Trustees v Wembley: Pandora's Box Opened?' (APL forum, February 2012). See also in Jersey the private trust case also overcoming the absence of a deed: *Re the Shirnovic Trust* [2012] JRC 081 (the Royal Court of Jersey).

[133] [1989] 1 WLR 1010 (Millett J).

[134] [1990] 1 WLR 1511 (Scott J). Cited by Henderson J in *Entrust* [2012] EWHC 3640 (Ch).

[135] [1993] OPLR 225 (Knox J).

[136] [2012] EWHC 447 (Ch) (Warren J).

[137] *Barber v Guardian Royal Exchange* (Case C-262/88), [1991] 1 QB 344, ECJ.

However, the courts construed this strictly, particularly following *Bestrustees v Stuart*, and held that, in order for such a change to be effective from the date of the announcement (rather than the later date of any confirming deed), there would need to be either an effective use of the amendment power at the time (or consent shown by the individual members) which may be difficult to show.   **17.160**

The Pensions Act 1995 also then came into play imposing a limitation, from 6 April 1997, in s 67 providing that 'accrued rights' could not be reduced without express written member consent. This led to an increased practice of employers and schemes arranging for amendments to be recorded on an interim basis (eg a deed of amendment attaching the relevant announcement) to satisfy the s 67 requirements.   **17.161**

This has still left a number of schemes where amendments have been announced (and put into action) but leaving formal issues regarding the effective date of the change.   **17.162**

In *Foster Wheeler v Hanley*,[138] the Court of Appeal confirmed that a later deed, purporting to backdate a change to an earlier date (the date of the announcement) was, although ineffective in backdating (because it was contrary to the amendment power and indeed s 67), could be effective as from the date of the deed. No 'blue pencil' rule would be applied, instead the deed could be considered to be subject to an implied limitation that it did not take effect retrospectively.   **17.163**

Obviously this was helpful in allowing the change to be made, but could still have effect to extend the '*Barber* window' of equalized benefits to apply from 1990 to the effective date of change (rather than the earlier date of the announcement).   **17.164**

A second problem also emerged in that it is unclear whether such a retrospective change (even if allowed by s 67 and the amendment power) is compatible with European law. The sex equalization obligations shown by the *Barber* case arose from the EU Treaty (Art 119 of the Treaty of Rome at that time).   **17.165**

In *Harland & Wolff Pension Trustees Ltd v Aon Consulting Financial Services Ltd*,[139] Warren J held that European law meant that an amendment could not be backdated to the date of the *Barber* decision (closing the *Barber* window altogether). This is unhelpful in removing the degree of flexibility that existed (at least before s 67 of the Pensions Act 1995 came into force in April 1997).   **17.166**

It is to be noted that the decision in *Harland & Wolff* related to an amendment that backdated to before any relevant announcement had been made to employees. It is therefore possible that such an extreme solution or answer would not apply if all the backdated deed was doing was taking the position back to the date of the relevant announcement.   **17.167**

Notifying Members

There is a statutory obligation on trustees in relevant schemes to notify members of benefit changes etc under the statutory Disclosure Regulations 1996 (see Chapter 18 (Disclosure obligations)).   **17.168**

---

[138] [2009] EWCA Civ 651, [2010] ICR 374, CA.
[139] [2009] EWHC 1557 (Ch), [2010] ICR 121 (Warren J).

17.169 However, some amendment powers also include a provision requiring trustees to notify members of any changes made by an amendment. This may be forgotten or not complied with. It may be considered to be onerous (eg the address for each member may not be known) and perform no good function (eg the requirement may not be limited to members affected by the amendment).

17.170 In practice the courts have interpreted this so that a failure to notify members promptly or by missing out some members does not invalidate the amendment—see *Betafence Ltd v Veys*,[140] where Lightman J held:

> In my judgment there is no basis for holding that the breach of duty by the Trustees in failing to notify in any way invalidated the 1993 Amendment. Neither the language of Rule 23 nor any rule of law lends any support to any argument in favour of invalidation. There may be a failure to notify members (or some of them) for any of a variety of reasons. The amendment may be for the member's advantage or disadvantage. The accident of a failure of notification cannot prejudice the legal effect of the amendment. What it might do is afford to members who are able to show that they have been prejudiced by the failure to communicate, the possible basis for a claim for compensation against the Trustees.

Over Execution

17.171 What if an amendment purports to go further than is allowed by reason of a limitation in the amendment power or by law. The courts have consistently held that the amendment will usually survive and be effective to the extent allowed.

17.172 For example, if an amendment purports to apply to all benefits (but applying to past service benefits is contrary to the amendment power or European law), the courts have held that the amendment can take effect for future benefits. See Neuberger J in *Bestrustees v Stuart*[141] and the Court of Appeal in *Foster Wheeler*.[142]

Express Limits in Amendment Powers

17.173 It is common for amendment powers also to include express limitations on what amendments can be made.

17.174 Common examples include:

(a) a prohibition on amendments that could have effect to reduce accrued rights of members (save with their consent); or

(b) a restriction prohibiting payment of any part of the funds of the pension scheme to the employer.

---

[140] [2006] EWHC 999 (Ch) at [67] (Lightman J). Followed by Vos J in *HR Trustees v Wembley* [2011] EWHC 2974 (Ch) at [69].

[141] [2001] OPLR 341 (Neuberger J). See also *Doyle v Manchester Evening News* (1985) [1989] PLR 47 (Judge Blackett-Ord V-C); *Betafence Ltd v Veys* [2006] EWHC 999 (Ch), (2006) 8 ITELR 917 at [68] and [69] (Lightman J). On severance of a pension scheme provision for being in restraint of trade, see *Re Prudential Assurance Co's Trust Deed, Horne v Prudential Assurance Co Ltd* [1934] Ch 338 (Eve J); *Bull v Pitney-Bowes Ltd* [1966] 3 All ER 384 (Thesiger J).

[142] *Foster Wheeler Ltd v Hanley* [2009] EWCA Civ 651, [2010] ICR 374, CA.

Accrued Rights Limitations

Many schemes have a limitation on changes that affect the 'accrued rights' of members. In practice this will normally be considered to be limited to their benefits (rather than other rights such as, for example, how trustees are appointed or investments). **17.175**

Two problems arise: (a) what are accrued rights? and (b) how is the test applied? **17.176**

Some difficulty arises as to the meaning of accrued rights for this purpose. Does it only apply, in a final salary scheme, to rights accrued up to the relevant date on a leaving service basis? Alternatively, must some regard be had to the possibility of future salary increases? **17.177**

In the *Courage* case,[143] Millett J (as he then was) held that such a limitation should be construed as protecting the rights of the members in relation to their service up to the date of the amendment. In a final salary scheme, where the ultimate pension depended on the period of service and the salary at the date of retirement (or leaving service), such an 'accrued right' would not be limited to the benefits based on the salary as at the date of the amendment, but instead should be based on ultimate final salary. **17.178**

In *Courage* two schemes provided that amendments must not 'reduce ... the accrued pension of any employed member'. 'The term, accrued pensions' was defined in the rules of these two schemes to mean pensions based on salary at the relevant date. However, the third scheme provided that amendments must not 'vary or affect any benefits already secured by past contributions in respect of any Member without his consent in writing'. **17.179**

Millett J referred to there being some dispute as to the interpretation of the restriction applicable to the third scheme and held (at p 543g) that: **17.180**

> In the absence of express definition, I see no reason to exclude any benefit to which a member is prospectively entitled if he continues in the same employment and which has been acquired by past contributions, and no reason to assume that he has retired from such employment on the date of the employer's cessation when he has not. The contrary argument places a meaning on 'secured' which is not justified.

Similarly, the New Zealand case, *Ritchie v Blakeley*.[144] This case appears to have concerned a money purchase scheme which provided that 'no such amendment shall be made which will reduce or adversely affect a Member's interest in the fund as established at the date of such amendment without the written consent of that individual member'. Because of a change in government requirements for tax approval, the trustees amended the scheme to remove a lump sum option available to employees on retirement. The lump sum option would remain in relation to the amount accrued to each individual member's account as at the date of the amendment but would not apply to later accruals by way of future contributions. The New Zealand Court of Appeal held (by a majority only) that the lump sum option could be removed in relation to future contributions. The dissenting judge thought that this was not the case and referred to: **17.181**

> the contributing member's proper and reasonable expectation in terms of the trust deed which he has embarked upon that future contributions will not be adversely interfered with without his consent.

---

[143] *Re Courage Group's Pension Schemes* [1987] 1 All ER 528 (Millett J).
[144] [1985] 1 NZLR 630, NZCA.

17.182 In considering the interpretation of such an express provision, it would appear that the fact that the company has the option to wind-up the scheme (in which case benefits would be calculated on a leaving service basis) is not relevant unless the scheme is in fact wound-up. See *Courage* at p 543g. Similarly in *Mettoy*,[145] counsel at one stage argued that the terms of the existing scheme were not relevant as the company could have terminated the existing scheme and set up a new scheme. However, Warner J held that this was irrelevant as this had not in fact been done.

17.183 When is the test applied in relation to a particular amendment?

17.184 In *Courage*, Millett J referred to the express restriction. He went on to hold that amendments made in relation to transfers of separated portions in the *Courage* schemes on a partial winding-up suffered from the defects that they did not adequately provide for the protection of the members' rights as envisaged by the express restrictions contained in the amendment powers, eg an employee was liable to be transferred to a different scheme under which the rules and entitlements were unspecified and did not provide for their rights to be protected in the future. This is perhaps an argument for saying that transfer powers may only be included if they make provision designed to comply with express restrictions on amendment powers.

17.185 It seems clear that the test of whether an amendment is valid must be made at the time of the amendment and not in light of later events—see *Stevens v Bell*[146] and *Mettoy*.[147]

17.186 This can cause some issues.[148] In practice it means that the scheme amendment power can be used to freeze a scheme by reference to pensionable service as at the date of the freezing, but still must usually include salary linkage in the form of the ultimate benefit needing to be calculated by reference to the member's salary on the date of leaving service (unless some other closure/freezing power is available[149]). In practice, salary linkage could also be ended with the agreement of the member or by the employer specifying that pensionable salary does not increase—see Chapter 15 (Contract overriding trust). The statutory amendment power in section 229 of the Pensions Act 2004 could also be used.

17.187 Having said that, it is likely that *Courage* would be followed (at least at first instance) in England. It was followed in *Walker Morris Trustees Ltd v Masterson*[150] and (in effect) in *Re IMG Pension Plan: HR Trustees v German*.[151] A different approach has been followed in Canada.[152]

No temporal limit?—'any benefits then provided' or 'benefits secured'

17.188 Some express amendment restrictions have been construed even wider. For example *Lloyds Bank*.[153]

---

[145] *Mettoy Pension Trustees Ltd v Evans* [1991] 2 All ER 513, [1990] 1 WLR 1587 (Warner J).
[146] [2002] EWCA Civ 672, CA.
[147] *Mettoy Pension Trustees Ltd v Evans* [1991] 2 All ER 513, [1990] 1 WLR 1587 (Warner J).
[148] See Ian Gordon, *'Battling with Courage'* (Practical Law for Companies, 2010).
[149] See eg the Pensions Ombudsman decision in *Barton* (2009) 21 December, 74532/2 (King PO).
[150] [2009] EWHC 1955 (Ch) (Peter Smith J).
[151] [2009] EWHC 2785 (Ch) (Arnold J).
[152] *CASAW v Alcan Smelters and Chemicals* 2001 DLR (4th) 504; *Dinney v Great-West Life Assurance Co* 2005 MBCA 36; *Patrick v Telus Communications* 2005 BCJ 2607, CA; and *Lloyd v Imperial Oil* 2008 ABQB 379.
[153] *Lloyds Bank Pension Trust Corpn Ltd v Lloyds Bank plc* [1996] OPLR 181 (Rimer J).

The expression 'any benefits then provided' was contained in an amendment power that was **17.189** widely interpreted in Australia in *Gas & Fuel Corpn of Victoria v Fitzmaurice*.[154] Hedigan J held that it covered future service benefits. Counsel contended that amendments would be prohibited only if they reduced benefits of members which had accrued at the date of the amendment.

Counsel argued that the word 'then' was:

> wholly temporal, relating to the date of the instrument which amended the deed.

But Hedigan J held that there should be a construction of the power of amendment clause:

> benign to the protection and preservation of the position of [members].

Hedigan J held that the correct construction of the clause was that any amendment which might have the effect of reducing the benefits of contributors which, but for the amendment, *might* accrue in the future was not authorized and was *ultra vires*.

Previous decisions on particular wording are not binding in cases on other deeds. First **17.190** instance decisions (even in the UK) are not binding on later first instance judges. But of course they are persuasive.

It may be material if a restriction refers to 'any' benefit—this was considered to be relevant **17.191** (because it suggests a very wide coverage of benefits) in the Australian cases, *Gas & Fuel*[155] and *Wilson v Metro Goldwyn Mayer*.[156]

The rationale of protecting benefits has also been applied in the UK: see the decision of Rimer **17.192** J in *Lloyds Bank*.[157] The wording of the protected clause there was different ('the pecuniary benefits secured'), but the rationale was the same. Rimer J referred to the *Gas & Fuel* case.[158]

In *Lloyds Bank*, leading counsel for the employer (Edward Nugee QC) argued that the courts **17.193** should look at the overall powers of the employer to terminate employment etc to emphasize that no employee joining a scheme can regard 'promised' benefits as more than uncertain or precarious. But Rimer J disagreed. He did not consider that those were relevant factors to look at when interpreting an amendment power. Rimer J held:

> 28 For his part, Mr Nugee pointed out that (i) no employer is obliged to provide a pension scheme for his employees, (ii) it would (in theory) be open to the bank and LMB to dismiss their employees and then to re-employ them only on terms that they did not join the Scheme, (iii) an employee's membership of a pension scheme has no effect on the employer's right to terminate his employment, so that any employee joining the Scheme can have no certainty that he will remain employed until NRD, but may be dismissed for misconduct, be made redundant, decide to leave, or die whilst in service, and (iv) even if the bank cannot do so, LMB can give notice at any time terminating its participation in the Scheme, so resulting in a winding-up of the Scheme as regards at any rate the LMB employees.
>
> 29 The intended collective thrust of these points was that an employer is not bound to make pension promises but, if he does, there are various ways in which his exposure under them can or may be limited. In consequence, no employee joining the bank and the Scheme can regard

---

[154] (1991) 22 ATR 10, [1991] PLR 137 (Hedigan J).
[155] (1991) 22 ATR 10, [1991] PLR 137 at [87]–[88] and [105] (Hedigan J).
[156] (1980) 18 NSWLR 730 at 736B.
[157] *Lloyds Bank Pension Trust Corpn Ltd v Lloyds Bank plc* [1996] OPLR 181 (Rimer J).
[158] But not to *Wilson v MGM* where the wording being considered looked more similar to that in *Lloyds Bank*.

the promised benefits as more than uncertain and precarious. These considerations, submits Mr Nugee, justify the court in approaching the interpretation of general rule 9 on the basis that it is likely to have been intended to confer a wide amendment power on the bank and the trustees.

30 I respectfully disagree. I am prepared for present purposes to accept Mr Nugee's points (i) to (iv) above (although I should record that Mr McDonnell challenged point (ii)), but I cannot see how they can be relevant to the interpretation of general rule 9. The purpose of that rule is to convey a message as to the nature of the amending power whilst the Scheme is still in being, and I do not consider that the meaning of that message can or should be governed by the sort of considerations to which Mr Nugee referred. The message means what it says, no more and no less. The issue is as to what that is.

17.194 In a later case in Victoria, *BHLSPF Pty Ltd v Brashs Pty Ltd*,[159] Warren J (as she then was) considered a scheme with a restriction in the amendment power that provided that 'no such modification rescission alteration or addition shall operate so as to detract from the benefits secured to a member by the contributions paid by him and by the Company in respect of him prior to the date of such modification rescission alteration or addition'. She held that this prohibited an amendment that sought to remove the discretion of the trustee to use any surplus remaining on a winding-up to increase members' benefits.

Does 'benefit' include a discretionary benefit?

17.195 The position should perhaps be contrasted with a definition that referred to rights or entitlements (eg under s 67 of the Pensions Act 1995).

17.196 *Wilson v MGM* is a case on future benefits being covered even if discretionary. In that case the court had to consider a clause stating that amendments would 'not prejudice any benefits secured by contributions made on behalf of any member'. Kearney J held that it covered future potential benefits (eg on a winding-up) payable at the discretion of the company.

17.197 In the *Gas & Fuel* case (on a restriction similar to that in the Scheme) Hedigan J held that the protection applied to any benefit that 'might' accrue in the future (this issue does not seem to be central to that case however).

17.198 *Lloyds Bank* does not seem to have been concerned with discretions.

17.199 Where an amendment power contained a restriction on changes that no amendment was to be made 'without a member's consent if the amendment would reduce or adversely affect that member's interest in the fund at the date of amendment', McGechan J in New Zealand held in *Cullen v Pension Holdings Ltd*[160] that this applied where changes were introduced in a DB scheme to the employer contribution rule.

Prohibition on Payments to the Employer

17.200 Such limitations were often included as a way of reinforcing the tax deductibility of payments to the scheme by the employer. The argument being that it could be pointed to as meaning that sums once paid into the scheme would not flow back to the employer and so a tax deduction should be given.

---

[159] [2001] VSC 512 (Warren J). Cited in *HR Trustees v German* at [122].
[160] [1992] PLR 135 (McGechan J).

The rationale for this limitation from a tax perspective fell away with change in Revenue **17.201**
practice in relation to taxation, and in particular following the Finance Act 1988 imposing a
specific tax charge on payments back to employers (see now s 207 of the Finance Act 2004).

Despite this change in the underlying circumstances, the courts have construed such provi- **17.202**
sions as continuing to apply.

In *Mettoy*,[161] Warner J construed a provision referring to an amendment which could 'lead to **17.203**
the transfer or payment of any part of the Pension Fund to the Principal Company'. Warner
J held that this did not prohibit a rule change authorizing a payment back to the employer
where at the time the amendment was made there was no immediate intention that such a
payment would be made. This seems very permissive.

By contrast, in *Harwood-Smart v Caws*,[162] Rimer J held that an amendment allowing a refund **17.204**
of surplus back to the employer was not valid because it had been made in contradiction of
a previous limitation in the amendment power (the amendment power could not be subsequently amended to delete this provision).

The extent of such limitations need to be considered carefully. Often they do not merely **17.205**
apply to surplus refunds back to an employer (see Chapter 20 (Employers and surpluses))
but also to any payment back to the employer—even if this is payment for services provided
by the employer or on an arm's length basis. This seems unnecessarily restrictive, but may be
the literal interpretation of the words involved.

The background tax position could perhaps be relevant in construing such limitations. If **17.206**
the limitation expressly refers to the tax position, then it may be that the limitation has now
fallen away given the tax changes. Contrary to *Harwood-Smart v Caws*, perhaps this could
be also found by a more relaxed interpretation in the light of changed circumstances—see
eg (in a non-pensions context) the Supreme Court in *Lloyds TSB Foundation for Scotland v
Lloyds Banking Group Plc*[163] (where a covenant to pay a percentage of profits was held to be
impliedly adjustable if the underlying accounting standards changed fundamentally in an
unforeseen way).

It is clear that a mere reduction in employer contributions (because there is a surplus in the **17.207**
scheme) does not amount to a repayment out of the scheme contrary to a relevant provision
in the amendment power. The House of Lords in *National Grid*[164] overturned a decision
to the contrary of Vinelott J in *British Coal Corpn v British Coal Staff Superannuation
Scheme*.[165]

A prohibition in an amendment power on (say) refunds to an employer cannot be avoided by **17.208**
using the transfer power so that a transfer can be made to another scheme without the restriction. This would be an improper purpose. See *Hillsdown*.[166] This probably only applies if
there is a surplus in the transferring scheme at the time of transfer—see *Bullard v Randall*.[167]

---

[161] *Mettoy Pension Trustees Ltd v Evans* [1991] 2 All ER 513, [1990] 1 WLR 1587 (Warner J).
[162] [2000] OPLR 227 (Rimer J).
[163] [2013] UKSC 3, [2013] 2 All ER 103, SC.
[164] *National Grid v Lawes and Mayes, International Power v Healy* [2001] UKHL 20, [2001] 2 All ER
417, HL.
[165] [1995] 1 All ER 912 (Vinelott J).
[166] [1997] 1 All ER 862, [1996] OPLR 291 (Knox J).
[167] *Re Vauxhall Motor Pension Fund* [1989] PLR 31 (Browne-Wilkinson V-C).

17.209 In *Harding v Joy Manufacturing Holdings Ltd*,[168] the Inner House of the Court of Session approved trustees entering into a merger proposal which would result in the transfer of surplus to a receiving scheme (which would not contain the same unilateral power for the trustees to increase benefits).

Proper Purpose

17.210 Amendments must be for a proper purpose—ie within the scope of the power as envisaged when the contract was made—see Chapter 9 (Trustee powers: proper purpose) and eg *Hole v Garnsey*[169] (industrial and provident society) and the *Pilots* case, *PNPF Trust Co v Taylor*[170] (pension scheme).

17.211 A similar rule applies to the amendment power given to companies in relation to their articles of association. It is clear that despite the wide statutory power given to members of a company to amend articles of association by special resolution, the courts have interpreted this as being subject to restrictions. In the leading case *Allen v Gold Reefs of West Africa*,[171] the Court of Appeal construed the statutory power and held that:

> Wide as the language of section 50 is, the power conferred by it, must, like all other powers, be exercised subject to those general principles of law and equity which are applicable to all the powers conferred on majorities and enabling them to bind minorities. It must be exercised not only in the manner required by law, but also bona fide for the benefit of the company as a whole, and it must not be exceeded. These conditions are always implied, and are seldom, if ever, expressed.

17.212 It is of interest to note that this constraint has been implied by the courts even where a trading and commercial entity such as a company is concerned and even where the persons affected (the shareholders) have consented by a large majority.

17.213 Similarly, in *Society of Lloyd's v Robinson*[172] the House of Lords followed both *Hole v Garnsey* and *Allen* as limits on an amendment power, but upheld the amendments concerned (retrospective amendments to a trust deed by the Society of Lloyd's amending to catch damages claims by Lloyd's names).

17.214 More recently in *Dalriada Trustees Ltd v Faulds*[173] Bean J commented:

> [75] ... In *Hole v Garnsey* [1930] AC 472, the House of Lords held that a power to amend (in that case, the rules of a society registered under the Industrial and Provident Societies Act 1893) cannot be used to make an amendment which was outside the 'reasonable contemplation of the parties' to the contract containing the power when that contract was made. Like 'fraud on the power', the expression 'reasonable contemplation of the parties' is a term of art, and does not mean what it may appear at first sight to mean. In *PNPF Trust Co Ltd v Taylor and others* [2010] EWHC 1573 (Ch) Warren J considered it in the context of amendments to a pension scheme. He said (at para 144):

---

168 2000 SLT 843, [2001] OPLR 235, CSIH. See discussion in Ch 20 'Employers and surpluses'.
169 [1930] AC 472, HL.
170 [2010] EWHC 1573 (Ch) (Warren J).
171 [1900] 1 Ch 671, CA.
172 [1999] 1 WLR 756, HL. Also citing the Australian cases, *Graham Australia Pty Ltd v Perpetual Trustees WA Ltd* (1989) 1 WAR 65, [1992] PLR 193 and *Kearns v Hill* (1990) 21 NSWLR 107.
173 [2011] EWHC 3391 (Ch), [2012] 2 All ER 734 (Bean J).

The 'reasonable contemplation' of the parties, or rather what can 'reasonably be considered to have been within the contemplation of the parties', imports an objective test. It is not, in my view, relevant to know what the parties did or did not actually consider. I am not, for instance, concerned with what the directors of any of the CHAs discussed in their boardroom or considered with their lawyers. That is consistent with descriptions of the restriction on the scope of a power to alter the objects or purposes of the trust; the amendment must not change the whole substratum of the trust (see in an analogous situation *Re Ball's Settlement Trusts* [1968] 1 WLR 899 and also *Kearns v Hill*) or its basic purpose (see *Bank of New Zealand v Board of Management of New Zealand Officers' Provident Association* [2003] UKPC 58).

[76] Here each Scheme is described, in the first recital in the deed, as a pension scheme within s 150 of the 2004 Act. The purpose of such a scheme is to provide benefits to or in respect of its members on retirement, death, reaching a particular age, the onset of serious ill-health or incapacity, or in similar circumstances. An amendment to allow unsecured loans to non-members in order to procure reciprocal loans to members alters the basic purpose of the scheme, or, as Warren J put it, the whole substratum of the trust.

In the pensions area, see also *ITS v Hope*[174] and the *Pilots* case[175] and *Stena*, discussed in Chapter 9 (Trustee powers: proper purpose).   **17.215**

In *Stena Line v Merchant Navy Ratings Pension Fund Trustees*,[176] Briggs J dealt with a pension scheme having a substantial funding deficit. The trustee had power to amend the scheme (no employer consent was needed) and proposed an amendment to the scheme to redress the deficit. Briggs J held that the trustee had the power to alter or replace the previous regime by imposing deficit repair contribution obligations on specified employers. On appeal,[177] Arden LJ (with whom Toulson and Rimer LJJ agreed) upheld this view.   **17.216**

---

[174] *Independent Trustee Services v Hope* [2009] EWHC 2810 (Ch), [2010] ICR 553 (Henderson J).
[175] *PNPF Trust Co Ltd v Taylor* [2009] EWHC 1693 (Ch) (Warren J).
[176] [2010] EWHC 1805 (Ch), [2010] All ER (D) 280 (Jul) (Briggs J).
[177] [2011] EWCA Civ 543.

18

DISCLOSURE OF DOCUMENTS BY TRUSTEES: *SCHMIDT V ROSEWOOD*

Introduction

There is a general rule for trusts that documents (and perhaps information) held by trustees are disclosable to beneficiaries on request[1]. This can also apply to other fiduciaries—eg directors.[2] It does not apply to non-fiduciaries such as employers.[3] **18.1**

The main English authority on this was, until 2003, a 1965 Court of Appeal case involving a private trust, *Re Londonderry*.[4] The *Londonderry* case is authority that disclosure should be made, but that this does not apply to documents that may reveal the reasons for the trustee making a decision. **18.2**

In 2003 in *Schmidt v Rosewood*,[5] the Privy Council[6] substantially recast the law on this point. Lord Walker gave the judgment. **18.3**

Application to Pensions—*Wilson v Law Debenture*

Before *Schmidt* in 1995, in *Wilson v Law Debenture Trust Corpn plc*[7] Rattee J (in an unreserved decision) held that this general trust law rule applied to pension trusts.[8] The main thrust of the decision was not whether the *Londonderry* rule applied, but whether or not the exception to the rule in relation to non-disclosure of the reasons for a decision applied to pension trusts. Rattee J held that there was no reason for applying an extended obligation on pension trustees on this point. **18.4**

The plaintiffs were former active members of the scheme. They had moved, on a sale of their employer, to a new scheme. The scheme rules gave the trustees a discretion to pay a transfer amount to the new scheme of such part of the assets of the scheme as the trustee 'determines **18.5**

---

[1] See Christopher McCall QC, '*Schmidt v Rosewood Trust Ltd*: The End of the Trust as a Disappearing Trick' [2003] PCB 358; Sir Gavin Lightman, 'The Trustees' Duty to Provide Information to Beneficiaries' [2004] PCB 23; Tsun Hang Tey, 'Letters of Wishes and Trustee's Duties' (2008) 22 TLI 126; Emily Campbell and Jonathan Hilliard, 'Disclosure of Information by Trustees' in David Hayton (ed), *The International Trust* 3rd edn (Jordans, 2011); Michael Gibbon, 'Beneficiaries' Information Rights' (2011) 17 Trusts and Trustees 27; and Rose-Marie Antoine, *Trusts and Related Tax Issues in Offshore Financial Law* (Oxford University Press, 2005) Ch 7. See also the APL talks by Sandeep Maudgil (October 2007); Hugh Arthur and Henrietta Sargant (May 2003); Jeremy Goodwin (July 2004); and Dan Schaffer (APL Conference, 2004 and APL Summer Conference, 2012). From Australia, see Tina Cockburn, 'Trustee Duties: Disclosure of Information' (2005) Murdoch University Electronic Journal of Law 13; JC Campbell, 'Access by Trust Beneficiaries to Trustees' Documents Information and Reasons' (2009) 3 J Eq 97; and Georgia Dawson, 'A Fork in the Road for Access to Trust Documents' (2009) 3 J Eq 39.

[2] An implied duty to disclose can also apply to directors faced with a request from a shareholder—see *CAS (Nominees) Ltd v Nottingham Forest plc* [2001] 1 All ER 954 (Evans-Lombe J) and Joan Loughrey 'Privileged Litigants: Shareholder Rights, Information Disclosure and Corporate Legal Professional Privilege' [2007] JBL 778.

[3] See Ch 11. In relation to non-disclosure by an employer, see the Jersey decision in relation to an employee benefits trust: *Re HHH Employee Trust* [2012] JRC 127B (JA Clyde-Smith, Commissioner and Jurats Le Breton and Milner).

[4] [1965] 1 Ch 918, CA.

[5] [2003] UKPC 26, [2003] 2 AC 709, PC.

[6] Privy Council authority will generally be followed in UK courts. But not always—see eg the Court of Appeal in *Sinclair Investments (UK) Ltd v Versailles Trade Finance Ltd (in admin)* [2011] EWCA Civ 347, [2012] Ch 453. The Court of Appeal can have problems when looking at conflicting decisions. See M Conaglen and R Nolan, 'Precedent from the Privy Council' (2006) 122 LQR 349 and R Nolan, 'Bribes: A Reprise' (2011) 127 LQR 19. On the Privy Council in Australia, see *Cook v Cook* [1986] HCA 73, (1986) 162 CLR 376 at 390.

[7] [1995] 2 All ER 337, [1995] OPLR 103 (Rattee J).

[8] See also Ch 2 (Pension trusts and general trust law) and Ch 3 (Pension trusts and statute).

to be appropriate'. The scheme had a surplus, but the trustee decided that no part of the surplus would transfer. The members sought disclosure by the trustee of relevant valuations and minutes in relation to this decision, including documents revealing the reason for the trustee's decision.[9] The trustee disclosed the valuation and minutes (redacted to black out items that would reveal the trustee's reasons). The trustee, relying on, in particular, the decision of the Court of Appeal in *Re Londonderry's Settlement*, refused to disclose those documents, on the basis that by virtue of the decision of the Court of Appeal it was not required to disclose documents which would disclose the trustee's reason for exercising its discretion.

18.6   Rattee J held:

> It would in my judgment be wrong in principle to hold that the long-established principles of trust law as to the exercise by trustees of discretions conferred on them by their trust instruments, in the context of which parties to a pension scheme such as the present entered into those schemes, no longer apply to them and that the trustees are under more onerous obligations to account to their beneficiaries than they could have appreciated when appointed, on the basis of the relevant trust law as it has stood for so long.
>
> I accept Mr Warren's submission that if any such amendment to the law of trusts as applied to pension schemes is to be made it should be made by the legislature, either by regulations made under or by the extension of s 113 of the Pension Schemes Act 1993[10] in which Parliament has already addressed the question of the extent to which members of a pension scheme should be entitled to information relating to the scheme's administration.

18.7   Subsequently Sir Robert Walker (speaking extra-judicially and before the decision in *Schmidt*) commented[11] that this conclusion of Rattee J seemed to treat *Re Londonderry* as a 'rather more precise and definitive statement of principle than it may be'.

Pensions Legislation on Disclosure

18.8   In the UK the pensions legislation also required disclosure by occupational pension scheme trustees of various documents and information.

18.9   The main provision is the Occupational Pension Schemes (Disclosure of Information) Regulations 1996.[12] These require pension trustees to disclose information to individual members (and prospective members) about the scheme, including their benefits (in some cases automatically, and at other times following a request by the member). This includes:

(a) (on request) copies of the documents constituting the scheme (reg 3), but only where relevant to the rights of the member—reg 3(5);

(b) basic information about the scheme (reg 4 and Sch 1);

(c) information about individual benefits (reg 5 and Sch 2);

---

[9]   In practice it may be difficult to challenge a trustee's decision on such a point—see *Wrightson Ltd v Fletcher Challenge Nominees Ltd* [2001] UKPC 23, [2001] OPLR 249, PC, but contrast a more recent UK case on transfers (oddly not referring to *Wrightson*), *Independent Trustee Services Ltd v Hope* [2009] EWHC 2810 (Ch), [2010] ICR 553 (Henderson J).

[10]   These are specific disclosure requirements on pension scheme trustees—mainly in relation to benefits—under regulations. Currently these are the Occupational Pension Schemes (Disclosure of Information) Regulations 1996 (SI 1996/1655 as amended).

[11]   'Some Trust Principles in the Pensions Context' in AJ Oakley (ed), *Trends in Contemporary Trust Law* (Clarendon Press, 1996).

[12]   SI 1996/1655 as amended.

(d) an annual report, including accounts (reg 6);

(e) copies of the funding documents (actuarial valuation, schedule of contributions etc under Pt 3 of the Pensions Act 2004, statement of investment principles under s 35 of the Pensions Act 1995).

There are potentially civil penalties (charged by the Pensions Regulator) for failure to comply with these regulations (reg 11). Some schemes are (broadly) exempted from the Disclosure Regulations, for example, schemes which are not tax approved.[13]   **18.10**

Trustees are also obliged to make available to the employer copies of actuarial valuations (within seven days of receipt)—s 224(7) of the Pensions Act 2004.   **18.11**

In practice trustees will disclose other documents to the employer. In particular, where the legislation requires the trustees to consult or agree with the employer (eg on the statement of investment principles,[14] scheme funding documents[15]), this implies that information has been given to the employer as well—*Pitmans Trustees Ltd v Telecommunications Group plc*.[16]   **18.12**

2003: The Law Moves: *Schmidt v Rosewood*

In 2003 the Privy Council decided *Schmidt v Rosewood*[17] on the disclosure issue in an appeal from the Isle of Man. The case concerned a discretionary family trust. The decision can be seen as substantially recasting the law on the disclosure obligation. There were many references to the Australian cases in this area, in particular *Hartigan Nominees v Rydge*[18] and *Roose v IOOF*.[19]   **18.13**

Unfortunately, the judgment of the Privy Council, given by Lord Walker, is quite difficult to apply. The general rule that the duty to disclose applies to all sorts of beneficiaries (including discretionary beneficiaries) is relatively clear. What is less clear are the comments that there is no general proprietary right to disclosure, instead it is more of a question of the court (or trustees?) exercising a discretion that a disclosure is appropriate.   **18.14**

Trust Law

Pre-*Schmidt*

Independently of any right of disclosure in litigation, the courts have long held that beneficiaries of a trust have a right to require trustees to disclose trust documents and information to them, reasoning that the beneficiary has a 'proprietary right' to inspect all trust documents: the documents are owned by the trust and, therefore, by the beneficiaries.   **18.15**

By contrast, potential beneficiaries under discretionary trusts were entitled only, on request, to information about the trust's assets.[20]   **18.16**

---

[13] Regulation 2(1)(a). In practice not registered for tax purposes under the Finance Act 2004.
[14] Occupational Pension Schemes (Investment) Regulations 2005 (SI 2005/3378), reg 2(2)(b).
[15] Pensions Act 2004, s 229.
[16] [2004] EWHC 181 (Ch), [2005] OPLR 1 at [56] (Sir Andrew Morritt V-C) citing Webster J in *R v Secretary of State for Social Services, ex parte Association of Metropolitan Authorities* [1986] 1 All ER 164 at 167g.
[17] [2003] UKPC 26, [2003] 2 AC 709, PC.
[18] (1992) 29 NSWLR 405, NSWCA.
[19] (1999) 73 SASR 484 (Full Court, South Australia).
[20] *Murphy v Murphy* [1998] 3 All ER 1 (Neuberger J).

18.17 The courts have long held that beneficiaries of a trust have a right to require trustees to disclose information to them. It is clear that this right arises independently of any right of disclosure as part of a litigation process ('discovery', or now called 'disclosure'). Thus in *O'Rourke v Darbishire*,[21] Lord Wrenbury held:

> If the plaintiff is right in saying that he is a beneficiary and if the documents are documents belonging to the executors as executors, he has a right to access to the documents which he desires to inspect upon what has been called in the judgments in this case a proprietary right. The beneficiary is entitled to see all trust documents because they are trust documents and because he is a beneficiary. They are in this sense his own. Action or no action, he is entitled to access to them. This has nothing to do with discovery. The right to discovery is a right to see someone else's documents. The proprietary right is right to access to documents which are your own.

18.18 But this approach, and an automatic right to disclosure, gave rise to two major issues:

(a) Does the disclosure right apply to discretionary beneficiaries as well as those with fixed interests? For example could a person who merely may become entitled to an interest if the trustees (or someone else) exercises a discretion have a right to disclosure of information? Does it matter if the individual may be the object of exercise of a power by the trustees or if he or she is a full-blown discretionary beneficiary?

(b) Is any right given to beneficiaries absolute? Ie does the beneficiary have the right to disclosure of the relevant information regardless of any other duties on the trustees (eg confidentiality) or of the interests or rights of other beneficiaries? Even if there is not an absolute right, what is the balance? Should trustees disclose unless they have a good reason not to?

18.19 Both of these issues were the subject of decision in English and commonwealth courts over recent years. This decision of the Privy Council gave some pretty authoritive guidance (although it has raised other questions).

18.20 Until the Privy Council decision in *Schmidt v Rosewood Trust Ltd*,[22] the leading modern English case on what constituted trust documents which the beneficiaries were entitled to inspect was the decision of the Court of Appeal in *Re Londonderry's Settlement*.[23] In *Londonderry*, the court decided that, provided the trustees of a family trust were acting in good faith, they were not obliged to disclose agendas and minutes of trustee meetings which disclosed the (confidential) deliberations of the trustees on how they should exercise their discretion, the reasons for the exercise of the trustees' discretion, or any material upon which those reasons were or might have been based.

18.21 The Court of Appeal noted, however, that if trustees do give reasons, their soundness can be considered by the court.[24] It therefore became common in drafting minutes to refer to the outcome of the exercise of a discretion 'after consideration of all the relevant matters' but not to state what those matters were, or what discussion took place. See further para 18.99 below.

---

[21] [1920] AC 581 at 626–7, HL.
[22] [2003] UKPC 26, [2003] 2 AC 709, PC.
[23] [1965] Ch 918, CA.
[24] This has been challenged by commentators. See Sir Gavin Lightman, 'The Trustees' Duty to Provide Information to Beneficiaries' [2004] PCB 23.

This did not, however, prevent trustees' decisions from being successfully challenged in the courts if the trustees could be shown to have acted improperly, whether from an improper motive or by taking account of factors which the trustee should not have taken into account or not taking into account factors which the trustee should have taken into account. **18.22**

Schmidt v Rosewood Trust Ltd

The decision in *Schmidt* of the Judicial Committee of the Privy Council, on appeal from the Isle of Man, concerned the right of beneficiaries of a discretionary family trust to disclosure of information by trustees.[25] As a Privy Council case, the decision is strictly binding only in the Isle of Man. However, in practice, it will almost certainly be followed by the English courts. **18.23**

Mr Schmidt was a potential beneficiary under discretionary trusts set up in the Isle of Man. He appealed against a court ruling that he was not entitled to disclosure of trust documentation and information because he was not a beneficiary but had only a discretionary interest or expectation. **18.24**

The Privy Council held that: **18.25**

(i) there is no absolute right for a beneficiary to request documents or information from trustees; and

(ii) there is no distinction to be drawn for this purpose between discretionary beneficiaries and absolute beneficiaries.

Lord Walker, giving the opinion of the Board, said that the test was simply whether disclosure should be ordered as part of the court's overall jurisdiction to supervise and intervene in the administration of trusts, discretionary or otherwise. The right to seek disclosure is simply one such area of intervention. **18.26**

The Privy Council cast doubt on cases which had interpreted *Re Londonderry* as meaning that there was a right to disclosure, saying that the more recent cases were to be regarded as only beginning to work out in some detail how the court should exercise its discretion where beneficiaries apply for disclosure. The Board has thus recast the approach as a balancing judgment by the trustees between the interests of the beneficiary requesting information and the interests of the other beneficiaries under the trust. **18.27**

The Board identified areas in which the court may have to form a discretionary judgment: **18.28**

(a) whether a discretionary object should be granted relief at all (the wishes of the settlor being but one relevant factor);

(b) what classes of documents should be disclosed, either completely or in an edited form;

(c) especially when there are issues of personal or commercial confidentiality, the court may have to balance the competing interests of different beneficiaries, the trustees themselves, and third parties; and

(d) what safeguards should be imposed (whether by undertakings to the court, arrangements for professional inspection, or otherwise) to limit the use which may be made of documents or information disclosed under the order of the court.

---

[25] [2003] UKPC 26, [2003] 2 AC 709, PC.

18.29 This decision will almost certainly be followed in England and Wales. Perhaps this will be on the basis that the Board is restating what the earlier cases were deciding: those cases were not wrong but instead examples of the factors to be considered (by trustees and the courts). Conversely it may be argued that *Schmidt* recasts this area of the law entirely to make disclosure generally a discretionary matter (instead of a right).

18.30 Lord Walker held that there is no difference for this purpose between the interests of potential discretionary beneficiaries and 'fixed' beneficiaries. He was pretty forthright in overturning the decision of the appellate court in the Isle of Man on this point.

18.31 Lord Walker was also dismissive of any claims that there should be any difference between the object of a power and the object of a discretionary trust. He held (at [51]) that:

> The right to seek the court's intervention does not depend on entitlement to a fixed and transmissible beneficial interest. The object of a discretion (including a near power) may also be entitled to protection from a court of equity, although the circumstances in which you may seek protection, and the nature of the protection he may expect to obtain, will depend on the court's discretion.[26]

18.32 In taking this line, Lord Walker followed the bulk of the commonwealth authority, in particular the decision of the New South Wales Court of Appeal in *Hartigan Nominees v Rydge*.[27]

What rights do beneficiaries have?

18.33 On the second question, Lord Walker went on to hold that there is *no* absolute right for a beneficiary to request documents or information from trustees. Lord Walker made it clear that there is no distinction for this purpose between discretionary beneficiaries and absolute beneficiaries. The Privy Council held (at [54]) that a proprietary vested interest is not determinative of the right:

> in the Board's view it is neither sufficient nor necessary.

18.34 Lord Walker held that any right of disclosure of information is proprietary in the sense that it arises out of a trust, which most would regard as being part of the law of property (see [50]).

18.35 Lord Walker referred to two earlier cases where even an absolute beneficiary was refused access to certain documents, citing the decisions of North J in *Re Cowin*[28] and Chitty J in *Re Tillott*.[29]

18.36 Lord Walker quoted at length from the judgment in Australia of Kirby P (as he then was) in *Hartigan Nominees v Rydge*,[30] in particular that it is a better test to allow beneficiaries a right to require access to information as part of the court's overall jurisdiction to ensure that trustees are complying with their fiduciary duties (eg to keep the beneficiary informed and to render accounts).

18.37 The comments in the previous cases about proprietary rights of disclosure, in particular the comments of Lord Wrenbury quoted above, look on first reading to mean that there was a *right* to disclosure, rather than any sort of exercise of a balancing judgment by the trustees.

---

[26] Here Lord Walker cited *Gartside v IRC* [1968] AC 553; *McPhail v Doulton* [1971] AC 424; *Re Manisty's Settlement* [1974] Ch 17 (Templeman J); and *Mettoy Pension Trustees v Evans* [1990] 1 WLR 1587 (Warner J).

[27] (1992) 29 NSWLR 405, NSWCA.

[28] (1886) 33 ChD 179 (North J).

[29] [1892] 1 Ch 86 (Chitty J).

[30] (1992) 29 NSWLR 405, NSWCA.

For example in *CAS Nominees v Nottingham Forest*,[31] Evans-Lombe J had held in 2001 that **18.38** a shareholder was entitled to disclosure of legal advice given to directors. He held (at [11]):

> The fundamental rule which governs an attempt by a shareholder to obtain the production of documents by a company in which he holds shares but which documents would otherwise be protected by legal professional privilege is to be found in the judgment of Phillimore LJ in *Woodhouse & Co (Ltd) v Woodhouse* (1914) 30 TLR 559. The report summarises his judgment as follows (at 590):
>
>> ... [the judge] had read the opinions, and they were taken on behalf of the company and not on behalf of others, two of them after the action began, and the third in preparation for the action. They had to consider the principle applicable where a shareholder was a plaintiff or a defendant in litigation with the company. To his mind, whether he was plaintiff or defendant was immaterial ... The principle was that if people had a common interest in property, an opinion having regard to that property, paid for out of the common fund, i.e., company's money or trust fund, was the common property of the shareholders, or cestuis que trust. But where the parties were sundered by litigation such an opinion obtained by one of them was privileged.

This approach did give rise to a whole degree of difficulty in determining what are 'trust' **18.39** documents and so arguably must be disclosed and what are not.

Lord Walker in *Schmidt* arguably cut through this issue and instead recast the approach. **18.40**

This echoes the comments of the full court of South Australia in *Rouse v IOOF Australia* **18.41** *Trustees*[32] when discussing the comments of Lord Wrenbury. Doyle CJ stated (at [89]):

> Some of the later decisions take what his Lordship said quite literally, and treat him as holding that a beneficiary has an actual proprietary interest in trust documents, and that the existence of that proprietary interest is the hallmark of what is a trust document. I doubt whether that is what His Lordship intended. I consider that the true position is as stated by Dawson and Toohey JJ in *Breen v Williams* (1996) 186 CLR 71 at 89:
>
>> But the right of access of a beneficiary to trust documents arises because of the beneficial interests of the beneficiary in the trust property and it is in that sense that the right may be described as proprietary.

In *Schmidt*, Lord Walker referred to the *IOOF* case in this case (but not on this point). **18.42**

Thus Lord Walker treated the 1965 decision of the Court of Appeal in *Re Londonderry's* **18.43** *Settlement*[33] and more recent cases as beginning to work out in some detail the way in which the court should exercise its discretion where beneficiaries apply for disclosure (see [54]).

Lord Walker held that there are three areas in which the court may have to form a discretion- **18.44** ary judgment:

(a) whether a discretionary object (or some other beneficiary with only remote or wholly defeasible interest) should be granted relief at all;
(b) what classes of documents should be disclosed, either completely or in a redacted form;
(c) what safeguards should be imposed (whether by undertakings to the court, arrangements for professional inspection, or otherwise) to limit the use which may be made of documents or information disclosed under the order of the court.

---

[31] [2001] 1 All ER 954 (Evans-Lombe J).
[32] (1999) 73 SASR 484 (Full Court, South Australia).
[33] [1965] Ch 918, CA.

18.45 In reaching the decision that discretionary beneficiaries (and objects of powers) were entitled to discovery, the Privy Council referred to various other cases on this point, in particular *Hartigan Nominees, Chain-Nickson v Bank of Ireland*[34] (a decision of Kenny J in Ireland), *Spellson v George*[35] and *A-G of Ontario v Stavro*.[36] He also mentioned the decision of Neuberger J in *Murphy v Murphy*.[37]

18.46 Ultimately the Privy Council held (at [67]) that:

> No beneficiary (and least of all a discretionary object) has any entitlement as of right to disclosure of anything which can plausibly be described as a trust document. Especially when there are issues as to personal or commercial confidentially, the court may have to balance the competing interests of different beneficiaries, the trustees themselves, and third parties. Disclosure may have to be limited and safeguards may have to be put in place. Evaluation of the claims of those beneficiaries (and especially of a discretionary object) may be an important part of the balancing exercise which the court has to perform on the materials placed before it. In many cases the court may have no difficulty in concluding that an applicant with no more than a theoretical possibility of benefit will not be granted any relief.

Comment on *Schmidt*

18.47 *Schmidt* marked a radical shift for those who had read *Re Londonderry* and the earlier *O'Rourke* case as giving a proprietary right to disclosure. Instead of a proprietary right to discovery (perhaps subject to some defences such as confidentiality), it appears that generally there is no absolute right.

18.48 But will a court be inclined to hold that documents should be disclosed unless there is some reason not to? Even the Australian cases (eg *Rouse v IOOF*[38]) started with a prima facie right to discovery, which was then subject to various defences.

18.49 So is this a fundamental shift so that instead there appears merely a balancing exercise? Will trustees feel able to agree to disclosure or will beneficiaries have to go to court?

18.50 Strictly, of course, this decision does not overrule the previous cases. But it will almost certainly be followed on the basis that Lord Walker is restating what the earlier cases were deciding. So the earlier cases were not wrong, but instead examples of the factors to be considered (by trustees and the courts). Factors that clearly need to be considered include:[39]

    (a)   confidentiality and wishes of the settlor—*Hartigan*;

    (b)   protecting trustees from the need to disclose reasons—*Londonderry*;

    (c)   the need to protect other beneficiaries as part of a litigation process—*IOOF*.[40]

Decisions After *Schmidt v Rosewood*

18.51 There have been various cases on disclosure following the decision of the Privy Council in *Schmidt v Rosewood*. But they do not, in the main, concern superannuation or pension trusts.

---

[34] [1976] IR 593 (Kenny J).
[35] (1987) 11 NSWLR 300.
[36] (1994) 119 DLR (4th) 750.
[37] [1998] 3 All ER 1 (Neuberger J).
[38] (1999) 73 SASR 484 (Full Court, South Australia).
[39] See further Emily Campbell and Jonathan Hilliard, 'Disclosure of Information by Trustees' in D Hayton (ed), *The International Trust* 3rd edn (Jordans, 2011).
[40] See also *Thomas v Secretary of State for India* (1870) 18 WR 312.

New Zealand—*Foreman v Kingstone* (2003)

In 2003 in New Zealand in *Foreman v Kingstone*[41] Potter J treated *Schmidt v Rosewood* as **18.52** binding but thought that the old categories of disclosure under the previous cases remained appropriate.

Foreman v Kingstone involved a number of related family discretionary trusts. The court was **18.53** asked to determine whether discretionary beneficiaries were entitled to information including the following:

(a) the reasons for amending and winding-up certain family trusts;
(b) copies of all communications between the trustees and their legal advisers in relation to various dispositions; and
(c) details of the advice which led the trustees to decline to provide the information and documents.

Potter J followed the approach in *Schmidt* and held that: **18.54**

> Beneficiaries are entitled to receive information which will enable them to ensure the accountability of the trustees in terms of the trust deed. They are entitled to have the trust property properly managed and to have the trustees account for their management. . . .

In determining whether the particular applicants should be granted disclosure, Potter J **18.55** adopted the factors enumerated by the Privy Council in *Schmidt*. She held that the Court may take into account the following:

(a) whether there are issues of personal or commercial confidentiality;
(b) the nature of the interests of the beneficiaries seeking disclosure;
(c) the impact on the trustees, other beneficiaries, or third parties;
(d) whether some or all of the documents can be withheld on full or redacted form;
(e) whether safeguards can be imposed on the use of trust documentation (eg undertakings, professional inspection etc);
(f) whether disclosure would be likely to embitter family feelings.

The position in New Zealand is that: **18.56**

- *Schmidt* is, as in Australia, often being followed rather than *Re Londonderry* in terms of the conceptual test for disclosure, ie it is a matter of Court supervisory discretion;
- *Schmidt* is not being extended to ordering disclosure of reasons for the exercise of a discretion; and
- Legal opinions will be disclosable if they do not relate to the exercise of discretions.

UK—*Breakspear v Ackland* (2008)

In *Breakspear v Ackland*[42] Briggs J (as he then was) had to decide whether or not the disclosure **18.57** of a letter of wishes in a private family trust was appropriate. Briggs J held that in general a letter of wishes from a settlor was to be considered as being confidential and there was no duty on the trustees to disclose it.

---

[41] [2004] NZLR 841, [2003] 6 ITELR 841, [2005] WTLR 823 (Potter J).
[42] [2008] EWHC 220 (Ch), [2009] Ch 32 (Briggs J). Noted in [2008] CLJ 252.

18.58 But in this case the trustees had indicated that they were intending to apply to the court for directions about how to exercise their discretion. In such a case the letter of wishes would need to be disclosed to both the court and the beneficiaries, so there was no point in maintaining confidentiality now.

18.59 Briggs J commented that he was bound to follow the decision in *Londonderry*. He considered the judgment of Lord Walker in *Schmidt* and commented that:

> 40. Apart from the conclusion that the grant or withholding of disclosure sought by a beneficiary is essentially a discretionary matter for the court, (rather than a matter of right depending upon 'bright dividing lines' or rigid categories of excluded documents), Lord Walker expressed no hint of disapproval at the manner in which the Court of Appeal explained in *Re Londonderry* the principled basis for refusing inspection on grounds of confidentiality. On the contrary, he described the need to protect confidentiality as 'one of the most important limitations on the right to disclosure of trust documents' (in paragraph 49) and commended *Re Londonderry* as an important case in the development of the principles regulating the exercise of discretion, in the passage in paragraph 54 which I have quoted above.
>
> 41. It seems to me inconceivable that the Privy Council can have approved of Kirby P's wholesale attack on the *Re Londonderry* approach to the preservation of confidentiality. Lord Walker's approval of the approach of Kirby P in *Hartigan Nominees* was limited to that part of his analysis with which Sheller JA concurred: see paragraph 61. Quite apart from the difficulty that I am bound by a decision of the Court of Appeal, it does not seem to me that *Schmidt v. Rosewood* justifies a departure from what I have described as the *Londonderry* principle. The obviously non-confidential nature of the documents of which disclosure was sought in *Schmidt v Rosewood* means that the statements in Lord Walker's judgment about the importance of confidentiality are, however persuasive, obiter dicta.

18.60 Ultimately Briggs J held that the confidentiality in a wishes letter in a private family trust should be respected and no disclosure ordered just on a request by a beneficiary. He held:

> 57. My reason for concluding that, regardless of my own opinion, I am bound to continue to treat the *Londonderry* principle as still being good law is simply because it formed part of the ratio of that decision, it has never been overruled, and because, if anything, it received a general endorsement rather than criticism in *Schmidt v Rosewood*.
>
> 58. I turn therefore to the question whether, and if so in what way, the *Londonderry* principle applies to wish letters. In that context I am content to limit myself to wish letters arising in the context of family discretionary trusts, rather than employee trusts, pension trusts or other business trusts, leaving for another occasion the manner in which the *Londonderry* principle is applicable to them. The defining characteristic of a wish letter is that it contains material which the settlor desires that the trustees should take into account when exercising their (usually dispositive) discretionary powers. It is therefore brought into existence for the sole purpose of serving and facilitating an inherently confidential process. It seems to me axiomatic that a document brought into existence for the sole or predominant purpose of being used in furtherance of an inherently confidential process is itself properly to be regarded as confidential, to substantially the same extent and effect as the process which it is intended to serve.

18.61 Thus Briggs J specifically excluded pension trust from his reasoning.

Ultimately Briggs J treated the issue of disclosure as one for the trustees (or ultimately the court) in exercising a discretion about whether or not to disclose. He finished (at [73]): **18.62**

> Before leaving this general legal analysis, I emphasise that the application of the *Londonderry* principle to wish letters in the way in which I have sought to explain them is not to be taken as something akin to a statutory code. The question begins and ends, both for trustees and for the court, a question of discretion, or of the review of the exercise of discretion. There are no fixed rules, and the trustees need not approach the question with any pre-disposition towards disclosure or non-disclosure. All relevant circumstances must be taken into account, and in all cases other than those limited to a strict review of the negative exercise of a discretion, both the trustees and the court have a range of alternative responses, not limited to the black and white question of disclosure or non-disclosure. The responses include all those identified by Lord Walker *in Schmidt's case* [2003] 3 All ER 76 at [67], and may include, in an appropriate case, a private reading of the wish letter by the judge to himself, a process which I think would have been undertaken by the Court of Appeal of New South Wales in the *Hartigan Nominees case* (1992) 29 NSWLR 405, had that avenue not been closed off by the decision of the trial judge in that case not to do so.

Ireland: *O'Mahony v McNamara*

Schmidt has been followed in Ireland in relation to a pension scheme. In *O'Mahony v McNamara*[43] Carroll J confirmed that a beneficiary's right to seek disclosure of trust documents is simply an aspect or incident of the court's inherent and fundamental jurisdiction to supervise and intervene in the administration of a trust. **18.63**

The plaintiffs, who were members of a staff retirement benefit scheme, sought an order for disclosure of all trust documents relating to the retirement benefit scheme. Carroll J held that the High Court, as part of its inherent jurisdiction to supervise and, if appropriate, intervene in the administration of a trust, could order the disclosure of trust documents. **18.64**

Australia

There have been various Australian cases[44]—eg *Crowe v Stevedoring Employees Retirement Fund*,[45] *Avanes v Marshall*,[46] and *McDonald v Ellis*.[47] **18.65**

Crowe v Stevedoring Employees Retirement Fund (2003)

In *Crowe v Stevedoring Employees Retirement Fund Pty Ltd*, Balmford J considered the extent of the obligation of superannuation trust funds to provide information to members. In *Crowe*, the plaintiff sought various items of information relating to defined benefits. Balmford J referred to *Schmidt v Rosewood* and reviewed the cases on whether or not the disclosure principles in *Re Londonderry* should apply to a superannuation scheme. She followed *Hartigan v Rydge* and held that they should ([37]). **18.66**

Balmford J held that the material relating to defined benefits sought by the fund member **18.67**

---

[43] [2005] IEHC 118, [2005] 1 IR 519 (Carroll J).
[44] Besides the cases discussed here, see the cases mentioned when discussing 'legal privilege' above.
[45] [2003] VSC 316, [2003] PLR 343 (Balmford J).
[46] [2007] NSWSC 91, (2007) 68 NSWLR 595 (Gzell J).
[47] [2007] NSWSC 1068 (Bryson AJ).

(eg actuarial valuations) would not contain evidence of the reasons why trustees made their decisions and so should be disclosed. The provision of the material was not prohibited by *Re Londonderry*.

Avanes v Marshall (2007)

18.68 *Avanes v Marshall*[48] concerned a testamentary family trust. Gzell J referred to *Schmidt v Rosewood* and considered that it required a reappraisal of *Re Londonderry*. The beneficiary had requested copies of correspondence with the lawyers. Gzell J read the documents and decided that they should not be disclosed (at [21]):

> In my view the documents do not relate to the exercise of any discretion or power the trustees possess under the settlement. Having no relevance to any discretion or power, the interests of the trustees in keeping confidential communications between their solicitors and counsel outweigh any requirement of openness between the trustees and the life tenant.

McDonald v Ellis (2007)

18.69 *McDonald v Ellis*[49] also involved a family trust in which the plaintiff had an interest in remainder. Bryson AJ was unconvinced of the merits of the more discretionary approach in *Schmidt v Rosewood* and refused to follow *Avanes v Marshall* on this point. Bryson AJ considered that it may be that *Schmidt* is limited to claims by a beneficiary.

Canada

Camosun College (2004)

18.70 In 2004 in *Camosun College Faculty Association v College Board*[50] the Court of Appeal of British Columbia dealt with a request by the Faculty Board and plan members of the college for copies of legal opinions in relation to a decision of the College pension plan trustees. The issue was the trustees' decision that a phased retirement provision in the collective agreement between the Faculty Association and the Camosun College did not meet the conditions for termination of employment in the Plan rules.

18.71 As part of the process to challenge this trustee decision an application was made to the Court for an order that the trustees produce a legal opinion obtained by them in the course of their duties in the administration of the College Plan. The applicants claimed that the opinion was relied upon by the trustees when the decision under review was made. The trustees declined the request citing *Re Londonderry's Settlement* and claiming solicitor and client privilege.

18.72 At first instance Vickers J considered that the legal opinion would be relevant in the main proceedings if the criteria for setting aside the trustees' decision was good faith and reasonableness. He therefore went on to consider whether the legal opinion was privileged as against beneficiaries or whether there was in fact common interest privilege on the basis that the trustees and members had a joint interest in the proper administration of the trust.

18.73 The trustees argued that joint interest in the proper administration of the trust did not equate with common interest privilege for two reasons. First, the trustees cited *Re Londonderry's*

---

48 [2007] NSWSC 91, (2007) 68 NSWLR 595 (Gzell J).
49 [2007] NSWSC 1068 (Bryson AJ).
50 2004 BCSC 1578 (British Columbia Court of Appeal). See Eileen Gillese, 'Pension Plans, Fiduciary Duties, and the Thorny Question of Disclosure' (2011) 90 Canadian Bar Review 517.

Settlement, Wilson v Law Debenture, and *Schmidt v Rosewood* to demonstrate that a court will not order trustees to disclose reasons for exercise of powers. Secondly, they cited *Rouse v IOOF Australia Trustees Ltd* [51] and *Alberta Ltd v First City Trust Co* [52] where the courts concluded that trustees could not effectively carry out their duties if they were required to disclose their hand with respect to litigation.

Vickers J rejected these two arguments on the basis that neither in his view applied to **18.74** Camosun and he held that the legal opinion was not protected by solicitor client privilege.

On appeal the Court of Appeal overturned the order for production of the legal opinion but **18.75** did so on different grounds. The Court of Appeal held that the challenge to the trustees' decision should be made out on whether or not they had power under the rules of the Plan not whether their decision was reasonable. Consequently it was an issue of pure construction. It was for the Court in the main proceedings to decide whether the trustees have power or not under the Plan rules to pay benefits on phased retirement.

Patrick v Telus Communications Inc (2005)

In *Patrick v Telus Communications Inc*,[53] beneficiaries of a pension scheme sought disclosure **18.76** of legal opinions obtained by the employer/administrator. Rogers J referred to *Londonderry*, *IOOF*, and *Schmidt* and held that legal opinions were disclosable to the beneficiaries once proceedings had started and the good faith of the trustee's exercise of discretion challenged.

Trustees Going Forward

So what should trustees now do when receiving a request from beneficiaries for documents **18.77** (eg a counsel's opinion)?

In practice, the courts are likely still to continue to treat beneficiaries as having a right to **18.78** such documents (unless it is clear they are not a beneficiary at all). If the opinion has been obtained at the expense of the trust then it is an asset of the trust and so should be available to the beneficiaries. There may of course be reasons why trustees do not consider that it is appropriate to disclose. These should be properly considered and given due weight.

Trustees are at risk as to their costs if they wrongfully refuse to disclose (ie the court takes a different view). In *Schmidt*, costs were awarded against the trustees (and the case sent back to the Isle of Man courts to decide whether or not the trustees could recover their costs from the fund).

Who is a Beneficiary?

It is clear from *Schmidt* that all beneficiaries (including those only the objects of a discretion) **18.79** may be able to require the disclosure of documents and information. In practice the more 'vested' and current the interest of the beneficiary, the more likely it is that disclosure will be ordered.

---

[51] (1999) 73 SASR 484, Full Court, South Australia.
[52] (1997) 10 CPC (4th) 255.
[53] 2005 BCSC 1762 at [39]–[40] (Rogers J). See also *MacPherson v MacPherson* 2005 BCSC 207 (Humphries J).

In practice it is considered that it is more difficult for a contingent beneficiary (eg a spouse or child of a living member who will only draw benefits if the member dies before them) to successfully claim for disclosure of information. Looking at the various categories of beneficiary in a pension scheme:

(a)   member (pensioner, deferred or active)—high claim;

(b)   spouse or dependant—low claim (member can be the primary claim);

(c)   potential discretionary recipient of a death benefit—low claim while member alive, higher after death;

(d)   employer—high claim as a beneficiary and scheme funder,[54] but any claim to disclosure may have some limits based on confidentiality and the interests of the scheme.

Confidential Information

18.80   The cases generally confirm that confidentiality is one factor that the courts will consider (and hence so should a trustee) when deciding whether or not to order disclosure to a beneficiary.

18.81   In practice there will often be cases where trustees have received information on a confidential basis (eg from a third party) as part of the investment of the trust assets or from the employer as part of its discussions with the trustees about funding (this will often involve a discussion about the strength of the employer's ability to support the scheme or 'covenant').

18.82   *Schmidt* supports this approach. As Austin J held in Australia in *Gray v Guardian Trust Australia*:[55]

> 38   In *Schmidt v Rosewood Trust Pty Ltd* IOM [2003] UK PC 26 (27 March 2003), where a person claiming to be a beneficiary sought access to the accounts of the trust, alleging a possible breach of trust, the Privy Council said (at paragraph [51]) that the correct approach was to regard the right to seek disclosure of trust documents as one aspect of the court's inherent jurisdiction to supervise, and if necessary to intervene in, the administration of trusts. Their Lordships rejected the idea that a beneficiary has a right to disclosure of everything that might plausibly be described as a trust document, and said that the court may have to balance competing interests of different beneficiaries, the trustees themselves, and third parties, especially where issues such as personal or commercial confidentiality are involved (at paragraph [61]).

18.83   Disclosure to beneficiaries of third party confidential information will usually not be in the interests of the trust (or pension scheme). The third party will be reluctant to make disclosure in the future.

18.84   In relation to pension schemes the Pensions Regulator has endorsed a confidentiality approach. The Pensions Regulator supported this approach in its 2005 clearance guidance:[56]

> **Confidentiality**
>
> 86.   Trustees must understand that information they receive in their position as trustees is confidential. This is particularly important when it comes to sensitive information—involving either

---

[54]   See Ch 10 (Trustees' duties to employers).
[55]   [2003] NSWSC 704 at [38] (Austin J).
[56]   Extract from TPR Guidance on clearance applications (April 2005).

scheme members or the employer. Trustees cannot expect to be given 'inside information' from the employer if they pass it on.

87. One way of ensuring that all parties understand the importance of confidentiality is to enter into a confidentiality agreement. This should ideally be done every time a new trustee joins the board, rather than waiting until there is an important issue which the employer is reluctant to discuss because of confidentiality issues.

[Footnote: The Regulator may remove trustees who are in breach of a confidentiality agreement as not fit and proper persons—section 3 of the Pensions Act 1995.]

It may be that trustees face a difficulty if they have received information under an obligation **18.85** of confidentiality (subject perhaps only to disclosure required by law). If they then disclose this to a beneficiary (or the Pensions Regulator) they may be at risk of a claim by the third party.[57] If they do not, they risk a claim by the beneficiary. Such confidentiality obligations are increasingly common in agreements with professional advisers (eg actuaries and accountants) who are attempting to reduce their potential exposure of liability to third parties by limiting distribution of their advice.

Pension trustees, of course, are under an obligation to disclose some documents (eg actuarial **18.86** valuations, copies of trust deeds etc). This arises under the statutory disclosure regulations made under the Pension Schemes Act 1993 and will override any implied confidentiality obligation.

For pension trustees the mere existence of this catalogue of statutory disclosure of obligations **18.87** could also be argued to limit the common law right of disclosure (see eg the unfair dismissal case *Johnson v Unisys*[58]). Conversely, the rights of pension trustees could be considered to be 'purchased' and so therefore to be greater than their family trust comprising volunteers. This was discussed in *Wilson v Law Debenture*, where Rattee J decided that no extension of normal trust law was needed.

Legal Advice/Privilege

Litigation

Disclosure (formerly 'discovery') in the context of litigation requires a court order.[59] A **18.88** normal court order would be for 'standard disclosure'.[60] This requires a party to disclose documents which are or have been in his control (eg with an agent such as an adviser) and are documents:

 (i) on which he relies; or
 (ii) which adversely affect his own case; or

---

[57] The statutory obligation under the Pensions Act 2004 to disclose some information to the Pensions Regulator will override any confidentiality obligation under English law. But this may not be a defence if there is a confidentiality obligation under a non-UK law—see eg the difficulties of the administrators in *Bloom v The Pensions Regulator* [2012] EWHC 1409 (Ch) (Mann J).

[58] [2003] 1 AC 518, HL and Ch 3 above.

[59] See Civil Procedure Rules 1998, Pt 31.

[60] See CPR r 31.5.

    (iii) which adversely affect another party's case; or

    (iv) which support another party's case; or

    (v) which he is required to disclose by a relevant practice direction.

Legal privilege

18.89 Under the rules of court, advice from a legal adviser to the client is normally exempt from being disclosed to the other party in legal proceedings.

18.90 Advice from a legal adviser regarding the trust may be a trust document and therefore subject to disclosure under the trust law principles above rather than being protected from disclosure by legal privilege. However, under the trust law principles, trustees do not generally have to disclose advice relating to a claim by a beneficiary to that beneficiary. The same would generally apply to a legal opinion obtained in contemplation of litigation (subject to the trust law principles described above if the opinion was paid for by the fund).[61]

18.91 It seems clear that legal privilege is not, of itself, a defence to a claim for disclosure by a beneficiary under the *Londonderry* principles.[62] For example in *Londonderry*, Salmon LJ held:[63]

> The position is quite different where the beneficiary seeks disclosure of documents from the trustees in the air, as in this case, from the position where the beneficiary seeks discovery of documents in an action in which allegations are being made against the bona fides of the trustees. If the documents in question are in the possession or power of the trustees and are relevant to the issues in the action, they must be disclosed whether or not they are trust documents. In some instances, however, the fact that they are trust documents may nullify the privilege that would otherwise exist, as, for example, if the document consists of counsel's opinion taken before the issue of the writ, clearly the beneficiary is entitled to see any opinion taken on behalf of the trust.

18.92 But it may be different if the beneficiary is claiming privileged documents where the beneficiary has an interest in separate proceedings (eg the beneficiary is connected with a third party involved in litigation with the trustee). In such cases, disclosure may well not be in the interests of the trust or scheme and so properly withheld—*IOOF* and *Schmidt*.

18.93 The various Australian cases also make the point that legal privilege is only a defence to a general litigation claim form disclosure or discovery as part of legal proceedings. It is not a defence to a claim by a beneficiary for disclosure under the *Londonderry* principle, unless disclosure is restricted by the need to keep the trustee's reasons confidential (*Londonderry*) or is otherwise in the interests of the trust (*IOOF* and *Schmidt*).

18.94 Recent cases[64] on this include *Silkman v Shakespeare Haney Securities*;[65] *Krok v Szaintop Homes Pty Ltd*;[66] *Avanes v Marshall*;[67] *Gray v BNY Trust Co of Australia Ltd*;[68] *Dura (Australia)*

---

[61] Eg *Rouse v IOOF Australia Trustees Ltd* (1999) 73 SASR 484.

[62] On privilege and pensions, see Emily Campbell, 'Privilege and Pensions Disputes' (APL seminar, June 2010) and Paul Lewis, Andrew Spink, and Hardeep Nahal, 'Privilege and Disclosure in a Pensions Dispute Context' (APL seminar, October 2009).

[63] [1965] Ch 918 at 938. Cited by Rogers J in British Columbia in *Patrick v Telus Communications* 2005 BCSC 1762.

[64] See Michael Vrikasis, 'How Should Trustees Commission Legal Advice?' (2013) 24 Australian Superannuation Law Bulletin 147 (March 2013).

[65] [2011] NSWSC 148 (Hammerschlag J).

[66] [2011] VSC 16 (Judd J).

[67] [2007] NSWSC 191, (2007) 68 NSWLR 595 (Gzell J).

[68] [2009] NSWSC 789, (2009) 76 NSWLR 586 (Bergin CJ in Eq).

Constructions Pty Ltd v Hue Boutique Living Pty Ltd;[69] and *Eastmark Holdings Pty Ltd v Kabraji (No 3)*.[70]

In *Gray v BNY Trust Co of Australia Ltd*,[71] Bergin CJ (in Eq) denied a beneficiary a right to **18.95** inspect documents containing legal advice provided to the trustee. The critical reason for denying the inspection, and the upholding of the privilege, was the nature of the relationship between the plaintiff beneficiary and defendant trustee. Bergin CJ held, at 601:

> ...It is necessary to focus on the relationship at the time the documents were created. There is no doubt that at the time the documents were created in relation to the main proceedings in which the plaintiff was suing the defendant the communications were privileged.

In *Dura (Australia) Constructions Pty Ltd v Hue Boutique Living Pty Ltd*[72] Macaulay J, refer- **18.96** ring to some of these cases, noted at [19]:

> As can be seen, the cases distinguish the situation in which the advice is sought and obtained by a trustee in the discharge of its obligation to properly administer the trust from that in which it seeks advice in its personal capacity. The same distinction was important in *Krok's case*. Judd J answered the question in favour of the beneficiary seeking production of the documents from the trustee '...because the advice sought and obtained by the trustee was in discharge of its obligation to administer the trust, and not for its own personal benefit.'

In New Zealand in *Foreman v Kingstone*,[73] having weighed up the factors Potter J declined to **18.97** order the trustees to disclose legal opinions giving the reasons for the exercise of their discretion to amend the trust and supporting legal advice. She held that:

> legal opinions obtained by the trustees for the purpose of the trust, funded by the trust funds, are prima facie trust documents and included in information that should generally be available to beneficiaries.... But because beneficiaries are not entitled to advice or information obtained by the trustees in relation to the management of trust property or to the future conduct concerning trust property nor advice directed to the trustees' reasons for the exercise of their discretions (as distinct from the information which informed their reasons), whether the beneficiaries are entitled to disclosure of the communications will depend on their nature.

She also declined the request for legal advice on disclosure on the basis: **18.98**

> While beneficiaries are entitled to information obtained by the trust which informs the trustees in the exercise of their discretions, they are not entitled to the reasons.

Reasons

The common law right (at least for private trusts) is that trustees can refuse to disclose **18.99** information that would give details of their reasons (*Londonderry*). However, in relation to pension trusts, the Pensions Ombudsman has strongly indicated in a number of his determinations that failure to disclose reasons could, in appropriate circumstances, be considered to be maladministration—see eg *Allen v TKM Group*.[74]

---

[69] [2011] VSC 477 (Macaulay J).
[70] [2012] NSWSC 1463 (Hallen J).
[71] [2009] NSWSC 789, (2009) 76 NSWLR 586 (Bergin CJ in Eq).
[72] [2011] VSC 477 (Macaulay J).
[73] [2004] NZLR 841, [2003] 6 ITELR 841, [2005] WTLR 823 (Potter J).
[74] L00370, [2002] PLR 333 (Laverick PO). See further below.

Do trustees have to give reasons?

18.100 It is clear that in a private trust context trustees are under no obligation to give reasons for the exercise of their discretions etc. The leading case here is the decision of the Court of Appeal in *Re Londonderry's Settlement*.[75] This case involved an application for disclosure of documents by trustees. However, the Court of Appeal clearly based its decision on disclosure on the principle that trustees are not obliged to give reasons for their decisions. Harman LJ stated (at p 928) that:

> trustees exercising a discretionary power are not bound to disclose to their beneficiaries the reasons actuating them in coming to a decision. This is a long-standing principle and rests largely I think on the view that nobody could be called upon to accept a trusteeship involving the exercise of a discretion unless, in the absence of bad faith, he will not be liable to have his motives or his reasons called in question either or by the beneficiaries or by the court.

18.101 This rule seems to be based on the fact that it 'might make the lives of the trustees intolerable should such an obligation rest upon them'—see Salmon LJ at p 937A.

18.102 This rule seems to follow from some old cases for example:

(a) in 1851 in *Re Beloved Wilkes's Charity*[76] Lord Chancellor Truro held that the trustees of a charity in relation to education of young men to be become ministers of the Church of England were not obliged to give reasons;

(b) in 1812 in *The King v The Archbishop of Canterbury*[77] Lord Ellenborough refused to review a decision not to licence a clerk to give a lecture in a Parish Church.

18.103 A similar rule was applied in relation to company directors where they have been given discretions under the company's articles of association. For example, in *Re Gresham Life Assurance Society, ex parte Penny*,[78] the Court of Appeal held that directors were not under any duty to give reasons for their refusal to register a share transfer. The directors stated that they had considered the matter carefully and the court appeared satisfied with this.

18.104 James LJ stated (at p 450):

> I cannot conceive that any director would choose to accept office, or exercise the power entrusted to him, if he were liable to be called upon to say what the particular reasons were or the particular motive was which influenced him in coming to the conclusion that any person was not eligible as a shareholder. I think therefore that these directors were well advised in not subjecting themselves to be cross-examined and interrogated at to what particular reasons they might have for personally objecting to this gentleman, and in confining themselves to saying, by their secretary, that the question was discussed by the board of directors, that the propriety of the transfer to the particular transferee was the subject matter for discussion, and having taken that into consideration, they arrived at the conclusion to which they had arrived. This conclusion, of course, in the absence of any suggestion to the contrary, or of any evidence to the contrary, we must take to be a bona fide conclusion on their part that, for some reason or other connected with the interests of the company they did not think fit to recognise that gentleman as a transferee.[79]

---

[75] [1965] Ch 918, CA.

[76] (1851) 3 Mac & G 440 (Lord Chancellor Truro).

[77] (1812) 15 East 117 (Lord Ellenborough).

[78] (1872) 8 Ch App 446, CA.

[79] On challenging decisions by directors not to register a transfer, see also the decision to the same effect of Laddie J in *Popely v Planarrive Limited* [1997] 1 BCLC 8.

Re Londonderry has been followed in pensions cases. In Australia, the full court in Queensland **18.105** has held it applicable to a pension scheme (although the deed here included an express provision requiring the trustees to 'observe strict secrecy in relation to the Plan')—*Tierney v King*.[80]

Similarly in the later case (involving a private trust) of *Hartigan Nominees Pty Ltd v Rydge*,[81] **18.106** the majority of the Court of Appeal in New South Wales also upheld the reasoning in *Re Londonderry* on this point.

Thus Mahoney JA stated (at p 438): **18.107**

> The law allows trustees to act without detailing their reasons, not to encourage secrecy, but to avoid litigation . . .

And Sheller JA (at p 442): **18.108**

> It is, I think, sensible in the context of a trust and absent bad faith, that the law allow discretionary powers to be exercised without the need for disclosure by trustees of their reasons. The principle was challenged in argument before us. It is, however, in my opinion, far too well settled as part of the law of trust for us not to accept and apply it.

This issue has been addressed in England in relation to pension schemes. In *Wilson v The* **18.109** *Law Debenture Trust Corpn*,[82] Rattee J heard arguments that the principles laid down in *Re Londonderry* should not apply to pension trusts on the basis they are commercial trusts and different from the private trusts envisaged by that case. Rattee J rejected this argument. He held (at p 111G):

> It would in my judgment be wrong in principle to hold that the long-established principles of trust law as to the exercise by trustees of discretions conferred on them by their trust instruments, in the context of which parties to a pension scheme such as the present entered into those schemes, no longer apply to them and that the trustees are under more onerous obligations to account to their beneficiaries than they could have appreciated when appointed, on the basis of the relevant trust law as it has stood for so long.

> I accept Mr Warren's submission that if any such amendment to the law of trusts as applied to pension schemes is to be made it should be made by the legislature. . .

The decision of Rattee J might be thought to finalize the position in England.[83] However, **18.110** it may be that other first instance judges will not follow that decision. In 1996, Robert Walker (then a High Court judge) gave a talk at a conference in Cambridge on 'Trends in Contemporary Trust Law'.[84] Sir Robert Walker drew a distinction between private trusts and trustees of a pension scheme for employees of a company. He stated that:

> There are, it seems to me, strong arguments that in such circumstances the trustees should be ready to justify their decisions to those whose interest they represent, subject to protection for what is truly confidential (whether for commercial or personal reasons). Whatever their strict obligations, pension trustees would in my view be well advised, in almost all circumstances,

---

[80] [1983] 2 QdR 580.
[81] (1992) 29 NSWLR 405, NSWCA.
[82] [1995] 2 All ER 337, [1995] OPLR 103 (Rattee J). Noted by Dan Schaffer in (1994) TLI 118.
[83] *Re Londonderry* has also been followed in a pensions context in New Zealand—see McGechan J in *Stuart v Armourguard Security* [1996] 1 NZLR 484 at 506.
[84] 'Some Trust Principles in the Pensions Context' in AJ Oakley (ed), *Trends in Contemporary Trust Law* (Clarendon Press, 1996). This talk is also in [1996] PLR 107.

to adopt a policy of the utmost openness. Secrecy breeds suspicion, and suspicion can lead to speculative actions for breach of trust, often at the expense either of trade union funds or of the legal aid fund.

18.111   Sir Robert then went on to refer to the decision in *Wilson v Law Debenture*. He said that the conclusion reached by Mr Justice Rattee:

> seems, with great respect, to treat *Re Londonderry* as a rather more precise and definitively statement of principle than it may be.
>
> It remains to be seen how far the law will develop, either by case law or by further legislative intervention. In administrative law the tide is running towards a general duty to give reasons for decisions, and decisions of pension trustees have at least too much in common with those of official bodies as with those of family trustees, at least as regards to the degree to which they depend on objective, rather than subjective judgment.

18.112   In relation to public bodies consider the decision of *R v Commonalty and Citizens of the City of London ex parte Matson*[85] a decision by the Court of Appeal holding that the Court of Aldermen in the City of London had to give reasons for rejecting an applicant.

18.113   In *Target Holdings*[86] in the House of Lords there are comments to the effect that commercial trusts should be governed by different rules compared to private trusts.

Should pension trustees give reasons?

18.114   It is said that Lord Mansfield, the Chief Justice from 1756–88, advised a friend who had been appointed governor of a Caribbean island and would be acting as a judge:[87]

> Tut, man, decide promptly, but never give any reasons for your decisions. Your decisions may be right, but your reasons are sure to be wrong.

18.115   Those advising trustees have long adopted a practice of suggesting that the trustees do not give reasons to beneficiaries as to why they have reached their decision. Although this may run against the natural inclination of trustees to be open in their dealings with beneficiaries, at least two reasons can be advanced for this practice:

(a)   It avoids the need to disclose confidential or embarrassing information where the private circumstances of the beneficiaries are concerned. This can arise in pension schemes for example in relation to lump sum death benefits or in relation to questions of establishing dependency etc. For example, a member may have requested that part of a lump sum death benefit and pension scheme be payable to (say) an illegitimate child. His wife may be unaware of the existence of the child and it may be embarrassing for the trustees to have to reveal it.

(b)   The second (and probably more important) reason is that generally it is considered that if the trustees give reasons it would be easier for the beneficiary to challenge the exercise of discretion by the trustees.

18.116   This second ground, that refusing to give reasons probably protects the trustees against challenge, is arguably a protection for the trustees and not the beneficiaries. Given that the trustees are meant to be acting solely in the best interests of the beneficiaries, it can be argued

---

[85]   [1996] 8 Admin LR 49, CA. Noted in the May 1996 issue of 'Commercial Lawyer' at 54.
[86]   [1996] 1 AC 421, HL.
[87]   Quoted by John Cordy Jeaffreson, *A Book About Lawyers* vol 1 (Hurst and Balckett, 1867) 85.

that self-protection is not a ground on which trustees should rely.

It is to be noted that there is some clear authority on this second point, beginning with Lord **18.117** Chancellor Truro in *Re Beloved Wilkes's Charity*,[88] citing Lord Ellenborough in *The King v The Archbishop of Canterbury*.[89]

In *Re Londonderry*,[90] Harman LJ discussed the rule that trustees are not obliged to give rea- **18.118** sons and went on to say:

> To this there is added a rider, namely, that if trustees do give reasons, their soundness can be considered by the court. Compare the observations of James LJ in *Re Gresham Life Assurance Society, ex parte Penny* (1872) 8 Ch App 446, 449, 450 on the analogous position of directors.

In Australia in *Karger v Paul*,[91] McGarvie J in the Victorian Supreme Court held that: **18.119**

> the exercise of a discretion in these terms will not be examined or reviewed by the Courts so long as the essential component parts of the exercise of the particular discretion are present. Those essential component parts are present if the discretion is exercised by the trustees in good faith, upon real and genuine consideration and in accordance with the purposes to which the discretion was conferred. The exception is that the validity of the trustees' reasons would be examined and reviewed if the trustees chose to state their reasons for their exercise of discretion.

As against this, the House of Lords in an appeal from Scotland *Dundee Hospitals v Walker*[92] **18.120** seems to have considered to the contrary. Lord Normand held:

> It was said for the appellants that the courts have greater liberty to examine and correct a decision committed by a testator to his trustees, if they chose to give reasons, than if they do not. In my opinion that is erroneous. The principles on which the court must proceed are the same whether the reasons for the trustees' decision are disclosed or not, but, of course, it becomes easier to examine a decision if the reasons for it have been disclosed.

This case was referred to by Sir Robert Walker in the Cambridge talk[93] already mentioned. **18.121** He commented:

> it would certainly be odd if the Court were more ready to intervene against trustees who are careful enough to obtain full written advice and keep full written minutes, and candid enough to disclose them to their members' scrutiny.

Further, in Australia, the Courts have started to review decisions of trustees even though **18.122** reasons have not been given—see *Vidovic v Email Superannuation Pty Ltd*,[94] a decision of Bryson J in the Supreme Court of New South Wales.

John Mesher's commentary on *Wilson v Law Debenture* in the back of the report in the **18.123** Occupational Pensions Law Reports (OPLR) series of reports is worth repeating:

> What in the past may have been the real barrier to the beneficiaries starting actions alleging breach of duty was the fear of liability for costs. The Court of Appeal's decision in *McDonald*

---

[88] (1851) 3 Mac & G 440 at 448 (Truro LC).
[89] (1812) 15 East 11 (Lord Ellenborough). Both these cases are cited by Sheller JA on this point in *Hartigan* at 442.
[90] At 928.
[91] [1984] VR 161 at 163 (McGarvie J).
[92] [1952] 1 All ER 896 at 900, HL.
[93] 'Some Trust Principles in the Pensions Context' in AJ Oakley (ed), *Trends in Contemporary Trust Law* (Clarendon Press, 1996). This talk is also in [1996] PLR 107.
[94] (1995) 3 March (Bryson J).

and others v Horn and others [1994] OPLR 281, given a few weeks after that in *Wilson*, has opened up the possibility of the making of prospective costs orders in cases of hostile litigation against pension scheme trustees under which beneficiaries can have their costs paid out of the pension fund. But the beneficiaries must show a sufficient case for further investigation before a prospective costs order can be made to cover even the costs of some independent investigation or of discovery. Hoffmann LJ said in *McDonald v Horn*, at [1994] OPLR 292, that members of an occupational pension scheme are entitled to openness in the way in which the scheme is run and that:

> trustees and employers who are concerned that the costs are coming out of *their* money will be more ready to save costs by providing full information and if necessary agreeing to an independent investigation of the plaintiffs' complaints at an early stage.

However, that statement must be set in the context of a sufficient case for further investigation having been made. It therefore does not undermine the rule confirmed in *Wilson*. It may, however, encourage dissatisfied beneficiaries to attempt to obtain an order for the costs of some form of independent investigation of all the circumstances, including the reasons for the exercise of discretions, to be met before having to satisfy the rigorous requirements for obtaining discovery under the *Re Londonderry* rules.

18.124   Given the tendency of the Courts to adopt a more rigorous approach to the situations in which it will review trustee decisions, from the trustee perspective the approach of advising trustees not to give reasons still has much to commend it. Giving reasons must increase the probability of a challenge by the beneficiary.

18.125   It must be quite easy to give a reason that seems perfectly reasonable to the trustee but is later considered by the Court (or the Pensions Ombudsman) to have been improper or immaterial. Particularly given the test that one of the grounds of reviewing the trustee's decision may still be that it has relied on factors which it should not have relied, this seems to be over-exposing the trustees.

18.126   This may go against the usual concept of being open and frank with beneficiaries. However, given the increasing tendency for decisions of trustees to be challenged, it seems rash to advise trustees that they should give reasons.[95]

18.127   Non-disclosure may also lead a court to draw adverse inferences—eg *Re Fairbairn*.[96] A similar approach could be developing in England: there are indications in the courts that they will look for trustees to give reasons or draw inferences if they do not—see for example the comments of Robert Walker J in *Scott v National Trust*[97] and of the Court of Appeal in *Edge v Pensions Ombudsman*.[98]

18.128   The position of pension trusts may perhaps be becoming considered to be similar to public authorities. But even with public authorities, the courts will not always require reasons to be given. In *R (on the application of The Asha Foundation) v Millennium Commission*,[99] the Court of Appeal refused to strike down a decision on the basis that no reason had been given. Lord

---

[95] This analysis is supported by an article by John Edstein in Australia in (1996) Superannuation Bulletin—Australian Tax Practice (29 March 1996).

[96] [1967] VR 633 at 639 (Gillard J).

[97] [1999] 4 All ER 705 at 718c. Followed in Australia in *Maciejewski v Telstra Super Pty Ltd* (1998) 44 NSWLR 601 (Young J).

[98] [2000] Ch 602, [1999] 4 All ER 546 at 571, CA.

[99] [2003] EWCA Civ 88, [2003] All ER (D) 81 (Jan) at [24], CA.

Woolf LCJ (with whom the other two members of the Court of Appeal agreed) held that for decisions by a public body:

> of the sort the Commission was making, as a matter of good administration and fairness, the body concerned should give such reasons as were appropriate and reasonable in the circumstances. This should be done (a) because the obligation to give reasons causes a decision-making body properly to focus its mind on the relevant considerations and (b) the exercise of giving reasons causes the body in turn to consider the relevant considerations.

However, that did not mean that in every case there would be a duty to give detailed reasons—it all depends on the circumstances.

The Pensions Ombudsman and reasons

As noted above, the common law right, according to *Re Londonderry*, seems to be for trustees to refuse to disclose information that would give details of their reasons. **18.129**

But pension schemes are also subject to the jurisdiction of the Pensions Ombudsman (under the Pension Schemes Act 1993) to make binding determinations both on disputes of fact or law and on 'maladministration causing injustice'. Is failing to give reasons maladministration? Can the Pensions Ombudsman order a remedy where the courts will not? The trend of determinations is to make an order. **18.130**

The Pensions Ombudsman has indicated in a number of determinations that failure to disclose reasons for exercising a discretion could, in appropriate circumstances, be considered to be maladministration, at least where the decision taken is adverse to the individual beneficiary and the individual could appeal that decision on the basis of the reasons for the decision. **18.131**

In *Allen v TKM Group Pension Trust Ltd*,[100] the Ombudsman (David Laverick) found that there had been maladministration on the part of the trustee in that it had: **18.132**

i. misdirected itself and failed properly to exercise its discretion to grant an unreduced early retirement pension; and
ii. failed to provide a copy of the minutes of the meeting at which they determined not to grant Mr Allen an unreduced early retirement pension.

Laverick PO commented that, although there is no legal duty on trustees to make copies of their minutes available to members, **18.133**

> . . . as a matter of good administrative practice Trustees should provide reasons for their decision to those with a legitimate interest in the matter and, subject to the need to preserve rights to privacy of individual members, should also make the minutes of their meeting available to scheme members. I can see no good reason for the Trustee not to have done so in this case and the failure of the Trustee to do this for Mr Allen was also maladministration. Not knowing the basis on which an adverse decision is taken is itself an injustice.

In July 1998, in *Blaney*,[101] the previous Ombudsman (Julian Farrand) disagreed with the trustee's assertion that, because of *Re Londonderry*, he was precluded from requiring the trustee to give the reasons for its decision regarding an incapacity pension. He said that, whatever the trust law position, he was entitled to find that a trustee's failure to give reasons constituted **18.134**

---

[100] L00370, [2002] PLR 333 (Laverick PO).
[101] *Blaney v BS Pension Fund Trustee* (1998) 15 July, GE00263 (Farrand PO).

maladministration insofar as that failure did not meet the standards of good administrative practice applied by, and expected of, pension scheme trustees. £100 was ordered to be paid as compensation.

18.135 In October 1998 in *Chloride*[102] the Ombudsman (Julian Farrand) looked at the arrangements that the trustee had made for winding-up a scheme and paying a refund to the employer. He held:

> It is not good trust administration for trustees to seek to make themselves unaccountable to their beneficiaries, myself or the courts by omitting to keep proper records of their decisions. It opens the way to conflict of interest, hidden negligence, and even corruption, although there is no suggestion of this on the part of the Trustee here. Trustees should keep proper records of their decisions (and the Pensions Act 1995 has now introduced such a requirement). Whilst there are circumstances, as set out in Re Londonderry's Settlement supra and Wilson -v- The Law Debenture plc [1994] PLR 141 why such records need not always be revealed to a beneficiary, this does not justify trustees in deliberately omitting to keep any record of their deliberations.

18.136 In 2003 in *Northern Telecom*[103] the Ombudsman held that it was not maladministration to fail to provide further details of benefit calculations following a failed challenge to the benefit levels:

> No useful purpose would have been served by providing the information because Mr Beale is no longer entitled to assert that his pension is wrongly calculated. The inevitable result of providing the information would simply have been to enable Mr Beale to pursue his already hostile correspondence with further vigour.

18.137 In *Digital Equipment*[104] in 2005, Laverick PO considered the trust cases, including *Londonderry* and *Schmidt* and held that a beneficiary was entitled to see legal advice given to the trustees.

18.138 In *Centrica*[105] in July 2007 the deputy Pensions Ombudsman held that it was maladministration for trustees to refuse to disclose information obtained by them for the purpose of distributing death benefits (under a discretionary trust). The trustees had accepted the evidence on a confidential basis, but it was held that they should have considered the ramifications of so doing.

18.139 In *Hedley*[106] (2008) the deputy Pensions Ombudsman, dealt with a claim for an ill-health pension. Although he did not uphold the complaint and therefore agreed with the trustees' decision not to award an ill-health pension, he made an award against the trustees for maladministration for not providing Mr Hedley with the reasons for their decision.

18.140 In 2011 *IBC Vehicles Pension Plan*[107] was a case concerning a complaint about the way a lump sum death benefit had been decided to be distributed by the trustees of a pension scheme. King PO referred to *Londonderry* and *Schmidt*, but noted that in the case concerned the trustees had not limited the complainants' access to their materials and minutes of reasons. But he upheld the complaint in the end based on what he saw as a failure of the trustees properly to consider whether the recipient qualified as being financially dependent.

---

[102] *Edwardes v Law Debenture Trust Corpn* (1998) 23 October, F00898 (Farrand PO).
[103] *Beale v Nortel Networks UK Pension Trust Ltd* (2003) 2 December, L00743 (Laverick PO).
[104] *Cameron v Digital Equipment Pension Plan* (2005) 4 April, M00949 (Laverick PO).
[105] *Mrs P v Centrica Staff Pension Trustees Ltd* (2007) 17 July, Q00486 (Gordon Deputy PO).
[106] *Hedley* (2008) 27 May, R00049 (Gordon Deputy PO). See also *Stone* (2007) 11 October, R00465 (Gordon Deputy PO) and *Raza* (2008) 6 November, 72522 (Gordon Deputy PO).
[107] *Ellaway v IBC Pension Trustees* (2011) 15 February, 80200/1 (King PO).

Case law generally indicates a reluctance by the courts to allow the Pensions Ombudsman **18.141** to make orders where the courts would not—*Legal & General Assurance Society Ltd v CCA Stationery Ltd.*[108]

Modification of Disclosure Rights by the Trust

Could a provision in the trust instrument limit any disclosure obligation? It is difficult to **18.142** see why not.[109] Emily Campbell and Jonathan Hilliard argue[110] that a restriction in the trust instrument may be followed by the courts if it strikes a reasonable balance between confidentiality and disclosure for a good reason. But they argue that the court retains an overriding discretion to order disclosure where this would be strongly in the interest of beneficiaries.[111]

The claim is sometimes made[112] that a limiting provision might be restricted by the principle[113] that there is an irreducible core minimum level of fiduciary duty which cannot be **18.143** excluded (otherwise there is no trust). But even if this exists, it is difficult to see why this would apply to disclosure obligations.[114]

These two points both emerged in 2013 in a private trust case in Bermuda. *In the Matter of* **18.144** *an Application for Information about a Trust*[115] involved a claim by beneficiary for disclosure of information by a trustee. The trust deed contained an express restriction on disclosure, save with the consent of the Protector. Kawaley CJ, the Chief Justice of Bermuda, held that:

(a) the restriction was valid and not incompatible with the irreducible core obligations of a trust; and

(b) the court had a discretion, as part of its supervisory jurisdiction, to order disclosure of some documents anyway (despite the limitation). The limitation was a factor for the court in deciding what should be disclosed.[116]

Minutes of Trustee Meetings

This section looks briefly at the law on disclosure of both the minutes of pension trustee **18.145** meetings and documentation on which pension trustee decisions may be based.

---

[108] [2003] EWHC 2989 (Ch), [2004] OPLR 207 (Laddie J), but see Julian Farrand 'Courts v Pensions Ombudsman—Stepping on Toes?' (2000) 14 TLI 146.

[109] See eg *Tierney v King* [1983] 2 QdR 580 at 582 and *Hartigan Nominees v Rydge* (1992) 29 NSWLR 405 at 446 (Sheller JA).

[110] Emily Campbell and Jonathan Hilliard, 'Disclosure of Information by Trustees' in David Hayton (ed), *The International Trust* 3rd edn (Jordans, 2011) 575 and 576.

[111] See in Guernsey, *Bathurst v Kleinwort Benson (Channel Islands) Trustees Ltd* [2007] WTLR 959 (Lieutenant Bailiff Patrick Talbot QC) at 1002 and in Cayman, *AN v Barclays Private Bank & Trust (Cayman) Ltd* [2007] WTLR 565 at 597 (Smellie CJ).

[112] DWM Waters, M Gillen, and LD Smith, *Waters' Law of Trusts in Canada* 3rd edn (Carswell, 2005) 1077; David Hayton, 'The Irreducible Core Content of Trusteeship' in AJ Oakley (ed), *Trends in Contemporary Trust Law* (Oxford University Press, 1996) 54.

[113] See *Armitage v Nurse* [1998] Ch 241, CA.

[114] See eg JRF Lehane, 'Trustees: The Duty to Provide Information and Documents and the Right to Withhold Reasons for the Exercise of Discretions' (1994) 3 Journal of International Trust and Corporate Planning 134. On the core obligation point, see also the discussion in Ch 14 (Trustee indemnities and exonerations).

[115] [2013] SC (Bda) 16 Civ (Kawaley CJ). An appeal is due to be heard in November 2013.

[116] Citing Schmidt J's list of relevant factors in *Foreman v Kingstone* [2004] 1 NZLR 841 at [90].

18.146 The sources of the law are both legislative and judicial. Assuming pension scheme members are to be allowed to inspect the trustees' minutes, a related issue is the extent to which those minutes should record the reasons for the trustees' decisions.

Disclosure Regulations

18.147 The Occupational Pension Schemes (Disclosure of Information) Regulations 1996[117] do not include a specific requirement to disclose trustee minutes.

Data Protection Act 1998

18.148 The subject access and privacy provisions of the Data Protection Act 1998 may be relevant depending on the material in the trustee minutes sought to be disclosed.

18.149 Under the Data Protection Act an individual has the right to be given by a data controller (in the case of a pension scheme, normally the trustees) details of any personal data relating to him, the purposes for which the data are held, and the recipients to whom data have been, or may be, disclosed. To obtain access to the data, the individual must make a request in writing (together with payment of a small fee). Certain personal data are exempt from disclosure, notably health records.

18.150 This obligation applies only to personal data held on a computer or, if in hard copy, in a filing system structured by reference to personal data, eg names. If the reasons for a trustee's decision relating to a member are held on that member's file, the member will be able to access that information. To avoid this problem, trustees' minutes might be kept separately from members' files in an unreferenced filing system.

18.151 If trustees are unable to comply with a request for access without disclosing information about a third party, they need only comply if that third party consents or if it is reasonable to comply without that consent. However, if a duty of confidentiality is owed to that third party, consent is likely to be required.

What should trustees do when beneficiaries request information?

18.152 In practice, the courts are likely still to continue to treat a beneficiary as having a right to inspect trust documents. If a legal opinion, for example, has been obtained at the expense of the trust then it is an asset of the trust and so the presumption is that it is available to the beneficiaries. If the trustees do not consider that it is appropriate to disclose the documents, their reasons should be properly considered and given due weight.

18.153 It seems that legal advice is disclosable. Legal professional privilege is still not by itself a defence to a disclosure request (unlike disclosure as part of litigation). However, the fact that legal advice may be confidential or relevant to some other litigation could still mean that disclosure is not appropriate.

18.154 It may be that trustees face a difficulty if they have received information under an obligation of confidentiality (subject only to disclosure required by law). If they then disclose this to a beneficiary they may be at risk of a claim by the third party. If they do not, they risk a claim by the beneficiary. Such confidentiality obligations are increasingly common in agreements with professional advisers (eg actuaries and accountants) who are attempting to reduce their potential exposure of liability to third parties by limiting distribution of their advice.

---

[117] SI 1996/1655 (as amended).

Trustees are at risk as to their costs if they wrongfully refuse to disclose (ie the court takes a different view). **18.155**

Conclusion

Following *Schmidt v Rosewood Trust*, trustees should: **18.156**

(a) give serious consideration to how decisions are recorded;

(b) consider when drafting minutes how much detail it is advisable to include especially, for example, where sensitive issues such as the distribution of lump sum death benefits are involved;

(c) when requested to disclose minutes, consider whether those minutes contain sensitive information which should not be disclosed; and

(d) consider whether to disclose on a case-by-case basis.

The table below is a summary of the considerations which could apply if pension scheme members seek to have the minutes of trustee meetings disclosed. Whether in a particular case trustee minutes must be disclosed will depend on the particular decisions and deliberations being recorded in those minutes and the surrounding facts. **18.157**

Issue	Factors relevant to disclosure
Disclosure Regulations	No specific requirement to disclose trustee minutes.
Litigation	Disclosure requires a court order, normally for 'standard disclosure'. Minutes of meetings could fall under such an order, and particular minutes would have to be defended from disclosure on the basis of the various defences set out below.
Trust law	Following *Schmidt v Rosewood* no 'right' to see trust documents, but the court has power to order disclosure. Whether a court would order trustee minutes to be disclosed would depend on, among other things, the nature of the interest of the particular beneficiary requiring disclosure, and the contents of the particular minutes sought. (If minutes relate not only to the member's but also to others' benefits, any confidential parts should be blanked out.) Parts of minutes setting out reasons may be blanked out—*Wilson v Law Debenture*.
Legal privilege	Legal advice regarding the trust may be a trust document and therefore subject to trust law principles, not legal privilege. However, trustees do not generally have to disclose: 1. advice relating to a claim by a beneficiary, to that beneficiary; or 2. a legal opinion obtained in contemplation of litigation, subject to trust law principles if the opinion was paid for by the fund.
Pensions Ombudsman's jurisdiction	The Pensions Ombudsman has taken the view that maladministration includes failure by trustees to disclose their reasons for exercising a discretion, at least where the decision taken is adverse to the individual beneficiary and the individual could appeal that decision on the basis of the reasons for the decision.
Data protection	The subject access and privacy provisions of the Data Protection Act 1998 may be relevant depending on the material in the trustee minutes sought to be disclosed.

18.158 Giving specific clear advice is quite difficult. Does this mean that if a beneficiary requests information or documents, then the trustees should only disclose if they have a court order approving? Probably not, but it is difficult to see how trustees should or should not act in individual circumstances.

18.159 Generally the implication is that there are some constraints so that there is not an absolute propriety right to a disclosure of documents or information if this would be inconsistent with the primary purpose of the trust etc seems helpful. This follows the useful decision in South Australia in the *IOOF* case.[118]

18.160 So this means that trustees can properly enter into confidentiality agreements and that beneficiaries cannot use the *Re Londonderry* principle to force trustees to disclose the information they have so received.

Letter of Wishes

18.161 It is common for pension schemes to provide for lump sum death benefits to be paid on the death of a member (in particular on the death of a member in current service with the employer). A discretion is given to the trustees (this aids flexibility in adapting to circumstances and makes the payment more clearly outside the member's estate for inheritance tax purposes). The list of potential beneficiaries will be set out in the trust deed and will usually include specific near relatives of the member, but also anyone nominated by the member in advance of his or her death.

18.162 Nominations forms are common. They have the dual purpose of potentially adding someone to the list of potential beneficiaries (if they were not already there) and giving some (non-binding) guidance to the trustees about how the member wanted the discretion to be exercised. The trustees will usually give great weight to this nomination (but take into account any known change in circumstances etc).

18.163 In these circumstances the position of a potential recipient looks very similar to the position of the discretionary beneficiaries in many of the family trust cases[119] (eg *Schmidt* itself). It is likely in these cases that if a potential recipient (eg a family member) requested a copy of the letter of wishes, a court would follow the discretionary approach in *Schmidt* and probably refuse to order disclosure—eg *Re Londonderry* and *Breakspear v Ackland*[120] (also following the majority in the Australian Court of Appeal in the earlier *Hartigan*[121] case).

18.164 A relevant factor may be if the member was told that the nomination form would be confidential.

---

[118] *Rouse v IOOF Australia Trustees Ltd* (1999) 73 SASR 484.

[119] See Tsun Hang Tey, 'Letters of Wishes and Trustee's Duties' (2008) 22 TLI 126 and Gerwyn Griffiths, 'An Inevitable Tension: The Disclosure of Letters of Wishes' (2008) 72 Conv 322.

[120] [2008] EWHC 220 (Ch), [2009] Ch 32 (Briggs J). See also to the same effect on non-disclosure of a letter of wishes, the Jersey case, *Re Rabaiotti 1989 Settlement* [2000] JLR 173 and the New Zealand case, *Foreman v Kingstone* [2004] 1 NZLR 841 (Schmidt J).

[121] (1992) 28 NSWLR 405 at 409, NSWCA.

Taking Copies and Costs

Generally a beneficiary, where there is a right to see documents, is limited to a right to inspect documents and not to be provided with copies. If the trustees allow copies to be taken, they are entitled to require the beneficiary to pay the costs of producing the information (and the copies). **18.165**

In Australia in *Marigold Pty Ltd v Belswan (Mandurah) Pty Ltd*,[122] a case involving a unit trust, White AUJ reviewed the various authorities, including the old English cases of *Ottley v Gilby*[123] and *Re Bosworth*.[124] He held that a beneficiary does not generally have a right to take copies of documents (even on tendering to pay costs). Both Ford and Lee, *Principles of the Law of Trusts*[125] and *Underhill and Hayton*[126] rely on these cases as establishing that a beneficiary must pay the costs of requiring copies of documents. **18.166**

For pension schemes, the 1996 Disclosure Regulations contain a similar obligation. A member (or trade union etc) is entitled to inspect copies of the constitutional documents of the scheme, annual report, and funding documents etc free of charge, but the trustee is entitled to make a charge for providing copies (save for the latest annual report). This charge is limited to the expense incurred in copying, posting, and packing such a copy.[127] **18.167**

---

[122] [2001] WASC 274 (White AUJ).

[123] [1845] EngR 494, (1845) 8 Beav 602, 50 ER 237 (Lord Langdale MR).

[124] (1889) 58 LJ Ch 432.

[125] Looseleaf (1996).

[126] *Underhill and Hayton: Law of Trusts and Trustees* 18th edn, ed David Hayton, Paul Matthews, and Charles Mitchell (LexisNexis, 2010) para 56.1.

[127] Disclosure Regulations 1996 (SI 1996/1655), regs 3(2), 6(4), and 8(3).

19

EMPLOYER-RELATED INVESTMENT

Overview

19.1 This chapter provides an overview of the issues raised by the limitation on employer-related investment imposed by s 40 of the Pensions Act 1995. It covers:

(a) an overview of the rationale for and history of employer-related investment restrictions and a summary of the current position;

(b) the current requirements in detail;

(c) the definition of employer-related investments and employer-related loans;

(d) transactions at an undervalue;

(e) how wide is the net: employer or connected or associated with an employer;

(f) exclusions from the regime, including small schemes;

(g) excluded assets; collective investment schemes; and insurance policies;

(h) transitional provisions;

(i) consequences of breach, including the civil penalty and criminal offence;

(j) scheme funding and s 75 debts.

Rationale and History

Why are employer-related investments a bad thing?

Segregation of a pension scheme's funds from the employer's assets, so that they will not be available to the employer's creditors, is a control mechanism in safeguarding the security of benefit provision by private sector funded pension schemes. **19.2**

Where trustees invest part of the pension fund in the sponsoring employer, the invested assets generally cease to be segregated and become part of the employer's general assets. As a result, the scheme's dependence on the ability of the employer to pay is increased. **19.3**

In practice that sort of issue could be dealt with to a degree without prohibiting or restricting such investments, for example by providing for investment in an employer not to count as assets for funding checks etc. However, the legislation has preferred to impose a limit on such investment. **19.4**

A Brief History of Employer-Related Investment Restrictions

First restrictions

Perhaps surprisingly, prior to 1992 there was no specific statutory regulation of self-investment (although various Inland Revenue controls were imposed as a tax matter in relation to small self-administered schemes). Scheme trustees were accordingly free to invest in the scheme employer subject only to: **19.5**

(a) their usual fiduciary duties; and

(b) the requirement under s 191 of the Financial Services Act 1986 that 'day-to-day' decisions concerning investments be made by an authorized person under that Act.

This was changed with effect from 9 March 1992 when the Occupational Pension Schemes (Investment of Scheme's Resources) Regulations 1992[1] (the 1992 Regulations) came into force. Those regulations were made under s 57A of the Social Security Pensions Act 1975, a section inserted by the Social Security Act 1990. This section was subsequently consolidated as s 112 of the Pension Schemes Act 1993. The sections gave a power for the DSS[2] to make regulations to limit the 'employer-related investments' of a pension scheme. **19.6**

---

[1] SI 1992/246.

[2] The DSS is the Department of Social Security, the predecessor of the Department for Work and Pensions (DWP).

19.7 The 1992 Regulations were broadly similar in scope to the current regime (save that the prohibition on employer-related loans was not included). They provided that not more than 5 per cent of the current market value of a scheme's resources could at any time be invested in 'employer-related investments'. However, there was uncertainty about the extent to which assets held within a collective investment schemes counted towards the 5 per cent limit.

Recommendations of the 1993 Pension Law Review Committee (Goode Committee)

19.8 In its report[3] the Goode Committee gave careful consideration to whether self-investment should be wholly prohibited. Noting that a variety of different views had been submitted in evidence, they decided to adopt what they termed an 'intermediate' position.

19.9 Whilst recognizing that some restrictions were required, the Goode Committee felt that a blanket exclusion extending to associated companies was wholly impractical and burdensome—it was hard to see how trustees making a small investment in, or leasing a few offices to, a particular company could be expected to make a search to ensure that the company in question was not a remote parent or subsidiary of the employer, or to engage in continuous monitoring to see that it did not become so later.

19.10 In these circumstances, and given that there had been insufficient time since its implementation to conclude whether the 5 per cent limit set out in the 1992 Regulations was appropriate, the Goode Committee recommended that it should be retained for the time being. However, the Goode Committee recommended that the legislation should prohibit altogether the provision of loans or other financial assistance to, and the giving of guarantees for, the employer and associated companies. In their view, the impracticability objection to a complete ban on employer-related investments did not apply to loans.

19.11 Finally, one of the principal limitations of the 1992 Regulations identified by the Goode Committee was the perceived lack of any effective sanction for failure to adhere to the prescribed limits of self-investment.

Introduction of section 40 of the Pensions Act 1995

19.12 Following the Goode Committee recommendations, s 112 of the Pension Schemes Act 1993 and the 1992 Regulations were repealed and replaced with s 40 of the Pensions Act 1995 and the 1996 Investment Regulations.[4] These came into force from 6 April 1997.

19.13 Section 40 of the Pensions Act 1995 restricts the extent to which the trustees (and fund managers) of occupational pension schemes may invest pension scheme assets in the sponsoring or participating employers of the scheme and their associated entities. Section 40(1) provides that the trustees or managers must:

> secure that the scheme complies with any prescribed restrictions with respect to the proportion of its resources which may at any time be invested in, or any description of, employer-related investments.

19.14 The 1996 Regulations:

(a) retained the 5 per cent limit on 'employer-related investments';

---

[3] Issued in September 1993, CM2342.
[4] The Occupational Pension Schemes (Investment) Regulations 1996 (SI 1996/3127).

(b) expanded the definition of 'employer-related investments' to make it clear that assets held in collective investment schemes were included (whilst providing for exclusions in certain cases);

(c) introduced a complete prohibition on 'employer-related loans'; and

(d) introduced express civil and criminal penalties for breach.[5]

IORP Directive 2003

EU Directive 2003/41/EC on the activities and supervision of institutions for occupa- **19.15**
tional retirement provision (the IORP Directive) includes specific provisions in relation to
self-investment. Article 18 ('Investment Rules') provides:

> 1. Member States shall require institutions located in their territories to invest in accordance
> with the 'prudent person' rule and in particular in accordance with the following rules . . . invest-
> ment in the sponsoring undertaking shall be no more than 5% of the portfolio as a whole
> and, when the sponsoring undertaking belongs to a group, investment in the undertakings
> belonging to the same group as the sponsoring undertaking shall not be more than 10% of
> the portfolio.
>   When the institution is sponsored by a number of undertakings, investment in these sponsoring
> undertakings shall be made prudently, taking into account the need for proper diversification.
>   Member States may decide not to apply the requirements referred to in points (e) and (f) to
> investment in government bonds.

Article 22(4) of the IORP Directive also contained an ability for member states to postpone **19.16**
until 23 September 2010 the application of Art 18(1)(f) to institutions located within their
territory (save for institutions operated on a cross-border basis).

Summary of the Current Position

The detail of the self-investment regime is currently contained in the Occupational Pension **19.17**
Schemes (Investment) Regulations 2005[6] (the 2005 Investment Regulations) and in particular
regs 10–17. These came into force on 30 December 2005 and replaced the 1996 Regulations.
The restrictions reflect and expand upon the obligations under the IORP Directive, but take
advantage of the Art 22(4) ability to postpone the application of the directive requirements
in this respect until 23 September 2010.[7]

Similarly to the 1996 Regulations, the 2005 Investment Regulations: **19.18**

(a) limit the proportion of a scheme's assets that may be invested in 'employer-related
investments' to a maximum of 5 per cent of the current market value of the scheme's
resources;[8]

(b) generally prohibit employer-related loans altogether;[9] and

---

[5] Note that the introduction of criminal penalties went further than the recommendations of the Goode
Committee, which had only proposed civil penalties for defaulting trustees.

[6] SI 2005/3378.

[7] This meant that the provisions of the 1996 Regulations relating to self-investment (regs 2–9) were broadly
carried forward (with a few changes) into the 2005 Investment Regulations (reg 10–16): see the explanatory
memorandum to the 2005 Investment Regulations at para 4.9.

[8] Regulation 12(2)(a).

[9] Regulation 12(2)(b).

(c) prohibit any employer-related investment which involves the trustees entering into a transaction at an undervalue.[10]

19.19 It should be noted that there is no express provision for how and when the 5 per cent limit is tested (eg by reference to the last accounts). As such, it is probably a test applicable at all times. This may make trustees extremely cautious about having any significant employer-related investment (unless well below the 5 per cent limit) as it will be extremely difficult to ensure that on a day-to-day basis the 5 per cent limit is not breached—in practice, the limit could be broken by either (or both of) the value of the employer-related investment going up or the value of the rest of the fund going down.[11]

19.20 Failure to comply with the restrictions in s 40 has the following consequences:

(a) **civil penalty**: s 10 applies (so that a civil penalty can be made) to any trustee who fails to take all such steps as are reasonable to secure compliance;[12] and

(b) **criminal offence**: it is a criminal offence for trustees to agree in the determination to make an investment in contravention of section 40;[13] and

(c) **unauthorized investment**: contravention of s 40 probably results in the investment being unauthorized, so that the trustees are liable for any losses resulting; and

(d) **does not count as an asset**: assets held in contravention of s 40 do not count for the purposes of funding valuations under Pt 3 of the Pensions Act 2004 or a s 75 deficit calculation (under the Pensions Act 1995).

19.21 The 2005 Investment Regulations were amended in 2010—by changes in the Occupational, Personal and Stakeholder Pensions (Miscellaneous Amendments) Regulations 2009.[14] Most of these changes took effect in September 2010 (to reflect requirements under the IORP Directive[15]).

What are 'Employer-Related Investments'?

19.22 The restrictions in s 40 and the 2005 Investment Regulations apply to 'employer-related investments'.

19.23 The term 'employer-related investment' is defined in s 40(2):

(a) shares or other securities issued by the employer or by any person who is connected with, or an associate of, the employer: s 40(2)(a); or

---

[10] Regulation 12(3).

[11] Meaning that, paradoxically, there is a greater risk of breach in circumstances where the employer-related investment was a good investment decision from a monetary perspective.

[12] Section 40(4).

[13] Section 40(5).

[14] Note that para 7.12 of the Explanatory Memorandum to the 2009 Regulations states that 'Regulation 19 also introduces a provision to permit employer-related loans (currently prohibited by the Investment Regulations) and, for employer-related investment purposes, requires that they comply with the 5% limit.' In fact, the 2009 Regulations do no such thing: see new reg 12(2A) which retains the prohibition on employer-related loans (subject to certain exceptions which were previously excluded from the employer-related investment regime altogether: see new reg 12(2B)).

[15] As the ability to postpone the application of Art 18(1)(f) expired on 23 September 2010: see Art 22(4).

(b) land occupied or used by, or leased to, the employer (or any connected or associated person): s 40(2)(b);[16] or

(c) property other than land which is used for the purposes of any business carried on by the employer (or any connected or associated person): s 40(2)(c);[17] or

(d) loans to an employer (or any connected or associated person): s 40(2)(d); or

(e) other prescribed investments: s 40(2)(e).

Regulation 11 of the 2005 Investment Regulations prescribes further categories of 'employer-related investment': **19.24**

(a) investments made through a collective investment scheme, which would have been prohibited had they been made directly: reg 11(a) (there are exemptions—see the discussion below); or

(b) any guarantee of, or security given to secure, obligations of the employer (or of any person who is connected with, or an associate of, the employer): reg 11(b); or

(c) any loan arrangement entered into with any person whereby 'the trustees' or managers' right to or expectation of repayment depends on the employer's actions or situation, unless it was not the trustees' or managers' purpose in entering into the arrangement to provide financial assistance to the employer': reg 11(c). This is presumably an anti-avoidance mechanism intended to catch indirect arrangements whereby money is lent to a third party but the economic interest is effectively that of the employer;[18] or

(d) investment in some insurance policies to the extent that the investments held under the policy would be employer-related investments if held directly by the scheme: regs 11(d) and (e). There are some exemptions—see the discussion below.

'Shares or Other Securities'

Definition

The term 'securities' is defined in s 40(2A) as meaning: **19.25**

(a) shares, instruments creating or acknowledging indebtedness, instruments giving entitlements to investments, certificates representing securities.

Section 40(2B) provides that subs 2A 'must be read with' s 22 of and Sch 2 to the Financial Services and Markets Act 2000 (FSMA 2000) and the relevant regulations. **19.26**

Importantly, the language used to define 'securities' in s 40(2A) tracks the exact language used in Sch 2 to FSMA 2000, which describes certain types of investments. **19.27**

What About OEICS and Unit Trusts?

An open-ended investment company[19] (OEIC) is a pooled investment vehicle. They are generally intended to be equivalent to unit trusts for investment purposes. However, their legal **19.28**

---

[16] Presumably on the basis that the value of such property will be intrinsically dependent on the employer (and would significantly lose value in an employer insolvency).

[17] Presumably for the same reasons as for land used by the employer.

[18] For example, a loan to a third party could be made on the basis that it was only repayable if the third party itself was repaid a loan that it had made to the employer.

[19] Section 236 (Open-ended investment companies) of the Financial Services and Markets Act 2000.

structure is different. They are established as corporate bodies—so investors acquire shares in the OEIC. In unit trusts the investor acquires an equitable interest in the underlying assets in the form of units.

19.29 It is clear that if a pooled arrangement is established as a unit trust, the fact that an employer (or connected or associated person) operates as its manager would not automatically categorize an investment by the trustees in the unit trust as an 'employer-related investment'. Instead, there would, broadly, be a 'look through' to any underlying assets held by such a collective investment scheme[20] so that the investment would only be employer-related to the extent of the proportion of any employer-related investments held by the unit trust. The 2005 Investment Regulations envisage a similar 'look through' in relation to all collective investment schemes (which includes an OEIC).[21]

19.30 However, if the pooled investment is established by an OEIC, there is a concern that, if the OEIC is itself connected with the employer (or associated or connected person), shares in the OEIC will automatically be employer-related investments.

19.31 The legal question that arises is whether an investment in shares in an OEIC constitutes an investment in 'shares or other securities' within s 40(2)(a) of the Pensions Act 1995.

19.32 The list in s 40(2A) refers to four types of 'investment' described in Sch 2 to FSMA 2000. It does not, however, refer to 'units in a collective investment scheme' (which expressly includes 'shares or securities of an open-ended investment company'[22]) which are a further type of 'investment' listed in Sch 2 to FSMA 2000.

19.33 However, the term 'shares' is not expressly defined in s 40. On a purposive approach, shares in an OEIC probably do *not* fall within s 40(2)(a). This is on the basis that:

(a) shares within OEICs are not within the definition of 'securities' for the purposes of this section, given the express list in subs (2A) and the requirement in subs (2B) that the list should be read with Sch 2 to the FSMA; and

(b) the use of the word 'other' in the phrase 'shares or other securities' suggests that the term 'shares' is also to be taken as limited only to the shares which fall within the definition of securities (ie excluding shares within OEICs). If this were not the case, then there would be no need to use the word 'other' in this phrase.

19.34 The counter-argument is, of course, that had Parliament wished to exclude shares in OEICs, it could have done this quite simply by merely referring to 'securities' and not used the term 'shares' at all. It is clear that shares within OEICs almost certainly constitute 'shares' within the meaning of that term if used on its own. It is only by the references in subss (2A) and (2B) that the exclusion for OEICs applies.

19.35 However, it is likely that the words 'shares or other' were added to clarify that the main form of employer-related investment (ie shares) were definitely caught (ie to make it clearer for those who did not realize that the term 'securities' includes shares).[23]

---

[20] See reg 11(a)—collective investment schemes are dealt with below.
[21] See the definition of collective investments schemes in reg 1(2) of the 2005 Investment Regulations, cross-referring to Pt 17 of the Financial Services and Markets Act 2000, which envisages that an OEIC is a collective investment scheme—see s 236(1).
[22] Paragraph 16(1) of Schedule 2 to FSMA 2000.
[23] In this context, note that 'securities' are defined in para 1 of Sch 2 to FSMA 2000 as 'shares in the stock or share capital of a company' and that an OEIC is expressly excluded from the definition of 'company' in this context.

Given these two possible interpretations, it is more likely that a court would follow the **19.36** purposive interpretation and interpret the phrase so that shares in OEICs are not included. Such an interpretation would have various merits (which may help a court to decide in its favour) including:

(a) it removes the anomaly that shares within an employer-affiliated OEIC could be considered to be employer-related investment, whereas units in an employer managed unit trust are not. Such a purposive approach would address the mischief at which the section is aimed. It would not give a blanket loop-hole, as investment within OEICs would still count as employer-related investments to the extent of any such investments held as part of the OEIC fund; and

(b) failure to comply with the limitations in s 40 can be a criminal offence (see below) on the part of any trustee who 'agreed in the determination to make the investment'. It is a general principle that criminal offences are construed strictly. The law leans against creating a criminal offence unless there are clear words.[24]

Both of these factors are reasons why a court would be likely to favour this interpretation and **19.37** consider that investment within an employer affiliated OEIC is not automatically caught by the employer-related investment provisions.[25]

What About Gilts?

The definition of securities appears to exclude gilts.[26] Although in the ordinary course of **19.38** things a gilt would fall within the natural meaning of 'security' it does not appear to fall within the specific definition within s 40(2A).

As noted above, s 40(2B) provides that s 40(2A) must be read in accordance with certain **19.39** provisions of FSMA 2000. Importantly, the language used to define 'securities' in s 40(2A) tracks the exact language used in Sch 2 to FSMA 2000, which describes certain types of investments.

Relevantly, s 40(2A) follows the order of the investments described in Sch 2 tp FSMA 2000 **19.40** except that it omits 'government and public securities', which, in Sch 2, appears before 'instruments giving entitlements to investments'.

This looks likely to be a deliberate policy decision by the legislation that gilts, which fall **19.41** within 'government and public securities' in FSMA 2000 are excluded from the meaning of 'securities' for the purposes of s 40 of the Pensions Act 1995. This also reflects the previous approach adopted in the earlier wording of s 40, before it was amended in 2001, which also

---

[24] See the discussion at para 1456 in the section on 'Statutes' in *Halsbury's Laws of England* vol 44(1) (4th edn, reissue, 1995).

[25] Freshfields wrote in 1999 to the Department for Social Security (as it then was) (DSS) and the then regulator, the Occupational Pensions Regulatory Authority (Opra). The DSS were sympathetic to our interpretation of the legislation, confirming that their legal advice was 'that shares in OEICs do not fall within section 40(2)(a) of the Pensions Act 1995'. However, there was a caveat that 'the contrary cannot be regarded as unarguable'. Opra also appeared to follow our view (and indeed referred to a Counsel's opinion they had obtained on the issue). Although the Opra letter also confirmed that their view was not definitive in practice, the letter was a strong indication that Opra's legal advice was likely to support a policy of not taking any action in the area.

[26] This is permitted by Art 18 of the IORP Directive. It may be relevant for a number of schemes, eg where the employer is a bank which is now wholly or partly state owned (eg Royal Bank of Scotland, Northern Rock).

expressly carved out the reference to government and public securities by reference to certain paragraphs in Sch 1 to the Financial Services Act 1986.

19.42 It could be argued that a gilt could fall within s 40(2)(d), as a loan to the employer, if the issuer of the gilt (ie HM Treasury) was the employer or connected or associated with the employer. However, this does not seem to be a sustainable interpretation of the provision.

19.43 As a general principle of statutory interpretation, where you have a list of general and specific items, if the subject matter falls within a specific item it was not intended to fall within the general item as well.

19.44 It seems reasonably clear that a gilt would ordinarily be regarded as a 'security' issued by the employer (as opposed to a loan) if the natural meaning was given to both terms. As discussed above, a gilt has been specifically excluded from the ordinary meaning of 'security' by virtue of the listed meaning of security in s 40(2A) and the reference to the FSMA.

19.45 As gilts appear to have been specifically excluded for the purposes of the better fitting term (ie security), it would not be a sensible or purposive interpretation of the legislation to then try and construe them as a 'loan to the employer'.

19.46 Accordingly, gilts cannot be an employer-related investment for the purposes of s 40, regardless of whether or not the issuer of the gilt is the employer in relation to the scheme.

19.47 It is also worth noting that the terms 'connected' and 'associated' for the purposes of s 40 are defined in ss 249 and 435 of the Insolvency Act 1986 (see below), neither of which has any express provision which provides a test for the connection or association of a company (eg an employer) to the state (ie HM Treasury).

What About Swaps?

19.48 Trustees are increasingly using more sophisticated investments to hedge their scheme's exposure to various risks. These may take the form of swap agreements. The question which arises is whether it would be acceptable for trustees to enter into a swap transaction where the counterparty is an employer (or a connected or associated person)—for example where the employer to the scheme is an investment bank.

19.49 Whether such an arrangement would amount to an 'employer-related investment' would need to be considered carefully on a case-by-case basis and will differ depending on the terms of the transaction and its overall effect.

19.50 However, in most cases, it is to be expected that a swap agreement would not create a debt but impose a contingent liability on the bank as counterparty. Arguably, this would not fall within the definition of 'employer-related investment'.

19.51 This is a somewhat surprising conclusion—given that the overall purpose of s 40 is to prevent a scheme from having a material financial exposure to the financial performance of its employer (other than, of course, the obligation of the employer to make contributions).

19.52 In August 2006, TPR confirmed by email (in response to a general query on a no-names basis) that, in their view, 'swaps themselves are not an investment as defined in the Occupational Pension Schemes (Investment) Regulations 2005'. However, the email also noted that this 'is a very complex area and it would be a matter of legal opinion . . . We therefore suggest that you consider the nature of the swap and whether the individual terms being swapped would fall within the definition'.

Employer Loans

Section 40(3) provides that to the extent that 'sums due and payable by a person to the trustees **19.53** or managers of an occupational pension scheme remain unpaid', this shall be treated as a loan and the resources of the scheme shall be treated as invested accordingly.

Although there are some exemptions from this (see below eg schedule of contributions), the **19.54** potential breadth of s 40(3) is significant. For example:

(a) given the breadth of the 'associated or connected' test, an accidental overpayment of benefits to a pensioner member who is drawing benefits whilst remaining in service with an employer results in a prohibited 'employer-related loan';
(b) any arrangement with an employer (or person associated or connected with an employer) which might result in a payment being due to the scheme from such a person would, if there was a default on the obligation, become a prohibited employer-related loan. This could include parent company guarantees and other contingent assets.

TPR Guidance on monitoring the employer covenant recognizes this: **19.55**

> Where assets are transferred directly (and particularly when it is through sophisticated SPV structures) the trustees need to clarify whether these investments may be classified as employer related investments. They may need specialist legal advice to help them in this regard. . .
> Trustees are likely to need specialist legal advice to ensure that any contingent asset is available when needed, is properly enforceable and on particular legal issues such as employer related investment.
> . . . When considering the issues which relate to contingent assets, non-cash transfers Special Purpose Vehicles or other arrangements for additional scheme support, the trustees are likely to require independent specialist legal advice . . . The trustees may need, amongst other things, to ask their lawyers:
> that the arrangement would be consistent with:
> . . . the employer related investment provisions in section 40 of the Pensions Act 1995 and the Occupational Pension Schemes (Investment) Regulations 2005 (SI 2005/3378).[27]

It should be noted that TPR has no power to validate arrangements which would otherwise **19.56** contravene the restrictions on employer-related investment, regardless of the merits of any particular proposal and the interests of scheme members.[28]

Collective Investment Schemes/Insurance Policies

Collective investment schemes and insurance policies are considered in more detail below **19.57** (with details of the applicable exemptions).

---

[27] The Pensions Regulator, 'Monitoring Employer support' <http://www.thepensionsregulator.gov.uk/guidance/monitoring-employer-support.aspx>.
[28] See Camilla Barry, 'Employer-related Investments: Financial Genius or Criminal Misconduct?' *Pensions Week* (20 July 2009).

Employer-Related Loans

Importance of the distinction

19.58 All 'employer-related loans' are 'employer-related investments', but not all 'employer-related investments' are 'employer-related loans'. However, the distinction is of crucial importance:

(a) reg 12(2)(a) broadly prohibits 5 per cent or more of the current market value of the resources of a scheme being invested in 'employer-related investments';

(b) however, where those 'employer-related investments' are also 'employer-related loans', reg 12(2)(b) provides for a *total prohibition* (subject to some limited exceptions).

What is an 'employer-related loan'?

19.59 The term 'employer-related loan' is defined in reg 12(4) and includes:

(a) loans to an employer (or a person connected or associated with an employer);[29]

(b) debentures, loan stock, bonds, certificates of deposit, or similar instruments (unless such securities are listed on a recognized stock exchange) of an employer (or connected or associated person);[30]

(c) guarantees or security given to secure the obligations of an employer (or a connected or associated person);[31]

(d) leaving amounts outstanding to a scheme which are due and payable by an employer (or a connected or associated person);[32] and

(e) a loan arrangement within reg 11(c)[33] – ie an indirect loan (where recovery is dependent on the employer or associate).

Listed on a Recognized Stock Exchange

19.60 Regulation 12 provides (in effect) that some instruments 'listed on a recognized stock exchange' will not be employer-related loans.

19.61 This is defined in reg 1(2) by reference to s 841 of the Income and Corporation Taxes Act 1988, which in turn leads to s 1005 of the Income Tax Act 2007.

19.62 Under s 1005 of the Income Tax Act 2007, HMRC is required to designate 'recognized stock exchanges' by Order (s 1014 states that this does not need to be done by statutory instrument). A list of 'recognized stock exchanges' is available at <http://www.hmrc.gov.uk/fid/rse.htm>. In the UK, the London Stock Exchange and the Plus-listed market are designated as recognized stock exchanges.

19.63 Under s 1005(3) of the Income Tax Act 2007, securities are *listed* which are:

(a) . . . admitted to trading on that exchange; and

(b) . . . included in the official UK list or are officially listed in a qualifying country outside the UK in accordance with provisions corresponding to those generally applicable in EEA states.

---

[29] Ie employer-related investments under s 40(2)(d): see reg 12(4)(a).
[30] Regulation 12(4)(b).
[31] Regulation 12(4)(c), applying Regulation 11(b).
[32] Pensions Act 1995, s 40(3).
[33] Regulation 12(4)(c), applying Regulation 11(c).

The securities on the official UK list (maintained by UKLA) can be found at <http://www. **19.64**
fsa.gov.uk/ukla/officialList.do>.

This means that, for example, securities listed on AIM are *not* included in the official list and **19.65**
so would still be prohibited employer-related loans.

Loans to Entities Who Later Become Employers (or Associates)

The 2005 Investment Regulations contain special provisions for dealing with the situation **19.66**
where loans or securities become employer-related following the initial grant due to changes
in ownership of the employer or person to whom a loan has been made.

Broadly, trustees may retain these arrangements until two years after the date at which the **19.67**
loan became employer-related or later if the trustees are contractually prevented from enforcing repayment of the loan (or disinvestment) earlier than this.[34] Note that this does not apply
to any sum regarded as a loan under s 40(3) (ie sums due and payable to the scheme but
which are unpaid).

There does not appear to be any similar provision for investments which are not loans (eg **19.68**
shares) where the investment becomes employer-related due to changes in ownership—
for example on the sale and purchase of an employer so that its associated and connected
companies change.[35] Presumably, there is less of a concern here as such 'employer-related
investments' are not prohibited outright (merely subject to the 5 per cent limit).

The position under the 2005 Investment Regulations was that these loans were excluded **19.69**
from being both employer-related loans *and* employer-related investments: see reg 12(2).
However, the 2009 Regulations[36] amended this with effect from 23 September 2010 so that,
whilst such loans continue to be exempt from the general prohibition on employer-related
loans, they are now counted as employer-related investments for the purposes of the 5 per cent
limit: see new reg 12(2B).

Transactions at Undervalue

The 2005 Investment Regulations also contain a blanket prohibition on employer-related **19.70**
investments where the making of the investment involves the trustees or managers entering into
a transaction at an undervalue.[37] The definition of an undervalue is taken from s 238(4) of the
Insolvency Act 1986.[38] It covers the following types of transaction:

(a) gifts;
(b) transactions which otherwise provide for no consideration to be received;

---

[34] Regulation 15(1).
[35] To give a fairly recent example, if a Cadbury pension scheme were to have had a significant investment in
Kraft before it took over Cadbury.
[36] Occupational, Personal and Stakeholder Pensions (Miscellaneous Amendments) Regulations 2009, SI
2009/615 (the 2009 Regulations).
[37] Regulation 12(3).
[38] Regulation 12(5).

(c) transactions whereby the value of the consideration received in money or money's worth is significantly less than the value, in money or money's worth, of the consideration provided.

19.71 This could, for example, occur where a trustee owns property which is leased to the employer (which would be an employer-related investment but would be permitted provided that it was within the 5 per cent limit) where the lease provided for significantly less than market rent to be paid by the employer.

Meaning of 'Employer or Connected or Associated with an Employer'

Why do we need to know?

19.72 As noted above, the restrictions on investment cover investment with:

(a) an employer; and
(b) a person who is 'connected or associated' with an employer.[39]

19.73 Trustees and managers will therefore need to understand which entities fall within these definitions in relation to their scheme to ensure that the restrictions are complied with.

Who is an employer?

General

19.74 The term 'employer' is quite wide. It means an 'employer of persons in the description or category of employment to which the scheme relates'—s 124(1) of the Pensions Act 1995. It appears that this can include a company which still participates in a scheme, even if it has ceased to employ any active members but either could do in future (because it continues to have employees who are eligible to join the scheme) or still employs deferred members of the scheme—*Cemex UK Marine Ltd v MNOPF Trustees Ltd*[40] and the Pilots case, *PNPF Trust Co Ltd v Taylor*.[41]

19.75 In a multi-employer scheme, former employers are also treated as remaining as employers.[42] An employer will remain as an employer for the purposes of s 40 unless both:

(a) they stopped being an employer before the scheme started to wind-up and while it still had some active members participating; and
(b) any relevant s 75 debt has been paid (or compromised).[43]

Frozen schemes

19.76 If the scheme has no active members (ie is frozen) the last set of employers before the freezing event are treated as employers.[44] Therefore, for a scheme which has no active members, every

---

[39] See the definition of 'employer-related investment' in s 40(2). Note that the IORP Directive does not have a similar concept: see the definition of 'sponsoring undertaking' in Art 6(c).

[40] [2009] EWHC 3258 (Ch) (Peter Smith J).

[41] [2010] EWHC 1573 (Ch) (Warren J).

[42] Regulation 1(5). See further D Pollard, *Corporate Insolvency: Employment and Pension Rights* 5th edn (Bloomsbury Professional, 2013) Ch 55 (Who is an employer under the pensions legislation?).

[43] Regulation 1(5)(b).

[44] Regulations 1(4) and 1(5)(a).

person who was an employer immediately before the scheme ceased to have active members will be treated as an employer for the purposes of s 40 unless both:

(a) a s 75 debt becomes due from that person to the scheme (eg under a notice under reg 9(4) of the Occupational Pension Schemes (Employer Debt) Regulations 2005); and

(b) any relevant s 75 debt has been paid (or compromised).[45]

Who is connected or associated?

General

The definitions of the terms 'connected' and 'associated' are taken from the Insolvency Act 1986[46] and are reasonably broad.   **19.77**

Obviously a holding company and subsidiary of an employer are treated as associated. Less obviously, some companies which are not subsidiaries (or in the same group) will also be treated as associated—for example a company in which the employer company holds one-third of the voting rights.[47]   **19.78**

Common directorships

As noted above, the definition of a connected or associated person is wide. In practice, trustees may well think that it is obvious when they have any 'employer-related investments'. They may assume that investment with a company outside the accounting group is not caught.   **19.79**

However, the definition used in the Insolvency Act is wide enough for two companies to be connected if they share just one common director. Investment in a company will be an employer-related investment if that company has one director who is also a director of one of the employer companies.   **19.80**

There is a specific exemption[48] in relation to the employer-related investment rules for companies connected only by reason of sharing a common director. This was introduced to recognize the fact that, given the importance of non-executive directors in the corporate governance field, the common director association might produce unintended limitations on the investments of pension schemes.   **19.81**

Taking an example from the listed arena, the 2008/09 British Airways (BA) Annual report confirmed that one of its non-executive directors (Maarten van den Bergh) is also the Deputy Chairman of the BT Group. This common directorship would, without the exemption in reg 10, mean that an investment by a BA pension scheme in the BT Group shares would be an employer-related investment (and so caught by the 5 per cent limit).   **19.82**

It should be noted that the reg 10 exemption is limited. It only applies if the connection is *solely* by reason of the common directorship. In practice, this may mean that it is only useful for common non-executive directors—if the director is also an employee (eg an executive director) the exemption may not apply.   **19.83**

---

[45] Regulation 1(5)(a).

[46] See s 123 of the Pensions Act 1995. Note that s 123(3) provides for modifications to these definitions for the purposes of s 40 to be prescribed in regulations—see further below and reg 10.

[47] For further analysis, see D Pollard, 'Who is "Connected" or "Associated"?' (2009) 22 Insolvency Intelligence 33 and Pollard, *Corporate Insolvency: Employment and Pension Rights* 5th edn (2013) Ch 70.

[48] See reg 10.

19.84 Trustees may need to check the other directorships held by each director of each of the participating employers (this information should be held with the register of directors in the company's statutory books and on file at the Companies Registry).

Multi-employer schemes

19.85 Where a pension scheme has more than one sponsoring employer, the way in which the restrictions apply will depend upon whether the scheme is asset sectionalized or not. Where the scheme is non-sectionalized, the 5 per cent limit applies to the entire scheme and an investment with any employer (or its associates etc) needs to be considered.

19.86 Where the scheme is sectionalized, each section is generally treated as a separate scheme (provided there is no cross-subsidy between the sections) and the 5 per cent limit applies to each section: see reg 16(1)–(4).

19.87 Where at least two of the employers are non-associated and various other (complex) conditions are met the overall level of employer-related investments must not exceed a prudent level and, in any event, 20 per cent of the current market value of the scheme assets.[49]

Exclusions from the section 40 regime

19.88 Section 40 only applies to an occupational pension scheme.[50] It does not apply to a personal pension scheme.

19.89 There are a number of statutory exclusions which take certain types of occupational pension scheme or investment outside the scope of the regime. A number of these exclusions are not permitted by the IORP Directive and so the 2009 Regulations made changes to the 2005 Investment Regulations with effect from 23 September 2010 (when the ability of Member States to postpone the IORP self-investment requirements expired[51]).

19.90 It should be noted that there is *no* exemption for money purchase schemes;[52] or schemes that are not tax registered.[53]

19.91 The employer-related investment restrictions do not apply to 'small schemes',[54] defined as schemes with less than 12 members where all the members are trustees and either all trustee decisions require unanimity among the trustees or the scheme has an independent trustee.[55] However, small schemes that undertake cross-border activities do fall within the s 40 restrictions.[56]

---

[49] Regulation 16(5)(a). Under the IORP Directive, there is no 20 per cent limit—the requirement in Art 18 where an institution is sponsored by a number of undertakings is that investment in these sponsoring undertakings shall be made prudently, taking into account the need for proper diversification.

[50] As defined in s1 of the Pension Schemes Act 1993 (as amended by the Pensions Act 2004). See s 124(5) of the Pensions Act 1995.

[51] Article 22(4) of the IORP Directive.

[52] Even though the value of members' notional accounts will be determined by the value of the members' own investment choices—and in contrast to the pre-2010 position on AVCs (see below).

[53] The restrictions in s 40 did not apply to schemes without tax approval until the 2005 Investment Regulations replaced the 1996 Investment Regulations (SI 1996/3127). The 1996 Regulations used to provide that they only applied to schemes with tax approval, but this was deleted when the 1996 Regulations were revoked and replaced by the 2005 Investment Regulations. The 2005 Investment Regulations presumably do not repeat this exemption as there is no provision in the IORP expressly allowing this.

[54] Regulation 12(1) of the 2005 Investment Regulations. The IORP Directive permits a much wider exclusion for schemes with less than 100 members: see Art 5.

[55] As referred to in s 23 of the Pensions Act 1995 (reg 1(2) of the 2005 Investment Regulations).

[56] Regulation 17(c).

A summary of the exemptions is: **19.92**

Exemption before 23 September 2010	Position following 23 September 2010
Small schemes (less than 12 members)	No change: exemption continues
Amounts due under the statutory schedule of contributions or s 75	No change: exemption continues
Additional Voluntary Contributions (AVCs) invested with member written agreement	Now count towards 5 per cent limit
Authorized bank and building society accounts	• Still do not count as a prohibited loan • Now count towards the 5 per cent limit
Excluded collective investment schemes	Exclusion removed
Excluded insurance policies	Now count towards the 5 per cent limit
Investments held prior to 6 April 1997	Exclusion removed

Excluded assets

Pre-2010 Current position

Certain investments do not count as 'employer-related investments' and do not need to be   **19.93**
taken into account for the purposes of the 5 per cent market value test or the prohibition on
employer-related loans. These included the following:

(a) Accounts with building societies or authorized banks.[57] Were it not for this exclusion,
    pension schemes of banks and building societies would be prohibited from holding
    accounts with that particular bank or building society. This exemption ceased to apply
    in 2010.
(b) Investments derived from a member's voluntary contributions which are invested in
    employer-related investments with the written agreement of the member concerned.[58]
    This exemption ceased to apply in 2010.
(c) Some investments in insurance policies issued by an insurer which is an employer.[59] The
    exemption here is complex (see below).
(d) Amounts due under the statutory schedule of contributions or s 75 of the Pensions
    Act 1995 (debt on employer).[60] Note that there is no exclusion for amounts that may
    become due under other statutory provisions, for example as a result of a contribu-
    tion notice or financial support direction issued by the Pensions Regulator under the
    Pensions Act 2004.

2009 Regulations: bank accounts

The 2009 Regulations removed the exemption in reg 13(3) (accounts with building societies   **19.94**
or authorized banks) with effect from 23 September 2010. Instead, new reg 15A (Deposits)
provides that the prohibition on employer-related loans[61] shall not apply to such accounts.[62]

---

[57] Regulation 13(3).
[58] Regulation 13(4).
[59] Regulation 13(2).
[60] Regulation 13(6).
[61] Which will be in new reg 12(2A).
[62] With the definition of account being mirrored from the previous exemption.

This means that deposits held in such accounts are now 'employer-related investments' for the purposes of the 5 per cent limit if the employer is connected or associated with the bank or building society.[63]

19.95 Given that most schemes do not tend to hold a significant proportion of their assets in cash, this may not be a concern on a day-to-day basis. However, it could cause concern in more unusual circumstances, for example:

(a) if there needs to be a significant realization of cash (eg to pay lump sum benefits on a significant early retirement/redundancy exercise or where a large executive benefit comes into payment);

(b) if a particularly large cash contribution is received from an employer (eg following the trigger of a s 75 debt).

19.96 There is no *de minimis* period for breach of the 5 per cent limit—so there would still be a breach of the employer-related investment requirements even though the limit might, in such circumstances, only be breached for a short period (until the benefits were paid out or the contribution invested elsewhere). Given the potentially serious consequences of breach,[64] this might mean that trustees should consider whether a non-employer account should be used for such payments.

19.97 The 2009 Regulations removed the reg 13(4) exemption in relation to member's voluntary contributions with effect from 23 September 2010. This was presumably to comply with the IORP Directive.[65]

Transitional provisions: pre-2010 position

19.98 The 2005 Investment Regulations contain various transitional provisions permitting the retention of employer-related loans and employer-related investments in excess of 5 per cent which were held prior to 6 April 1997: reg 14.

19.99 The consultation draft of the 2009 Regulations had proposed removing the transitional protection relating to employer-related investments[66] with effect from September 2010 to comply with the IORP Directive.[67] However, due to responses to the consultation, these provisions were removed from the 2009 Regulations on the same basis as the changes relating to the exemption for collective investment schemes (see below). The deletions were however later made by the Occupational Pension Schemes (Investment) (Amendment) Regulations 2010.[68]

19.100 The transitional protection given to employer-related loans has been amended by the 2009 Regulations so that, whilst such loans continue to be exempt from the general prohibition on employer-related loans, they are now counted as employer-related investments for the purposes of the 5 per cent limit: see new reg 12(2B).

---

[63] To comply with the IORP Directive: see para 21 of the December 2008 DWP consultation on the draft regulations. See new reg 12(2B).

[64] See below.

[65] See para 20 of the December 2008 DWP consultation.

[66] Ie it had proposed removing regs 14(1)(b) and 14(2)(e).

[67] See para 20 of the December 2008 DWP consultation on the draft regulations.

[68] SI 2010/2161.

Collective investment schemes and insurance policies

There are also exemptions relating to collective investment schemes and insurance policies (see below).   **19.101**

(a) pooled investments;
(b) investment through Collective Investment Schemes.

Pre-2010 position

Pension schemes often make investments through a collective investment schemes (CIS) such as a unit trust or open-ended investment company (OEIC). For this purpose a CIS is as defined in Pt 17 of FSMA 2000, but also includes some arrangements that would not otherwise be a CIS.[69]   **19.102**

If the CIS has investments[70] which would have been employer-related investment if made by the scheme, then the relevant proportion of the CIS is treated as employer-related investment.[71]   **19.103**

So if the CIS has (say) an investment in shares of the employer worth £1m and the scheme owns (say) 40 per cent of the CIS, the scheme will be treated as having employer-related investment worth £400k.   **19.104**

There was, before 2010, an exemption in reg 13(7): investments made by the operator of a CIS are not taken into account provided that: **19.105**

(a) the CIS is operated by an authorized person (within s 31 of the FSMA 2000);
(b) the CIS has at least ten participants;[72]
(c) not more than 10 per cent of the assets of the CIS are attributable directly (or indirectly through an intervening CIS) to the pension scheme's resources (adding in any pension schemes of the same group[73]); and
(d) not more than 10 per cent of the investments of the CIS are invested in securities which fall within para 11 of Sch 2 to the FSMA 2000 (shares or stock in the share capital of a company) and issued by any one issuer (or group[74]). Note that there is no need for this concentration to be in shares of the employer (or an associate).

Before 2010, pension schemes needed to check if a particular CIS qualified for this exemption to apply.   **19.106**

2010 changes

The consultation draft of the 2009 Regulations proposed the removal of reg 13(7) with effect from 23 September 2010 to comply with the IORP Directive.[75] However, the government response to the consultation in April 2009 noted that the great majority of consultation   **19.107**

---

[69] See the definition of CIS in reg 1(2), expressly including in the definition arrangements in paras 4 and 9 of the FSMA 2000 (Collective Investment Schemes) Order 2001 (SI 2001/1062). Paragraph 4 would otherwise exclude arrangements operated otherwise than by way of business. Paragraph 9 would otherwise exclude arrangements entered into for commercial purposes wholly or mainly related to existing business. Note that the para 10 exclusion from being a CIS still applies (arrangements with each participant a body corporate in the same group as the operator).

[70] Strictly this only applies to investments made by the operator of the CIS—see reg 11(a)(i)—but it is difficult to see how the CIS could hold investments which have not be made by the operator.

[71] Regulation 11(a).

[72] With schemes where the employers are in the same group counting as one participant for these purposes: see regs 13(8)(a) and 13(9).

[73] Regulations 13(8)(b) and 13(9).

[74] Regulations 13(8) and 13(9).

[75] See para 20 of the December 2008 DWP consultation on the draft regulations.

responses it had received were concerned about the way in which employer-related investments in CISs were affected. As a result:

> Given that the Directive does not have to be fully transposed until September 2010, some of the amendments relating to CISs...have been removed...The Government will look to see if there is a better way of ensuring that the investment regulations fully comply with article 18 of the IORP...
>
> The Government accept there are complex issues arising from the removal of the exemption relating to CISs. Given the sheer weight of the response this has generated and the fact that the changes do not need to come into force until September 2010, the Government has decided to put the removal of the existing exemptions for CISs on a separate track.[76]

19.108 However, although the 2009 Regulations left the CIS exemption intact, the consultation response emphasized that this 'should not be taken as an indication that the exemptions are to remain indefinitely, and further changes to remove them may be included in a separate instrument'.

19.109 The CIS exemption was later removed by the Occupational Pension Schemes (Investment) (Amendment) Regulations 2010.[77]

Insurance policies

Pre-2010 Current position

19.110 Regulations 11(d) and (e) deal with investment in insurance policies:[78]

> For the purposes of [section 40], the following are prescribed as employer-related investments:
>
> (d) where any of a scheme's resources are invested in an insurance policy the terms of which permit—
> (i) the premiums or other consideration for the rights acquired under the policy, or
> (ii) any monies otherwise credited to or for the benefit of the trustees or managers or the members,
>   to be invested in a fund created only for the purposes of that policy, the proportion of the scheme's resources invested in that policy which is the same proportion as B is of A where:
>   A represents all the assets of the insurer held in the fund, and B represents that part of A which would, if invested by the scheme, be employer-related investments: and
> (e) where any of a scheme's resources are invested in an insurance policy (not being resources invested in a fund created only for the purposes of that policy) the terms of which permit the trustees of managers or the employer to direct that—
> (i) some or all of the premiums or other consideration for the rights acquired under the policy, or
> (ii) any monies otherwise credited to or for the benefit of the trustees or managers or the members,
>   are invested in employer-related investments, any investments made by the insurer from those premiums or other consideration or monies, which would have been employer-related investments if they had been made by the scheme.

---

[76] See pp 9–11 of the response to consultation.
[77] SI 2010/2161.
[78] Note that 'insurance policy' is defined for these purposes in reg 1(2) as a contract of a kind referred to in Art 2 of the Life Directive (Directive 2002/83EC) but excluding a contract of a kind referred to in Art 2(2)(c) and (d) of that directive.

This means that, in a similar manner to CISs, generally there is a look through to the underlying **19.111** investments where either:

    (a) the underlying fund of the insurer is created for the purpose of the policy (reg 11(d)); or
    (b) where the trustees or employer can direct that the underlying investments owned by the insurer are invested in employer-related investments (regulation 11(e)).

Such policies will count as employer-related investment to the extent that the investments **19.112** held under the policy would be employer-related investment if held directly by the scheme.

However, where (say) a scheme invests in a general with-profits or pooled policy of an insurer, **19.113** any investment held by the insurer with the employer will not count as employer-related investments.

There is an exemption in reg 13(2) for policies within reg 11(e) (but not reg 11(d)—ie where **19.114** the fund under the policy is *not* created only for the purposes of the insurance policy) where:

    (a)   the policy is a 'specified qualifying insurance policy';[79] and
    (b)   the policy is issued by an insurer which is the employer.

This exemption only for reg 11(e) seems to be designed to allow schemes of an insurer to **19.115** be able to use certain policies issued by the insurer and then to direct that all or part of the investments are with the insurer.

2010 change

The 2009 Regulations removed the reg 13(2) exemption with effect from 23 September **19.116** 2010.

Timing for test

How does the test work?

The 5 per cent share limit is by value of the fund (not shareholding in the employer). So **19.117** the scheme could hold (say) 90 per cent of the employer, provided that it has other assets so that the shareholding is not over 5 per cent of the fund value (including the shares in the employer).

This means that the limit can be broken by: **19.118**

    (a)   the value of employer going up; or
    (b)   the value of the rest of the fund going down.

There is no express provision for how and when the limit is tested, but: **19.119**

    (a)   it probably means at all times (eg not by looking at the last accounts); and
    (b)   it requires a look at the market value of investments.

One issue is whether restrictions in s 40 on the proportion of resources in employer-related **19.120** investments:

    (a)   only applies to the making of an investment (ie at the moment when the trustees made the investment), or
    (b)   applies to the state of the investment of the scheme's assets from time to time.

---

[79] Which is defined in reg 1(2) by reference to FSMA 2000.

19.121 Section 40 and the 2005 Regulations are somewhat contradictory on this issue:

(a) s 40(1) refers to a scheme complying with prescribed restrictions with respect to the proportion of its resources 'that may at any time be invested in' employer-related investments;

(b) s 40(4) applies civil penalties to 'any trustee who fails to take all such steps as are reasonable to secure compliance';

(c) s 40(5) applies criminal penalties to 'any trustee or manager who agreed in the determination to make the investment';

(d) the language of reg 12(2)(a) refers to the 'current market value of the resources of the scheme';

(e) reg 14 deals with transitional provisions and permits already-existing arrangements potentially in breach of the rules on employer-related investments to continue; and

(f) reg 15 deals with loans that become employer-related and permits them to be retained for a period.

19.122 Although it could perhaps be argued that the use of the term 'invested in' in s 40(1) perhaps points to a test at the time of making the investment only, the use of the phrase 'at any time' negates this. The better view is that the restrictions on employer-related investments are not solely restrictions which apply at the time when the scheme makes the investment. They are restrictions on the proportion of the scheme's resources that at any one time are held as investments (ie what investments the scheme has).

19.123 For example in *Wright v Ginn*[80] (a case under the slightly differently worded regulations under s 112 of the Pension Schemes Act 1993, the predecessor to s 40), Millett J (as he then was) noted the then restriction was that 'not more than 5 per cent per cent of the current market value of the resources of a scheme may be invested on employer-related investments' and commented that:

> It is plain in my judgment that the expression 'be invested' does not mean 'be laid out' in but 'be represented by'. This follows from the provisions of reg 5 and particularly reg 5(3) and the principal Act.

19.124 But this distinction is relevant for the purposes of civil and criminal penalties:

(a) s 40(4) applies civil penalties in respect of investments which the scheme holds from time to time (and which may have become prohibited investments);

(b) s 40(5) applies criminal penalties to the decision to make an investment which is a prohibited investment.

Loans and enforcement of outstanding amounts

19.125 Section 40 is clear that if an amount is outstanding from an employer (or associate) and is unpaid on the due date, then this must be treated as an employer-related loan—s 40(3) and see above.

19.126 This means that trustees need to think what will happen if such amounts become due and payable, but are not paid. This would not matter if the amounts are due under the schedule of contributions (or s 75 etc) as these amounts are exempt from s 40. But other amounts

---

[80] [1994] OPLR 83 at 86A (Millett J).

could give a concern—for example if a parent company of an employer gives a guarantee or amounts become due under an investment (eg a dividend on shares).

The trustee should not be liable for a civil penalty if he or she takes 'reasonable steps' to enforce and recover the debt. **19.127**

As noted above, the Pensions Regulator has noted this issue in its guidance on contingent assets.[81] **19.128**

Consequences of breach

Overview

There are potentially severe civil and criminal penalties for trustees who invest (or who allow investment to be retained) in breach of these restrictions:[82] **19.129**

(a) a criminal offence which may lead to a fine or imprisonment or both;
(b) civil penalties;
(c) an investment which contravenes s 40 probably also counts as being unauthorized by the terms of the trust. In that case there is a potential for a member to bring a claim against the trustees for losses flowing from the unauthorized investment.[83]

As noted above, the Pensions Regulator has no power to validate arrangements which would otherwise contravene the restrictions on employer-related investment, regardless of the merits of any particular proposal and the interests of scheme members. **19.130**

There are also other issues arising out of a breach to consider: **19.131**

(a) scheme funding;
(b) scheme accounts;
(c) s 75 debts;
(d) notification requirements to the Pensions Regulator.

Civil penalties

Section 40(4) provides that, in the case of a trust scheme, any trustee who fails to take all reasonable steps to ensure the scheme complies with any prescribed limits on the level of permitted employer-related investment may be fined by the Pensions Regulator, in accordance with s 10. Section 10 provides for a maximum fine of £5,000 for an individual or £50,000 for a company. **19.132**

Although s 40(1) appears to impose an absolute duty on scheme trustees or managers by requiring that they 'must secure' that the scheme complies with any prescribed restrictions, s 40(4) qualifies this duty for the purpose of establishing whether the trustee is liable to civil penalty. **19.133**

Liability will not be attracted by any trustee who shows that he has taken 'all such steps as are reasonable to secure compliance'. **19.134**

This could be the case where, for example, an individual trustee is outvoted by the others and he can demonstrate that he used all reasonable steps to persuade the others to disinvest.

---

[81] See <http://www.thepensionsregulator.gov.uk>.
[82] Pensions Act 1995, s 40(5) and (6).
[83] Even if this is not the case, an employer-related investment may be more likely to be found to have been made in breach of general investment/fiduciary duties: see below.

19.136 Another example might be where reasonable investigation has not revealed that an investment has in fact been made with an associate. Nevertheless, the burden on the trustee is likely to remain a relatively high one and it will be up to the trustee to demonstrate that he has taken all such steps as are reasonable.

19.137 If a corporate trustee is liable for a civil penalty under s 10, then a 'director, manager, secretary or other similar officer' of the corporate trustee can also be liable if the relevant act or omission was done with his or her consent, connivance or is attributable to his or her neglect—s 10(5) and (6) of the Pensions Act 1995.[84]

Criminal liability

19.138 Criminal liability will arise if any resources of an occupational pension scheme are invested in contravention of s 40(1), in which case any trustee or manager who agreed in the determination to make the investment is guilty of an offence and liable:

(a) on summary conviction, to a fine not exceeding the statutory maximum (currently £5,000[85]); and

(b) on conviction on indictment, to a fine or imprisonment (the maximum sentence is currently two years), or both.

19.139 Curiously, s 40 of the Pensions Act 1994 does not state the maximum term of imprisonment for conviction on indictment.[86] However, s 77 of the Powers of Criminal Courts (Sentencing) Act 2000 states that:

> Where a person is convicted on indictment of an offence against any enactment and is for that offence liable to be sentenced to imprisonment, but the sentence is not by any enactment either limited to a specified term or expressed to extend to imprisonment for life, the person so convicted shall be liable to imprisonment for not more than two years.

19.140 Although those not involved in any determination will not be liable, there is no reasonable steps defence for any trustee or manager who has actually been involved at any stage in the investment decision.

19.141 It seems that liability will arise even where the trustee or manager is unaware that the proposed investment is employer-related. Given the potential difficulties highlighted above of identifying certain employer related investments, this provision seems harsh.

19.142 What happens, for instance, where sudden market fluctuations cause the limit to be exceeded, or, if following an acquisition, a sizeable 'ordinary' investment is automatically converted into a self-investment?

19.143 The criminal offence should not then arise. When the initial investment was made, it was below the limit. A later rise may bring into play the civil penalty, but not the criminal offence.

---

[84] For a general review of this extended liability, see Pollard, *Corporate Insolvency: Employment and Pension Rights* 5th edn (2013) Ch 15.

[85] Magistrates' Courts Act 1980, s 32.

[86] Compare this with, for example, s 80 of the Pensions Act 2004 (offence of providing false or misleading information) which states that on indictment a person shall be imprisoned for a 'term not exceeding two years . . .'.

This is supported by the comments made in Parliament at the time of the Pensions Bill in **19.144**
1995. The then DSS Minister of State, Lord Mackay of Ardbrecknish commented[87] that:

> Amendment No. 64 tightens the criminal offence in Clause 35 so that it is more serious than
> the breach that carries a civil penalty. It makes it a criminal offence for a trustee or manager
> of an occupational pension scheme to agree to a determination to make an investment that
> breaches the provisions on employer related investments. We believe that those who agree to
> use scheme assets in breach of these provisions should be liable to prosecution. Such action is
> in many ways equivalent to theft, and there must be a strong deterrent.

Example: **19.145**

If (say) shares in an employer are acquired by a scheme, various scenarios occur:

the shares are worth less than 5 per cent of the scheme's assets at the date of acquisition, but later grow to over 5 per cent (eg other assets reduce or the shares increase)	No breach of s 40 on first investment Later breach when value rises to more than 5 per cent —civil penalty

the shares are worth more than 5 per cent of the scheme's assets at the date of acquisition	Breach of s 40 on first investment
	   -criminal penalty
	   -civil penalty

If an investment is made which brings the level of self-investment above the prescribed limit, **19.146**
liability will presumably only attach to those of the trustees involved in the determination to
make the investment that brings the level of self-investment above the prescribed limit (and
not those who were involved in the earlier non-breaching investments).

If there is a criminal offence by a corporate trustee, then a 'director, manager, secretary or **19.147**
other similar officer' of the corporate trustee is also criminally liable if the breach is due to his
or her consent, connivance or neglect—s 115 of the Pensions Act 1995.[88]

Liability of non-trustees

The criminal offence in s 40(4) only applies to a trustee. The civil penalty in s 40(5) applies **19.148**
to a trustee or manager. But the term 'manager' is defined in s 124(1) as follows:

> managers, in relation to an occupational pension scheme other than a trust scheme, means the
> persons responsible for the management of the scheme.

Accessory criminal liability?

As noted above, the primary offence is a concern for the trustees or managers of a scheme. **19.149**
Further, under s 40, a civil penalty can only be issued against a trustee (see also above).

As a result, employers might consider that the employer-related investment regime does not **19.150**
concern them, for example, in seeking to persuade the trustees to invest in employer-related
investments or enter into contingent asset arrangements that could amount to employer-related
investments (save to the extent that the trustees may be unwilling to enter into such arrangements if there is a risk that the restrictions might be breached). However, given the potential

---

[87] Hansard, House of Lords, 12 July 1995, col 1686.
[88] For a general review of this extended liability, see Pollard *Corporate Insolvency: Employment and Pension
Rights* 5th edn (2013) Ch 15.

criminal liability, it seems at least possible that there could be secondary criminal liability for employers in these circumstances.

19.151 As a general rule, provided that they have the necessary intention, any third party who 'aids, abets, counsels or procures' (a Secondary Party) the commission of an indictable offence or a summary offence is liable to be punished as a principal offender.[89] For a Secondary Party to be convicted, it must be proved that the act which constituted the aiding, abetting, counselling, or procuring was done:

(a) intentionally, in the sense that he did it deliberately (and not accidentally), knowing that his act was capable of encouraging the commission of an offence; and

(b) with intent to assist or encourage the perpetrator (and not to obstruct or hinder him).[90]

19.152 Although it must be proved that a Secondary Party had the intention set out above, it does not have to be proved that it was his purpose or desire that this crime be committed.[91]

19.153 A Secondary Party must also be aware of all the essential circumstances which make the act done a crime but he need not have known that the act amounted in law to a crime. In other words, the employer must simply be aware that the trustee is investing scheme resources in employer-related investments and not that by doing so the trustee is committing a criminal offence.

19.154 Finally, a Secondary Party must have foreseen as a real possibility that the principal was acting with an intention to invest resources of the Scheme in employer-related investments.[92]

19.155 On this basis (and subject to the act of the Secondary Party constituting 'aiding, abetting, counselling or procuring'), if a Secondary Party assists in the investment of scheme resources by the trustee of such a scheme, and intended to do so (rather than by doing so mistakenly), it appears very possible that a Secondary Party could be criminally liable under s 40(5).

19.156 In deciding whether any given act amounts to 'aiding, abetting, counselling or procuring', the Court of Appeal held in *A-G's Reference (No 1 of 1975)*[93] that such words should be construed in their ordinary meaning and not in a technical sense. The ordinary meaning of 'aids, abets, counsels or procures' was further discussed by Lord Widgery CJ in that case:

(a) The natural meaning of 'to aid' is to 'give help, support or assistance to'. It is not necessary to prove that there was any agreement between the principal and the Secondary Party.

(b) The natural meaning of 'to abet' is 'to incite, instigate or encourage' and this can only be committed by a Secondary Party who is present when the crime is committed. This implies either an express or implied agreement between the parties.

(c) The ordinary meaning of 'to counsel' is 'to encourage' and most often covers advice, information, encouragement, or the supply of equipment before the commission of

---

[89] See s 8 of the Accessories and Abettors Act 1861 (as amended by s 65(4) of the Criminal Law Act 1977).

[90] See *R v Bryce* [2004] EWCA Crim 1231, CA which held that it is not necessary for a secondary party to be certain of the act which the perpetrator commits; it is enough that the secondary party is aware that there is a real possibility that the perpetrator *may* do the act in question or a similar act.

[91] *National Coal Board v Gamble* [1959] 1 QB 11, DC.

[92] In *R v Powell, R v English* [1999] 1 AC 1 the House of Lords held that 'foresight of real possibility' means foresight of a risk which is not foreseen as so remote that the secondary party 'dismissed it as altogether negligible'.

[93] [1975] QB 773, CA.

a crime and implies agreement with the principal.[94] In the case of aiding, abetting, or counselling there is no need to prove any causative link between the act and the commission of the offence. This is subject to, in the case of counselling, the offence that was committed being within the scope of the counselling.[95]

(d) The ordinary meaning of 'to procure' means 'to produce by endeavour, by setting out to see that it happens and taking the appropriate steps to produce that happening'. In contrast to aiding, abetting, and counselling, a causal link is required between the procuring and the commission of the offence by the principal offender, and the Secondary Party will be liable even if the principal is entirely 'innocent' of the Secondary Party's act.

If a third party commits an act that does fall within the scope of 'aiding, abetting, counselling or procuring' as a question of fact, it is possible that they could also be criminally liable for a breach of s 40(1) by a trustee of a Scheme, subject to them also having the necessary intention (as outlined above).   **19.157**

Civil liability to scheme members—breach of trust

Another interesting question is whether a breach of the statutory duty in s 40 could also give rise to a civil right of action by an affected person, in addition to the sanctions expressly specified by s 40.   **19.158**

It seemed clear that the effect of the predecessor of s 40, s 112 of Pension Schemes Act 1993 (which prescribed no specific sanction), was to impose a specific statutory duty on trustees which was enforceable by individual beneficiaries. So, if a scheme failed (or its trustees failed) to comply with the prohibition in s 112, this could be treated as a breach of trust, actionable by beneficiaries of the trust.   **19.159**

This was confirmed by Millett J (as he then was) in 1994 in his decision in *Wright v Ginn*,[96] a case which considered the interrelation of s 112 and s 4 of the Trustee Act 1925. Section 4 (now repealed[97]) provided some relief for trustees who would otherwise be liable for breach of trust in relation to unauthorized investments. Millett J held that s 4 was equally applicable to questions of breach of s 112.   **19.160**

However, it seems arguable that this no longer remains the case given the change to the wording in s 40(1) (as opposed to that found in s 112(1)) and the specific sanctions set out in s 40(4) and (5). The position is unhelpfully unclear.   **19.161**

Generally it is often a difficult question of law as to whether or not an independent civil remedy (eg for breach of statutory duty) is given to affected persons where a statute imposes a   **19.162**

---

[94] In *R v Clarkson* [1971] 3 All ER 344 the Courts Martial Appeal Court held that counselling or advising must have an effect on the mind of the principal so as to constitute the necessary encouragement in fact.
[95] In *R v Calhaem* [1985] 2 All ER 266, CA, the court held that the offence actually committed must be within the scope of the counselling, ie the principal does not deliberately depart from the plan.
[96] [1994] OPLR 83 (Millett J). See Ian Greenstreet, 'The New Use for Section 4 of the Trustee Act 1925: A Little Used One-Hundred Year Old Statutory Provision Applied in a Modern Context' (1994) 8 TLI 56.
[97] See the Trustee Act 2000, s 40(1), (3), Sch 2, Pt II, para 18, coming into force on 1 February 2001: see SI 2001/49, art 2. It is not clear why s 4 of the 1925 Act was repealed. It is not discussed in the Law Commission consultation paper 146 (of June 1997)—see <http://www.lawcom.gov.uk/docs/cp146.pdf>, nor in the final Law Commission report (260, July 1999).

duty or requirement. The presumption is that no such separate duty arises if the statute itself provides for a penalty or means of enforcement.[98] See generally:

(a) *Lonrho v Shell Petroleum*;[99]
(b) *Scally v Southern Heath Board*[100] (failure to issue statutory statement of terms to employee liable to sanction in employment tribunal. No civil claim);
(c) *Richardson v Pitt-Stanley*[101] (failure to take out employer liability insurance is a criminal offence. No civil claim); and
(d) *X (Minors) v Bedfordshire County Council*[102] (no civil duty of care in exercise of statutory discretions).

19.163 It may be relevant that s 117 of the Pensions Act 1995 provides that the provisions of Pt 1 of the Act (which includes s 40) generally override the provisions of pension schemes. This issue does not seem to have been tested in the courts.

19.164 There may of course be an express restriction on employer-related investment in the scheme rules or perhaps the statement of investment principles (SIP).

19.165 If there is a restriction in the SIP, the relevant investment managers may be liable for any infringement—see s 36(5) of the Pensions Act 1995 requiring a fund manager to exercise powers of investment with a view to giving effect to the SIP.

19.166 If a breach of the employer-investment limits was a breach of trust, then any person who dishonestly assists in the breach may also incur a liability—see eg *Barlow Clowes International Ltd v Eurotrust*[103] and *Twinsectra Ltd v Yardley*.[104]

PO jurisdiction

19.167 The Pensions Ombudsman generally has jurisdiction to make determinations dealing with a dispute of fact or law or in relation to maladministration causing injustice. However, the regulations expressly exclude from the Ombudsman's jurisdiction matters relating to a breach of s 40.

19.168 The Ombudsman is not allowed[105] to:

> make any findings of fact to the effect that a person responsible for the management of an occupational pension scheme has failed to comply with the requirements under... section 40 of the Pensions Act 1995.

19.169 In the determination relating to the *Greenup and Thompson Ltd Pension Scheme*,[106] the Deputy Pensions Ombudsman noted this limitation, stating (at para 3):

> **JURISDICTION**
>
> 3. I am aware that, from an early stage, the Pensions Regulator has been involved in investigating the circumstances of the Loan in relation to a potential breach of Section 40 of the Act.

---

[98] See Freshfields, *The Guide to the Pensions Act 1995* (Tolley Publishing, 1995) Ch 19 (Penalties).
[99] [1982] AC 173, HL.
[100] [1992] 1 AC 294, HL.
[101] [1995] QB 123, CA.
[102] [1995] 2 AC 633, HL.
[103] [2006] 1 WLR 1476, [2006] 1 All ER 333, PC.
[104] [2002] AC 164, HL.
[105] The Personal and Occupational Pension Schemes (Pensions Ombudsman) Regulations 1996 (SI 1996/2475), reg 4(2)(c).
[106] (2008) 9 July, Q00623 (Gordon Deputy PO).

Regulation 4(2)(c) of The Personal and Occupational Pension Schemes (Pensions Ombudsman) Regulations 1996 prevents me from making a finding to the effect that the Trustees breached Section 40 of the Act. However, the Pensions Regulator has confirmed to this office that, in advancing the Loan, the Trustees breached Section 40 of the Act, which is a criminal offence.

Having said that, the Deputy Ombudsman held that the trustees were in breach of trust in making an unsecured loan to the employer. But this seems to have been based only partly on the potential breach of s 40. The Ombudsman held (at para 50) that: **19.170**

50. The 1999 Rules provide the Trustees with a broad discretion when making investments, including loans, subject to the provisions of Section 40 of the Act. Section 40 of the Act, and its accompanying regulations, are plain. The view of the Pensions Regulator is that the loans made by the Trustees to the Company are illegal: advancing the Loan was a criminal offence. However, even ignoring the illegality of the Loan, there are many other reasons why, in my opinion, prudent trustees would not have advanced it.

And later at paras 67–9: **19.171**

67. In order to protect trustees from being made personally liable for a breach of trust, it is common for pension scheme rules to contain a clause affording such protection in certain circumstances. The 1999 Rules are no different. Rule 8(1) (the 'Exemption Clause'), exonerates the Trustees from liability save for those acts which occur due to their own wilful neglect or default.

68. However, Section 33 of the Act renders the Exemption Clause void. This is because Section 33 denies any attempt to afford protection where the Trustees, in exercising an investment function (advancing the Loan), have failed to take care and exercise skill. Here, (a) the Loan was illegal and (b) the Trustees did not meet the 'prudent man' test.

69. In my view therefore the Trustees cannot rely on the Exemption Clause contained in Rule 8(1). Neither can they rely on the provisions of Section 34(4) of the Act, namely, that they have delegated their investment functions to a fund manager. For the reasons given in paragraph 66 above, Section 34(4) does not apply.

Other implications: funding/tax

Employer-related investment which is contrary to the trusts in s 40 will be ignored when calculating the assets of the scheme for the purposes of scheme specific funding (under Pt 3 of the Pensions Act 2004) or for the employer debt provisions (under s 75 of the Pensions Act 1995). **19.172**

Scheme accounts

Scheme accounts are required to include a statement giving the percentage of the scheme's resources which are invested in employer-related investments (within the meaning of s 40(2) of the Pensions Act 1995) at the end of the scheme year.[107] **19.173**

Note that this obligation applies to all employer-related investment, not just any in contravention of the s 40 limits. **19.174**

There is no requirement for the accounts to exclude any employer-related investment over the s 40 limits from being included in the assets of the scheme (contrast scheme specific funding and s 75 noted below). **19.175**

---

[107] Paragraph 5(a) of the Schedule to the Occupational Pension Schemes (Requirement to Obtain Audited Accounts and a Statement from the Auditor) Regulations 1996 (SI 1996/1975, as amended by SI 1997/786 and SI 2005/2426).

Scheme annual report

19.176 Trustees are required to include in their annual report details of the percentage of assets invested in employer-related investment as at the year end and, if this exceeds any limit in s 40, what steps and when they have been taken or propose to take to comply.

19.177 Paragraph 16 of Sch 3 to the Occupational Pension Schemes (Disclosure of Information) Regulations 1996[108] states that the annual report must include:

> 16 Where the scheme has employer-related investments (within the meaning of section 40(2) of the 1995 Act), a statement—
>
> (a) as to the percentage of the scheme's resources invested in such investments at the end of the scheme year;
>
> (b) if that percentage exceeds 5 per cent, as to the percentage of the scheme's resources which are investments to which regulation 6 of the Occupational Pension Schemes (Investment) Regulations 1996[109] (investments not subject to restrictions) applies; and
>
> (c) if any resources of the scheme are then invested in contravention of subsection (1) of section 40 of the 1995 Act—
>
>   (i) as to the steps the trustees or managers have taken or propose to take to secure that the scheme complies with that section, and
>
>   (ii) as to the time when any proposed steps will be taken.

Scheme specific funding

19.178 Amounts invested in contravention of the limits in s 40 are to be disregarded when looking at the assets of the scheme for the purposes of the scheme specific funding provisions in Pt 3 of the Pensions Act 2004.

19.179 Regulation 3(1)(a) of the Occupational Pension Schemes (Scheme Funding) Regulations 2005[110] states:

> (1) The assets of a scheme to be taken into account for the purposes of Part 3 of the 2004 Act are the assets attributed to the scheme in the relevant accounts, excluding—
>
> (a) any resources invested (or treated as invested by or under section 40 of the 1995 Act) in contravention of section 40(1) of the 1995 Act (employer-related investments).

19.180 It is unclear if the reference to assets 'treated as invested' under s 40 is intended to be a reference to the excess assets over the 5 per cent limit even if when first invested the limit was not infringed.

19.181 If (say) shares in an employer are acquired by a scheme, various scenarios occur:

the shares are worth less than 5 per cent of the scheme's assets at the date of acquisition, but later grow to over 5 per cent (eg other assets reduce or the shares increase)	No breach of s 40 on first investment
	Later breach when value rises to more than 5 per cent—civil penalty
	Only excess over 5 per cent is ignored in SSF valuation

(Continued)

---

[108] SI 1996/1655, as amended by SI 1997/786.

[109] The cross-reference is still to the 1996 Investment Regulations. This should now be read as a reference to reg 13 of the 2005 Investment Regulations.

[110] SI 2005/3377.

Continued	
the shares are worth more than 5 per cent of the scheme's assets at the date of acquisition	Breach of s 40 on first investment
	- criminal penalty
	Only excess over 5 per cent is ignored in SSF valuation

There is no reason why any investment up to the 5 per cent level should not still be included in the relevant valuation. It is only the excess that is contrary to s 40 and if the level was reduced back to less than 5 per cent, the whole employer-related investment remaining would be counted.   **19.182**

Millett J commented in *Wright v Ginn*[111] (a case on the predecessor section, s 112 of the Pension Schemes Act 1993) that if at any time the 5 per cent limit was exceeded, 'the excess would cease to be an authorised investment', thus impliedly confirming that the balance below 5 per cent was not so affected.   **19.183**

Section 75 debts

The question of valuing any employer-related (self-) investment is difficult in the context of a debt due from an employer under s 75 of the Pensions Act 1995, particularly if there is an insolvency. If (say) the scheme owns shares in the employer, the value of those shares might (in extreme circumstances) depend on the level of the debt obligation owed under s 75, which would itself depend on the value of the shares! Obviously a circularity can occur.   **19.184**

There is a similar problem if there is already a debt outstanding from the employer to the pension scheme outside the statutory liability under s 75 such as an unpaid contribution or a loan previously made from the scheme to the employer.   **19.185**

The actuary and the trustees must either: **19.186**

(a) ignore the value of the employer's debt when calculating the value of the assets of the scheme; or
(b) try to assess the value of the debt

Option (a), ignoring the value of the employer's debt when calculating the value of the assets of the scheme, seems, in the absence of statutory provision to allow it, to be unjustified as it ignores the value of what is an asset.   **19.187**

In addition, an element of 'double proof' would arise as the scheme would be proving in the liquidation for both the original debt and the liability under s 75, which to a degree represents the same debt. This is not allowed in a liquidation as a matter of general insolvency law. In *Re Oriental Commercial Bank, ex parte European Bank*,[112] Mellish LJ stated that 'There is only to be one dividend in respect of what is in substance the same debt'. See also *Re Fenton*,[113] *Barclays Bank plc v TOSG Trust Fund*,[114] and *Re Glen Express Ltd*.[115]   **19.188**

---

[111] [1994] OPLR 83 at 86D (Millett J).
[112] (1871) LR 7 Ch App 99 at 103, CA.
[113] [1931] 1 Ch 85, CA.
[114] [1984] AC 626, HL.
[115] [2000] BPIR 456, 19 October 1999 (Neuberger J).

19.189   In *Bishopsgate Investment Management Ltd v Homan*,[116] Vinelott J at first instance refused (at p 194) to allow trustees to have a 'double dipping claim', ie to claim from the employer in relation to a shortfall in scheme assets both under a provision in the scheme and under the Social Security Pensions Act 1975, s 58B (the predecessor of the Pensions Act 1995, s 75). This would infringe the rule against double proofs or double dividends in an insolvent winding up. The point was not raised in the Court of Appeal.

19.190   Option (b) is to try to assess the value of the debt. If the employer is insolvent then the value attributable to the debt will be less than 100 pence in the pound, but must reflect the likely amount to be recovered, presumably by way of dividend in the insolvency.

19.191   The problem with this is that the amount which is likely to be recovered may well depend on the amount of the liability owed to the pension scheme under s 75. The circularity problem arises again.

19.192   Since April 2008, the Employer Debt Regulations[117] now provide for the same exclusion as in the Scheme Funding Regulations (see above), ie simply that assets invested or treated as invested in contravention of the employer-related investment provisions in the Pensions Act 1995, s40 are ignored. Regulation 5(4) provides:

> (4) Subject to paragraph (15), the assets of a scheme to be taken into account by the trustees or managers are the assets attributable to the scheme in the relevant accounts, excluding:
>> (a) any resources invested (or treated as invested by or under section 40 of the 1995 Act) in contravention of section 40(1) of the 1995 Act (employer-related investments).

19.193   This is subject to reg 5(15) which provides that any Amount B due under a withdrawal arrangement under the Employer Debt Regulations can still count as an asset (if the scheme is not winding-up at the s 75 applicable time):

> (15) If at the applicable time the scheme has not commenced winding-up and a withdrawal arrangement or an approved withdrawal arrangement is in force before the applicable time, the Amount B treated as a debt due under the arrangement shall be included as an asset of the scheme, provided that the trustees or managers are reasonably satisfied that, as at the applicable time, the guarantors have sufficient financial resources to be likely to pay Amount B.

19.194   Before April 2008 the MFR Regulations and the Employer Debt Regulations contained some provisions expressly excluding the value of some employer-related investment (as defined in the Pensions Act 1995, s 40 and the 2005 Investment Regulations). These provisions are still relevant for debts arising before 6 April 2008:

    (a) Resources invested in contravention of s 40 were ignored.[118] This would catch all employer-related loans[119] and other investment if over 5 per cent of the scheme's assets,[120] subject to transitional provisions.

    (b) After 6 April 2007, employer-related loans were excluded even if allowed under the transitional provisions in the 1996 Regulations.[121]

---

[116] [1994] PLR 179 (Vinelott J).

[117] The Occupational Pension Schemes (Employer Debt) Regulations 2005 (SI 2005/678, as amended).

[118] The Occupational Pension Schemes (Minimum Funding Requirement and Actuarial Valuations) Regulations 1996 (SI 1996/1536), reg 6(1)(a).

[119] Employer Debt Regulations 2005, reg 12(1)(b).

[120] Employer Debt Regulations 2005, reg 12(1)(a).

[121] MFR Regulations, reg 6(2).

(c) After a scheme has started to wind-up, the 5 per cent limit in reg 5(1)(a) of the 2005 Investment Regulations was to 'be disregarded'.[122] The effect of disregarding reg 5(1)(a) was that all employer-related investment, save for employer-related loans within reg 5(1)(b), should be counted. The effect of disregarding reg 5(1)(a) seems to be that all such investment is allowed, it is no longer limited by reg 5(1) and so would no longer contravene s 40. See s 40(1) containing the main requirement that a scheme complies with any 'prescribed restrictions'. This is certainly how the Institute and Faculty of Actuaries read this provision in the past, see para 3.2 of GN19 (version 4.7).

Contracting-out of S2P

Among the new requirements for contracted-out schemes imposed by the Pensions Act 1995 was that the Secretary of State (now the Inland Revenue) must be satisfied that restrictions on employer-related investment in s 40 apply to the scheme in question and that the scheme complies with these restrictions. This restriction is now found in s 9(2B)(b) of the Pension Schemes Act 1993. **19.195**

Tax issues

An investment in employer-related investment will often involve a transaction between the scheme and the employer. This may not always be the case (eg if the scheme purchases shares of the employer on a market from a third party). **19.196**

Tax issues need to be considered on payments or transactions between a tax registered pension scheme and an employer (or associate). **19.197**

Under the Finance Act 2004, the only payments which a registered occupational pension scheme makes to a sponsoring employer (or former sponsoring employer) which count as authorized payments (and so do not trigger a tax charge) are those listed at s 175 of the Finance Act, which include 'scheme administration payments', as defined in s 180. **19.198**

Section 180 is as follows: **19.199**

---

180 Scheme administration employer payments

(1) A 'scheme administration employer payment' is a payment made—
   (a) by a registered pension scheme that is an occupational pension scheme, and
   (b) to or in respect of a [person who is or has been a] sponsoring employer, for the purposes of the administration or management of the pension scheme.
(2) But if a payment falling within subsection (1) exceeds the amount which might be expected to be paid to a person who was at arm's length, the excess is not a scheme administration employer payment.
(3) Scheme administration employer payments include in particular—
   (a) the payment of wages, salaries or fees to persons engaged in administering the pension scheme, and
   (b) payments made for the purchase of assets to be held for the purposes of the pension scheme.

---

[122] See reg 5(7) of the (pre-2008) Employer Debt Regulations (previously reg 3(4) of the Deficiency Regulations 1996).

(4) A loan to or in respect of a [person who is or has been a] sponsoring employer is not a scheme administration employer payment.

(5) Payments made to acquire shares in a sponsoring employer are not scheme administration employer payments if, when the payment is made—

    (a) the market value of shares in the sponsoring employer held for the purposes of the pension scheme is equal to or greater than 5% of the aggregate of the amount of the sums, and the market value of the assets, held for the purposes of the pension scheme, or

    (b) the total market value of shares in sponsoring employers held for the purposes of the pension scheme is equal to or greater than 20% of the aggregate of the amount of the sums, and the market value of the assets, held for the purposes of the pension scheme.

(6) Regulations made by the Board of Inland Revenue may provide that payments of a description specified in the regulations are, or are not, scheme administration employer payments.

19.200 Some further discussion is contained in the HMRC Manual: *Registered Pension Schemes Manual* RPSM04102050 (payments for the administration or management of a scheme should be made on an arm's length, commercial basis; an amount over the expected arm's length price will be treated as an unauthorized member payment and taxed accordingly).

RPSM7105020 (the percentage of shares which can be held in one company is not restricted providing that the sums invested are less than 5 per cent of the fund value).

RPSM07105020—Technical Pages: Investments: Equities: Limits

Limits on shares in sponsoring employer companies [s180(5)]

    There are restrictions on the amounts in which a registered pension scheme may invest in shares of a sponsoring employer.

    A registered pension scheme may acquire shares in a sponsoring employer providing that at the time the payment is made the market value of the shares is less than 5 per cent of the total of the cash sums and the market value of the net assets held for the purpose of the pension scheme.

    The scheme may acquire shares of more than one sponsoring employer of the scheme providing that at the time the payment is made the market value of the shares is less than 20% of the total of the sums and the market value of the assets held for the purpose of the pension scheme. The shares in any one sponsoring employer of the scheme should be less than 5%.

    The market value is tested at the time the payment is made for the shares and will not be re-tested at a later date, if for example the scheme assets lose their value, unless new shares in the sponsoring employer are acquired.

    There are no restrictions with regard to the percentage of shares which can be held in one company (for example a registered pension scheme could potentially own 100% of the share capital of a company) providing that the sums invested are less than 5% of the fund value mentioned above.

    Where the above 5% or 20% limits are exceeded, the amount will be subject to an unauthorised payments charge on the employer (see RPSM07108010). The scheme will also be subject to a scheme sanction charge (see RPSM07108030).

19.201 Note that under reg 15 of the Pension Protection Fund (Tax) Regulations 2006 (SI 2006/575), these sections do not apply in relation to the Pension Protection Fund.

Pensions law implications of a payment

Under section 37 of the Pensions Act 1995, trustees may only exercise a power to make pay- **19.202**
ments to the employer out of funds held for the purposes of the scheme if certain conditions
at s 37(3) are met, which include obtaining a written valuation and an actuarial certificate
and giving notice of the proposal to exercise the power to members.

Section 37 was replaced on 6 April 2006 (under s 250 of the Pensions Act 2004[123]), but the **19.203**
new s 37 did not retain the exemption previously in s 37(7)[124] for payments not caught to tax.
This seems to have been an error. It may perhaps be possible to construe s 37 as not applying
as a matter of general interpretation to investment payments by a scheme, eg to purchase
shares or make a loan (which are not refunds of surplus). Section 37 is headed 'Payment of
surplus to an employer', but in fact refers to a 'power . . . to make payments to the employer
out of funds held for the purposes of the scheme'.

Section 130 of the Pensions Act 2008 re-introduced the exemption. Section 37 now includes **19.204**
a new s 37(1A) stating that it does not apply to payments authorized under s 175(c)–(f) of
the Finance Act 2004, including scheme administration employer payments.

However, this provision did not come into force until 6 April 2009,[125] so between 6 April **19.205**
2006 and 6 April 2009 there was a risk that trustees would have to comply with s 37 if
making payments to an employer (or former employer).

Company law implications

Where there is a corporate trustee, that trustee company will often be a subsidiary of the **19.206**
employer. Sections 136–140 of the Companies Act 2006[126] contain provisions relating to
subsidiaries owning shares in their holding company.

Section 136 contains a general prohibition on a body corporate from being a shareholder in **19.207**
its holding company.

This is subject to an exception in s 138(1) which provides that the prohibition does not apply **19.208**
where the subsidiary is concerned as a trustee unless the holding company or a subsidiary of it is
'beneficially entitled' under the trust.

In determining whether the holding company or a subsidiary are 'beneficially entitled', a **19.209**
number of things are disregarded:

(a) Any rights the subsidiary (ie the trustee company) has in its capacity as trustee, in particular any right to recover expenses or be remunerated out of the trust property and
any right to be indemnified out of trust property for liabilities resulting from the performance of trustee duties (s 138(2)(c)).
(b) Where shares in a company are held on trust for the purposes of a pension scheme:
(i) any 'residual interest' that has not vested in possession (s 139(1)). Residual interest for

---

[123] See SI 2006/560, art 2(1)(b), Sch, Pt 1.
[124] See s 37(7), as originally enacted, but not included in the new s 37 substituted by the Pensions Act 2004
from 6 April 2006.
[125] See SI 2009/82, Art 2(2)(c).
[126] Companies Act 2006, ss 138–140, replacing, from 1 October 2009, s 23 of and Sch 2 to the Companies
Act 1985. Schedule 2 itself replaced provisions originally added by the Companies (Beneficial Interests) Act
1983. See Ch 4 (Corporate trustees).

these purposes broadly means an ability to return surplus to an employer (whether in an ongoing scheme or in a wind-up situation): see s 139(2).

(ii) Any charge or lien on, or set-off against, scheme benefits enabling the employer to obtain discharge of a monetary obligation due to it from a member: see s 140.

Scheme provisions

19.210 There is, of course, a need to check if the scheme provisions allow for payment to an employer. Often there is a limitation in the scheme's amendment power on such payments (not limited to 'surplus' refunds). If so, it is likely that the limitation will be treated as applying to the investment provision, even if not expressly included (see *National Grid Co plc v Mayes*[127] and the BA case, *Stevens v Bell*[128]).

General fiduciary duties

19.211 The trustees will need to consider their general fiduciary duties:

(a) Do they have power to make the investment under the scheme rules?
(b) Is this an investment they should make and are they acting for a proper purpose? For example, are they being influenced by the interest of the employer rather than members?
(c) Have any conflicts of interest been appropriately managed?

19.212 See the determinations of the Pensions Ombudsman in *Re ES Group Pension Scheme*[129] (there is no mention here of any breach of s 40) and in *Went*.[130]

Other legislative considerations

19.213 There are also general financial services/pensions provisions that should be considered, for example:

(a) insider trading;
(b) general investment duties (prudence, diversification etc);
(c) trustees must not make day-to-day investment decisions;
(d) investments need to be managed by a fund manager;
(e) investments need to comply with the pension scheme's statement of investment principles and be made on written advice;
(f) A trustee cannot rely on exoneration clause in relation to investment matters: s 33 of the Pensions Act 1995.[131]

Conclusion

19.214 Employer-related investment is a complex minefield, both in legal terms and in the practical consequences of the legal requirements. It is important for trustees to consider (and keep under review):

(a) who falls within the 'employer' and 'connected and associated' net for their scheme;

---

[127] [2001] UKHL 20, [2001] 2 All ER 417, HL.
[128] [2002] EWCA Civ 672, CA.
[129] *Adams* (2009) 11 March, M00358-370 [2009] PLR 153 (King PO).
[130] (2008) 14 August, L00575 (Gordon Deputy PO).
[131] See Ch 14 (Trustee indemnities and exonerations).

(b) all transactions with such persons to consider whether the employer-related investment restrictions may be breached; and

(c) when investments held without a breach of the restrictions might subsequently breach the restrictions (whether because of changes in the connected and associated 'net' or because of changes in the investments held).

In practice, these issues are likely to arise more frequently (especially with the increase in **19.215** the use of contingent assets). Although raising employer-related investment issues may not make pensions lawyers popular (both with trustees, employers, and with other parties interested in securing a particular transaction—especially where it appears to otherwise be a good deal for the scheme), the potential for both criminal and personal liability generally tends to focus trustee minds.

20

EMPLOYERS AND SURPLUSES

Introduction[1]

20.1 This chapter looks at surpluses in pension schemes, in particular at:

(a) who owns the surplus—introduction;
(b) money purchase surpluses;
(c) defined benefit surpluses;
(d) surpluses on a winding-up;
(e) how does a surplus arise;
(f) using surplus in an on-going scheme;
(g) paying surplus to employers.

---

[1] See generally Kris Weber and Sian Williams, 'Pension scheme surpluses' in *Tolleys Pensions Law* (looseleaf) Ch G2A; Richard Nobles, *Pensions Employment and the Law* (Clarendon Press, 1993), esp Ch 7; Lord Browne-Wilkinson, 'Equity and its Relevance to Superannuation Today' (1992) 6 TLI 119; Philip Bennett, *Pension Fund Surpluses* (Sweet & Maxwell, 1994); Lord Millett 'Pension Funds and the Law of Trusts: The Tail Wagging the Dog?' (2000) 14 TLI 66; David Pollard, 'Pensions Law and Surpluses: A Fair Balance Between Employer and Members?' (2003) 17 TLI 2; and Noel Davis, 'Surpluses in Superannuation Funds—Where Are We Now?' (2001) 15 TLI 130. Also Nigel Inglis-Jones, 'Surplus: Where Are We Now?' (APL conference, 1998) and Mark Greenlees, 'The Treatment of Surpluses: An Exercise in Horsetrading?' (APL conference, 1991). In Canada, see Douglas Rienzo, 'Trust Law and Access to Pension Surplus' (2005) 25 Estates Trusts & Pensions Journal 14; and Mary Louise Dickson QC, 'Pension surplus' in TG Youdan (ed), *Equity, Fiduciaries and Trusts*

In the current economic conditions, surpluses in pension schemes are much less common. **20.2** But the issue of use of surpluses may well become more relevant again in the future. It raises interesting questions of trust law and pension scheme interpretation.

Who Owns the Surplus?

The 2001 Myners review on institutional investment[2] suggested that the law on ownership **20.3** of surplus within a pension scheme is unclear and that the issue should be referred to the Law Commission:

> 7.29 It has often been perceived that the interests of employers and scheme members diverge over the surplus. This is clearly true in a narrow sense: at any one time, more for one party to a particular fund clearly means less for the other.
>
> 7.30 But even for a single fund this may well not be true over the long term, and it is certainly not true across pension funds in general. Employers with a clear entitlement to part of the surplus are more likely to continue providing defined benefit schemes; and they are more likely to give those schemes the resources they need to be managed effectively.
>
> 7.32 Second, even where direct extraction of surplus might be considered, the sponsor may still face the possibility of extended litigation and uncertainty. This prospect serves nobody well. Its main effect is to weaken sponsors' interest in their schemes and to accelerate the move away from defined benefit provision. Greater certainty about access to at least a proportion of the surplus would help to maintain the viability of defined benefit schemes. It may be that no further clarification is possible here—and that some uncertainty is inevitable. But given the importance of the issue, this question should be thoroughly investigated.

The review recommended that the Law Commission should be asked to review whether the **20.4** objective of maximum clarity over ownership of the surplus can be achieved through legal change.

But in its 2002 Green Paper on pensions,[3] the then government announced that it was not **20.5** going to take this forward:

> A related issue, raised in the Myners report, is the ownership of scheme surplus. The Government has obtained Law Commission advice. This indicates that, from a legal perspective, the relevant issue in an ongoing scheme is not 'ownership' of a surplus but rather how the trustees are permitted or obliged by the trust deed and scheme rules to deal with any surplus. We believe that legislative intervention in this area would result in more, rather than less, complexity. In view of this, we are not proposing to legislate further.

This must be right. The issue when surpluses exist is whether the law on pension fund sur- **20.6** pluses strikes a fair balance between the interests of members and the rights of the employer (or its creditors where the employer is insolvent). The answer to this question requires a view to be taken as to what is a 'fair balance' in the context of surpluses in a pension scheme.

(a) Employers argue that they have paid contributions higher than was necessary and so they should be entitled to benefit from any surplus.

(Carswell, 1989). From Australia, Anthea Nolan, 'The Role of the Employment Contract in Superannuation; An Analysis Focusing on Surplus Repatriation Powers Conferred on Employers' (1996) 24 ABLR 341.

[2] 'Institutional investment in the UK: a review', report to HM Treasury by Paul Myners (6 March 2001).
[3] Page 57 of the Green Paper 'Simplicity, Security and Choice: Working and Saving for Retirement' (Cm 5677) issued on 17 December 2002.

(b) Conversely employees argue that pension schemes are set up primarily to provide them with benefits, that any surplus results from a good investment performance and that the surplus should be used entirely for their benefit.

20.7 The courts have, not surprisingly, sought to avoid this overall issue and instead taken refuge in the wording of the scheme concerned.[4]

20.8 Clearly it is possible to draft an occupational pension scheme that expressly provides for any surplus assets to be used to provide extra benefits for the members.[5]

20.9 Similarly, a scheme can be drafted to provide for the benefit of any surplus to pass to the employer (and be under its control),[6] subject to various limitations in the pensions legislation, in particular on payments to the employer in the Pensions Act 1995[7] and on on-going funding in the Pensions Act 2004.

20.10 Save to this extent, Parliament has not intervened to say that contribution holidays or refunds of surplus are not possible (and there has been a lot of legislation in the area in the last 25 years). Indeed, it is a fairly simple analysis to show that providing for surpluses to 'belong' to members will almost certainly discourage employers from setting up pension schemes on a final salary (or defined benefit) basis.

20.11 Thus Robert Walker J (as he then was) commented in National Grid[8] (at first instance):

> Parliament does have power to intervene, and has to a limited extent done so by s.37 of the Pensions Act 1995. It is open to debate whether more drastic legislative intervention would be in the best long-term interests of beneficiaries under pension schemes. As I have said, it is a matter of real concern that the destination of surplus should depend, as it often seems to depend, on subtle and complex arguments about the meaning of the scheme documents. But any general exclusion of employers from surplus would tend to make employers very reluctant to contribute to their pension schemes more than the bare minimum that they could get away with. That would be unfortunate, and it would be even more unfortunate if employers were driven to abandon final-salary, balance-of-cost schemes and were instead to turn to money-purchase schemes which may in the long term prove less advantageous to the beneficiaries.

20.12 Cory J in Canada in the Supreme Court in *Schmidt v Air Products*[9] was not convinced:

> It is suggested that if employers are not able to retrieve surpluses, they will be tempted to fund existing plans less generously. I cannot agree. First, unless the terms of the plan specifically preclude it, an employer is entitled to take a contribution holiday. Second, most pension plans require the level of employer contribution to be determined by an actuary. The employer will not be able to reduce the level of contribution unilaterally below that required according to standard actuarial practice. Third, employers are required by legislation to make up any unfunded liability. Finally, the fact that some employers cannot recoup surplus on termination is unlikely to influence the conduct of employers as a whole. In order to obtain registration, plans

---

[4] See eg Walton J in *Re Imperial Foods* [1986] 2 All ER 802 and Vinelott J in *Taylor v Lucas Pensions Trust* [1994] OPLR 29.

[5] But before 2006 (when the tax rules changed) subject to the limits on benefits imposed by the Inland Revenue if the scheme was to qualify for tax approval.

[6] Eg by the availability of a contribution holiday or refund to the employer.

[7] For example, the minimum funding requirement in ss 56–61, and the provisions on repayment to employers in ss 37 and 76.

[8] *National Grid Co plc v Laws* [1997] OPLR 207 at 230 (Robert Walker J). Eventually upheld on appeal in the House of Lords [2001] UKHL 20, [2001] 2 All ER 417, HL.

[9] [1994] 2 SCR 611, [1995] OPLR 283, [1995] PLR 75, Can SC.

created since 1981 must make provision for distribution of surplus on termination. It is generally only in pre-existing plans that the problem of ownership of surplus arises and, as the results of these appeals demonstrate, even then the employee entitlement to the surplus is not automatic.

This looks unconvincing in a UK context. It allows for contribution holidays or reductions by an employer, but seeks to prohibit actual refunds (which are much rarer). **20.13**

The problem arises where the provisions of the scheme are not clear on these points (or at least not clear enough to overcome any presumptions about scheme interpretation that the courts may have). The courts then have to construe the trust documents. It is at this point that the issue of a 'fair balance' can perhaps be said to arise. **20.14**

This chapter looks at the attitude that the courts have taken in this analysis. It concludes that, if anything, the courts are leaning too far towards the interests of employees and away from those of employers. This would reinforce the shift by employers away from final salary pension schemes and towards money purchase only. This is probably not an efficient use of resources for an ageing population (collective saving can be much more efficient than individual[10]). **20.15**

Primary obligation on the trust

As discussed in Chapter 1 ('What is an occupational pension scheme?'), generally UK occupational pension schemes are established so that the primary obligation to provide the relevant retirement benefits (pension/lump sum) rests with the trustees and not with the employer. **20.16**

The structure could, fairly easily, have been framed instead so that the trust assets were a security device. The primary obligation to pay the pensions could have rested with the employer, with the trust merely providing a funded form of security to ensure that obligation was ultimately met. **20.17**

This alternative structure can be seen in: **20.18**

(a) the German pension system (where pensions payable by employers are generally simple debt obligations, although with security in the form of compulsory insurance); and
(b) in some UK state pensions (eg the Civil Service Pension Scheme, the Teachers Pension Scheme, the Fire Services Pension Scheme etc) where there are no underlying assets and the pension remains an unsecured obligation of the relevant state body.

A defined benefit occupational pension scheme will have a trust liability to pay benefits at a particular level to members of the pension scheme (employees and ex employees) and to their spouses and dependants. Usually this involves a pension for life. **20.19**

These obligations are generally payable at some time in the future. The actual amount that will be needed to meet the obligation is not known at today's date (at least in the case of defined benefits as opposed to defined contribution benefits). **20.20**

It is clear that at any one time the level of assets held within the pension scheme (shares and land etc) may, on an actuarial estimate, be considered to be more (or less) than the underlying anticipated future liability. This gives rise to a potential surplus or deficit in the fund. **20.21**

---

[10] Lower charges, more expert investment, more risk-taking and so (in theory) higher returns.

Money Purchase Surpluses

20.22   A money purchase (or defined contribution) pension scheme usually involves benefits being calculated by reference to a notional account of the member concerned.[11] This account is credited with payments into the scheme (whether by the member or by the employer in respect of the member).

20.23   The payments in are then usually invested by the trustees (within a range) as part of the assets of the scheme, commonly with an element of choice by the member concerned. Investment gains and losses are credited to the account and, when the member retires (or dies or seeks a transfer etc), the assets are realized. An amount equal to the net amount realized is used to provide the relevant benefits.

20.24   At that stage the benefits can either be paid in cash or, if (say) a pension is to be provided, the relevant benefits secured by purchasing an insurance policy that provides the relevant benefits (often outside the scheme). Thus at all stages of this process it is possible for the trustees precisely to match the underlying liability.

20.25   However, at this accumulation phase surpluses (and deficits) can arise. The scheme and trustees can incur liabilities not matched by underlying assets (eg if they give misleading advice, fail to invest quickly enough etc).

Investment issues

20.26   Liabilities can also arise if the trustees do not completely match the actual investments with the notional investments in the member's account. This may be deliberate, although this would be fairly unusual in the UK.

20.27   It is more common in the US for these arrangements to be set up as 'accumulation funds'. This means that a particular level of return is promised, although the trustees can choose to invest the underlying assets in something else. For example, an interest rate based on a bank rate could be promised as a benefit, but the trustees could decide to use the money to try and beat the promise by investing (say) in equities. This is rather like the position of a bank in relation to a depositor, offering a fixed interest rate and assuming that it can use the money received to earn more elsewhere.

20.28   The original definition of 'money purchase benefits' in the pensions legislation only referred to benefits being linked to amounts contributed. There was no requirement for the relevant notional fund to be matched with an underlying asset.[12]

20.29   Surpluses can also arise in money purchase arrangements:

(a)   if the member leaves within the first two years—UK pensions law[13] currently allows for the scheme to provide for the employer's contributions to be forfeited and not be used

---

[11] See the definition in s 181 of the Pension Schemes Act 1993. This definition has caused some difficulties—see *Bridge Trustees Ltd v Houldsworth* [2011] UKSC 42, [2012] 1 All ER 659, SC and the retrospective amendments (not yet in force) envisaged by s 29 of the Pensions Act 2011.

[12] *Bridge Trustees Ltd v Houldsworth* [2011] UKSC 42, [2012] 1 All ER 659, SC overruling the earlier Court of Appeal decision in *AON Trust Corpn Ltd v KPMG* [2005] EWCA Civ 1004, [2006] 1 All ER 238 on this point. The amendments in s 29 of the Pensions Act 2011 to the relevant definition are intended to put the position back so that matching is required in order to qualify as a money purchase benefit for statutory purposes (potentially with retrospective effect).

[13] The preservation provisions in the Pension Schemes Act 1993.

to provide benefits for that member. The member's contributions would (normally) be refunded (less a tax charge). The employer's contributions usually remain in the fund and are used to cancel out ('frank') other contributions otherwise due from the employer;[14]

(b) if the member dies with no relevant beneficiaries, the value of the account cannot be used to provide benefits;

(c) similarly, before April 2006, the conditions of approval of an occupational pension scheme by the Inland Revenue included a restriction on the amount of benefits that could be paid.[15] If the amount in the member's account would be able to be used to purchase benefits greater than this level, the excess benefits could not be paid (and the relevant amount would remain in the scheme). This would mean that the entire value of the member's account was not able to be used to provide benefits to or in respect of that member;[16]

(d) forfeiture of benefits (and paying debts owed to the employer) are allowed in limited circumstances.[17] These are mainly limited to cases where the employee owes an obligation to the employer arising through a 'criminal, negligent or fraudulent act or omission' by the member.[18] Similarly, if the member is a trustee and has committed a breach of trust and so owes an obligation to the scheme, forfeiture is also allowed.[19]

Deficits or surpluses can also arise in what would otherwise look to be a money purchase **20.30** scheme if the ultimate pension benefit is not secured through the purchase of an annuity with an insurance company. If, instead, the annuity is provided within the scheme (ie the scheme actually pays out the pension, taking the risk as to whether or not the funding is actually sufficient to provide it), in effect the scheme is converted to a defined benefit scheme (although it still may remain within the definition of a money purchase scheme within the current pensions legislation[20]).

Defined Benefit Schemes: Surpluses

Final salary (or defined benefit) occupational schemes are more complex. Prior to a **20.31** winding-up of the scheme, the level of benefits provided by the scheme is usually independent of the level of assets within it.[21] There is no direct correlation between the level of assets within the scheme and the benefits to be provided.

---

[14] It is prudent to ensure that the trust deed makes it clear that this is possible—see Neuberger J in *Barclays Bank v Holmes* [2001] OPLR 37.

[15] The tax rules changed on and from 6 April 2006, when the tax rules in the Finance Act 2004 came into force. It was still possible for schemes to retain a benefit limit (as a matter of scheme design) on the same lines as the previous tax limits. In practice many schemes removed the limits in the case of money purchase benefits.

[16] In practice the maximum level of benefits was relatively high (and add-on benefits could be included—eg full indexation, large spouse pension).

[17] See ss 91–95 of the Pensions Act 1995 and *Freshfields on Corporate Pensions Law 2013* (ed Pollard and Magoffin) (Bloomsbury Publishing, 2013) Ch 14.

[18] Pensions Act 1995, s 91(5)(d).

[19] Pensions Act 1995, s 91(5)(e).

[20] *Bridge Trustees Ltd v Houldsworth* [2011] UKSC 42, [2012] 1 All ER 659, SC overruling the earlier Court of Appeal decision in *AON Trust Corpn Ltd v KPMG* [2005] EWCA Civ 1004, [2006] 1 All ER 238 on this point. The amendments in s 29 of the Pensions Act 2011 to the relevant definition are intended to put the position back so that matching is required in order to qualify as a money purchase benefit for statutory purposes (potentially with retrospective effect).

[21] One exception is the ability of the trustees to reduce statutory transfer payments (following a request by the member) where the scheme is underfunded—reg 7D of the Occupational Pension Schemes (Transfer

20.32 Instead the benefits are defined, usually by reference to a formula based on salary at the date of retiring or leaving employment. The standard benefit is an annual pension from age 60 or 65 of 1/60th of 'Final Pensionable Salary' (as defined in the scheme deeds) for every year of pensionable service within the scheme.

Measuring funding

20.33 It is obviously important for the relevant parties to have some idea of how well (or badly) a scheme is funded. The funding provides (as a minimum) security for the benefits. The more funding there is, the more likely it is that there will be sufficient assets when benefits actually start to be drawn.

20.34 Conversely, if there is not enough funding, then ultimately either the benefits must be reduced or additional funding provided (usually by the employer).

20.35 The Inland Revenue used (before 2006) also to be concerned to ensure that there was not too a great a level of funding within the scheme. Assets within the scheme are generally held tax-free and so the Revenue is losing (or at least deferring) tax that it would otherwise gain. Accordingly the tax legislation[22] used to impose limits on the assets that it allowed to be retained within occupational pension schemes with the benefit of this tax exemption. If these limits were exceeded, then either the surplus amount needed to be reduced within a time scale acceptable to the Inland Revenue or tax reliefs were (to an extent) withdrawn. There was no overriding provision in the tax legislation requiring a scheme to get rid of the surplus. The only sanction was that the scheme may suffer tax.

20.36 It is the job of the scheme's actuary to estimate, using suitable actuarial assumptions, the current level of the funding of the scheme. Clearly, in order to do this, the actuary needs to use various assumptions. The amount of money needed today to provide a pension for an individual (which may not start for a number of years) will depend on various factors, including:

(a) how long the member will live;

(b) whether he or she has a spouse or dependants who will receive a pension following the member's death (and if so how long they will live);

(c) how much is assumed as an investment return between today and the date the pension actually is payable;

(d) what level of increases to the pension is given (either as an increase to the pension once in payment or as a revaluation amount before it starts being paid);

(e) the relevant 'annuity rate' assumed once the pension actually starts coming to payment; and

(f) what options the member may choose (eg to commute part of his pension at retirement or to take a transfer to another scheme).

20.37 There is a relatively wide range of assumptions that can be used by the actuary in these circumstances. A wide range of answers can result from the range of assumptions used. No one of these answers is 'right'. They may fall within a reasonableness band. What for one actuary

---

Values) Regulations 1996 (SI 1996/1847). In addition, in some circumstances trustees will consider the level of scheme funding when deciding on discretionary benefits—see eg the Pensions Ombudsman determination in *Brown* (2011) 28 October, 83842/1 (Irvine Deputy PO).

[22] See Sch 22 to the Income and Corporation Taxes Act 1988. This was repealed from 6 April 2006 by the Finance Act 2004.

is a surplus can be another actuary's deficit. The end result depends on how cautious or optimistic the actuary is (or is instructed to be).

Different solvency tests

There are four main funding tests[23] currently in use in relation to defined benefit occupational pension schemes. **20.38**

Most actuarial valuation methods now look at the assets within the scheme as the market value of those assets on the valuation date (ignoring any employer covenant or employer-related investment). **20.39**

The main variation between the methods is then within the assessment of the liabilities—in effect the net current value of the anticipated liabilities. The critical component in any actuarial valuation is the discount rate used—how are the anticipated future benefit payments discounted to a net current value?[24] The larger the discount rate (or rate of return on investments), the smaller the net present value capital amount of the benefit liabilities and so more likely for there to be an actuarial 'surplus'. **20.40**

This is a crucial issue when looking at actuarial valuations. **20.41**

Valuation method	Discount rate
Company accounts (FRS 17/IAS 19)	AA corporate bonds
Scheme specific funding (Pt 3 of the Pensions Act 2004)	As agreed with trustees (usually) (NB The Pensions Regulator says it is generally looking for more caution than in FRS 17)
Pension Protection Fund (PPF) valuation (s 179 of the Pensions Act 2004)	Buyout (see below) approximation using defined assumptions—but only valuing PPF protected benefits
Buyout (s 75 of the Pensions Act 1995)	Insurance company discount rates (usually government gilts less a margin)

If a surplus is estimated, it may well only be transient. It could be affected by (say) a change in asset values or a change in benefit liabilities (eg longevity or change in interest rates). **20.42**

Surplus in company accounts

In recent years, the combination of: **20.43**

(a) a reduction in yield on government bonds (gilts) (used commonly in assessing buy-out rates, and, more commonly, recently, in relation to scheme-specific funding); and

(b) rising AA corporate bond yields,

have meant that in many cases a surplus can be shown in a sponsoring company's accounts (under the relevant accounting standards, FRS 17 or IAS 19) but that the valuation used by

---

[23] Less relevant now are some older measures—eg the statutory minimum funding requirement (MFR) basis under the Pensions Act 1995 applicable until replaced by scheme specific funding (from December 2005) under the Pensions Act 2004. Also, the Government Actuary Department (GAD) basis applicable for tax surplus checking purposes under ICTA 1988 (and now not applicable under the Finance Act 2004 rules).

[24] See the summary of the methods taken from the expert actuary's evidence in *Alitalia-Linee Aeree Italiane SPA v Rotunno* [2008] EWHC 185 (Ch) at [33]–[38] (Henderson J).

trustees when agreeing scheme-specific funding for an ongoing valuation (and also any s 75 buy-out valuation) still shows a significant deficit.

20.44 In these circumstances, a surplus on an accounting basis could still mean a deficit on the scheme-funding basis, so that there needs to be a recovery plan with deficit contributions and that the trustees are not likely to allow contribution holidays, etc.

20.45 A surplus on the accounting measure can still result in an increase in the company's net assets as shown in its accounts. Whether or not such a surplus is shown as an asset in the company's accounts can depend on the operation of an accounting interpretation, IFRIC 14.[25] This interpretation is difficult to analyse as a legal matter, (accounting advice is needed) but broadly IFRIC 14 states that the employer needs to have an unconditional right to use the surplus at some point during the life of the plan or on its wind-up for a surplus to be recognized in the employer's accounts.

20.46 Even if a surplus appears, it seems not to be a realized profit when calculating distributable reserves (a deficit is probably a realised loss).[26]

Surplus on the PPF basis

20.47 Surplus on the Pension Protection Fund (PPF) basis[27] can be helpful in that:

(a) it can reduce the risk-based PPF levy;
(b) it can mean that various events are no longer notifiable to the Pensions Regulator under the notifiable events regime;[28]
(c) it can make it easier for the employer to agree corporate transactions with the Pensions Regulator or the trustees; and
(d) there are some (complicated) provisions allowing trustees to agree settlement or discharge of a debt on an employer arising under s 75 of the Pensions Act 1995 without prejudicing the scheme's ultimate eligibility to enter the PPF. Notification to, and validation by, the board of the PPF is required.[29]

Surplus on scheme-specific funding basis

20.48 Surplus on the scheme-specific funding basis (under Pt 3 of the Pensions Act 2004) may well be useful in that:

(a) there will be no need for a recovery plan (under s 226);
(b) if there is no recovery plan, the other funding documents do not have to be provided to the Pensions Regulator,[30] although they may well be requested by the Pensions Regulator anyway—for example, as part of its annual return mechanics;

---

[25] International Financial Reporting Interpretations Committee (IFRIC) issued an Interpretation, IFRIC 14, in July 2007 on 'IAS 19—the limit on a defined benefit asset, minimum funding requirements and their interaction'.
[26] See the ICAEW Technical Release: TECH50/04 'Guidance on the effect of FRS 17 "Retirement benefits" and IAS 19 "Employee benefits" on realised profits and losses' issued in November 2004—see <http://www.icaew.com>.
[27] As shown in an actuarial valuation under s 179 of the Pensions Act 2004.
[28] Pensions Act 2004, s 69.
[29] Pension Protection Fund (Entry Rules) Regulations 2005 (SI 2005/590) reg 2(3).
[30] Under Pensions Act 2004, s 226(6).

(c) it may mean that there is not a 'relevant deficit' when considering the need for clearance from the Pensions Regulator in relation to its moral hazard powers under ss 38–51 of the Pensions Act 2004. Various employer-related events (eg change of structure, return of capital) could (without a surplus) otherwise be potentially 'Type A' events (and so may involve considering whether clearance from the Pensions Regulator would be desirable). A surplus may mean that there is less need for clearance;[31] and

(d) it may well be possible to agree with the trustees that any surplus can be used to offset ongoing contributions—for example, for future service benefits or, potentially, even to fund money purchase sections (see *Barclays Bank* case discussed at para 20.101 below).

Buy-out basis (or winding-up basis)

Lastly, the funding could be assessed by estimating how much it would cost to purchase annuities from an insurance company that would match the current liabilities of the scheme (assuming it wound-up on the day in question). This would allow the benefits to be (in effect) fully secured by purchase outside the scheme (although they would, of course, depend on the solvency of the relevant insurance company). There is still some degree of variation in the amount. The rates quoted by insurers vary from day to day (depending on how keen they are to accept this sort of business). **20.49**

The statutory debt on an employer arising under s 75 of the Pensions Act 1995[32] in certain situations (eg the scheme starting to wind-up, the employer entering an insolvency process etc) has, since 2 September 2005, needed to be calculated with benefit liabilities being estimated on a buy-out basis. **20.50**

The buy-out basis (involving the purchase of insurance annuities) is usually more expensive than the basis used for ongoing funding.[33] This is because the insurance company will be committing to a long-term liability. It will be cautious about the level of growth it assumes on the underlying assets to meet that liability (contrast the position where it does not guarantee a particular pension but instead merely offers to manage the underlying assets). **20.51**

In addition, the rates quoted will include an allowance for the expenses and profits of the insurance company, as well as a solvency reserve requirement imposed by the government as part of the regulation of insurers. **20.52**

Broadly, one reason for employers setting up a pension scheme is because the costs of purchasing relevant annuities from insurance companies are higher than might be anticipated had the scheme remained ongoing and used its ongoing actuarial assumptions. In effect, occupational pension schemes could be seen as a sort of 'do it yourself' insurance company, which had lighter regulation (and hence is hoped to be less expensive) when compared to an insurance product. **20.53**

Surplus on a Scheme Winding-Up

On a winding-up of a pension scheme (eg because the scheme no longer needs to be continued or the employer becomes insolvent), ultimately the trustees must use the available assets to **20.54**

---

[31] TPR's clearance guidance (June 2009) at para 49.
[32] On s 75, see D Pollard, *Corporate Insolvency: Employment and Pension Rights* 5th edn (Bloomsbury Professional, 2013) Chs 57–62.
[33] See *Alitalia-Linee Aeree Italiane SPA v Rotunno* [2008] EWHC 185 (Ch) at [37]–[38] (Henderson J).

provide the benefits. If there is a deficit, a debt may arise on the employer under s 75 of the Pensions Act 1995 and the pension protection fund under the Pensions Act 2004 may apply. Subject to this, the trustees will look to secure the benefits through the purchase of annuities with insurance companies (to match the underlying benefit liabilities). Members have a right to transfer to other arrangements (taking a cash equivalent), but they cannot usually be forced to convert to a money purchase arrangement.

20.55 On a winding-up, discretionary benefits are not allowed for. For example, future pay rises (for active members) or any discretionary benefits such as discretionary increases to pensions in payment. Some levels of discretionary pension increases may be guaranteed (eg inflation up to 5 per cent) either by the trust deed or by statute,[34] but pension rises over and above this will be discretionary, usually only with the consent of the employer and the trustees. These discretionary benefits are not included within the amounts allowed for on a winding-up.

20.56 Commonly this used to mean that on a winding-up, schemes were pretty well funded and had sufficient to buy-out the accrued benefits (ignoring discretionary benefits). Although buy-out costs tended to be greater than ongoing costs, there would be no future salary increases to be taken into account nor the discretionary benefits.

20.57 Scott J (as he then was) gave a good analysis in 1990 in *Davis v Richards & Wallington Industries Ltd*:[35]

> The 1975 scheme... was one in which each employee's pension entitlement was based on the level of his or her final salary. In the nature of things an individual's salary tends to rise during the course of his or her employment, both by reason of annual salary rises and by reason of promotion. In any one year, an employee's 5 per cent contribution to the fund would be based on the salary for that year, but the funding of the expectant pension on retirement would be based on the expected higher level of the salary at the time of retirement. The employer's contribution in each year would be based on an actuarial calculation of the sum necessary to fund a pension on that higher salary level. So where a pension scheme based on final salary level terminates, there will almost inevitably be a surplus. Each employee who is under retirement age will be entitled to benefits payable in the future but based on his or her salary at the date of termination. But the funding of the benefits and the employer's contributions before the termination date will have been based on the higher level of his or her expected final salary. So on the termination there is bound to be a surplus in the fund.
>
> One of the options open to an employee of the group when leaving his or her employment with less than five years' qualifying service[36] was, subject to certain specified limits, to have a refund of his or her contributions to the scheme. Both before and after the execution of the definitive deed a number of employees availed themselves of this option. Their contributions were refunded to them. But, of course, the contributions paid on their behalf by their employers remained in the scheme and enhanced the size of the surplus.

20.58 But in recent years, the cost of purchasing annuities with insurance companies has risen (and assets may have not kept pace). So deficits are more common. Even if there is thought to be a surplus on initial start of winding-up, this can change over time (eg as market interest rates, annuity rates, and asset values vary).[37]

---

[34] See Pensions Act 1995, s 50.

[35] [1990] 1 WLR 1511 at 1528 (Scott V-C).

[36] This is now reduced to two years' qualifying service—see the preservation legislation in the Pension Schemes Act 1993.

[37] For examples of changes in funding positions, see *BESTrustees plc v Kaupthing Singer & Friedlander Ltd* [2012] EWHC 629 (Ch), [2012] 3 All ER 874 (Sales J) (big variation in buy-out costs over time, but did not

If there is a surplus on a scheme winding-up, the question will arise as to what happens to it. **20.59** It is more common than in an ongoing situation for trustees to have a discretion to use surplus to increase benefits for members (up to Inland Revenue limits, if retained by the relevant scheme after the tax changes in April 2006). Any ultimate surplus arising after the exercise of the trustee's discretion will usually revert to the employer. On the issues in relation to the exercise of discretion by trustees, see para 20.132 below.

Other schemes may not include a discretion on member benefit increases for the trustee, but **20.60** instead one for the employer. Usually this will not be a fiduciary power in the hands of the employer, but can be exercised in its own interests.[38]

A resulting trust may be implied if there is no express provision.[39] **20.61**

Closed schemes

Trustees have the power, in some circumstances, to defer the actual purchase of annuities. **20.62** In effect they can defer a winding-up and choose to continue the pension scheme as a closed scheme,[40] paying benefits as they fall due. This may be attractive for large occupational pension schemes where the amount of annuity to be bought will, in fact, be larger than many insurance companies. There is, however, a risk for the trustees—what if the investments underperform?

The trustees run the risk of a later challenge as having made the wrong decisions. Given that **20.63** trustees are generally unpaid, they are often reluctant to do this.

The power to continue the scheme as closed in these circumstances can be contained within **20.64** the trust deed or, in certain circumstances, under s 38 of the Pensions Act 1995.

How Does a Surplus Arise Over Time?

Clearly, the relevant actuarial assumptions need to look to the long term. A 20-year-old who **20.65** starts work may not draw her pension for 40 years and may then live for another 30 years. The financial market (and the law) does generally not have many examples of such long-term obligations.

The assumptions used by the actuary are almost certainly likely to prove mistaken. It is not **20.66** in fact possible for someone to estimate accurately matters such as likely final salary, date of death, numbers of members married, level of investment return etc.

For this reason actuarial valuations are carried out at intervals (under the Pensions Act at **20.67** least every three years). In effect, a check is made to see how the actual circumstances of the scheme have matched the assumptions previously envisaged. If the liabilities are less than the assets (eg because pay rises have not been as high as envisaged or there have been a number

---

affect s 75 debt) and, from Canada, *Kidd v The Canada Life Assurance Co* 2013 ONSC 1868 (Perell J) (surplus severely reduced as partial winding-up continued).

[38] See the discussion on this, in particular in relation to *Mettoy*, in Ch 11 (Employer powers—non-fiduciary).
[39] *Air Jamaica v Charlton* [1999] 1 WLR 1399, PC.
[40] Ie closed to the entry of new members and, probably, with the cessation of accrual of further pensionable service (and hence benefits). See s 38 of the Pensions Act 1995 for a statutory power in some (limited) circumstances.

of redundancies) or, conversely, there are more assets than envisaged (eg because the stock market is booming), the valuation on an ongoing basis will show a surplus. It is important to note that there could easily be a surplus on one basis (eg the FRS17 accounting number), but deficit on a buy-out basis.

20.68 In 1999 in the Supreme Court of South Africa in *TEK Corpn Provident Fund v Lorentz*,[41] Marais JA held:

> Defined benefit pension funds do not exist to generate surpluses but they may arise when reality and actuarial expectation do not coincide. In assessing the financial health of a pension fund an actuary is gazing into the proverbial crystal ball to see what the future will hold. The use of the metaphor is not intended to demean the exercise; it is highly sophisticated and requires considerable training and skill, yet it remains, when all is said and done, an exercise in prophecy. Some of the data available may be relatively immutable and provide a secure foundation for predictions. Much of it is not. There are a host of factors about which assumptions have to be made because they lie in the future. Examples are rates of return upon different categories of investment, the rate of inflation, governmental fiscal policy, increases in salary, mortality rates for active and retired members, the rate of employee turnover, the incidence of disability, and the extent to which early retirement options may be exercised. The list is not exhaustive but it suffices to show the very considerable role that assumption plays in the assessment of the financial soundness of a pension fund and explains why even the most meticulously assessed valuation may be confounded by subsequent experience. While it is obviously so that the funds necessary to ensure that the defined benefits which the pension fund must provide are paid and will continue to be paid, are sacrosanct and may not be used for the benefit of the employer, that is not necessarily so of funds which are plainly surplus to that requirement. I say 'plainly' advisedly because the existence of a surplus at any particular point in the history of a fund may be so potentially transitory that it would be imprudent to diminish the fund by eliminating the surplus.

20.69 Clearly then, if an actuarial valuation shows a surplus, the issue arises as to whether this should be applied for the benefit of the employer or the members or someone else or not applied at all. In order to examine this question it is necessary to have some regard to the funding of pension schemes.

20.70 Commonly occupational pension schemes which provide defined benefits will envisage only a fixed level of contribution by members (say 5 per cent of salary). The scheme will envisage (either in a discretionary or binding form) contribution of the 'balance of costs' by the employer.

20.71 In effect the employer will be the 'funder' of last resort.

(a) Some schemes will include within the trust deed an obligation on the employer to make up this funding: eg where the trustee has a right to require funding at a level 'necessary to provide the benefits' or 'as determined by the actuary'.

(b) Other schemes will not have included an obligation on the employer. Instead they allow the employer the discretion as to whether or not to fund (but they often include a provision entitling the trustees to wind-up the fund if they are not satisfied with the funding level).

(c) Some other schemes (particularly those which relate to the public sector or privatized companies) envisage that the employer will always contribute a multiple of the contributions of the members/employees.

---

[41] 1999 (4) SA 884 (SCA), [1999] OPLR 137, SC South Africa.

It may be that the scheme also envisages that employee contributions can rise as well if fund- **20.72**
ing is needed. Examples of this are the Electricity Pension Schemes, the National Coal Board
Scheme and others. It is not coincidental that these have been the subject of relatively recent
litigation.[42]

How Does Surplus Affect Benefits?

It would be odd for an employer to allow trustees to have a discretion over the level of benefits **20.73**
being provided, particularly given that the employer is the funder of last resort.

However, there are some occupational schemes that do provide for discretions to be given **20.74**
to trustees (eg in the form of a unilateral amendment power or power to increase benefits[43]).
However, it is far more common for these powers to require the employer's consent or to be
a unilateral power in the hands of the employer alone.

The main exception to this common position is that some schemes include a unilateral power **20.75**
for trustees to increase benefits if there is a surplus revealed on the ultimate winding-up of a
scheme. Many (older) schemes envisage that the trustees have a discretion to use any funds
remaining after mainstream benefits have been secured to increase those benefits (subject to
limits imposed by the Inland Revenue). Other schemes do not give a unilateral discretion to
the trustees in this situation. Instead, they either require the consent of the employer or give
the discretion to the employer itself (or instead provide for the monies to form the excess
funds to be repaid to the employer).

Using Surplus in an Ongoing Scheme

There are four main methods in which a surplus can be utilized in an ongoing scheme:[44] **20.76**

(a) it could be left in the scheme (as a buffer for future variations);
(b) it could be used to reduce future employer contributions;
(c) it could be used to increase benefits for some or all members (some variants of this are to
     be allowed to reduce future member contributions or to refund money to members[45]); or
(d) it could be paid to the employer.

As Lord Hoffmann said in the *National Grid*[46] case: **20.77**

> There are only two ways of dealing with an actuarial surplus. You can pay more money out of
> the scheme or you can reduce the amount of money coming in.

---

[42] See *Cowan v Scargill* [1985] Ch 270 (Megarry V-C); *British Coal Corpn v British Coal Staff Superannuation Fund Scheme Trustees* [1995] 1 All ER 912 (Vinelott J); *National Grid v Laws & Mayes* [2000] ICR 174, CA; [2001] 2 All ER 417, HL.
[43] See eg the schemes in *Aitken v Christy Hunt* [1991] PLR 1 (Ferris J) and *Law Debenture Trust plc v Lonrho Africa* [2002] EWHC 2732 (Ch), [2003] OPLR 167 (Patten J).
[44] See para 4.3.21 of the Goode Report (1993).
[45] Refunding money to members (save for a refund of member contributions if no vested benefits are provided) is generally not allowed as an authorized payment under the tax rules in the Finance Act 2004 (or before 2006 by the Inland Revenue out of approved schemes).
[46] *National Grid v Lawes & Mayes* [2001] UKHL 20, [2001] 2 All ER 417 at [7], HL.

20.78 In deciding which of these courses of actions can be taken, it is crucial to examine the terms of the underlying trust instrument. This is crucial in determining not only who has the decision-making power (does it require the agreement of the trustee and the employer or is it unilateral in one or the other?) but also as to whether this specific action is allowed at all. Does the deed (for example) expressly prohibit payments back to the employer?

20.79 The case law in this area inevitably develops based on the construction of the individual documents. Knox J in *LRT Pension Fund Trustee v Hatt*[47] quoted with approval the words of Sir Robin Cooke P (as he then was) in the Court of Appeal in New Zealand:[48]

> Consideration of the merits are of little importance. What must be decisive are the terms of the trust constituted by the particular scheme.

20.80 When surpluses were more common, the issue became fairly political. Battles were waged in the newspapers involving complaints by members (and some unions) that 'our money has been stolen' by an employer taking contribution holidays.

20.81 In *TEK Corpn Provident Fund v Lorentz*[49] in South Africa, Marais JA commented:

> [17] It has often been argued that in a situation like the present (sometimes described as 'balance of cost' pension schemes) where the employer is the ultimate guarantor of the financial soundness of the fund, any surplus should enure to its benefit as the members of the fund carry no risk in that regard. The contention seems to me to be unduly simplistic but whatever its merits (if any) may be in equity, it begs the question whether any such entitlement exists in law. As Warner J observed in *Mettoy Pension Trustees Ltd v Evans* [1991] 2 All ER 513 (Ch) at 551b 'One cannot in my opinion, in construing the rules of a "balance of cost" pension scheme relating to surplus, start from an assumption that any surplus belongs morally to the employer.' Once a surplus arises it is *ipso facto* an integral component of the fund. Unless the employer can point to a relevant rule of the fund or statutory enactment or principle of the common law which confers such entitlement or empowers the trustees to use the surplus for its benefit, the employer has no right in law to the surplus. It goes without saying that whatever negotiations may be taking place behind the scenes to cater for such situations by way of legislation, as has been done in some other countries, this court can judge the matter only in accordance with existing law. In *Schmidt v Air Products Canada Ltd* [1994] 2 SCR 611 Cory J, writing for the majority, said: 'Regrettably a comprehensive approach to the issues arising from pension surplus has yet to be enacted in any part of this country. The courts have on a number of occasions been required to determine the allocation of pension surplus. Yet the courts are limited in their approach by the necessity of applying the sometimes inflexible principles of contract and trust law. The question of entitlement to surplus raises issues involving both social policy and taxation policy. The broad policy issues which are raised by surplus disputes would be better resolved by legislation than by a case-by-case consideration or individual plans. Yet that is what now must be undertaken.' (At 652d–e). I echo those sentiments.

20.82 Similarly, Knox J in *LRT Pension Fund Trustee v Hatt*[50] approved the comments in the consultation document issued in September 1992 by the Pension Law Review Committee (the Goode Committee). That committee stated:

> 9.5 In a defined benefit scheme, the object is to ensure that there are sufficient assets to match the scheme's liabilities as they arise. If this matching of assets and liabilities could be done

---

[47] [1993] OPLR 225, [1993] PLR 227 (Knox J).
[48] *Re UEB Industries Pension Plan* [1992] 1 NZLR 294 at 298, NZCA. See also *Stevens v Bell* [2002] EWCA Civ 672, [2002] OPLR 207, CA and the discussion in Ch 17 (Amendment powers).
[49] 1999 (4) SA 884, SC Sth Africa.
[50] [1993] OPLR 225 at 266 (Knox J).

with perfect foresight, all the assets of the fund would always be required to meet the liabilities (which are individuals' actual or prospective entitlement to pension benefits), there would no surpluses and deficits, and the question of ownership would, to that extent be less problematic.

9.6 In practice, however, it is impossible to assess the level of contributions to a pension fund with sufficient precision to ensure that assets and liabilities always match, simply because there is no practical possibility of predicting economic performance and the individual behaviour of scheme members with the accuracy which would be required. Because of the uncertainties inherent in forecasting the value of future assets and liabilities, and because of the tendency of deficits and surpluses to appear and disappear within relatively short periods of time, it is normal for assumptions to be made which are deliberately conservative. Rather than aiming at a perfect balance, and an equal probability that the fund will turn out to be in deficit as in surplus, it is usual to aim for a situation where the probability of a scheme's being in surplus is greater than its being in deficit. In recent years, large pension surpluses have arisen, largely because of dramatic and unexpected increases in the actuarially assessed value of equities in which pension funds are invested, but also because of lower than expected preserved pension costs resulting from the contraction of industrial employment. But since these trends may be reversed, one year's surplus may easily become the following year's deficit.

9.7 The existence of surpluses and deficits also depends heavily on the methodology used by the scheme actuary and on the assumptions which underpin the assessed value of the scheme's assets. The difference between a fund's assets and its liabilities (the surplus or deficit) tends to be small relative to the size of the assets and liabilities themselves. This means that small variations in the assumptions underpinning the actuarial assessment of the value of assets and liabilities can result in disproportionately large changes in the surplus or deficit, or in the conversion of one into the other. Because there is no single method for assessing the state of a fund, it is possible for a scheme to be in deficit on one approach whilst simultaneously in surplus on another.

9.8 Trustees cannot approve the return of a surplus to the employer unless they are given the power to do so in the trust deed. Where the power does not exist, it may be introduced either through the scheme's own powers of amendment or by a modification order authorised by the OPB. So long as the scheme is active, the trust fund must be kept intact to meet present and future liabilities. On the other hand, there is usually nothing to prevent the employer from taking a contribution holiday, for this does not involve the removal of trust assets, it merely defers their augmentation.

9.9 For all these reasons the question of whether a continuing fund is in surplus or in deficit cannot be answered with any precision, (though it is no less important for that), and the concept of ownership of a surplus is even more uncertain than that of ownership of the fund as a whole. Nevertheless, trustees and actuaries are required to take a view on the existence of surpluses and deficits during the lifetime of the scheme, if only because tax legislation requires surpluses arising under an approved scheme to be eradicated over a given period. The position is further complicated by the fact that surplus in a continuing scheme may mean one thing for Inland Revenue purposes, another for Department of Social Security and OPB purposes and a third from the view point of the actuary.

9.10 Where the scheme rules provide, employers may be required to make good deficits. The scheme rules may also empower the trustees, with or without the consent of the employer, to utilise surpluses to improve benefits. There are provisions in social security legislation which will require limited indexation of pensions in payment and accrued pension rights to be the first charge on any surplus. These provisions have not yet been brought into effect, except that schemes may not pay any part of surplus to the employer unless limited price indexation has been introduced.

The position of the trustees in terms of applying trust rules in this situation is difficult. The **20.83** courts are not particularly helpful in giving clear guidance.

Partly this is because each situation does depend on the particular circumstances of the **20.84** scheme, in particular its individual rules. Having said that, there had, until the early part of this century, been a clear failure by the courts to give some sort of guidance as to the presumptions they will apply when interpreting pension scheme documents.[51] Would they, for example:

(a) always lean in favour of the beneficiaries on the basis that it will be the employer who initially drew up the document?;[52]

(b) always regard a trust as being irrevocable (and so no payment back to the employer) unless there are clear words making it revocable?;[53]

(c) construe powers given to employers as being fiduciary[54] or as subject to an implied duty of trust and confidence?[55]

20.85 In practice, the courts have moved towards a more literal approach, saying that there is no one philosophy to adopt when interpreting trust deeds—see Chapter 17 ('Amendment Powers'). In *Stevens v Bell*,[56] Arden LJ held:

> At the end of the day, the function of the court is to construe the document without any predisposition as to the correct philosophical approach.

20.86 Looking at the trust implications of the four routes in turn:

Leave Surplus within the Scheme

20.87 Clearly, a surplus in the scheme gives more security for the ultimate provision of benefits to members. Unless the scheme mandates or requires something else (and some schemes do envisage a requirement on trustees to use surplus for benefit improvements etc) it may well be a permitted use of surplus to allow it remain within the scheme and for the ultimate position to be seen as the scheme progresses.

20.88 Having said that, if a surplus arises and the trustees are satisfied about the security of the scheme to provide benefits, the presumption must be that the employer's wishes in relation to use of the surplus (eg for a contribution reduction) would need to be given great weight by the trustees. It is not a proper part of their role to build up unnecessary surpluses.[57]

Reduce Future Employer or Member Contributions

20.89 The terms of the actual contribution rule is crucial here. If the rule provides that the employer has the discretion about the amount contributed or must contribute up to a certain minimum

---

[51] See generally on this, R Nobles, *Pensions Employment and the Law* (Clarendon Press, 1993) Ch 2.

[52] See the decision of the Court of Appeal in *National Grid* [1999] PLR 37. Later overturned by the House of Lords.

[53] See the decision of the Canadian Supreme Court in *Schmidt v Air Products* [1994] 2 SCR 611, [1995] OPLR 283.

[54] See Ch 11 (Employer powers—non-fiduciary) and Browne-Wilkinson V-C in *Imperial Tobacco* [1991] 2 All ER 597 at 604j; Robert Walker J in *National Grid* [1997] PLR 157 at [88] (doubting whether the decision of Warner J in *Mettoy* [1990] 1 WLR 1587 that an employer power was fiduciary would be so held today); Knox J in *Hillsdown* [1997] 1 All ER 862, [1996] PLR 427 at 448; and Waddell CJ in *Lock v Westpac* (1991) 25 NSWLR 593, [1991] PLR 167 at 177—noted by John Gover (1992) 9 Australian Bar Review 172. Contrast Cooke P in New Zealand in *Cullen v Pension Holdings* (1991) 1 NZSC 40,233 at 40,298.

[55] See *Imperial Tobacco* [1991] 2 All ER 597, [1991] 1 WLR 589.

[56] [2002] EWCA Civ 672, [2002] OPLR 207, CA.

[57] See eg *Alitalia-Linee Aeree Italiane SPA v Rotunno* [2008] EWHC 185 (Ch) at [87], (Henderson J): 'to require the Trustees to request contributions from Alitalia by reference to the buy-out basis, even when the

level decided by the trustees (or the actuary) 'as being necessary to secure the benefits' then if there is a surplus it is likely that the employer will be able to insist on reducing the contribution rate below that which it would have otherwise have paid had there not been a surplus.[58]

The correct analysis is that there is not a cancellation of a debt obligation or a payment back **20.90** to the company of the surplus that is being used to reduce the 'normal' contribution rate. Instead, the reduced rate is the only rate that is payable. This is important. It means that such a reduction in contributions is not in contravention of a provision that prohibits payments back to the employer.[59]

An example of the analysis on this is the decision of the Supreme Court in South Africa in **20.91** *TEK Corpn Provident Fund v Lorentz*.[60] Marais JA held:

> [23] While on this topic it would be as well to correct a misconception which led Navsa J to hold that it was not permissible for the employer to avoid making contributions by reliance upon the existence of a surplus save to the extent that the surplus was attributable to past over contribution from the employer. With respect to the learned judge, I do not think that is correct. It overlooks the distinction between a defined benefit scheme in which the employer's contribution is fixed and must be paid irrespective of the state of the fund, and a scheme like the present in which it is not and liability to contribute arises only when it is necessary in the estimation of the fund's actuary to ensure the financial soundness of the fund. In the former class of case there is an existing and continuing liability to contribute and using the existence of a surplus to avoid the making of contributions could not be justified. In the latter class of case, of which the present is an example, there is no predetermined and continuing liability to contribute. The liability arises only when need arises. Present a surplus, absent a need and absent a liability. The employer is therefore not being relieved of a liability and is receiving no benefit to the detriment of the fund or its members. It is irrelevant how the surplus arose and whether or not it is attributable to over contribution in the past by the employer. There is simply no liability to contribute in such circumstances.

Similarly, in Canada Cory J in *Schmidt v Air Products*:[61] **20.92**

> I can see no objection in principle to employers' taking contribution holidays when they are permitted to do so by the terms of the pension plan. When permission is not explicitly given in the plan, it may be implied from the wording of the employer's contribution obligation. Any provision which places the responsibility for the calculation of the amount needed to fund promised benefits in the hands of an actuary should be taken to incorporate accepted actuarial practice as to how that calculation will be made. That practice currently includes the application of calculated surplus funds to the determination of overall current service cost. It is a practice that is in keeping with the nature of a defined benefits plan, and one which is encouraged by the tax authorities. . . . An employer's right to take a contribution holiday must also be determined on a case by case basis. The right to take a contribution holiday can be excluded either explicitly or implicitly in circumstances where a plan mandates a formula for calculating employer contributions which removes actuarial discretion. Contribution holidays may also be permitted by the terms of the plan. When the plan is silent on the issue, the right to take a contribution holiday is not objectionable so long as actuaries continue to accept the application of existing surplus to current service costs as standard practice. These principles apply

---

Scheme is operating on an ongoing basis and there are no doubts about the employer's solvency, would make no commercial sense, and would also be methodologically unsound'.

[58] See eg *Alitalia-Linee Aeree Italiane SPA v Rotunno* [2008] EWHC 185 (Ch) (Henderson J).
[59] Neither does it trigger benefit improvements under s 37 of the Pensions Act 1995 containing a requirement for limited price indexation of pensions in payment if such a payment back is envisaged.
[60] 1999 (4) SA 884, SC South Africa.
[61] [1994] 2 SCR 611, SC Can.

whether or not the pension fund is subject to a trust. Because no money is withdrawn from the fund by the employer, the taking of a contribution holiday represents neither an encroachment upon the trust nor a reduction of accrued benefits. These general considerations are, of course, subject to applicable legislation.

20.93 Conversely, it seems that if there was a pre-existing obligation on the employer to pay an amount to the scheme (eg if there had been a prior redundancy and this was required to be funded by a payment by the employer) it may not be possible to cancel this existing amount by using surplus. This was the point of the extensive (and expensive) litigation in the *National Grid* case.

20.94 In *National Grid*, Robert Walker J overturned the Pensions Ombudsman and held that this was permitted. However, the Court of Appeal thought that it was not permitted by the rules concerned. It felt (without giving a particularly good analysis of why it felt this) that the power allowing the employer to 'make arrangements' to deal with the surplus did not allow it to cancel out pre-existing debt obligations (at least not with the agreement of the trustees).[62]

20.95 The House of Lords in *National Grid v Lawes; International Power v Healy*[63] held that the limitations in the clause containing the amendment power (against paying monies of the scheme to the employer) applied to the arrangement power (in a different clause) as well. However, the House of Lords held that a cancellation of a debt due from the employer to the scheme (but not yet received by the scheme) was not within the limitation. Accordingly, it was possible for the employer to use the arrangement power to cancel the outstanding payments (although it is unclear whether a formal deed of amendment is needed—Lord Scott indicates that it is, Lord Hoffmann seems to say that it is not—in any event, the employers here had already executed retrospective deeds of amendment confirming what had happened).

20.96 The House of Lords overruled the decision of Vinelott J in *British Coal*.[64] He had held that an amendment could not be made to allow a surplus to be used to cancel existing contribution obligations owed by the employer. This would contravene a limitation on the amendment power prohibiting payments back to the employer.

20.97 The boundary for this distinction was always fairly unclear. When does the cancellation of a debt become equivalent to a payment back as opposed to a recalculation of the original debt itself? This was in danger of dragging the courts again down the difficult area of cancellation and reduction of obligations—similar to that envisaged by the litigation on whether bankers can take security in the form of a charge over deposits made with them—see *Re Charge Card Services*[65] for a good explanation by Millett J (as he then was) as to why a charge is conceptually impossible. This line was not followed by a rather confused decision of Lord Hoffmann in the House of Lords in *Re BCCI (No 8)*[66] considering that it was not conceptually impossible.

---

[62] Strangely, *Schmidt v Air Products* was not cited.
[63] Before Lords Slynn, Steyn, Hoffmann, Clyde, and Scott. *National Grid v Lawes; International Power v Healy* [2001] UKHL 20, [2001] 2 All ER 417, HL.
[64] [1995] 1 All ER 912 (Vinelott J).
[65] [1987] Ch 150 (Millett J). See D Pollard, 'Credit Balances as Security' [1988] Journal of Business Law 127.
[66] [1998] AC 214, HL.

DC offset

The increasing closure of schemes both to new members and to future accrual of defined **20.98** benefits can often mean that the ability of employers to use surpluses by reducing future defined benefit contributions is getting more limited.

An alternative is that an offset would still usually be possible if the employer had included a **20.99** defined contribution (DC or money purchase) arrangement within the same scheme as the defined benefit (DB) arrangement.

Unless the rules of the scheme prohibit, then the contributions that would otherwise be **20.100** payable by the employer to the scheme for the DC members could be met by a reduction of surplus (in effect a transfer from the DB section to the DC section).

It is preferable if such a cost transfer provision is expressly allowed under the scheme's rules. **20.101** Such a provision was upheld by Neuberger J (as he then was) in *Barclays Bank v Holmes*.[67] See also the determination of the Pensions Ombudsman in the *IBM* case.[68]

Increase Benefits for Members

Schemes will usually allow benefits for members to be increased. This will be in the form of **20.102** increases to underlying benefits or of discretionary increases to pensions in payments. Even before 2006, provided the (relatively generous) Inland Revenue limits on benefits were not exceeded, the Inland Revenue had no issues with this. The tax rules now envisage that benefits can be paid above any limit, but that there will be increased tax charges (on the member) if his or her benefits exceed the 'lifetime allowance'.

Again, from a trust law perspective, the issue will depend on who has control of this particu- **20.103** lar power. If it is given to the employer alone, then it is likely that it will be very difficult for members to challenge the failure by the employer to exercise the power. The most that could be done would be to challenge it based on a breach of the mutual implied duty of trust and confidence. This is a difficult area of developing law in relation to pension schemes (and the implied duty itself).[69]

The same issues will arise if the power to augment benefits is one that requires the consent **20.104** of the trustees. Often the trust instrument envisages that the trustees must, in effect agree to benefit augmentations if relevant funding is provided. This tends to mean that if there is a surplus they may have no grounds on which to refuse augmentation of benefits even if these have the indirect effect of assisting the employer. For example:

(a) the employer may agree to benefit improvements only for current active members (as part of a salary package so that it has to increase direct salary costs less); or
(b) it may decide to increase benefits only for senior executives or it may decide to increase benefits for those it is making redundant (so that it has to pay less by way of redundancy payments).

---

[67] [2001] OPLR 37 (Neuberger J), distinguishing *Kemble v Hicks* [1998] 3 All ER 154 (Rimer J).
[68] (2004) 22 October, K00516 (Laverick PO).
[69] See the decision of the House of Lords in *Malik v BCCI* [1998] AC 20 and Ch 13 (Employer powers: the implied duty of trust and confidence).

20.105 It is much less common to find that there is a unilateral power for trustees to agree to benefit improvements in these circumstances (although it is not completely unknown[70]).

Pay to the Employer

20.106 Payments back to an employer are not outside the main purpose of a scheme. In the *National Grid* case, *International Power v Healy*,[71] Lord Hoffmann held:

> On the other hand, some of the matters put forward as relevant by Mr Inglis-Jones QC on behalf of the National Grid members seemed to me of marginal significance. For example, he said that the main purpose of the scheme was to provide pensions for the employees. That I would certainly accept. But then he said that it would be inconsistent with such a purpose to make payments or the equivalent of payments to the employer. In relation to a surplus, this does not seem to me to follow. A surplus is (by definition) money in excess of what is needed to effect the main purpose of the scheme.

20.107 Similarly, Timothy Lloyd J at first instance in *Stevens v Bell: Re Airways Pension Scheme*.[72]

20.108 Until the 1970s, it was unclear whether the Inland Revenue would allow payments back to the employer as being consistent with Revenue approval for occupational pension schemes. However, from 1986 onwards, a free-standing tax (now of 35 per cent[73]) is levied on such payments back. Under the discretionary tax approval regime in place (under the Income and Corporation Taxes Act 1988) before 2006 the Revenue had no objections to payments back either on a winding-up or where the scheme was over-funded on a Government Actuary Department (GAD) basis. In effect, they increase the tax that is received. A surplus refund payment to an employer can now be an authorized payment under the Finance Act 2004 tax regime.

20.109 Section 37 of the Pensions Act 1995 (substituted from 6 April 2006 by the Pensions Act 2004) deals with when surplus refunds can be made out of an ongoing scheme. The section overrides scheme rules to the effect that any surplus refund can only be made with the agreement on the trustees (even if the rules provide a unilateral power for the employer to pay surplus refunds). The section states:

(a) any surplus refund cannot exceed the amount of the surplus on a buy-out basis;

(b) that actuarial advice and certificates must be given;

(c) the trustees must be satisfied that it is in the interest of the members that the proposal is exercised; and

(d) notices have been given to the members in advance.

20.110 The relevant regulations are the Occupational Pension Schemes (Payment to Employers) Regulations 2006.[74] They set out the relevant notification requirements both to members and to the Pensions Regulator. The regulations also deal with assessing how a refundable

---

[70] See eg the schemes in *Aitken v Christy Hunt* [1991] PLR 1 (Ferris J) and *Law Debenture Trust plc v Lonrho Africa* [2002] EWHC 2732 (Ch), [2003] OPLR 167 (Patten J).

[71] [2001] 2 All ER 417, [2001] UKHL 20 at [16].

[72] [2001] All ER (D) 193, [2001] PLR 99. Upheld by the Court of Appeal [2002] EWCA Civ 672, [2002] PLR 247.

[73] Now under s 207 of the Finance Act 2004. This was reduced from 40 per cent in May 2001.

[74] SI 2006/802.

surplus can be calculated—they require the s 75 insurance buy-out methodology to be used.

If a refund is to be made from an ongoing scheme (so that s 37 applies) (this is now pretty rare), a relevant resolution may need to be passed under the transitional provisions in s 251 of the Pensions Act 2004 (as amended by the Pensions Act 2011). **20.111**

The House of Lords considered s 37 in the *National Grid*[75] case and decided that it did not apply to a cancellation of debts (as opposed to the payment of monies already held by the scheme). **20.112**

Do the rules prohibit a refund?

Older schemes often contain an express prohibition on payments back to the employer or, at least, amendments that allow payments back to the employer. In this case such payments will not be practical, save by obtaining (before April 2006) a modification order under statute.[76] **20.113**

In *Harwood-Smart v Caws*,[77] Rimer J rejected the argument that such a limitation in a pension scheme trust deed was only there to allow the scheme to comply with what was then thought to be Revenue requirements so that it should be regarded as being only within the scheme to the extent it was still currently required to comply with Revenue requirements. Counsel argued that this would be a 'purposive' approach to the interpretation of the scheme. However, this was rejected by Rimer J on the basis that the language of the scheme was clear, conveyed a non-ambiguous meaning and did not produce a commercially absurd result. **20.114**

The decision in *Harwood-Smart* is probably not affected by the later decision of the House of Lords in the *National Grid* case. But there may be more scope for arguing that the change in the underlying tax rules should be taken into account, following *Lloyds TSB Foundation for Scotland v Lloyds Banking Group Plc*[78] where the Supreme Court upheld a changed interpretation of a deed where the underlying account rules changed in a way 'wholly outside the parties' original contemplation and is something they would not have accepted had they foreseen it'. **20.115**

A prohibition on refunds (or payments) to the employer within scheme rules cannot be avoided by the scheme arranging a transfer to another scheme (which does not contain the restriction).[79] **20.116**

Similarly, a restriction in the amendment power may mean that a rule already in the scheme that could otherwise be used to arrange a refund cannot be used. It may be impliedly subject to the limitation in the amendment power.[80] **20.117**

---

[75] *National Grid v Lawes & Mayes* [2001] UKHL 20, [2001] 2 All ER 417, HL.
[76] Either from the Occupational Pensions Board or, from April 1997, from the Occupational Pensions Regulatory Authority (Opra)—see s 69(3)(a) of the Pensions Act 1995. This power was repealed by the Pensions Act 2004 from 6 April 2006.
[77] [1999] All ER(D) 1369, [2000] PLR 101 (Rimer J).
[78] [2013] UKSC 3, [2013] 2 All ER 103, SC.
[79] *Hillsdown Holdings plc v Pensions Ombudsman* [1997] 1 All ER 862 (Knox J).
[80] *National Grid v Mayes, International Power v Healy* [2001] UKHL 20, [2001] 2 All ER 417, HL and *Stevens v Bell* [2002] EWCA Civ 672, [2002] OPLR 207, CA (sometimes cited as *British Airways Pension Trustees Ltd v British Airways plc*).

Trustee Discretion

20.118 For those schemes which allow such refunds (or allow a power to be included by amendment), the questions for the trustees are:

(a) Is it a proper exercise of the relevant power to allow a surplus refund (or exercise of the amendment power of the scheme to allow this)?

(b) Is it a power they should be exercising in the current circumstances?

20.119 It might be thought that surplus refunds were not a proper use of powers under pension schemes. It could be argued that the sole purpose of the scheme is to provide relevant benefits to members and not to pay an amount to the employer. In addition, many schemes are set up under an 'irrevocable' trust.

20.120 There was little case law in the UK as to whether it is appropriate or possible for there to be surplus refunds to employers. In Australia in *Lock v Westpac* the New South Wales courts allowed a surplus refund as part of an agreed 'package' including the employers' consent to benefit improvements.

20.121 Conversely, in Canada, in *Schmidt v Air Products*[81] the Supreme Court of Canada held that such a use of the amendment power to get rid of a provision saying there should be no refund to the employer was contrary to the purpose of the scheme and should not be allowed. In effect, it was making an irrevocable trust into a revocable trust.

20.122 The position in the UK is that such refunds would be allowed.

20.123 Millett J (as he then was) in *Courage* [82] considered that it would be appropriate for trustees to bargain with employers for benefit improvements in the circumstances. He held:

> It will, however, only be in rare cases that the employer will have any legal right to repayment of any part of the surplus. Regulations shortly to be made under s 64 of the Social Security Act 1973, as amended by para 3 of Sch 10 to the Social Security Act 1986, are expected to confer power on the Occupational Pensions Board to authorise modifications to pension schemes in order to allow repayment to employers. Repayment will, however, still normally require amendment to the scheme, and thus co-operation between the employer and the trustees or committee of management. Where the employer seeks repayment, the trustees or committee can be expected to press for generous treatment of employees and pensioners, and the employer to be influenced by a desire to maintain good industrial relations with its workforce.
>
> It is, therefore, precisely in relation to a surplus that the relationship between 'the company' as the employer and the members as its present or past employees can be seen to be an essential feature of a pension scheme. In the present case, the members of these schemes object to being compulsorily transferred to a new scheme of which they know nothing except that it has a relatively small surplus. While they have no legal right to participate in the surpluses in the existing schemes, they are entitled to have them dealt with by consultation and negotiation between their employers with a continuing responsibility towards them and the committee of management with a discretion to exercise on their behalf, and not to be irrevocably parted from these surpluses by the unilateral decision of a take-over raider with only a transitory interest in the share capital of the companies which employ them.

---

[81] [1994] 2 SCR 611, Can SC.
[82] [1987] 1 WLR 495 (Millett J).

In the *National Grid*[83] case, Lord Hoffmann referred to this main purpose argument and **20.124** dismissed it. He held:

> On the other hand, some of the matters put forward as relevant by Mr Inglis-Jones on behalf of the National Grid members seemed to me of marginal significance. For example, he said that the main purpose of the scheme was to provide pensions for the employees. That I would certainly accept. But then he said that it would be inconsistent with such a purpose to make payments or the equivalent of payments to the employer. In relation to a surplus, this does not seem to me to follow. A surplus is (by definition) money in excess of what is needed to effect the main purpose of the scheme.

The existence of the refund provisions in the tax legislation (now the Finance Act 2004) and **20.125** the provisions in the Pensions Act 1995 dealing with surplus refunds (s 37 and s 69) indicate that from a UK perspective such surplus funds are permitted. The issue for trustees in these circumstances is whether they should agree to what is being proposed by the employer.

Negotiations between Employer and Trustees

A distinction must be drawn between: **20.126**

(a) those situations where the consent of the employer is needed (ie the trustees have no unilateral power to act on their own without the consent of the employer);
(b) where the trustees have unilateral power (eg to increase benefits or to amend the scheme) so that they can act without the consent of the employer.

In the first case, clearly an agreement with the employer is needed. Otherwise, as men- **20.127** tioned by Millett J in *Courage*,[84] the surplus will remain 'in baulk'. In practice, trustees in this situation are advised that they should seek the best bargain that they can achieve with the employer. Broadly, they should envisage themselves as looking after the interests of the members of the scheme in these circumstances (leaving the employer to look after its own interests). This finesses, to a degree, the question of whether or not the trustees should be considering the interests of the employer as well (see below).

Having reached the position of having got what they think to be the best offer from the **20.128** employer, the trustees must then decide whether or not it is in the best interest of the beneficiaries of the scheme (members etc) to accept that offer. Effectively they have the choice either to agree to the proposal (in which case there will presumably be benefit improvements, but a loss of security in the sense that the solvency level of the scheme will go down) or not. Which do they think is in the long-term best interests of all the members of the scheme?

One difficulty is knowing how far they should seek to negotiate to push for benefit improve- **20.129** ments 'across the board'. Is it legitimate of the employer to say that it would not agree to an existing benefit for pensioners (say because he thought they were very good and currently fully indexed) but instead would want any benefit improvements to be limited to current active members and deferred pensioners?

This was the precise situation faced by the trustees in litigation involving the industrial **20.130** training board pension scheme, culminating in the decision of the Court of Appeal in *Edge*

---

[83] *National Grid v Lawes & Mayes* [2001] UKHL 20, [2001] 2 All ER 417 at [16], HL.
[84] See also Knox J in *LRT v Hatt* [1993] OPLR 225 at 267.

v Pensions Ombudsman.[85] The Pensions Ombudsman considered that the trustees, in agreeing to no benefit improvement for pensioners, had acted improperly. They had not acted in an impartial manner. The Pensions Ombudsman accordingly ordered the trustees to reverse their decision. This determination of the Pensions Ombudsman was reversed on appeal both by the Vice Chancellor and by the Court of Appeal. They both considered that it was appropriate for the trustees to consider the attitude of the employer in these circumstances. The trustees had not acted unreasonably and arbitrarily as it was not their duty to be impartial as regards different categories of beneficiary of a pension scheme (perhaps a contrast can be made here with the investment powers) and so the decision of the Pension Ombudsman was overturned.

20.131 The trustees in *Edge* did not have a unilateral power. They were being asked to agree to a proposal made by the employer (whose consent for benefit changes was needed). But the decision gives useful guidance for trustees in relation to the position where they have a unilateral power. The reasoning in the *Edge* case seems to be equally as applicable to unilateral powers. Various issues arise here:

(a) How far do the trustees owe a duty to exercise powers reasonably as regards the employer as well as the other members of the scheme? Can it be argued that the employer is also a beneficiary of the scheme or at the very least interested in the assets of the scheme and hence if there is a deficit later on it can be called to provide funding (not least under s 75 of the Pensions Act 1995). Does the trustee owe a duty solely to the members of the scheme or is it also owed to the employers? Can it be argued that the purpose of the power is only to advance the position of the employer? In effect there is no overriding obligation of the trustee to push benefits to the extent of prejudicing the employer.[86]

(b) A lesser version of this duty would entail looking at the position should the employer strongly object to a position being taken by the trustees. Can the employer terminate the scheme and terminate contributions? Does the risk of this mean that the trustee could be said to not be acting in the interests of members if it exercised the power in a way that prejudices the employer?

20.132 These are difficult areas. See more generally the discussion in Chapter 10 ('Trustees' duties to employers'). The *Edge* decision itself gives a strong indication that trustees are not expected blindly to act in the interests of members and employees etc to the exclusion of consideration of any of the interests of the employers.

Trustee Discretion—Proper Purpose

20.133 Where trustees have a discretion in relation to use of surplus (eg on a winding-up) the leading decision is that of Nicholls V-C (as he then was) in *Threlis Ltd (1974) Pension Scheme v Lomas.*[87] This involved a scheme that was winding-up. There was a surplus available after all required benefits had been provided. The employer was the sole trustee and the liquidator (recognizing a conflict) surrendered his power to augment benefits to the Court. The Vice

---

[85] [2000] Ch 602, CA.
[86] See Ch 10 (Trustees' duties to employers) and Edward Nugee QC, 'The Duties of Pension Scheme Trustees to the Employer' (1998) 12 TLI 216 and SEK Hulme QC, 'The Basic Duties of Trustees of Superannuation Trusts—Fair to One, Fair to All?' (2000) 14 TLI 30.
[87] [1992] OPLR 22 (Nicholls V-C).

Chancellor decided that the Court would exercise the discretion to increase benefits in the manner in which a trustee could be expected to act, having regard to all the material circumstances. These circumstances included the position of the employer.

Nicholls V-C listed the material circumstances as including: **20.134**

(i) the scope of the power;
(ii) the purpose of the power;
(iii) the source of the surplus;
(iv) the size of the surplus and the impact of the statutory pension indexation provisions;
(v) the financial position of the employer; and
(vi) the needs of the members of the scheme.

More recently, in *Alexander Forbes Trustee Service Ltd v Halliwell*[88] Hart J accepted (in the   **20.135** context of use of a surplus in a winding-up) the argument that the trustees are required to consider the interests of the employer was applied:

> It was submitted that the Ombudsman had overlooked the fact that in exercising its discretion over surplus the trustees were not bound solely to consider the interest of the members but were entitled and indeed bound to consider the interests of the employers as well: indeed, if its obligation was solely to consider the interests of the members it was difficult to see how any surplus could have been allowed to return to the employers at all.[89]

> In my judgment those criticisms of the Ombudsman's determination are justified.[90]

In practice, trustees in this position would have a wide discretion.[91]   **20.136**

In *Harding v Joy Manufacturing Holdings Ltd*,[92] the Inner House of the Court of Session con-   **20.137** sidered an application to court by trustees in relation to a merger proposal. The scheme was in surplus on a winding-up basis and the trustees had a unilateral power to increase pensions in payment and deferred pensions, after consulting the employer. The Inner House referred to Scott V-C in *Edge* and held that it would be proper for the trustees to agree to a 'deal' with the employer for 1/3rd of a surplus to be used for benefit improvements, but for the whole fund to be transferred to a new scheme (which did not contain a power for the trustees to increase benefits unilaterally).

The Inner House held: **20.138**

> Recognising that the trustees are vested with a considerable measure of discretion as to how they should deal with the surplus in the fund, we are satisfied that, even though the trustees express disappointment about the amount of the surplus to be made available to existing members, it cannot be said that no reasonable trustees could accept the proposals and exercise their powers in the manner contemplated by the trustees. The following factors appear relevant.
>
> First, the company's proposals mean that one-third of the surplus calculated on an ongoing basis, or roughly half of the surplus if calculated on a cessation basis, will be made available exclusively for the existing members of the Scheme.

---

[88] [2003] EWHC 1685 (Ch), [2003] OPLR 355 (Hart J).
[89] At [22].
[90] At [23].
[91] See eg *NBPF Pension Trustees Ltd v Warnock-Smith* [2008] EWHC 455 (Ch), [2008] 2 All ER (Comm) 740 (Floyd J) and the Pensions Ombudsman in *Hobbs* (2008) 19 May, S00129 (King PO) (exercise of discretion: trustees' surplus allocation 'at margins of rationality' but could not be overturned).
[92] 2000 SLT 843, [2001] OPLR 235, CSIH.

Secondly, the distribution is to be pro rata to the liabilities.

Thirdly, the proposals involve no detriment to the existing members of the Scheme, since the Scheme will be closed to new members.

Fourthly, on transfer of the assets to the HIPS, they remain ring-fenced for members of the Scheme.

Finally, while the proposals doubtless involve general advantages to Harnischfeger [the employer] by virtue of the merger of the funds with their pension scheme, one effect of the proposals will be that, by increasing the liabilities to the members of the Scheme, they will reduce the funds on the strength of which the company would be otherwise entitled to take a contributions holiday. Having regard to these aspects of the proposals, it is impossible to say that no reasonable trustees could accept them as an appropriate way of dealing with the surplus in the fund.

20.139 See also (to the same effect) in Australia *Re AMP Superannuation*.[93] In this case, an employer of a multi-employer pension plan decided to terminate the plan and distribute the surplus before doing so. There was a surplus of Aus$1.5m and the trustee proposed to improve the four remaining members' benefits. The employer refused to consent, arguing the improvements should be more modest, and the members of the plan refused to agree, arguing the benefits should be improved further. The trustees applied to the court for approval of their proposals.

20.140 Windeyer AJ held that trustees can take into account the requirements of an employer sponsor when deciding upon the application of surplus and there is no automatic requirement to apply such surplus to the benefit of employee members exclusively. The trustee had power to implement the employer proposal, and it is open to it the trustee to be satisfied that implementation of the proposal is reasonable. If, after considering the reasons given by the court, the trustee formed the opinion it should no longer pursue the implementation of the original proposal it would be justified in implementing the employer's proposal.

Avoiding a Blocked Surplus

20.141 In the absence of an ongoing funding obligation (DB or DC), then the primary method for an employer to obtain immediate value out of a surplus in an occupational pension scheme would be by a cash refund out of the scheme. However, the terms of the scheme may not allow this and pensions (and tax) legislation is not helpful here (see above).

20.142 In practice, it will often be better for employers (who look as though they may be getting towards a surplus) to consider reducing contributions to reduce the risk of 'overshooting': in effect trying to reduce deficit contributions paid into the scheme (until they are needed) rather than ending up with a surplus that cannot be refunded (or can only be refunded with a tax charge).

20.143 Trustees may well be concerned about the impact on security for benefits under the scheme if such course is followed. One option can be for an employer to seek to negotiate with the trustees:

(a) the removal or cancellation of unhelpful protective provisions—for example, a provision in the scheme that provides for the trustee to be required (or have a discretion) to use a surplus on winding-up to augment benefits instead of repaying to the employers; or

---

[93] [2012] 002 PBLR; [2011] NSWSC 1439 (Acting Justice Windeyer). See also *Invensys Australia Superannuation Fund Pty Ltd v Austrac Investments Ltd* [2006] VSC 112, (2006) 15 VR, (2006) 198 FLR 302

(b) to agree that instead of contributions being made in to the scheme (where they would run the risk of being 'trapped'), security is instead given by the company—for example a contribution is paid into a separate account or fund over which a mortgage or charge is given to the trustees. The Pensions Regulator has suggested that this route should be considered where schemes are at or close to their funding targets and the trustees and employer consider that market changes and contributions may lead to surplus funding.[94]

This would then help with any security concerns of the trustees. This practice is sometimes called an escrow account route, but the precise legal status of an escrow account can be unclear and using a trust can give rise to difficult tax consequences. A mortgage or charge is a more tax transparent and easier solution in many cases. **20.144**

One issue for employers would be that payments into a mortgaged account or fund will generally not attract tax relief until such time as they are in fact paid in to the underlying registered pension scheme. **20.145**

Conclusion

If anything, the risk was that courts may have been leaning too far towards the interests of employees and away from those of employers. There was a real risk that employers would shift away from final salary pension schemes and towards no pension provision at all or money purchase only. **20.146**

This is probably not an efficient use of resources for an ageing population. Collective saving is often much more efficient than individual—the trustees will be able to rely on the backing of the employer to spread investments, take more expert advice, reduce costs by dealing direct with fund managers etc, and take a more aggressive investment structure. This should result in a bigger pension for each £1 invested (by the employer or by the employee) when compared to more individual structures. **20.147**

The courts ran the risk of upsetting that balance if they push the situation too much towards the member. This has probably not happened yet (although the decision of the Court of Appeal in *National Grid* runs close). If it did happen, the risk is that members of well-funded schemes may benefit—but at the expense of those in less well-funded schemes and at the cost of future pension provision. **20.148**

A good example of this has been the (political) saga in relation to the National Bus pension scheme. This scheme was due to be wound up. The trustees were concerned that it may not have enough assets to be able to buy out all its liabilities by purchasing annuities with insurance companies. **20.149**

The government agreed to step in and guarantee the scheme's funding, but only on condition that if there was in fact a surplus in the scheme it was payable to the government. The trustees also agreed to amend the scheme to convert a right to have pension increase set by reference to increases in national earnings. This was thought to be too difficult for an insurer to match **20.150**

(Byrne J); and *Macedonian Orthodox Community Church Saint Peter Incorporated v His Eminence the Diocesan Bishop of Macedonian Orthodox Diocese of Australia and New Zealand* [2008] HCA 42, (2008) 237 CLR 66, HC Aus.

[94] Paragraph 15 of the TPR statement on Pension Scheme Funding in the Current Environment, April 2012.

and was converted instead to a right to increase based on a percentage above price inflation instead. This was intended to be broadly comparable.

20.151   As it happened, the stock market turned and a surplus resulted. The members had their benefits secured and the surplus was paid to the government. Some years later some members complained about this.

20.152   The Pensions Ombudsman held[95] that the arrangements were invalid. The change to the indexation provisions contravened the amendment power in the rules, but, more crucially, he held that the agreement between the trustees and the government was based on the premise that the government could exercise its power to terminate contributions and leave the scheme in deficit. He held that this would not have been a proper use of the termination power and would have been a breach of the implied duty of mutual trust and confidence.

20.153   This seems very unhelpful. The net effect is that employers will be put off making arrangements with trustees that are designed to help members. There must be lots of employees who would appreciate a government guarantee of their benefits.

---

[95]   (1996) 6 September, A10113, [1997] PLR 1 (Farrand PO).

USEFUL WEBSITES

Organization and website	Details
APL: <http://www.apl.org.uk>	Association of Pension Lawyers: The APL has a website and most of the papers given at its conferences find their way on to it. But you have to be a member to access them.
Austlii <http://www.austlii.edu.au>	Australasian Legal Information Institute: Materials include copies of Australian cases (including state courts).
BAILII: <http://www.bailii.org>	The newer British Isles equivalent of Austlii. It contains British and Irish case law and legislation, European Union case law, Law Commission reports, and other law-related British and Irish material.
CANLII <http://www.canlii.org/en/index.php>	Canadian Legal Information Institute: It provides copies of Canadian cases, including from the provinces.
Cardiff Index to Legal Abbreviations <http://www.legalabbrevs.cardiff.ac.uk>	Case citation index from Cardiff University.
ECJ <http://curia.europa.eu/jurisp/cgi-bin/form.pl?lang=en>	Judgments of the European Court of Justice from 1997 (earlier caselaw is also available). The link is to the search form.
Freshfields Bruckhaus Deringer LLP <http://www.freshfields.com>	Publications page includes copies of various briefings. Includes many on employment and pensions issues.
House of Lords <http://www.publications.parliament.uk/pa/ld/ldjudgmt.htm>	This page lists html versions of all House of Lords' judgments delivered since 14 November 1996. Not searchable (but try BAILII). From October 2009, see the Supreme Court website.
Legislation: Office of Public Sector Information <http://www.opsi.gov.uk/legislation>	This site provides links to the full text of all UK Parliament Public General Acts (from 1988 onwards) and all statutory instruments (from 1987 onwards) as they were originally enacted. For more recent legislation, the explanatory memorandum is also available.
NZLII <http://www.nzlii.org>	The New Zealand equivalent of Austlii and Bailii. Includes New Zealand court decisions.
Pensions Ombudsman <http://www.pensions-ombudsman.org.uk>	Includes determinations of the Ombudsman in a searchable form.
Pensions Regulator <http://www.thepensionsregulator.gov.uk>	Includes various codes of practice and guidance. Also the decisions of the determinations panel.

(Continued)

Continued

Organization and website	Details
Privy Council <http://www.jcpc.gov.uk> (from 2009) <http://www.privy-council.org.uk> (1999 to 2009)	Privy Council judgments since 1999 (there are still some appeals, notably from the Isle of Man, the various Channel Isles, Jamaica, Mauritius, the Cayman Islands, Bermuda, Gibraltar and Brunei).
National Archive Legislation Database <http://www.legislation.gov.uk>	The National Archive (which includes HMSO) publishes copies of the official version of legislation. In the main this is as originally enacted, but in some cases references to later amendments are included.
Supreme Court <http://www.supremecourt.gov.uk>	The Supreme Court took over from the House of Lords in relation to legal appeals from October 2009. Supreme Court decisions are on this website.
Trust Law Committee <http://www.kcl.ac.uk/law/research/centres/trustlawcommittee/index.aspx>	The Trust Law Committee was set up in 1994 as a group of leading academics and practitioners dedicated to researching weaknesses of trust law in England and Wales and ways of improving it.

BOOKS AND ARTICLES: SHORT BIBLIOGRAPHY

Arthur, Hugh 'Exoneration Clauses After Armitage v Nurse—Where Are We Now?' (APL Seminar, April 1998)

Asplin, Sarah and Nugee, Christopher 'Retires, Retiring, Retired' (APL Seminar, April 2004)

Atiyah, PS 'Common Law and Statute Law' (1985) 48 MLR 1

Atkinson, Mark 'That's Not What We Meant. . . Rectification, Mistake and Estoppel' (APL Spring Conference, May 2001)

Atkinson, Mark 'Goalkeepers are Different. What About Pension Scheme Trustees?' (2003) 17 TLI 25

Beatson, J 'Has the Common Law a Future?' [1997] CLJ 291

Beatson, J 'The Role of Statute in the Development of Common Law Doctrine' (2001) 117 LQR 247

Bennett, Philip 'Trustees' Indemnities, Insurance and Exoneration Clauses' (APL Conference, 1996)

Bennett, Philip 'Coping With Conflict' (2004) The Treasurer 27 (May)

Birks, Peter 'Accessory Liability' (1996) LMCLQ 1

Birks, Peter and Pretto, Arianna (eds) *Breach of Trust* (Hart Publishing, 2002)

Browne-Wilkinson, Lord 'Equity and Its Relevance to Superannuation Today' (1992) 6 TLI 119

Burrows, Andrew 'Common Law and Statute' (2012) 128 LQR 232

Butler, Lisa 'A Reply to the Changing Winds of Superannuation—Relief for Employers?' (2000) 11 Journal of Banking and Finance Law and Practice 284

Campbell, Emily 'Dishonest Assistance: To Plead or Not to Plead', Trusts & Estates Journal, December 1998

Campbell, Emily and Hilliard, Jonathan 'Disclosure of Information By Trustees' in *The International Trust* (3rd edn, David Hayton (ed), Jordan Publishing, 2011)

Campbell, JC 'Access by Trust Beneficiaries to Trustees' Documents Information and Reasons' (2009) 3 J Eq 97

Conaglen, Matthew and Nolan, Richard 'Precedent From the Privy Council' (2006) 122 LQR 349

Conaglen, Matthew *Fiduciary Loyalty* (Hart Publishing, 2010)

Dal Pont, Gino 'The Amendment of Trust Deeds—A Super(Annuation) Gloss?' (2008) 31 Australian Bar Review 1

Davis, Noel 'Surpluses in Superannuation Funds—Where Are We Now?' (2001) 15 TLI 130

Davis, Noel 'Conflicts of Interest' (2013) 24 ASLB 164

Dawson, Georgia 'A Fork in the Road for Access to Trust Documents' (2009) 3 J Eq 39

Edmundson, Peter 'Express Limitation of a Trustee's Rights of Indemnity' (2011) 5 J Eq 77

Farrand, Julian 'Courts v Pensions Ombudsman—Stepping On Toes?' (2000) 14 TLI 146

Finn, Paul *Fiduciary Obligations* (Law Book Co, Sydney, 1977)

Finn, Paul 'Statutes and the Common Law' (1992) 22(1) University of Western Australia Law Review 7

Fischel, Daniel and Longbein, John H 'ERISA's Fundamental Contradiction: The Exclusive Benefit Rule' (1983) 55 University Of Chicago Law Review 1105

Fitzsimons, Malcolm 'Managing Pension Scheme Trustee Conflicts of Interest' (2006) 20 TLI 211

Ford HAJ and Hardingham IJ 'Trading Trusts: Rights and Liabilities of Beneficiaries' in PD Finn (ed), *Equity and Commercial Relationships* (Law Book Co, Sydney, 1987)

Ford, HAJ and Lee, WA *Principles of the Law of Trusts* (Law Book Co, Looseleaf, 1996)

Fox, DM 'Disclosure of a Settlor's Wish Letter in a Discretionary Trust' [2008] CLJ 252

France, Isabel 'Pension Scheme Rule Amendments—Getting It Right' (2004) 18 TLI 202

Freshfields, *The Guide to the Pensions Act 1995* (Tolley Publishing, 1995)

Freshfields On Corporate Pensions Law 2013 (ed Pollard And Magoffin, Bloomsbury Professional, 2013)

Gordon, Ian *Battling with Courage* (Practical Law for Companies, 2010)

Greenlees, Mark 'The Treatment of Surpluses: An Exercise in Horsetrading?' (APL Conference, 1991)

Greenstreet, Ian 'The New Use for Section 4 of the Trustee Act 1925: A Little Used One-Hundred Year Old Statutory Provision Applied in a Modern Context' (1994) 8 TLI 56

Greenstreet, Ian 'Should Trustees Be More Like Bankers?: The Changing Role of Occupational Pension Scheme Trustees' (2005) 19 TLI 3

Greenstreet, Ian 'Voting for Christmas—The Legal Issues' (APL Conference, June 2005)

Greenstreet, Ian 'Practical Issues When Updating Your Pension Scheme Documentation' (APL Conference, 2007)

Gummow, William 'The Common Law and Statute' in *Change and Continuity: Statute, Equity And Federalism* (Clarendon Press, 1999)

Ham, Robert 'Trustees' Liability' (1995) 9 TLI 21

Hanrahan, PF 'Directors' Liability in Superannuation Trustee Companies' (2008) 2 J Eq 204

Hayton, David 'Trust Law and Occupational Pension Schemes' [1993] Conv 283

Hayton, David 'The Irreducible Core Content of Trusteeship' in *Trends In Contemporary Trust Law* (ed AJ Oakley, Clarendon Press, 1996)

Hayton, David 'Pension Trusts and Traditional Trusts, Drastically Different Species of Trust' [2005] Conv 229

Heath, Dawn and Pollard, David 'One of the Criminal Ones: An Overview of Section 40 of the Pensions Act 1995, Employer-Related Investment' (2010) 24 TLI 13

Heath, Dawn and Pollard, David 'The Power of Employers to Appoint or Remove Trustees of Occupational Pension Schemes: Is It Fiduciary?' (2011) 25 TLI 184

Hilliard, Jonathan 'On the Irreducible Core Content of Trusteeship—A Reply to Professors Matthews and Parkinson' (2003) 17 TLI 144

Hilliard, Jonathan 'The Flexibility of Fiduciary Doctrine in Trust Law: How Far Does it Stretch in Practice' (2009) 23 TLI 119

Hilliard, Jonathan and Campbell, Emily 'Disclosure of Information by Trustees' in *The International Trust* (3rd edn, ed David Hayton, Jordan Publishing, 2011)

Hilliard, Jonathan and Ham, Robert 'A Runaway Train or Stuck in the Sidings? South West Trains v Wightman After Bradbury and IBM' (APL Seminar, 2012)

Hood, Parker *Principles of Lender Liability* (Oxford University Press, 2012)

Hooley, Richard 'Controlling Contractual Discretion' [2013] CLJ 65

Howard, Mark 'Pension Trustee Liability Insurance' (2011) 25 TLI 99

Hulme, SEK 'The Basic Duties of Trustees of Superannuation Trusts—Fair to One, Fair To All?' (2000) 14 TLI 130

Jacobs, Michael 'To Be Or Not To Be…Trustee Act 1925, S37(1)(c) Revisited Again' (1993) 7 TLI 73

Jeaffreson, John Cordy *A Book About Lawyers* (Hurst and Balckett, 1867, Vol 1)

Lewin on Trusts (18th edn, Sweet & Maxwell, 2008) by Lynton Tucker, Nicholas Le Poidevin, and James Brightwell

Lightman, Sir Gavin 'The Trustees' Duty to Provide Information to Beneficiaries' [2004] PCB 23

Lindsay, Mr Justice 'The Implied Term of Trust and Confidence' [2001] ILJ 1

Lingren, Kevin 'A Superannuation Fund Trustee's Right of Indemnity' (2010) 4 J Eq 85

Mcalister, Pam 'Accrued Benefits—In Search of a Legal Meaning' (2000) 11 ASLB 73

Maclean, David *Trusts and Powers* (Sweet & Maxwell, 1989)

Maclean, David 'Effect of an Invalid Deed of Amendment of a Superannuation Fund Trust Deed' (2001) 76 ALJ 158

Marsh, DR *Corporate Trustees* (Europa Publications, 1952)

Matthews, Paul 'The Efficacy of Trustee Exemption Clauses in English Law' (1989) 42 Conv 44

Matthews, Paul 'The New Trust: Obligations Without Rights?' in AJ Oakley (ed), *Trends in Contemporary Trust Law* (Clarendon Press, 1996)

Matthews, Paul 'The Comparative Importance of the Rule in Saunders v Vautier' (2006) 122 LQR 266.

Maudgil, Sandeep 'Trustee Disclosure—Do Members Have a Right to Know?' (APL Conference, 2007)

Maudgil, Sandeep 'Benefit Changes and the Employment Contract' (APL Conference, 2009)

Millett, Peter 'The Quistclose Trust: Who Can Enforce It?' (1985) 101 LQR 269

Millett, Lord 'Pension Schemes and Trusts—The Tail Wagging the Dog?' (2000) 14 TLI 66

Mitchell, Charles 'Assistance' in Peter Birks and Arianna Pretto (eds), *Breach of Trust* (Hart Publishing, 2002)

Moffatt, Graham 'Pension Funds: A Fragmentation of Trust Law' (1993) 56 MLR 471

Newman, Paul 'HR Trustees v Wembley: Pandora's Box Opened?' (APL Forum, February 2012)

Nicholls, Lord 'Trustees and Their Broader Community: Where Duty, Morality and Ethics Converge' (1996) 70 ALJ 205

Nobles, Richard *Pensions Employment and the Law* (Clarendon Press, 1993)

Nolan, Anthea 'The Role of the Employment Contract in Superannuation; an Analysis Focusing on Surplus Repatriation Powers Conferred on Employers' (1996) 24 ABLR 341

Nolan, Anthea and Godding, Steve 'Employers' Rights and Duties in Respect of the Funds They Sponsor' (Superannuation Conference 2010)

Nolan, Richard 'Shopping for Defendants: Worthless Trust Companies and Their Directors' [2008] CLJ 472

Nolan, Richard 'Controlling Fiduciary Power' [2009] CLJ 293

Nugee, Christopher and Asplin, Sarah 'Retires, Retiring, Retired' (APL Seminar, April 2004)

Nugee, Edward 'The Duties of Pension Scheme Trustees to the Employer' (1998) 12 TLI 216

O'Dea, Geoff, Long, Julian, and Smyth, Alexandra *Schemes of Arrangement: Law and Practice* (Oxford University Press, 2012)

Penner, James 'Exemptions' in Birks and Pretto (eds), *Breach of Trust* (Hart Publishing, 2002)

Pittaway, Ian 'Pension Funds—Is a Separate Branch of Trust Law Evolving?' (1990) 4 Trust Law & Practice 156

Pollard, David 'The Unfair Contract Terms Act: Points When Drafting Contracts' (1987) Business Law Review 131

Pollard, David 'Credit Balances as Security' [1988] JBL 127

Pollard, David 'Appointment and Removal of Trustees—A Fiduciary Power?' (1991) 37 British Pension Lawyer 1

Pollard, David 'Lock v Westpac Banking Corporation' (1992) 42 British Pension Lawyer 7

Pollard, David 'Occupational Pension Schemes: Disclosure of Interests in Shares Under Part VI of the Companies Act 1985' (1996) 17 Company Lawyer 272

Pollard, David 'Employers' Powers in Pension Schemes: The Implied Duty of Trust and Confidence' (1997) 11 TLI 93

Pollard, David 'Re Joy Manufacturing Holdings Limited' (1999) 13 TLI 255

Pollard, David 'Pension Schemes: Corporate Trustees' (2000) 14 TLI 2

Pollard, David 'Section 68: The Forgotten Section?' (APL Seminar, February 2001)

Pollard, David and Randall, Nicholas 'Pensions as a Contractual Right' (Industrial Law Society Seminar, 2002)

Pollard, David 'Employers' Liens on Pension Benefits' (2002) Journal of Pensions Management (June)

Pollard, David 'Pension Trusts: The Position of Spouses and Dependants' (2002) 16 TLI 74

Pollard, David 'Pensions Law and Surpluses: A Fair Balance Between Employer and Members?' (2003) 17 TLI 2

Pollard, David 'Schmidt v Rosewood Trust' (2003) 17 TLI 90

Pollard, David 'Pensions and Tupe' (2005) 24 ILJ 127

Pollard, David 'Trustees' Duties to Employers: The Scope of the Duty of Pension Trustees' (2006) 20 TLI 21

Pollard, David 'Corporate Trustees' in *Tolley's Pensions Law* (LexisNexis)

Pollard, David and Heath, Dawn 'One of the Criminal Ones: An Overview of Section 40 of the Pensions Act 1995, Employer-Related Investment' (2010) 24 TLI 13

Pollard, David and Heath, Dawn 'The Power of Employers to Appoint or Remove Trustees of Occupational Pension Schemes: Is It Fiduciary?' (2011) 25 TLI 184

Pollard, David *Corporate Insolvency: Employment and Pension Rights* (5th edn, Bloomsbury Professional, 2013)

Prophet, Clifton 'Protecting Pension Trustees and Fiduciaries—Exoneration and Indemnity' (2001) 15 TLI 194

Scott Donald, M 'What Contribution Does Trust Law Make to the Regulatory Scheme Shaping Superannuation In Australia?'—Australian Prudential Regulatory Authority (APRA)

Scott Donald, M 'Best Interest' (2008) 2 J Eq 245

Simmonds, Andrew 'The Pension Protection Fund—18 Months On' (2007) 21 TLI 150

Stafford, Andrew and Ritchie, Stuart *Fiduciary Duty—Directors and Employees* (Jordans, 2008)

Stannard, Paul 'Pensions as an Employment Right' (APL Conference, 1992)

Stone, Margaret 'The Superannuation Trustee: Are Fiduciary Obligations and Standards Appropriate?' (2007) J Eq 167

Sweet and Maxwell's Law of Pension Schemes by Simmons & Simmons Pension Group, Nigel Inglis-Jones and Martin Jenkins (Sweet & Maxwell, Looseleaf)

Tennet, Michael 'Pensions Cases That Time Forgot' (2007) 21 TLI 125

Thomas, Geraint *Thomas on Powers* 2nd edn (Oxford University Press, 2012)

Thomas, Geraint and Hudson, Alastair *The Law of Trusts* 2nd edn (Oxford University Press, 2010)

Underhill and Hayton: The Law of Trusts and Trustees 18th edn (ed David Hayton, Paul Matthews, and Charles Mitchell) (LexisNexis, 2010)

Vann, Vicki 'No Such Thing as a Judicious Breach of Trust?' (1998) 12 TLI 44

Vinelott, Sir John 'Pensions Law and the Role of the Courts' (1994) 8 TLI 35

Vrisakis, Michael 'The Best Test of (or the 'Bestest') Interests of Members' (2006) 17(9) ASLB 138

Vrikasis, Michael 'How Should Trustees Commission Legal Advice?' (2013) 24 ASLB 147 (March 2013)

Walker, Sir Robert 'Some Trust Principles in the Pensions Context' in AJ Oakley (ed) *Trends In Contemporary Trust Law* (Clarendon Press, 1996)

Warren, Nicholas 'Trustee Risk and Liability' (1999) 13 TLI 226

Warren, Nicholas and Newman, Paul 'Joint Opinion On Section 67' (Institute And Faculty Of Actuaries, April 2000).

Weber, Kris and Williams, Sian 'Pension Scheme Surpluses' in *Tolley's Pensions Law* (LexisNexis)

Young, PW, Croft, C, and Smith, M *On Equity* (Lawbook Co, Sydney, 2009)

INDEX